Lecture Notes in Computer Science 12820

Advanced Research in Computing and Software Science
Subline of Lecture Notes in Computer Science

More information about this subseries at http://www.springer.com/series/7407

Leonel Sousa · Nuno Roma ·
Pedro Tomás (Eds.)

Euro-Par 2021:
Parallel Processing

27th International Conference
on Parallel and Distributed Computing
Lisbon, Portugal, September 1–3, 2021
Proceedings

Editors
Leonel Sousa (iD)
Universidade de Lisboa
Lisbon, Portugal

Nuno Roma (iD)
Universidade de Lisboa
Lisbon, Portugal

Pedro Tomás (iD)
Universidade de Lisboa
Lisbon, Portugal

ISSN 0302-9743   ISSN 1611-3349   (electronic)
Lecture Notes in Computer Science
ISBN 978-3-030-85664-9   ISBN 978-3-030-85665-6   (eBook)
https://doi.org/10.1007/978-3-030-85665-6

LNCS Sublibrary: SL1 – Theoretical Computer Science and General Issues

This Springer imprint is published by the registered company Springer Nature Switzerland AG
The registered company address is: Gewerbestrasse 11, 6330 Cham, Switzerland

Preface

This volume contains the papers presented at Euro-Par 2021, the 27th International European Conference on Parallel and Distributed Computing, held between September 1–3, 2021. Although Euro-Par 2021 had been planned to take place in Lisbon, Portugal, it was organized as a virtual conference, as a result of the COVID-19 pandemic.

For over 25 years, Euro-Par has brought together researchers in parallel and distributed computing. Founded by pioneers as a merger of the two thematically related European conference series PARLE and CONPAR-VAPP, Euro-Par started with the aim to create the main annual scientific event on parallel and distributed computing in Europe and to be the primary choice of professionals for the presentation of their latest results.

Since its inception, Euro-Par has covered all aspects of parallel and distributed computing, ranging from theory to practice; scaling from the smallest to the largest parallel and distributed systems; from fundamental computational problems and models to full-fledged applications; and from architecture and interface design and implementation to tools, infrastructures, and applications. Euro-Par's unique organization into topics provides an excellent forum for focused technical discussion as well as interaction with a large, broad, and diverse audience of researchers in academic institutions, public and private laboratories, and commercial stakeholders. Euro-Par's topics have always been oriented towards novel research issues and the current state of the art. Most topics have become constant entries, while new themes have emerged and been included in the conference. Euro-Par selects new organizers and chairs for every event, giving the opportunity to young researchers and leading to fresh ideas while ensuring tradition. Organizers and chairs of previous events support their successors. In this sense, the conference also promotes networking across borders, leading to the unique spirit of Euro-Par.

Previous conferences took place in Stockholm, Lyon, Passau, Southampton, Toulouse, Munich, Manchester, Paderborn, Klagenfurt, Pisa, Lisbon, Dresden, Rennes, Las Palmas, Delft, Ischia, Bordeaux, Rhodes, Aachen, Porto, Vienna, Grenoble, Santiago de Compostela, Turin, Göttingen, and Warsaw.

Thus, Euro-Par in Portugal followed the well-established format of its predecessors. The 27th Euro-Par conference was organized with the support of INESC-ID and Instituto Superior Técnico (Tecnico Lisboa) -the Faculty of Engineering of the University of Lisbon. Tecnico Lisboa is a renowned place for research in engineering, including in all fields related to electrical and computer engineering and computer science.

The topics of Euro-Par 2021 were organized into 10 tracks, namely:

- Compilers, Tools, and Environments
- Performance and Power Modeling, Prediction and Evaluation

- Scheduling and Load Balancing
- Data Management, Analytics, and Machine Learning
- Cluster, Cloud, and Edge Computing
- Theory and Algorithms for Parallel and Distributed Processing
- Parallel and Distributed Programming, Interfaces, and Languages
- Multicore and Manycore Parallelism
- Parallel Numerical Methods and Applications
- High-performance Architectures and Accelerators

Overall, 136 papers were submitted from 37 countries. The number of submitted papers, the wide topic coverage, and the aim of obtaining high-quality reviews resulted in a careful selection process involving a large number of experts. As the joint effort of the members of the Program Committee and of the 121 external reviewers, a total of 218 reviewers from 33 countries submitted 540 reviews: 10 papers received three reviews, 122 received four reviews, and 4 received 5 or more. On average, each paper received 4 reviews. The accepted papers were chosen after offline discussions in the reviewing system followed by a lively discussion during the paper selection meeting, which took place via video conference on April 19, 2021. As a result, 38 papers were selected to be presented at the conference and published in these proceedings, resulting in a 27.9% acceptance rate.

To increase reproducibility of the research, Euro-Par encourages authors to submit artifacts, such as source code, data sets, and reproducibility instructions. Along with the notification of acceptance, authors of accepted papers were encouraged to submit their artifacts. A total of 6 papers were complemented with their artifacts. These artifacts were then evaluated by the Artifact Evaluation Committee (AEC). The AEC managed to successfully reproduce the results of all of the 6 papers. These papers are marked in the proceedings by a special stamp; and the artifacts are available on-line in the Figshare repository.

In addition to the technical program, we had the pleasure of hosting three keynotes held by:

- Manish Parashar, University of Utah, USA,
- Alba Cristina Melo, University of Brasilia, Brazil,
- Keshav Pingali, University of Texas, USA.

Although Euro-Par 2021 was converted into a virtual event, it encouraged interaction and on-line discussions, in order to make it a successful and friendly meeting.

The conference program started with two days of workshops on specialized topics. Dora Blanco Heras and Ricardo Chaves ensured coordination and organization of this pre-conference event as workshop co-chairs. After the conference, a selection of the papers presented at the workshops will be published in a separate proceedings volume.

We would like to thank the authors, chairs, PC members, and reviewers for contributing to the success of Euro-Par 2021. Similarly, we would like to extend our appreciation to the Euro-Par Steering Committee for its support. Our mentor, Fernando Silva, devoted countless hours to this year's event, making sure we were on time and on track with all the (many) key elements of the conference. Our virtual task force led by Tiago Dias took care of various aspects of moving a physical conference to cyberspace.

August 2021   Leonel Sousa
                                                              Nuno Roma
                                                              Pedro Tomás

Organization

The Euro-Par Steering Committee

Full Members

Luc Bougé (SC Chair)	ENS Rennes, France
Fernando Silva (SC Vice-Chair)	University of Porto, Portugal
Dora Blanco Heras (Workshops Chair)	CiTIUS, University of Santiago de Compostela, Spain
Marco Aldinucci	University of Turin, Italy
Emmanuel Jeannot	Inria, Bordeaux, France
Christos Kaklamanis	Computer Technology Institute, Patras, Greece
Paul Kelly	Imperial College London, UK
Thomas Ludwig	University of Hamburg, Germany
Tomàs Margalef	Autonomous University of Barcelona, Spain
Wolfgang Nagel	Dresden University of Technology, Germany
Francisco Fernàndez Rivera	CiTIUS, University of Santiago de Compostela, Spain
Krzysztof Rzadca	University of Warsaw, Poland
Rizos Sakellariou	University of Manchester, UK
Henk Sips (Finance Chair)	Delft University of Technology, The Netherlands
Leonel Sousa	Universidade de Lisboa, Portugal
Domenico Talia	University of Calabria, Italy
Massimo Torquati (Artifacts Chair)	University of Pisa, Italy
Phil Trinder	University of Glasgow, UK
Denis Trystram	Grenoble Institute of Technology, France
Felix Wolf	Technical University of Darmstadt, Germany
Ramin Yahyapour	GWDG, Göttingen, Germany

Honorary Members

Christian Lengauer	University of Passau, Germany
Ron Perrott	Oxford e-Research Centre, UK
Karl Dieter Reinartz	University of Erlangen-Nürnberg, Germany

General Chair

Leonel Sousa	INESC-ID, IST, Universidade de Lisboa, Portugal

Workshop Chairs

Ricardo Chaves	INESC-ID, IST, Universidade de Lisboa, Portugal
Dora Blanco Heras	University of Santiago de Compostela, Spain

PhD Symposium Chairs

Aleksandar Ilic	INESC-ID, IST, Universidade de Lisboa, Portugal
Didem Unat	Koç University, Turkey

Submissions Chair

Nuno Roma	INESC-ID, IST, Universidade de Lisboa, Portugal

Publicity Chairs

Gabriel Falcão	IT, Universidade de Coimbra, Portugal
Maurício Breternitz	ISCTE, Instituto Universitário de Lisboa, Portugal

Web Chairs

Pedro Tomás	INESC-ID, IST, Universidade de Lisboa, Portugal
Helena Aidos	LASIGE, FCUL, Universidade de Lisboa, Portugal

Local Chairs

Tiago Dias	INESC-ID, ISEL, Instituto Politécnico de Lisboa, Portugal
Ricardo Nobre	INESC-ID, Portugal

Artifact Evaluation Committee

Nuno Neves	INESC-ID, Universidade de Lisboa, Portugal
Massimo Torquati	University of Pisa, Italy

Scientific Organization

Topic 1: Compilers, Tools, and Environments

Global Chair

Frank Hannig	Friedrich-Alexander-Universität Erlangen-Nürnberg, Germany

Local Chair

Gabriel Falcão	Instituto de Telecomunicações, Universidade de Coimbra, Portugal

Members

Izzat El Hajj	American University of Beirut, Lebanon
Simon Garcia Gonzalo	Barcelona Supercomputing Center, Spain
Hugh Leather	Facebook AI Research and The University of Edinburgh, UK
Josef Weidendorfer	TU München, Germany

Topic 2: Performance and Power Modeling, Prediction and Evaluation

Global Chair

Didem Unat	Koç University, Turkey

Local Chair

Aleksandar Ilic	INESC-ID, IST, Universidade de Lisboa, Portugal

Members

Laura Carrington	EP Analytics, USA
Milind Chabbi	Uber Technologies, USA
Bilel Hadri	KAUST Supercomputing Lab, Saudi Arabia
Jawad Haj-Yahya	ETH Zurich, Switzerland
Andreas Knüpfer	TU Dresden, Germany
Alexey Lastovetsky	University College Dublin, Ireland
Matthias Mueller	RWTH Aachen University, Germany
Emmanuelle Saillard	CRCN, Inria Bordeaux, France
Martin Schulz	Technical University Munich, Germany

Topic 3: Scheduling and Load Balancing

Global Chair

Oliver Sinnen	University of Auckland, New Zealand

Local Chair

Jorge Barbosa	Universidade do Porto, Portugal

Members

Giovanni Agosta	Politecnico di Milano, Italy
Bertrand Simon	University of Bremen, Germany
Luiz F. Bittencourt	University of Campinas, Brazil
Lúcia Drummond	Universidade Federal Fluminense, Brazil
Emmanuel Casseau	University of Rennes, Inria, CNRS, France
Fanny Dufossé	Inria Grenoble, France
Henri Casanova	University of Hawaii at Manoa, USA

Loris Marchal	CNRS, University of Lyon, LIP, France
Maciej Malawski	AGH University of Science and Technology, Poland
Malin Rau	Universität Hamburg, Germany
Pierre-Francois Dutot	Université Grenoble Alpes, France
Rizos Sakellariou	The University of Manchester, UK
Lucas Mello Schnorr	Federal University of Rio Grande do Sul, Brazil
Gang Zeng	Nagoya University, Japan

Topic 4: Data Management, Analytics, and Machine Learning

Global Chair

| Alex Delis | University of Athens, Greece |

Local Chair

| Helena Aidos | LASIGE, Universidade de Lisboa, Portugal |

Members

Angela Bonifati	Lyon 1 University, France
Pedro M. Ferreira	LASIGE, Universidade de Lisboa, Portugal
Panagiotis Liakos	University of Athens, Greece
Jorge Lobo	Universitat Pompeu Fabra, Spain
Paolo Romano	INESC-ID, Universidade de Lisboa, Portugal
Jacek Sroka	University of Warsaw, Poland
Zahir Tari	Royal Melbourne Institute University, Australia
Goce Trajcevski	Iowa State University, USA
Vassilios Verykios	Hellenic Open University, Greece
Demetris Zeinalipour	University of Cyprus, Cyprus

Topic 5: Cluster, Cloud, and Edge Computing

Global Chair

| Radu Prodan | University of Klagenfurt, Austria |

Local Chair

| Luís Veiga | INESC-ID, Universidade de Lisboa, Portugal |

Members

Juan J. Durillo	Leibniz Supercomputing Centre (LRZ), Germany
Felix Freitag	Polytechnic University of Catalonia, Spain
Aleksandar Karadimche	University for Information Science and Technology "St. Paul the Apostle", Macedonia
Attila Kertesz	University of Szeged, Hungary
Vincenzo de Maio	Technical University of Vienna, Austria
Joan-Manuel Marquès	Universitat Oberta de Catalunya, Spain

Rolando Martins   University of Porto, Portugal
Hervé Paulino   Universidade Nova de Lisboa, Portugal
Sasko Ristov   University of Innsbruck, Austria
José Simão   INESC-ID, ISEL, Portugal
Spyros Voulgaris   Vrije Universiteit Amsterdam, The Netherlands

Topic 6: Theory and Algorithms for Parallel and Distributed Processing

Global Chair

Andrea Pietracaprina   Università di Padova, Italy

Local Chair

João Lourenço   Universidade Nova de Lisboa, Portugal

Members

Adrian Francalanza   University of Malta, Malta
Ganesh Gopalakrishnan   University of Utah, USA
Klaus Havelund   NASA's Jet Propulsion Labratory, USA
Ulrich Meyer   Goethe-Universität Frankfurt, Germany
Emanuele Natale   Université Côte d'Azur, Inria-CNRS, France
Yihan Sun   University of California, Riverside, USA

Topic 7: Parallel and Distributed Programming, Interfaces, and Languages

Global Chair

Alfredo Goldman   University of São Paulo, Brazil

Local Chair

Ricardo Chaves   INESC-ID, IST, Universidade de Lisboa, Portugal

Members

Ivona Brandic   Vienna University of Technology, Austria
Dilma Da Silva   Texas A&M University, USA
Laurent Lefevre   Inria, France
Dejan Milojicic   HP Labs, USA
Nuno Preguiça   Universidade Nova de Lisboa, Portugal
Omer Rana   Cardiff University, UK
Lawrence Rauchwerger   University of Illinois at Urbana Champaign, USA
Noemi Rodriguez   PUC-Rio, Brazil
Stéphane Zuckerman   ETIS Laboratory, France

Topic 8: Multicore and Manycore Parallelism

Global Chair

Enrique S. Quintana Ortí   Universitat Politècnica de València, Spain

Local Chair

Nuno Roma   INESC-ID, IST, Universidade de Lisboa, Portugal

Members

Emmanuel Jeannot   Inria, France
Philippe A. Navaux   Federal University of Rio Grande do Sul, Brazil
Robert Schöne   TU Dresden, Germany

Topic 9: Parallel Numerical Methods and Applications

Global Chair

Stanimire Tomov   University of Tennessee, USA

Local Chair

Sergio Jimenez   Universidad de Extremadura, Spain

Members

Hartwig Anzt   Karlsruhe Institute of Technology, Germany
Alfredo Buttari   CNRS/IRIT Toulouse, France
José M. Granado-Criado   University of Extremadura, Spain
Hatem Ltaief   King Abdullah University of Science and Technology,
    Saudi Arabia
Álvaro Rubio-Largo   University of Extremadura, Spain

Topic 10: High-performance Architectures and Accelerators

Global Chair

Samuel Thibault   Université de Bordeaux, France

Local Chair

Pedro Tomás   INESC-ID, IST, Universidade de Lisboa, Portugal

Members

Michaela Blott   Xilinx, Ireland
Toshihiro Hanawa   University of Tokyo, Japan
Sascha Hunold   Vienna University of Technology, Austria
Naoya Maruyama   NVIDIA, USA
Miquel Moreto   Barcelona Supercomputing Center, Spain

PhD Symposium

Chairs

Didem Unat	Koç University, Turkey
Aleksandar Ilic	INESC-ID, IST, Universidade de Lisboa, Portugal

Members

Mehmet Esat Belviranli	Colorado School of Mines, USA
Xing Cai	Simula Research Laboratory, Norway
Anshu Dubey	Argonne National Lab, USA
Francisco D. Igual	Universidad Complutense de Madrid, Spain
Sergio Santander-Jiménez	University of Extremadura, Spain
Lena Oden	FernUniversität Hagen, Germany

Artifacts Eavaluation

Chairs

Nuno Neves	INESC-ID, IST, Universidade de Lisboa, Portugal
Massimo Torquati	University of Pisa, Italy

Members

Diogo Marques	INESC-ID, IST, Universidade de Lisboa, Portugal
Alberto Martinelli	Università degli Studi di Torino, Italy
João Bispo	INESCTEC, Faculty of Engineering, University of Porto, Portugal
João Vieira	INESC-ID, IST, Universidade de Lisboa, Portugal
Iacopo Colonnelli	Università di Torino, Italy
Ricardo Nobre	INESC-ID, IST, Universidade de Lisboa, Portugal
Nuno Paulino	INESCTEC, Faculty of Engineering, University of Porto, Portugal
Luís Fiolhais	INESC-ID, IST, Universidade de Lisboa, Portugal

Additional Reviewers

Ahmad Abdelfattah	Hamza Baniata	Adrien Cassagne
Prateek Agrawal	Raul Barbosa	Sebastien Cayrols
Kadir Akbudak	Christian Bartolo Burlò	Daniel Chillet
Mohammed Al Farhan	Naama Ben-David	Terry Cojean
Maicon Melo Alves	Jean Luca Bez	Soteris Constantinou
Alexandra Amarie	Mauricio Breternitz	João Costa Seco
Filipe Araujo	Rafaela Brum	Nuno Cruz Garcia
Cédric Augonnet	Rocío Carratalá-Sáez	Arthur Carvalho Cunha
Alan Ayala	Caroline Caruana	Alexandre Denis
Bartosz Balis	Pablo Carvalho	Nicolas Denoyelle

Vladimir Dimić
Petr Dobias
Panagiotis Drakatos
Anthony Dugois
Lionel Eyraud-Dubois
Pablo Ezzatti
Carlo Fantozzi
Johannes Fischer
Sebti Foufou
Emilio Francesquini
Gabriel Freytag
Giulio Gambardella
João Garcia
Afton Geil
Anja Gerbes
Fritz Goebel
David Gradinariu
Yan Gu
Amina Guermouche
Harsh Vardhan
Changwan Hong
Sergio Iserte
Kazuaki Ishizaki
Marc Jorda
Nikolaos Kallimanis
Ioanna Karageorgou
Alexandros Karakasidis

Dimitrios Karapiperis
Raffi Khatchadourian
Cédric Killian
Andreas Konstantinides
Orestis Korakitis
Matthias Korch
Sotiris Kotsiantis
Thomas Lambert
Matthew Alan Le Brun
Lucas Leandro Nesi
Ivan Lujic
Piotr Luszczek
Manolis Maragoudakis
Andras Markus
Roland Mathà
Miguel Matos
Kazuaki Matsumura
Narges Mehran
Aleksandr Mikhalev
Lei Mo
Lucas Morais
Grégory Mounié
Paschalis Mpeis
Pratik Nayak
Alexandros Ntoulas
Ken O'Brien
Cristobal Ortega

Yiannis Papadopoulos
Marina Papatriantafilou
Miguel Pardal
Maciej Pawlik
Lucian Petrica
Geppino Pucci
Long Qu
Vinod Rebello
Tobias Ribizel
Rafael Rodríguez-Sánchez
Evangelos Sakkopoulos
Matheus S. Serpa
João A. Silva
João Soares
João Sobrinho
Nehir Sonmez
Philippe Swartvagher
Antonio Teofilo
Luan Teylo
Yu-Hsiang Tsai
Volker Turau
Jerzy Tyszkiewicz
Manolis Tzagarakis
Yaman Umuroglu
Alejandro Valero
Huijun Wang
Jasmine Xuereb

Euro-Par 2021 Invited Talks

Big Data and Extreme-Scales: Computational Science in the 21st Century

Manish Parashar

University of Utah, USA
manish.parashar@utah.edu

Extreme scales and big data are essential to computational and data-enabled science and engineering in the 21st, promising dramatic new insights into natural and engineered systems. However, data-related challenges are limiting the potential impact of application workflows enabled by current and emerging extreme scale, high-performance, distributed computing environments. These data-intensive application workflows involve dynamic coordination, interactions and data coupling between multiple application processes that run at scale on different resources, and with services for monitoring, analysis and visualization and archiving, and present challenges due to increasing data volumes and complex data-coupling patterns, system energy constraints, increasing failure rates, etc. In this talk I will explore some of these challenges and investigate how solutions based on data sharing abstractions, managed data pipelines, data-staging service, and in-situ/in-transit data placement and processing can be used to help address them. This research is part of the DataSpaces project at the Scientific Computing and Imaging (SCI) Institute, University of Utah.

HPC for Bioinformatics: The Genetic Sequence Comparison Quest for Performance

Alba Cristina Melo

University of Brasilia, Brazil
`alves@unb.br`

Genetic Sequence Comparison is an important operation in Bioinformatics, executed routinely worldwide. Two relevant algorithms that compare genetic sequences are the Smith-Waterman (SW) algorithm and Sankoff's algorithm. The Smith-Waterman algorithm is widely used for pairwise comparisons and it obtains the optimal result in quadratic time - $O(n^2)$, where n is the length of the sequences. The Sankoff algorithm is used to structurally align two sequences and it computes the optimal result in $O(n^4)$ time. In order to accelerate these algorithms, many parallel strategies were proposed in the literature. However, the alignment of whole chromosomes with hundreds of millions of characters with the SW algorithm is still a very challenging task, which requires extraordinary computing power. Likewise, obtaining the structural alignment of two sequences with the Sankoff algorithm requires parallel approaches. In this talk, we first present our MASA-CUDAlign tool, which was used to pairwise align real DNA sequences with up to 249 millions of characters in a cluster with 512 GPUs, achieving the best performance in the literature in 2021. We will present and discuss the innovative features of the most recent version of MASA-CUDAlign: parallelogram execution, incremental speculation, block pruning and score-share balancing strategies. We will also show performance and energy results in homogeneous and heterogeneous GPU clusters. Then, we will discuss the design of our CUDA-Sankoff tool and its innovative strategy to exploit multi-level wavefront parallelism. At the end, we will show a COVID-19 case study, where we use the tools discussed in this talk to compare the SARS-CoV-2 genetic sequences, considering the reference sequence and its variants.

Knowledge Graphs, Graph AI, and the Need for High-performance Graph Computing

Keshav Pingali

Katana Graph & The University of Texas at Austin, USA
pingali@cs.utexas.edu

Knowledge Graphs now power many applications across diverse industries such as FinTech, Pharma and Manufacturing. Data volumes are growing at a staggering rate, and graphs with hundreds of billions edges are not uncommon. Computations on such data sets include querying, analytics, and pattern mining, and there is growing interest in using machine learning to perform inference on large graphs. In many applications, it is necessary to combine these operations seamlessly to extract actionable intelligence as quickly as possible. Katana Graph is a start-up based in Austin and the Bay Area that is building a scale-out platform for seamless, high-performance computing on such graph data sets. I will describe the key features of the Katana Graph Engine that enable high performance, some important use cases for this technology from Katana's customers, and the main lessons I have learned from doing a startup after a career in academia.

Euro-Par 2021 Topics Overview

Topic 1: Compilers, Tools and Environments

Frank Hannig and Gabriel Falcao

This topic addresses programming tools and system software for all kinds of parallel computer architectures, ranging from low-power embedded high-performance systems, multi- and many-core processors, accelerators to large-scale computers and cloud computing. Focus areas include compilation and software testing to design well-defined components and verify their necessary structural, behavioral, and parallel interaction properties. It deals with tools, analysis software, and runtime environments to address the challenges of programming and executing the parallel architectures mentioned above. Moreover, the topic deals with methods and tools for optimizing non-functional properties such as performance, programming productivity, robustness, energy efficiency, and scalability.

The topic received eight submissions across the subjects mentioned before. The papers were thoroughly reviewed by the six program committee members of the topic and external reviewers. Each submission was subjected to rigorous review from four peers. After intensely scrutinizing the reviews, we were pleased to select two high-quality papers for the technical program, corresponding to a per-topic acceptance ratio of 25%.

The first accepted paper "ALONA: Automatic Loop Nest Approximation with Reconstruction and Space Pruning" by Daniel Maier et al. deals with approximate computing. More specifically, the contribution advances the state-of-the-art in pattern-based multi-dimensional loop perforation. The second paper "Automatic low-overhead load-imbalance detection in MPI applications" by Peter Arzt et al. presents a method for detecting load imbalances in MPI applications. The approach has been implemented into the Performance Instrumentation Refinement Automation (PIRA) framework.

We would like to thank the authors who responded to our call for papers, the members of the Program Committee and the additional external reviewers who, with their opinion and expertise, ensured a program of the highest quality. Many thanks to Leonel Sousa for the tremendous overall organization of Euro-Par 2021 and his engaging interaction.

Topic 2: Performance and Power Modeling, Prediction and Evaluation

Didem Unat and Aleksandar Ilic

In recent years, a range of novel methods and tools have been developed for the evaluation, design, and modeling of parallel and distributed systems and applications. At the same time, the term 'performance' has broadened to also include scalability and energy efficiency, and touching reliability and robustness in addition to the classic resource-oriented notions.

The papers submitted to this topic represent researchers working on different aspects of performance modeling, evaluation, and prediction, be it for systems or for applications running on the whole range of parallel and distributed systems (multi-core and heterogeneous architectures, HPC systems, grid and cloud contexts etc.). The accepted papers present novel research in all areas of performance modeling, prediction and evaluation, and help bringing together current theory and practice.

The topic received 14 submissions, which were thoroughly reviewed by the 11 members of the topic program committee and external reviewers. Out of all submissions and after a careful and detailed discussion among committee members, we finally decided to accept 3 papers, resulting in a per-topic acceptance ratio of 21%.

We would like to thank the authors for their submissions, the Euro-Par 2021 Organizing Committee for their help throughout all the process, and the PC members and the reviewers for providing timely and detailed reviews, and for participating in the discussion we carried on after the reviews were received.

Topic 3: Scheduling and Load Balancing

Oliver Sinnen and Jorge Barbosa

New computing systems offer the opportunity to reduce the response times and the energy consumption of the applications by exploiting the levels of parallelism. Modern computer architectures are often composed of heterogeneous compute resources and exploiting them efficiently is a complex and challenging task. Scheduling and load balancing techniques are key instruments to achieve higher performance, lower energy consumption, reduced resource usage, and real-time properties of applications.

This topic attracts papers on all aspects related to scheduling and load balancing on parallel and distributed machines, from theoretical foundations for modelling and designing efficient and robust scheduling policies to experimental studies, applications, and practical tools and solutions. It applies to multi-/manycore processors, embedded systems, servers, heterogeneous and accelerated systems, HPC clusters as well as distributed systems such as clouds and global computing platforms.

A total of 23 full submissions were received in this track, each of which received at least three reviews, the large majority four. Following a thorough and lively discussion of the reviews among the 16 PC members, 7 submissions were accepted, giving an acceptance rate of 30%.

The chairs would like to sincerely thank all the authors for their high quality submissions, the Euro-Par 2021 Organizing Committee for all their valuable help, and the PC members for their excellent work. They all have contributed to making this topic and Euro-Par an excellent forum to discuss scheduling and load balancing challenges.

Topic 4: Data Management, Analytics and Machine Learning

Alex Delis and Helena Aidos

Many areas of science, industry, and commerce are producing extreme-scale data that must be processed — stored, managed, analyzed – in order to extract useful knowledge. This topic seeks papers in all aspects of distributed and parallel data management and data analysis. For example, cloud and grid data-intensive processing, parallel and distributed machine learning, HPC in situ data analytics, parallel storage systems, scalable data processing workflows, and distributed stream processing were all in the scope of this topic.

This year, the topic received 20 submissions, which were thoroughly reviewed by the 12 members of the track program committee and external reviewers. Out of all the submissions and after a careful and detailed discussion among committee members, we finally decided to accept 4 papers, resulting in a per-topic acceptance ratio of 20%.

We would like to express our thanks to the authors for their submissions, the Euro-Par 2021 Organizing Committee for their help throughout all the process, the PC members and the external reviewers for providing timely and detailed reviews, and for participating in the discussion we carried on after the reviews were received.

Topic 5: Cluster, Cloud and Edge Computing

Radu Prodan and Luís Veiga

While the term Cluster Computing is hardware-oriented and determines the organization of large computer systems at one location, the term Cloud Computing usually focuses on using these large systems at a distributed scale, typically combined with virtualization technology and a business model on top. Despite their differences, there exist many complementary interdependencies between both fields that need further exploration. This topic of the Euro-Par conference is open to new research, which spans across these two related areas. In both Cluster and Cloud Computing, much relevant research works focus on performance, reliability, energy efficiency, and the impact of novel processor architectures. Since Cloud Computing tries to hide the hardware and system software details from the users, research issues include various forms of virtualization and their impact on performance, resource management, and business models that address system owner and user interests.

In the last years, and primarily due to the increasing number of IoT applications, the combination of local resources and Cloud Computing, also referred to as Fog and Edge Computing, has received growing interest. This concept has led to many research questions, like an appropriate distribution of subtasks to the available systems under various constraints.

This year, 14 papers were submitted to this track and received at least four reviews from the 13 program committee members. Following the thorough discussion of the reviews, the conference chairs decided to include five submissions to the track in the overall conference program. The accepted papers address relevant and timely topics such as cloud computing, fault-tolerance, edge computing, energy efficiency.

The track chairs thank all the authors for their submissions, the Euro-Par 2021 Organizing Committee for their help throughout the process, the PC members, and the reviewers to provide timely and detailed reviews and participate in the discussions.

Topic 6: Theory and Algorithms for Parallel and Distributed Processing

Andrea Pietracaprina and João M. Lourenço

Nowadays parallel and distributed processing is ubiquitous. Multicore processors are available on smartphones, laptops, servers and supercomputing nodes. Also, many devices cooperate in fully distributed and heterogeneous systems to provide a wide array of services. Despite recent years have witnessed astonishing progress in this field, many research challenges remain open concerning fundamental issues as well as the design and analysis of efficient, scalable, and robust algorithmic solutions with provable performance and quality guarantees.

This year, a total of 12 submissions were received in this track. Each submission received four reviews from the eight PC members. Following the thorough discussion of the reviews, four original and high quality papers have been accepted to this general topic of the theory of parallel and distributed algorithms, with the acceptance rate of 33%.

We would like to thank the authors for their excellent submissions, the Euro-Par 2021 Organizing Committee for their help throughout all the process, and the PC members and the external reviewers for providing timely and detailed reviews, and for participating in the discussions that helped reach the decisions.

Topic 7: Parallel and Distributed Programming, Interfaces, and Languages

Alfredo Goldman and Ricardo Chaves

Parallel and distributed applications require appropriate programming abstractions and models, efficient design tools, parallelization techniques and practices. This topic attracted papers presenting new results and practical experience in this domain: efficient and effective parallel languages, interfaces, libraries and frameworks, as well as solid practical and experimental validation.

The accepted papers emphasize research on high-performance, resilient, portable, and scalable parallel programs via appropriate parallel and distributed programming model, interface and language support. Contributions that assess programming abstractions and automation for usability, performance, task-based parallelism or scalability were valued.

This year, the topic received 14 submissions, which were thoroughly reviewed by the 11 members of the track program committee and external reviewers. After careful and detailed discussion among committee members, we decided to accept 5 of the submissions, giving a per-topic acceptance ratio of 36%.

The topic chairs would like to thank all the authors who submitted papers for their contribution to the success of this track, the Euro-Par 2021 Committee for their support, and the external reviewers for their high-quality reviews and their valuable feedback.

Topic 8: Multicore and Manycore Parallelism

Enrique S. Quintana Ortí and Nuno Roma

Modern homogeneous and heterogeneous multicore and manycore architectures are now part of the high-end, embedded, and mainstream computing scene and can offer impressive performance for many applications. This architecture trend has been driven by the need to reduce power consumption, increase processor utilization, and address the memory-processor speed gap. However, the complexity of these new architectures has created several programming challenges, and achieving performance on these systems is often a difficult task. This topic seeks to explore productive programming of multicore and manycore systems, as well as stand-alone systems with large numbers of cores and various types of accelerators; this can also include hybrid and heterogeneous systems with different types of multicore processors. It focuses on novel research and solutions in the form of programming models, frameworks and languages; compiler optimizations and techniques; lock-free algorithms and data structures; transactional memory advances; performance and power trade-offs and scalability; libraries and runtime systems; innovative applications and case studies; techniques and tools for discovering, analysing, understanding, and managing multicore parallelism; and in general, tools and techniques to increase the programmability of multicore, manycore, and heterogeneous systems, in the context of general-purpose, high-performance, and embedded parallel computing.

This year 7 papers covering some of these issues were submitted. Each of them was reviewed by four reviewers. Finally, one regular paper was selected. It proposes an extension to the oneAPI programming model in order to provide the ability to exploit multiple heterogeneous devices when executing the same kernel following a co-execution strategy. It also discusses the implementation of common load-balancing schemes, including static and dynamic allocation.

We would like to express our gratitude to all the authors for submitting their work. We also thank the reviewers for their great job and useful comments. Finally, we would like to thank the Euro-Par organization and steering committees for their continuous help, and for producing a nice working environment to smooth the process.

Topic 9: Parallel Numerical Methods and Applications

Stanimire Tomov and Sergio Jimenez

The need for high-performance computing is driven by the need for large-scale simulation and data analysis in science and engineering, finance, life sciences, etc. This requires the design of highly scalable numerical methods and algorithms that are able to efficiently exploit modern computer architectures. The scalability of these algorithms and methods and their ability to effectively use high-performance heterogeneous resources is critical to improving the performance of computational and data science applications.

This conference topic provides a forum for presenting and discussing recent developments in parallel numerical algorithms and their implementation on current parallel architectures, including many-core and hybrid architectures. The submitted papers address algorithmic design, implementation details, performance analysis, as well as integration of parallel numerical methods in large-scale applications.

This year, the topic received 14 submissions, which were thoroughly reviewed by the 7 members of the track program committee and a number of external reviewers. Each submission received four reviews. After careful and constructive discussions among committee members, we decided to accept five papers, resulting in a per-topic acceptance ratio of 36%.

We would like to sincerely thank all the authors for their submissions, the Euro-Par 2021 Organizing Committee for all their valuable help, and the reviewers for their excellent work. They all have contributed to making this topic and Euro-Par an excellent forum to discuss parallel numerical methods and applications.

Topic 10: High-performance Architectures and Accelerators

Samuel Thibault and Pedro Tomás

Various computing platforms provide distinct potentials for achieving massive performance levels. Beyond general-purpose multi-processors, examples of computing platforms include graphics processing units (GPUs), multi-/many-core co-processors, as well as customizable devices, such as FPGA-based systems, streaming data-flow architectures or low-power embedded systems. However, fully exploiting the computational performance of such devices and solutions often requires tuning the target applications to identify and exploit the parallel opportunities.

Hence, this topic explores new directions across this variety of architecture possibilities, with contributions along the whole design stack. On the hardware side, the scope of received papers spans from general-purpose to specialized computing architectures, including methodologies to efficiently exploit the memory hierarchy and to manage network communications. On the software side, the scope of received papers included libraries, runtime tools and benchmarks. Additionally, we also received application-specific submissions that contributed with new insights and/or solutions to fully exploit different high-performance computing platforms for signal processing, big data and machine learning application domains.

The topic received 10 submissions, which were thoroughly reviewed by the 7 members of the track program committee and external reviewers. Out of all the submissions and after a careful and detailed discussion among committee members, we finally decided to accept 2 papers, resulting in a per-topic acceptance ratio of 20%.

The topic chairs would like to thank all the authors who submitted papers for their contribution to the success of this topic, the Euro-Par 2021 Committee for their support, as well as all the external reviewers for their high-quality reviews and their valuable feedback.

Contents

Data Management, Analytics and Machine Learning

Cluster, Cloud and Edge Computing

Theory and Algorithms for Parallel and Distributed Processing

Parallel and Distributed Programming, Interfaces, and Languages

Compilers, Tools and Environments

ALONA: Automatic Loop Nest Approximation with Reconstruction and Space Pruning

Daniel Maier[1](✉), Biagio Cosenza[2], and Ben Juurlink[1]

[1] Technische Universität Berlin, Berlin, Germany
daniel.maier@tu-berlin.de
[2] University of Salerno, Fisciano, Italy

Abstract. Approximate computing comprises a large variety of techniques that trade the accuracy of an application's output for other metrics such as computing time or energy cost. Many existing approximation techniques focus on loops such as loop perforation, which skips iterations for faster, approximated computation. This paper introduces ALONA, a novel approach for automatic loop nest approximation based on polyhedral compilation. ALONA's compilation framework applies a sequence of loop approximation transformations, generalizes state-of-the-art perforation techniques, and introduces new multi-dimensional approximation schemes. The framework includes a reconstruction technique that significantly improves the accuracy of the approximations and a transformation space pruning method based on Barvinok's counting that removes inaccurate approximations. Evaluated on a collection of more than twenty applications from PolyBench/C, ALONA discovers new approximations that are better than state-of-the-art techniques in both approximation accuracy and performance.

1 Introduction

Many real-world applications can trade the accuracy of an application's result for other metrics, typically performance or energy. Approximate computing is an emerging paradigm that explicitly exploits this gap. Prior work investigates both hardware and software techniques [23]. Software techniques include soft slices [31] and mixed-precision tuning [8]. A popular approach is to attack the problem at loop level. Loop perforation [33] is a general-purpose technique that lowers the accuracy of loops by skipping loop iterations. Similarly, loop perforation can also be applied to data-parallel kernels executed on GPUs. Paraprox [30] is a framework for the approximation of data-parallel programs that operates on commodity hardware systems. More recently, these perforation techniques have been augmented with a reconstruction phase that improves the accuracy of perforated kernels [21].

While loops are generally an important target for both approximation and optimization techniques, e.g., loop-level parallelization, existing loop-level

ⓒ Springer Nature Switzerland AG 2021
L. Sousa et al. (Eds.): Euro-Par 2021, LNCS 12820, pp. 3–18, 2021.
https://doi.org/10.1007/978-3-030-85665-6_1

approximation techniques focus on one loop and a specific dimension instead of taking the whole iteration domain of all loop nests into consideration.

Polyhedral compilation has been proven to be an effective way to reason about loops. Polyhedral techniques can potentially target any affine loop nest, and perform a variety of tasks such as the efficient application of code transformations [4,27], the accurate modeling of performance and other metrics [1,15], and automatic parallelization [3,5].

We explore how the polyhedral model can be effectively used for the implementation of automatic approximation techniques targeting loop nests. In particular, we use it to efficiently handle a sequence of code transformations, which in our case includes loop perforation, and to filter the large set of possible approximations using a metric based on Barvinok's counting of the number of the exact and approximate loop iterations [2]. Furthermore, we provide a signal reconstruction step implemented as a post-processing technique that improves the accuracy by reconstructing missing values in the final result and provides an interface for application-specific reconstruction.

Our approach is fully compatible with existing polyhedral techniques that focus on automatic parallelization, and, in fact, extends existing state-of-the-art perforation frameworks such as Paraprox [30] and Sculptor [20] in terms of supported approximation schemes, and improves them in terms of accuracy and performance.

The contributions of this work are:

1. We introduce ALONA, the first compiler approach for automatic approximation of affine loop nests based on polyhedral techniques. ALONA generalizes existing state-of-the-art perforation techniques and can model multi-dimensional approximation schemes (Sect. 3.2, evaluated in Sect. 6.2).
2. ALONA's accuracy is significantly improved by supporting signal reconstruction techniques that mitigate the error by reconstructing missing values in the output (Sect. 4, evaluated in Sect. 6.3).
3. To efficiently handle the large transformation space, ALONA proposes an approximation space pruning technique based on Barvinok's counting of loop iterations (Sect. 5, evaluated in Sect. 6.4).
4. We experimentally evaluate the proposed polyhedral perforation framework on a collection of more than twenty benchmarks from PolyBench and Paraprox (Sect. 6). Results show that ALONA discovers new approximations and outperforms state-of-the-art methods.

2   Related Work

Approximate computing is an emerging paradigm where accuracy is traded for a gain in performance or a reduction in energy consumption. This trade-off is feasible because there is often a gap between the accuracy provided by a system and the accuracy required by an application. Research in approximate computing exploits this gap using a variety of approaches, ranging from hardware-supported techniques such as Truffle [11], CADE [16] and Replica [12], to pure software methods, including compilers and APIs, which we review in this section.

The Approxilyzer framework [35] quantifies the significance of instructions in programs when considering the output accuracy; given a program and an end-to-end quality metric, it selects a set of instructions as candidates for approximation by introducing bit errors. TAFFO [8] is a dynamic assistant for floating to fixed point conversion. A general-purpose software technique, extended and refined in many recent works [19–21], is *loop perforation* [33]. Loops are the bottleneck in many applications. Loop perforation skips loop iterations (or part of loop iterations) in order to reduce the compute load and to gain performance. Paraprox [30] is a framework for the approximation of data-parallel programs. It uses approximation techniques specifically tailored to specific data-parallel patterns. For instance, stencil patterns are approximated using center, row, and column value approximation. Maier et al. [21] extend these patterns with an additional reconstruction phase that exploits GPU's local memory for better approximation accuracy. Sculptor [20] moves the scope of perforation from loop iterations to individual statements and explores dynamic perforation, e.g., a perforation pattern that changes during the runtime of a program. Different phases during program execution with individual sensitivity towards approximation were explored by Mitra et al. [22]. Lashgar et al. [19] extend the OpenACC programming model with support for loop perforation. Relaxation of synchronizations is studied in the parallelizing compiler HELIX-UP [7] and by Deiana et al. [10] who propose a C++ language extension for non-deterministic programs. Some approaches focus on other parallel semantics, e.g., speculative lock elision [18], task discarding [29], and breakable dependence [34].

Polyhedral compilation has been proven as an effective way to reason about loops, both in terms of transformation and modeling. Polyhedral techniques target affine loop nests and can be used for a variety of tasks such as the efficient application of code transformations or the design of performance models. The polyhedral approach is nowadays in use by several automatic parallelization compilers, notable examples are Pluto [3,6], Pluto+ [5], PPCG [36], Polly [14], and speculative parallelization [17]. High-level loop transformations are critical for performance; however, finding the best sequence of transformations is difficult, and resulting transformations are both machine- and program-dependent. As optimizing compilers often use simplistic performance models, iterative compilation [13,25,26] is widely used to maximize performance. Adaptive Code Refinement [32] is a semi-automatic approach that relies on the polyhedral representation of stencil programs to apply transformations and to generate an approximated version of the code.

3   ALONA

We show the compilation workflow of our framework in Fig. 1 and it comprises of eight steps. (1) Starting from the accurate program the SCoPs are extracted. (2) Create the approximation space by generating perforated SCoPs for each SCoP.

(3) In the next step, the Barvinok score of each approximation is calculated. (4) The approximated SCoPs are sorted based on the score. (5) The approximation space is pruned. (6) From the remaining approximated SCoPS, the source code is synthesized. (7) The selected programs are compiled and executed while recording performance and accuracy. (8) Finally, Pareto-optimal solutions are selected. Optionally, a reconstruction phase is performed after step 6.

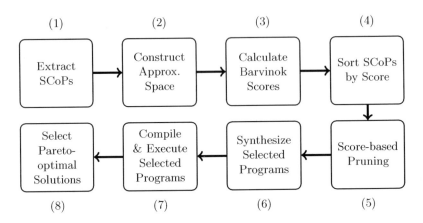

Fig. 1. ALONA's Compilation Workflow.

3.1 Polyhedral Loop Nest Perforation

Loop perforation is the technique of skipping parts of a loop. ALONA implements loop nest perforation with the tools provided by the polyhedral model. Loop perforation transforms loops to execute a subset of their iterations in order to reduce the amount of computational work [33]. This transformation can be accomplished, e.g., by changing the increment of the loop variable or by modifying the loop start and end. Listing 1.2 shows the perforated loop of Listing 1.1: the loop variable i is incremented by 2 instead of 1 and, therefore, every other loop iteration is perforated.

```
for(i=0; i<=7; i++) {
    /* work() */
}
```

```
for(i=0; i<=7; i+=2) {
    /* work() */
}
```

Listing 1.1. Original Loop.   **Listing 1.2.** Perforated Loop.

3.2 Polyhedral Model

The polyhedral model represents loops by convex polyhedra and uses parametric integer programming for analysis and transformation. A polyhedron is a convex set of points in a lattice, i.e., a set of points in a $\mathbb{Z}$ vector space that is bounded by affine inequalities. Loop nests, in their algebraic representation, are called *static control parts* (SCoP). A SCoP contains all information about control and data flow. Loop nests are usually required to have a statically defined control flow. A SCoP is a maximal set of consecutive statements where loop bounds and conditionals only depend on invariants and global parameters. The global parameters are constant but statically unknown and only available during runtime.

```
for(i=0; i<=7; i++) {
S1:  C[i] = 0;
        for(j=0; j<=7; j++) {
S2:      C[i] += A[i][j] * B[j];
        }
}
```

Listing 1.3. Accurate Loop Nest.

Listing 1.3 shows an exemplary loop nest that computes the matrix-vector product $C = A \cdot B$, and which we use throughout this section to provide examples of iteration domain and memory access functions. The loop nest contains two SCoPs: $S1$ and $S2$. The outer loop runs from $i = 0$ to $i \leq 7$, incrementing i for every iteration and initializing $C[i] = 0$. The inner loop runs from $j = 0$ to $j \leq 7$, incrementing j, reading from $C[i]$, $A[i][j]$ and $B[j]$ and writing to $C[i]$.

The *iteration domain* represents the iterations of a statement in a loop nest and describes the dynamic instances of all statements in the SCoP. A set of affine inequalities defines all possible values of the surrounding loop iterators. Each instance of a statement S is identified by (S, i) where i is the *iteration vector* that contains the values of the loop indices of the surrounding loops.

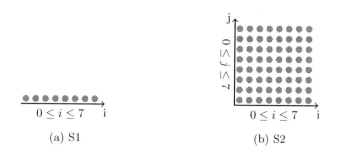

(a) S1   (b) S2

Fig. 2. Iteration Domain for the Loop Nest in Listing 1.3.

The set of inequalities for SCoP $S1$ in Listing 1.3 consists of $0 \leq i \leq 7$. The inequalities bounding the iteration domain of $S2$ are $0 \leq i \leq 7$ and $0 \leq j \leq 7$. The iteration domain defined by these inequalities is shown in Fig. 2. While $S1$ is one-dimensional, $S2$ has two dimensions spanned by i and j.

Memory access functions describe the locations of data that is accessed by statements. Memory accesses are performed through array references. For each statement S, two sets $\mathcal{L}^S$ and $\mathcal{R}^S$ exist, each containing (M, f) pairs. Each pair is a reference to a variable M that is accessed (written $\mathcal{L}$ or read $\mathcal{R}$) and a data access function f that maps the iteration vector in $\mathcal{D}^S$ to the memory location in the variable M. The arrow $\rightarrow$ denotes the mapping of a statement $S(i)$ with iteration vector i to variable $M(i)$ where i denotes the location in M. The memory access functions for Listing 1.3 are $\mathcal{L}^{S1} = S1(i) \rightarrow C(i)$, $\mathcal{R}^{S1} = \emptyset$ and $\mathcal{L}^{S2} = S2(i) \rightarrow C(i)$, and $\mathcal{R}^{S2} = S2(i,j) \rightarrow A(i,j), B(j), C(i)$.

Polyhedral Transformations are accomplished in the polyhedral representation of a loop nest. These transformations are constructed out of a set of transformation primitives that mostly correspond to simple polyhedral operations. By composition of an arbitrary number of transformations, complex optimizations can be built. The actual code generation happens after all transformations have been applied and this step is independent of the actual transformations.

3.3   Polyhedral Loop Perforation

Polyhedral loop perforation is implemented in two steps: shrinkage of the iteration domain, and adjustment of the memory accesses.

(1) The iteration domain is bounded by affine inequalities and, in order to shrink the size of the iteration domain, we alter these inequalities. First, the dimension which should be reduced in size has to be identified together with the loop variable, i.e., i. Next, we alter the inequalities to reflect the new size of the iteration domain. Although this can be done in many ways, we explain here for reasons of simplicity the following approach: In the inequalities, we multiply all occurrences of i with the perforation factor $f = 2$. Consider again SCoP S2 in Fig. 2b. First, we shrink the iteration domain by the perforation factor. The resulting iteration domain is visualized in Fig. 3a. The iteration domain is now half the size in the i-dimension and the inequality for i is updated.

(2) We adjust the memory accesses. Otherwise, a whole chunk of loop instances is perforated instead of every other instance. The adjustment of the memory accesses is closely related to the perforation factor f. In fact, in each memory access, all occurrences of the loop index variable are multiplied by the loop perforation factor, i.e., i becomes 2*i. Using this approach, we achieve the effect of a perforated iteration domain, while the iteration domain is in fact dense and convex. Recall the memory access functions for SCoP S2 from Sect. 3.2: $\mathcal{L}^{S2} = S2(i) \rightarrow C(i)$, and $\mathcal{R}^{S2} = S2(i,j) \rightarrow A(i,j), B(j), C(i)$. We multiply every occurrence of i with 2 in order to adjust the memory accesses. We use $\mathcal{L}_p$ and $\mathcal{R}_p$ to denote the perforated memory access functions: $\mathcal{L}_p^{S2} = S2(i) \rightarrow C(2i)$, and $\mathcal{R}_p^{S2} = S2(i,j) \rightarrow A(2i,j), B(j), C(2i)$. The result is depicted in Fig. 3b.

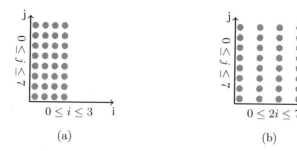

Fig. 3. The intermediate steps of polyhedral loop perforation.

3.4   Extensions to Classical Loop Perforation

Classical loop perforation [33] has been refined to include parallel programs [30], to perforate on statement-level and using non-static pattern [20], or to perforate threads on GPUs [21]. This section shows how our approach generalizes existing approximation schemes, which are all covered by our framework.

Paraprox [30] uses three schemes to approximate stencil data access patterns: the center scheme that uses the center value in a stencil to approximate the neighboring values; the rows scheme that perforates two out of three rows by using one row to approximate the row above and the row below; and the column scheme that is a 90° rotated row scheme. The rows and columns scheme can be implemented straightforwardly using polyhedral perforation on the corresponding inner or outer loop. The center scheme can be obtained by applying first a perforation of rows and successively a perforation of columns.

Sculptor [20] extends the perforation from loop iterations to individual statements and uses dynamic perforation patterns instead of being limited to fixed patterns for the whole loop. Sculptor operates on LLVM bitcode, while we operate on high-level C code. Our approach is able to perforate on an individual statement level, and it is able to employ different perforation patterns for different statements. We support different perforation patterns in a loop by first applying loop splitting, which splits a loop into two sub-loops. Then, we perforate the new loops individually.

Multi-dimensional Schemes: As a result of using the polyhedral model and performing perforation at SCoP level, ALONA supports multi-dimensional perforation of loop nests, which is not supported by previous work.

4   Reconstruction

By post-processing the results of an approximated application, the error introduced by the approximation technique can be mitigated. As this process depends heavily on the application, the *reconstruction phase* requires an application-specific or data-specific approach to achieve optimal results. However, in some cases, even a general approach can be beneficial. The impact of a general and simple reconstruction approach is also shown by related work [21]. Therefore, we introduce our reconstruction phase that prevents uninitialized values in the results of applications.

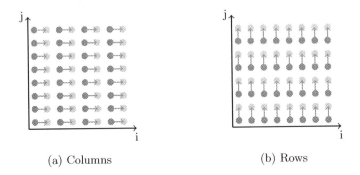

(a) Columns   (b) Rows

Fig. 4. Reconstruction.

Consider a loop where one output element is calculated in each iteration. After perforating every other loop iteration, every other output element is correct, but the remaining output elements are not written at all and, therefore, have high error. Data often contains redundancy, e.g., spatial redundancy in images, where pixels close to each other are very likely to have a similar value. We exploit this redundancy to reconstruct missing data. In our approach, a reconstruction phase is implemented together with the perforation of SCoPs as this allows us to easily identify the perforated elements and replace them with nearby approximations. We apply the reconstruction only to the output SCoPs, i.e., when the final result is written, while we apply normal (non-reconstructed) perforation to all other SCoPs. As the reconstruction is performed in a post-processing step outside the polyhedral model, it does not influence polyhedral transformations.

The reconstruction phase comprises two steps: (1) identify perforations of the output SCoP of the application, and (2) synthesize code to reconstruct all missing output elements. This can be done, e.g., using the nearest neighbor output element that was not perforated. However, also more complex interpolation is possible. For a two-dimensional loop nest that is perforated in both dimensions, the perforation is separated for each dimension. This example is depicted in Fig. 4. First, the i-dimension is reconstructed (a); then, the j-dimension of the loop is reconstructed (b). Arrows indicate the source and target of the reconstruction. Bright points indicate reconstructed data copied from adjacent dark points. While ALONA includes a generic framework for reconstruction, it is also possible to integrate application-specific reconstruction phases.

5   Approximation Space Pruning

ALONA generates many approximated code versions. The number of approximated code versions depends on the number of loop nests, their depth, and the number of supported skip factors. For example, in Listing 1.3, the approximation space for a given skip factor and scheme, consists of three approximations: (1) perforate S1; (2) perforate S2; (3) perforate S1 and S2. Considering different scheme and factor, the number of possible approximated code versions can be very large. This section introduces ALONA's approximation space pruning technique, which is able to find approximated code versions with low error, therefore reducing the number of version to be executed, e.g., by search-based autotuners.

5.1   Approximation Ordering

Accurately modeling the error of an approximated program is a complex task, because the error profile of an application is not only application-specific, but it depends also on the input data. Instead of trying to accurately model the error, our approach solves an easier task: ranking each approximated code version so that, e.g., only those with higher rank are evaluated. The idea to focus on an ordering problem instead of an accurate (regression) model has been previously used for performance tuning [9]; here, we use it to filter the most accurate code versions that are later executed.

Our method establishes an ordering of the possible loop nest approximations based on the observation that a code version with more perforated iterations is likely to have a higher error than a code version with fewer perforated iterations. We calculate this ordering by computing, for each code version, the ratio of loop iterations that are perforated, which ranges from 0 (all loop iterations perforated) to 1 (accurate program). For instance, for a program with one loop that is perforated for every other loop iteration, this ratio equals to 0.5.

5.2   Barvinok Counting Based Pruning

We use pruning to reduce the number of code versions to be tested. Our approach is based on the observation that there is a connection between the amount of work removed and speedup for many applications. We use Barvinok counting to calculate both the size of the original accurate iteration domain and the size of the approximated perforated domain. We use the ratio of the cardinality of the iteration domain of the perforated program and the cardinality of the iteration domain of the original program. In order to calculate this score, we count the number of instances in the iteration domain of each SCoP. We compute the sum of the cardinality of $\mathfrak{D}_p^i$ of the perforated program and

$$Score(\mathfrak{D}_p) = \frac{\sum\limits_{\forall i} |\mathfrak{D}_p^i|}{\sum\limits_{\forall i} |\mathfrak{D}^i|}$$

divide it by the sum of the cardinality $\mathfrak{D}^i$ for the original program. The resulting ratio is the amount of perforated loop instances of all SCoPs of the program. This number is independent of the problem size.

Pruning is used to reduce the optimization time by lowering the number of configurations considered. First, we apply score-based pruning where configurations below a certain score are discarded. Then, exhaustive search is used to select optimal solutions.

6   Experimental Evaluation

We evaluate the accuracy and performance of ALONA and compare it to Paraprox [30], the state-of-the-art perforation technique. Our set of configurations also include those used in Sculptor [20]; however, we are unable to label the specific configurations, as we do not know Sculptor's algorithmic decisions.

We use a set of well-known and well-tested tools for the experimental evaluation of our approach. We use the Polyhedral Compiler Collection [28] for the extraction of the SCoP (clan), which is extended by our framework to implement the SCoP perforation. Furthermore, we use the Barvinok library to retrieve the size of the iteration domain. Finally, Cloog is used for code generation and gcc 7.4.0 (-O3) to compile the synthesized code.

6.1   Benchmark Setup

We measure runtime and accuracy of 22 applications from PolyBench/C 4.1 [24] and three additional applications also used by Paraprox. Our measurements were conducted on an Intel Core i7-3930K (3.20 GHz). The accuracy of an application is heavily influenced by the input data and can span a wide range. We evaluate the applications with their default input and, therefore, the error is not representative for all possible inputs. However, when comparing different perforation configurations, the accuracy trend shows which perforation schemes deliver higher accuracy. We report the *mean relative error* (MRE) of the element-wise difference of true and approximated results.

6.2   Discovered Solutions

In Fig. 5, we show detailed speedup and error for six applications. Orange and red points indicate state-of-the-art techniques. Blue points show approximations discovered by ALONA. Using the green dashed line, we indicate Pareto-optimal configurations. We show how ALONA is able to outperform Paraprox both in terms of accuracy and speedup and, in fact, that many superior solutions are discovered.

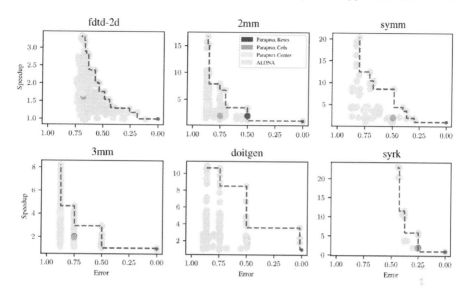

Fig. 5. Configurations discovered by ALONA and state-of-the-art techniques.

For the FDTD-2D application, there are 26 Pareto-optimal configurations. ALONA generates approximated programs that are nearly twice as fast when compared to Paraprox for the same error budget. Many configurations outperform Paraprox in both speedup and error. 2MM has 17 Pareto-optimal approximations, and they result in three clusters of approximately the same error. The application is very sensitive to approximation and all points result in an error of at least 50%. Here, ALONA outperforms state-of-the-art techniques in terms of speedup. There are 12 Pareto-optimal configurations for SYMM. ALONA yields a more than 4× higher speedup than state of the art, and it is also able to provide a lower speedup for the same performance. The clustering of the points of 3MM is similar to the 2MM application as it performs a similar calculation. 12 configurations are Pareto-optimal and ALONA improves on both error and speedup. While most configurations generated by ALONA for DOITGEN have an error of 50% or higher, there are 3 configurations that have a much lower error of around 2% and a speedup that outperforms Paraprox' by 2×. 14 configurations are Pareto-optimal. SYRK has 11 Pareto-optimal configurations and ALONA is able to improve on the speedup.

Overall, the results show that as our approach generalizes existing perforation schemes, it is capable to discover new approximation schemes, and many of those newly found solutions are also Pareto-optimal.

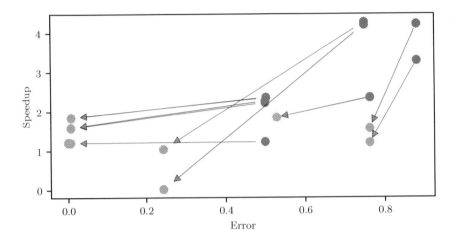

Fig. 6. Effects of reconstruction.

6.3   Reconstruction

We evaluate a case study detailing the effects of the reconstruction for the BICG application. The prospects of reconstruction and the importance of application-specific reconstruction techniques are outlined in Sect. 4. In our case study, we use a post-processing step to replace all missing data values in the result with adjacent data values.

The experimental results are shown in Fig. 6. There are 14 different approximated code versions. For each of the different approximated programs, we measure error and speedup, respectively with and without reconstruction. Some approximations being very similar in performance and accuracy and thus the points are overlapping. Blue points indicate approximations *without* reconstruction. Orange points connected by arrows show the same approximations *with* reconstruction enabled. Ideally, the arrows are horizontal lines (same speedup, accuracy improvement). All arrows are pointing to the bottom left, as the error is reduced and the speedup is affected. In all cases where the non-reconstructed results are affected by error, utilizing the reconstruction lowers the error, in many cases significantly. The speedup is affected moderately in many cases. However, there are also cases where the speedup decreases sharply, or the approximated application is slowed down in comparison to the baseline. On average, we are able to improve the error by approx. 30% while retaining approx. 60% of the speedup by employing reconstruction.

These results emphasize the importance of reconstruction in order to minimize the error: even when using a basic reconstruction technique, there is big potential to improve the accuracy by an order of magnitude while retaining most of the performance.

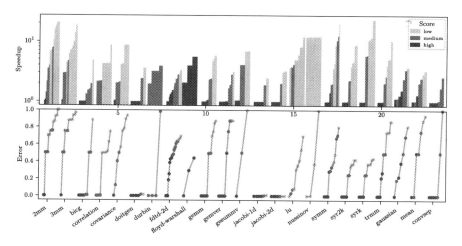

Fig. 7. Speedup and accuracy of pareto-optimal configurations discovered by ALONA.

6.4   Evaluation of Perforation Configurations

Depending on the application, i.e., the number of nested loops, the space of possible perforation configurations can be very large. There is no single configuration that is superior to all other configurations, because the target of optimization is multi-objective: the two goals are high performance and low error.

In Fig. 7, we compare Pareto-optimal perforation schemes for all applications. The figure is built from two related subplots: In the upper bar chart, we show the speedup of all Pareto-optimal configurations; and in the lower part we show the *corresponding* error. We use three color shades from light to dark that indicate the score. Darker points/bars have a higher score and brighter points have a lower score. All configurations use no reconstruction. For most of the applications, the majority of the Pareto-optimal solutions has a low score. A notable exception is FLOYD-WARSHALL, which has only a small number of Pareto-optimal solutions. Solutions with a small speedup have a darker shade, a medium speedup is indicated by a medium shade and high speedups are usually brighter shaded. This can be explained by the rationale that perforating a smaller part leads to a smaller speedup and perforating a larger part of an application leads to a larger speedup. A similar trend can be observed for the accuracy.

It should be noted that PolyBench is not curated as an approximate computing benchmark suite. Therefore, its applications are not necessarily resilient to approximation. Furthermore, in this specific experiment, the results are not improved by our reconstruction approach as we do not have application-specific reconstruction routines for all applications. This can be clearly observed, as there are some applications where the error for most of the configurations is rather high, e.g., applications with low resilience like 2MM and 3MM.

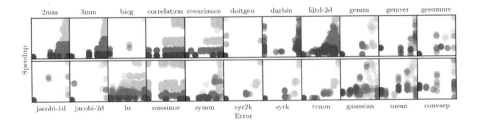

Fig. 8. Speedup and accuracy in relation to score.

Nonetheless, ALONA is able to find some solutions with low error and a speedup larger than 1 for almost all applications. There are also applications, where almost all solutions have a low error, e.g., BICG, DOITGEN, DURBIN, JACOBI-1D, JACOBI-2D, or CONVSEP, which indicates that these applications are more resilient to approximation.

6.5   Approximation Space Pruning

In Fig. 8, the results of our Barvinok-based approximation space pruning are shown. Each subfigure plots speedup (y-axis) and error (x-axis) for all configurations individually for each application. We calculate the Barvinok-based score as detailed in Sect. 5. The brightness of the points indicates the score. Notably, for most applications, the set of solutions can clearly be divided into three large sets with respectively low, medium, and high speedup. This observation is useful in the context of performing a static pre-filtering of the approximation space to significantly reduce the number of approximations, e.g., to one third of all approximations.

Exemplary, for the 2MM application, the *time to solution* is 99 s for the compilation and 4213 s (approx. 72 min) for executing all application variants. By using our score-based filtering, we are able to reduce this time to 768 s (approx. 13 min). This time is composed of 39 s for compilation and 729 s for the execution of the applications.

7   Conclusions and Future Work

ALONA is a new approximation framework that automatically approximates affine loop nests. By using polyhedral analysis, ALONA extends state-of-the-art loop perforation techniques and applies perforation and reconstruction on multi-dimensional loop nests. It also features an optional processing step that reconstructs missing results and significantly improves the accuracy of the approximated applications. The large number of approximated code variants constructed by ALONA are tackled with an approximation space pruning technique, which filters code variants with larger error thanks to a Barvinok's counting-based approximation metric. This technique can be combined with search heuristics and iterative compilation, providing an efficient tool to identify fast code versions with low error and overall reducing the time to solution. Experimental results show that ALONA is capable of discovering new approximations that are Pareto-dominant with respect to approximations found by state-of-the-art approximation schemes. In particular, whenever we have the same approximation accuracy as state-of-the-art approaches, ALONA's performance is better.

In future work, we plan to integrate ALONA with existing polyhedral optimizers and in combination with automatic parallelization.

Acknowledgement. This research has been partially funded by MIUR PON Ricerca e Innovazione 2014–2020 (grant number AIM1872991-1).

References

1. Bao, W., Krishnamoorthy, S., Pouchet, L.N., Sadayappan, P.: Analytical Modeling of Cache Behavior for Affine Programs. Lang, ACM Program (2017)
2. Barvinok, A.I.: A polynomial time algorithm for counting integral points in polyhedra when the dimension is fixed. Mathematics of Operations Research (1994)
3. Baskaran, M.M., Ramanujam, J., Sadayappan, P.: Automatic C-to-CUDA code generation for affine programs. In: Proceedings of CC (2010)
4. Benabderrahmane, M., Pouchet, L., Cohen, A., Bastoul, C.: The polyhedral model is more widely applicable than you think. In: Proceedings of CC (2010)
5. Bondhugula, U., Acharya, A., Cohen, A.: The pluto+ algorithm: a practical approach for parallelization and locality optimization of affine loop nests. ACM TOPLAS (2016)
6. Bondhugula, U., Baskaran, M.M., Krishnamoorthy, S., Ramanujam, J., Rountev, A., Sadayappan, P.: Automatic transformations for communication-minimized parallelization and locality optimization in the polyhedral model. In: Proceedings of CC (2008)
7. Campanoni, S., Holloway, G.H., Wei, G., Brooks, D.M.: HELIX-UP: relaxing program semantics to unleash parallelization. In: Proceedings of CGO (2015)
8. Cherubin, S., Cattaneo, D., Chiari, M., Agosta, G.: Dynamic Precision Autotuning with TAFFO. TACO (2020)
9. Cosenza, B., Durillo, J.J., Ermon, S., Juurlink, B.: Autotuning stencil computations with structural ordinal regression learning. In: Proceedings of IPDPS (2017)
10. Deiana, E.A., St-Amour, V., Dinda, P.A., Hardavellas, N., Campanoni, S.: Unconventional Parallelization of Nondeterministic Applications. SIGPLAN Not. (2018)
11. Esmaeilzadeh, H., Sampson, A., Ceze, L., Burger, D.: Architecture support for disciplined approximate programming. In: Proceedings of ASPLOS (2017)
12. Fernando, V., Franques, A., Abadal, S., Misailovic, S., Torrellas, J.: Replica: a wireless manycore for communication-intensive and approximate data. In: Proceedings of ASPLOS (2019)
13. Ganser, S., Größlinger, A., Siegmund, N., Apel, S., Lengauer, C.: Speeding up iterative polyhedral schedule optimization with surrogate performance models. TACO (2018)
14. Grosser, T., Größlinger, A., Lengauer, C.: Polly - Performing Polyhedral Optimizations on a Low-Level Intermediate Representation. Parallel Proc, Letters (2012)
15. Gysi, T., Grosser, T., Brandner, L., Hoefler, T.: A fast analytical model of fully associative caches. In: Proceedings of PLDI (2019)

16. Imani, M., Garcia, R., Huang, A., Rosing, T.: CADE: configurable approximate divider for energy efficiency. In: Proceedings of DATE (2019)
17. Jimborean, A., Clauss, P., Pradelle, B., Mastrangelo, L., Loechner, V.: Adapting the polyhedral model as a framework for efficient speculative parallelization. In: Proceedings of PPoPP (2012)
18. Khatamifard, S.K., Akturk, I., Karpuzcu, U.R.: On approximate speculative lock elision. IEEE Trans. Multi-Scale Comput. Syst. 4(2) (2018)
19. Lashgar, A., Atoofian, E., Baniasadi, A.: Loop perforation in OpenACC. In: Proceedings of ISPA (2018)
20. Li, S., Park, S., Mahlke, S.: Sculptor: Flexible approximation with selective dynamic loop perforation. In: Proceedings of ICS (2018)
21. Maier, D., Cosenza, B., Juurlink, B.: Local memory-aware kernel perforation. In: Proceedings of CGO (2018)
22. Mitra, S., Gupta, M.K., Misailovic, S., Bagchi, S.: Phase-aware optimization in approximate computing. In: Proceedings of CGO (2017)
23. Mittal, S.: A Survey of Techniques for Approximate Computing. ACM Comput. Surv. (2016)
24. Pouchet, L.N.: Polybench/c 3.2. http://www.cse.ohio-state.edu/~pouchet/software/polybench/
25. Pouchet, L.N., Bastoul, C., Cohen, A., Cavazos, J.: Iterative Optimization in the Polyhedral Model: Part II. Multidimensional Time, SIGPLAN Not (2008)
26. Pouchet, L.N., Bastoul, C., Cohen, A., Vasilache, N.: Iterative optimization in the polyhedral model: Part i, one-dimensional time. In: Proceedings of CGO (2007)
27. Pouchet, L., Bondhugula, U., Bastoul, C., Cohen, A., Ramanujam, J., Sadayappan, P., Vasilache, N.: Loop transformations: convexity, pruning and optimization. In: Proceedings of POPL (2011)
28. Pouchet, L.N., Bondhugula, U., Bastoul, C., Cohen, A., Ramanujam, R., Sadayappan, P.: Hybrid iterative and model-driven optimization in the polyhedral model (2009)
29. Rinard, M.: Probabilistic accuracy bounds for fault-tolerant computations that discard tasks. In: Proceedings of ICS (2006)
30. Samadi, M., Jamshidi, D.A., Lee, J., Mahlke, S.: Paraprox: pattern-based approximation for data parallel applications. In: Proceedings of ASPLOS (2014)
31. Sampson, A., Dietl, W., Fortuna, E., Gnanapragasam, D., Ceze, L., Grossman, D.: Enerj: approximate data types for safe and general low-power computation. In: Proceedings of PLDI (2011)
32. Schmitt, M., Helluy, P., Bastoul, C.: Automatic adaptive approximation for stencil computations. In: Proceedings of CC (2019)
33. Sidiroglou-Douskos, S., Misailovic, S., Hoffmann, H., Rinard, M.: Managing performance vs. accuracy trade-offs with loop perforation. In: Proceedings of ESEC (2011)
34. Udupa, A., Rajan, K., Thies, W.: ALTER: exploiting breakable dependences for parallelization. In: Proceedings of PLDI (2011)
35. Venkatagiri, R., Mahmoud, A., Hari, S.K.S., Adve, S.V.: Approxilyzer: Towards a systematic framework for instruction-level approximate computing and its application to hardware resiliency. In: Proceedings of MICRO (2016)
36. Verdoolaege, S., Carlos Juega, J., Cohen, A., Ignacio Gómez, J., Tenllado, C., Catthoor, F.: Polyhedral parallel code generation for CUDA. ACM TACO (2013)

Automatic Low-Overhead Load-Imbalance Detection in MPI Applications

Peter Arzt⬢, Yannic Fischler⬢, Jan-Patrick Lehr$^{(\boxtimes)}$⬢,
and Christian Bischof⬢

Scientific Computing, Department of Computer Science,
Technical University of Darmstadt, Darmstadt, Germany
peter.arzt@stud.tu-darmstadt.de,
{yannic.fischler,jan-patrick.lehr,
christian.bischof}@tu-darmstadt.de

Abstract. Load imbalances are a major reason for efficiency loss in highly parallel applications. Hence, their identification is of high relevance in performance analysis and tuning. We present a low-overhead approach to automatically identify load-imbalanced regions and filter out irrelevant ones based on new selection heuristics in our PIRA tool for automatic instrumentation refinement for the Score-P measurement system. For the LULESH mini-app as well as the Ice-sheet and Sea-level System Model simulation package we, thus, correctly identify existing load imbalances while maintaining a runtime overhead of less than 10% for all but one input. Moreover, the traces generated are suitable for Scalasca's automatic trace analysis.

Keywords: Score-P · Load imbalance · HPC · Performance analysis

1 Introduction

Load imbalances, i.e., the uneven distribution of work across compute units, are a major source of inefficiencies in parallel and high-performance computing (HPC). Moreover, the increasing degree of parallelism multiplies the severity of existing load imbalance, should the target applications be scaled to larger processor counts. Hence, load-imbalance analysis is, unsurprisingly, a task performed frequently in performance analysis and tuning.

Tools such as *HPCToolkit* [1] or *Score-P* [8] are used as measurement systems for highly parallel applications to enable subsequent performance and load-imbalance analysis. Score-P, in particular, has been created as a common infrastructure across multiple *client* applications that analyze its data. An often-used client to visually uncover performance issues with *Message Passing Interface (MPI)* applications is *Vampir* [14]. *Scalasca* [6] offers automatic root-cause analysis for typical MPI problems, e.g., late sender issues, using trace analysis.

A significant impediment to many of the Score-P client tools is the significant runtime overhead that an instrumented application can suffer from, caused by

© Springer Nature Switzerland AG 2021
L. Sousa et al. (Eds.): Euro-Par 2021, LNCS 12820, pp. 19–34, 2021.
https://doi.org/10.1007/978-3-030-85665-6_2

measurement hooks inserted by Score-P. Also, the capturing of many events leads to trace files impractically large for analysis. Moreover, the hooks are not distributed evenly, hence, the measurement system itself changes the timing behavior of the target application significantly and the resulting profile data may be useless. Therefore, analysts use *filtering* of functions when working with Score-P to reduce the runtime impact of the measurement system. While being a rather mechanical process, the filtering is typically carried out manually.

In this paper, we address this impediment and propose *PIRA LIDe* to automatically detect load imbalances and refine the Score-P instrumentation to cover only such imbalanced code sections. It extends the existing PIRA [11] automation with new selection heuristics for load imbalances and adds automatic filtering of irrelevant MPI functions. We show its effectiveness by identifying existing load imbalances in the mini-app *LULESH* [7] and a Greenland ice-sheet simulation employing the *Ice-sheet and Sea-level System Model (ISSM)* [9]. Moreover, we use the resulting low-overhead instrumentation with Scalasca's existing load-imbalance analysis and compare its results to a manually performed analysis.

The paper is structured as follows: Sect. 2 outlines related work w.r.t. load-imbalance detection. Section 3 introduces the basics of PIRA before Sect. 4 explains load imbalance and our approach PIRA LIDe to detect it. Subsequently, Sect. 5 evaluates the approach, followed by a discussion in Sect. 6. Finally, Sect. 7 concludes and outlines further avenues of research.

2   Related Work

Tools to detect load imbalances in parallel applications have been proposed in the past, with fundamental differences in complexity and measurement technology. Early work on automatic load-imbalance detection was presented in 2007 by DeRose et al. [4] who presented load-imbalance quantifying metrics implemented as an extension to Cray's performance-analysis infrastructure. In their paper, the authors describe scanning call-graph profiles for load imbalance by comparing function runtimes. Results were reported and visualized automatically.

Other approaches shift the focus from solely detecting load imbalance, and, additionally, introduce ideas to analyze the root cause of such inefficiencies to provide more concrete feedback to the analyst. The work in the Scalasca framework [3] is based on *replaying* the target program's execution traces. This facilitates a detailed analysis of its communication patterns and allows for precise classification of wait states or the exact quantification of negative effects.

A major challenge with trace-based approaches is the lack of scalability as the size of the data generated grows proportionally with the degree of parallelism and execution time. This challenge is particularly prominent in instrumentation-based measurement approaches, as they generate millions of events per second unless filtering is applied [13]. HPCToolkit [16] addresses this and relies on statistical sampling instead of instrumentation for measurement. Moreover, HPC-Toolkit uses call-path profiles instead of traces, and an algorithm that identifies so-called *balance points* to quantify the efficiency loss. In addition, *blame shifting* is introduced to identify locations, potentially responsible for the load imbalance.

Recently, *Hatchet* [2] was proposed as an infrastructure to represent, process and visualize profiling data from various tools. It provides a set of abstract operations on the profile data that allows a user to implement arbitrary analyses of program behavior, such as the automatic evaluation of load-imbalance metrics.

All aforementioned approaches analyze previously captured profiling or tracing data of the target program's execution for signs of load imbalance. Therefore, the most important commonality is their dependence on high-quality measurements as their input. In particular, this means that before being able to use these approaches, the analyst is required to provide measurements, perturbed as lightly as possible, to ensure the reliability of automatic analyses. This is especially apparent for trace-based approaches, such as Scalasca.

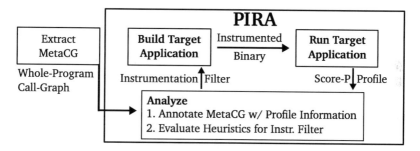

Fig. 1. PIRA constructs and analyzes a whole-program call-graph (CG) to create instrumentation filters. The initial analysis uses source-code features only, whereas subsequent analyses use dynamic, i.e., profile information, in addition.

3   PIRA

PIRA [11] is a set of tools for automatic instrumentation refinement on top of Score-P [8]. This means that it focuses measurements automatically on relevant parts of the target application and frees a performance analyst from the tedious task of manual filter creation. PIRA has been used successfully to detect and focus on application runtime hot-spots [11] and to create instrumentation filters that focus the measurement on those kernels that impact scaling behavior by showing increasing runtime with increasing problem size using empirical performance modeling [10]. It uses a whole-program call-graph (CG) representation, called *MetaCG* [12], to evaluate different static and dynamic analysis heuristics during its *build–run–analyze* cycle, Fig. 1. The heuristics are implemented in the *profile-guided instrumentation selection* (PGIS) tool and create instrumentation filters that are subsequently used in the back-end instrumentation tool Score-P. Hence, PIRA's automation is independent of the particular heuristics and can be extended to evaluate other metrics by extending PGIS with new selection heuristics. The back-end uses compile-time selective instrumentation, meaning that a target application needs to be recompiled once the instrumentation filter changes.

3.1   MPI Function Filtering

An important advancement in PIRA is the automatic selective MPI function filtering, as it can significantly contribute to runtime-overhead reductions. This is particularly relevant for target codes that use asynchronous communication and many calls to, e.g., MPI_Iprobe, as these would result in large runtime overheads. Moreover, these overheads can prohibitively influence the recorded characteristics of the target application, i.e., obscuring existing load imbalances. PIRA scans the instrumentation filter created and recognizes MPI functions that have been marked for measurement. Thereafter, it uses *wrap* [5] to generate wrapper functions for all other MPI functions. These wrappers are automatically compiled and added to the application's invocation. They immediately call into the PMPI interface and, hence, circumvent Score-P's MPI measurement mechanics. An important detail is that certain MPI functions, e.g., MPI_Init and MPI_Finalize, are never filtered to guarantee the integrity of the measurement.

4   Automatic Load-Imbalance Detection

Our approach extends PIRA to automatically refine the instrumentation towards code sections that show particular load imbalances during execution. The subsequent sections present (1) a definition of load imbalance, (2) the metric used to quantify load imbalance, and (3) the principal approach of PIRA LIDe.

4.1   Load Imbalance

Load imbalance is commonly defined as an "uneven distribution of work that forces some processes to idle between synchronization points" [16]. This definition, Fig. 2 for a visualization, includes two essential components for a load imbalance. Most importantly, an unbalanced distribution of work must be present. This leads to some processes requiring more time to complete specific code regions than others. When followed by synchronization, processes that received less work are forced to wait until the synchronization completes and cannot perform useful work in the meantime. Naturally, this leads to an undesirable decrease of overall system efficiency, as computational time is allocated but wasted. Load imbalance is a major cause for scaling problems: Since a single slow process can defer the completion of a synchronization routine, potential waiting time, i.e., the efficiency decrease, increases with the number of processes involved. Hence, it is likely for load imbalance to become a relevant performance issue when software is employed to a higher degree of parallelism, e.g., due to a new generation of hardware. The analysis of a target software for existing load imbalances is, thus, an important task for performance analysts.

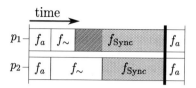

(a) Example call graph. The main function calls a function f_a which invokes an imbalanced function $f_\sim$ and a synchronization routine f_{Sync}, e.g., `MPI_Barrier`.

(b) Example trace of f_a and its children. p_1 reaches f_{Sync} (gray area) first and is forced to wait for p_2. The induced idle time is represented by the hatched area. After f_{Sync} the execution continues in a balanced fashion.

Fig. 2. Minimal example for load imbalance with two parallel MPI-processes p_1, p_2. Note that, due to the synchronization in f_{Sync}, f_a is itself balanced although a load imbalance is present in $f_\sim$.

4.2 Quantifying Load Imbalance

We use the established *Imbalance Percentage* [4] metric to quantify the severeness of a potential load imbalance for a given node in the MetaCG representation., i.e., a function. Assume n is the number of MPI processes working on a function f and $T_{\max}$ and T_{avg} are the maximum and average of the processes' inclusive runtime in function f, respectively. Then the metric value is defined as follows:

$$M_{\text{Imbalance Percentage}} = \frac{T_{\max} - T_{\text{avg}}}{T_{\max}} \cdot \frac{n}{n-1}$$

The metric maps the degree of imbalance to the interval $[0, 1]$, with 0 being a perfectly balanced execution. The worst-case, in which all but one process are forced to idle over the entire function runtime, is indicated with a value of 1. The imbalance threshold can be configured by the analyst, but our experiments with the ISSM and LULESH proved 5% to be a reasonable choice.

4.3 Load-Imbalance Detection Extension in PIRA

Our approach, PIRA LIDe, defines new analysis heuristics that enable load-imbalance detection as an extension to PIRA. As a prerequisite, we implement a mechanism in the analysis infrastructure that enables PIRA to enrich MetaCG's node representation with additional information that is available in all following iterations. Moreover, the internal graph-node representation is extended to account for multiple execution locations, e.g., different MPI processes. This allows the evaluation of differences in execution times across the processes involved.

The metric described in Sect. 4.2 is used in a newly created dynamic analysis heuristic, and enables the iterative refinement towards load-imbalanced sections, Fig. 3 for an example. It is designed to search for load imbalances in the target application iteratively while keeping the measurement overhead as low as possible. We refer to the general approach as *iterative descent*, as the algorithm starts at the top of the target application's call-hierarchy, e.g., main for C/C++, *cf.* step 1 in Fig. 3. The instrumentation is subsequently advanced further down by one step per PIRA iteration. The load-imbalance metric is calculated for each node for which profile information is available to detect an uneven work distribution. As soon as a function is assessed to be imbalanced, the finding is reported back to the analyst.

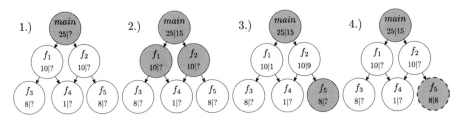

Fig. 3. Four iterations of iterative descent without context handling. Gray nodes are instrumented in the next iteration. A dotted circle denotes detected load imbalance. The labels within the nodes denote: the function name, the inclusive statement count and the inclusive runtime. A question mark denotes missing information. Function f_1 does not pass the runtime threshold so the iterative descent is not advanced to its children. f_4 has too few statements and is not instrumented at all. Assume that f_5 is a function with uneven work distribution.

The main-function is instrumented in every iteration to provide information about the total execution time. Two different mechanisms are used to keep irrelevant functions from being instrumented in order to minimize measurement overhead. First, a function's inclusive runtime needs to exceed a configurable fraction of the entire program's execution time. If this threshold is not surpassed, a function is marked as irrelevant and is excluded from instrumentation in all subsequent iterations, *cf.* function f_1 in Fig. 3. Additionally, the iterative descent is not advanced into the node's children. Second, in the case of a function surpassing the runtime threshold but showing a balanced work-distribution, the function itself will not be included in the instrumentation, but the iterative descent is performed into its children, i.e., all potentially called functions. However, a second mechanism is applied to inhibit the descent into very small functions that can potentially induce critical measurement overhead. We use the inclusive statement count of a function, i.e., the statically calculated number of statements in a function and all its descendants, as a rough estimate of the amount of work performed in a function. Children whose inclusive statement count does not surpass a statement threshold are not considered for the descent, *cf.* function f_4 in Fig. 3. This threshold is calculated as the maximum of a fixed number of statements (*child constant threshold*) and a fraction of the whole program's inclusive statement count (*child fraction*). Both values, along with the *relevance threshold* and *imbalance threshold*, can be configured as parameters.

Context Handling: Merely detecting the uneven distribution of work in parallel program execution is, however, only the first step to provide useful aid in the search for load imbalance. PIRA LIDe is designed to act as a basis for more detailed methods of performance analysis. Commonly, it is of interest in which calling contexts a load imbalance actually occurs. As PIRA currently relies on call-graph profiles, which by design use accumulated information, context differentiation cannot be performed by PIRA LIDe's analysis. Instead, two different modes of context handling are supported to facilitate the subsequent interpretation and utilization of PIRA LIDe's output. Both of them extend the list of instrumented functions to produce more complete measurements that can then be used for further analysis. For any node which has been detected as imbalanced, `MajorPathsToMain` instruments all functions on all paths to `main` which have not been previously marked as irrelevant. As a result, the analyst can distinguish the different calling contexts when inspecting the Score-P profiles. `FindSynchronizationPoints` is designed to enable the creation of useful traces using the instrumented binaries created by PIRA LIDe. To that end, for every sub-graph in which a load imbalance has been detected, all MPI-functions are instrumented using PIRA's call-site instrumentation feature in order to capture the synchronization routine in which forced waiting time occurs.

5   Evaluation

We apply the load-imbalance detection to the MPI-parallel LULESH [7] mini-app as well as the Ice-sheet and Sea-level System Model (ISSM) [9] in version 4.18. We use the LULESH mini-app as it allows to adjust the amount of load imbalance present in the execution, which makes it well suited to study PIRA LIDe's capabilities. In addition, we use the ISSM to simulate the ice sheet behavior of a Greenland model [15], and evaluate whether PIRA LIDe is able to detect load imbalance in production software. Our evaluation focuses on the runtime overhead introduced by PIRA LIDe and compares it to out-of-the-box Score-P instrumentation. In addition, we generate traces and apply Scalasca's analyzer to perform a critical path and its imbalance-impact analysis.

LULESH: LULESH is a mini-app that implements a simplified 3D Lagrangian hydrodynamics on an unstructured mesh model. We use version 2.0, which adds optional artificial load imbalance by modifying the computational cost of various material properties and their respective equation of state. About half the regions have no additional cost, whereas 45% have an additional cost that corresponds to the load-imbalance parameter b. The remaining 5% of the regions have an additional cost of ten times the cost of b. For more details, please see [7].

Ice-sheet and Sea-level System Model (ISSM): The ISSM [9] simulates the evolution of ice shields by taking into account the relevant physical models, e.g., stress of the ice, changes in temperature, falling snow, etc. Each physical component is computed in its own kernel, called core or analysis. These kernels are executed in predefined sequences, e.g., the *transient solution*, and the ISSM is synchronized at the end of each kernel, i.e., each kernel is a closed system w.r.t. load imbalance.

We use a Greenland ice-shield model, which uses the *transient solution* with higher-order approximation (HO) of the Stokes equation and linear finite elements (P1) on an unstructured pentahedron (triangular prism) mesh. The mesh resolutions are denoted by the elements' minimal edge-length e, i.e., smaller numbers mean higher resolution. The coarser mesh, $e = 4000$ (not viable to study physical phenomena), has $1,055,572$ elements and the finer mesh, $e = 500$ (desired for simulation), has $10,282,132$ elements. For more details, see [15].

Experiment Setup: All experiments are conducted on a dedicated compute node of the Lichtenberg HPC system with a 96-core Intel Xeon Platinum 9242 processor and 384GB of main memory. Unless stated otherwise, we run five repetitions for vanilla, Score-P and PIRA LIDe experiments.

We run LULESH without OpenMP using 8, 27, and 64 MPI processes and the load-imbalance parameter b set to the values 0, 1, and 2. The remaining parameters are left with their default values. For the ISSM, we use 27, 64, and 96 MPI processes to keep the runtime within reasonable limits, and use two different mesh resolutions. We run 1 and 10 timesteps of the coarser mesh (G4000/1, G4000/10), while for the finer mesh we run only 1 timestep (G500/1). PIRA LIDe uses its default configuration: Imbalance threshold: 5%, relevance threshold: 2%, child constant threshold: 150, child fraction: $3 \cdot 10^{-5}$, PIRA iterations: 20, context handling strategy: MajorPathsToMain. However, for trace generation, PIRA LIDe's FindSynchronizationPoints context handling is used.

Table 1. PIRA LIDe's execution result on LULESH and the ISSM for different inputs using 64 MPI processes. *Sections* is the number of section reported as load imbalanced. *Metric* is the largest imbalance-percentage value in the last PIRA iteration. *Ttl. time* denotes the total PIRA runtime (including initial build, CG extraction, analysis, profiling, etc.) in seconds. Notation: μ (mean) $\pm \sigma$ (std. deviation)

Benchmark		Sections	Metric [%]	Ttl. time [sec.]
LULESH	-b 0	4 ± 1	45	$3,532 \pm 29$
	-b 1	3 ± 0	56	$3,599 \pm 52$
	-b 2	4 ± 1	61	$3,658 \pm 12$
ISSM	G4000/1	4 ± 0	23	$15,413 \pm 349$
	G4000/10	4 ± 0	21	$18,623 \pm 362$
	G500/1	4 ± 0	13	$22,181 \pm 106$

Table 2. Profiling overhead measured during PIRA LIDe's execution on different LULESH and ISSM inputs compared to runs with no instrumentation (*Vanilla*) and Score-P-filtered instrumentation respectively. *Time* is the runtime of a single execution in seconds and *Ovh.* the corresponding relative overhead. For PIRA LIDe, the maximum overhead across PIRA iterations in noted. Notation: μ (mean) $\pm \sigma$ (std. deviation)

Benchmark		Vanilla	PIRA LIDe		Score-P filtered	
		Time [sec.]	Time [sec.]	Ovh. [%]	Time [sec.]	Ovh. [%]
LULESH	-b 0	165 ± 0	163 ± 1	-1.1 ± 0.2	297 ± 3	55 ± 1
	-b 1	171 ± 1	167 ± 1	-1.9 ± 0.4	300 ± 1	56 ± 1
	-b 2	173 ± 1	169 ± 1	-1.9 ± 0.3	307 ± 1	55 ± 1
ISSM	G4000/1	25 ± 1	29 ± 0	14.9 ± 4.9	272 ± 3	900 ± 12
	G4000/10	142 ± 1	152 ± 1	6.4 ± 0.4	$1,948 \pm 22$	$1,154 \pm 7$
	G500/1	349 ± 9	362 ± 5	3.9 ± 1.8	$2,727 \pm 31$	644 ± 11

5.1 Experimentation Results

Table 1 shows that PIRA LIDe identifies four imbalanced sections in the ISSM. For LULESH the number of reported sections varies by one across repetitions. Analyzing PIRA LIDe's output shows that this is due to a LULESH function with a computed Imbalance Percentage around the threshold used. Hence, depending on measurement variation, the function is included or excluded.

As expected, the metric value for the imbalanced region in LULESH increases with the parameter for artificial load imbalance. However, even when disabling artificial load imbalance, PIRA LIDe reports sections as imbalanced. Manual analysis shows that this is correct, as $b = 0$ does not perfectly balance a LULESH execution. Interestingly, we consistently observe negative runtime overhead for LULESH, i.e., the PIRA LIDe version runs faster than a vanilla version.

For the ISSM, the maximum value for the imbalance percentage is moderate compared to the one observed for LULESH. Nevertheless, PIRA LIDe identifies multiple load-imbalanced sections in the ISSM, independent of the model configuration used.

We compare PIRA LIDe's overhead to Score-P's automatic instrumentation options. *Score-P full* is a full instrumentation of the target application, i.e., every function is instrumented. *Score-P filtered* applies an **inline**-filter, i.e., only functions that are not inlined by the compiler are instrumented. Table 2 shows the respective runtimes along with vanilla measurements. Figure 4 and Fig. 5 depict the relative overhead compared to both of these instrumentation modes for the ISSM and LULESH, respectively. It is visible in Fig. 6 that the overhead does only increase marginally across the different iteration of iterative descent.

PIRA LIDe reduces the ISSM runtime overhead by a factor of at least 14 (26) compared to Score-P filtered (Score-P full). Also, it exceeds 20% of runtime overhead in only one case for the ISSM, *cf.* Fig. 5, G4000/1. Interestingly, this

Table 3. Results of tracing experiments with different ISSM and LULESH inputs using instrumentation generated by PIRA LIDe and Score-P filtered, respectively. *Tracing time* denotes the runtime of a single tracing run and *Trace size* the size of the resulting trace file. *Impr.* is the relative improvement of PIRA LIDe instrumentation when compared to Score-P filtered. Values in brackets are estimated by Score-P.

Benchmark		Tracing time [sec.]			Trace size [GB]		
		PIRA LIDe	Score-P filt.	Impr.	PIRA LIDe	Score-P filt.	Impr.
LULESH	-b 0	161	440	2.7×	1.1	927	843×
	-b 1	166	433	2.6×	1.1	927	843×
	-b 2	167	478	2.9×	1.1	927	843×
ISSM	G4000/1	28	461	16.5×	1.3	1,879	1,445×
	G4000/10	150	N/A	N/A	11	(14,000)	(1,273×)
	G500/1	353	N/A	N/A	12	(20,000)	(1,667×)

overhead is not noticed for larger models. We found that this is partially caused by constant setup overhead of the measurement system. Such overhead imposes a larger impact for shorter running targets, e.g., smaller models. A typical overhead of less than ≈ 10% is maintained for every other benchmark variant. While Score-P filtered can reduce the excessive overhead of Score-P full drastically in both cases, it never achieves an acceptable runtime overhead without further manual filtering. Finally, the measurements show that the overhead barely increases with the number of MPI processes.

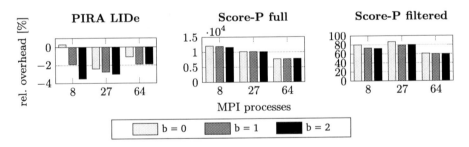

Fig. 4. Relative runtime overhead for PIRA LIDe (one repetition) and Score-P on LULESH.

PIRA LIDe's overhead reduction is accompanied by a substantial increase in total runtime, *cf.* Table 1. In the case of the ISSM (G500/1-model), the total PIRA runtime accumulates to ≈ 6h (initial build ≈ 2min, CG collection ≈10 min, *Build* ≈25 min, *Run* ≈2 h, *Analyze* ≈3.5 h), which is significantly longer than one run using Score-P's filtered instrumentation. Two major runtime contributors in the analysis step are (1) the graph construction, and, (2) the graph annotation with profile information.

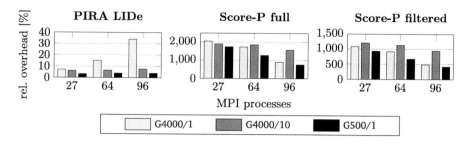

Fig. 5. Relative runtime overhead for PIRA LIDe (one repetition) and Score-P on the ISSM.

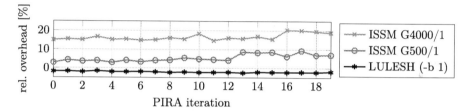

Fig. 6. Relative runtime overhead per iteration with 64 MPI processes for a single PIRA LIDe execution.

5.2 Scalasca Trace Analysis

Table 3 lists the trace size for LULESH and the ISSM running with 64 MPI processes. Scalasca's analysis requires the trace information to reside in main memory for its analyses. Hence, traces obtained by Score-P full and ISSM traces obtained by Score-P filtered cannot be analyzed with Scalasca as they exceed the 384GB of main memory available in nodes of the Lichtenberg cluster. PIRA LIDe reduces the trace sizes for LULESH and the ISSM by multiple orders of magnitude, *cf.* Table 3, significantly speeding-up or enabling a Scalasca analysis.

Table 4. Scalasca analysis for PIRA LIDe traces of LULESH for $b = \{0, 1\}$ and 64 MPI processes. Imbalance Impact is Scalasca's Critical-path Imbalance Impact.

LULESH	$b = 0$		$b = 1$	
Region	Critical Path	Imbalance Impact	Critical Path	Imbalance Impact
LagrangeLeapFrog	116.5	18.8	118.3	52.5
LagrangeElements	13.9	6.5	13.7	2.2
CalcQForElems	12.7	55.3	11.1	5.4
ApplyMaterialProp...	19.7	459.6	24.7	872.0

The most significant values for Scalasca's *critical-path* and *critical-path imbalance impact* metrics are shown in Table 4 for a LULESH execution with 64 MPI processes and PIRA LIDe's final instrumentation. Higher values reflect more significance, and the functions are listed top to bottom according to the call context, i.e., LagrangeLeapFrog calls LagrangeElements, etc. While the critical-path metric changes only slightly between the results for $b = 0$ and $b = 1$, i.e., artificially introduced load imbalance, the imbalance-impact metric changes significantly for two functions. The value for the LagrangeLeapFrog increases from 18.8 to 52.5 and the value for ApplyMaterialPropertiesForElems from 459.6 to 872, i.e., their imbalance is much more pronounced for $b = 1$.

Table 5. Scalasca analysis for PIRA LIDe traces of the ISSM and 64 MPI processes. Imbalance Impact is Scalasca's Critical-path Imbalance Impact.

ISSM	Imbalanced G4000/1		Imbalanced G500/1		Improved G500/1
Region	Critical Path	Imbal. Impact	Critical Path	Imbal. Impact	Imbal. Impact
SbA::CreateKMatrixHO	8.5	108.0	84.1	601.0	279.9
SbA::CreatePVector	1.0	11.2	10.1	72.7	60.9
EA::CreatePVector	1.3	16.2	12.7	89.7	40.9

Table 5 lists the respective Scalasca metric values for the sections in the ISSM identified by PIRA LIDe. The metric values suggest that imbalances with comparable impact exist in code sections of LULESH and the ISSM. More importantly, the load imbalance becomes apparent for the physically relevant model G500/1 in case of the *original* imbalanced version of the ISSM for all sections identified. As part of our work, these load imbalances have been addressed, *cf.* Table 5 most right column, and are discussed in Sect. 6.2.

6   Discussion

In the subsequent sections, we discuss the findings of PIRA LIDe for the two target applications and compare the results to a manual analysis. Also, we reflect on the strengths of our approach as well as its limitations.

6.1   LULESH

Scalasca computes all metrics for every function in the trace. Hence, it identifies several potential load imbalances in the Score-P-generated trace. In comparison, PIRA LIDe iteratively focuses the measurement on a single function, which is not present in the Score-P-generated trace. Generally, Scalasca's results confirm that the region PIRA LIDe identified is indeed load-imbalanced. This function is marked **inline**, hence, filtered in the Score-P-generated trace. According to the

LULESH description [7] and manual source-code analysis, PIRA LIDe identifies the function that introduces artificial load imbalance into LULESH. Moreover, the severeness of the load imbalance significantly increases for larger values of the load-imbalance parameter b. We consider the result of PIRA LIDe better than the result of the Score-P measurement, as it points to the particular function that applies the artificial load-imbalance penalty.

The varying number of reported sections, *cf.* Sect. 5.1, is a consequence of our threshold-based approach in combination with small variances in the measurement data. However, all of the reported sections are called in direct succession of each other and, thus, point the analyst to the same underlying problem. Thus, we do not consider this to degrade the value of PIRA LIDe's output.

The consistent occurrence of negative measurement overhead, i.e., application speedup, is surprising. As of now, we hypothesize that the instrumentation prevents the compiler from performing non-beneficial optimizations. However, a detailed analysis is beyond the scope of this paper and is left for future research.

6.2 ISSM

Full Score-P instrumentation of the ISSM leads to significant runtime overhead. Since additional overhead is generated by each function call, the overhead in individual regions is dependent on the varying number of functions calls, which leads to distorted results. Thereby analysis of profiles generated by an instrumented code might lead to the assumption, that sections, which in reality are insignificant for the runtime, seem to have a significant impact. On the other hand filtered builds, as generated by our approach, results in less overhead and depict reality more precisely.

Due to the overhead, models finer than G4000 cannot be analyzed by present instrumentation based tools without hand-written filters, but since we have seen that the load imbalance becomes apparent on larger models, it is worthwhile to take them into account. The low maximum relative overhead of our approach enables us to analyze small models as well as large models or multiple time steps, which are used for real simulation runs. Thereby we are able to show that the load-imbalanced regions do not change in the larger model, but the imbalance impact increases significantly.

We have proven our findings by a manual analysis of the code, which leads us to the same findings. The load imbalance occurs in the construction of the system of equations and is caused by early exits in the computation of some elements. However, writing meaningful filters for a large unknown frameworks like the ISSM takes up to a few days. Even experienced performance engineers need to iterate the sequence of filter adaption, profiling and analysis a few times to achieve a good result. Our approach does these iterations automatically and leads to an overhead of 3.9% (G500/1), while the hand written filter shows slightly less overhead of about 3.1% (G500/1). The main advantage of the manual analysis is the use of Score-P user regions, which enables the analyst to handle the iterative computation of all results as one section instead of instrumenting the call to the inner calculation function, which is called for each element. This improvement of the instrumentation is easily applicable to the automatically generated filter of PIRA LIDe.

Although we were not able to analyze Score-P traces of the ISSM with Scalasca because of the trace size, the filter generated by PIRA LIDe leads to manageable traces and Scalasca was able to report and quantify the load imbalance, *cf.* Table 5. Based on a meaningful instrumentation we were able to adjust the load balancing of the ISSM by passing new weights to the mesh partitioning. Further experiments have shown that adjusting these parameters decreases the load imbalance in the stress balance and the enthalpy core but increases the runtime of other cores of the ISSM. Our approach facilitates an automated analysis of the new behavior without any manual adaption of, e.g., filter lists and an iterative optimization.

6.3   PIRA LIDe

As described in the previous sections, PIRA LIDe produces correct and viable results for both LULESH and ISSM. However, currently, PIRA LIDe requires a considerable amount of time to complete a run. For instance, 20 PIRA iterations with 64 MPI processes for ISSM take ≈6 h to complete. At the moment, the long runtime is necessary to achieve minimal overhead. Although a single run takes substantially longer than, for example, Score-P filtered, PIRA LIDe's output is equally more valuable due to its high measurement quality. Hence, we do not think this time requirement impedes PIRA LIDe's potential to support performance analysis significantly, especially when compared to a manually performed analysis. Nevertheless, we see room for improvement. The current graph-construction implementation in PGIS results in long analysis times for the ISSM. Additionally, the total time requirement is determined by two factors. First, the current implementation of iterative descent is conservative, as it advances the instrumentation only by one level per iteration. More aggressive deepening, or other static heuristics, may reduce the number of required iterations. Second, PIRA's approach uses compile-time filtering of functions, which requires recompiling the entire target application in each iteration. Techniques such as binary rewriting or partial recompilation can address this issue.

Furthermore, the statement count, which is used as a rough estimate of work during the analysis, is highly approximating, especially w.r.t. nested loops and recursive functions. While static information is unable to reflect the program behavior completely, further optimization should be able to improve its accuracy.

At present, PIRA relies on relatively simple call-graphs as its internal representation. While this allows for fast processing, it implies that the load-imbalance detection operates on runtime data that has been accumulated over all calling contexts. Hence, the detection is context-agnostic. This limits the metric's ability to distinguish load imbalance between different contexts and quantify its effect precisely. A conceivable approach to more contextual analysis is to associate profile data with call-graph edges instead of nodes. However, the full context information can only be obtained using traces. To overcome the typical large overhead of traces, we have chosen to combine both concepts by using PIRA LIDe's instrumentation as a basis for Scalasca trace analysis.

7   Conclusion

We presented PIRA LIDe to automatically detect load imbalanced sections in MPI-parallel applications. The approach iteratively refines Score-P filters to include relevant sections in the measurement and exclude irrelevant ones to reduce runtime overhead. In its load-imbalance analysis it considers the differences in execution times across MPI ranks to compute an imbalance percentage.

We evaluated the approach on the LULESH mini-app, which allows to introduce artificial load imbalance, and on the Ice-sheet and Sea-level System Model (ISSM) simulating an ice-sheet model of Greenland. Compared to plain Score-P measurements with and without `inline`-filter, PIRA LIDe reduces the overhead by more than $14\times$ and typically achieved $< 10\%$. The identified load-imbalanced sections were validated manually for both LULESH and ISSM. Moreover, the resulting target binary can be used for tracing and subsequent application of the Scalasca automatic analyzer.

PIRA LIDe is available as part of PIRA starting from version 0.3.0 and released at https://github.com/tudasc/pira. As next steps, we plan to investigate mechanisms to remove the need to recompile a target application for every PIRA iteration, which would significantly reduce the total time-to-solution of PIRA LIDe. Also, we plan to improve the analyzer's internal representation, to allow for more fine-grain analysis and heuristics evaluation.

Acknowledgments. This work was funded by the Hessian LOEWE initiative within the Software-Factory 4.0 project and the Deutsche Forschungsgemeinschaft (DFG, German Research Foundation) – Project-ID 265191195 – SFB 1194. Calculations for this research were conducted on the Lichtenberg high-performance computer of Technical University of Darmstadt.

Contributions. Conception: Jan-Patrick Lehr; Funding: Christian Bischof; Investigation: Peter Arzt and Yannic Fischler; Methodology: Peter Arzt; Software: Peter Arzt; Supervision: Jan-Patrick Lehr; Validation: Yannic Fischler; Writing: Peter Arzt, Jan-Patrick Lehr, Yannic Fischler and Christian Bischof.

References

1. Adhianto, L., Banerjee, S., Fagan, M., Krentel, M., Marin, G., Mellor-Crummey, J., Tallent, N.R.: HPCToolkit: tools for performance analysis of optimized parallel programs. Concurr. Comput. Practice Exp. **22**(6), 685–701 (2010). https://doi.org/10.1002/cpe.1553
2. Bhatele, A., Brink, S., Gamblin, T.: Hatchet: pruning the overgrowth in parallel profiles. In: Proceedings of the International Conference for High Performance Computing, Networking, Storage and Analysis, SC 2019, pp. 1–21. Association for Computing Machinery (2019). https://doi.org/10.1145/3295500.3356219

3. Böhme, D., Geimer, M., Arnold, L., Voigtlaender, F., Wolf, F.: Identifying the root causes of wait states in large-scale parallel applications. ACM Trans. Parallel Comput. **3**(2), 11:1–11:24 (2016). https://doi.org/10.1145/2934661

4. DeRose, L., Homer, B., Johnson, D.: Detecting application load imbalance on high end massively parallel systems. In: Kermarrec, A.-M., Bougé, L., Priol, T. (eds.) Euro-Par 2007. LNCS, vol. 4641, pp. 150–159. Springer, Heidelberg (2007). https://doi.org/10.1007/978-3-540-74466-5_17

5. Gamblin, T.: wrap.py - A PMPI Wrapper. https://github.com/LLNL/wrap

6. Geimer, M., Wolf, F., Wylie, B.J.N., Ábrahám, E., Becker, D., Mohr, B.: The Scalasca performance toolset architecture. Concurr. Comput. Practice Exp. **22**(6), 702–719 (2010). https://doi.org/10.1002/cpe.1556

7. Karlin, I., Keasler, J., Neely, R.: LULESH 2.0 updates and changes. Technical report, Lawrence Livermore National Lab (LLNL) (2013). https://computing.llnl.gov/projects/co-design/lulesh2.0_changes1.pdf

8. Knüpfer, A., Rössel, C., Mey, D.a., Biersdorff, et al., S.: Score-P: a joint performance measurement run-time infrastructure for periscope, Scalasca, TAU, and Vampir. In: Tools for High Performance Computing 2011, pp. 79–91. Springer (2012). https://doi.org/10.1007/978-3-642-31476-6_7

9. Larour, E., Seroussi, H., Morlighem, M., Rignot, E.: Continental scale, high order, high spatial resolution, ice sheet modeling using the Ice Sheet System Model (ISSM). J. Geophys. Res. Earth Surface **117**(F1) (2012). https://doi.org/10.1029/2011JF002140

10. Lehr, J.P., Calotoiu, A., Bischof, C., Wolf, F.: Automatic Instrumentation Refinement for Empirical Performance Modeling. In: 2019 IEEE/ACM Intl. Workshop on Programming and Performance Visualization Tools (ProTools). pp. 40–47. IEEE (2019). https://doi.org/10.1109/ProTools49597.2019.00011

11. Lehr, J.P., Hück, A., Bischof, C.: PIRA: performance instrumentation refinement automation. In: 5th ACM SIGPLAN International Workshop on Artificial Intelligence and Empirical Methods for Software Engineering and Parallel Computing Systems, AI-SEPS 2018, pp. 1–10. ACM (2018). https://doi.org/10.1145/3281070.3281071

12. Lehr, J.P., Hück, A., Fischler, Y., Bischof, C.: MetaCG: annotated call-graphs to facilitate whole-program analysis, pp. 3–9. Association for Computing Machinery, New York (2020). https://doi.org/10.1145/3427764.3428320

13. Lehr, J.P., Iwainsky, C., Bischof, C.: The influence of HPCToolkit and Score-p on hardware performance counters. In: Proceedings of the 4th ACM SIGPLAN International Workshop on Software Engineering for Parallel Systems, SEPS 2017, pp. 21–30. ACM, New York (2017). https://doi.org/10.1145/3141865.3141869

14. Nagel, W.E., Arnold, A., Weber, M., Hoppe, H.C., Solchenbach, K.: VAMPIR: visualization and analysis of MPI resources. Supercomputer 63 **12**(1), 69–80 (1996)

15. Rückamp, M., Greve, R., Humbert, A.: Comparative simulations of the evolution of the Greenland ice sheet under simplified Paris Agreement scenarios with the models SICOPOLIS and ISSM. Polar Sci. **21**, 14–25 (2019). https://doi.org/10.1016/j.polar.2018.12.003

16. Tallent, N.R., Adhianto, L., Mellor-Crummey, J.M.: Scalable identification of load imbalance in parallel executions using call path profiles. In: SC 2010: Proceedings of the 2010 ACM/IEEE International Conference for High Performance Computing, Networking, Storage and Analysis, pp. 1–11 (2010). https://doi.org/10.1109/SC.2010.47, ISSN: 2167-4337

Performance and Power Modeling, Prediction and Evaluation

Trace-Based Workload Generation and Execution

Yannis Sfakianakis[1,2]([⊠]), Eleni Kanellou[1], Manolis Marazakis[1], and Angelos Bilas[1,2]

[1] Institute of Computer Science, Foundation for Research and Technology – Hellas (FORTH), Heraklion, Greece
{jsfakian,kanellou,maraz,bilas}@ics.forth.gr
[2] Department of Computer Science, University of Crete, Heraklion, Greece

Abstract. Although major cloud providers have captured and published workload executions in the form of traces, it is not clear how to use them for workload generation on a wide range of existing platforms. A methodological challenge that remains is to generate and execute realistic datacenter workloads on any infrastructure, using information from available traces. In this paper, we propose *Tracie*, a methodology addressing this challenge, and introduce the tool supporting its implementation. We present all the necessary steps starting from a trace up to workload execution: analysis of datacenter traces, extraction of parameters, application selection, and scaling of a workload to match the capabilities of the underlying infrastructure. Our evaluation validates that *Tracie* can generate executable workloads that closely resemble their trace-based counterparts. For validation, we correlate the recorded system metrics of a trace against the actual execution. We find that the average system metrics of synthetic workloads differ at most 5% compared to the trace and that they are highly correlated at 70% on average.

Keywords: Trace · Workload · Simulation · Cloud computing · Benchmarking

1 Introduction

The generation and execution of realistic cloud workloads constitute a significant methodological challenge in cloud computing. There have been two main directions towards addressing this challenge: (1) benchmark suites with popular cloud applications [10,19] and (2) simulators that rely on workload descriptions extracted from publicly available datacenter traces [2]. The first approach has the advantage that one can execute the workload on an existing platform, making it amenable to parameter tuning for specific purposes. However, the correlation of the resulting workload to the available datacenter traces is unclear and generally remains the responsibility of the user to validate and demonstrate it. The second approach directly connects to datacenter workloads; however, given only a trace, it is not possible to execute on an existing platform, limiting its applicability.

L. Sousa et al. (Eds.): Euro-Par 2021, LNCS 12820, pp. 37–54, 2021.
https://doi.org/10.1007/978-3-030-85665-6_3

This paper presents a robust and practical methodology, *Tracie*, to generate executable workloads from datacenter traces and sets of sample applications. The resulting workloads match key statistical characteristics derived from the respective traces. Towards this goal, we first determine which trace parameters characterize the trace and we include them in the generated actual executions. Parameter selection is not straightforward because each trace contains hundreds of parameters, such as job start time, number of tasks per job, etc. Second, we develop models of these parameters for the generation of the datacenter workload. Finally, we define a trace-specific application pool for the execution of the generated workloads. Workload execution is a real challenge because traces do not contain all the necessary variables to execute a workload. For example, we do not know the application types that were executed during trace creation.

To determine which variables of the trace are significant, we organize them into three categories: (1) variables that are *inherent* to the workload, for example, the arrival time of an application; i.e. workload variables, (2) variables that are *induced* to the workload, for example, the CPI of an application; i.e. execution variables, and (3) variables that refer to the infrastructure, for example, number of cores of server in the infrastructure; i.e. infrastructure variables. Then, we select the workload variables for the workload generation and the execution variables for the workload execution. Variables concerning the infrastructure are not crucial for describing the workload; hence, we omit them from further consideration. We model the workload as a random set of instances of the selected variables. Hence, we consider that each variable follows a different probability distribution function (PDF) and we estimate each PDF by processing the trace.

For workload execution, it is not feasible to precisely select the types of applications and the corresponding data, since this information is not part of the trace. Realistically, the best approximation we can achieve is to choose applications with similar micro-architectural characteristics, e.g. cycles per instruction (CPI). Towards this objective, we first estimate the PDF of each micro-architectural parameter available in the trace. We then measure the micro-architectural characteristics of several applications, executing them individually. Finally, we select from the available pool of application kernels the subset that best matches the micro-architectural characteristics extracted from the trace.

Overall, *Tracie* provides the methodology for the generation, execution, and validation of datacenter workloads resembling the source traces. Unlike prior related work, *Tracie* manages to generate realistic workloads on a wide range of existing platforms, starting from an analysis of a datacenter trace and leading up to the actual execution and monitoring of units of work selected from a pool of available application kernels. For validation, we define a method to statistically compare how close the execution of a workload generated by *Tracie* matches the original one captured in the trace. This is essential because the workload execution is affected by execution variables not included in the trace, e.g. interference of co-located applications and the dependencies of tasks belonging to an application.

In our evaluation, we use three types of containerized applications: (1) services that execute for a long time, e.g. a web server, (2) client applications that emulate the incoming requests of a service, e.g. the ab benchmark [1] issuing requests to a web server, and (3) batch applications that perform a specific amount of work, e.g. running a machine learning algorithm. Our evaluation shows that our PDF estimations of workload and execution characteristics match closely the histograms of these characteristics as captured in the traces. Correlation is 75% on average for workload parameters and 70% on average for micro-architectural parameters of applications.

The main contributions of this paper are as follows:

- Extraction of common parameters for datacenter traces that unify the description of traces from different cloud providers.
- A method for selecting a representative subset of parameters from a pool of available application kernels to match micro-architectural characteristics of applications used by traces.
- A method to validate that workload generated by *Tracie* match the execution of the captured workload trace, particularly in terms of key micro-architectural characteristics.
- A practical and easy to use workload generator that can generate executable workloads starting from a set of applications, or kernels.

2   Trace Analysis

We summarize the notions used in a trace as follows:

- A *task* is an indivisible unit of work that executes on a single processing unit. Task duration may vary significantly across tasks, from milliseconds to hours.
- A *job* is a set of tasks. For instance, in a web server, each user request is a job and consists of many tasks. Different Spark jobs in a Spark application appear in the trace as individual jobs.
- An *application* is a set of jobs that execute in batch mode, i.e. we are interested in the completion time of the full application and not individual jobs or tasks.
- A *service* is a set of user-facing jobs, i.e. we are interested in the completion time of individual jobs, as well as the job rate. Typically, services are assumed to run continuously.
- A *workload* is a set of applications and services.

Starting with the traces Google 2011 [29], Alibaba [24], and Google 2019 [30], we summarize the main events captured as follows:

- *Job events* represent changes in the state of a job, e.g. when a job is submitted or begins execution.
- *Task events* represent changes in the state of a task, similar to jobs. Task events may also contain constraints, e.g. when a task should (not) run on a specific server or task affinity with data.

– *Machine events* represent changes in the hardware or the software of the infrastructure, e.g. when a server is added, a kernel is updated, or a server fails. Machine, events, may also contain machine attributes, e.g. the amount of DRAM available in a server.
– *Resource events* represent the resources reserved or used by jobs and tasks within the interval, e.g. average CPU utilization over 10s. We exclude from this category events that refer to cumulative machine use, and instead, we include these in machine events.

Job, task, machine, and resource reservation events are point events, whereas resource usage events are periodic and refer to intervals. The above categorization, which is the default in traces, mixes inherent workload events with events that depend on the infrastructure and the scheduler. In the context of this paper, such categorization does not help because workload events originate exclusively from users, while the rest depend on the executing environment. Apart from that, there is information in the trace that does not add value to a workload generator, e.g., the user's username that submitted a job. Therefore, propose a different categorization for the trace that is more suitable for our goal:

– *Workload events*, about *inherent* workload characteristics. They include the submission times of jobs and tasks.
– *Execution events*, with information about the *induced* execution in a specific environment. They include the schedule time and the finish time of a job/task.

2.1 Workload and Execution Events

Next, we show how to select the workload and execution events, focusing on the Google'11 trace for illustration purposes. We follow the same procedure for all traces, and summarize our findings in Table 1.

Table 1. Selected events of Google'11, Alibaba, and Google'19 traces.

Category	Type	Information
Workload	Job submitted	[time, job-id, sched class]
Execution	Job scheduled, finished	[time, job-id, priority]
	Job usage	[start, end, job-id, task-id, resources, metrics]
	Task submitted, scheduled, finished	[time, job-id, task-id, resources]

Job submit events are affected neither by the underlying infrastructure nor by the job/task scheduler. They originate from user requests and are static to recorded workloads. Therefore, we consider the job submit as workload events, while the rest as execution events. We choose only the events in the common path of a workload execution from the rest events, i.e. job "schedule, finish" and task "submit, schedule, finish" events. Additionally, we select information about the event time, and the type of the jobs, either batch or UF, for the submit events. For the schedule and finish events, we select information about the event time, the resource usage, and the system metrics they cause. We omit the events that concern failures or kill events, as they are specific to the recorded workload.

3   *Tracie* Model

We model a workload as a set of running tasks with certain parameters. To simplify the modeling procedure and without loss of generality, we consider that a workload is a mix of independent, batch (abbreviated as B, below), and user-facing jobs (abbreviated as UF), originating either from applications or services. We also assume that all tasks in each job are identical, therefore, tasks have the same duration and execute the same code. Typically jobs today, repetitively perform similar tasks. For instance, a Spark job contains tasks that perform the same computation on different partitions of a Resilient Distributed Dataset (RDD) [33]. Different jobs consist of different tasks.

We consider that the aforementioned assumptions still leave enough flexibility for expressing other types of workloads. For example, a job that contains tasks that are not identical can be modelled by *Tracie* as a collection of jobs, one for each type of task it contains. If we wish to model a job where all tasks are of a different type, we can do so by replacing it with as many one-task jobs as the different task types in the original job.

Therefore, our model consists of the following entities:

– A *workload* W is a list of jobs along with their arrival time $[Job, J_{AT}]$.
– A *job* J is a tuple $[J, J_N, J_D, B/UF, (Task, T_{AT})]$, where J is the job type, J_N is the number of job tasks, J_D is the duration of the job, B/UF indicates if a job is batch or UF, and $[Task, T_{AT}]$ is a list of task instances along with their arrival time.
– A *task* T is a tuple $[T, T_D, T_R]$, where T is the task type, T_D is the duration of the task, and T_R are the resource allocation requests.

Table 2 summarizes the parameters we use in our model and their correspondence to trace events. $J_{AT}[UF]$ and $J_{AT}[B]$ parameters correspond to the timestamp of a submit job event of UF and batch jobs. $J_N[UF]$ and $J_N[B]$ parameters correspond to the number of finish events of tasks belonging to the same UF and batch job. $T_{AT}[UF]$ and $T_{AT}[B]$ parameters are the timestamps of a submit UF and batch task event. Finally, $T_D[UF]$, $T_D[B]$, $J_D[UF]$, and $J_D[B]$ are calculated as the difference in the timestamp of schedule and finish events for UF and batch tasks and jobs respectively.

Table 2. Parameter definition and PDF estimation for Google 11, Alibaba, and Google 19 traces.

	Params	Desc	Trace event	Google'11	Alibaba	Google'19
Workload	$J_{AT}[UF]$	UF job arrival	Timestamp of submit job event	$Chi^2(0.3, -1.5e^{-10}, 1.3e^{15})$	$N(1.3e^{12}, 7.2e^{11})$	$B(0.9, 1.1, -8.14e^{-11}, 2.5e^{12})$
	$J_{AT}[B]$	Batch job arrival		$R(2, 1.3e^{12}, 1.3e^{12})$	$R(713, 80, 2.4e^4)$	$B(0.4, 4565, -7.4e^{-11}, 1.7e^5)$
	$J_N[UF]$	UF job task cnt	Task finish event of the same job	$T(0.2, -1.5e^5, 6.6e^7)$	$Exp(-2.5e^{12}, 2e^{12})$	$N(-5e^{11}, 7.64e^{11})$
	$J_N[B]$	Batch job task cnt		$T(0.3, 1, 1.5e^{-20})$	$KDE(N, 2)$	$KDE(N, 2)$
Execution	$T_{AT}[UF]$	UF task arrival	Timestamp of submit task event	$T(0.5, 0.006, 0.006)$	$B(212, 2.6e^4, -4.8e^{15}, 5.8e^{17})$	$N(6.8e^{13}, 6.8e^{14})$
	$T_{AT}[B]$	Batch task arrival		$KDE(N, 2.5)$	$KDE(B, 1.6)$	$KDE(N, 1.8)$
	$T_D[UF]$	UF task duration	Difference in the timestamp of	$KDE(N, 1.9)$	$KDE(B, 23)$	$KDE(N, 1.98)$
	$T_D[B]$	Batch task duration	schedule and finish task events	$KDE(N, 2.1)$	$KDE(B, 2.1)$	$KDE(N, 2.09)$
	$J_D[UF]$	UF job duration	Difference in the timestamp of	$B(0.3, 4e^3, -2.3e^{-27}, 3.7e^3)$	$Chi^2(0.2, -1.1e^{-25}, 21)$	$N(1.3, 11)$
	$J_D[B]$	Batch job duration	schedule and finish job events	$T(0.2, -1.9e^5, 6.8e^6)$	$B(8506, 16.6, -2.2e^{17}, 2.2e^{17})$	$N(-1.9e^{13}, 5.1e^{14})$

Next, we use the traces to extract appropriate values for each parameter. We model parameters as independent random variables. For each trace, we extract the histograms of the events that correspond to our parameters. Then, we identify the PDFs that best fit the histogram in whole or piece-wise and we use these PDFs as the value distributions of our model parameters. Table 2 summarizes the PDF that corresponds to each model parameter for each trace.

Depending on the histogram, we follow two different methods. If the histogram matches a common probability distribution, such as Normal, R, Chi-squared, T, Beta, Log-normal, Gamma, F, Exponential, Cauchy, Laplace, log-gamma, Chi, we apply Parametric Density Estimation (PDE) [14,31] to calculate its specific parameters, such as mean value and variance. To figure out which PDF to use, we perform multiple PDE tests with different PDF types and select the best fitting PDF that exhibits the minimum distance (least squares) with the given data-set. If the minimum distance is above 0.5, we consider that the histogram does not match a single probability distribution, and we resort to a Non-parametric Density Estimation (NDE) [20] technique, Kernel Density Estimation (KDE). KDE [16] models random variables as the concatenation of multiple instances of a single PDF kernel. KDE divides the histogram into fixed-size intervals (*bandwidth*), with each interval represented by the same kernel and different kernel parameters. KDE first identifies the kernel and bandwidth from the histogram [17] and then identifies the kernel parameters similar to PDE for each interval.

For Google 2011, we find that $J_{AT}[UF]$ follows a Chi-squared distribution with parameters $(0.31, -1.5e^{-10}, 1.26e15)$. $J_{AT}[UF]$ follows a R distribution with parameters $(1.98, 1.25e^{12}, 1.25e^{12})$. $J_N[UF], J_N[B], T_{AT}[UF]$, and $J_D[B]$ follow a T-distribution with parameters $(0.16, -1.45e^5, 6.63e^7)$, $(0.25, 1.0, 1.53e^{-20})$,

$(0.48, 0.006, 0.006)$, and $(0.18, -1.91e^5, 6.8e^6)$. $J_D[UF]$ follows a beta distribution with parameters $(0.18, -1.91e^5, 6.8e^6)$. Finally, for $T_{AT}[B], T_D[UF]$, and $T_D[B]$, we apply KDE because they do not map well to any of PDF types we use for PDE. We find that these parameters match a Gaussian kernel, with respective bandwidths 2.46, 1.91, and 2.1.

3.1   Workload Scaling

We intend to run the generated workloads on different setups and infrastructure sizes. Therefore, there is a need to scale the workloads to match the intended infrastructure. The model parameters and their value distributions as extracted from available traces typically refer to large scale infrastructures, with task and job durations that exceed hours or even days, which is not practical or possible to follow on research prototypes and specific research problems. Running the workload on a different infrastructure requires scaling the workload to adjust the number of jobs, job durations, job arrival times, or data-set sizes. To achieve workload scaling, we introduce the following scaling factors:

– The total number of jobs in a workload, W_N. With W_N, we control the number of jobs per server and per time unit.
– A parameter for the scaling of job arrival times, W_{SAT}. With W_{SAT}, we control how loaded the servers will be during execution.
– A parameter for the scaling of the duration of batch and UF jobs, J_{SD}. J_{SD} parameter changes the dynamics of the batch and UF jobs in a workload. This parameter is useful to investigate how the infrastructure and the system software copes with changes in the behavior of the workload. For instance, when throughput is more important than latency, i.e. when the duration of batch jobs is significantly higher than UF jobs and vice versa.

3.2   Application Selection

In this step, we select the application types that will be used for executing the trace-based workload. We base the selection of applications on several trace events and the characteristics they represent: 1) maximum and average CPU, 2) memory, disk, and network utilization, 3) cycles per instruction and 4) memory accesses per instruction. First, we process each trace individually to generate histograms for these parameters. Then we perform dimensionality reduction, using Principal Component Analysis (PCA) [21]. This step is essential for application selection because of the large number of parameters, which complicates application type estimation. After dimensionality reduction, we perform PDF estimation, similar to our model parameters (Sect. 3). Table 3 shows the resulting parameters with their corresponding PDF type and parameters for each trace. The procedure to define the trace application pool requires access to various application types. For the purposes of this work, we select the batch applications from the Rodinia benchmark suite [9] and the TPC family [26]. Also, we select services among the following cloud services: NGINX [27], Redis [5], CouchDB [3], and Memcached [4]. However, it is not in the scope of this work to provide representative UF or batch applications. We assume that users provide suitable application pools depending on their use cases. In addition, we do not further differentiate the importance of some application types over others. Therefore, during workload execution, we uniformly select an application out of such a pool.

Table 3. Application selection features extracted for WTs.

Params	Desc	Google'11	Alibaba	Google'19
ACU	Avg. CPU	$T(0.8, 2e^{-11}, 2.7e^{-11})$	$T(1, 1e^{-11}, 3.7e^{-11})$	$T(0.3, 3, 1.3e^{-9}, 6.6e^{-11})$
MU	Avg. Mem	$Norm(0.01, 0.05)$	$B(0.5, 674, -6.3e^{-30}, 2.2)$	$B(0.05, -3.5e^{-32}, 1.2)$
MM	Max Mem	$G(0.05, -3.5e^{-32}, 1.2)$	$Exp(0.0, 4.4)$	N/A
N_{IN}	Net in	N/A	$Exp(0.03, 0.2)$	$Exp(0.5, 0.8)$
N_{OUT}	Net out	N/A	$B(0.2, 11.3, -1.2e^{-25}, 1.4)$	$B(0.5, 203, -3.5e^{-33}, 5.4)$
IO	IO	$B(0.6, 172, -6.7e^{-33}, 1.56)$	N/A	$B(0.3, 490, -9.9e^{-33}, 0.9)$
PG	Page cache	$Exp(0.02, 0.03)$	N/A	N/A
PG	Page cache	N/A	N/A	$G(0.6, -1.1e^{-31}, 0.07)$

3.3   Similarity Validation

To validate the similarity of the generated execution-based workloads to the corresponding trace characteristics, we capture system metrics from the actual execution of the generated workload and compare them to the trace events, for each model parameter. To compare the two data-sets, trace vs. measured, we use the Pearson correlation coefficient [8].

$$r_{xy} = \frac{\sum_{i=1}^{n}(x_i - \overline{x})(y_i - \overline{y})}{\sqrt{\sum_{i=1}^{n}(x_i - \overline{x})^2}\sqrt{\sum_{i=1}^{n}(y_i - \overline{y})^2}}, \tag{1}$$

where n is the total number of samples for both data-sets, x_i is the i-th sample of the first data-set and $\overline{x}$ its corresponding mean value, y_i is the i-th sample of the second data-set and $\overline{y}$ its corresponding mean value. The range of values that r_{xy} can take is $[-1, 1]$.

For this computation, the two data-sets need to have the same size. Therefore, we randomly divide the data-set of the trace to N subsets with a size equal to the synthetic workload data-set, and calculate their Pearson correlation coefficients. N is the quotient of the size of the trace data-set to the size of the synthetic data-set. We then calculate the mean value of the resulting r_{xy} coefficients. If r_{xy} is close to 1 (or -1), then the two data-sets are highly correlated (positively or negatively). If r_{xy} is close to 0, the two data-sets are not linearly correlated.

4   Implementation

Tracie is a Python script that produces executable workloads. The user can generate a workload based on one of the trace profiles of *Tracie*. A profile mainly contains the type of PDFs and their parameters for the random variables of Table 2. Each profile is stored in a separate directory which becomes a parameter to *Tracie*, e.g. ./wlGenerator.py –profile = "Google 2011". We expect that *Tracie* will be augmented over time with additional profiles from new traces, based on our methodology of Sect. 3. After specifying a profile, users can scale the workload to match their setup with three parameters: 1) the number of jobs, 2) factor for job arrival time, and 3) factor for the job duration of batch and UF jobs. The number of jobs defines how many jobs the generator will create, e.g. ./wlGenerator.py $-n = 80$, will create 80 jobs. The factor for job arrival time is a number that is multiplied by the arrival time of a job, e.g. ./wlGenerator.py –wSat $= 2$, will double the arrival times of jobs. Finally, the factor for the duration of the jobs is a number that changes the number of tasks to change the duration of jobs, e.g. ./wlGenerator.py –jSD $= 2$, will double the number of job tasks. Therefore, *Tracie* allows users to execute diverse workloads of the same load factor and run a workload at different load factors (scales). The emphasis in the former is that every time the generator selects different tasks and other parameters (based on PDF profiles). In the latter case, users can fix other parameters and change the induced load. In both cases, the generated loads will run on the given infrastructure using the sample applications provided along with *Tracie*.

Tracie consists of two main modules: the *workload generator* and the *workload executor*. The workload generator receives as input the workload profile, encoded in custom data type **wlProfile**. Further inputs are J, which is the number of desired jobs in the workload. The workload generator (Pseudocode 1) produces a *job sequence* as output. This output contains a sequence of job instances, specifying the characteristics for each instance. The workload generator is used offline to produce a job trace before a test run is performed.

To calculate a job duration J_D, we create by $N = J_D/T_D$ tasks. The output of the *workload generator* is two files: (1) a sequence of jobs where each line describes a single job, i.e. $J = [J_A T, J_T, T]$ and (2) a sequence of tasks per job, where each line is list of timestamps defining their arrival time within jobs. The workload executor parses the generated job sequence and the task arrival sequence to generate and execute the tasks for each job. The tasks within a job execute the same code on the same data.

Algorithm 1. Workload generation.

1: **procedure** WLGENERATOR(**wlProfile** WP, **int** J, **int** F)
2:     **int** $jc, N := 0$ ▷ job counter, number of tasks, respectively
3:     **time** $ts, t_{total}, J_D, A_D := 0$ ▷ job timestamp, total time, job dura-
                                                                    tion, application duration, respec-
                                                                    tively
4:     **Boolean** S ▷ scheduling class, may either be **B**, indicating batch job, or **UF**,
                                       indicating user-facing job
5:     **appType** T ▷ Application name, out of pool of codes available to the tool
6:     **jobTypeSeq** W ▷ A sequence of jobs, the workload to output
7:     **while** $jc < J$ **do**
8:         $rand := random\ number\ between\ 0\ and\ 100$
9:         **if** $rand < P_B$ **then**
10:            $< T, J_N, ts > := \text{generateJob}(B, WP, t_{total})$
11:        **else**
12:            $< T, J_N, ts > := \text{generateJob}(UF, WP, t_{total})$
13:        **end if**
14:        $t_{total} := ts$
15:        $W.append(< jc, T, J_N, F, ts >)$
16:    **end while**
17:    **return** W
18: **end procedure**

Workload execution

19: **function** EXECUTEWORKLOAD(**Boolean** S, **wlProfile** WP, **time** t_{total})
20:    **if** $S = batch$ **then**
21:        $J_D = WP.J_D[B](WP.\lambda_B)$
22:    **else**
23:        $J_D = WP.J_D[UF](WP.\lambda_{UF})$
24:    **end if**
25:    $Select\ an\ app\ A\ of\ type\ T\ and\ its\ configuration\ out\ of\ pool\ of\ available\ apps,$
       $determine\ its\ duration\ A_D.$
26:    $J_N = J_D/T_D$
27:    $ts = t_{total} + WP.J_{AT}(WP.\lambda_{AT})$
28:    **return** $< J, J_N, ts >$
29: **end function**

---

5   Experimental Evaluation

In this section, we first evaluate our methodology for PDE, KDE, and application selection. Afterwards, we use *Tracie* to reproduce synthetic workloads based on Google and Alibaba traces. In our experiments, we use a server with three 16-core AMD Opteron 6200 64-bit processors, running at 2.1 GHz, and 48 GB of DDR-III DRAM. For storage, we use a Samsung EVO 850 128 GB SSD.

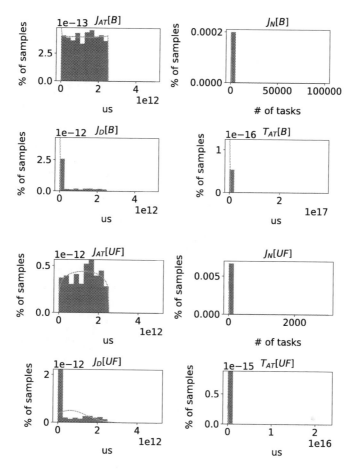

Fig. 1. Histogram and estimated PDFs using PDE for Google'11.

Table 4. Parameter similarity of PDFs and histograms (Google'11).

Parameter	$J_{AT}[B]$	$J_N[B]$	$J_D[B]$	$T_{AT}[B]$	$J_{AT}[UF]$	$J_N[UF]$	$J_D[UF]$	$T_{AT}[UF]$
Similarity (%)	94%	88%	72%	61%	91%	78%	55%	59%

5.1 Evaluating PDE

This section evaluates the accuracy of the PDFs computed by *Tracie* concerning the histograms of the corresponding parameters extracted from traces. Figure 1 compares the histograms of Google'11 parameters with the corresponding PDFs of *Tracie*. We observe that only the $J_D[UF]$ parameter is not very close to the histogram. To measure the similarity between PDFs and histograms, we compute their mean square distance. Table 4, shows the percentage of differences between histograms and PDFs. *Tracie* achieves the best distance for parameter $J_{AT}[B]$, for which the PDF and the histogram are 94% similar. The worst case is

$J_D[UF]$, for which the PDF is only 55% similar to the histogram, and on average, the PDFs are 75% similar to their histograms. Therefore, the characteristics of synthetic workloads of *Tracie* are quite close to the ones of the originating trace.

5.2   Dimensionality Reduction for Application Pools

Tracie reduces a large number of event types in each trace to a smaller number that can be used for application selection using PCA. Table 5 summarizes the importance of each event type as characterized by PCA. Event coefficients in bold indicate the most critical event types for each trace. We show with bold font the events of the traces that we select for application selection. The parameters average CPU and average memory usage are significant for all traces. Apart from that, max memory usage is critical for Google'11 and Alibaba traces while net in and net out for Alibaba and Google'19 trace. Finally, page cache usage and max IO usage are significant for Google'11 trace, while max CPU usage for Google'19. At most 6 parameters are sufficient to represent at least 75% of the micro-architectural characteristics of all traces. Cloud applications are diverse and can vary in all of these characteristics significantly. To reduce the parameter space, we focus only on the trace critical micro-architectural parameters.

Table 5. Applying PCA on execution parameters.

Parameter	avg_cpu	mem_usage	page_cache	max_mem	avg_disk_IO	disk_space	max_cpu
Google'11	**0.242**	**0.162**	**0.1**	**0.168**	0.0783	**0.095**	0.024
Alibaba	**0.176**	**0.12**	0.0718	**0.12**	0.053	0.078	0.018
Google'19	**0.136**	**0.098**	N/A	0.054	**0.099**	0.035	**0.24**
Parameter	max_IO	net_in	net_out	cpi	mai	cpu_distr	cpu_tail_distr
Google'11	**0.113**	N/A	N/A	0.005	0.018	N/A	N/A
Alibaba	0.075	**0.124**	**0.147**	0.004	0.013	N/A	N/A
Google'19	0.049	**0.107**	**0.103**	0.003	0.01	0.014	0.052

Table 6. Applying PCA on execution parameters: Importance of each parameter selected for workload execution.

Parameter	avg_cpu	mem_usage	page_cache	max_mem	avg_disk_IO	disk_space	max_cpu
Google'11	0.791	0.5	0.623	0.886	0.614	0.463	0.838
Alibaba	0.696	0.74	0.877	0.645	0.841	0.837	0.822
Parameter	max_IO	net_in	net_out	cpi	mai	cpu_distr	cpu_tail_distr
Google'11	0.5	0.655	0.613	0.706	0.531	0.77	0.734
Alibaba	0.834	0.655	0.568	0.757	0.636	0.739	0.829

5.3   Emulating the Google and the Alibaba Trace

This section generates and executes synthetic workloads of *Tracie*, based on Google and Alibaba. We then validate how representative the execution of these workloads is by comparing the system metrics of the synthetic workload execution to the ones in the trace. Figure 2 shows the results of two experiments, where we execute a workload based on the Google trace and a workload based on the Alibaba trace. By applying our validation methodology in both traces, we get a similarity coefficient among all usage parameters above 0.46 and, on average, 0.69. Table 6 shows the correlation coefficients for all parameters, for both workloads. Additionally, comparing the two synthetic workloads, we observe that the Alibaba workload is more bursty than the Google trace, which is why it results in a worse tail latency for the user-facing tasks. Moreover, we observe that the workload of the Alibaba trace has 100% load in the first 120 s and afterwards cools down, while in the Google trace load is more balanced over time.

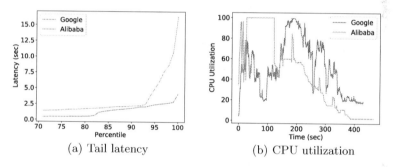

(a) Tail latency   (b) CPU utilization

Fig. 2. Two Workloads inspired by the Google and Alibaba traces, emulating the average server in each trace. (a) Tail latency of the tasks, (b) CPU utilization.

Google: According to the Google trace analysis [28], the average server is 50% utilized, the batch to user-facing job duration ratio is 0.5, and has 38% batch jobs. We create a workload using *Tracie* that follows the statistics of the Google trace for a single server and set 35 s as the average batch job duration. To scale down the workload, we estimate the scaling factors of *Tracie*, i.e. number of jobs, job arrival time, duration ratio of batch vs. UF jobs, by calculating the corresponding average values of Google servers. *Tracie* produces a workload with 52% CPU utilization and an average job arrival time of 10 s.

The trace released by Google has been studied extensively in several publications e.g. [6,11,12,22,23,25,28,29]). The trace has over 670,000 jobs and 25 million tasks executed over 12,500 hosts during 1-month time period [13]. Around 40% of submissions recorded are less than 10 ms after the previous submission even though the median arrival period is 900 ms. The tail of the arrival times distribution is power-law-like, though the maximum job arrival period is only 11 min. Jobs shorter than two hours account represent more than 95% of the jobs, and half of the jobs run for less than 3 min. The majority of jobs runs for less than 15 min [23].

Alibaba: Correspondingly, in Alibaba trace, the average server is 40% utilized, the batch to user-facing job duration ratio is 0.05, and it contains 53% batch jobs. Similarly, we create a workload with *Tracie*, selecting 4 s for the average batch job duration. The workload results in 45% CPU utilization and average job arrival time 680 ms. In both cases, the workload generated by *Tracie* is very close to the average statistics of servers as per the original traces.

The Alibaba trace is analyzed in [24]. It contains 11089 user-facing jobs and 12951 batch jobs, which run over a time period of 12 h. This places the batch job versus the user-facing job ratio at 53.9% to 46.1%. User-facing jobs in the Alibaba trace are long-running service jobs, in this particular case spanning the entire duration of the trace. On the contrary, batch jobs in the trace are predominantly short-running, with about 90% of batch jobs running in less than 0.19 of an hour, while a total of 98.1% of batch jobs runs in less than an hour. Overall, 47.2% of total jobs are long, whether batch or user-facing.

5.4   Investigating How Scaling Affects the Tail Latency

Finally, we show that with *Tracie* we can easily explore how the workload is affected when we change one of its scaling factors. In this experiment, we produce a workload that emulates the workload of a Google server according the Google trace on average. We examine how scaling the job arrival time affects the tail latency of jobs by running the workload 3 times with a different value scaling factor of J_{AT}. Figure 3 summarizes these three runs. Figure 3(a) shows the tail latency of all the user-facing tasks starting from 70th to the 100th percentile, while Fig. 3(b) shows the corresponding CPU utilization. In the first experiment (green line), we target a load of 25% on average. In the second (orange line), we target 50%, and in the third (blue line), we target 100%. The average utilization of the system is 31%, 46%, and 95% respectively, which indicates that we can successfully control the utilization of the system with *Tracie*, by just changing

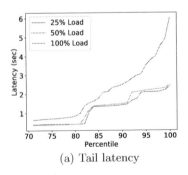
(a) Tail latency

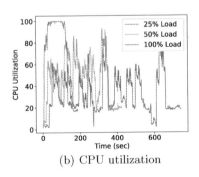
(b) CPU utilization

Fig. 3. Trade-off between CPU utilization and tail latency: (a) Tail latency of user-facing applications, for increasing system load. (b) CPU utilization.

the J_{AT} scaling factor. Moreover, the total execution time of the experiment changes almost in reverse proportion to the load of the system. The experiment finishes in 700 s for 25% load, 400s for 50% load, and 200 s for 100% load. Tail latency is not affected for the runs with 25% and 50% load. However, for the case with 100% load, tail latency suffers a 2× deterioration as we approach the 100-percentile of the tasks. It is not straightforward to increase the utilization of the system while still achieving low tail latency for the user-facing tasks.

6 Related Work

We classify prior work on workload generation in two main categories: (a) Benchmark suites with popular cloud applications to generate workloads mixes.

Benchmark Suites: BigDataBench [15] is a benchmark suite that provides benchmarks for online services, offline analytics, graph analytics, AI, data warehouse, NoSQL, and streaming. Contrary to our work, which focuses on using kernels as computation units, BigDataBench combines commonly occurring data characteristics (data motifs) with a set of micro-benchmarks to form computational building blocks. Subsequently, it uses the most common data motifs to compose complex workloads for a real-life software stack. DCMIX [32] combines a set of characteristic computation units to come up with a collection of benchmarks. DCMIX resembles *Tracie* in that it provides the functionality to execute a workload, as specified in a configuration file. However, *Tracie* also provides the capability to create arbitrary synthetic workloads, and goes one step further by profiling real-life datacenter traces to provide a collection of realistic parameter values. HiBench [19] is a benchmark suite for Hadoop. Compared to *Tracie*, BigDataBench, DCMIX, and HiBench do not consider real-life datacenter traces to provide parameter values based on realistic loads.

Workload Traces and Trace Generators: Several synthetic workload generators provide benchmarks that target specific operation aspects of a datacenter. BigBench [10] is a work that, similarly to ours, deals with the extraction of characteristics of realistic workloads and their use to generate synthetic workloads. However, BigBench focuses on a particular use case, a system handling the transactions of a big retailer, both physical and online. As such, the result is rather restricted to workloads that consist of database queries, contrary to our work, which aims at producing synthetic workloads for a more generic application domain. Some more generic efforts to produce synthetic workloads with realistic characteristics appear elsewhere in the literature. Due to the wide-spread use of this particular computing paradigm, two prominent synthetic workload generation examples, [7] and [2], deal with the synthesis of MapReduce workloads. GridMix [7] is a benchmarking tool by Apache Hadoop, which creates synthetic workloads suitable for testing Hadoop clusters. These traces are used as input to GridMix, which in turn outputs a synthetic workload. The load can be scaled up or down by adjusting the intervals between job submission. Several inherent and run-time characteristics of the jobs, such as memory usage, input data size, or job type, can be modeled. Similarly, SWIM [2] generates synthetic workloads based on the traces released by Facebook in 2009 and 2010. SWIM aims to produce workloads of shorter duration than the original traces while still maintaining their essential characteristics. CloudMix [18] is a benchmarking tool that synthesizes cloud workloads with realistic characteristics. Similar to our use of a pool of kernels, CloudMix relies on a repository of *reducible workload blocks* (RWBs), representing different mixes of assembly-level computations designed to mimic micro-architectural usage characteristics of tasks found in the Google trace. Workload scale-down is possible by reducing job and trace durations. Unlike our work, CloudMix is more concerned with reproducing the run-time behavior (in terms of micro-architectural characteristics) observed in the trace.

7   Conclusions

In this paper, we determine characteristics that describe datacenter workload traces. We use these characteristics to develop a methodology for generating synthetic workloads to execute on existing systems. We implement this methodology in *Tracie* and validate that the execution of applications in such workloads exhibits similar micro-architectural characteristics as the ones captured in the original trace. The flexibility of our methodology and *Tracie* lies in that they are not designed to mimic one particular datacenter workload. Instead, they can be configured to reproduce any desired profile, starting from a set of statistical characteristics extracted from traces. Furthermore, while we employ a specific set of application kernels as sample binaries for task execution, neither the methodology nor the supporting tools are hard-wired to this selection.

Acknowledgments. We thankfully acknowledge the support of the European Commission under the Horizon 2020 Framework Programme for Research and Innovation through the EVOLVE H2020 project (Grant Agreement Nr 825061).

References

1. ab Benchmark - Apache HTTP server benchmarking tool. https://httpd.apache.org/docs/2.4/programs/ab.html
2. Swim. https://github.com/SWIMProjectUCB/SWIM/wiki/Workloads-repository
3. The Apache CouchDB. https://couchdb.apache.org/
4. The Memcached I/O cache. https://memcached.org/
5. The Redis Database. https://redis.io/
6. Abdul-Rahman, O.A., Aida, K.: Towards understanding the usage behavior of Google cloud users: the mice and elephants phenomenon. In: IEEE International Conference on Cloud Computing Technology and Science (CloudCom 2014)
7. Apache: GridMix. https://hadoop.apache.org/docs/r1.2.1/gridmix.html
8. Benesty, J., Chen, J., Huang, Y., Cohen, I.: Pearson correlation coefficient. In: Noise Reduction in Speech Processing. Springer Topics in Signal Processing, vol. 2, pp. 1–4. Springer, Heidelberg (2009). https://doi.org/10.1007/978-3-642-00296-0_5

9. Che, S., et al.: Rodinia: a benchmark suite for heterogeneous computing. In: Proceedings of the 2009 IEEE International Symposium on Workload Characterization (IISWC)

10. Chen, Y., Alspaugh, S., Katz, R.: Interactive analytical processing in big data systems: A cross-industry study of mapreduce workloads. arXiv preprint arXiv:1208.4174 (2012)

11. Chen, Y., Ganapathi, A.S., Griffith, R., Katz, R.H.: Analysis and lessons from a publicly available Google cluster trace. Technical report. UCB/EECS-2010-95, EECS Department, University of California, Berkeley, June 2010. http://www2.eecs.berkeley.edu/Pubs/TechRpts/2010/EECS-2010-95.html

12. Di, S., Kondo, D., Cappello, F.: Characterizing and modeling cloud applications/jobs on a Google data center. J. Supercomput. **69**, 139–160 (2014). https://doi.org/10.1007/s11227-014-1131-z

13. Di, S., Kondo, D., Cirne, W.: Characterization and comparison of cloud versus grid workloads. In: IEEE Cluster (2012)

14. Efron, B., Tibshirani, R., et al.: Using specially designed exponential families for density estimation. Ann. Stat. **24**(6), 2431–2461 (1996)

15. Gao, W., et al.: Bigdatabench: A scalable and unified big data and ai benchmark suite. arXiv preprint arXiv:1802.08254 (2018)

16. Gray, A.G., Moore, A.W.: Nonparametric density estimation: toward computational tractability. In: Proceedings of the 2003 SIAM International Conference on Data Mining, pp. 203–211. SIAM (2003)

17. Guidoum, A.C.: Kernel estimator and bandwidth selection for density and its derivatives. The Kedd package, version 1 (2015)

18. Han, R., Zong, Z., Zhang, F., Vazquez-Poletti, J.L., Jia, Z., Wang, L.: Cloudmix: generating diverse and reducible workloads for cloud systems. In: 2017 IEEE 10th International Conference on Cloud Computing (CLOUD)

19. Huang, S., Huang, J., Dai, J., Xie, T., Huang, B.: The hibench benchmark suite: characterization of the mapreduce-based data analysis. In: 2010 IEEE 26th International Conference on Data Engineering Workshops (ICDEW). IEEE (2010)

20. Izenman, A.J.: Review papers: recent developments in nonparametric density estimation. J. Am. Stat. Assoc. **86**(413), 205–224 (1991)

21. Karamizadeh, S., Abdullah, S.M., Manaf, A.A., Zamani, M., Hooman, A.: An overview of principal component analysis. J. Signal Inf. Process. **4**(3B), 173 (2013)

22. Liu, B., Lin, Y., Chen, Y.: Quantitative workload analysis and prediction using Google cluster traces. In: 2016 IEEE Conference on Computer Communications Workshops (INFOCOM WKSHPS),pp. 935–940 (2016)

23. Liu, Z., Cho, S.: Characterizing machines and workloads on a Google cluster. In: Proceedings of the 2012 41st International Conference on Parallel Processing Workshops, ICPPW 2012, IEEE Computer Society, Washington, DC

24. Lu, C., Ye, K., Xu, G., Xu, C.Z., Bai, T.: Imbalance in the cloud: an analysis on Alibaba cluster trace. In: 2017 IEEE International Conference on Big Data (Big Data), pp. 2884–2892. IEEE (2017)

25. Moreno, I.S., Garraghan, P., Townend, P., Xu, J.: An approach for characterizing workloads in Google cloud to derive realistic resource utilization models. In: SOSE, pp. 49–60. IEEE Computer Society (2013)

26. Nambiar, R., Wakou, N., Carman, F., Majdalany, M.: Transaction Processing Performance Council (TPC), State of the council (2010)

27. Nedelcu, C.: Nginx HTTP Server: Adopt Nginx for Your Web Applications to Make the Most of Your Infrastructure and Serve Pages Faster Than Ever. Packt Publishing Ltd., Birmingham (2010)

28. Reiss, C., Tumanov, A., Ganger, G.R., Katz, R.H., Kozuch, M.A.: Heterogeneity and dynamicity of clouds at scale: Google trace analysis. In: Proceedings of the Third ACM Symposium on Cloud Computing (2012)
29. Reiss, C., Tumanov, A., Ganger, G.R., Katz, R.H., Kozuch, M.A.: Towards understanding heterogeneous clouds at scale: Google trace analysis (2012)
30. Tirmazi, M., et al.: Borg: the next generation. In: Proceedings of the Fifteenth European Conference on Computer Systems, pp. 1–14 (2020)
31. Varanasi, M.K., Aazhang, B.: Parametric generalized gaussian density estimation. J. Acoust. Soc. Am. **86**(4), 1404–1415 (1989)
32. Xiong, X., et al.: DCMIX: generating mixed workloads for the cloud data center. In: Zheng, C., Zhan, J. (eds.) Bench 2018. LNCS, vol. 11459, pp. 105–117. Springer, Cham (2019). https://doi.org/10.1007/978-3-030-32813-9_10
33. Zaharia, M., Chowdhury, M., Franklin, M.J., Shenker, S., Stoica, I., et al.: Spark: cluster computing with working sets. HotCloud **10**(10), 95 (2010)

Update on the Asymptotic Optimality of LPT

Anne Benoit[1], Louis-Claude Canon[2(✉)], Redouane Elghazi[2],
and Pierre-Cyrille Héam[2]

[1] LIP, ENS Lyon, Lyon, France
[2] FEMTO-ST, University
of Franche-Comté, Besançon, France
louis-claude.canon@univ-fcomte.fr

Abstract. When independent tasks are to be scheduled onto identical processors, the typical goal is to minimize the makespan. A simple and efficient heuristic consists in scheduling first the task with the longest processing time (LPT heuristic), and to plan its execution as soon as possible. While the performance of LPT has already been largely studied, in particular its asymptotic performance, we revisit results and propose a novel analysis for the case of tasks generated through uniform integer compositions. Also, we perform extensive simulations to empirically assess the asymptotic performance of LPT. Results demonstrate that the absolute error rapidly tends to zero for several distributions of task costs, including ones studied by theoretical models, and realistic distributions coming from benchmarks.

1 Introduction

We revisit the classical problem of scheduling n independent tasks with costs $p_1, \ldots, p_n$ onto m identical processors. The goal is to minimize the total execution time, or *makespan*, usually denoted by $C_{\max}$. This problem, denoted $P||C_{\max}$ in Graham's notation [15], has been extensively studied in the literature, and greedy heuristics turn out to have theoretical guarantees and to perform well in practice. In particular, we focus on the *Longest Processing Time (LPT)* heuristic, where the longest task will be scheduled first, on the processor where it can start the earliest. This heuristic is very simple and has a low complexity, while exhibiting good worst-case performance [16], and excellent empirical one. With a large number of tasks, LPT appears to be almost optimal.

Since the worst-case performance exhibits cases where LPT is further from the optimal, many different approaches have tried to fill the gap between this worst-case performance and the excellent practical performance. The goal is to provide performance guarantees of different kinds, for instance by studying the average-case complexity, some generic-case complexity, or convergence results.

Hence, many convergence results have been proposed in the literature. They state that LPT ends up providing an optimal solution when the number of tasks grows towards infinity. Some of these results even provide asymptotic rates that

© Springer Nature Switzerland AG 2021
L. Sousa et al. (Eds.): Euro-Par 2021, LNCS 12820, pp. 55–69, 2021.
https://doi.org/10.1007/978-3-030-85665-6_4

quantify the speed with which LPT tends to optimally. These results depend on assumptions on the probability distribution of the costs of the tasks, and on the definition of distance to optimality. However, the literature lacks a definitive answer on the convergence to optimality and its rate when faced with difficult cost distributions. In particular, this work is the first to consider dependent random costs with a constraint on the minimum cost.

First, Sect. 2 synthesizes the existing contributions and their limitations. Then, we revisit LPT and propose an update to these asymptotic optimality results, both from a theoretical perspective and from an empirical one. We also consider related heuristics, in particular a novel strategy recently proposed in [8]. Our contribution is twofold:

1. We derive a new convergence (in probability) result when the distribution of task costs is generated using uniform integer compositions, hence leading to a novel probabilistic analysis of the heuristics for this problem (Sect. 3);
2. We perform a thorough empirical analysis of these heuristics, with an extended range of settings to study particular distributions but also distributions coming from real applications (Sect. 4).

2   Related Work

Theoretical Studies. There are several theoretical works studying the rate of convergence of LPT. Coffman et al. [4] analyze the average performance of LPT under the assumption that costs are uniformly distributed in the interval $(0, 1]$. They show that the ratio between the expected makespan obtained with LPT and the expected optimal one with preemption is bounded by $O(1 + \frac{m^2}{n^2})$, where m is the number of processors and n is the number of tasks.

Frenk and Rinnooy Kan [14] bound the *absolute error* (i.e., the difference between the achieved makespan and the optimal one) of LPT using order statistics of the processing times when the cost distribution has a cumulative distribution function of the form $F(x) = x^a$ with $0 < a < \infty$. The results also stand when this constraint is relaxed into $F(x) = \Theta(x^a)$. They prove that the absolute error goes to 0 with speed $O\left(\left(\frac{\log\log(n)}{n}\right)^{\frac{1}{a}}\right)$ as the number of tasks n grows. For higher moments, of order q, a similar technique gives a speed of $O\left(\left(\frac{1}{n}\right)^{\frac{a}{q}}\right)$.

Frenk and Rinnooy Kan [13] also study uniform machines ($Q||C_{\max}$) in the more general case where costs follow a distribution with finite moment and the cumulative distribution function is strictly increasing in a neighbourhood of 0. They show that LPT is asymptotically optimal almost surely in terms of absolute error. When it is the second moment that is finite instead, they show that LPT is asymptotically optimal in expectation. For the more specific cases where the costs follow either a uniform distribution or a negative exponential distribution, they provide additional convergence rates.

Another theoretical study is done by Loulou [20], providing a comparison between LPT and a less sophisticated heuristic, RLP (Random List Processing), also called LS (List Scheduling) in this paper. This heuristic is simpler than

LPT because the jobs are considered in an arbitrary order instead of a sorted order. These algorithms are studied under the assumption that the costs are independent and identically distributed (i.i.d.) random variables with finite first moment. Under this assumption, the absolute error of RLP with at least three processors and LPT are both stochastically bounded by a finite random variable. The author also proves that the absolute error of LPT converges in distribution to optimality with rate $O(1/n^{1-\epsilon})$.

Coffman et al. [6] list various results and techniques that are useful for the study of the problems of scheduling and bin packing. They consider both theoretical optimal results, and heuristic algorithm results. LPT is one of the algorithms they study, in terms of both relative error (LPT/OPT) and absolute error (LPT − OPT). They also reuse the specific probability distribution used by Frenk and Rinnooy Kan [14] of the form $F(x) = x^a$, with $0 < a < \infty$. They present a heuristic adapted from a set-partitioning problem with a better convergence on this distribution.

Piersma and Romeijn [22] have considered the $R||C_{\max}$ problem (with unrelated machines), and they propose an LP relaxation of the problem, followed by a Lagrange relaxation. Assuming that the processing times are i.i.d. random vectors of $[0,1]^m$, they prove that $\frac{1}{n}$OPT converges almost surely to a value θ that they give (it depends on the Lagrange relaxation). Using a previous convergence result [14], they infer that the makespan of LPT also converges a.s. to $n\theta$.

Dempster et al. [9] consider an objective function also depending on the machine cost, and they propose a heuristic in two steps, where they first choose the machines to be bought with knowledge of the distribution of the jobs, and then schedule the jobs on the machines that were bought in the first step. For identical machines, assuming that the processing times are i.i.d. random variables with finite second moment, they prove that the relative error of their heuristic converges to 0 in expectation and probability when the number of jobs goes to infinity. For uniform machines, they need more assumptions to reach results.

Table 1 summarizes the main results that are known about LPT.

Table 1. For each main result, the problem may consider uniform processors (P) or processors with speeds $(Q$ or $R)$. A result on the absolute difference is stronger than on the ratio. OPT is the optimal makespan, whereas OPT* is the optimal makespan with preemption.

	Problem	Distribution	Studied quantity	Convergence/rate
[4]	$P||C_{\max}$	$\mathcal{U}(0,1)$	$E[\text{LPT}]/E[\text{OPT}^*]$	$1 + O(m^2/n^2)$
[14]	$P||C_{\max}$	$F(x) = x^a, 0 < a < \infty$	LPT − OPT	$O((\log\log(n)/n)^{\frac{1}{a}})$ almost surely (a.s.)
[14]	$P||C_{\max}$	As above	$E[(\text{LPT} - \text{OPT})^q]$	$O((1/n)^{\frac{a}{q}})$
[13]	$Q||C_{\max}$	Finite 1st moment	LPT − OPT	a.s.
[13]	$Q||C_{\max}$	Finite 2nd moment	LPT − OPT	In expectation
[13]	$Q||C_{\max}$	$\mathcal{U}(0,1)$ or $Exp(\lambda)$	LPT − OPT	$O(\log n/n)$ a.s.
[13]	$Q||C_{\max}$	$\mathcal{U}(0,1)$	$E[\text{LPT}] - E[\text{OPT}]$	$O(m^2/n)$
[20]	$P||C_{\max}$	Finite 1st moment	LPT − OPT	Bounding finite RV
[20]	$P||C_{\max}$	$\mathcal{U}(0,1)$	LPT − OPT	$O(1/n^{1-\epsilon})$ in dist
[6]	$P||C_{\max}$	$\mathcal{U}(0,1)$	$E[\text{LPT} - \text{OPT}]$	$O(m/(n+1))$
[22]	$R||C_{\max}$	$\mathcal{U}(0,1)$	OPT	$n\theta$ a.s.

Beyond LPT. Even though LPT has interesting properties in terms of convergence, other heuristics have been designed for the multiprocessor scheduling problem. For independent tasks and makespan minimization, the problem is actually close to a bin-packing problem, where one would like to create m bins of same size. Hence, the MULTIFIT heuristic [5] builds on techniques used in bin-packing, and it provides an improved worst-case bound.

Then, a COMBINE heuristic was proposed [19], combining MULTIFIT and LPT to get the best of these two heuristics. Another alternative, LISTFIT, was proposed in [17], still with the goal to minimize the makespan on identical machines.

Building on the Largest Differencing Method of Karmarkar and Karp [21], a novel heuristic was proposed, outperforming LPT and MULTIFIT from an average-case perspective.

More recently, Della Croce and Scatamacchia [8] revisit LPT to propose yet another heuristic, SLACK, by splitting the sorted tasks in tuples of m consecutive tasks (recall that m is the number of processors), and then sorting tuples by non-increasing order of the difference between the largest and smallest task in the tuple. A list-scheduling strategy is then applied with tasks sorted in this order. Moreover, LPT last step is enhanced to reach a better worst-case approximation ratio.

Empirical Studies. An empirical comparison of LISTFIT with MULTIFIT, COMBINE and LPT is proposed in [17]. Several parameters are varied, in particular the number of machines, number of jobs, and the minimum and maximum values of a uniform distribution for processing times. No other distribution is considered. LISTFIT turns out to be robust and returns better makespan values than previous heuristics.

Behera and Laha [1] consider the three heuristics MULTIFIT, COMBINE and LISTFIT, and propose a comprehensive performance evaluation. While LISTFIT outperforms the two other heuristics, this comes at a price of an increased time complexity. They do not consider instances with more than 300 tasks, and no comparison with LPT is done.

An empirical evaluation of LPT was proposed in [18], showing that LPT consumes less computational time than the competitors (MULTIFIT, COMBINE, LISTFIT), but returns schedules with higher makespan values. However, here again, there is no study of the convergence, and no comparison of LPT with other simpler algorithms.

Finally, an evaluation of SLACK is done in [8]: this variant of LPT turns out to be much better than LPT on benchmark literature instances, and it remains competitive with the COMBINE heuristic that is more costly and more difficult to implement.

Beyond Independent Tasks. While we have been focusing so far on independent tasks, there have also been some empirical analysis of list scheduling for general directed acyclic graphs (DAGs), i.e., with dependencies. For instance, Cooper et al. [7] evaluate various list schedulers on benchmark codes, pointing out cases where a basic list scheduling algorithm works well, and where more sophisticated approaches are helpful. In this paper, we focus on independent tasks to study the convergence of LPT and other heuristics.

3   Convergence Results for Integer Compositions

In this section, we derive new convergence results for four heuristics that are first described in Sect. 3.1. These results apply when the distribution of task costs is generated following an integer composition method. In contrast to related work where the number of tasks n is known beforehand, this consists in considering that the total amount of work W is fixed (costs are thus dependent random variables). We detail how tasks are generated among possible decompositions of this work (Sect. 3.2). We finally perform the probabilistic analysis in two different settings, depending whether the minimum cost of tasks is one (Sect. 3.3) or greater (Sect. 3.4).

The proofs of the results in this section are mainly based on combinatorics techniques. The reader is referred to [11] for more information. All the detailed proofs are available in the companion research report [3].

3.1   Algorithms

We consider four different list scheduling algorithms: they order the tasks in some way, and then successively assign tasks in a greedy manner, to the processor that has the lowest current finishing time (or makespan). Hence, tasks are always started as soon as possible, and for independent tasks, there is no idle time in the schedule.

The four algorithms differ in the way they first order the tasks:

- LS: List Scheduling is the basic list scheduling algorithm that does not order the tasks, but rather considers them in an arbitrary order. The time complexity of LS is $O(n \log m)$.
- LPT: Largest Processing Time orders the tasks from the largest to the smallest. The time complexity of LPT is $O(n \log n)$.
- MD: Median Discriminated is an attempt to find an intermediate solution between LPT and LS. The tasks are not completely sorted, but the median of the execution times is computed so that the first $\frac{n}{2}$ processed tasks are larger than the median, while the next $\frac{n}{2}$ are smaller. The time complexity of MD is $O(n \log m)$.
- SLACK: as defined by Della Croce and Scatamacchia in [8], it makes packs of m tasks and defines for each of these packs the slack, which is the difference between the largest and the smallest task of the pack. The packs are then sorted from the largest to the smallest slack and the tasks are ordered in the order incurred by the order of the packs. The time complexity of SLACK is $O(n \log n)$.

3.2   Tasks Random Generation

A W-composition is a finite sequence $p_1, \ldots, p_n$ of strictly positive integers such that $p_1 + \ldots + p_n = W$.

Let $\mathbb{D}_W$ be the uniform distribution over W-compositions and $\mathbb{D}_{W,p_{\min}}$ the uniform distribution over W-compositions satisfying for each i, $p_i \geq p_{\min}$. In particular, $\mathbb{D}_{W,1} = \mathbb{D}_W$. For instance, $\mathbb{D}_4$ is the uniform distribution over the eight elements $(1,1,1,1)$, $(1,1,2)$, $(1,2,1)$, $(1,3)$, $(2,1,1)$, $(2,2)$, $(3,1)$, (4); $\mathbb{D}_{4,2}$ is the uniform distribution over $(2,2)$ and (4). Note that for $\mathbb{D}_4$, the probability that $p_1 = 1$ is $1/2$ and the probability that $p_1 = 3$ is $1/8$.

In practice, random generation is performed using the recursive method [12].

For a list L of task costs, we denote by $\mathrm{LPT}(L, m)$ the makespan $C_{\max}$ returned by LPT on m machines. We define as well $\mathrm{LS}(L, m)$, $\mathrm{MD}(L, m)$ and $\mathrm{SLACK}(L, m)$ for the other heuristics. The optimal (minimum) $C_{\max}$ that can be obtained by any algorithm is similarly denoted $\mathrm{OPT}(L, m)$.

3.3   Probabilistic Analysis of List-Scheduling Heuristics For $\mathbb{D}_W$

Ratio for $\mathbb{D}_W$. In this setting, we know the total workload W, but the number of tasks n is not fixed and there is no minimum task cost. Let $L[W] = (p_1, \ldots, p_n)$ be a sequence of positive integers such that $\sum_{i=1}^{n} p_i = W$, hence a W-composition.

According to [16],

$$\frac{\mathrm{LS}(L[W], m)}{\mathrm{OPT}(L[W], m)} \leq 1 + (m-1)\frac{p_{\max}}{\sum_{i=1}^{n} p_i} = 1 + (m-1)\frac{p_{\max}}{W},$$

where $p_{\max} = \max\{p_i\}$.

Following [11, page 310], for $\mathbb{D}_W$ and for any y,

$$\mathbb{P}\left(p_{\max} \geq 2\log_2 W + y\right) = O\left(\frac{e^{-2y}}{W}\right). \tag{1}$$

Since by definition of OPT, $\mathrm{OPT}(L[W], m) \leq \mathrm{LS}(L[W], m)$, for any fixed m,

$$\mathbb{P}\left(\frac{\mathrm{LS}(\mathbb{D}_W, m)}{\mathrm{OPT}(\mathbb{D}_W, m)} \leq 1 + 2(m-1)\frac{\log_2(W)}{W}\right) \xrightarrow[W \to +\infty]{} 1. \tag{2}$$

It is also known, see [11, Proposition V.I.], that for the distribution $\mathbb{D}_W$, $E[p_{\max}] \sim \log_2 W$. By linearity of expectations, the following result holds:

$$E\left[\frac{\mathrm{LS}(\mathbb{D}_W, m)}{\mathrm{OPT}(\mathbb{D}_W, m)}\right] \xrightarrow[W \to +\infty]{} 1.$$

The results also hold for LPT, MD and SLACK, which are particular list-scheduling heuristics.

Absolute Error for $\mathbb{D}_W$. The *absolute error* of a heuristic is the difference between its result and the optimal result. A first obvious upper bound is that $LS(L, m) - OPT(L, m) \leq p_{\max}$ (for any set of tasks L), and previous results on $p_{\max}$ can be used to bound the error (but not proving it tends to 0). Furthermore, we prove the following theorem:

Theorem 1. *Algorithms LPT and SLACK are optimal for $\mathbb{D}_W$, with probability $1 - O\left(\frac{1}{W}\right)$. For any fixed m, for L generated according to $\mathbb{D}_W$,*

$$\mathbb{P}(\text{LPT}(L, m) = \text{OPT}(L, m)) = 1 - O\left(\frac{1}{W}\right), \quad and$$

$$\mathbb{P}(\text{SLACK}(L, m) = \text{OPT}(L, m)) = 1 - O\left(\frac{1}{W}\right), \quad and$$

$$\mathbb{P}(\text{MD}(L, m) \leq \text{OPT}(L, m) + 1) = 1 - O\left(\frac{1}{W}\right).$$

The proof is building upon two lemmas, and can be found in the companion research report [3]. Note that the result for MD is almost similar, but up to 1 to the optimal.

Theorem 1 can be reformulated in a convergence in probability result:

Corollary 1. *For every $\varepsilon > 0$, for the distributions $\mathbb{D}_W$,*

$$\lim_{W \to +\infty} \mathbb{P}(|\text{LPT}(L, m) - \text{OPT}(L, m)| \geq \varepsilon) = 0, \quad and$$

$$\lim_{W \to +\infty} \mathbb{P}(|\text{SLACK}(L, m) - \text{OPT}(L, m)| \geq \varepsilon) = 0, \quad and$$

$$\lim_{W \to +\infty} \mathbb{P}(|\text{MD}(L, m) - \text{OPT}(L, m)| \geq 1 + \varepsilon) = 0.$$

Proof. $\mathbb{P}(|\text{LPT}(L, m) - \text{OPT}(L, m)| \geq \varepsilon) = \mathbb{P}(\text{LPT}(L, m) - \text{OPT}(L, m) \geq \varepsilon) \leq \mathbb{P}(\text{LPT}(L, m) - \text{OPT}(L, m) > 0) = 1 - \mathbb{P}(\text{LPT}(L, m) - \text{OPT}(L, m) = 0) = O\left(\frac{1}{W}\right)$. The proof is similar for SLACK and MD. $\square$

3.4   Analysis for $\mathbb{D}_{W, p_{\min}}$

Let $\min\{p_i\} = p_{\min} \geq 2$. Let $\alpha_{W, p_{\min}}$ be the number of p_i's equal to $p_{\min}$ in a decomposition $(p_1, \ldots, p_k)$ satisfying $\sum p_i = W$ and for every i, $p_i \geq p_{\min}$. The random variable $\alpha_{W, p_{\min}}$ is studied for the $\mathbb{D}_{W, p_{\min}}$ distribution. Let also $\gamma_{p_{\min}, k}$ be the number of p_i's greater than or equal to k (with $k \geq p_{\min}$).

Theorem 2. *Let m be a fixed number of machines. One has, for L generated according to $\mathbb{D}_{W, p_{\min}}$, $\mathbb{P}(|\text{LPT}(L, m) - \text{OPT}(L, m)| \leq p_{\min}) \xrightarrow[W \to +\infty]{} 1$ and $\mathbb{P}(|\text{SLACK}(L, m) - \text{OPT}(L, m)| \leq p_{\min}) \xrightarrow[W \to +\infty]{} 1$.*

Here again, the proof, based on two lemmas, can be found in the companion research report [3]. Note that we do not have yet any theoretical results for MD for $\mathbb{D}_{W,p_{\min}}$, but experimental results explored in Sect. 4 are encouraging. Finally, we obtain the following corollary:

Corollary 2. *For every $\varepsilon > 0$, every $p_{\min} \geq 2$, for the distributions $\mathbb{D}_{W,p_{\min}}$,*

$$\lim_{W \to +\infty} \mathbb{P}(|\mathrm{LPT}(L,m) - \mathrm{OPT}(L,m)| < p_{\min} + \varepsilon) = 0, \quad and$$

$$\lim_{W \to +\infty} \mathbb{P}(|\mathrm{SLACK}(L,m) - \mathrm{OPT}(L,m)| < p_{\min} + \varepsilon) = 0.$$

4   Empirical Study

The objective of this section is threefold: first, evaluate the tightness of the convergence rate proposed in [14] (Sect. 4.2); then, assess the performance of the four heuristics when generating costs with the integer composition approach (Sect. 4.3); finally, quantifying the convergence for realistic instance (Sect. 4.4). We first detail the experimental setting in Sect. 4.1. All the algorithms were implemented in Python 3, and the code is available on figshare[1].

4.1   Experimental Setting

Synthetic Instances. We consider two kinds of synthetic instances: (1) i.i.d. execution times with cumulative distribution function $F(x) = x^a$ for some $a > 0$. This distribution has an expected value of $\frac{a}{a+1}$ and a variance of $\frac{a}{(a+1)^2 \cdot (a+2)}$. These values can be seen as a function of a in Fig. 1. Note that for $a = 1$, this is a uniform distribution $\mathcal{U}(0,1)$. (2) The integer composition distribution considered in Sect. 3, that is to say a uniform distribution on all possible ways to decompose a total amount of work into integer values.

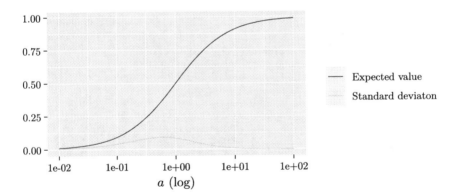

Fig. 1. Expected value and standard deviation of a random variable with cumulative distribution function $F(x) = x^a$ as a function of a with $0 < a < \infty$.

---

[1] https://doi.org/10.6084/m9.figshare.14755296.

Realistic Instances. We also compare the four algorithms of Sect. 3.1 using real logs from the Parallel Workloads Archive, described in [10] and available at https://www.cs.huji.ac.il/labs/parallel/workload/. More specifically, we took the instances called KIT ForHLR II with 114 355 tasks and NASA Ames iPSC/860 with 18 239 tasks. The profiles of the task costs in these instances are presented in Fig. 2.

In order to also get instances for which the number of tasks n could change, we build new instances from these two instances. In the new instances, the tasks are i.i.d. random variables with an empirical cumulative distribution function that is computed from the distribution of the two original instances.

Optimality Transform. When studying the absolute error of an algorithm, we consider the difference of its makespan to the optimal one to measure the convergence when the number of tasks n goes to infinity. The optimal makespan is computationally hard to get, so as a first approach, we can take a lower bound instead of the actual optimal value. However, there is a risk of actually measuring the quality of the lower bound instead of the quality of the algorithm.

To address this problem, we transform the instances so that we know the optimal makespan. This transformation is described as follows:

- we take an instance with n tasks;
- we perform a random List Scheduling on this instance;
- from this schedule, we add a total of at most $m - 1$ tasks so that all of the processors finish at the same time;
- we randomize the order of the tasks to avoid adding a bias to the heuristics;
- we end up with an instance with at most $n+m-1$ tasks such that the optimal makespan equals the sum of the execution times divided by the number of processors (OPT $= \frac{W}{m}$).

As we are interested in the asymptotic behavior of the algorithms, m is small compared to n, and we expect this transformation to alter the task distribution only marginally. However, studying the precise distribution of the added tasks is left to future work.

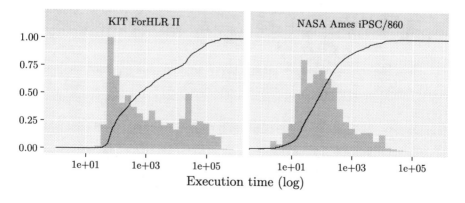

Fig. 2. Empirical cumulative distributions and histograms of task costs for the KIT ForHLR II and NASA Ames iPSC/860 instances.

4.2   Rate Tightness

We experimentally verify the bound given in [14]: if the tasks are independent and have cumulative distribution function $F(x) = x^a$ with $a > 0$, then the absolute error is a $O((\frac{\log\log(n)}{n})^{\frac{1}{a}})$ almost surely.

Figure 3 depicts the absolute error of LPT and related heuristics (LS, MD and SLACK) for different values of n. The instance contains $n - m + 1$ costs generated with the considered distribution and is then completed with the optimality transform. Moreover, we plot $C \cdot (\frac{\log\log(n)}{n})^{\frac{1}{a}}$, where C is the lowest constant such that all of LPT values are under the bound.

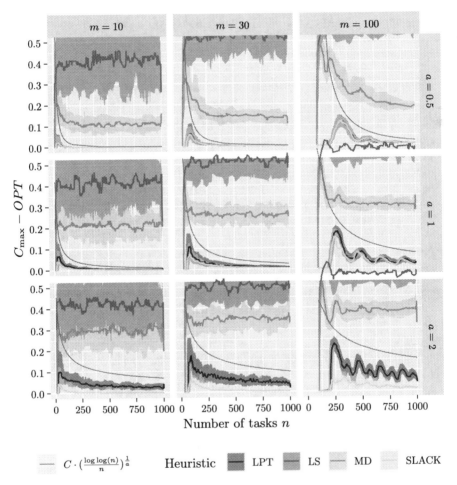

Fig. 3. Absolute error with a distribution of the form $F(x) = x^a$ with $a > 0$ (instances are transformed to obtain OPT). Smoothed lines are obtained by using a rolling median with 45 values (each value is set to the median of the 22 values on the left, the 22 on the right and the current one). The ribbons represent the rolling 0.1- and 0.9-quantiles.

We can see that the bound seems to be rather tight for LPT, which confirms that the convergence rate of [14] is strong. Also, we can see that the absolute error of SLACK seems to converge to 0 at a similar rate than LPT, but with a lower multiplicative constant. On the other side, the absolute errors of LS and MD do not seem to converge to 0 at all, but MD performs significantly better than LS.

4.3   Uniform Integer Compositions

Some experiments have been performed for the distributions described in Sect. 3: a total workload W is fixed as well as a fixed number m of machines. Then, the list of task costs is uniformly picked among all the possible lists for the distribution $\mathbb{D}_W$; and among all the possible lists with a minimum cost p_{min} for the distribution $\mathbb{D}_{W,p_{min}}$.

For $\mathbb{D}_W$, an instance has been generated for all W from 10 to 9999, for $m = 10$, $m = 30$, and $m = 100$. Instances are not transformed to avoid changing the total work W. Thus, we compare the makespan obtained by the heuristics to the lower bound on the optimal value OPT: $\max(\lceil \frac{W}{m} \rceil, p_{max})$. In all cases (about 30 000), LPT and SLACK always reach this bound, which indicates that they are both optimal and the bound is tight with these instances. Results for LS and MD are reported in Table 2. The average absolute error for MD is 0.35 for this experiment with a standard deviation of 0.6. Moreover MD is optimal in 67.6% of the samples and up to 1 from the optimum in 98% of the samples. LS is optimal in 3.3% of the cases and the average error is 3.75 (s.d. 2.15).

Similar tests have been done for $\mathbb{D}_{W,p_{min}}$ with $W \in \{10, \ldots, 9999\}$, $p_{min} \in \{3, 5, 7, 10\}$ and $m \in \{10, 30, 100\}$ (see Table 3). We now focus on the difference δ between C_{max} and the lower bound. In each case, the maximal value of δ is reported, as well as its average and standard deviation. Note that for each sample, both SLACK and LPT ensure that $\delta < p_{min}$, and MD ensures it in more than 99% of cases. The LS heuristic is less effective since for $p_{min} = 3$, only 42%

Table 2. Distribution in percentages of the absolute errors observed for LS and MD with W from 10 to 9999 and $m \in \{10, 30, 100\}$.

abs. err	LS	MD	abs. err	LS	MD
0	3.4	67.7	6	9.1	0.04
1	10.7	30.3	7	5.0	<0.01
2	17.0	0.96	8	2.7	0
3	18.1	0.58	9	1.5	0
4	17.3	0.28	10	0.7	0
5	13.7	0.08	>10	0.6	0

Table 3. Results on the difference between the $C_{\max}$ computed by the heuristics and a lower bound of the optimal makespan OPT. Each line is related to different $D_{W,p_{\min}}$. The first number is the maximum difference observed for all the samples, the second one is the average difference, and the last one is the standard deviation of this difference. Each value is obtained with W from 10 to 9999 and for $m \in \{10, 30, 100\}$.

$p_{\min}$	LPT	LS	MD	SLACK
3	$2 - 0.93 - 0.70$	$21 - 2.54 - 0.91$	$5 - 1.48 - 0.56$	$2 - 0.93 - 0.70$
5	$4 - 1.84 - 1.23$	$26 - 4.21 - 1.48$	$9 - 2.69 - 0.87$	$4 - 1.84 - 1.23$
7	$6 - 2.71 - 1.80$	$48 - 6.02 - 2.08$	$13 - 3.65 - 1.15$	$6 - 2.71 - 1.80$
10	$9 - 3.99 - 2.65$	$37 - 8.42 - 3.12$	$15 - 5.23 - 1.80$	$9 - 3.99 - 2.65$

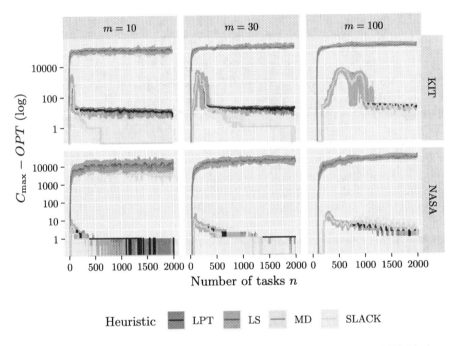

Fig. 4. Absolute error with costs derived from the KIT ForHLR II and NASA Ames iPSC/860 instances (after optimality transformation). Smoothed lines are obtained by using a rolling median with 45 values (each value is set to the median of the 22 values on the left, the 22 on the right and the current one). The ribbons represent the rolling 0.1- and 0.9-quantiles.

of the samples satisfy $\delta < p_{\min}$; 49% for $p_{\min} = 5$, 53% for $p_{\min} = 7$ and 58% for $p_{\min} = 10$. Results for the SLACK and LPT heuristics are very close. Over the about 120 000 samples, SLACK is strictly better than LPT only 46 times, when LPT is strictly better than SLACK only 46 times. Each time, the difference is either 1 or 2. On these distributions, SLACK and LPT seem to compete equally.

4.4 Realistic Workloads

In Fig. 4, we present experiments similar to those with synthetic instances in Sect. 4.2, but with the realistic instances.

As we can see when comparing LS and MD, treating the $\frac{n}{2}$ largest tasks first only marginally decreases the makespan of LS. We can also see that when n grows, the absolute error of LPT seems to be on par with the one of SLACK. In [8], SLACK was found to perform generally better than LPT for some synthetic instances, which differs from the results we get with more realistic instances. Finally, LPT seems to converge even faster to the optimal with these instances than with the synthetic ones, as the absolute error quickly becomes close to 0.

5 Conclusion

Given various probability distributions, we have evaluated the performance of four heuristics, among which the classical LPT heuristic and the more recent SLACK one. The literature already contains important theoretical results either in the form of different kinds of stochastic convergence to optimality or with a convergence rate. To the best of our knowledge, this paper is the first to empirically assess the tightness of a theoretical convergence rate for LPT. Furthermore, we focus on a novel definition of uniformity for the cost distribution: for a given total work, any integer composition can be drawn with the same probability, which leads to dependent random costs. This distribution is further enhanced by considering a subset of the decompositions that constrains the minimum cost. This paper proves the convergence in probability of LPT and similar heuristics with these distributions as well. Finally, we empirically analyze the convergence with realistic distributions obtained through traces. All these results contribute to understand the excellent performance of LPT in practice.

Future work will consist in obtaining stronger convergence theoretical results. For instance, existing results only consider that the number of tasks n tends to infinity. The impact of a varying number of processors m could be explored. Also, this work is the first attempt to consider dependent cost distributions, but many such distributions exist and could be explored. For instance, the same application consisting of a given set of tasks can be executed with different input size. The tasks could thus often have the same profile to a given multiplying factor. Finally, the novel distribution in this paper presents a minimum cost. Existing convergence results for independent distributions could probably be extended to consider costs with a similar minimum value. For instance, the worst-case ratio for LPT is achieved with costs $\frac{1}{3}$ and $\frac{1}{2}$. The uniform distribution $\mathcal{U}(\frac{1}{3}, \frac{1}{2})$ could thus present some challenges.

Acknowledgements and Data Availability Statement. The datasets and code generated during and/or analyzed during the current study are available in the Figshare repository: https://doi.org/10.6084/m9.figshare.14755296 [2].

This work has been supported by the EIPHI Graduate School (contract ANR-17-EURE-0002).

References

1. Behera, D.K., Laha, D.: Comparison of heuristics for identical parallel machine scheduling. Adv. Mater. Res. **488–489**, 1708–1712 (2012)
2. Benoit, A., Canon, L.C., Elghazi, R., Héam, P.C.: Artifact and instructions to generate experimental results for the Euro-Par 2021 paper: "Update on the Asymptotic Optimality of LPT". https://doi.org/10.6084/m9.figshare.14755296
3. Benoit, A., Canon, L.C., Elghazi, R., Héam, P.C.: Update on the Asymptotic Optimality of LPT. Research report, Inria (2021). https://lccanon.github.io/report_LPT_conv.pdf
4. Coffman, E.G., Frederickson, G.N., Lueker, G.S.: Probabilistic analysis of the LPT processor scheduling heuristic. In: Dempster, M.A.H., Lenstra, J.K., Rinnooy Kan, A.H.G. (eds.) Deterministic and Stochastic Scheduling. NATO Advanced Study Institutes Series (Series C – Mathematical and Physical Sciences), vol. 84, pp. 319–331. Springer, Dordrecht (1982). https://doi.org/10.1007/978-94-009-7801-0_18
5. Coffman, E.G., Garey, M.R., Johnson, D.S.: An application of bin-packing to multiprocessor scheduling. SIAM J. Comput. **7**, 1–17 (1978)
6. Coffman, Jr., E.G., Lueker, G.S.: Asymptotic methods in the probabilistic analysis of sequencing and packing heuristics. Manage. Sci. **34**(3), 266–290 (1988)
7. Cooper, K.D., Schielke, P.J., Subramanian, D.: An Experimental Evaluation of List Scheduling. Technical report 98-326, Rice Computer Science (1998)
8. Della Croce, F., Scatamacchia, R.: The longest processing time rule for identical parallel machines revisited. J. Sched. **23**(2), 163–176 (2020). https://doi.org/10.1007/s10951-018-0597-6
9. Dempster, M.A.H., et al.: Analysis of heuristics for stochastic programming results for hierarchical scheduling problems. Math. Oper. Res. **8**(4), 525–537 (1983)
10. Feitelson, D.G., Tsafrir, D., Krakov, D.: Experience with using the parallel workloads archive. J. Parallel Distrib. Comput. **74**(10), 2967–2982 (2014)
11. Flajolet, P., Sedgewick, R.: Analytic Combinatorics. Cambridge University Press, Cambridge (2009)
12. Flajolet, P., Zimmermann, P., Cutsem, B.V.: A calculus for the random generation of labelled combinatorial structures. Theor. Comput. Sci. **132**(2), 1–35 (1994)
13. Frenk, J.B.G., Rinnooy Kan, A.H.G.: The asymptotic optimality of the LPT rule. Math. Oper. Res. **12**(2), 241–254 (1987)
14. Frenk, J.B.G., Rinnooy Kan, A.H.G.: The rate of convergence to optimality of the LPT rule. Discrete Appl. Math. **14**(2), 187–197 (1986)
15. Graham, R.L., Lawler, E.L., Lenstra, J.K., Kan, A.H.G.R.: Optimization and approximation in deterministic sequencing and scheduling: a survey. Ann. Discrete Math. **5**, 287–326 (1979)
16. Graham, R.L.: Bounds on multiprocessing timing anomalies. SIAM J. Appl. Math. **17**(2), 416–429 (1969)
17. Gupta, J.N.D., Ruiz-Torres, A.J.: A LISTFIT heuristic for minimizing Makespan on identical parallel machines. Prod. Plan. Control **12**(1), 28–36 (2001)
18. Laha, D., Behera, D.K.: A comprehensive review and evaluation of LPT, MULTIFIT, COMBINE and LISTFIT for scheduling identical parallel machines. Int. J. Inf. Commun. Technol. (IJICT) **11**(2), 151–165 (2017)
19. Lee, C.Y., David Massey, J.: Multiprocessor scheduling: combining LPT and MULTIFIT. Discrete Appl. Math. **20**(3), 233–242 (1988)
20. Loulou, R.: Tight bounds and probabilistic analysis of two heuristics for parallel processor scheduling. Math. Oper. Res. **9**(1), 142–150 (1984)

21. Michiels, W., Korst, J., Aarts, E., van Leeuwen, J.: Performance ratios for the Karmarkar-Karp differencing method. Electron. Notes Discrete Math. **13**, 71–75 (2003)
22. Piersma, N., Romeijn, H.E.: Parallel machine scheduling: a probabilistic analysis. Naval Res. Logist. (NRL) **43**(6), 897–916 (1996)

E2EWatch: An End-to-End Anomaly Diagnosis Framework for Production HPC Systems

Burak Aksar[1][(✉)] ⓘ, Benjamin Schwaller[2], Omar Aaziz[2], Vitus J. Leung[2], Jim Brandt[2], Manuel Egele[1], and Ayse K. Coskun[1]

[1] Boston University, Boston, MA 02215, USA
{baksar,megele,acoskun}@bu.edu
[2] Sandia National Laboratories, Albuquerque, NM 87123, USA
{bschwal,oaaziz,vjleung,brandt}@sandia.gov

Abstract. In today's High-Performance Computing (HPC) systems, application performance variations are among the most vital challenges as they adversely affect system efficiency, application performance, and cost. System administrators need to identify the anomalies that are responsible for performance variation and take mitigating actions. One can perform manual root-cause analysis on telemetry data collected by HPC monitoring infrastructures to analyze performance variations. However, manual analysis methods are time-intensive and limited in impact due to the increasing complexity of HPC systems and terabyte/day-sized telemetry data. State-of-the-art approaches use machine learning-based methods to diagnose performance anomalies automatically. This paper deploys an end-to-end machine learning framework that diagnoses performance anomalies on compute nodes on a 1488-node production HPC system. We demonstrate job and node-level anomaly diagnosis results with the Grafana frontend interface at runtime. Furthermore, we discuss challenges and design decisions for the deployment.

Keywords: HPC · Anomaly diagnosis · Machine learning · Telemetry.

1 Introduction

High-Performance Computing (HPC) systems offer invaluable computing resources for a range of scientific and engineering applications, such as national security, scientific discovery, and economic research. Following the massive growth in data and computing power, system infrastructure has grown more complex, and effective management of HPC systems has become more challenging. Many researchers report *anomalies* that cause performance variations due to network contention [9], hardware problems [23], memory-related problems (e.g., memory leak) [2], shared resource contention (e.g., reduced I/O bandwidth) [8,17], or CPU-related problems (e.g., CPU throttling, orphan processes) [13]. Performance anomalies do not necessarily terminate the execution, but often increase job execution times by greater than 100% [22,32,37].

© Springer Nature Switzerland AG 2021
L. Sousa et al. (Eds.): Euro-Par 2021, LNCS 12820, pp. 70–85, 2021.
https://doi.org/10.1007/978-3-030-85665-6_5

System administrators continuously collect and analyze system telemetry data with rule-based heuristics (e.g., [3,13]) to determine the causes behind performance variations. Due to the highly complex infrastructure and massive volumes of telemetry data (e.g., billions of data points per day), rule-based methods are incapable of effective management and analysis. Thus, researchers use machine learning (ML)-based tools more often to detect and diagnose performance variations automatically [4,11,15].

In this paper, we propose *E2EWatch*, an end-to-end anomaly diagnosis framework for production HPC systems. *E2EWatch* detects and diagnoses previously seen performance anomalies in compute nodes at runtime based on a recently proposed ML-based approach [33]. We design an end-to-end architecture for deployment and deploy this framework on a 1488-node HPC production system to display job and node level analysis results with an easy-to-interpret user interface. Our specific contributions are as follows:

- Deployment of a state-of-the-art anomaly diagnosis framework on a 1488-node production HPC system;
- Visualization and analysis of job and node-level anomaly diagnosis results on-the-fly;
- Demonstration of the effectiveness of our framework under a variety of experimental scenarios and discussion of deployment challenges and techniques.[1]

The rest of the paper is organized as follows. Section 2 provides a brief overview of related work; Sect. 3 describes the methodology in detail; Sect. 4 describes experimental scenarios; Sect. 5 presents our results, and we conclude in Sect. 6.

2 Related Work

Performance variation has been an important research topic for large-scale computing systems. Especially as we move towards the exascale computing era, it will remain a substantial challenge. This section briefly reviews the latest anomaly detection and diagnosis research in three categories: rule-based statistical methods, ML-based methods, and deployment.

Rule-Based Statistical Methods: These methods are widely used in large-scale production systems since they are generally easier to design and deploy in practice compared to more sophisticated ML-based methods. Some example methods use manually selected threshold values for important system metrics [3,18]. Some researchers investigate the statistical correlation between features and performance issues instead of solely assigning thresholds. Brandt et al. track systems and components' operational behaviors over time and analyze their correlations with various causes, such as aging components [13]. Agelastos et al. leverage system-wide resource utilization data and investigate specific metrics to detect I/O congestion and out-of-memory cases [2]. Even though many rule-based statistical methods are easy to implement for the administration side,

---

[1] Our implementation is available at: https://github.com/peaclab/E2EWatch.

their efficacy is highly dependent on system properties (e.g., operating system, underlying hardware configurations).

ML-Based Methods for Performance Analytics: Some researchers focus on predicting node or application-level failures using ML models trained on system monitoring data and logs [16,20,35]. Ates et al. use ML models to detect applications running on supercomputers by leveraging applications' resource utilization characteristics [5]. Anomaly detection (for a broader range of events than failures) is widely popular in the HPC and cloud domains [10,26,36]. However, most anomaly detection focuses on detecting anomalies instead of providing information on the anomaly type. Several ML approaches have been proposed to detect anomalous behavior in applications and compute nodes using historical *normal* data [4,11,15,21,31]. Tuncer et al. leverage historical telemetry data to diagnose previously observed performance anomalies on compute nodes during an application run, but do not demonstrate a runtime deployment [33]. In addition to node-level anomaly detection and diagnosis, Xie et al. train a one-class support vector machine on vector embeddings to detect anomalous function executions using call stack trees [34]. In another work, Denis and Vadim use a Long Short Term Memory (LSTM) network to detect abnormal and suspicious behavior during an application run [31].

Deployment: Operational Data Analytics (ODA) solutions provide runtime system insights for users and system administrators and complement monitoring frameworks [12,27,30]. Some important application areas of ODA are application fingerprinting, scheduling and allocation, performance variation detection. Netti et al. demonstrate the use of several ML models to forecast compute node power and identify outliers and anomalous behavior using power, temperature, and CPU metrics on an HPC cluster at runtime [27]. Borghesi et al. propose an autoencoder-based semi-supervised approach to detect anomalous behaviors in compute nodes and deploy them to their 45-node HPC system [11].

In production systems, the size of a system can substantially affect the deployment because a production HPC system might have thousands (e.g., Sierra, Astra) to tens of thousands (e.g., Cori, Blue Waters) compute nodes. For example, Borghesi et al. train node-specific models that use monitoring data from a specific node and a node-agnostic model that uses monitoring data from all compute nodes during training [11]. Using node-specific models could be feasible for small computing clusters; however, it infers high training and maintenance costs, e.g., selecting a new detection threshold for each model is time-consuming. The abovementioned approaches (e.g., [11,27]) only collect data when the system behaves in the normal state, which requires constant system assessment by a system administrator. A manual assessment approach may not be feasible considering the complexity of HPC systems. Another aspect is evaluating models' performance against scenarios where there are unknown applications and unknown application inputs in order to guarantee they perform as intended. However, neither of the methods covers real-world deployment scenarios. Even though Netti et al. and Borghesi et al. have online deployment components, they solely focus on detecting anomalies rather than classifying their type [11,27]. To the best of our knowledge, none of the prior methods provide an end-to-end anomaly diagnosis framework running on a large-scale production HPC system.

3   Methodology

The main goal of *E2EWatch* is to diagnose the root cause of previously observed performance anomalies in compute nodes during application runs. We provide diagnosis results in a dashboard that enables users or system administrators to track their applications' status and interfere when necessary. Figure 1 shows an overview of *E2EWatch*. In this paper, we focus on anomalies that cause performance variability (e.g., CPU contention and memory problems) in different sub-systems instead of faults that terminate the execution of a program prematurely. Our framework can diagnose the anomaly type and provide easy-to-interpret results to users while an application is still running.

3.1   *E2EWatch* Overview

E2EWatch is an end-to-end anomaly diagnosis framework similar to Tuncer et al.'s framework, and we deploy the framework on a production HPC system [33]. *E2EWatch* has a user interface and works with labeled data that system administrators or automated methods can generate. In this work, we collect system telemetry data from compute nodes while running applications with and without synthetic anomalies that produce well-known performance variations (e.g., CPU contention, memory leakage). Specifically, we collect resource usage (e.g., free memory, CPU utilization) and performance counter telemetry data (e.g., CPU interrupt counts, flits) across a set of applications. After the data collection phase, we apply statistical preprocessing techniques (e.g., feature selection) to raw time series data to extract useful information and then train supervised ML models. We compare the performance of a set of ML models in the test data and deploy the best model to the *monitoring server*. At runtime, a user queries a specific job-id assigned by the monitoring server. We provide a summary across all compute nodes, and drill-down analysis for each node, used by the application. In the upcoming sections, we explain each phase in detail.

3.2   Offline Data Collection

The goal of offline data collection is to collect high-fidelity monitoring data to train ML models. We use Lightweight Distributed Metric Service (LDMS) to collect telemetry data across different subsystems [1]. We run controlled experiments with synthetic anomalies from the HPC Performance Anomaly Suite (HPAS) with three real and three proxy applications to mimic performance anomalies [6]. We perform data cleaning and interpolation for missing hardware metrics and increasing counter values. We provide the details of the anomalies, applications, and data preprocessing in Sect. 4.

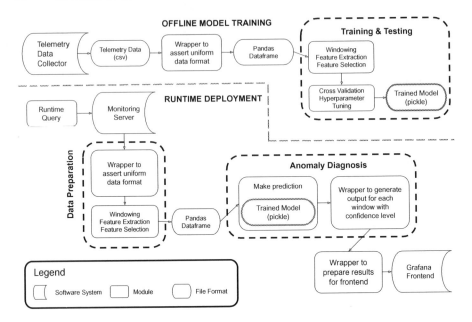

Fig. 1. The high-level architecture of *E2EWatch*. The top flow contains the offline training phase, and the bottom flow contains the online anomaly diagnosis phase. We train ML models with known normal and anomalous application telemetry data and find the best parameters with hyperparameter tuning for each model. We deploy the best-performing model to the monitoring server. A user sends a query with the specific application ID at runtime, and our framework displays node-by-node diagnosis results in the Grafana frontend interface.

3.3 Offline Data Preparation

After the offline data collection, we divide raw time series into multiple equal-length overlapping windows with 15-s skip intervals (e.g., [0–45], [15–60]). While the windowing operation substantially increases the amount of training data, it also enables us to provide results without waiting for an application to run to completion. Then, we calculate the following statistical features of each window: "minimum and maximum; 5th, 25th, 50th, 75th, 95th percentile values; mean, variance, skewness and kurtosis" [33]. Each 2D window transforms into a 1D vector after the feature extraction stage. This approach brings substantial savings in computational power and memory while preserving the main characteristics of time series.

After we extract statistical features, we adopt the feature selection process proposed by Tuncer et al. [33]. We calculate the cumulative distribution functions (CDF) of each feature when running the application with and without an anomaly. We use *the Kolmogorov-Smirnov* (KS) test to compare each feature's CDF [24]. CDFs of normal and anomalous metric values show a high statistical difference if the anomaly substantially affects metric values. We repeat the abovementioned procedure and concatenate the selected features for each application and anomaly pair.

3.4   Offline Training and Testing

The goal of this stage is to find the best-performing model before deploying the model to the monitoring server. After the offline data preparation phase, we perform hyperparameter tuning for each ML model and test their performance using multiple cross-validation folds. We label each equal-sized window for our anomaly diagnosis task according to the node's label it belongs to. For example, if we run an anomaly on a compute node, we label it according to the type of the anomaly; otherwise, it is labeled *normal*.

3.5   Deployment and Runtime Diagnosis

We use the model trained during the offline training phase for runtime diagnosis. We store the trained model on the monitoring server of our target system (see Sect. 4 for details) along with other back-end components such as data storage and visualization. At runtime, a user sends a query to the monitoring server with the desired application ID assigned by the HPC system scheduler, and our runtime analysis module presents results in the Grafana frontend. For the job-level breakdown, we calculate how many anomalous windows are diagnosed for each anomaly across the compute nodes used by the application (e.g., 75% of windows have "cachecopy" anomaly). In Fig. 2, we demonstrate a job-level diagnosis summary for one example application run. The user can see all anomalies diagnosed over time along with the classifier's prediction confidence for the selected application ID. We explain the calculation of the prediction confidences in Sect. 5. Furthermore, it is possible to perform drill-down analysis for the selected compute nodes.

4   Experimental Methodology

We detail the target system and the monitoring framework in the first section. Next, we describe the synthetic anomalies we use to create performance variation. In the last section, we explain the implementation details of *E2EWatch*.

4.1   Target System and Monitoring Framework

To demonstrate the efficacy of *E2EWatch*, we conduct experiments and deploy the framework on Eclipse, a production HPC system with 1488 compute nodes located at Sandia National Laboratories (SNL). Each node has 128 GB memory and two sockets, where each socket has 18 E5-2695 v4 CPU cores with 2-way hyperthreading [29]. System administrators use LDMS to monitor the system health of Eclipse, and LDMS is actively running on all compute nodes. LDMS

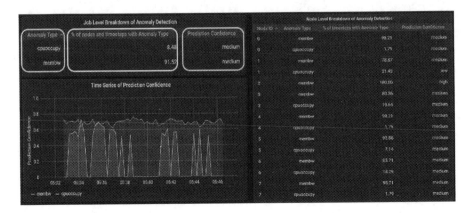

Fig. 2. An example SWFFT application run with the *membw* anomaly. We provide diagnosed anomaly types (orange box) and their percentage across all windows (yellow box) as well as model's prediction confidences (green box) in the job-level breakdown. The time series plot shows the average confidence level of each anomaly across all the compute nodes used by the application. We also provide the node-level breakdown composed of the same analyses we provide in the job-level breakdown. (Color figure online)

can collect thousands of different resource usage metrics and performance counters from compute nodes at sub-second granularity. From LDMS, we use 160 system metrics sampled 1 Hz while running six applications with and without synthetic anomalies. The applications used are listed in Table 1. SNL has a separate monitoring server, referred to here as HPCMON, for data storage, analysis, and visualization. HPCMON is a four-node cluster with 48 Intel Xeon Gold 6240 CPUs, 750 GB of memory, and 28 TB of NVMe raided storage. Eclipse telemetry data is sent to HPCMON and is queryable through a Grafana frontend interface. A user specifies the time range and application ID of interest, and the corresponding telemetry data is sent through our ML models at query time. The model output is then summarized and formatted for Grafana visualization [30].

4.2   Synthetic Anomalies

We use open-source synthetic anomalies from High-Performance Anomaly Suite (HPAS) [6]. HPAS has 8 performance anomalies that create contention across different subsystems such as memory, network, and I/O. We use the following anomalies: *memleak*, which mimics memory leakage by allocating an array of characters of a given size without storing the addresses; *membw* mimics memory bandwidth contention, which prevents data from being loaded into the cache; *cpuoccupy* mimics excessive CPU utilization; *cachecopy* mimics cache contention by allocating two-arrays and swapping their contents repeatedly for a specific cache level, e.g., L3 cache. We have 3 different input configurations for each

Table 1. We run 3 real and 3 proxy applications during offline data collection phase.

Benchmark	Application	Description
ECP proxy suite	ExaMiniMD	Molecular dynamics
	SWFFT	3D Fast Fourier Transform
	sw4lite	Numerical kernel optimizations
Real applications	LAMMPS	Molecular dynamics
	HACC	Cosmological simulation
	sw4	Seismic modeling

application, which corresponds to 4, 8, and 16 node application runs, respectively. On each node, we allocate one core for LDMS, one core for an anomaly, and 32 cores for an application (Table 2).

Table 2. A list of anomalies and their configurations.

Anomaly type	Configuration
cpuoccupy	-u 100%, 80%
cachecopy	-c L1,-m 1/-c L2 -m 2
membw	-s 4K, 8K, 32K
memleak	-s 1M, -p 0.2/-s 3M -p 0.4/-s 10M -p 1

4.3 Implementation Details

We fill out missing metric values with linear interpolation because some metric values can be missing while telemetry data is being collected. We also take the difference of cumulative counters in every step because we care about the increase, not the raw value. We strip out the first and last 60 s of the collected time-series data to prevent fluctuations during the initialization and termination phases of applications. We experiment with 45 and 60-s windows since we want to provide effective results while minimizing the delay. In the end, we choose 60-s windowing since it led to a better F1-score, anomaly miss rate, and false alarm rate during evaluation.

We use the "Min-Max" scaler on training data and scale the test data using the same scaler during the model training to minimize possible data leakage. After the training, the scaler is saved as a Python *pickle* object, and the same scaler is used during runtime diagnosis. We split the dataset into 5-folds and iteratively fit the model on the remaining folds while holding the remaining one for validation. While splitting the data, we use stratified sampling where the class distribution matches with the whole dataset in each fold.

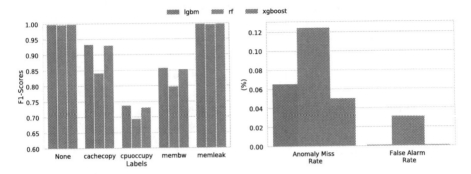

Fig. 3. Macro average F1-scores of LGBM, Random Forest, and XGBoost models. LGBM and XGBoost perform up to 10% better in cachecopy, cpuoccupy, and membw anomalies than Random Forest. LGBM and XGBoost are 2x better than Random Forest in anomaly miss rate while achieving near zero false alarm rate.

We experiment with Random Forest and Gradient Boosting Machines. Random Forest is composed of multiple decision trees, and it generally combines the average of each decision tree or applies majority voting during prediction. We use the implementation in *scikit-learn* that uses majority voting for the classification tasks [28]. Gradient Boosting Machines are decision-tree-based classifiers and use gradient boosting, which produces a prediction result using an ensemble of weak prediction models. We use *Extreme Gradient Boosting (XGBoost)* [14] and *Light Gradient Boosting Machine (LGBM)* [19] implementations. Even though XGBoost and LGBM are part of the gradient boosting machines, they have different techniques while splitting the nodes. We use the LGBM as a final classifier due to high performance in F1-score, anomaly miss rate, and false alarm rate.

5   Evaluation

We evaluate our model under 3 different experimental scenarios and report F1-score, false alarm rate (i.e., false-positive rate), and anomaly miss rate (i.e., false-negative rate). F1-score is defined as the harmonic mean of precision and recall, where precision shows what percentage of positive class predictions were correct and recall shows what percentage of actual positive class samples were identified correctly. Equation 1 shows the false alarm rate, which corresponds to the percentage of normal runs identified as one of the anomaly types. Equation 2 shows the anomaly miss rate, which corresponds to the percentage of anomalous runs (any anomaly) identified as normal.

$$False\ Alarm\ Rate = \frac{False\ Positives}{False\ Positives + True\ Negatives} \tag{1}$$

$$Anomaly\ Miss\ Rate = \frac{False\ Negatives}{False\ Negatives + True\ Positives} \tag{2}$$

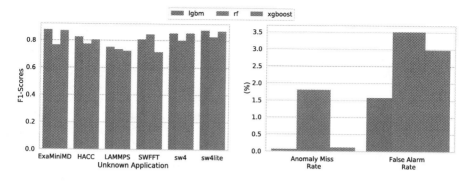

Fig. 4. Macro average F1-score of models when an unknown application exists in the test set. LGBM is 8% and 4% better than Random Forest and XGBoost in F1-score on average, respectively. LGBM and XGBoost achieve lower false alarm and anomaly miss rates than Random Forest.

5.1 Anomaly Diagnosis Scores

We present anomaly diagnosis results for each anomaly type with anomaly miss rate and false alarm rate in Fig. 3. Average F1-scores are 0.91, 0.90, and 0.87, for LGBM, XGBoost, and Random Forest, respectively. All models achieve an almost perfect diagnosis F1-score for windows without anomalies. LGBM and XGBoost outperform Random Forest in terms of F1-score in all cases. It is expected to see a similar performance among XGBoost and LGBM since they are fundamentally similar. XGBoost and LGBM miss 0.05% of anomalous windows and achieve almost zero false alarm rates. The F1-scores of *cpuoccupy* anomaly are lower than other anomalies because all classifiers confuse *cpuoccupy* with *membw* anomaly due to similar CPU utilization characteristics.

5.2 Unknown Applications

In a production system scenario, it is likely to encounter applications that do not exist in the training data, so we evaluate the model's performance with scenarios where unknown applications exist in the test data while keeping all the anomalies. First, we remove all runs of the selected application from the training set and then include only the removed application to the test set. We repeat this setup for each application and report average F1-scores, anomaly miss rate, and false alarm rate in Fig. 4. Except for SWFFT, XGBoost and LGBM are up to 10% better than Random Forest in F1-scores, and LGBM is the best performing one, including for anomaly miss rate and false alarm rate.

5.3 Unknown Application Inputs

Another common scenario in production systems is running the same application with different input decks. In our dataset, we have three input sizes (small, medium, large) for each application, and each input size corresponds to the different number of compute nodes we run the application. We evaluate the model's performance with scenarios where unknown application inputs exist in test data. First, we remove all runs of the selected input size from the training set and then include only the removed input size in the test set. We repeat this setup for each input size and report average F1-scores along with anomaly miss rate and false alarm rate in Fig. 5. For all unknown input types, LGBM and XGBoost can diagnose anomalies with F1-scores over 0.75. LGBM is the most robust one to unknown input sizes in terms of anomaly miss rate and false alarm rate.

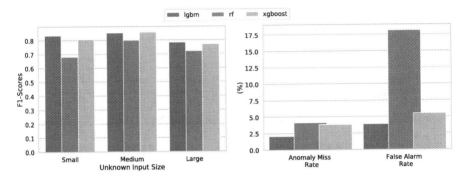

Fig. 5. Macro average F1-score of models when an unknown application input exists in the test set. LGBM and XGBoost are 13% better than Random Forest in F1-scores. While models have comparable anomaly miss rates, LGBM is 8x, and XGBoost is 4x better than Random Forest in false alarm rate.

5.4   Discussion on Deployment

At SNL, HPCMON hosts the analysis and visualization pipeline for understanding HPC system data. The pipeline uses the Scalable Object Store (SOS) database that has unique indexing to efficiently manage structured data, including time series [30]. The first advantage of SOS is that we can query the data of interest instead of getting the whole data and selecting afterward. This enables E2EWatch to provide anomaly diagnosis results without waiting for the completion of an application. The second advantage is that SOS enables easy configuration for user-derived metrics, hence supports a flexible analysis development cycle. This feature enables the easier development of new models for different classification tasks as new needs arise. At a high level, *E2EWatch* requires the following components to provide diagnosis results at runtime in another production system:

1. **Monitoring framework** that can collect numeric telemetry data from compute nodes while applications are running. Even though we only experiment

with LDMS, it can be adapted to other popular monitoring frameworks such as Ganglia [25], Examon [7] by modifying the wrappers in the data collection phase.

2. **Labeled data** that is composed of anomalous and normal compute node telemetry data. It is possible to create labeled data sets using a suite of applications and synthetic anomalies. Another option is to use telemetry data labeled by users.

3. **Backend web service** that can provide telemetry data on the fly to the trained model. We use the existing Django web application deployed on the monitoring server [30]. It is possible to use other backend web services that can handle client requests and query data from the database. If runtime diagnosis is not necessary, it is also possible to run the pickled model after the application run is completed.

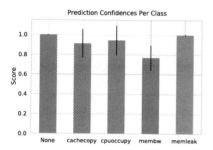

Fig. 6. The deployed model's prediction confidence for each anomaly type. Error bars show one standard deviation above and below. Except *membw* anomaly, the model has very high confidence for each class. The confidence translation table provides a way for a user to interpret prediction results easily.

We calculate the model's prediction confidence in the test data for correctly classified samples and provide the statistical distribution in Fig. 6. Prediction confidences are also necessary to monitor possible *concept drift* and *data drift*. Concept drift happens when the statistical properties of the target variable change, e.g., some anomalies might start showing different characteristics. Data drift occurs when the statistical properties of streaming data change. Especially in HPC systems, seasonality and user trends could change according to usage, e.g., conference deadlines and periodic system upgrades. For example, suppose we observe a sudden decrease in prediction confidences of samples predicted *normal*. In that case, it can point out a possible drift scenario.

We implement two filtering techniques to increase robustness against false alarms and anomaly misses for runtime anomaly diagnosis. The first one is *consecutive filtering*, where we keep the original prediction label if it persists in C consecutive windows; otherwise, we replace it with *the normal* label. Even though this approach reduces false alarms, it increases the anomaly miss rate since we

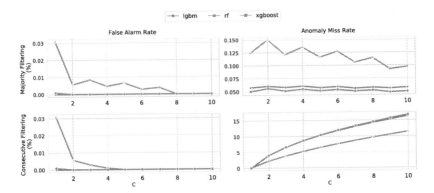

Fig. 7. The first row shows majority filtering results, and the second row shows consecutive filtering results for different C values. LGBM and XGBoost maintains a constant false alarm rate in both filtering techniques, whereas Random Forest's false alarm rate is reduced almost three times.

replace anomalies directly with the normal label. The second one is *majority filtering*, where we replace the original prediction label with the most frequent class label in C consecutive windows. Majority filtering generally reduces false alarms and anomaly miss rates. As an example, using the following window predictions, [memleak, memleak, membw, memleak, memleak], majority filtering will return [memleak,memleak, memleak,memleak,memleak], whereas consecutive filtering will return [normal,normal,normal,memleak,memleak] when C equals 3. In Fig. 7, we show the effect of these two filtering techniques on all classifiers. While consecutive filtering increases anomaly miss rate in all classifiers, it significantly reduces Random Forest's false alarm rate. On the other hand, LGBM and XGBoost have almost constant false alarm rates and anomaly miss rates with both techniques.

6   Conclusion and Future Work

Automatic and online diagnosis of performance anomalies has been increasingly important as we move towards the Exascale computing era; however, transitioning from research to real-world applications is challenging. In this paper, we demonstrated *E2EWatch*, an end-to-end anomaly diagnosis framework, on a 1488-node HPC production machine. *E2EWatch* provides job and node-level visualizations in an easy-to-interpret dashboard. Our future work includes creating a data set that is composed of a large set of popular HPC applications and evaluating the framework with a scenario where the scale of the number of applications and input decks is comparable to production systems. The second direction is to conduct user studies and evaluate the performance of our framework in a real-world setting. The third direction we plan to explore is deployment process for production systems that have compute nodes with GPUs.

Acknowledgment. This work has been partially funded by Sandia National Laboratories. Sandia National Laboratories is a multimission laboratory managed and operated by National Technology and Engineering Solutions of Sandia, LLC., a wholly owned subsidiary of Honeywell International, Inc., for the U.S. Department of Energy's National Nuclear Security Administration under Contract DE-NA0003525. This paper describes objective technical results and analysis. Any subjective views or opinions that might be expressed in the paper do not necessarily represent the views of the U.S. Department of Energy or the United States Government.

References

1. Agelastos, A., et al.: The lightweight distributed metric service: a scalable infrastructure for continuous monitoring of large scale computing systems and applications. In: Proceedings of the International Conference for High Performance Computing, Networking, Storage and Analysis (SC), pp. 154–165 (2014)
2. Agelastos, A., et al.: Toward rapid understanding of production HPC applications and systems. In: IEEE International Conference on Cluster Computing, pp. 464–473 (2015)
3. Ahad, R., Chan, E., Santos, A.: Toward autonomic cloud: automatic anomaly detection and resolution. In: International Conference on Cloud and Autonomic Computing, pp. 200–203 (2015)
4. Arzani, B., Ciraci, S., Loo, B.T., Schuster, A., Outhred, G.: Taking the blame game out of data centers operations with NetPoirot. In: Proceedings of the ACM SIGCOMM Conference, pp. 440–453 (2016)
5. Ates, E., et al.: Taxonomist: application detection through rich monitoring data. In: Aldinucci, M., Padovani, L., Torquati, M. (eds.) Euro-Par 2018. LNCS, vol. 11014, pp. 92–105. Springer, Cham (2018). https://doi.org/10.1007/978-3-319-96983-1_7
6. Ates, E., Zhang, Y., Aksar, B., et al.: HPAS: an HPC performance anomaly suite for reproducing performance variations. In: Proceedings of the 48th International Conference on Parallel Processing, pp. 1–10. ACM, August 2019
7. Bartolini, A., et al.: The DAVIDE big-data-powered fine-grain power and performance monitoring support. In: Proceedings of the 15th ACM International Conference on Computing Frontiers, pp. 303–308 (2018)
8. Bhatele, A., Mohror, K., Langer, S.H., Isaacs, K.E.: There goes the neighborhood: performance degradation due to nearby jobs. In: SC 2013: Proceedings of the International Conference on High Performance Computing, Networking, Storage and Analysis, pp. 1–12 (2013)
9. Bhatele, A., et al.: The case of performance variability on dragonfly-based systems. In: IEEE International Parallel and Distributed Processing Symposium (IPDPS), pp. 896–905 (2020)
10. Bhuyan, M.H., Bhattacharyya, D., Kalita, J.K.: NADO: network anomaly detection using outlier approach. In: Proceedings of the International Conference on Communication, Computing and Security, pp. 531–536 (2011)
11. Borghesi, A., Bartolini, A., Lombardi, M., Milano, M., Benini, L.: A semisupervised autoencoder-based approach for anomaly detection in high performance computing systems. Eng. Appl. Artif. Intell. **85**, 634–644 (2019)
12. Bourassa, N., et al.: Operational data analytics: optimizing the national energy research scientific computing center cooling systems. In: Proceedings of the 48th International Conference on Parallel Processing: Workshops, pp. 1–7 (2019)

13. Brandt, J.M., et al.: Enabling advanced operational analysis through multi-subsystem data integration on trinity. Technical report, Sandia National Lab. (SNL-CA), Livermore, CA (United States) (2015)
14. Chen, T., Guestrin, C.: XGBoost: a scalable tree boosting system. In: Proceedings of the ACM International Conference on Knowledge Discovery and Data Mining, pp. 785–794 (2016)
15. Dalmazo, B.L., Vilela, J.P., Simoes, P., Curado, M.: Expedite feature extraction for enhanced cloud anomaly detection. In: IEEE/IFIP Network Operations and Management Symposium, pp. 1215–1220 (2016)
16. Das, A., Mueller, F., Rountree, B.: Aarohi: making real-time node failure prediction feasible. In: 2020 IEEE International Parallel and Distributed Processing Symposium (IPDPS), pp. 1092–1101 (2020)
17. Dorier, M., Antoniu, G., Ross, R., Kimpe, D., Ibrahim, S.: CALCioM: mitigating i/o interference in HPC systems through cross-application coordination. In: IEEE International Parallel and Distributed Processing Symposium, pp. 155–164 (2014)
18. Jayathilaka, H., Krintz, C., Wolski, R.: Performance monitoring and root cause analysis for cloud-hosted web applications. In: Proceedings of the 26th International Conference on World Wide Web, pp. 469–478 (2017)
19. Ke, G., et al.: Lightgbm: a highly efficient gradient boosting decision tree. Adv. Neural. Inf. Process. Syst. **30**, 3146–3154 (2017)
20. Klinkenberg, J., Terboven, C., Lankes, S., Müller, M.S.: Data mining-based analysis of HPC center operations. In: IEEE International Conference on Cluster Computing (CLUSTER), pp. 766–773 (2017)
21. Lan, Z., Zheng, Z., Li, Y.: Toward automated anomaly identification in large-scale systems. IEEE Trans. Parallel Distrib. Syst. **21**(2), 174–187 (2009)
22. Leung, V.J., Bender, M.A., Bunde, D.P., Phillips, C.A.: Algorithmic support for commodity-based parallel computing systems. Technical report, Sandia National Laboratories (2003)
23. Marathe, A., Zhang, Y., Blanks, G., Kumbhare, N., Abdulla, G., Rountree, B.: An empirical survey of performance and energy efficiency variation on intel processors. In: Proceedings of the 5th International Workshop on Energy Efficient Supercomputing, pp. 1–8 (2017)
24. Massey, F.J., Jr.: The Kolmogorov-Smirnov test for goodness of fit. J. Am. Stat. Assoc. **46**(253), 68–78 (1951)
25. Massie, M.L., Chun, B.N., Culler, D.E.: The ganglia distributed monitoring system: design, implementation, and experience. Parallel Comput. **30**(7), 817–840 (2004)
26. Nair, V., et al.: Learning a hierarchical monitoring system for detecting and diagnosing service issues. In: Proceedings of the ACM SIGKDD International Conference on Knowledge Discovery and Data Mining, pp. 2029–2038 (2015)
27. Netti, A., et al.: DCDB wintermute: enabling online and holistic operational data analytics on HPC systems. In: Proceedings of the 29th International Symposium on High-Performance Parallel and Distributed Computing, pp. 101–112 (2020)
28. Pedregosa, F., et al.: Scikit-learn: machine learning in Python. J. Mach. Learn. Res. **12**, 2825–2830 (2011)
29. Sandia National Laboratories: HPC capacity cluster platforms (2017). https://hpc.sandia.gov/HPC%20Production%20Clusters/index.html
30. Schwaller, B., Tucker, N., Tucker, T., Allan, B., Brandt, J.: HPC system data pipeline to enable meaningful insights through analysis-driven visualizations. In: IEEE International Conference on Cluster Computing (CLUSTER), pp. 433–441 (2020)

31. Shaykhislamov, D., Voevodin, V.: An approach for dynamic detection of inefficient supercomputer applications. Procedia Comput. Sci. **136**, 35–43 (2018)
32. Skinner, D., Kramer, W.: Understanding the causes of performance variability in HPC workloads. In: Proceedings of the IEEE Workload Characterization Symposium, pp. 137–149 (2005)
33. Tuncer, O., et al.: Online diagnosis of performance variation in HPC systems using machine learning. IEEE Trans. Parallel Distrib. Syst. **30**(4), 883–896 (2018)
34. Xie, C., Xu, W., Mueller, K.: A visual analytics framework for the detection of anomalous call stack trees in high performance computing applications. IEEE Trans. Vis. Comput. Graph. **25**(1), 215–224 (2018)
35. Zasadziński, M., Muntés-Mulero, V., Solé, M., Carrera, D., Ludwig, T.: Early termination of failed HPC jobs through machine and deep learning. In: Aldinucci, M., Padovani, L., Torquati, M. (eds.) Euro-Par 2018. LNCS, vol. 11014, pp. 163–177. Springer, Cham (2018). https://doi.org/10.1007/978-3-319-96983-1_12
36. Zhang, X., Meng, F., Chen, P., Xu, J.: TaskInsight: a fine-grained performance anomaly detection and problem locating system. In: IEEE International Conference on Cloud Computing (CLOUD), pp. 917–920 (2016)
37. Zhang, Y., Groves, T., Cook, B., Wright, N.J., Coskun, A.K.: Quantifying the impact of network congestion on application performance and network metrics. In: IEEE International Conference on Cluster Computing (CLUSTER), pp. 162–168 (2020)

Scheduling and Load Balancing

Collaborative GPU Preemption via Spatial Multitasking for Efficient GPU Sharing

Zhuoran Ji[(⊠)] and Cho-Li Wang

The University of Hong Kong, Hong Kong, China
{zrji2,clwang}@cs.hku.hk

Abstract. GPUs have been widely used in data centers and are often over-provisioned to satisfy the stringent latency targets of latency-sensitive (LS) jobs. The GPU under-utilization provides a strong incentive to share GPUs among LS jobs and batch jobs. Preemptive GPU prioritization is costly due to the large contexts. Many novel GPU preemption techniques have been proposed, exhibiting different trade-offs between preemption latency and overhead. Prior works also propose collaborative methods, which intelligently select the preemption techniques at preemption time. However, GPU kernels usually adopt code transformation to improve performance, which also impacts the preemption costs. As kernel transformation is performed before launching, the preemption technique choices are also determined then. It is impractical to select a preemption technique arbitrarily at preemption time if code transformation is adopted. This paper presents *CPSpatial*, which combines GPU preemption techniques via GPU spatial multitasking. *CPSpatial* proposes preemption hierarchy and SM-prefetching, achieving both low latency and high throughput. Evaluations show that *CPSpatial* also has zero preemption latency like the traditional instant preemption techniques, and at the time, achieves up to $1.43\times$ throughput. When dealing with sudden LS job workload increasing, *CPSpatial* reduces the preemption latency by 87.3% compared with the state-of-the-art GPU context switching method.

Keywords: GPU · GPU sharing · Collaborative GPU preemption

1 Introduction

Data centers have been adopting GPUs to meet the demand of emerging massively data-parallel applications, which consist of both latency-sensitive jobs (LS jobs) and batch jobs [15,16]. LS jobs have stringent Quality-of-Service (QoS) requirements, while batch jobs prefer cost-efficient throughput. GPUs are often over-provisioned to satisfy the stringent QoS targets of LS jobs, causing GPU under-utilization for most of the time [15]. Idle computing capacities can be donated to batch jobs to improve GPU utilization. When LS jobs come, batch jobs should instantly release GPUs to avoid blocking LS jobs.

© Springer Nature Switzerland AG 2021
L. Sousa et al. (Eds.): Euro-Par 2021, LNCS 12820, pp. 89–104, 2021.
https://doi.org/10.1007/978-3-030-85665-6_6

Preemptive GPU prioritization is costly due to the large contexts of GPU kernels. Prior studies have proposed many novel GPU preemption techniques [8,9,12], with different trade-offs between preemption latency and overhead. Some studies also propose collaborative methods [9], which dynamically select preemption techniques when preemption occurs. However, GPU kernels usually adopt various kernel transformations, such as persistent threads programming style [4] and kernel fusion [3], to improve performance. Some of them also impact preemption costs, which then influence or even determine the techniques that can be selected at preemption time. Moreover, many sophisticated software preemption techniques themselves also transform kernels for runtime support [7,14]. Kernel transformation methods are determined before launching, so should be the preemption technique choices. It is impractical to arbitrarily select a preemption technique during preemption if considering kernel transformation.

This paper presents *CPSpatial* (**C**ollaborative GPU **P**reemption via **Spatial** Multitasking) for efficient GPU sharing among LS jobs and batch jobs. *CPSpatial* considers the impact of code transformation and proposes to combine different preemption methods via GPU spatial multitasking. It partitions GPUs into several virtual zones and assigns each zone a preemption technique. For a thread block launched to a zone, its adopted code transformation technique needs and only needs to be compatible with this zone's preemption technique. Prior collaborative methods determine the preempted thread block first and then intelligently select a preemption technique for it. Differently, *CPSpatial* selects the preemption technique first and then finds the thread blocks that can be preempted with the selected preemption technique (i.e., belonging to the corresponding zone).

CPSpatial selects preemption techniques for the virtual zones so that these preemption techniques form a preemption hierarchy. Like memory hierarchy, the higher the zone, the shorter the preemption latency and the lower the throughput. *CPSpatial* takes advantage of the preemption hierarchy to schedule LS jobs and batch jobs, providing both low latency and high throughput. SM-prefetching is proposed to make the preemption hierarchy's latency more robust to sudden LS job workload increasing. It assigns each zone a threshold, below which SM-prefetching is invoked. SM-prefetching proactively preempts thread blocks of the next lower zone and converts them to this zone. It provides a buffer period for the preemption, avoiding the next incoming LS job suffering from the whole preemption latency of the lower zones. The middle zone is most critical for the preemption hierarchy, as it serves as a buffer. We specially design a checkpoint-based preemption technique for the middle zone, which stores checkpoints in both on-chip resources and device memory in a heterogeneous manner.

The main contributions of this paper are summarized as follows:

1. We identify the impact of kernel transformation on GPU preemption and propose *CPSpatial*, a collaborative GPU preemption framework compatible with kernel transformation.
2. We propose preemption hierarchy, with which the whole system shows both low latency and high throughput regardless of the LS job workload.

3. We propose SM-prefetching to help maintain the preemption hierarchy structure. It makes the preemption latency more robust to abrupt LS job workload increasing.

This paper is organized as follows: Sect. 2 introduces the background and related work. Section 3 discusses the motivation. Then, Sect. 4 presents the architecture of *CPSpatial*, and Sect. 5 presents the preemption hierarchy. Section 6 evaluates the performance of *CPSpatial*. Conclusion and future work directions are discussed in Sect. 7.

2 Background and Related Work

Prior GPU Preemption Techniques. There are many novel GPU preemption techniques, with various trade-offs between preemption latency and overhead. The preemption latency refers to the elapsed time before releasing the GPU, which determines the waiting time. The overhead contains preemption overhead and runtime overhead. The preemption overhead is the additional work caused by preemption and resuming, while the runtime overhead is the extra work for preemption support regardless of whether preemption occurs.

SM-draining [12] stops dispatching new thread blocks when receiving the preemption signal and waits until the dispatched thread blocks finish. It reduces the preemption overhead, but the preemption latency can be as long as the kernel execution time. *SM-flushing* [9] drops the running thread blocks immediately if the idempotent condition holds. The preempted thread blocks are restarted from the beginning during resuming. It achieves instant preemption but may incur considerable preemption overhead. Preemptive GPU context switching [8] has also been studied, showing a mid-range preemption latency and overhead. Chimera [9] combines these hardware preemption techniques by intelligently selecting them when preemption occurs.

Prior works also propose many software GPU preemption techniques, which need no hardware extensions and can implement much more sophisticated logic. Moreover, software solutions allow each GPU kernel to have a dedicated preemption strategy. Lin et al. [8] propose to ignore the preemption signal temporarily and continue the execution. The context is switched until reaching an instruction with a small context. This method (denoted as *CS-Defer*) significantly reduces the preemption overhead but is not friendly to QoS-required systems due to its long and undetermined preemption latency. Prior studies also propose checkpoint-based GPU soft error resilience mechanisms [6], which can be adapted for GPU preemption. The preempted thread blocks can resume from the checkpoints, which reduces the preemption overhead. However, saving contexts as checkpoints involves device memory access, incurring non-trivial overhead.

GPU Kernel Transformations. The grid size of a batch job is usually much larger than the maximal parallelism of GPUs (maximal concurrent threads). Persistent Thread (PT) programming style [4] is usually adopted to improve throughput, which consolidates a batch of independent threads into a single persistent thread. It improves data reuse and reduces launching costs. More importantly, PT allows the compilers to unroll the loops and fuse the instructions, which increases instruction-level parallelism to hide memory latency.

Kernel fusion [3] is also a widely used kernel transformation technique, which combines multiple kernels into a single one. It improves the overall performance if these kernels share some data, especially when one kernel's output is another kernel's input. The intermediate result is allowed to reside in on-chip memory and thus does not need to be swapped to/from device memory.

These GPU kernel transformation techniques can significantly improve throughput, especially for kernels with low arithmetic intensity. As a side effect, the execution time of a single thread block is prolonged. The long execution time and large context impact the cost of many preemption techniques.

GPU Spatial Multitasking. Most GPUs support concurrent kernel execution, which allows different kernels to co-locate on the same GPU. It improves GPU utilization, especially when co-locating memory-intensive and compute-intensive kernels [13]. Many studies also explore co-locating LS jobs and batch jobs [15,16]. SMGuard [15] avoids batch jobs blocking LS jobs by limiting resource usage of batch jobs so that enough resources are reserved for LS jobs. Laius [16] proposes to allocate "just-enough" resources for LS jobs and donate the remaining resources to batch jobs. CLITE [10] further proposes to incrementally adjust the resource usage of LS jobs based on the observed performance.

Unlike the above methods, *CPSpatial* does not use spatial multitasking to isolate LS jobs and batch jobs for prioritization. Instead, *CPSpatial*'s objective of spatially partitioning GPUs is to combine preemption techniques. *CPSpatial* allows batch jobs to occupy the whole GPU, as LS jobs can preempt them almost immediately with collaborated preemption techniques. It achieves both low latency and high throughput without the need for precise LS job workload prediction.

3 Motivation

GPU kernels often adopt code transformation to improve performance, such as kernel fusion [3] and persistent thread programming style [4]. Some of them also affect preemption costs, impacting the dynamic preemption technique selection at preemption time. Figure 1 shows the throughput and single thread block execution time of PT kernels (relative to non-PT kernels). The selected benchmarks are described in Sect. 6. PT kernels show 28.1% throughput improvement on average and up to 78.1% compared with non-PT kernels. PT usually significantly prolongs the execution time of a single thread block: 7.54× on average and up to 13.9×. The long execution time of persistent thread blocks makes *SM-flushing* and *SM-draining* very costly so that persistent thread blocks can almost only be preempted by context switching. In summary, adopting PT kernels achieves higher throughput but limits the preemption technique choices,

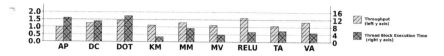

Fig. 1. Compare PT kernels and non-PT kernels

incurring high preemption costs if preemption occurs. In contrast, non-PT kernels have much lower preemption costs, but at the same time, lower throughput, decreasing the overall throughput if no preemption occurs.

Kernels are transformed before launching, or more specifically, before compilation. Due to the critical impact on preemption cost, the code transformation almost determines the feasible preemption techniques. It is impractical to combine preemption techniques simply via dynamic selection at preemption time if kernel transformation is adopted. Moreover, many sophisticated software preemption techniques also transform the kernel code for runtime support. For example, checkpoint-based GPU preemption techniques [6] allow preempted thread blocks to restart from a checkpoint. The checkpoints must be saved during normal execution, which also should be determined before launching. It inspires us to design a collaborative preemption method, which considers the impact of code transformation.

4   *CPSpatial* Architecture

CPSpatial is a collaborative preemption framework designed for efficient GPU sharing among LS jobs and batch jobs. It combines different preemption techniques via GPU spatial multitasking. The GPUs are partitioned into several virtual zones, and each zone is assigned a code transformation method (Fig. 2a). Thread blocks launched to each zone are transformed accordingly, determining the preemption techniques that can be selected when these thread blocks are preempted. The key idea of *CPSpatial* is that, when preemption occurs, it selects the preemption technique first and then preempts the thread blocks that can be preempted with the selected technique. Even if the feasible preemption techniques for each thread block have been determined before launching, *CPSpatial* still enables collaborative preemption by selecting the thread blocks.

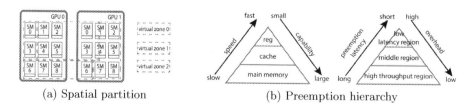

(a) Spatial partition   (b) Preemption hierarchy

Fig. 2. Basic idea of *CPSpatial*

Preemption techniques exhibit various trade-offs between preemption latency and overhead. *CPSpatial* organizes the preemption techniques of the virtual zones to form a preemption hierarchy. Like memory hierarchy, the highest zone has the shortest preemption latency but the lowest throughput, while the lowest zone causes the longest preemption latency but with the highest throughput (Fig. 2b). *CPSpatial* takes advantage of the preemption hierarchy to schedule LS jobs and batch jobs. The preemption hierarchy makes the whole system show both low latency and high throughput.

Figure 3 shows the overview architecture of *CPSpatial*. It consists of a scheduler that implements the scheduling logic, a zone monitor that adjusts the preemption hierarchy structure, and a kernel transformer that transforms kernels according to the scheduler's requirements.

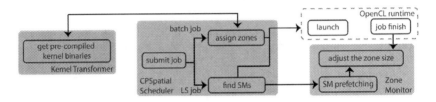

Fig. 3. Architecture of *CPSpatial*

4.1 *CPSpatial* Scheduler

When an LS job comes, the scheduler first figures out its resource usage. Many studies have discussed the resource allocation problem for GPU jobs with QoS requirements [10,16]. If idle Streaming Multiprocessors (SMs) are not enough, the scheduler preempts thread blocks of batch jobs to release resources for the LS job. The highest zone is preempted first and then the lower zones. The highest zone has the least preemption latency, which usually achieves instant preemption. The lower zones have long preemption latency, but their thread blocks are rarely preempted. SM-prefetching further reduces the expected waiting time caused by preempting lower zones. After launching the LS job, the scheduler updates the tracking information of the size of each zone and invokes the zone monitor. The latter adjusts the preemption hierarchy structure if needed.

On the other hand, when launching a batch job, the scheduler first assigns virtual zones for each of its thread blocks. The zones are assigned based on the tracking information of the size and the occupation of each zone. The objective is to maintain the preemption hierarchy structure. The scheduler prefers to allocate thread blocks of batch jobs to the lowest zone first for high throughput. Until the lowest zone is full, the scheduler allocates the thread blocks to higher zones. After that, *CPSpatial* invokes the kernel transformer to get the transformed code. It then launches the thread blocks and updates the tracking information of the occupation of each zone.

LS jobs are not transformed based on the preemption hierarchy. *CPSpatial* has almost no impact on the execution time of LS jobs. The prioritization among LS jobs can follow the real-time GPU kernel scheduling strategies, such as [5].

4.2   Virtual Zone Monitor

When the LS job workload is high, many thread blocks of the highest zone have been preempted and occupied. As the highest zone shrinks, the remaining thread blocks may not be enough for future incoming LS jobs. These LS jobs need to preempt thread blocks of lower zones, which have relatively long preemption latency. SM-prefetching is proposed to reduce the preemption latency when the LS job workload suddenly increases. It assigns each zone a threshold. When the zone is smaller than its threshold, SM-prefetching proactively preempts some thread blocks of the next lower zone and allocates the released SMs to this zone.

Even though the lower zones' preemption latency is relatively long, it does not directly impact the waiting time of LS jobs. As shown in Fig. 4, SM-prefetching is invoked at T_{PF}, the next LS job arrives at T_{LS}, and the preemption latency of the second-highest zone is t_{pl}. SM-prefetching reduces the waiting time of the LS job from t_{pl} to $\max(0, t_{pl} - (T_{LS} - T_{PF}))$.

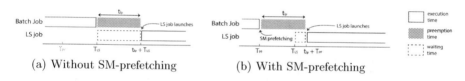

(a) Without SM-prefetching   (b) With SM-prefetching

Fig. 4. Waiting time of LS jobs with and without SM-prefetching

The time $T_{LS} - T_{PF}$ is a buffer period for the preemption. SM-prefetching makes the system more robust when the LS job workload increases suddenly. Even if the remaining SMs of the highest zone are not enough for the current LS job workload, the first affected LS job, if any, does not need to wait a whole preemption time of the second-highest zone.

The zone monitor is also responsible for allocating the SMs released by finished jobs to the preemption hierarchy. The released SMs are allocated to higher zones first to reduce the frequency of SM-prefetching.

4.3   Kernel Transformer

GPUs are partitioned into virtual zones. "Virtual" indicates that there is no need to really partition the GPU. As long as a thread block is transformed with a transformation technique, the SM, which accommodates this thread block, can be regarded as belonging to the corresponding zone. A thread block can be assigned to any SM so that *CPSpatial* does not affect the cache locality.

The kernel transformer is responsible for transforming the kernels. For example, to support persistent thread, the kernel transformer should be able to transform a kernel to its PT version based on the requirement from the scheduler. The number of thread blocks should also be adjusted accordingly [4]. Many software GPU preemption mechanisms also need to transform the kernel code for runtime support [7]. The transformation strategies should also be implemented in the kernel transformer.

The kernel transformer can either be online or offline. The online transformer transforms the kernel codes after receiving the requirement from the scheduler. The transformed code is then compiled and returned to the scheduler. The advantage is that only the necessary transformation and compilation is performed. In contrast, the offline transformer applies all possible transformations to a kernel regardless of whether the scheduler needs them. When invoked by the scheduler, it can immediately return the pre-compiled kernels, which incurs no runtime overhead. However, a transformation may be applied even if it is not used at all. In practice, the preemption hierarchy only contains a few transformation techniques. Applying all code transformation techniques is not very costly. Thus, *CPSpatial* adopts the offline transformer.

5   Preemption Hierarchy

CPSpatial implements a three-level preemption hierarchy to demonstrate the idea, whereas more levels usually offer better performance. The highest zone influences the preemption latency of the preemption hierarchy the most, as preemption mainly occurs in this zone. It adopts *SM-flushing*, which incurs almost no preemption latency. Correspondingly, non-PT kernels are used, whose execution time is usually short, to reduce the expected useful work waste incurred by *SM-flushing*. As non-PT kernels have much lower throughput for some applications, the highest zone has low throughput if no preemption occurs.

On the other hand, the lowest zone should provide high throughput, even at the expense of higher preemption costs. The lowest zone adopts PT kernels, which provides up to 1.78× throughput for the selected benchmarks. *CPSpatial* assigns *CS-Defer* (described in Sect. 2) to the lowest zone. As a context switching style technique, *CS-Defer* is less sensitive to the long execution time of persistent thread blocks. Moreover, *CS-Defer* needs no runtime support and thus incurs no runtime overhead. The lowest zone provides high throughput because of the low runtime overhead and preemption overhead. However, the preemption latency is relative long as the contexts are saved at preemption time.

As the middle zone serves as a buffer, its preemption technique is most critical for the preemption hierarchy. It needs to carefully trade-off the preemption latency and throughput overhead. Even if LS jobs rarely preempt the middle zone directly, SM-prefetching still proactively preempts its thread blocks to prepare for the LS job workload increasing. If its preemption latency is too long, SM-prefetching may fail to adjust the preemption hierarchy structure in time. On the other hand, SM-prefetching is not as frequent as preemption. The middle zone cannot blindly trade higher overhead for lower latency. Otherwise, the overall throughput of the preemption hierarchy decreases. The buffer period provided by SM-prefetching allows the middle zone to have a relatively long preemption latency, which can be used to trade-off for lower preemption overhead.

5.1   Checkpoint-Based GPU Context Switching

CPSpatial adapts the checkpoint-based GPU fault tolerance mechanisms for preemption (named *CKPT-CW*). *CKPT-CW* proactively saves the context as checkpoints. The preempted thread blocks can then resume from the checkpoints. As preemption is more frequent than soft errors (1/day in 16 nm [6]), *CKPT-CW* needs a much shorter checkpoint interval to avoid incurring high resuming costs. It enables much more frequent checkpoints via heterogeneous checkpoint storage.

If the free on-chip resources are enough for the largest checkpoint, $ckpt_{onchip}$ is set to the size of the largest checkpoint, and all checkpoints are stored in on-chip resources. Otherwise, $ckpt_{onchip}$ is selected so that it is enough to store most of the selected checkpoints. The size is determined by the quartile of the checkpoint sizes. As shown in Fig. 5, for a checkpoint that is smaller than $ckpt_{onchip}$, all of its variables are saved in on-chip resources. For a checkpoint, whose size is larger than $ckpt_{onchip}$, *CKPT-CW* saves $ckpt_{onchip}$ variables of the checkpoint in on-chip resources, while the others are saved into device memory.

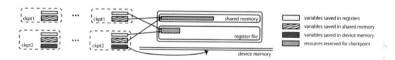

Fig. 5. Heterogeneous checkpoint storing

The on-chip resources are selected based on the resource usage of the kernel to minimize the occupation decreasing. If the shared memory usage is the bottleneck, registers are mainly used to store the on-chip part of the checkpoint. In contrast, most of the on-chip part is stored in the shared memory if the occupation is limited by the register usage. In reality, the unused shared memory is usually enough to store the on-chip part. Some studies [9] report the under-utilization of shared memory for most GPU kernels, and the checkpoints are selected at the instructions with small contexts. However, when free on-chip resources are not enough to store the on-chip part of the checkpoint, the occupation is decreased until getting enough free on-chip resources.

Heterogeneous checkpoint storing incurs much less runtime overhead as on-chip resource access is much faster. However, the on-chip part still needs to be saved into device memory if preemption occurs, contributing to the preemption latency. Whereas *CKPT-CW* does not achieve instant preemption, its preemption latency is much shorter and more predictable than *CS-Defer*. *CKPT-CW* does not need to defer the preemption and only needs to save at most $ckpt_{onchip}$ variables into device memory for each preempted warp during preemption. As an expense, *CKPT-CW* incurs non-trivial runtime overhead, including potential occupation decreasing and on-chip resource access. It is less useful on a standalone basis but matches the requirements of the middle zone. As only a few SMs belong to the middle zone, the induced runtime overhead is not significant from the perspective of the whole system.

For non-idempotent kernels, each idempotent zone also needs a checkpoint. Some idempotent zones are too small to find a satisfying checkpoint, incurring high runtime overhead. Prior studies optimize checkpoint selection for non-idempotent kernels [6], while *CPSpatial* chooses not to assign thread blocks of non-idempotent kernels to the middle zone. Only few popular kernels are non-idempotent [9], and data centers usually host many kinds of kernels. *CPSpatial* can launch thread blocks of other kernels to the middle zone. If there is no idempotent kernel, *CPSpatial* leaves the highest zone and the middle zone idle.

5.2   Zone Size and Threshold

The size and threshold of each zone can be adjusted dynamically and incrementally. *CPSpatial* offers short waiting time and high throughput with the preemption hierarchy. Dynamically adjusting the size and threshold eases the preemption hierarchy structure maintenance.

Long average waiting time indicates that the highest zone is small, so that many LS jobs preempt thread blocks of the lower zones. *CPSpatial* should increase the size of the highest zone for the current LS job workload.

Another possible situation is that the average waiting time is acceptable, while several LS jobs suffer long waiting time. *CPSpatial* then adjusts the preemption hierarchy structure based on how frequent SM-prefetching is invoked. If SM-prefetching is rarely invoked, it means that the highest zone is large enough for the current workload, while SM-prefetching is not invoked in time to prepare for the small workload peaks. *CPSpatial* then sets a lower threshold for the highest zone to make SM-prefetching easier to trigger. On the other hand, the preemption latency outliers are due to the small size of the middle zone. *CPSpatial* needs to preempt thread blocks of the lowest zone to adjust the preemption hierarchy structure. It then converts some SMs from the lowest zone to the middle zone.

When the highest zone becomes over-large due to workload decreasing, or the thread blocks preempted by SM-prefetching is much less than the number of SMs of the middle zone, *CPSpatial* converts some of their SMs to the lowest zone. When converting SMs to lower zones, *CPSpatial* does not proactively preempt thread blocks but waits for them to finish. The goal of increasing the ratio of lower zones is to increase throughput. The overhead incurred by preemption is usually more than the runtime overhead of higher zones.

CPSpatial uses the workload statistic to adjust the preemption hierarchy structure rather than using it to assign thread blocks to zones. The preemption technique assignment is based on the current occupation status of the preemption hierarchy. Moreover, the difference between history and future workload does not necessarily lead to poor performance. SM-prefetching and preemption hierarchy reduce the impact of under-estimating and over-estimating the LS workload, much like the cache to the memory hierarchy.

6 Experiment and Result

This section evaluates *CPSpatial*[1] on an AMD Radeon VII graphics card [1]. *CPSpatial* is implemented as a wrapper of OpenCL runtime with the help of ROCdbgapi (ROCm v3.7). *CKPT-CW* is implemented based on LLVM (version 12), a compiler framework that supports the AMDGPU backend.

6.1 Experimental Setup

We select a wide range of OpenCL kernels from BLAS (Basic Linear Algebra Subprograms) libraries, deep learning libraries, and Rodinia benchmarks [2], including average pooling (AP), direct convolution (DC), dot product (DOT), K-means (KM), matrix-matrix multiplication (MM), matrix-vector multiplication (MV), ReLU activation (RELU), tangent activation (TA), and vector addition (VA). Among them, RELU, DC, and DOT are also selected as LS kernels. The input size of LS jobs is selected so that their execution time is around 1–2 ms. Many studies [15] report that the execution time of typical latency-sensitive GPU applications is about 1–2 ms. MLPerf [11] also shows that the neural network inference time is in the order of hundred microseconds to milliseconds.

We evaluate four GPU preemption frameworks. The first is *non-PT+DS* (**D**ynamic **S**election), which adopts non-PT kernels for all batch jobs. It dynamically selects from *SM-flushing* and *CS-Defer* when preemption occurs. *PT+DS* is the same as *non-PT+DS*, except that it adopts PT kernels. *PT+CS-Defer* also adopts PT kernels for all batch jobs but always chooses *CS-Defer* when preemption occurs. *CPSpatial* is the collaborative preemption framework presented in this paper. In our experiments, all evaluated preemption frameworks rank the preemption technique candidates with the preemption latency so that *non-PT+DS* and *PT+DS* almost always choose *SM-flushing*. The goal of sharing GPUs with batch jobs is to improve utilization. Batch jobs should not block LS jobs, as LS jobs are sensitive to latency and usually have high priority.

Our experiments assume each LS job occupies $\frac{1}{16}$ of the GPU, and there are always enough batch jobs. The arrival times of LS jobs are sampled from Poisson distributions, and their expected occurrence rates determine the LS job workload. The experiments evaluate each preemption framework's performance when the LS job workload (average arrival interval) suddenly changes from 320 μs to 20 μs, 80 μs, 320 μs (unchanged), 1.28 ms, 5.12 ms, and 20.48 ms. The scheduling frameworks have no prior knowledge about the abrupt workload change, which is the most challenging situation. The evaluation metrics are the waiting time of LS jobs and the throughput of batch jobs.

---

[1] https://github.com/jizhuoran/cpspatial.

Most GPU drivers do not support thread-block-grained launching. Our experiment launches the thread blocks as independent kernels to ease the preemption-resuming and throughput calculation while supporting it by hardware is not costly nor challenging. Moreover, the preemption routine and resuming routine are also launched as separate kernels when measuring the time. In production environments, the preemption latency and throughput do not need to be precisely measured so that conventional signal handling mechanisms can be used.

6.2   Latency

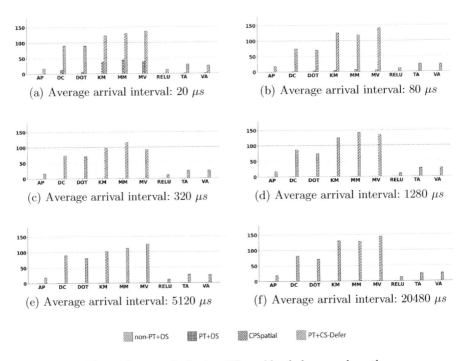

(a) Average arrival interval: 20 μs

(b) Average arrival interval: 80 μs

(c) Average arrival interval: 320 μs

(d) Average arrival interval: 1280 μs

(e) Average arrival interval: 5120 μs

(f) Average arrival interval: 20480 μs

non-PT+DS   PT+DS   CPSpatial   PT+CS-Defer

Fig. 6. Latency (μs) when LS workload changes abruptly

Figure 6 shows the preemption latency when the LS job workload suddenly changes from 320 μs to other arrival intervals, ranging from 20 μs to 20.48 ms. The preemption latency is measured from the device side and only counts the waiting time of LS jobs that are blocked by batch jobs. The objective of the experiments is to evaluate the scheduling frameworks' performance when sharing GPUs among LS jobs and batch jobs, while the prioritization within LS jobs is studied by other works, such as [5].

As *SM-flushing* directly flushes the running thread blocks, *PT+DS* and *non-PT+DS* show almost zero preemption latency regardless of the workload. In contrast, *PT+CS-Defer* shows relatively constant and long preemption latency under different LS job workloads, as it always preempts batch jobs with *CS-Defer*. The preemption latency is 82.3 μs on average and up to 143.8 μs. Considering the average execution time of LS jobs (1–2 ms), the waiting time caused by *PT+CS-Defer* is non-trivial.

CPSpatial achieves short preemption latency by combining preemption techniques via spatial multitasking. With preemption hierarchy and SM-prefetching, *CPSpatial* incurs only 22.7 μs and 2.94 μs preemption latency when the LS job arrival interval changes to 20 μs and 80 μs, respectively. Compared with *PT+CS-Defer*, it reduces the preemption latency by 87.3% on average. The LS job workload increasing is abrupt and unknown to the scheduling frameworks. *CPSpatial* does not change the preemption hierarchy structure during the experiment. The size of the highest zone is chosen based on the original LS job arrival interval (320 μs), which is not enough when the arrival interval suddenly increases by a factor of 16 (i.e., 20 μs). Thus, the LS jobs need to preempt thread blocks of the middle zone and even of the lowest zone. However, *CPSpatial* still achieves almost instant preemption for $\frac{4}{9}$ benchmarks with the help of SM-prefetching. On the other hand, when the LS job workload decreases or remains unchanged, *CPSpatial* shows almost zero preemption latency for all benchmarks.

For *CKPT-CW* and *CS-Defer*, the preemption latency is highly correlated with the context size of the preempted thread block. The contexts of MM and MV are relatively large, and thus *CKPT-CW* and *CS-Defer* incur long preemption latency when dealing with them. In contrast, RELU and VA have relatively small contexts, whose preemption latencies are short when preempted by *CKPT-CW* and *CS-Defer*. For RELU, the preemption latency of *CPSpatial* is almost 0 even when the LS job arrival interval drops to 20 μs.

6.3 Throughput

Collaborative preemption also improves throughput. Figure 7 shows the normalized throughput of batch jobs. The baseline is the throughput of the PT kernels executing without preemption. When the average arrival interval equals 20 μs, LS jobs almost occupy the whole GPU, and thus the throughput of batch jobs is almost zero. However, *PT+CS-Defer* still has quite a high throughput, as *CS-Defer* defers the preemption. The instructions, which are executed before context switching, are useful work and contribute to the throughput. *CPSpatial* achieves 71.3% throughput of *PT+CS-Defer* without compromising the preemption latency. The lowest zone contributes to the throughput as it adopts *CS-Defer*, while the highest zone offers low latency preemption.

PT+DS has a much lower throughput under frequent preemption due to the considerable useful work waste caused by flushing PT kernels. When the LS job arrival interval is 80 μs, the throughput of *non-PT+DS* is 11.5× of *PT+DS* on average. The throughput gap is about the same as the relative execution time of a single thread block between PT kernels and non-PT kernels. With preemption hierarchy, *CPSpatial* achieves 2.0× throughput of *non-PT+DS*, which is 23.1× of *PT+DS*. When the LS job workload is 320 μs, *non-PT+DS* achieves 1.15×

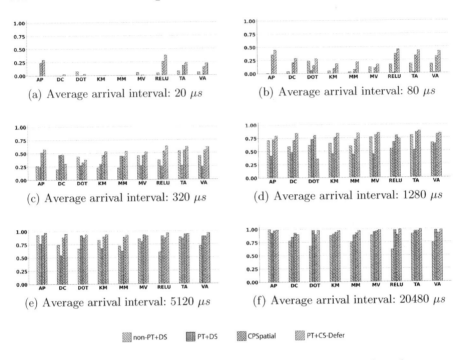

(a) Average arrival interval: 20 μs

(b) Average arrival interval: 80 μs

(c) Average arrival interval: 320 μs

(d) Average arrival interval: 1280 μs

(e) Average arrival interval: 5120 μs

(f) Average arrival interval: 20480 μs

non-PT+DS   PT+DS   CPSpatial   PT+CS-Defer

Fig. 7. Normalized throughput when LS workload changes abruptly

throughput of $PT+DS$ on average, and up to 2.06×. In this case, the preemption overhead incurred by flushing PT kernels still outweighs the throughput gap between the PT version and non-PT version for most kernels. $CPSpatial$ breaks the trade-off between the waiting time of LS jobs and the overall throughput of batch jobs. It achieves 1.37× throughput of $non-PT+DS$. Achieving almost zero preemption latency, the throughput of $CPSpatial$ is 91.7% of $PT+CS-Defer$, while the latter's average preemption latency is 73.1 μs under this LS job workload.

Adopting non-PT kernels, $non-PT+DS$ suffers significant throughput degradation when the LS job workload is low, or in other words, when batch jobs are rarely preempted. When the average arrival interval ≥ 5.12 ms, the throughput of $non-PT+DS$ is only 78.7% of the baseline, while $PT+DS$ achieves 85.4% throughput of the baseline. Even without prior knowledge of the sudden and drastic LS job workload decreasing, $CPSpatial$ still achieves 91.4% throughput of the baseline. It suffers less preemption overhead and runtime overhead. The highest zone adopts non-PT kernels, wasting less useful work when preempted; the lower zones adopt PT kernels, which achieve high throughput and will not be preempted when the LS job workload is low. While $PT+CS-Defer$ achieves the highest throughput (95.5%), it is at the expense of long waiting time for LS jobs. It violates the objective of sharing GPUs among LS jobs and batch jobs. If the LS job workload dropped to an even lower level, $PT+DS$ and $PT+CS-Defer$

would have about the same throughput, as all of their thread blocks adopt PT kernels. In this case, the preemption overhead is negligible, and the throughput is determined by the adopted kernel transformation techniques.

CPSpatial has higher throughput than *non-PT+DS* and *PT+DS* in most of the experiments. Compared with *PT+CS-Defer*, its throughput degradation is acceptable, even when the LS job workload suddenly drops to a very low level. Moreover, if the LS job workload keeps low, some SMs of the highest zone will be re-allocated to lower zones. It further narrows the throughput gap between *CPSpatial* and *PT+CS-Defer*.

7 Conclusion

This paper identifies the impact of kernel transformation on GPU preemption. We propose *CPSpatial*, a collaborative GPU preemption framework for efficient GPU sharing among LS jobs and batch jobs. It considers the impact of kernel transformation and proposes to combine preemption techniques via spatial partition. The preemption techniques are organized to form a preemption hierarchy, providing both low preemption latency and high throughput. *CPSpatial* adopts SM-prefetching to make the preemption latency more robust to sudden LS job workload increasing. We have evaluated *CPSpatial* with comprehensive benchmarks. When the LS job workload increases, *CPSpatial* reduces the preemption latency by 87.3% compared with *PT+CS-Defer*, and achieves 1.1× and 1.2× throughput of *PT+DS* and *non-PT+DS*. When the preemption hierarchy structure exactly matches the LS job workload, *CPSpatial* achieves almost zero preemption latency; at the time, it achieves 91.7% throughput of *PT+CS-Defer*, whose average preemption latency is 73.1 μs.

As future work, we plan to support more preemption techniques and GPU kernel transformation techniques to improve the preemption hierarchy. In addition, we would like to evaluate *CPSpatial* in a realistic multiuser and multitasking environment with a large-scale cluster. We are also interested in using reinforcement learning to adjust the zone size and the threshold.

Acknowledgements. This research is supported by Hong Kong RGC Research Impact Fund R5060-19. We appreciate EURO-PAR reviewers for their constructive comments and suggestions.

References

1. AMD: Vega instruction set architecture reference guide (2017). https://developer. amd.com/wp-content/resources/Vega_Shader_ISA_28July2017.pdf
2. Che, S., et al.: Rodinia: a benchmark suite for heterogeneous computing. In: 2009 IEEE International Symposium on Workload Characterization (IISWC), pp. 44–54. IEEE (2009)
3. Chen, T., et al.: {TVM}: an automated end-to-end optimizing compiler for deep learning. In: 13th {USENIX} Symposium on Operating Systems Design and Implementation ({OSDI} 18), pp. 578–594 (2018)

4. Gupta, K., Stuart, J.A., Owens, J.D.: A study of persistent threads style GPU programming for GPGPU workloads. IEEE (2012)
5. Kato, S., Lakshmanan, K., Rajkumar, R., Ishikawa, Y.: Timegraph: GPU scheduling for real-time multi-tasking environments. In: Proceedings of USENIX ATC, pp. 17–30 (2011)
6. Kim, H., Zeng, J., Liu, Q., Abdel-Majeed, M., Lee, J., Jung, C.: Compiler-directed soft error resilience for lightweight GPU register file protection. In: Proceedings of the 41st ACM SIGPLAN Conference on Programming Language Design and Implementation, pp. 989–1004 (2020)
7. Li, C., Zigerelli, A., Yang, J., Zhang, Y., Ma, S., Guo, Y.: A dynamic and proactive GPU preemption mechanism using checkpointing. IEEE Trans. Comput.-Aided Des. Integr. Circ. Syst. **39**(1), 75–87 (2018)
8. Lin, Z., Nyland, L., Zhou, H.: Enabling efficient preemption for SIMT architectures with lightweight context switching. In: SC 2016: Proceedings of the International Conference for High Performance Computing, Networking, Storage and Analysis, pp. 898–908. IEEE (2016)
9. Park, J.J.K., Park, Y., Mahlke, S.: Chimera: Collaborative preemption for multi-tasking on a shared GPU. ACM SIGARCH Comput. Archit. News **43**(1), 593–606 (2015)
10. Patel, T., Tiwari, D.: Clite: efficient and qos-aware co-location of multiple latency-critical jobs for warehouse scale computers. In: 2020 IEEE International Symposium on High Performance Computer Architecture (HPCA), pp. 193–206. IEEE (2020)
11. Reddi, V.J., et al.: Mlperf inference benchmark. In: 2020 ACM/IEEE 47th Annual International Symposium on Computer Architecture (ISCA), pp. 446–459. IEEE (2020)
12. Tanasic, I., Gelado, I., Cabezas, J., Ramirez, A., Navarro, N., Valero, M.: Enabling preemptive multiprogramming on GPUS. ACM SIGARCH Comput. Archit. News **42**(3), 193–204 (2014)
13. Wang, Z., Yang, J., Melhem, R., Childers, B., Zhang, Y., Guo, M.: Simultaneous multikernel: fine-grained sharing of GPUS. IEEE Comput. Archit. Lett. **15**(2), 113–116 (2015)
14. Wu, B., Liu, X., Zhou, X., Jiang, C.: Flep: enabling flexible and efficient preemption on GPUS. ACM SIGPLAN Not. **52**(4), 483–496 (2017)
15. Yu, C., et al.: Smguard: a flexible and fine-grained resource management framework for GPUS. IEEE Trans. Parallel Distrib. Syst. **29**(12), 2849–2862 (2018)
16. Zhang, W., et al.: Laius: towards latency awareness and improved utilization of spatial multitasking accelerators in datacenters. In: Proceedings of the ACM International Conference on Supercomputing, pp. 58–68 (2019)

A Fixed-Parameter Algorithm
for Scheduling Unit Dependent Tasks
with Unit Communication Delays

Ning Tang[(✉)] and Alix Munier Kordon

Sorbonne Université, CNRS, LIP6, 75005 Paris, France
{Ning.Tang,Alix.Munier}@lip6.fr

Abstract. This paper considers the minimization of the makespan for a set of dependent tasks with unit duration and unit communication delays. Given an upper bound of the makespan, release dates and deadlines of the tasks can be computed. Time windows are defined accordingly. We prove that our scheduling problem is fixed-parameter tractable; the parameter is the maximum number of tasks that are schedulable at the same time considering time windows.

A fixed-parameter algorithm based on a dynamic programming approach is developed and proved to solve this optimization problem. This is, as far as we know, the first fixed-parameter algorithm for a scheduling problem with communication delays.

Keywords: Scheduling · Communication delays · Makespan · Fixed-parameter algorithm

1 Introduction

This paper tackles a basic scheduling problem with communication delays defined as follows: a set $\mathcal{T} = \{1, 2, \ldots, n\}$ of n tasks is to be executed on an unlimited number of machines (sometimes also called as processors). Each machine can process at most one task at a time and each task is processed once. Tasks have a unit execution processing time and are partially ordered by a precedence graph $\mathcal{G} = (\mathcal{T}, \mathcal{A})$. Let t_i be the starting time of the task i. For any arc $(i, j) \in \mathcal{A}$, the task i must finish its execution before the task j starts executing, i.e. $t_i + 1 \leq t_j$. If tasks i and j are assigned to different processors, a unit communication delay must be added after the execution of the task i, to send data to task j and thus $t_i + 2 \leq t_j$. The problem is to find a feasible schedule that minimizes the makespan; it is referred to $\overline{P}|prec, p_i = 1, c_{ij} = 1|C_{max}$ using standard notations [12].

The development of fixed-parameter algorithms for NP-complete problems is a way to get polynomial-time algorithms when some parameters are fixed [7,9]. More formally, a fixed-parameter algorithm solves any instance of a problem of size n in time $f(k) \cdot \text{poly}(n)$, where f is allowed to be a computable superpolynomial function and k the associated parameter.

L. Sousa et al. (Eds.): Euro-Par 2021, LNCS 12820, pp. 105–119, 2021.
https://doi.org/10.1007/978-3-030-85665-6_7

Mnich and van Bevern [14] surveyed main results on parameterized complexity for scheduling problems and identified 15 open problems. However, there is no result of parameterized complexity for scheduling problems with communication delays.

The purpose of this paper is to present the first fixed-parameter algorithm for the problem $\overline{P}|prec, p_i = 1, c_{ij} = 1|C_{max}$. We observe that, to any upper bound $\overline{C}$ of the minimum makespan, feasible release dates r_i and deadlines d_i can be associated for any task $i \in \mathcal{T}$ considering the precedence graph $\mathcal{G}$. The parameter considered for our algorithm is the pathwidth, denoted by $pw(\overline{C})$, and corresponds to the maximum number of tasks minus one that can be executed simultaneously if we only consider the intervals $\{(r_i, d_i), i \in \mathcal{T}\}$.

The pathwidth $pw(\overline{C})$ can be interpreted as a simple measure of the parallelism of the instance considered for a fixed makespan $\overline{C}$. One can observe that $pw(\overline{C})$ is the pathwidth of the interval graph associated with the set of intervals $\{(r_i, d_i), i \in \mathcal{T}\}$ [4].

We prove in this paper that the scheduling problem with communication delays $\overline{P}|prec, p_i = 1, c_{ij} = 1|C_{max}$ can be solved in time $\mathcal{O}(n^3 \cdot pw(\overline{C}) \cdot 2^{4pw(\overline{C})})$ using a dynamic programming approach. A multistage graph where paths model feasible schedules is partially built until a complete feasible schedule is obtained. Our algorithm is inspired from the work of Munier [15] which developed a fixed-parameter algorithm for the problem $P|prec, p_i = 1|C_{max}$.

This paper is organised as follows. Section 2 presents related work. Section 3 defines the problem and the notations. It also recalls the modeling of our problem using an integer linear program. Section 4 presents some important dominance properties considered to characterize the structure of the solutions. Section 5 is dedicated to the description of the algorithm and its validity proof. The complexity of our algorithm is studied in Sect. 6. Section 7 is our conclusion.

2   Related Work

The scheduling problem $P|prec, p_i = 1, c_{ij} = 1|C_{max}$ with a limited number of processors was first introduced by Rayward-Smith [18]. Basic scheduling problems with communication delays were intensively studied since the 1990s due to the importance of applications, see. the surveys [6,10,11,21].

Hoogeveen et al. [13] have shown that a polynomial-time algorithm without duplication exists for solving the problem $\overline{P}|prec, p_i = 1, c_{ij} = 1|C_{max}$ when the makespan is bounded by 5, but it is NP-complete when the makespan is bounded by 6. This problem was also proved to be polynomial-time solvable for some special classes of graphs such as trees [5], series-parallel graphs [16] and generalized n-dimensional grid task graphs [3].

Many authors considered scheduling problems with communication delays for a limited number of processors. An exact dynamic programming algorithm of time complexity $\mathcal{O}(2^{w(G)}.n^{2w(G)})$ was developed by Veltman [22] for $P|prec, p_i = 1, c_{ij} = 1|C_{max}$. The parameter $w(G)$ is the width of the precedence graph G defined as the size of its largest antichain. This algorithm can clearly be considered for solving the problem without limitation of the number of machines by setting the number of machines equal to the number of tasks. We can observe that it is not a fixed-parameter algorithm. Zinder et al. [24] have developed an exact branch-and-bound algorithm which converges to an optimal schedule for the problem $P|prec, p_i = 1, c_{ij} = 1|C_{max}$. For the more general problem $P|prec, c_{ij}|C_{max}$, Sinnen et al. in [20] have developed an enumerative A^* algorithm coupled with pruning methods. Orr and Sinnen [17] have developed an original techniques to reduce the space of exploration and to speed up branch-and-bound methods.

Several authors also considered integer linear programming formulations (ILP in short) to solve exactly scheduling problems with communications delays and a limited number of processors. Davidović et al. in [8] tackled the scheduling problems for a fixed network of processors; communications are proportional to both the amount of exchanged data between pairs of dependent tasks and the distance between processors in the multiprocessor architecture. They developed two formulations and they compared them experimentally. Later, Ait El Cadi et al. [2] improved this approach by reducing the size of the linear program (number of variables and constraints) and by adding cuts; they compared positively to the previous authors. Venugopalan and Sinnen in [23] provided a new ILP formulation for the usual problem $P|prec, c_{ij}|C_{max}$ and comparison with [8] for several classes of graphs and fixed number of processors.

Extensions of usual problems with communication delays were extensively studied. For example, the survey of Giroudeau and Koenig [11] considered a hierarchical communication model where processors are grouped into clusters. Shimada et al. [19] developed two heuristic based methods to consider both malleable tasks and communications delays for executing a program on an homogeneous multi-core computing system. Ait-Aba et al. [1] provided complexity results for an extension of the basic communication model for scheduling problems on an heterogeneous computing systems with two different resources.

3 Problem Definition and Notations

In this section, we first recall that our scheduling problem can be modelled using an integer linear program. The computation of release dates and deadlines of tasks are expressed depending on the precedence graph and a fixed upper bound of minimum makespan $\overline{C}$. The associated pathwidth is defined, and a necessary condition for feasible schedules is provided. They will be both considered in next sections for our fixed-parameter algorithm.

3.1 Problem Definition

An instance of our scheduling problem $\overline{P}|prec, p_i = 1, c_{ij} = 1|C_{max}$ is defined by a directed acyclic graph $\mathcal{G} = (\mathcal{T}, \mathcal{A})$. For each task $i \in \mathcal{T}$, let $\Gamma^+(i)$ (resp. $\Gamma^-(i)$) be the set of successors (resp. predecessors) of i, i.e. $\Gamma^+(i) = \{j \in \mathcal{T}, (i,j) \in \mathcal{A}\}$ and $\Gamma^-(i) = \{j \in \mathcal{T}, (j,i) \in \mathcal{A}\}$.

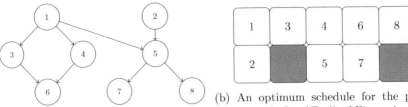

(a) A precedence graph $\mathcal{G} = (\mathcal{T}, \mathcal{A})$.

(b) An optimum schedule for the precedence graph $\mathcal{G} = (\mathcal{T}, \mathcal{A})$ of Figure 1a.

Fig. 1. A precedence graph $\mathcal{G} = (\mathcal{T}, \mathcal{A})$ and an associated optimum schedule.

Our scheduling problem can easily be modelled by a integer linear program P defined below. For any task $i \in \mathcal{T}$, we note t_i the starting time of the execution of task i. For any arc $e = (i, j) \in \mathcal{A}$, we note x_{ij} the communication delay between the tasks i and j. We set $x_{ij} = 0$ if the task j is executed just after the task i on the same processor; in this case, there is no communication delay between them. Otherwise, $x_{ij} = 1$.

$$
(P) \begin{cases}
\min C \\
\forall e = (i, j) \in \mathcal{A}, t_i + 1 + x_{ij} \le t_j & (1) \\
\forall i \in \mathcal{T}, t_i + 1 \le C & (2) \\
\forall i \in \mathcal{T}, \sum_{j \in \Gamma^+(i)} x_{ij} \ge |\Gamma^+(i)| - 1 & (3) \\
\forall i \in \mathcal{T}, \sum_{j \in \Gamma^-(i)} x_{ji} \ge |\Gamma^-(i)| - 1 & (4) \\
\forall i \in \mathcal{T}, t_i \in \mathbb{N} \\
\forall e = (i, j) \in \mathcal{A}, x_{ij} \in \{0, 1\}
\end{cases}
$$

Variables are the starting times $t_i, \forall i \in \mathcal{T}$ of the tasks, the communication delays $x_{ij}, \forall (i, j) \in \mathcal{A}$ and the makespan C. Inequalities (1) express precedence relations and communication delays between tasks executions. Inequalities (2) define the makespan. Inequalities (3) express that any task has at most one successor performed at its completion time on the same processor. Similarly, inequalities (4) express that any task has at most one predecessor performed just before its starting time on the same processor.

Any feasible schedule $\sigma(\mathcal{G})$ corresponds to a feasible solution of P and is thus defined by two vectors: starting times $t^\sigma \in \mathbb{N}^{|\mathcal{T}|}$ and communication delays $x^\sigma \in \{0, 1\}^{|\mathcal{A}|}$.

Now, one can observe that x is the decision variable of P, and thus from a practical point of view, we can consider the starting time $t \in (\mathbb{R}^+)^n$. Anyway, we will limit in this paper starting times to non negative integer values.

Let us consider for example the precedence graph presented by Fig. 1a for $\mathcal{T} = \{1, 2, \ldots, 8\}$. Figure 1b presents an associated feasible schedule $\sigma(\mathcal{G})$ of makespan 5. Associated starting times and communication delays are respectively $t^\sigma = (0, 0, 1, 2, 2, 3, 3, 4)$ and $x^\sigma = (x_{13}^\sigma, x_{14}^\sigma, x_{15}^\sigma, x_{25}^\sigma, x_{36}^\sigma, x_{46}^\sigma, x_{57}^\sigma, x_{58}^\sigma) = (0, 1, 1, 0, 1, 0, 0, 1)$.

3.2   A Necessary Condition on Feasible Schedules

A time window (r_i, d_i) associated to the task $i \in \mathcal{T}$ is given by a release date $r_i \in \mathbb{N}$ and a deadline $d_i \in \mathbb{N}$ such that the task i must be completed during the time interval (r_i, d_i), i.e. $t_i \geq r_i$ and $t_i + 1 \leq d_i$.

Let us suppose that the predecessors $j_1, \ldots, j_p$ of any task $i \in \mathcal{T}$ are numbered in decreasing order of the release times, i.e. $r_{j_1} \geq r_{j_2} \geq \cdots \geq r_{j_p}$. Then, the release date r_i can be calculated recursively as follows:

$$r_i = \begin{cases} 0 & \text{if } |\Gamma^-(i)| = 0 \\ r_{j_1} + 1 & \text{if } |\Gamma^-(i)| = 1 \text{ or } (|\Gamma^-(i)| > 1 \text{ and } r_{j_1} > r_{j_2}) \\ r_{j_1} + 2 & \text{if } |\Gamma^-(i)| > 1 \text{ and } r_{j_1} = r_{j_2}. \end{cases} \quad (1)$$

Now, let $\overline{C}$ be an upper bound of the minimum makespan for the graph $\mathcal{G} = (\mathcal{T}, \mathcal{A})$. Deadlines of tasks can similarly be computed as follows. Let us suppose that the successors $k_1, k_2, \ldots, k_q$ of any task $i \in \mathcal{T}$ are numbered in the increasing order of the deadlines, i.e. $d_{k_1} \leq d_{k_2} \leq \cdots \leq d_{k_q}$. The deadline d_i can be calculated by the following recursive function:

$$d_i = \begin{cases} \overline{C} & \text{if } |\Gamma^+(i)| = 0 \\ d_{k_1} - 1 & \text{if } |\Gamma^+(i)| = 1 \text{ or } (|\Gamma^+(i)| > 1 \text{ and } d_{k_1} < d_{k_2}) \\ d_{k_1} - 2 & \text{if } |\Gamma^+(i)| > 1 \text{ and } d_{k_1} = d_{k_2}. \end{cases} \quad (2)$$

Clearly, for any schedule $\sigma(\mathcal{G})$ of makespan bounded by $\overline{C}$, $t_i^\sigma \in [r_i, d_i)$. For any value $\alpha \in \{0, \ldots, \overline{C}-1\}$, we note X_α as the set of tasks that can be scheduled at time α following release times and deadlines, i.e. $X_\alpha = \{i \in \mathcal{T}, r_i \leq \alpha, \alpha+1 \leq d_i\}$. We also denote by Z_α the set of tasks than must be completed at or before time $\alpha + 1$, i.e. $Z_\alpha = \{i \in \mathcal{T}, d_i \leq \alpha + 1\}$. The pathwidth of $\mathcal{G}$ associated to the length $\overline{C}$ is the defined as $pw(\overline{C}) = \max_{\alpha \in \{0, \ldots, \overline{C}-1\}}(|X_\alpha| - 1)$.

Figure 2a shows the release time and deadline of tasks from the graph presented by Fig. 1a with the upper bound of the makespan $\overline{C} = 6$. Figure 2b shows the associated sets X_α and Z_α for $\alpha \in \{0, 1, \ldots, 5\}$. For this example, $pw(\overline{C}) = |X_3| - 1 = 5$.

Let us consider that $\sigma(\mathcal{G})$ is a feasible schedule of makespan $C \leq \overline{C}$. For every integer $\alpha \in \{0, \ldots, C - 1\}$, we set $\mathcal{T}_\alpha^\sigma = \{i \in \mathcal{T}, t_i^\sigma = \alpha\}$. The following lemma will be considered further to reduce the size of the tasks sets built at each step of our algorithm.

Lemma 1. *Let $\sigma(\mathcal{G})$ be a feasible schedule of $\mathcal{G}$. For any $\alpha \in \{0, \ldots, C - 1\}$,*

$$\bigcup_{\beta=0}^{\alpha} \mathcal{T}_\beta^\sigma - Z_\alpha \subseteq X_\alpha \cap X_{\alpha+1}.$$

Proof. Since $\sigma(\mathcal{G})$ is feasible, for any $\alpha \in \{0, \ldots, C - 1\}$, $\mathcal{T}_\alpha^\sigma \subseteq X_\alpha$ and thus, $\forall i \in \bigcup_{\beta=0}^{\alpha} \mathcal{T}_\beta^\sigma$, $r_i \leq \alpha$. Moreover, each task $i \notin Z_\alpha$ satisfies $d_i \geq \alpha + 2$.

Thus, for any task $i \in \bigcup_{\beta=0}^{\alpha} \mathcal{T}_\beta^\sigma - Z_\alpha$, $[\alpha, \alpha + 2] \subseteq [r_i, d_i]$. Therefore $\bigcup_{\beta=0}^{\alpha} \mathcal{T}_\beta^\sigma - Z_\alpha \subseteq X_\alpha \cap X_{\alpha+1}$, and the lemma is proved. $\qquad\square$

tasks	1	2	3	4	5	6	7	8
r_i	0	0	1	1	2	3	3	3
d_i	3	3	5	5	4	6	6	6

(a) Release times r_i and deadlines d_i of all tasks from Figure 1a for $\overline{C} = 6$.

α	X_α	Z_α
0	$\{1,2\}$	$\emptyset$
1	$\{1,2,3,4\}$	$\emptyset$
2	$\{1,2,3,4,5\}$	$\{1,2\}$
3	$\{3,4,5,6,7,8\}$	$\{1,2,5\}$
4	$\{3,4,6,7,8\}$	$\{1,2,3,4,5\}$
5	$\{6,7,8\}$	$\{1,2,3,4,5,6,7,8\}$

(b) Sets X_α and Z_α, $\alpha \in \{0,\dots,5\}$.

Fig. 2. Release times, deadlines, and sets X_α and Z_α, $\alpha \in \{0,\dots,5\}$ for the instance presented by Fig. 1a and $\overline{C} = 6$.

For our example presented by Fig. 2 and $\alpha = 3$, we have $Z_3 = \{1,2,5\}$ and $X_3 \cap X_4 = \{3,4,6,7,8\}$. For the schedule showed in Fig. 1, we have $\bigcup_{\beta=0}^{3} T_\beta^\sigma = \{1,2,3,4,5,6,7\}$. We observe that $\bigcup_{\beta=0}^{3} T_\beta^\sigma - Z_3 = \{3,4,6,7\} \subseteq X_3 \cap X_4$.

4   Dominance Properties

In this section, we express two properties of optimal schedules, which can narrow the search space.

4.1   Coherent Schedules

We can associate to any execution time vector $t^\sigma \in \mathbb{N}^n$ of a feasible schedule a communication vector x^σ, where each element $x_i^\sigma \in \{0,1\}$ in x^σ is of maximum value. The schedule obtained is said to be coherent, as defined as follows:

Definition 1 (Coherent schedule). *A schedule $\sigma(\mathcal{G})$ is **coherent** if for any arc $e = (i,j) \in \mathcal{A}$, if $t_i^\sigma + 2 \leq t_j^\sigma$, then $x_{ij}^\sigma = 1$.*

Next Lemma is a consequence of the ILP formulation of our scheduling problem:

Lemma 2 (Coherent schedule property). *Let $\sigma(\mathcal{G})$ be a feasible schedule of $\mathcal{G}$. Then, there exists a coherent feasible schedule $\sigma'(\mathcal{G})$ with $t_i^{\sigma'} = t_i^\sigma, \forall i \in \mathcal{T}$.*

Proof. Let us suppose that $\sigma(\mathcal{G})$ is a non-coherent feasible schedule. Then, we build a schedule $\sigma'(\mathcal{G})$ by setting:

1. for every task $i \in \mathcal{T}$, $t_i^{\sigma'} = t_i^\sigma$;
2. for every arc $(i,j) \in \mathcal{A}$, if $t_i^{\sigma'} + 2 > t_j^{\sigma'}$, then $x_{ij}^{\sigma'} = 0$, otherwise, $x_{ij}^{\sigma'} = 1$.

We show that $\sigma'(\mathcal{G})$ is feasible. Let us consider an arc $e = (i,j) \in \mathcal{A}$. Two cases are considered:

1. if $t_i^\sigma + 2 > t_j^\sigma$, then $x_{ij}^\sigma = 0 = x_{ij}^{\sigma'}$ and $t_i^{\sigma'} + 1 \leq t_j^{\sigma'}$, the constraint is thus fulfilled by $\sigma'(\mathcal{G})$.
2. Now, if $t_i^\sigma + 2 \leq t_j^\sigma$, we get $x_{ij}^{\sigma'} = 1 \geq x_{ij}^\sigma$ and $t_i^{\sigma'} + 1 + x_{ij}^{\sigma'} \leq t_j^{\sigma'}$ is true.

Moreover, for every arc $(i, j) \in \mathcal{A}$, $x_{ij}^{\sigma'} \geq x_{ij}^\sigma$. Thus $\sigma'(\mathcal{G})$ is a coherent feasible schedule and we proved the lemma. □

4.2   Preferred Sons

Let us consider that $\sigma(\mathcal{G})$ is a feasible coherent schedule of makespan $C \leq \overline{C}$. For every integer $\alpha \in \{0, \ldots, C-1\}$, we set $W_\alpha = \bigcup_{\beta=0}^{\alpha} \mathcal{T}_\beta^\sigma$ and $B_\alpha = \mathcal{T}_\alpha^\sigma$. The set W_α contains all the tasks that are performed during the interval $[0, \alpha + 1]$, and B_α contains all the tasks that are executed at time α. We show hereafter that, if a task $i \in \mathcal{T}$ has one or more successors schedulable at time $t_i^\sigma + 1$ (called the preferred sons of i), then we can always impose that exactly one of them is executed at time $t_i^\sigma + 1$ on the same processor as the task i.

Definition 2 (Preferred sons). *For every integer $\alpha \in \{0, \ldots, C-1\}$, a task $j \in \mathcal{T}$ is a **preferred son** of a task $i \in B_\alpha$ if j is a successor of i that is schedulable at time $\alpha + 1$. The set of the **preferred sons** of i with respect to W_α and B_α is defined as $PS_{W_\alpha, B_\alpha}(i) = \{j \in \Gamma^+(i), \Gamma^-(j) \subseteq W_\alpha \text{ and } \Gamma^-(j) \cap B_\alpha = \{i\}\}$.*

Definition 3 (Preferred sons property). *A coherent feasible schedule $\sigma(\mathcal{G})$ satisfies the **preferred sons property** if, for every integer $\alpha \in \{0, \ldots, C-1\}$, each task $i \in B_\alpha$ such that $PS_{W_\alpha, B_\alpha}(i) \neq \emptyset$ has exactly one preferred son executed at time $\alpha + 1$.*

Let us consider as example the precedence graph and the feasible schedule presented by Fig. 1. For $\alpha = 0$, $W_0 = B_0 = \{1, 2\}$, $PS_{W_0, B_0}(1) = \{3, 4\}$ and $PS_{W_0, B_0}(2) = \emptyset$. Thus, we can enforce that exactly one task in $\{3, 4\}$ would be executed at time 1.

Lemma 3. *Let $\sigma(\mathcal{G})$ be a coherent feasible schedule. There exists a corresponding coherent feasible schedule $\sigma'(\mathcal{G})$ that satisfies the preferred sons property and such that for any task $i \in \mathcal{T}$, $t_i^{\sigma'} \leq t_i^\sigma$.*

Proof. We can suppose without loss of generality that tasks are scheduled by $\sigma(\mathcal{G})$ as soon as possible following the communication delay vector x^σ of $\sigma(\mathcal{G})$, i.e. $\forall i \in \mathcal{T}$, $t_i^\sigma = \max(0, \max_{j \in \Gamma^-(i)}(t_j^\sigma + 1 + x_{ji}^\sigma))$.

Let us suppose that $\sigma(\mathcal{G})$ does not verify the preferred sons property. Let then $\alpha \in \{0, \ldots, C-1\}$ be the first instant for which the property is not fulfilled, and $i^\star \in B_\alpha$ a corresponding task with $PS_{W_\alpha, B_\alpha}(i^\star) \neq \emptyset$. We show that, for every task $j \in \Gamma^+(i^\star)$, $x_{i^\star j}^\sigma = 1$.

- Since $i^\star$ is performed at time α, $i^\star$ cannot have two successors scheduled at time $\alpha + 1$. So, every task $j \in PS_{W_\alpha, B_\alpha}(i^\star)$ satisfies $t_j^\sigma \geq t_{i^\star}^\upsilon + 2$ and by coherence of $\sigma(\mathcal{G})$, $x_{i^\star j}^\sigma = 1$.

– Now, any task $j \in \Gamma^+(i^\star) - PS_{W_\alpha, B_\alpha}(i^\star)$ is not schedulable at time $\alpha + 1$, thus $t_j^\sigma \geq t_{i^\star}^\sigma + 2$ and by coherence of $\sigma(\mathcal{G})$, $x_{i^\star j}^\sigma = 1$.

Now, any task $j \in PS_{W_\alpha, B_\alpha}(i^\star)$ has all its predecessors in W_α, thus $\forall k \in \Gamma^-(j)$, $t_k^\sigma + 2 \leq t_{i^\star}^\sigma + 2 \leq t_j^\sigma$, and by coherence of $\sigma(\mathcal{G})$, $x_{kj}^\sigma = 1$. We build another coherent schedule $\sigma'(\mathcal{G})$ as follows:

1. We first choose a task $j^\star \in PS_{W_\alpha, B_\alpha}(i^\star)$. We then set $x_{i^\star j^\star}^{\sigma'} = 0$ and for each arc $e = (k, \ell) \in \mathcal{A} - \{(i^\star, j^\star)\}$, $x_{k\ell}^{\sigma'} = x_{k\ell}^\sigma$.
2. We set $\forall i \in \mathcal{T}$, $t_i^{\sigma'} = \max(0, \max_{j \in \Gamma^-(i)}(t_j^{\sigma'} + 1 + x_{ji}^{\sigma'}))$.

For every task $i \in \mathcal{T}$, $t_i^{\sigma'} \leq t_i^\sigma$. Now, we get $\sum_{\ell \in \Gamma^+(i^\star)} x_{i^\star \ell}^{\sigma'} = \sum_{\ell \in \Gamma^+(i^\star) - \{j^\star\}} x_{i\ell}^{\sigma'} + x_{i^\star j^\star}^{\sigma'} = |\Gamma^+(i^\star)| - 1$. Similarly, we get $\sum_{\ell \in \Gamma^-(j^\star)} x_{\ell j^\star}^{\sigma'} = \sum_{\ell \in \Gamma^-(j^\star) - \{i^\star\}} x_{\ell j^\star}^\sigma + x_{i^\star j^\star}^{\sigma'} = |\Gamma^-(j^\star)| - 1$, and thus $x^{\sigma'}$ is feasible.

Each task $i^\star$ is considered at most once and thus this transformation is done at most n times. So, it gives a feasible coherent schedule that satisfies the preferred sons property without increasing the makespan, thus the lemma holds. □

4.3 Limitation of the Feasible Schedules Set

The following theorem is a simple consequence of Lemma 2 and 3.

Theorem 1. *Let $\sigma(\mathcal{G})$ be a feasible schedule. Then, there exists a feasible coherent $\sigma'(\mathcal{G})$ that satisfies the preferred sons property and such that, for each task $i \in \mathcal{T}$, $t_i^{\sigma'} \leq t_i^\sigma$.*

5 Presentation of the Algorithm

This section provides our fixed-parameter algorithm. We start with the description of the multistage graph. We present then our algorithm and we show its correctness.

5.1 Description of the Multistage Graph

Let us consider a precedence graph $\mathcal{G} = (\mathcal{T}, \mathcal{A})$ and an upper bound $\overline{C}$ of the makespan. We build an associated multistage graph $S(\mathcal{G}) = (N, A)$ with $\overline{C}$ stages which maximum paths represent all the feasible schedules following the condition of Theorem 1.

Nodes of $S(\mathcal{G})$. Elements of N are partitioned into $\overline{C}$ stages. For any value $\alpha \in \{0, \dots, \overline{C} - 1\}$, N_α is the set of nodes at stage α. A node $p \in N$ is a couple $(W(p), B(p))$, where $B(p) \subseteq W(p) \subseteq \mathcal{T}$. If $p \in N_\alpha$, tasks from $W(p)$ have to be completed at time $\alpha + 1$, while those from $B(p)$ are scheduled at time α. N_0 contains only one node p_0 with $B(p_0) = \{i \in \mathcal{T}, \Gamma^-(i) = \emptyset\}$ and $W(p_0) = B(p_0)$.

Observe that, for any value $\alpha \in \{0, \dots, \overline{C} - 1\}$, all tasks from Z_α must be completed at time $\alpha + 1$, thus for any node $p \in N_\alpha$, $Z_\alpha \subseteq W(p)$. Moreover, by Lemma 1, $W(p) - Z_\alpha \subseteq X_\alpha \cap X_{\alpha+1}$.

Arcs of $S(\mathcal{G})$. For any $\alpha \in \{0, 1, \ldots, \overline{C} - 2\}$ and $(p, q) \in N_\alpha \times N_{\alpha+1}$, the arc $(p, q) \in A$ if there exists a feasible schedule such that tasks from $W(q)$ are all completed at time $\alpha + 2$ with tasks from $B(q)$ executed at time $\alpha + 1$ and those from $B(p)$ at time α. The nodes p and q satisfy then the following conditions:

A.1 Since p is associated to a partial schedule of q, $W(p) \cup B(q) = W(q)$ and since tasks can only be executed once, $W(p) \cap B(q) = \emptyset$.

A.2 Any task $i \in B(q)$ must be schedulable at time $\alpha+1$, thus all its predecessors must belong to $W(p)$. Then, $B(q) \subseteq \{i \in X_{\alpha+1}, \Gamma^-(i) \subseteq W(p)\}$.

A.3 Any task $i \in B(q)$ cannot have more than one predecessor scheduled at time α, thus $B(q) \subseteq \{i \in X_{\alpha+1}, |\Gamma^-(i) \cap B(p)| \leq 1\}$.

A.4 Any task $i \in X_{\alpha+1} - W(p)$ for which all its predecessors are completed at time α must be scheduled at time $\alpha + 1$. Thus, if $\Gamma^-(i) \subseteq W(p) - B(p)$, then $i \in B(q)$.

A.5 For any task $i \in B(p)$, if $PS_{W(p),B(p)}(i) \cap X_{\alpha+1} \neq \emptyset$, then by Definition 2, these successors of i are schedulable at time $\alpha + 1$. Following Theorem 1, we impose that exactly one among them is executed at time α on the same processor than i and thus $|PS_{W(p),B(p)}(i) \cap B(q)| = |\Gamma^+(i) \cap B(q)| = 1$. Otherwise, if $PS_{W(p),B(p)}(i) \cap X_{\alpha+1} = \emptyset$, no successor of i can be scheduled at time $\alpha + 1$ which corresponds to $|\Gamma^+(i) \cap B(q)| = 0$.

Remark 1. The preferred sons of a task $i \in \mathcal{T}$ were initially defined with respect to two sets of tasks W_α and B_α built from a feasible schedule. Here, for any node $p \in N_\alpha$, the definition of PS is extended to consider the sets $W(p)$ and $B(p)$ simply by assuming that tasks from $W(p)$ (resp. $B(p)$) are those which are completed at time $\alpha + 1$ (resp. performed at time α).

Figure 3 is the multistage graph associated with the precedence graph of Fig. 1a and $\overline{C} = 6$. We observe that the path $(p_0, p_1^1, p_2^1, p_3^1, p_4^1)$ corresponds to the schedule shown in Fig. 1b. On the same way, the path $(p_0, p_1^0, p_2^0, p_3^0, p_4^0)$ corresponds to the schedule shown by Fig. 4.

5.2 Description of the Algorithm

Algorithm 1 builds iteratively the multistage graph $S(\mathcal{G}) = (N, A)$. This algorithm returns false if there is no feasible schedule of makespan bounded by $\overline{C}$, otherwise it returns the optimum makespan. For any set of tasks $X \subseteq \mathcal{T}$, let $\mathcal{P}(X)$ be the power set of X, i.e. the set of all subsets of X including the empty ones. This algorithm is composed by three main sections. Lines 1–6 correspond to the initialization step. Lines 7–9 build all the possible nodes. Lines 10–17 build the arcs and delete all the non connected nodes.

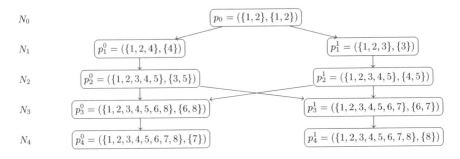

Fig. 3. The multistage graph associated with the precedence graph of Fig. 1a and $\overline{C} = 6$.

Fig. 4. An optimum schedule corresponding to the path $(p_0, p_1^0, p_2^0, p_3^0, p_4^0)$ of Fig. 3.

5.3   Validity of the Algorithm

Lemma 4. *Any feasible schedule $\sigma(\mathcal{G})$ of makespan $C \leq \overline{C}$ corresponds to a path of $S(\mathcal{G})$ ending with a node p with $W(p) = \mathcal{T}$.*

Proof. Let suppose that $\sigma(\mathcal{G})$ is a feasible schedule of makespan $C \leq \overline{C}$. By Theorem 1, we can suppose that $\sigma(\mathcal{G})$ is coherent and satisfies the preferred sons property. We can also suppose that $\sigma(\mathcal{G})$ is an as-soon-as-possible schedule, i.e. for any task $i \in \mathcal{T}$, $t_i^\sigma = \max(0, \max_{i \in \Gamma^-(j)}(t_j^\sigma + 1 + x_{ji}))$.

Let us consider the sequence $q_\alpha = (W(q_\alpha), B(q_\alpha))$ defined as $W(q_\alpha) = \bigcup_{\beta=0}^{\alpha} \mathcal{T}_\beta^\sigma$ and $B(q_\alpha) = \mathcal{T}_\alpha^\sigma$ for $\alpha \in \{0, \ldots, C-1\}$.

For $\alpha = 0$, $W(q_0) = \mathcal{T}_0^\sigma = \{i \in \mathcal{T}, t_i^\sigma = 0\} = \{i \in \mathcal{T}, \Gamma^-(i) = \emptyset\} = W(p_0)$ and thus $q_0 = p_0$.

Since $\sigma(\mathcal{G})$ is feasible, for every value $\alpha \in \{0, \ldots, C-1\}$, $\mathcal{T}_\alpha^\sigma \subseteq X_\alpha$. According to Lemma 1, $\bigcup_{\beta=0}^{\alpha} \mathcal{T}_\beta^\sigma - Z_\alpha \subseteq X_\alpha \cap X_{\alpha+1}$. So the node $q_\alpha = (W(q_\alpha), B(q_\alpha))$ has been built at stage α.

We prove then that, for every value $\alpha \in \{0, \ldots, C-2\}$, $(q_\alpha, q_{\alpha+1}) \in A$.

- $W(q_{\alpha+1}) = \bigcup_{\beta=0}^{\alpha+1} \mathcal{T}_\beta^\sigma = \bigcup_{\beta=0}^{\alpha} \mathcal{T}_\beta^\sigma \cup \mathcal{T}_{\alpha+1}^\sigma = W(q_\alpha) \cup B(q_{\alpha+1})$. Moreover, $W(q_\alpha) \cap B(q_{\alpha+1}) = \bigcup_{\beta=0}^{\alpha} \mathcal{T}_\beta^\sigma \cap \mathcal{T}_{\alpha+1}^\sigma = \emptyset$. Thus, $A.1$ is verified.
- Since $\sigma(\mathcal{G})$ is feasible, tasks from $B(q_{\alpha+1})$ are schedulable at time $\alpha+1$ and thus, properties $A.2$ and $A.3$ are verified.
- Since $\sigma(\mathcal{G})$ is an as-soon-as-possible schedule, property $A.4$ is fulfilled.
- Lastly, since $\sigma(\mathcal{G})$ satisfies the preferred sons property, $A.5$ is fulfilled.

Algorithm 1: Optimum makespan $C \leq \overline{C}$ if it exists, false otherwise.

Input: A precedence graph $\mathcal{G} = (\mathcal{T}, \mathcal{A})$, an upper bound of the makespan $\overline{C}$
Output: Optimum makespan $C \leq \overline{C}$ if it exists, false otherwise

1 **for** $i \in \mathcal{T}$ **do**
2 $\quad\lfloor$ Calculate r_i and d_i

3 **for** $\alpha \in \{0, 1, \ldots, \overline{C} - 1\}$ **do**
4 $\quad\lfloor$ Calculate X_α and Z_α

5 The set of arcs $A = \emptyset$
6 Let $N_0 = \{p_0\}$ with $B(p_0) = \{i \in \mathcal{T}, \Gamma^-(i) = \emptyset\}$ and $W(p_0) = B(p_0)$
7 **for** $\alpha \in \{1, 2, \ldots, \overline{C} - 1\}$ **do**
8 $\quad\big|$ Build the sets $\mathcal{P}(X_\alpha \cap X_{\alpha+1})$ and $\mathcal{P}(X_\alpha)$
9 $\quad\lfloor$ $N_\alpha = \{p = (W, B), W = Y \cup Z_\alpha, Y \in \mathcal{P}(X_\alpha \cap X_{\alpha+1}), B \in \mathcal{P}(X_\alpha), B \subseteq W\}$

10 **for** $\alpha \in \{0, 2, \ldots, \overline{C} - 2\}$ **do**
11 $\quad\big|$ **for** $(p, q) \in N_\alpha \times N_{\alpha+1}$ **do**
12 $\quad\big|\quad\big|$ **if** *conditions A.1, A.2, A.3, A.4, A.5 are met for* (p, q) **then**
13 $\quad\big|\quad\big|\quad\big|$ $A = A \cup \{(p, q)\}$
14 $\quad\big|\quad\big|\quad\big|$ **if** $W(q) = \mathcal{T}$ **then**
15 $\quad\big|\quad\big|\quad\big|\quad\lfloor$ **return** $\alpha + 2$

16 $\quad\lfloor$ Delete all the vertices $p \in N_{\alpha+1}$ without predecessor

17 **return** False

We conclude that $(q_0, q_1, \ldots, q_{C-1})$ is a path of $S(\mathcal{G})$. Moreover, since $\sigma(\mathcal{G})$ is of makespan C, $W(q_{C-1}) = \mathcal{T}$, and thus the lemma is verified. $\square$

Lemma 5. *Let* $C \leq \overline{C}$ *and* $(p_0, p_1, \ldots, p_{C-1})$ *a path of* $S(\mathcal{G})$ *with* $W(p_{C-1}) = \mathcal{T}$. *Then, for each task* $i \in \mathcal{T}$, *there exists a unique value* $\alpha \in \{0, \ldots, C-1\}$ *such that* $i \in B(p_\alpha)$.

Proof. According to the definition of $S(\mathcal{G})$, $W(p_0) \subset W(p_1) \subset \cdots \subset W(p_{C-1})$. Moreover, by assumption, $W(p_{C-1}) = \mathcal{T}$. Thus, for each task $i \in \mathcal{T}$, there is a unique $\alpha \in \{0, \ldots, C-1\}$ with $i \in W(p_\alpha)$ and $i \notin W(p_{\alpha-1})$. Since $W(p_{\alpha-1}) \cup B(p_\alpha) = W(p_\alpha)$, we get $i \in B(p_\alpha)$. $\square$

Lemma 6. *Every path* $(p_0, p_1, \ldots, p_{C-1})$ *of* $S(\mathcal{G})$ *with* $C \leq \overline{C}$ *and* $W(p_{C-1}) = \mathcal{T}$ *is associated to a feasible schedule of makespan* C.

Proof. Let $(p_0, p_1, \ldots, p_{C-1})$ be a path of $S(\mathcal{G})$ with $C \leq \overline{C}$ and $W(p_{C-1}) = \mathcal{T}$. A schedule $\sigma(\mathcal{G})$ of makespan C is defined as follows:

- By Lemma 5, for any task $i \in \mathcal{T}$, there exists a unique value $\alpha \in \{0, \ldots, C-1\}$ with $i \in B(p_\alpha)$. Thus, we set $t_i^\sigma = \alpha$.
- For any arc $(i, j) \in \mathcal{A}$, we set $x_{ij}^\sigma = 1$ if $t_j^\sigma > t_i^\sigma + 1$, otherwise $x_{ij}^\sigma = 0$.

We prove that the schedule $\sigma(\mathcal{G})$ satisfies the equations of the integer linear program P, and thus is feasible.

According to the condition $A.2$, we get $\Gamma^-(i) \subseteq W(p_{\alpha-1})$, so $t_j^\sigma + 1 \leq t_i^\sigma, \forall (j,i) \in \mathcal{A}$. Following the definition of x^σ, we observe that equations (1) are true.

Now, by definition of $\sigma(\mathcal{G})$, $t_i^\sigma \leq C - 1, \forall i \in \mathcal{T}$ and thus equations (2) are validated.

According to the condition $A.5$, for any task $i \in B(p_\alpha)$, $\alpha \in \{0, \ldots, C-2\}$

$C.1$ If $PS_{W(p_\alpha),B(p_\alpha)}(i) \cap X_{\alpha+1} \neq \emptyset$, then there is exactly one task $j^\star \in \Gamma^+(i) \cap B(p_{\alpha+1})$, i.e. such that $t_{j^\star}^\sigma = \alpha + 1 = t_i^\sigma + 1$. The task $j^\star$ is thus the unique successor of i for which $x_{ij^\star}^\sigma = 0$ and $\forall j \in \Gamma^+(i) - \{j^\star\}$, $x_{ij}^\sigma = 1$. Thus, $\forall i \in \mathcal{T}, \sum_{j \in \Gamma^+(i)} x_{ij}^\sigma = |\Gamma^+(i)| - 1$.

$C.2$ If $PS_{W(p_\alpha),B(p_\alpha)}(i) \cap X_{\alpha+1} = \emptyset$, then no successor of i is scheduled at time $\alpha + 1$, thus $\forall j \in \Gamma^+(i)$, $x_{ij}^\sigma = 1$ and $\sum_{j \in \Gamma^+(i)} x_{ij}^\sigma = |\Gamma^+(i)|$.

Therefore, equations (3) are checked. Lastly, according to the condition $A.3$, any task $i \in B(p_{\alpha+1})$ cannot have more than one predecessor in $B(p_\alpha)$, thus i has at least one predecessor $j^\star$ such that $x_{j^\star i}^\sigma = 0$. Therefore, $\forall i \in \mathcal{T}, \sum_{j \in \Gamma^-(i)} x_{ji}^\sigma \geq |\Gamma^-(i)| - 1$ and equations (4) are validated. We conclude that $\sigma(\mathcal{G})$ is a feasible schedule, and the lemma is proved. □

Theorem 2 (Validity of Algorithm 1). *Algorithm 1 returns the minimum makespan C of a feasible schedule if $C \leq \overline{C}$, false otherwise.*

Proof Let us suppose first that our algorithm returns $C \leq \overline{C}$, then the minimum path from p_0 to a node p with $W(p) = \mathcal{T}$ is of length C. By Lemma 6 this path is associated to a feasible schedule of makespan C and thus this schedule is optimal.

Now, let us suppose that such a path does not exist; in this case, Algorithm 1 returns false. By Lemma 4, there is no feasible schedule of makespan $C \leq \overline{C}$ and the theorem is proved. □

6   Complexity Analysis

We prove in this section that Algorithm 1 is a fixed-parameter algorithm.

Lemma 7. *Let us denote by n the number of tasks and $pw(\overline{C})$ the pathwidth of the interval graph built with the upper bound $\overline{C}$ of the minimum makespan. The number of nodes $|N|$ of the multistage graph $S(\mathcal{G}) = (N, A)$ is $\mathcal{O}(n \cdot 2^{2pw(\overline{C})})$ and the number of arcs $|A|$ is $\mathcal{O}(n \cdot 2^{4pw(\overline{C})})$.*

Proof. According to Algorithm 1, each node $p \in N_\alpha$ is such that $p = (W(p), B(p))$ with $W(p) = Y(p) \cup Z_\alpha$ and $Y(p) \subseteq X_\alpha \cap X_{\alpha+1}$. The number of possibilities for $Y(p)$ is thus bounded by $2^{|X_\alpha \cap X_{\alpha+1}|} \leq 2^{|X_\alpha|}$. Now, since $B(p) \subseteq X_\alpha$, the number of possibilities for $B(p)$ is bounded by $2^{|X_\alpha|}$. Then, the number of nodes in N_α for $\alpha \in \{0, \ldots, \overline{C} - 1\}$ is bounded by $2^{2|X_\alpha|}$.

By definition of the pathwidth, the value $|X_\alpha|$ is bounded by $pw(\overline{C}) + 1$, thus the number of nodes $|N_\alpha|$ is $\mathcal{O}(2^{2pw(\overline{C})})$. Now, since $\overline{C} \leq n$, the number of nodes

$|N|$ is $\mathcal{O}(n \cdot 2^{2pw(\overline{C})})$. Moreover, the size of $N_\alpha \times N_{\alpha+1}$ for $\alpha \in \{0, \ldots, \overline{C} - 1\}$ is $\mathcal{O}(2^{4pw(\overline{C})})$, thus the whole number of arcs $|A|$ is $\mathcal{O}(n \cdot 2^{4pw(\overline{C})})$, and we get the lemma. □

Lemma 8. *For any $\alpha \in \{0, \ldots, \overline{C} - 2\}$, the time complexity of checking the conditions A.1 to A.5 for a couple of nodes $(p, q) \in N_\alpha \times N_{\alpha+1}$ is $O(n^2 \cdot pw(\overline{C}))$.*

Proof. The time complexity for checking the condition *A.1* is $O(n)$. For the condition *A.2*, we need to build the set $\{i \in X_{\alpha+1}, \Gamma^-(i) \subseteq W(p)\}$. If we denote by m the number of arcs of $\mathcal{G}$, building this set requires to enumerate all the successors of tasks in $X_{\alpha+1}$, which is in time complexity equal to $\mathcal{O}(m)$. Since $m \le n^2$, the time complexity for checking the condition *A.2* is thus $O(n^2 \cdot pw(\overline{C}))$. For the same reasons, time complexity for checking the conditions *A.3* and *A.4* is also $O(n^2 \cdot pw(\overline{C}))$. For condition the *A.5*, the time complexity of the computation of the preferred sons of a task $i \in B(p)$ is also $O(n^2)$, and thus checking this condition also takes $\mathcal{O}(n^2 \cdot pw(\overline{C}))$, and the lemma holds. □

Theorem 3 (Complexity of Algorithm 1). *The time complexity of Algorithm 1 is $\mathcal{O}(n^3 \cdot pw(\overline{C}) \cdot 2^{2pw(\overline{C})})$, where $pw(\overline{C})$ is the pathwidth of the interval graph associated to the time windows $[r_i, d_i], i \in \mathcal{T}$.*

Proof. The time complexity of the computation of the release dates and deadlines (lines $1 - 2$) and the sets X_α and Z_α for $\alpha \in \{0, \ldots \overline{C}\}$ (lines $3 - 4$) is $\mathcal{O}(n^2)$ since $\overline{C}$ is bounded by n. The time complexity for building N at lines $7 - 9$ is $\mathcal{O}(n \cdot 2^{2pw(\overline{C})})$ by Lemma 7. Following Lemma 7 and 8, the complexity of building arcs of $S(\mathcal{G})$ in lines $10 - 17$ is $\mathcal{O}(n^3 \cdot pw(\overline{C}) \cdot 2^{4pw(\overline{C})})$, thus the theorem holds. □

7 Conclusion

We have shown in this paper that the problem $\overline{P}|prec, p_i = 1, c_{ij} = 1|C_{max}$ is fixed-parameter tractable. The parameter considered is the pathwidth associated with an upper bound $\overline{C}$ of the makespan. For this purpose, we have developed a dynamic programming algorithm of complexity $\mathcal{O}(n^3 \cdot pw(\overline{C}) \cdot 2^{4pw(\overline{C})})$. This is, as far as we know, the first fixed-parameter algorithm for a scheduling problem with communication delays.

This work opens up several perspectives. The first one is to test experimentally the efficiency of this algorithm, and to compare it to other exact methods such as integer linear programming or dedicated exact methods [17, 20]. A second perspective is to study the extension of this algorithm to more general problems in order to get closer to applications and to evaluate if these approaches can be considered to solve real-life problems.

References

1. Ait Aba, M., Munier Kordon, A., Pallez (Aupy), G.: Scheduling on two unbounded resources with communication costs. In: Yahyapour, R. (ed.) Euro-Par 2019. LNCS, vol. 11725, pp. 117–128. Springer, Cham (2019). https://doi.org/10.1007/978-3-030-29400-7_9
2. Ait El Cadi, A., Ben Atitallah, R., Hanafi, S., Mladenović, N., Artiba, A.: New MIP model for multiprocessor scheduling problem with communication delays. Optimization Letters **11**(6), 1091–1107 (2014). https://doi.org/10.1007/s11590-014-0802-2
3. Andronikos, T., Koziris, N., Papakonstantinou, G., Tsanakas, P.: Optimal scheduling for UET/UET-UCT generalized n-dimensional grid task graphs. J. Parallel Distrib. Comput. **57**(2), 140–165 (1999)
4. Bodlaender, H.L.: A tourist guide through treewidth. Acta Cybern. **11**, 1–21 (1992)
5. Chrétienne, P.: A polynomial algorithm to optimally schedule tasks on a virtual distributed system under tree-like precedence constraints. Eur. J. Oper. Res. **43**(2), 225–230 (1989)
6. Chrétienne, P., Picouleau, C.: Scheduling with communication delays: a survey, pp. 65–90 (1995)
7. Cygan, M., et al.: Parameterized Algorithms. Springer, Cham (2015). https://doi.org/10.1007/978-3-319-21275-3
8. Davidović, T., Liberti, L., Maculan, N., Mladenovic, N.: Towards the optimal solution of the multiprocessor scheduling problem with communication delays. In: MISTA Conference (2007)
9. Downey, R.G., Fellows, M.R.: Fundamentals of Parameterized Complexity. TCS. Springer, London (2013). https://doi.org/10.1007/978-1-4471-5559-1
10. Drozdowski, M.: Scheduling for Parallel Processing. Springer, Heidelberg (2009). https://doi.org/10.1007/978-1-84882-310-5
11. Giroudeau, R., Koenig, J.C.: Scheduling with communication delays. In: Levner, E. (ed.) Multiprocessor Scheduling, chap. 4. IntechOpen, Rijeka (2007)
12. Graham, R.L., Lawler, E., Lenstra, J., Rinnooy Kan, A.: Optimization and approximation in deterministic sequencing and scheduling: a survey. In: Hammer, P., Johnson, E., Korte, B. (eds.) Discrete Optimization II, Annals of Discrete Mathematics, vol. 5, pp. 287–326. Elsevier (1979)
13. Hoogeveen, J., Lenstra, J., Veltman, B.: Three, four, five, six, or the complexity of scheduling with communication delays. Oper. Res. Lett. **16**(3), 129–137 (1994)
14. Mnich, M., Van Bevern, R.: Parameterized complexity of machine scheduling: 15 open problems. Comput. Oper. Res. **100**, 254–261 (2018)
15. Munier Kordon, A.: A fixed-parameter algorithm for scheduling unit dependent tasks on parallel machines with time windows. Discrete Appl. Math. **290**, 1–6 (2021)
16. Möhring, R.H., Schäffter, M.W.: Scheduling series-parallel orders subject to 0/1-communication delays. Parallel Comput. **25**(1), 23–40 (1999)
17. Orr, M., Sinnen, O.: Optimal task scheduling benefits from a duplicate-free state-space. J. Parallel Distrib. Comput. **146**, 158–174 (2020)
18. Rayward-Smith, V.: UET scheduling with unit interprocessor communication delays. Discrete Appl. Math. **18**(1), 55–71 (1987)
19. Shimada, K., Taniguchi, I., Tomiyama, H.: Communication-aware scheduling for malleable tasks. In: 2019 International Conference on Platform Technology and Service (PlatCon), pp. 1–6 (2019)

20. Sinnen, O.: Reducing the solution space of optimal task scheduling. Comput. Oper. Res. **43**, 201–214 (2014)
21. Veltman, B., Lageweg, B., Lenstra, J.: Multiprocessor scheduling with communication delays. Parallel Comput. **16**(2), 173–182 (1990)
22. Veltman, B.: Multiprocessor scheduling with communication delays. Ph.D. thesis, Eindhoven University of Technology (1993)
23. Venugopalan, S., Sinnen, O.: ILP formulations for optimal task scheduling with communication delays on parallel systems. IEEE Trans. Parallel Distrib. Syst. **26**(1), 142–151 (2015)
24. Zinder, Y., Su, B., Singh, G., Sorli, R.: Scheduling UET-UCT tasks: branch-and-bound search in the priority space. Optim. Eng. **11**, 627–646 (2010)

Plan-Based Job Scheduling for Supercomputers with Shared Burst Buffers

Jan Kopanski[✉][iD] and Krzysztof Rzadca[✉][iD]

Institute of Informatics,
University of Warsaw, Stefana
Banacha 2, 02-097 Warsaw, Poland
jan@kopanski.eu,
krzadca@mimuw.edu.pl

Abstract. The ever-increasing gap between compute and I/O performance in HPC platforms, together with the development of novel NVMe
storage devices (NVRAM), led to the emergence of the burst buffer
concept—an intermediate persistent storage layer logically positioned
between random-access main memory and a parallel file system. Despite
the development of real-world architectures as well as research concepts, resource and job management systems, such as Slurm, provide
only marginal support for scheduling jobs with burst buffer requirements,
in particular ignoring burst buffers when backfilling. We investigate the
impact of burst buffer reservations on the overall efficiency of online job
scheduling for common algorithms: First-Come-First-Served (FCFS) and
Shortest-Job-First (SJF) EASY-backfilling. We evaluate the algorithms
in a detailed simulation with I/O side effects. Our results indicate that the
lack of burst buffer reservations in backfilling may significantly deterio-
rate scheduling. We also show that these algorithms can be easily extended
to support burst buffers. Finally, we propose a burst-buffer–aware plan-
based scheduling algorithm with simulated annealing optimisation, which
improves the mean waiting time by over 20% and mean bounded slowdown
by 27% compared to the burst-buffer–aware SJF-EASY-backfilling.

Keywords: High performance computing (HPC) · EASY backfilling ·
Online job scheduling · Multi-resource scheduling · Simulated
annealing · Nonvolatile memory · Simulation

1 Introduction

With the deployment of Fugaku [5], supercomputing has already exceeded the
threshold of exascale computing. However, this significant milestone only empha-
sised the challenge of a constantly growing performance gap between compute
and I/O [16]. HPC applications typically alternate between compute-intensive
and I/O-intensive execution phases [10], where the latter is often characterised

© Springer Nature Switzerland AG 2021
L. Sousa et al. (Eds.): Euro-Par 2021, LNCS 12820, pp. 120–135, 2021.
https://doi.org/10.1007/978-3-030-85665-6_8

by emitting bursty I/O requests. Those I/O spikes produced by multiple parallel jobs can saturate network bandwidth and eventually lead to I/O congestion, which effectively stretches the I/O phases of jobs resulting in higher turnaround times. The development of novel storage technologies, such as NVRAM, paves the way to solve the issue of bursty I/O by introducing burst buffers [20].

A burst buffer is an intermediate, fast and persistent storage layer, which is logically positioned between the random-access main memory in compute nodes and a parallel file system (PFS) in a far (backend) storage. Burst buffers absorb bursty I/O requests and gradually flush them to the PFS, which facilitates, e.g., more efficient checkpointing, data staging or in-situ analysis [11].

Many recent supercomputers were equipped with burst buffers, including the leading TOP500 machines: Fugaku [22], Summit, and Sierra [24]. In Summit and Sierra, storage devices are installed locally in each compute node – the *node-local* architecture. The main advantages of this architecture are (a) the linear scaling of I/O bandwidth; and (b) exclusive, consistent and predictable access of jobs to the storage devices, which results in lower variation in I/O performance. An alternative is the *remote shared* architecture (in, e.g., Cori [2] and Trinity [12]). There are several sub-types of remote shared architectures depending on the placement of burst buffers, which may be located in (1) selected compute nodes, (2) specialised I/O nodes, (3) specialised network-attached storage nodes or (4) in a backend storage system [11]. Compared to node-local architectures, shared architectures provide data resiliency and longer residency times, making them more suitable for data staging. An additional benefit of specialised network-attached storage nodes (3) is a transparent maintenance of the super-computing cluster—replacement of a storage device can be performed without causing downtime of any compute or I/O node. Our paper focuses on shared burst buffer architectures (and our results can be applied to any of the sub-type listed above) because, as we will show later, shared burst buffers challenge the efficiency of modern HPC schedulers.

HPC platforms are managed by middleware, Resources and Jobs Management Systems (RJMS) such as Slurm [25], responsible for scheduling and executing jobs submitted by users. A user submitting a job specifies the binary with all the arguments, but also parameters used for scheduling: the number of requested nodes and the walltime – an upper bound on the processing time. RJMSs usually implement some sort of backfilling algorithm for scheduling [8]. Perhaps the most common is the First-Come-First-Served (FCFS) EASY-backfilling (aggressive backfilling) [23], in which jobs are queued according to their arrival time (sometimes weighted by the job's or the user's priority, but this is orthogonal to our approach). Another common scheduling policy is the Shortest-Job-First (SJF; SPF) EASY-backfilling [3] that sorts pending jobs by their walltime. SJF usually improves user-centric metrics such as mean waiting time or mean slowdown. Regardless of the ordering, the EASY-backfilling algorithm may backfill (execute a job out of order) whenever there are enough free nodes, and the backfilled job would not delay the job at the head of the queue.

The current approach to managing burst buffers by RJMS seems to just extend the user-provided job description by the requested volume of burst buffer storage. This requested volume is then granted for the job's entire duration (just as compute nodes are granted for the entire duration). However, when we analysed backfilling in Slurm, we noticed that these burst buffer requests are treated quite differently from compute nodes. Slurm documentation explains this phase as: "After expected start times for pending jobs are established, allocate burst buffers to those jobs expected to start earliest and start stage-in of required files." It means that the burst buffers are allocated after backfilling, which may starve jobs requiring burst buffers.

Contributions. We address the problem of efficient online job scheduling in supercomputers with shared burst buffer architecture as follows:

1. By simulation, we show that in the EASY-backfilling algorithm, the Slurm-like decoupling of burst buffer reservations from processor reservations leads to heavy-tailed distribution turnaround times.
2. We point to a possible starvation issue of jobs with burst buffer requirements in Slurm backfilling implementation.
3. We show a simple extension of EASY-backfilling which significantly improves scheduling efficiency by considering both burst buffers and processors.
4. We propose a burst-buffer–aware plan-based scheduling algorithm with simulated annealing optimisation, which improves the mean waiting time by over 20% and mean bounded slowdown by 27% compared to the SJF EASY-backfilling with burst buffer reservations.

Source code associated with this paper is available at:
https://github.com/jankopanski/Burst-Buffer-Scheduling

2   Related Work

Scheduling in HPC is a vast research area. Below, we review only the papers addressing the problem of scheduling with burst buffer resources.

FCFS and EASY-backfilling are examples of queue-based scheduling algorithms. Queue-based schedulers periodically attempt to launch jobs based on only the current state of a system. An alternative is plan-based scheduling which creates an execution plan of all pending jobs [15]. Zheng *et al.* [26] used simulated annealing for finding an optimal execution plan. However, they only considered standard, CPU jobs. Our proposed plan-based algorithm (Sect. 3.3) extends their approach with burst buffer requirements and introduces several improvements to their simulated annealing optimisation, significantly reducing the number of iterations required to find a near-optimal solution.

Efficient job scheduling in platforms with shared burst buffer architecture was studied by Lackner, Fard and Wolf [19]. A job waiting for burst buffers may end up with a higher turnaround time than if it started earlier, but without fast persistent storage (which could increase its runtime). [19] proposed an extension to backfilling by estimating job's turnaround times with and without the access to burst buffers. In general, their solution is complementary to ours and could be incorporated into our plan-based scheduling.

Fan *et al.* [7] formulated the multi-resource scheduling problem as a multi-objective integer linear program (ILP), which maximises both compute and storage utilisation. The ILP is optimised by a genetic algorithm generating a Pareto front. To limit the computational complexity, they perform the optimisation only on a fixed-size window at the front of a waiting queue. A potential problem in their algorithm may arise in the step of resource allocation. For instance, in a Dragonfly cluster topology, we prefer to allocate nodes for a job within a single group. Such topology-awareness is not readily reflected in the proposed ILP. In contrast, our plan-based approach is as generic as backfilling and thus does not impose any limitations on resource allocation.

Herbein *et al.* [13] considered I/O contention between burst buffers and PFS. They modified EASY-backfilling by allowing it to start only those jobs that do not oversaturate network links and switches. While this change solves the issue of stretching I/O phases, it might result in underutilisation of the network bandwidth. Consequently, although the job running time is minimised, the waiting time may increase, leading to a higher turnaround time.

A hybrid solution that combines detailed information from RJMS with low-level I/O requests scheduling was proposed by Zhou *et al.* [27]. They presented an I/O-aware scheduling framework for concurrent I/O requests from parallel applications. It enables the system to keep the network bandwidth saturated and keep a uniform stretch of I/O phases of jobs, improving average job performance. In that sense, it is an alternative solution to Herbein *et al.* However, as Zhou *et al.* approach does not require any modification of the main scheduling algorithm, it can be incorporated into our burst-buffer–aware plan-based scheduling.

3   Scheduling Algorithms

3.1   Example

We start with an illustrative example of how a burst buffer reservation may impact the FCFS EASY-backfilling schedule. Suppose we are executing jobs as defined by Table 1 on a small cluster with 4 nodes (denoted by CPUs) and 10 TB of shared burst buffer storage. For simplicity, walltime of each job is equal to its runtime (perfect user runtime estimates). The BB column

Table 1. Example of jobs with an inefficient schedule with the standard EASY-backfilling.

Job	Submit[m]	Runtime[m]	CPU	BB[TB]
1	0	10	1	4
2	0	4	1	2
3	1	1	3	8
4	2	3	2	4
5	3	1	3	4
6	3	1	2	2
7	4	5	1	2
8	4	3	2	4

denotes the total amount of burst buffer requested by a job. The scheduler runs periodically at every minute. The first iteration of scheduling starts at time 0 and also includes jobs submitted at time 0. For comparison of algorithms, we present how this set of jobs would be scheduled by EASY-backfilling without (Fig. 1) and with (Fig. 2) burst buffer reservations. Filled rectangles represent started jobs; stripped represent future FCFS reservations.

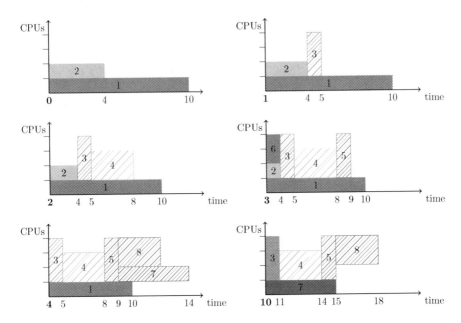

Fig. 1. FCFS EASY-backfilling *without* future burst buffer reservations may delay all jobs in a queue behind the first job (3), which received a reservation of processors. Job 3 cannot start at its scheduled time (t = 4 min, bottom-left) as there are not enough burst buffers until job 1 completes. Note that subfigures show the schedule in subsequent time moments (t = 0 min top-left, t = 1 top-right, t = 2 middle-left, etc.)

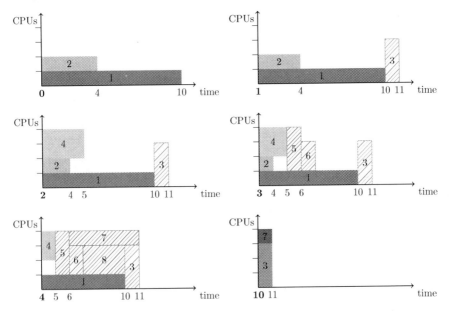

Fig. 2. Schedule by FCFS EASY-backfilling *with* burst buffer reservations. Job 3 is scheduled after job 1 completes, which permits backfilling all the remaining jobs.

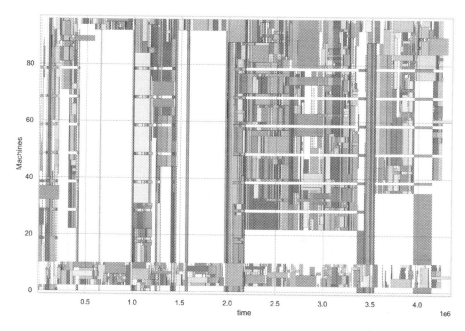

Fig. 3. Gantt chart of the first 3500 jobs executed by FCFS EASY-backfilling without future reservations of burst buffers. The large empty spaces in the chart, which are immediately followed by tall jobs, indicate significantly underutilised compute resources.

Let us focus our attention on job 3. Figure 1 shows the schedule created by the backfilling without burst buffer reservations. At the time 0 (top-left), two jobs are submitted and started immediately. After a minute (top-right), job 3 is submitted, but there are not enough available processors to start it. Concerning only CPUs, jobs 1 and 3 would be able to run in parallel after the completion of job 2. However, their summarised burst buffer requirements exceed the total capacity of 10 TB available in the cluster. As the standard EASY-backfilling does not consider burst buffers in scheduling, it would schedule job 3 just after job 2. At time 2 (middle-left), job 4 is submitted. Despite having enough free processors and burst buffers, it cannot be launched instantly as it would delay job 3, which is at the front of the waiting queue and hence received a reservation of 3 CPUs for the time period 4–5. The same situation applies to job 5, which given the resources, could be backfilled in place of job 3, but would then delay its scheduled execution. It is not the case for job 6, which can be backfilled before job 3. An unusual situation happens at time 4 (bottom-left). Job 3 does not have enough burst buffers to start the execution and prevents all other jobs from starting. It causes most of the processors in the cluster to remain idle until the completion of job 1. Indeed, job 3 behaves like a barrier in the scheduling of other jobs. The last time step presents the moment just after the completion of job 1. Job 3 is finally able to start. Additionally, job 7 is backfilled ahead of jobs 4 and 5 as it has enough processors and burst buffers to start immediately.

Figure 2 shows how FCFS EASY-backfilling *with burst buffer reservations* schedules the same set of jobs. The first difference from the previous algorithm appears at time step 1. Although the newly arrived job 3 cannot start at that time, its burst buffer requirements are recognised and it is scheduled after job 1 completes. Thus, job 4 can start immediately when submitted, as it will not delay job 3. At time 4, all the new jobs 5, 6, 7, 8 can be backfilled ahead of job 3. Lastly, at time 10, there are only left jobs 3 and 7.

Although this example may seem artificial, it distils the problem we observed when simulating a larger set of jobs (see Fig. 3).

3.2   Burst Buffer Reservations in Backfilling

In this section, we show how to extend EASY-backfilling with burst buffer reservations. Algorithm 1 shows the pseudocode of EASY-Backfilling. Jobs in the waiting queue Q are stored in the order of arrival. At the beginning, the algorithm attempts to launch jobs according to FCFS policy until the first job J for which there are not enough free resources (processors or burst buffers). The reservation for processors is acquired for J at the earliest possible time in the future. Next, the remaining jobs in Q are backfilled ahead of J under the condition that they would not delay the scheduled execution of J.

The standard EASY-Backfilling does not include the part presented in the square brackets (line 14). This minor change—a future reservation of burst buffers together with processors prior to the backfilling process—solves the problem presented in the example in Sect. 3.1.

Algorithm 1. EASY-Backfilling scheduling

1: **procedure** FCFS(Q)   ▷ Q - queue of pending jobs
2:     **for** $J \in Q$ **do**
3:         **if** there are enough free processors and burst buffers for J **then**
4:             Launch J and remove it from Q ▷ Allocations cannot overlap
5:         **else**
6:             Break
7: **procedure** BACKFILL(Q)
8:     **for** $J \in Q$ **do**   ▷ Allocations cannot overlap with reservations
9:         **if** there are enough free processors and burst buffers for J **then**
10:             Launch J and remove it from Q
11: **procedure** EASY-BACKFILLING(Q)
12:     FCFS(Q)
13:     $J \leftarrow$ pop the first job from Q
14:     Reserve compute [and storage] resources for J at the earliest time in the future
15:     **if** SJF **then**
16:         Sort Q ascending by walltime
17:     BACKFILL(Q)
18:     Remove reservations for J ▷ Will be reacquired in the next scheduling
19:     Push back J at the front of Q

In principle, Slurm implements conservative backfilling. However, there is an issue in Slurm implementation of burst buffer support, which could possibly lead to starvation of jobs with burst buffer requirements. Slurm allows to delay a job requesting burst buffer if it has not started a stage-in phase. In this case, the job does not receive a reservation of processors. Therefore, other jobs can be backfilled ahead of it. In our experimental workload, every job requires burst buffers, thus every job can be arbitrarily delayed. Assuming that all jobs require burst buffers and each job is executed right after the stage-in phase, as in our model (Fig. 4), Slurm backfilling works similarly to backfilling without any future reservations— procedure Backfill at line 7 (but without the reservation in line 14). There are still some differences between Slurm scheduling and the Backfill procedure. First, Slurm decouples allocation of burst buffers and allocation of processors. Slurm also has an FCFS scheduling loop running concurrently to backfilling.

In conclusion, the large empty spaces visible in Fig. 3 only happen in the theoretical EASY-backfilling without future reservations of burst buffers. The current, greedy scheduling in Slurm solves this but at the expense of potentially arbitrary delays of jobs with burst buffer requirements. A simple extension of backfilling with future simultaneous processor and burst buffer reservations eliminates both problems.

3.3   Plan-Based Scheduling

The general idea of plan-based scheduling is to create an execution plan for all jobs in the waiting queue. An execution plan is an ordered list of jobs with their scheduled start times and assigned resources. Naturally, only a few jobs could be launched immediately. Others are provided with non-overlapping reservations of resources at different points of time in future for the duration of their walltimes. The easiest way to create the execution plan is to iterate over the queue of jobs and for each job find the earliest point in time when sufficient resources are available. The quality of the obtained plan depends on the order of jobs. Therefore, it is possible to define an optimisation objective and perform a search over permutations of jobs.

We further investigate and extend the plan-based approach to scheduling with simulated annealing optimisation proposed by Zheng et al. [26]. First, we extend the reservation schema with the reservations for burst buffer requests. Second, we apply several modifications to the simulated annealing. Our plan-based scheduling is presented in Algorithm 2. The input parameters Q, r, N, M denote the waiting queue, cooling rate, number of cooling steps and constant temperature steps respectively.

As the optimisation objective, we minimise a sum of waiting times of jobs weighted by an exponent $\alpha \in \mathbb{R}^+$ (definition of the waiting time is given in Fig. 4). For a permutation P, let W_j^P denote the waiting time of the j-th job in Q according to the execution plan created based on P.

$$\min_P \sum_{j \in Q} (W_j^P)^\alpha \tag{1}$$

Algorithm 2. Plan-based scheduling

1: **procedure** PLAN-BASED(Q, r, N, M)
2:     **if** Q is small (≤ 5 jobs) **then**
3:         Perform exhaustive search over all permutations
4:         Reserve resources; Launch jobs; Return
5:     $P_{\text{best}}, S_{\text{best}} \leftarrow$ find a permutation with the lowest score among candidates
6:     $P_{\text{worst}}, S_{\text{worst}} \leftarrow$ find a permutation with the highest score among candidates
7:     **if** $S_{\text{best}} \neq S_{\text{worst}}$ **then**   ▷ Simulated annealing
8:         $T \leftarrow S_{\text{worst}} - S_{\text{best}}$ ▷ Initial temperature
9:         $P \leftarrow P_{\text{best}}$
10:         **for** N iterations **do**
11:             **for** M iterations **do**
12:                 $P' \leftarrow$ swap two jobs at random positions in P
13:                 Create execution plans for P and P' ▷ Details in Section 3.3
14:                 $S \leftarrow$ calculate score for P based on the execution plan
15:                 $S' \leftarrow$ calculate score for P' based on the execution plan
16:                 **if** $S' < S_{\text{best}}$ **then**
17:                     $S_{\text{best}} \leftarrow S'; P_{\text{best}} \leftarrow P'$
18:                     $S \leftarrow S'; P \leftarrow P'$
19:                 **else if** random$(0, 1) < e^{(S-S')/T}$ **then**
20:                     $S \leftarrow S'; P \leftarrow P'$
21:             $T \leftarrow r \cdot T$ ▷ Temperature cooling
22:     Launch jobs and reserve resources according to the execution plan of P_{best}

We denote the sum in the above formula as a score S of the execution plan of P. Zheng *et al.* observed that for small values, such as $\alpha = 1$, this objective allows one job to be significantly postponed in favour of other jobs as long as the total waiting time of all jobs improves, which eventually may even lead to starvation. The higher is the value of α, the more penalised is the objective function for delaying a job. Plan-based scheduling does not ensure as strict fairness criteria as reservations in EASY-backfilling, but increasing the value of α may be perceived as a soft mechanism for ensuring fair resource sharing.

We enhance the simulated annealing algorithm of [26] as follows. First, we introduce a set of candidates I for the initial permutation used to generate the best and worst initial scores ($S_{\text{best}}, S_{\text{worst}}$), which allow us to set an optimal initial temperature T according to the method proposed by [1]. We define the set of 9 initial candidates by sorting jobs according to 9 different criteria: (1) the order of submission (FCFS); (2) ascending and (3) descending by the requested number of processors, (4) ascending and (5) descending by the requested size of burst buffer per processor, (6) ascending and (7) descending by the ratio of the requested size of burst buffer per processor to the requested number of processors, (8) ascending and (9) descending by walltime.

Second, we make the search space exploration faster by (1) introducing exhaustive search over all possible permutations for small queues (up to 5 jobs); (2) faster cooling ($r = 0.9$, $N = 30$, $M = 6$); and (3) skipping the annealing if it is unlikely to find a better permutation—when the scores of the best and the worst initial candidates are the same ($S_{\text{best}} = S_{\text{worst}}$). As a result, our algorithm finds a near-optimal permutation in only $N \cdot M + |I| = 189$ iterations, compared to $\lceil 100 \log_{0.9}(0.0001) \rceil = 8742$ iterations by Zheng *et al.* The number of iterations has principal importance in online job scheduling, where the time available for scheduling is limited.

4   Simulation

4.1   Method

To evaluate and compare scheduling algorithms, we created a detailed supercomputer simulator. We extended Batsim [6,21]—a simulator framework of RJMS based on SimGrid [4], which is capable of simulating I/O contention and I/O congestion effects. We used Pybatsim scheduler to implement our algorithms and manage I/O side effects.

Platform Model: Our simulated cluster is modelled according to a Dragonfly topology. It consists of 108 nodes divided into 3 groups, each group contains 4 chassis, each chassis has 3 routers, and there are 3 nodes attached to each router. However, only 96 of the nodes are compute nodes. The other 12 nodes are assigned a storage role. That is, a single node in every chassis is dedicated to being a burst buffer node. This type of shared burst buffer architecture resembles the architecture of Fugaku, where one of every 16 compute nodes contains SSDs for burst buffers [22]. In our model, a single compute node is equivalent to a single processor/CPU. While our simulated cluster has a limited size (only 108 nodes), we consider it sufficient to show the effects of the proposed scheduling policies. We could not scale to more nodes due to a technical issue with Batsim reporting errors on larger SimGrid Dragonfly clusters.

The bandwidth of a compute network is set to model 10 Gbit/s Ethernet. The compute network is connected with a single shared link to one additional node which represents PFS. We set the bandwidth of this link to 5 GB/s, based on data from the IO500 list, to make I/O side effects noticeable. We set the total burst buffer capacity to the expected total burst buffer request when all nodes are busy, which we calculate based on the average of the fitted log-normal distribution of burst buffer request per processor (described below). We divide this capacity equally among the storage nodes.

Job Model: We consider parallel, non-preemptive and rigid jobs. Our simulated job model (Fig. 4) includes data staging and checkpointing as burst buffer use cases, which are interleaved with computation and communication phases. A job is divided into a variable number of phases (from 1 to 10) based on the specified number of computing operations. They are interleaved by I/O phases which simulate checkpointing—one of the major use cases of burst buffers. When a job checkpoints, it transfers data from compute nodes to the assigned burst buffer nodes; meanwhile, the job's computations are suspended. After the checkpoint completes, data transfer from burst buffers to PFS is triggered, and the next computation phase starts concurrently. Furthermore, jobs start and complete with data staging phases between PFS and burst buffers. The size of the data transfers is equal to the requested burst buffer size.

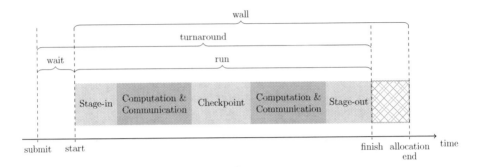

Fig. 4. Job execution model used in simulations and job's performance metrics. After the job starts, it get the data from PFS (stage-in), then performs between 1 and 10 computation phases; after each, but last, computation phase, the job checkpoints. After the last computation phase, the job transfers the results to PFS (stage-out).

Workload Model: In order to perform experiments on a realistic work-load, we decided to transform the KTH-SP2-1996-2.1-cln log from the Parallel Workload Archive (PWA) [9] into the Batsim input format, resulting in the workload with 28453 jobs. We selected this log as it was recorded on a cluster with 100 nodes, the closest to our simulated cluster. From the log, we extract submission times, walltimes and the requested number of processors. The requested memory size would be especially valuable for modelling burst buffer requests, but this data is not available in this log. We use the log in two different settings: first, we perform some experiments on the complete log; second, we split the workload into 16 non-overlapping, three-week-long parts to measure the variability of our results.

Burst Buffer Request Model: As workloads in PWA do not contain information on burst buffer requests, researchers either collect new logs [7] or create probabilistic workload models [13,19]. As the log from [7] was unavailable, we supplemented jobs from the KTH-SP2-1996-2.1-cln log with a probabilistic distribution of burst buffer requests. Under the assumption that a burst buffer request size is equal to the main memory request size, we created a model of burst buffer request size per processor based on the METACENTRUM-2013-3 log. Burst buffer request size equal to the requested RAM size is a representative case for modelling data staging and checkpointing (saving a distributed state of an entire job).

At first, we investigated a cross-correlation between the requested memory size and the number of processors. According to empirical cumulative distribution functions, it appears only for large jobs with at least 64 processors. However, large jobs contribute to only 11% of processor time. Therefore we model burst buffer requests per processor independently from the job size. We fitted several long-tail distributions to empirical data, which resulted in the best fit achieved by a log-normal distribution. We validated the quality of fitting with 5-fold cross-validation and Kolmogorov-Smirnov D-statistic test.

4.2   Results

We evaluate and compare the following scheduling policies:

fcfs FCFS without backfilling;

fcfs-easy FCFS EASY-backfilling without reservations for burst buffers;

filler Perform the backfill procedure from Algorithm 1 but without reserving resources for queued jobs in future (without line 14);

fcfs-bb FCFS EASY-backfilling with simultaneous reservations for processors and burst buffers;

sjf-bb SJF EASY-backfilling with simultaneous reservations for processors and burst buffers;

plan-α burst-buffer–aware plan-based scheduling; the number in the policy name (e.g., plan-2) is a value of the parameter α from Eq. (1).

We show mean waiting time (Fig. 5) and mean bounded slowdown (Fig. 6, bounded for jobs shorter than 10 min). The small black bars in these plots show 95% confidence intervals.

Figure 5 and Fig. 6 show the first surprising result: excluding the baseline fcfs, fcfs-easy has *two orders of magnitude higher* mean waiting time and bounded slowdown than other policies. The simple extension of the FCFS-backfilling to explicitly reserve burst buffers (fcfs-bb) results in significant improvements. When the scheduler is additionally able to change the ordering of the jobs (sjf-bb), the gains are even higher. fcfs-easy shows better distribution than fcfs for the majority of jobs. However, it changes for the last 32-quantile. The explanation for this observation is visible in the tail distribution plot Fig. 9, which for each policy presents individual values for 3000 jobs with the highest waiting times. We see there an extremely significant dispersion of waiting times of fcfs-easy, which also affects the bounded slowdown (Fig. 10). Overall, fcfs-easy on average achieves better results than fcfs, but it can considerably delay numerous jobs. These results quantitatively confirm the example from Sect. 3.1.

The simple filler shows good distribution of waiting times and bounded slowdown, also in the quantile plots (Fig. 7 and Fig. 8 are boxenplots, also called letter-value plots [14], with a logarithmic scale). However, the tail distribution plots (Fig. 9 and Fig. 10) show that filler is likely to disproportionately delay some jobs—pointing to their near-starvation, which we hinted at in Sect. 3.2.

Our proposed plan-based scheduling algorithm, plan-2, outperforms all other policies. As opposed to queue-based scheduling, plan-based scheduling may leave a cluster underutilised at a given moment to enable earlier execution of jobs in the future. Although this behaviour can result in a higher median waiting time, it should improve higher-order quantiles as seen in Fig. 7. However, as plan-1 has much flexibility in reordering jobs, it is likely to fully utilise the cluster by taking jobs from any position in the queue for instant execution. This flexibility comes at the cost of significant delay of selected jobs, as shown in Fig. 9.

For a more robust comparison between the algorithms, we split the workload into 16 three-week-long parts. We compute the average for each part and each policy, and then normalise it by the corresponding average from the sjf-bb policy.

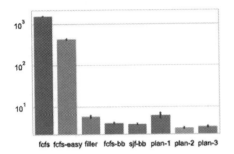

Fig. 5. Mean waiting time [hours].

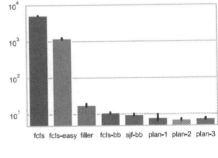

Fig. 6. Mean bounded slowdown.

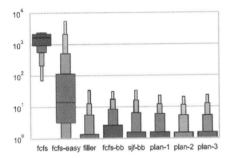

Fig. 7. Waiting time quantiles [h].

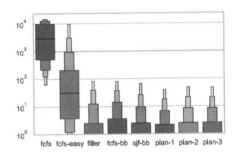

Fig. 8. Bounded slowdown quantiles.

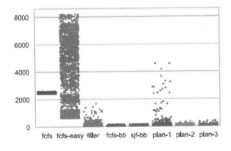

Fig. 9. Waiting time tail distribution [h].

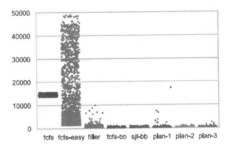

Fig. 10. Bounded slowdown tail dist.

We chose sjf-bb as the reference policy, because on the whole workload, its mean waiting time is smaller by 4.5% than fcfs-bb. Boxplots in Fig. 11 and Fig. 12 show statistics. Moreover, the 16 dots on each box correspond to the 16 averages, one for each three-week-long part. These results might be interpreted in the following way: the lower the boxplot, the better the scheduling efficiency. This analysis confirms our results on the whole trace: in most cases, filler has a higher mean than non-starving, burst-buffer–aware policies; and plan-based scheduling outperform greedy list scheduling. Additionally, in the shorter workloads, plan-1 outperforms plan-2 because of the limited capability of delaying jobs.

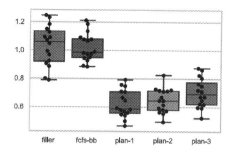
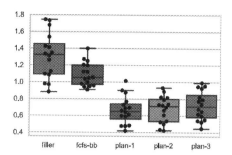
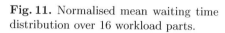

Fig. 11. Normalised mean waiting time distribution over 16 workload parts.

Fig. 12. Normalised mean bounded slowdown distribution over 16 workload parts.

5   Conclusion

The lack of reservations of burst buffers acquired simultaneously with processors in backfilling can cause significant inefficiency in online job scheduling. Slurm overcomes this issue by allowing to delay jobs with burst buffer requirements which may cause their starvation. Although this issue is not commonly visible in the current systems due to relatively low utilisation of the intermediate storage, it may become more critical in the future with further adoption of burst buffers.

We proposed a relatively simple change to the EASY-backfilling which eliminates this inefficiency. In our experiments, this amended EASY-backfilling results in consistently good performance. In initial experiments, we tested a few other reasonable local heuristics, like dynamic prioritising of jobs to balance utilisation of burst buffers and processors. However, none of these approaches strongly dominated this amended EASY-backfilling. To get even better results, we had to employ a relatively more complex approach, the plan-based scheduling. The presented plan-based scheduling not only solves the basic inefficiencies but also improves overall efficiency in terms of waiting time and bounded slowdown. Furthermore, it does not impose any requirements on resource allocation, so it may be easily generalised to other kinds of resources such as main memory (RAM), High Bandwidth Memory, GPUs, FPGAs or software licenses. However, the plan-based approach requires more changes in the cluster scheduler; and is also more computationally-intensive (although our enhancements kept the limited number of iterations of the global optimisation loop).

Data Availability Statement

The datasets and code generated during and/or analysed during the current study are available in the Figshare repository: https://doi.org/10.6084/m9.figshare.14754507 [18].

Acknowledgements. This research is supported by a Polish National Science Center grant Opus (UMO-2017/25/B/ST6/00116).

The MetaCentrum workload log [17] was graciously provided by Czech National Grid Infrastructure MetaCentrum. The workload log from the KTH SP2 was graciously provided by Lars Malinowsky.

References

1. Ben-Ameur, W.: Computing the initial temperature of simulated annealing. Comput. Optim. Appl. **29**, 369–385 (2004). https://doi.org/10.1023/B:COAP.0000044187.23143.bd
2. Bhimji, W., et al.: Accelerating science with the NERSC burst buffer early user program (2016)
3. Carastan-Santos, D., De Camargo, R.Y., Trystram, D., Zrigui, S.: One can only gain by replacing EASY Backfilling: a simple scheduling policies case study. In: CCGrid. IEEE (2019)
4. Casanova, H., Giersch, A., Legrand, A., Quinson, M., Suter, F.: Versatile, scalable, and accurate simulation of distributed applications and platforms. J. Parallel Distrib. Comput. **74**, 2899–2917 (2014)
5. Dongarra, J.: Report on the Fujitsu Fugaku system. Tech. Rep. ICL-UT-20-06, University of Tennessee, June 2020
6. Dutot, P.F., Mercier, M., Poquet, M., Richard, O.: Batsim: a realistic language-independent resources and jobs management systems simulator. In: JSSPP Workshop (2016)
7. Fan, Y., et al.: Scheduling beyond CPUs for HPC. In: HPDC 2019. ACM (2019)
8. Feitelson, D.G.: Experimental analysis of the root causes of performance evaluation results: a backfilling case study. TPDS **16**, 175–182 (2005)
9. Feitelson, D.G., Tsafrir, D., Krakov, D.: Experience with using the parallel workloads archive. J. Parallel Distrib. Comput. **74**, 1982–2967 (2014)
10. Gainaru, A., Aupy, G., Benoit, A., Cappello, F., Robert, Y., Snir, M.: Scheduling the I/O of HPC applications under congestion. In: IPDPS, Proceedings IEEE (2015)
11. Harms, K., Oral, H.S., Atchley, S., Vazhkudai, S.S.: Impact of burst buffer architectures on application portability (2016)
12. Hemmert, K.S., et al.: Trinity: architecture and early experience (2016)
13. Herbein, S., et al.: Scalable I/O-aware job scheduling for burst buffer enabled HPC clusters. In: HPDC 2016. ACM (2016)
14. Hofmann, H., Wickham, H., Kafadar, K.: Letter-value plots: boxplots for large data. J. Comput. Graph. Stat. **26**, 469–477 (2017)
15. Hovestadt, M., Kao, O., Keller, A., Streit, A.: Scheduling in HPC resource management systems: queuing vs. planning. In: Feitelson, D., Rudolph, L., Schwiegelshohn, U. (eds.) JSSPP 2003. LNCS, vol. 2862, pp. 1–20. Springer, Heidelberg (2003). https://doi.org/10.1007/10968987_1
16. Isakov, M., et al.: HPC I/O throughput bottleneck analysis with explainable local models. In: SC20. IEEE (2020)
17. Klusáček, D., Tóth, Š, Podolníková, G.: Real-life experience with major reconfiguration of job scheduling system. In: Desai, N., Cirne, W. (eds.) JSSPP, pp. 83–101. Springer International Publishing, Cham (2017). https://doi.org/10.1007/978-3-319-61756-5_5
18. Kopanski, J., Rzadca, K.: Artifact and instructions to generate experimental results for the Euro-par 2021 paper: plan-based job scheduling for supercomputers with shared burst buffers, August 2021. https://doi.org/10.6084/m9.figshare.14754507

19. Lackner, L.E., Fard, H.M., Wolf, F.: Efficient job scheduling for clusters with shared tiered storage. In: CCGRID, IEEE/ACM, pp. 321–330 (2019)
20. Liu, N., et al.: On the role of burst buffers in leadership-class storage systems. In: MSST, Proceedings IEEE (2012)
21. Poquet, M.: Simulation approach for resource management. Theses, Université Grenoble Alpes, December 2017
22. RIKEN Center for Computational Science: Post-k (fugaku) information (2020). https://postk-web.r-ccs.riken.jp/spec.html. Accessed 04 Aug 2020
23. Srinivasan, S., Kettimuthu, R., Subramani, V., Sadayappan, P.: Selective reservation strategies for backfill job scheduling. In: Feitelson, D.G., Rudolph, L., Schwiegelshohn, U. (eds.) JSSPP 2002. LNCS, vol. 2537, pp. 55–71. Springer, Heidelberg (2002). https://doi.org/10.1007/3-540-36180-4_4
24. Vazhkudai, S.S., et al.: The design, deployment, and evaluation of the coral pre-exascale systems. In: SC18, Proceedings IEEE (2018)
25. Yoo, A.B., Jette, M.A., Grondona, M.: SLURM: simple Linux utility for resource management. In: Feitelson, D., Rudolph, L., Schwiegelsohn, U. (eds.) JSSPP 2003. LNCS, vol. 2862, pp. 44–60. Springer, Heidelberg (2003). https://doi.org/10.1007/10968987_3
26. Zheng, X., Zhou, Z., Yang, X., Lan, Z., Wang, J.: Exploring plan-based scheduling for large-scale computing systems. In: CLUSTER, Proceedings IEEE (2016)
27. Zhou, Z., et al.: I/O-aware batch scheduling for petascale computing systems. In: CLUSTER. IEEE (2015)

Taming Tail Latency in Key-Value Stores: A Scheduling Perspective

Sonia Ben Mokhtar[1], Louis-Claude Canon[2(✉)], Anthony Dugois[3],
Loris Marchal[3], and Etienne Rivière[4]

[1] LIRIS, Lyon, France
sonia.benmokhtar@insa-lyon.fr
[2] FEMTO-ST Institute, Besançon, France
louis-claude.canon@femto-st.fr
[3] LIP, Lyon, France
{anthony.dugois,
loris.marchal}@ens-lyon.fr
[4] ICTEAM, UCLouvain,
Louvain-la-Neuve, Belgium
etienne.riviere@uclouvain.be

Abstract. Distributed key-value stores employ replication for high availability. Yet, they do not always efficiently take advantage of the availability of multiple replicas for each value, and read operations often exhibit high tail latencies. Various replica selection strategies have been proposed to address this problem, together with local request scheduling policies. It is difficult, however, to determine what is the absolute performance gain each of these strategies can achieve. We present a formal framework allowing the systematic study of request scheduling strategies in key-value stores. We contribute a definition of the optimization problem related to reducing tail latency in a replicated key-value store as a minimization problem with respect to the maximum weighted flow criterion. By using scheduling theory, we show the difficulty of this problem, and therefore the need to develop performance guarantees. We also study the behavior of heuristic methods using simulations, which highlight which properties are useful for limiting tail latency: for instance, the EFT strategy—which uses the earliest available time of servers—exhibits a tail latency that is less than half that of state-of-the-art strategies, often matching the lower bound. Our study also emphasizes the importance of metrics such as the stretch to properly evaluate replica selection and local execution policies.

Keywords: Online scheduling · Key-value store · Replica selection · Tail latency · Lower bound

1 Introduction

Online services are used by a large number of users accessing ever-increasing amounts of data. One major constraint is the high expectation of these users in terms of service responsiveness. Studies have shown that an increase in the average latency has direct effects on the use frequency of an online service,

© Springer Nature Switzerland AG 2021
L. Sousa et al. (Eds.): Euro-Par 2021, LNCS 12820, pp. 136–150, 2021.
https://doi.org/10.1007/978-3-030-85665-6_9

e.g., experiments at Google have shown that an additional latency of 400 ms per request for 6 weeks reduced the number of daily searches by 0.6% [6].

In modern cloud applications, data storage systems are important actors in the evolution of overall user-perceived latency. Considerable attention has been given, therefore, to the performance predictability of such systems. Serving a single user request usually requires fetching multiple data items from the storage system. The overall latency is often that of the slowest request. As a result, a very small fraction of slow requests may result in overall service latency degradation for many users. This problem is known as the *tail latency problem*. In large-scale deployments of cloud applications, it has been observed that the 95th and 99th percentiles in the query distribution show latency values that can be several orders of magnitude higher than the median [1,8].

In this study, we focus on the popular class of storage systems that are key-value stores, where each value is simply bound to a specific key [9,16]. These systems scale horizontally by distributing responsibility for fractions of the key space across a large number of storage servers. They ensure disjoint-access parallelism, high availability and durability by relying on data *replication* over several servers. As such, read requests may be served by any of these replica.

Replica selection strategies [13,15,23] dynamically schedule requests to different replicas in order to reduce tail latency. When the request reaches the selected replica, it is inserted into a queue and a local queue scheduling strategy may decide to prioritize certain requests over others. These combinations of global and local strategies are well adapted to the distributed nature of key-value stores, as they assume no omniscient or real-time knowledge of the status of each replica, or of concurrently-scheduled requests. It remains difficult, however, to systematically assess their potential. On the one hand, there is no clear upper bound on the performance that a global, omniscient strategy could theoretically achieve. On the other hand, it is difficult to determine what is the impact of using only local or partial information on achievable performance. Our goal in this paper is to bridge this gap, and equip designers of replica selection and local scheduling strategies with tools enabling their formal evaluation. By modeling a corresponding scheduling problem, we develop a number of guarantees that apply to a variety of designs.

Outline. We make the following contributions:

- a formal model to describe replicated key-value stores and the scheduling problem associated to the minimization of tail latency (Sect. 3);
- a polynomial-time offline algorithm, a $(2 - \frac{1}{m})$-approximation guarantee and a NP-completeness result for related scheduling problems (Sect. 4);
- online heuristics to solve the online optimization of maximum weighted flow, representing compromises in locally available information at the different servers of the key-value store (Sect. 5);
- the comparison of these heuristics in extensive simulations (Sect. 6).

The algorithms, the related code, data and analysis are available online[1].

---

[1] https://doi.org/10.6084/m9.figshare.14755359.

2   Related Work

We provide here a short review of related studies. An extended survey can be found in our companion research report [3].

Key-Value Stores. Key-value stores implement data partitioning for horizontal scalability, typically using consistent hashing. This consists of treating the output of a hash function as a ring; each server is then assigned a position on this circular space and becomes responsible of all data between it and its predecessor (the position of a data item is decided by hashing the corresponding key) [9,16]. Replication is implemented on top of data partitioning, by duplicating each data item on the successors of its assigned server.

Replica selection strategies [13,15,23] generally target the reduction of tail latency. They seek to avoid that a request be sent to a busy server when a more available one would have answered faster. The server receiving a request (the *coordinator*) is generally not the one in charge of the corresponding key. All servers know, however, the partitioning and replication plans. Coordinators can, therefore, associate a key with a list of replicas and select the most appropriate server to query. Cassandra uses Dynamic Snitching [16], which selects the replica with the lowest average load over a time window. This strategy is prone to instabilities, as lowly-loaded servers tend to receive swarm of requests. C3 [23] uses an adaptive replica selection strategy that can quickly react to heterogeneous service times and mediate this instability. Dynamic snitching and C3 both assume that values are served with the same latency. Héron [13] addresses the problem of head-of-line blocking arising when values have heterogeneous sizes: requests for small values may be scheduled behind requests for large values, increasing tail latency. It propagates across the cluster the identity of values whose size is over a threshold, together with load information and pending requests to such large values. Size-aware sharding [10] avoids head-of-line blocking on a specific server, by specializing some of its cores to serve only large values. Other systems, such as REIN [22] or TailX [14], focus on the specific case of multi-get operations, whereby multiple keys are read in a single operation. We intend to consider multi-get queries in our future work, as an extension of our formal models.

All the solutions mentioned above empirically improve tail latency under the considered test workloads. There is, however, no strong evidence that no better solution exists as the proposed heuristics are not compared to any formal ground. In contrast, and similarly to our objective, Li *et al.* [21] propose a *single-node* model of a complete hardware, application and operating system stack using queuing theory. This allows determining expected tail latencies in the modeled system. The comparison of the model and an actual hardware and software stack shows important discrepancies. The authors were able to identify performance-impacting factors (e.g. request re-ordering, limited concurrency, non-uniform memory accesses, etc.) and address them, matching close to optimal performance under the knowledge of predictions from the model. Our goal is to be an enabler for such informed optimization and development for the case of distributed (*multi-node*) storage services.

Flow Minimization in Scheduling. Minimization of latency—the time a request spends in the system—is commonly approached as the optimization of flow time in theoretical works, and a great diversity of scheduling problems deal with this criterion. The functions that usually constitute the objective to minimize are the max-flow ($F_{\max}$) and the sum-flow ($\sum F_i$). It is well-known that the max-flow criterion is minimized by the FIFO (First In First Out) strategy on a single-machine, and it has also been proven $(3 - \frac{2}{m})$-competitive on m machines [4].

Sometimes the maximum weighted flow $\max w_i F_i$ is considered in order to give more importance to some requests. For example Bender *et al.* introduced the stretch, where the weight is the inverse of the request serving time ($w_i = 1/p_i$), to express and study the notion of fairness for scheduling HTTP requests in web servers [4]. Bender *et al.* derive an $O(\sqrt{\Delta})$-competitive algorithm from the EDF (Earliest Deadline First) strategy, with Δ being the ratio between the largest processing time to the smallest one ($\Delta = \frac{\max p_i}{\min p_i}$). Later, Legrand *et al.* presented a polynomial-time algorithm to solve the offline minimization of max weighted flow time on unrelated machines when preemption is allowed [18].

Optimizing the average performance is obtained through minimizing the sum flow time criterion. However, this optimization objective may lead to starvation: some requests may be infinitely delayed in an optimal solution [4].

Replication in Scheduling. An important consequence of replication is that a given request cannot be executed by any server; it must be processed by a server in the subset of replicas able to handle it. This constraint is commonly known as "multipurpose machines". Brucker *et al.* proposed a formalization and analyzed the complexity of some of these problems [5]. They show for example that minimizing the sum flow on identical multipurpose machines can be solved in polynomial time. To the best of our knowledge, there exists no work considering replication for the minimization of the maximum (weighted) flow.

3   Formal Model

We propose a formal model of a distributed and replicated key-value store. This section describes the theoretical framework and states the optimization problem related to the minimization of tail latency.

Application and Platform Models. We start by defining a key-value map (K, V) as a set of associations between keys and values. We associate c keys $K = \{K_1, \ldots, K_c\}$ to c values $V = \{V_1, \ldots, V_c\}$: each unique key K_l refers to a unique value V_l whose size is $z_l > 0$.

The considered problem is to schedule a set of n requests $T = \{T_1, \ldots, T_n\}$ on m parallel servers $M = \{M_1, \ldots, M_m\}$ in a replicated key-value store. The set K is spread over these servers. For one server M_j, the function Ψ gives the subset of keys $\Psi(M_j) \subseteq K$ that is owned by M_j. Each request T_i carries a key that will be used to retrieve a specific value in the store. For one request T_i, the function φ gives this key $\varphi(T_i) = K_l$. The same key can be carried by different requests. Figure 1 shows the relationship between requests, keys and values. A server M_j may execute a request T_i if and only if $\varphi(T_i) \in \Psi(M_j)$, i.e., M_j holds the value for the carried key of T_i.

All requests are independent: no request has to wait for the completion of another request, and no communication occurs between requests. We limit ourselves to the non-preemptive problem, as real implementations of key-value stores generally do not interrupt requests.

In addition, each request T_i has a processing time $p_i = \alpha z_l + \beta$, where $\alpha, \beta > 0$ (with $\varphi(T_i) = K_l$). Processing time is equal to the average network latency β plus data sending time, which is proportional to the size of the value this request is looking for (factor α represents the inverse of the bandwidth). A request is also unavailable before time $r_i \geq 0$ and its properties are unknown as well.

As a server M_j may execute a request T_i only if it holds the key $\varphi(T_i)$, we treat the multipurpose machines scheduling problem where the set $\mathcal{M}_i \subseteq M$ represents the set of machines able to execute the request T_i, i.e., $\mathcal{M}_i = \{M_j \mid \varphi(T_i) \in \Psi(M_j)\}$. In the Graham $\alpha|\beta|\gamma$ notation of scheduling problems, this constraint is commonly denoted by $\mathcal{M}_i$ in the β-part. This aspect of the problem models data replication on the cluster. Key-value stores tend to express the replication factor, i.e., the number of times the same data is duplicated, as a parameter k of the system. Therefore, we have $|\mathcal{M}_i| = k$.

Problem Statement. There is no objective criterion that can straightforwardly represent the formal optimization of tail latency, as there is no formal definition of this system concept. Different works consider the 95th percentile, the 99th percentile, or the maximum, and it should be highlighted that we do not want to degrade average performance too much. We propose to approach the tail latency optimization by minimizing a well-known criterion in online scheduling theory: the maximum time spent by requests in the system, also known as the maximum flow time $\max F_i$, where $F_i = C_i - r_i$ expresses the difference between the completion time C_i and the release time r_i of a request T_i.

However, it seems unfair to wait longer for a request for a small value to complete than for a large one: for example, we know that a user's tolerance for

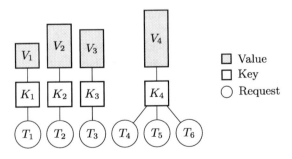

Fig. 1. A bipartite graph showing relations between requests, keys and values. Different requests may hold the same key (e.g. K_4).

the response time of a real system is greater when a process considered to be heavy is in progress. Hence, the latency should be weighted to emphasize the relative importance of a given request; we are looking for a "fairness" property. To formalize this idea, we associate a weight w_i to each T_i. The definition of this weight is flexible, in order to allow the key-value store system designer to consider different kinds of metrics. We focus on two weighting strategies in our simulations. First, the flow time ($w_i = 1$) gives an importance to each request that is proportional to its cost, which favors requests for large values. Second, the stretch ($w_i = \frac{1}{p_i}$) gives the same importance to each request, but this favors requests for small values because they are more sensitive to scheduling decisions.

In summary, our optimization problem consists in finding a schedule minimizing the maximum weighted flow time $\max w_i F_i$ under the following constraints:

- P: there are m parallel identical servers.
- $\mathcal{M}_i$: each request T_i is executable by a subset of servers.
- online-r_i: each request T_i has a release time $r_i \geq 0$ and request characteristics (r_i, p_i and w_i) are not known before r_i.

A solution to this problem ($P|\mathcal{M}_i, \text{online-}r_i| \max w_i F_i$) is to find a schedule Π, which, for a request T_i, gives its executing server and starting time. Then we define a pair $\Pi(T_i) = (M_j, \sigma_i)$, where the server M_j executes T_i at time $\sigma_i \geq r_i$. Server M_j must hold the required value ($M_j \in \mathcal{M}_i$), and there are no simultaneous executions: two different requests cannot be executed at the same time on the same server.

As mentioned earlier, we are also interested in minimizing the average latency ($\sum w_i F_i$) as a secondary objective; even if the main goal is to reduce tail latency, it would not be reasonable to degrade average performance doing so. This bi-objective problem could be approached by the optimization of the more general ℓ_p-norm function of flow times [2], but it is left for future work.

4 Maximum Weighted Flow Optimization

In order to evaluate the performance of replica selection heuristics, it would be interesting to derive optimal or guaranteed algorithms for the offline version of our problem, namely the minimization of the maximum weighted flow time of requests, or even for restricted variants. We show here that we can derive optimal or approximation algorithms when tasks are all released at time 0, but as soon as we introduce release dates, the problem gets harder to tackle. Nevertheless, a lower bound can be computed.

Without Release Times. We first focus on the non-preemptive problem of minimizing the maximum weighted flow time on a single server when there is no release times, i.e., all requests are available at time 0. Remark that in this case, the more common completion times equivalently replace flow times (i.e., $C_i = F_i$). We consider a simple algorithm named SINGLE-SIMPLE which schedules requests by non-increasing order of weights w_i, to solve this scheduling problem.

Theorem 1. SINGLE-SIMPLE *solves* $1|| \max w_i C_i$ *in polynomial time.*

Proof. Let OPT be an optimal schedule. If all requests are ordered by non-increasing weight, then SINGLE-SIMPLE is optimal. If they are not, we can find two consecutive requests T_j and T_k in OPT such that $w_j \leq w_k$. Then, their contribution to the objective is $\mathcal{C} = \max(w_j C_j, w_k(C_j + p_k)) = w_k(C_j + p_k)$ because $w_j C_j \leq w_j(C_j + p_k) \leq w_k(C_j + p_k)$. If we swap the requests, then the contribution becomes $\mathcal{C}' = \max(w_k C'_k, w_j(C'_k + p_j))$ where C'_k is the completion time of request T_k in this new schedule. By construction, $C_j + p_k = C'_k + p_j$. We have $w_k C'_k \leq w_k(C'_k + p_j)$, $w_j(C'_k + p_j) \leq w_k(C'_k + p_j)$ and $w_k(C'_k + p_j) = w_k(C_j + p_k) = \mathcal{C}$. Therefore, $\max(w_k C'_k, w_j(C'_k + p_j)) = \mathcal{C}' \leq \mathcal{C}$.

It follows that if two consecutive requests are not ordered by non-increasing weight in OPT, we can switch them without increasing the objective. By repeating the operation request by request, we transform OPT in another optimal schedule where requests are sorted by non-increasing w_i. Hence, SINGLE-SIMPLE is optimal. □

SINGLE-SIMPLE does not extend to m parallel machines in the general case. However, it solves the case where all requests have homogeneous size p. The proof of this result (available in the companion report [3]) follows a similar argument as the previous proof.

Theorem 2. SINGLE-SIMPLE *solves* $P|p_i = p| \max w_i C_i$ *in polynomial time.*

For m machines when processing times are not identical, the problem is trivially NP-hard even with unit weights because $P||C_{\max}$ is NP-hard [19]. We prove that SINGLE-SIMPLE is an approximation algorithm.

Theorem 3. SINGLE-SIMPLE *computes a* $(2 - \frac{1}{m})$-*approximation for the problem* $P|| \max w_i C_i$, *and this ratio is tight.*

Proof. Let us consider a schedule S built by SINGLE-SIMPLE and an optimal schedule OPT. We denote by T_j the request for which $w_j C_j = \max w_i C_i^S$, i.e., the request that reaches the objective in S. Then we remove from S and OPT all T_i such that $w_i < w_j$ (it does not change the objective $\max w_i C_i^S$ in S and can only decrease $\max w_i C_i^{OPT}$ in OPT). Let $C_{\max}^*$ denote the optimal makespan when scheduling only the remaining requests. As S is a list-scheduling (in the sense of Graham), we have $C_{\max}^S \leq (2 - \frac{1}{m}) \cdot C_{\max}^*$ [12], where $C_{\max}^S$ is the completion time of the last request in S (i.e., $C_j = C_{\max}^S$). Let T_k be the last completed request in OPT, such that $C_k = C_{\max}^{OPT}$. This makespan is bounded by the optimal one (i.e., $C_{\max}^* \leq C_k^{OPT}$). Therefore,

$$\max w_i C_i^S = w_j C_j^S = w_j C_{\max}^S \leq \left(2 - \frac{1}{m}\right) \cdot w_j C_{\max}^* \leq \left(2 - \frac{1}{m}\right) \cdot w_j C_k^{OPT}$$

$$\leq \left(2 - \frac{1}{m}\right) \cdot \frac{w_j}{w_k} \cdot w_k C_k^{OPT} \leq \left(2 - \frac{1}{m}\right) \cdot \frac{w_j}{w_k} \cdot \max w_i C_i^{OPT}.$$

As we removed all requests weighted by a smaller value than w_j, we have $\frac{w_j}{w_k} \leq 1$ and it follows that $\max w_i C_i^S \leq \left(2 - \frac{1}{m}\right) \cdot \max w_i C_i^{OPT}$. We now prove that this bound is asymptotically tight, by considering the instance with m machines and $n = m(m-1) + 1$ requests $T_{1 \leq i \leq n}$ with the following weights and processing times:

- $w_i = W + 1$, $p_i = 1$ for all $1 \leq i < n$;
- $w_n = W$, $p_n = m$.

Request T_n will be scheduled last in S, which gives an objective of $\max w_i C_i^S = (2m - 1)W$, whereas an optimal schedule starts this request at time 0 and has an objective of $\max w_i C_i^{OPT} = m(W + 1)$. On this instance, the approximation ratio $\left(2 - \frac{1}{m}\right) \cdot \frac{W}{W+1}$ tends to $2 - \frac{1}{m}$ as $W \to \infty$. $\qquad\square$

Offline Problem with Release Times. Legrand *et al.* solved the scheduling problem $R|r_i, pmtn| \max w_i F_i$ in polynomial time using a linear formulation of the model [18]. This offline problem is very similar to the one we are interested in, as the platform relies on unrelated machines, which generalizes our parallel multipurpose machines environment ($P|\mathcal{M}_i| \max w_i F_i$ is a special case of $R|| \max w_i F_i$ [20]). In fact, it only differs on one specific aspect: it allows preempting and migrating jobs, which we do not permit in our model.

We establish below the complexity of the problem $P|r_i, pmtn^*| \max w_i F_i$, where non-migratory[2] preemption is allowed. Interestingly, preventing migration makes the problem NP-complete. The proof of this result (available in the report [3]) consists in a reduction from the NP-complete problem $P||C_{\max}$ [19].

Definition 1 (NonMigratory-Dec(T, M, B)). *Given a set of requests T, a set of machines M and a bound B, if we define the deadline $d_i = r_i + \frac{B}{w_i}$ for all T_i, is it possible to build a non-migratory preemptive schedule where each request meets its deadline?*

Theorem 4. *The problem* NonMigratory-Dec(T, M, B) *is NP-complete.*

Online Problem. We now study problems in an online context, where properties of requests are not known before their respective release time. We prove that there exists no optimal online algorithm for the minimization of maximum weighted flow even on the very simple case of a single machine and unit request sizes, as outlined in the following theorem. The corresponding proof (available in the companion report [3]) consists in a well-chosen example for which no algorithm can make an optimal choice without knowing the tasks that will be submitted in the future.

Theorem 5. *No online algorithm can be optimal for the scheduling problem* $1|online\text{-}r_i, p_i = 1| \max w_i F_i$.

We now present an adaptation of Single-Simple to the online case, restricted to unit tasks, Single-Unit: at each time step, we consider all submitted requests

---

[2] We express non-migratory preemption as $pmtn^*$ in the β-part, not to be confused with the classic $pmtn$ constraint.

at this time and schedule the one whose flow (if processed now) is the largest. This gives priority to the currently most impacting requests. Unfortunately, even on unit size tasks, this strategy does not lead to an approximation algorithm, as outlined by the following theorem (see proof in the report [3]).

Theorem 6. *The competitive ratio of* SINGLE-UNIT *is arbitrarily large for the scheduling problem* $1|\text{online-}r_i, p_i = 1|\max w_i F_i$.

Lower Bound. We have seen that our initial scheduling problem, with heterogeneous processing times, no preemption and in an online setting is far from being solvable or even approximable. This motivates the search of lower bounds to constitute a formal baseline and derive performance guarantees. The solution to $R|r_i, pmtn|\max w_i F_i$ provides such a lower bound, which is found by performing a binary search on a Linear Program [18], followed by the reconstruction scheme from Lawler *et al.* [17]. The whole process is detailed in the companion report [3]. This bound is used to assess the performance of practical heuristics in Sect. 6.

5   Online Heuristics

We recall that a solution to our problem consists, for each request, in choosing a server among the ones holding a replica of the requested data as well as a starting time for each request. These two decisions appear at different places in a real key-value store: the selection strategy R used by the coordinator gives a replica $R(T_i) = M_r$, whose execution policy E_r defines the request starting time $E_r(T_i) = \sigma_i$. This section describes several online replica selection heuristics and execution policies that we then compare by simulation.

5.1   Replica Selection Heuristics

We consider several replica selection heuristics with different levels of knowledge about the cluster state. Some of these levels are hard to achieve in a real system; for instance, the information about the load of a given server will often be slightly out of date. Similarly, the information about the processing time can only be partial, as the size of the requested value cannot be known by the coordinator for large scale data sets, and practical systems generally employ an approximation of this metric, e.g., by keeping track of size *categories* of values using Bloom filters [13]. However, we exploit this exact knowledge in our simulations to estimate the maximal performance gain that a given type of information allows. We now describe selection heuristics, whose properties are shown in Table 1.

RANDOM. The replica is chosen uniformly at random among compatible servers: $M_r = \text{rand}\mathcal{M}_i$. This strategy has no particular knowledge.

LEASTOUTSTANDINGREQUESTS *(LOR)*. Let $\mathcal{R}(M_j)$ be the number of outstanding requests sent to M_j, i.e., the number of sent requests that received no response yet. This strategy choses the replica that minimizes $\mathcal{R}(M_j)$. It is easy to implement, as it only requires local information; in fact, it is one of the most commonly used in load-balancing applications [23].

HÉRON. We also consider an omniscient version of the replica selection heuristic used by Héron [13]. It identifies requests for values with size larger than a threshold, and avoids scheduling other requests behind such a request for a large value by marking the chosen replica as *busy*. When the request for a large value completes, the replica is marked *available* again. The replica is chosen among compatible servers that are *available* according to the scoring method of C3 [23].

EARLIESTFINISHTIME *(EFT)*. Let FINISHTIME(M_j) denote the earliest time when the server M_j becomes available, i.e., the time at which it will have emptied its execution queue. The chosen replica is the one with minimum FINISHTIME(M_j) among compatible servers. Knowing FINISHTIME is hard in practice, because it assumes the existence of a mechanism to obtain the exact current load of a server. A real system would use a degraded version of this heuristic.

EARLIESTFINISHTIME-SHARDED *(EFT-S)*. For this heuristic, servers are specialized: we define small servers, which execute only requests for small values, and large servers, which execute all requests for large values and some requests for small values when possible (similarly to size-aware sharding [10]). Once the server is chosen, each request is scheduled using the EFT strategy.

For the following experiments, we define large servers as the set of servers $\{M_b\}_{1 \le b \le m}$ such that $b \mod k = 0$ (recall k is the replication factor). This makes sure that one server in each interval $\mathcal{M}_i$ is capable of treating requests for large values. We define a threshold parameter ω to distinguish between requests for small and large values: requests with duration larger than ω are treated by large servers only, while others can be processed by all available servers. We derive the threshold ω from the size distribution, by choosing the parameter ω so that the total work is k times larger than the work on large servers on average (see details in the companion research report [3]).

5.2 Local Queue Scheduling Policies

We now present scheduling policies locally enforced by replicas. Each replica handles an execution queue $\mathcal{Q}$ in which coordinators send requests, and then decides of the order of executions. In a real key-value store, these policies should be able to extract exact information on the local values, and in particular their sizes, as a single server is responsible for a limited number of keys. We consider the following local policies, summarized in Table 1.

FIRSTINFIRSTOUT *(FIFO)*. This is a classic strategy, which is commonly used as a local scheduling policy in key-value stores (e.g., Cassandra [16]). The requests in $\mathcal{Q}$ are ordered by non-increasing insertion time, i.e., the first request that entered the queue (the one with the minimum r_i) is the first to be executed.

MAXSTRETCH. We propose another strategy, which locally reorders requests. When a server becomes available at time t, the next request T_i to be executed is the one in $\mathcal{Q}$ whose stretch $(t + p_i - r_i)/p_i$ is the highest. This favors requests for small values in front of requests for large ones, and thus is a way to mitigate the

Table 1. Properties of replica selection and local queue scheduling heuristics. ACK-DONE denotes the need to acknowledge the completion of sent requests. FINISHTIME is the knowledge of available times of each server. p_i denotes the processing times of local requests and r_i their release times. N is the number of local requests in Q and m is the total number of servers.

Replica selection			Local policy		
Heuristic	Knowledge	Complexity	Heuristic	Knowledge	Complexity
RANDOM	None	$O(1)$	FIFO	None	$O(1)$
LOR	ACK-DONE	$O(m)$	MAXSTRETCH	p_i, r_i	$O(N)$
HÉRON	ACK-DONE, $p_i \geq \omega$	$O(m)$			
EFT	FINISHTIME	$O(m)$			
EFT-S	FINISHTIME, $p_i \geq \omega$	$O(m)$			

problem of head-of-line blocking. Note that in any case, starvation is not a concern: focusing on the maximum stretch ensures that all requests will eventually be processed [4].

6   Simulations

We analyse the behavior of previously described strategies and compare them with each other in simulations. We built a discrete-event simulator based on salabim 21.0.1 for this purpose, which mimics a real key-value store: coordinators receive user requests and send them to replicas in the cluster, which execute these requests. Each request is first headed to the queue of a server holding a replica of the requested data by the selection heuristic. Then, the queue is reordered by the local execution policy and requests are processed in this order.

Workload and Settings. We designed a synthetic heterogeneous workload to evaluate our strategies: value sizes follow a Weibull distribution with scale $\eta = 32\,000$ and shape $\theta = 0.5$; these parameters yield a long-tailed distribution that is consistent with existing file sizes characterizations [11]. User requests arrive at coordinators according to a Poisson process with arrival rate $\lambda = m\mathcal{L}/\bar{p}$, where m is the number of servers, $\mathcal{L}$ is the wanted average server load (defined as the average fraction of time spent by servers on serving requests), and $\bar{p}$ is the mean processing time of requests. Each key has the same probability of being requested, i.e., we do not model skewed popularity. The cluster consists in $m = 12$ servers and we set the replication factor to $k = 3$, which is a common configuration in real implementations [9,16]. The network bandwidth is set to $1/\alpha = 100$ Mbps and the average latency is set to $\beta = 1$ ms. The threshold between small and large values is set to $\omega = 26$ ms, resulting in a proportion of 5% of requests for large values in the workload. Each experiment is repeated on 15 different scenarios; a given scenario defines the processing times p_i, the release times r_i, and the replication groups $\mathcal{M}_i$ according to described settings.

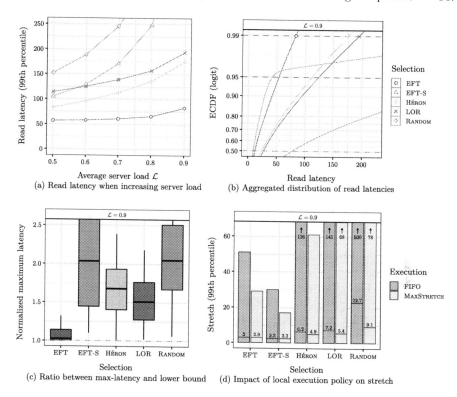

Fig. 2. Distributions of the objective functions for 5 replica selection heuristics. For Fig. (a), (b) and (d), simulations run over 120 s. For Fig. (c), simulations are launched over 1000 requests.

Results. Figure 2(a) shows the 99th quantile of read latency (in milliseconds) as a function of average server load for each selection heuristic and for load values ranging from 0.5 to 0.9, with FIFO as local policy. In this context, the maximum of the distribution is impacted by rare events of varying amplitude, which makes this criterion unstable. The stability of the 99th quantile allows comparing more confidently the performance between scenarios with identical settings. For an average load $\mathcal{L} = 0.9$, Fig. 2(b) shows Empirical Cumulative Distribution Functions (ECDF) of read latencies for each selection heuristics. The dashed horizontal lines respectively represent median, 95th and 99th percentile. The comparison of selection heuristics with the lower bound introduced in Sect. 4 is shown in Fig. 2(c). We normalize the max-latency obtained by a selection heuristic with this lower bound. Each boxplot represents the distribution of these normalized maximums among the 15 different scenarios. Horizontal red line locates the lower bound. Figure 2(d) illustrates the effect of different local execution policies on the 99th quantile of stretch. Horizontal lines represent median values.

We see in Fig. 2(a) that the choice on selection heuristic is critical for read latency, as the 99th quantile can often be improved by a factor 2 compared to state-of-the-art strategies LOR and HÉRON, without increasing median performance as confirmed in Fig. 2(b). This highlights the fact that knowing the current load of a server, and thus its earliest available time, as used in the EFT strategy, allows to get very close to the lower bound. Figure 2(c) also shows that EFT yields the most stable maximums between scenarios, as more than 50% of normalized values range from 1.0 to 1.15. This improves the confidence that this strategy will perform well in a majority of cases. For the stretch metric, where latencies are weighted by processing times, EFT-S performs even better than EFT (Fig. 2(d)), yielding a 99th quantile of 30 (resp. 18) when coupled with FIFO (resp. MAXSTRETCH). This is due to the nature of EFT-S that favors requests for small values, which are in majority in the workload. However, EFT-S does not perform well for the last quantiles in the latency distribution; this corresponds to the 5% of requests for large values that are delayed in order to avoid head-of-line blocking situations. Figure 2(d) also illustrates the significant impact of local execution policies on the stretch metric: local reordering according to MAXSTRETCH favors requests for small values, which results in an improvement for all selection strategies, even on the median values. Note that this does not necessarily improve latency, as FIFO is well-known to be the optimal strategy for max-flow on a single machine [4].

7   Conclusion

This study defines a formal model of a key-value store in order to derive maximal performance achievable by a real online system, and states the associated optimization problem. We also provide theoretical results on various problems related to our main scheduling problem. After showing the difficulty of this problem, we describe some investigations on a lower bound. We develop online heuristics and compare them with state-of-the-art strategies such as LOR, HÉRON [13] or size-aware sharding [10] using simulations. This allows understanding more finely the impact of replica selection and local execution on performance metrics. We hope that our work will help practitioners draw new scheduling strategies. We plan to continue to improve on a lower bound, for example by using resource augmentation models, and we propose to formally analyze EFT with various techniques such as competitive analysis. We wish to study the effect of various assumptions on scheduling, e.g., the impact of skewed key popularity, and to extend the model with multi-get operations [14, 22].

Acknowledgements and Data Availability Statement. The datasets and code generated during and/or analyzed during the current study are available in the Figshare repository: https://doi.org/10.6084/m9.figshare.14755359 [7].

References

1. Atikoglu, B., Xu, Y., Frachtenberg, E., Jiang, S., Paleczny, M.: Workload analysis of a large-scale key-value store. In: ACM SIGMETRICS Performance Evaluation Review, vol. 40, pp. 53–64. ACM (2012)
2. Bansal, N., Pruhs, K.: Server scheduling in the l_p norm: a rising tide lifts all boat. In: ACM STOCS (2003)
3. Ben Mokhtar, S., Canon, L.C., Dugois, A., Marchal, L., Rivière, E.: Taming Tail latency in key-value stores: a scheduling perspective (extended version). Tech. rep. (2021). https://hal.inria.fr/hal-03144818
4. Bender, M.A., Chakrabarti, S., Muthukrishnan, S.: Flow and stretch metrics for scheduling continuous job streams. In: ACM-SIAM Symposium on Discrete Algorithms (1998)
5. Brucker, P., Jurisch, B., Krämer, A.: Complexity of scheduling problems with multi-purpose machines. Ann. Oper. Res. **70**, 57–73 (1997)
6. Brutlag, J.: Speed matters for google web search (2009)
7. Canon, L.C., Dugois, A., Marchal, L.: Artifact and instructions to generate experimental results for the euro-par 2021 paper: "taming tail latency in key-value stores: a scheduling perspective". https://doi.org/10.6084/m9.figshare.14755359
8. Dean, J., Barroso, L.A.: The tail at scale. Commun. ACM **56**(2), 74–80 (2013)
9. DeCandia, G., et al.: Dynamo: amazon's highly available key-value store. ACM SIGOPS Oper. Sys. Rev. **41**, 205–220 (2007)
10. Didona, D., Zwaenepoel, W.: Size-aware sharding for improving tail latencies in in-memory key-value stores. In: NSDI, pp. 79–94 (2019)
11. Feitelson, D.G.: Workload Modeling for Computer Systems Performance Evaluation. Cambridge University Press (2015)
12. Graham, R.L.: Bounds for certain multiprocessing anomalies. Bell Syst. Tech. J. **45**(9), 1563–1581 (1966)
13. Jaiman, V., Ben Mokhtar, S., Quéma, V., Chen, L.Y., Rivière, E.: Héron: taming tail latencies in key-value stores under heterogeneous workloads. In: SRDS. IEEE (2018)
14. Jaiman, V., Ben Mokhtar, S., Rivière, E.: TailX: Scheduling Heterogeneous Multi-get Queries to Improve Tail Latencies in Key-Value Stores. In: Remke, A., Schiavoni, V. (eds.) DAIS 2020. LNCS, vol. 12135, pp. 73–92. Springer, Cham (2020). https://doi.org/10.1007/978-3-030-50323-9_5
15. Jiang, W., Xie, H., Zhou, X., Fang, L., Wang, J.: Haste makes waste: the on-off algorithm for replica selection in key-value stores. JPDC **130**, 80–90 (2019)
16. Lakshman, A., Malik, P.: Cassandra: a decentralized structured storage system. ACM SIGOPS Oper. Syst. Rev. **44**(2), 35–40 (2010)
17. Lawler, E.L., Labetoulle, J.: On preemptive scheduling of unrelated parallel processors by linear programming. J. ACM (JACM) **25**(4), 612–619 (1978)
18. Legrand, A., Su, A., Vivien, F.: Minimizing the stretch when scheduling flows of divisible requests. J. Sched. **11**(5), 381–404 (2008)
19. Lenstra, J.K., Kan, A.R., Brucker, P.: Complexity of machine scheduling problems. Stud. Integer Program. **1**, 343–362 (1977)
20. Leung, J.Y.T., Li, C.L.: Scheduling with processing set restrictions: a survey. Int. J. Prod. Econ. **116**(2), 251–262 (2008)
21. Li, J., Sharma, N.K., Ports, D.R., Gribble, S.D.: Tales of the tail: Hardware, OS, and application-level sources of tail latency. In: ACM Symposium Cloud Computing (2014)

22. Reda, W., Canini, M., Suresh, L., Kostić, D., Braithwaite, S.: Rein: taming tail latency in key-value stores via multiget scheduling. In: EuroSys (2017)
23. Suresh, L., Canini, M., Schmid, S., Feldmann, A.: C3: cutting tail latency in cloud data stores via adaptive replica selection. In: NSDI (2015)

A Log-Linear $(2 + 5/6)$-Approximation Algorithm for Parallel Machine Scheduling with a Single Orthogonal Resource

Adrian Naruszko⬛, Bartłomiej Przybylski$^{(\boxtimes)}$ ⬛,
and Krzysztof Rządca⬛

Institute of Informatics,
University of Warsaw,
Warsaw, Poland
an371233@students.mimuw.edu.pl,
{bap,krzadca}@mimuw.edu.pl

Abstract. As the gap between compute and I/O performance tends to grow, modern High-Performance Computing (HPC) architectures include a new resource type: an intermediate persistent fast memory layer, called burst buffers. This is just one of many kinds of renewable resources which are orthogonal to the processors themselves, such as network bandwidth or software licenses. Ignoring orthogonal resources while making scheduling decisions just for processors may lead to unplanned delays of jobs of which resource requirements cannot be immediately satisfied. We focus on a classic problem of makespan minimization for parallel-machine scheduling of independent sequential jobs with additional requirements on the amount of a single renewable orthogonal resource. We present an easily-implementable log-linear algorithm that we prove is $2\frac{5}{6}$-approximation. In simulation experiments, we compare our algorithm to standard greedy list-scheduling heuristics and show that, compared to LPT, resource-based algorithms generate significantly shorter schedules.

Keywords: Parallel machines · Orthogonal resource · Burst buffers · Rigid jobs · Approximation algorithm

1 Introduction

In a simplified model of parallel-machine scheduling, independent jobs can be freely assigned to processors if only at most one job is executed by each processor at any moment. Thus, the only resource to be allocated is the set of processors. However, this simple model does not fully reflect the real-life challenges. In practice, jobs may require additional resources to be successfully executed. These

© Springer Nature Switzerland AG 2021
L. Sousa et al. (Eds.): Euro-Par 2021, LNCS 12820, pp. 151–166, 2021.
https://doi.org/10.1007/978-3-030-85665-6_10

resources may include—among others—fast off-node memory, power, software licenses, or network bandwidth. All of these example resources are renewable, i.e. once a job completes it returns the claimed resources to the common pool (in contrast to consumable resources such as time or fuel).

Some of the resources may be orthogonal which means that they are allocated independently of other resources. For example, in standard High-Performance Computing (HPC) scheduling, node memory is not orthogonal as a job claims all the memory of the node on which it runs. On the other hand, in cloud computing, node memory is an orthogonal resource, as it is partitioned among containers or virtual machines concurrently running at the node. Thus, node memory (and also network bandwidth) is managed in a similar manner to the processors.

The results presented in this paper are directly inspired by the practical problem of parallel-machine scheduling of jobs in HPC centers with an orthogonal resource in a form of a burst buffer. A burst buffer is a fast persistent NVRAM memory layer logically placed between the operational memory of a node and the slow external file system. Burst buffers are shared by all the jobs running in a cluster and thus they are orthogonal to processors. They can be used as a cache for I/O operations or as a storage for intermediate results in scientific workflows.

The main contribution of this paper is a log-linear $2\frac{5}{6}$-approximation algorithm for a parallel-machine scheduling problem with independent, sequential and rigid jobs, a single orthogonal resource and makespan as the objective. We thus directly improve the classic $(3 - \frac{3}{m})$-approximation algorithm by Garey and Graham [6]. Although a $(2+\varepsilon)$-approximation algorithm [21] and an asymptotic FPTAS [14] are known, their time and implementation complexities are considerable. Our algorithm can be easily implemented and it runs in log-linear time. Additionally, it can be combined with known fast heuristics, thus providing good average-case results with a guarantee on the worst case.

The paper is organized as follows. In Sect. 2, we define the analysed problem and review the related work. Then, in Sect. 3 we present a $2\frac{5}{6}$-approximation algorithm and prove its correctness. In Sect. 4 we simulate our algorithm, compare its performance to known heuristics, and discuss its possible extensions. Finally, in Sect. 5, we make general conclusions.

2   Problem Definition and Related Work

We are given a set of m parallel identical machines, a set of n non-preemptable jobs $\mathcal{J} = \{1, 2, \ldots, n\}$, and a single resource of integer capacity R. Each job $i \in \mathcal{J}$ is described by its processing time p_i and a required amount of the resource $R_i \le R$. We use the classic rigid job model [5] in which the processing time does not depend on the amount of the resource assigned. Our aim is to minimize the time needed to process all the jobs (or, in other words, the maximum completion time). Based on the three-field notation introduced in [10] and then extended in [3], we can denote the considered problem as $\text{P}|res1\cdot\cdot|C_{\max}$. Here, the three values after the '*res*' keyword determine: (1) the number of resources (one in this case); (2) the total amount of each resource (arbitrary in this case); (3) the maximum resource requirement of a single job (arbitrary in this case). This problem is $\mathcal{NP}$-Hard as a generalization of P$||C_{\max}$ [7]. However, both the problems have been deeply analyzed in the literature. Moreover, different machine, job, and resource characteristics have been considered in the context of various objective functions. We refer the reader to [4] for the most recent review on resource-constrained scheduling.

In case of the variant without additional resources – P$||C_{\max}$ – it was proved that the LPT strategy leads to a $\left(\frac{4}{3} - \frac{1}{3m}\right)$-approximation algorithm [9] while any arbitrary list strategy provides a $\left(2 - \frac{1}{m}\right)$-approximation [8]. A classic result on polynomial-time approximation scheme (PTAS) for P$||C_{\max}$ was presented in [11]. In general, an efficient polynomial-time approximation scheme (EPTAS) for the Q$||C_{\max}$ problem (with uniform machines) is known [12,13]. As the P$||C_{\max}$ problem is strongly $\mathcal{NP}$-Hard, there exists no fully polynomial-time approximation scheme unless $\mathcal{P} = \mathcal{NP}$.

When orthogonal resources are introduced, the upper-bounds increase. Given s additional resources and more than two machines, any arbitrary list strategy leads to a $\left(s + 2 - \frac{2s+1}{m}\right)$-approximation algorithm [6] and this general bound is tight for $m > 2s + 1$. For $s = 1$, i.e. in the case of a single resource, this ratio becomes $3 - \frac{3}{m}$. We also get $\lim_{m \to \infty} \left(3 - \frac{3}{m}\right) = 3$.

For the P$|res1\cdot1, p_i = 1|C_{\max}$ problem with unit processing times, binary resource requirements and an arbitrary amount of the resource, the optimal $C_{\max}$ can be found in constant time [17]. The more general P$|res1\cdot1, r_i, p_i = 1|C_{\max}$ problem with ready times can be solved in linear time [1], while the P2$|res\cdot\cdot, r_i, p_i = 1|C_{\max}$ problem with just two machines and no limits on resource requirements of a single job is already $\mathcal{NP}$-Hard [2].

A number of heuristic and approximation algorithms has been developed for the P$|res1\cdot\cdot|C_{\max}$ problem and its close variants. A polynomial-time $\frac{4}{3}$-approximation algorithm for the P$|res1\cdot\cdot, p_i = 1|C_{\max}$ problem was shown in [18]. On the other hand, a $(3.5 + \varepsilon)$-approximation algorithm is known for the P$|res1\cdot\cdot, Int|C_{\max}$ problem [15], i.e. for resource-dependent job processing times. In [21], a $(2 + \varepsilon)$-approximation algorithm for the P$|res1\cdot\cdot|C_{\max}$ problem is presented. This algorithm can be transformed into a PTAS if the number of machines or the number of different resource requirements is upper-bounded by a constant. Further, an asymptotic FPTAS for the P$|res1\cdot\cdot|C_{\max}$ problem was shown [14]. Although the latter results have a great theoretical impact on the problem considered in this paper, the complexity of the obtained algorithms prevents them from being efficiently implemented.

3   Approximation Algorithm

In this section, we present a log-linear $2\frac{5}{6}$-approximation algorithm for the P$|res1\cdot\cdot|C_{\max}$ problem. In order to make our reasoning easier to follow, we normalize all the resource requirements. In particular, for each job $i \in \mathcal{J}$ we use its relative resource consumption $r_i := R_i/R \in [0,1]$. Thus, for any set of jobs $J \subseteq \mathcal{J}$ executed at the same moment it must hold that $\sum_{i \in J} r_i \leq 1$. We also denote the length of an optimal schedule with OPT.

Before we present algorithm details, we introduce some definitions and facts. We will say that job $i \in \mathcal{J}$ is *light* if $r_i \leq \frac{1}{3}$. *medium* if $\frac{1}{3} < r_i \leq \frac{1}{2}$, and *heavy* if $r_i > \frac{1}{2}$. Thus, each job falls into exactly one of the three disjoint sets, denoted by $\mathcal{J}_{\text{light}}, \mathcal{J}_{\text{medium}}, \mathcal{J}_{\text{heavy}}$, respectively. Note that—whatever the job resource requirements are—not more than one heavy and one medium, or two medium jobs can be executed simultaneously.

Given a subset of jobs $J \subseteq \mathcal{J}$, we define its total resource consumption as $R(J) := \sum_{i \in J} r_i$. We say that a set J is *satisfied* with θ resources, if for each subset $J' \subseteq J$ such that $|J'| \leq m$ we have $R(J') \leq \theta$. In such a case, we write $R_m(J) \leq \theta$.

The set of all the scheduled jobs will be denoted by $\mathcal{J}_{\text{scheduled}}$. For a scheduled job $i \in \mathcal{J}_{\text{scheduled}}$, we denote its start and completion times by S_i and C_i, respectively. We say that job i was *executed* before moment t if $C_i \leq t$, is being executed at moment t if $S_i \leq t < C_i$, and will be executed after moment t if $S_i > t$. The set of jobs executed at moment t will be denoted by $\mathcal{J}(t)$ and the total resource consumption of jobs in set $\mathcal{J}(t)$ by $R(t)$. We present a brief summary of the notation in Table 1.

Table 1. Summary of the notation

Symbol	Meaning
$\mathcal{J}$	The set of all the jobs
$\mathcal{J}(t)$	The set of all scheduled jobs i such that $S_i \leq t < C_i$
$J \subseteq \mathcal{J}$	Subset of all the jobs
$R(J)$	Total resource requirement of the jobs in J
$R_m(J)$	Total resource requirement of m most consumable jobs in J
$R(t)$	Total resource requirement of jobs in $\mathcal{J}(t)$

Let us start with the following lemmas, which are the essence of our further reasoning. In the algorithm, we will make sure that the assumptions of these lemmas are met, so we can use them to prove the general properties of the solution.

Lemma 1. *If $R(t) \geq \frac{2}{3}$ for all $t \in [t_a, t_b)$, then $t_b - t_a \leq \frac{3}{2}OPT$.*

Proof. It holds that $OPT \geq \sum_{i \in \mathcal{J}} r_i \cdot p_i$, as the optimal schedule length is lower-bounded by a total amount of resources consumed by all jobs in time. As $R(t) \geq \frac{2}{3}$, we obtain

$$\frac{2}{3} \cdot (t_b - t_a) \leq \int_{t_a}^{t_b} R(t)\, dt \leq \sum_{i \in \mathcal{J}} r_i \cdot p_i \leq OPT,$$

and thus $t_b - t_a \leq \frac{3}{2}OPT$. $\square$

Lemma 2. Let $J_1, J_2 \subseteq \mathcal{J}$. If $R_m(J_1) < \theta_1$ and $R_m(J_2) < \theta_2$, then $R_m(J_1 \cup J_2) < \theta_1 + \theta_2$.

Proof. Let us notice that, given any set of jobs J, the value of $R_m(J)$ is determined by m most resource-consuming jobs in J. Thus, the value of $R_m(J_1 \cup J_2)$ is determined by m most resource-consuming jobs from sets J_1 and J_2. As a consequence, it holds that $R_m(J_1 \cup J_2) \leq R_m(J_1) + R_m(J_2) < \theta_1 + \theta_2$.   □

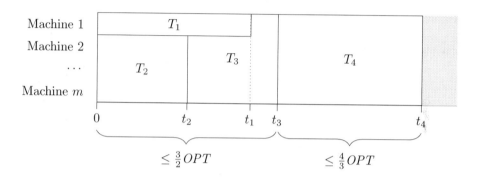

Fig. 1. The structure of a resulting schedule T.

3.1   The Idea

Our approximation algorithm consists of four separate steps that lead to a resulting schedule T. In each of the steps we generate a part of a schedule denoted by T_1, T_2, T_3 and T_4, respectively. A general structure of schedule T is presented in Fig. 1. Note that some time moments are marked by t_1, t_2, t_3 and t_4. These values are found while the algorithm is being executed. However, our algorithm guarantees that $0 \leq t_2 \leq t_1 \leq t_3 \leq t_4$. We also state that $t_3 \leq \frac{3}{2}OPT$ and that $t_4 - t_3 \leq \frac{4}{3}OPT$. As it is so, we get $C_{\max}(T) \leq \frac{3}{2}OPT + \frac{4}{3}OPT = 2\frac{5}{6}OPT$. The algorithm is structured as follows.

Step 1. Schedule all heavy jobs on the first machine in the weakly decreasing order of their resource requirements. As a consequence, it holds that $t_1 = \sum_{i \in \mathcal{J}_{\text{heavy}}} p_i$ and thus $t_1 \leq OPT$.

Step 2. Schedule selected light jobs starting from moment 0 in such a way that $t_2 \leq t_1$ and $R(t) \geq \frac{2}{3}$ for all $t < t_2$.

Step 3. Schedule all medium jobs and selected not-yet scheduled light jobs starting from moment t_2 in such a way that $t_3 \leq \frac{3}{2}OPT$.

Step 4. Schedule all the remaining jobs using an LPT list strategy, starting from moment t_3. In Steps (2) and (3), we selected jobs to be scheduled in such a way that now all non-scheduled jobs form a set J such that $R_m(J) \leq 1$. Thus, $t_4 - t_3 \leq \frac{4}{3}OPT$.

As Step (1) is self-explanatory, we will not discuss it in details. However, we present its pseudocode in Algorithm 1A. Steps (2) and (3) share a subroutine SCHEDULE-2/3 presented in Algorithm 2. Given a set J of jobs to be scheduled and a starting time t_s, the procedure schedules some (perhaps none) of the jobs from J and returns t_c such that $R(t) \geq \frac{2}{3}$ for all $t \in [t_s, t_c)$. If $t_s = t_c$, then $[t_s, t_c) = \emptyset$ and the statement remains true. Note that the time complexity of the SCHEDULE-2/3 subroutine is $O\left(|J| \log |J|\right)$.

Algorithm 1A. Approximation algorithm—Step 1 out of 4

SCHEDULE all the jobs from the $\mathcal{J}_{\text{heavy}}$ set in a weakly decreasing order of r_i, on the first machine, starting from moment 0

$t_1 \leftarrow \sum_{i \in \mathcal{J}_{\text{heavy}}} p_i$

Algorithm 2.

---

procedure SCHEDULE-2/3(J, t_s)

    $t_c \leftarrow t_s$

    SORT J in a weakly decreasing order of r_i

    for $i \in J$ **do**

        $t_c \leftarrow \min\{t \colon t \geq t_c \text{ and } R(t) < \frac{2}{3}\}$

        if job i can be feasibly scheduled in the $[t_c, t_c + p_i)$ interval **then**

            SCHEDULE job i in the $[t_c, t_c + p_i)$ interval on any free machine

        else break

    return $\min\{t \colon t \geq t_c \text{ and } R(t) < \frac{2}{3}\}$

3.2   The Analysis of the Algorithm

In Step (2) of the algorithm, we partially fill the T_2 block of the schedule in such a way that at least $\frac{2}{3}$ of the resource is consumed at any point in the $[0, t_2)$ interval. As we expect t_2 to be less or equal to t_1, this step does not apply if $t_1 = 0$ or, equivalently, if $\mathcal{J}_{\text{heavy}} = \emptyset$. The procedure itself is presented in Algorithm 1B and its time complexity is $O(|\mathcal{J}_{\text{light}}| \log |\mathcal{J}_{\text{light}}|)$. Note that when it is finished, there might exist one or more scheduled jobs $i \in \mathcal{J}_{\text{light}}$ such that $C_i > t_2$, i.e. $\mathcal{J}(t_2) \cap \mathcal{J}_{\text{light}}$ might be a non-empty set.

Proposition 1. *Let $t_1 > 0$. After Step (2) is finished, the following statements hold:*

(a) If $t_1 = t_2$, then $R(\mathcal{J}(t_2) \cap \mathcal{J}_{\text{light}}) < \frac{1}{3}$.
(b) If $t_1 > t_2$, then $R(\mathcal{J}(t_2) \cap \mathcal{J}_{\text{light}}) < \frac{1}{6}$ and $R_m\left(\mathcal{J}_{\text{light}} \setminus \mathcal{J}_{\text{scheduled}}\right) < \frac{1}{3}$.

Proof (1a). Assume that $t_1 = t_2$ and let $h \in \mathcal{J}_{\text{heavy}}$ be the last heavy job scheduled in Step (1). Note that, in particular, $C_h = t_1$. If $\mathcal{J}(t_2) \cap \mathcal{J}_{\text{light}} = \emptyset$, then obviously $R(\mathcal{J}(t_2) \cap \mathcal{J}_{\text{light}}) = 0 < \frac{1}{3}$. Otherwise, each job in the $\mathcal{J}(t_2) \cap \mathcal{J}_{\text{light}}$ set

---

Algorithm 1B. Approximation algorithm—Step 2 out of 4

$t_2 \leftarrow 0$
if $\mathcal{J}_{\text{heavy}} \neq \emptyset$ **then**
    $t_c \leftarrow$ SCHEDULE-2/3$(\mathcal{J}_{\text{light}}, 0)$
    $t_2 \leftarrow \min\{t_1, t_c\}$
    if $t_1 = t_2$ **then**
        UNSCHEDULE jobs $i \in \mathcal{J}_{\text{light}}$ for which $S_i \geq t_2$

---

must have been started before t_2. Consider a moment $t = t_2 - \varepsilon$, for an arbitrarily small ε. The set $\mathcal{J}(t)$ consists of job h, zero or more light jobs $i \in \mathcal{J}_{\text{light}}$ for which $C_i = t_2$, and all the jobs from the $\mathcal{J}(t_2) \cap \mathcal{J}_{\text{light}}$ set.

Select job $j \in \mathcal{J}(t_2) \cap \mathcal{J}_{\text{light}}$ that was scheduled as the last one. Be reminded that in Step (2), light jobs are scheduled in the decreasing order of their resource requirements. From the construction of the algorithm we conclude that $R(t) - r_j < \frac{2}{3}$. If $r_j \geq \frac{1}{6}$, then it must be the only job in the $\mathcal{J}(t_2) \cap \mathcal{J}_{\text{light}}$ set, as $r_h + r_j > \frac{2}{3}$. Thus, $\frac{1}{6} \leq R(\mathcal{J}(t_2) \cap \mathcal{J}_{\text{light}}) < \frac{1}{3}$. If $r_j < \frac{1}{6}$, then $R(t) - r_j - r_h < \frac{2}{3} - \frac{1}{2} = \frac{1}{6}$, so $R(t) - r_h < \frac{1}{6} + r_j < \frac{1}{3}$. Thus, $R(\mathcal{J}(t_2) \cap \mathcal{J}_{\text{light}}) < \frac{1}{3}$. $\qquad\square$

Proof (1b). Assume that $t_1 > t_2$ and let $h \in \mathcal{J}_{\text{heavy}}$ be the heavy job executed at the moment t_2. The value returned by the SCHEDULE-2/3 subroutine guarantees that $R(t) \geq \frac{2}{3}$ for $0 \leq t < t_2$. At the same time, it must hold that $\frac{1}{2} < R(t_2) < \frac{2}{3}$. Thus, at moment t_2 we have $R(\mathcal{J}(t_2) \cap \mathcal{J}_{\text{light}}) + r_h < \frac{2}{3}$ and, as a consequence, $R(\mathcal{J}(t_2) \cap \mathcal{J}_{\text{light}}) < \frac{1}{6}$.

Now, we will show that $R_m(\mathcal{J}_{\text{light}} \setminus \mathcal{J}_{\text{scheduled}}) < \frac{1}{3}$. There are two cases to be considered: either all the machines are busy at the moment t_2 or not. If not all the machines are busy, then all the light jobs were scheduled. Otherwise, any remaining light job would be scheduled on a free machine before the SCHEDULE-2/3 subroutine would end. Thus, $\mathcal{J}_{\text{light}} \setminus \mathcal{J}_{\text{scheduled}} = \emptyset$ and $R_m(\mathcal{J}_{\text{light}} \setminus \mathcal{J}_{\text{scheduled}}) = 0$.

Now, assume that all the machines are busy at the moment t_2, i.e. $|\mathcal{J}(t_2) \cap \mathcal{J}_{\text{light}}| = m - 1$. As the light jobs were scheduled in the weakly decreasing order of their resource requirements and $R(\mathcal{J}(t_2) \cap \mathcal{J}_{\text{light}}) < \frac{1}{6}$, which was proven before, we have

$$\max\{r_i \colon i \in \mathcal{J}_{\text{light}} \setminus \mathcal{J}_{\text{scheduled}}\} \leq \min\{r_i \colon i \in \mathcal{J}(t_2) \cap \mathcal{J}_{\text{light}}\} < \frac{1}{6}.$$

As $R(\mathcal{J}(t_2) \cap \mathcal{J}_{\text{light}}) < \frac{1}{6}$ and $|\mathcal{J}(t_2) \cap \mathcal{J}_{\text{light}}| < m$, we conclude that $R_{m-1}(\mathcal{J}(t_2) \cap \mathcal{J}_{\text{light}}) = R(\mathcal{J}(t_2) \cap \mathcal{J}_{\text{light}}) < \frac{1}{6}$ and $R_{m-1}(\mathcal{J}_{\text{light}} \setminus \mathcal{J}_{\text{scheduled}}) \leq R_{m-1}(\mathcal{J}(t_2) \cap \mathcal{J}_{\text{light}}) < \frac{1}{6}$. Finally,

$$R_m(\mathcal{J}_{\text{light}} \setminus \mathcal{J}_{\text{scheduled}}) \leq R_{m-1}(\mathcal{J}_{\text{light}} \setminus \mathcal{J}_{\text{scheduled}}) + \max\{r_i \colon i \in \mathcal{J}_{\text{light}} \setminus \mathcal{J}_{\text{scheduled}}\} < \frac{1}{6} + \frac{1}{6} = \frac{1}{3}. \qquad\square$$

Before Step (3) is started, all heavy jobs and some (perhaps none) light jobs are scheduled. At this point, we ignore all the jobs from the $\mathcal{J}(t_2) \cap \mathcal{J}_{\text{light}}$ set, i.e.

the scheduled light jobs for which $S_i \leq t_2 < C_i$. Being ignored, they are treated as scheduled jobs that do not occupy machines and do not use any resources. Thus, we will not schedule these jobs in Step (3). These jobs will be rescheduled in Step (4). As a consequence, at any point $t \geq t_2$ not more than a single heavy job is actually executed. In Step (3), we first schedule all the medium jobs using a standard list scheduling approach, and then, if $t_1 = t_2$, we try to schedule not-yet scheduled light jobs using the SCHEDULE-2/3 routine. This intuition is formalized in Algorithm 1C. Note that the time complexity of Algorithm 1C is $O(|\mathcal{J}| \log |\mathcal{J}|)$.

Algorithm 1C. Approximation algorithm—Step 3 out of 4

IGNORE all the jobs from the $\mathcal{J}(t_2) \cap \mathcal{J}_{\text{light}}$ set
Use a standard list scheduling approach to SCHEDULE all the jobs from $\mathcal{J}_{\text{medium}}$ in a weakly increasing order of r_i, starting from moment t_2
$t_g \leftarrow \sup\{t\colon R(t) \geq \frac{2}{3}\}$
if $t_1 = t_2$ **then**
$\qquad t_g \leftarrow$ SCHEDULE-2/3$(\mathcal{J}_{\text{light}} \setminus \mathcal{J}_{\text{scheduled}}, t_g)$
$t_c \leftarrow \max\{C_i\colon i \in \mathcal{J}_{\text{scheduled}}\}$
$t_3 \leftarrow \max\{t_g, t_1\}$

Proposition 2. *Let t_c and t_g be defined as in Algorithm 1C. After Step (3) is finished, the following statements hold:*

(a) If $t_c = t_1$, then $R_m(\mathcal{J} \setminus \mathcal{J}_{scheduled}) < \frac{1}{3}$.
(b) If $t_c > t_1 = t_2$, then $R_m\left(\mathcal{J}(t_g) \cup (\mathcal{J} \setminus \mathcal{J}_{scheduled})\right) < \frac{2}{3}$.
(c) If $t_c > t_1 > t_2$, then $R_m\left(\mathcal{J}(t_g) \cup (\mathcal{J} \setminus \mathcal{J}_{scheduled})\right) < \frac{5}{6}$.

Proof (2a). If $t_c = t_1$ and $t_1 = t_2$, then no jobs were scheduled in Step (3) and thus $|\mathcal{J} \setminus \mathcal{J}_{\text{scheduled}}| = 0$. On the other hand, if $t_c = t_1$ and $t_1 > t_2$, then all medium jobs are finished before or at t_1. The only jobs that were not scheduled yet are light jobs. According to Proposition 1(b), we had $R_m\left(\mathcal{J}_{\text{light}} \setminus \mathcal{J}_{\text{scheduled}}\right) < \frac{1}{3}$ after Step (2), so now it must hold that $R_m(\mathcal{J} \setminus \mathcal{J}_{\text{scheduled}}) < \frac{1}{3}$. □

Proof (2b). Notice that $R(t_g) < \frac{2}{3}$ and thus at most one medium job is being executed at t_g. If no medium jobs are being executed at t_g, then either there were no medium jobs to be scheduled or light jobs made the value of t_g increase. In both cases, as $t_c > t_1 = t_2$, there are only light jobs being executed at t_g and only light jobs are left to be scheduled. Thus, $R_m\left(\mathcal{J}(t_g) \cup (\mathcal{J} \setminus \mathcal{J}_{\text{scheduled}})\right) < \frac{2}{3}$. Otherwise, the value of t_g would be even larger. Notice that if exactly one medium job is being executed at t_g, then this medium job is the last one executed. Consider two cases. If not all the machines are busy at t_g, then there are no light jobs left to be scheduled and thus $\mathcal{J} \setminus \mathcal{J}_{\text{scheduled}} = \emptyset$ and $R_m\left(\mathcal{J}(t_g) \cup (\mathcal{J} \setminus \mathcal{J}_{\text{scheduled}})\right) = R(t_g) < \frac{2}{3}$. On the other hand, if all the machines are busy at t_g, then a medium job and $m - 1$ light jobs are executed at this moment. As the medium job has larger resource requirement than any light job, and light jobs were scheduled in a weakly decreasing order of their resource requirements, it must hold again that $R_m \left(\mathcal{J}(t_g) \cup (\mathcal{J} \setminus \mathcal{J}_{\text{scheduled}}) \right) = R(t_g) < \frac{2}{3}$. $\qquad\qquad\qquad\square$

Proof (2c). From the assumption that $t_c > t_1 > t_2$, we conclude that at least one medium job was scheduled in Step (3) and $t_3 \geq t_g > \max_{i \in \mathcal{J}_{\text{scheduled}}} S_i \geq t_2$. As all the light jobs for which $S_i \geq t_2$ were unscheduled in Step (2), all the light jobs for which $C_i > t_2$ were ignored, and $t_1 \neq t_2$, no light jobs are executed at moment t_g. If two non-light jobs, i and j, were executed at t_g, then it would hold that $r_i + r_j > \frac{2}{3}$ which contradicts the fact that $t_g \geq \sup\{t : R(t) \geq \frac{2}{3}\}$. Finally, if a heavy job was executed at t_g, then it would hold that $t_c = t_1$ which contradicts the assumption that $t_c > t_1$. Thus, at most one medium job can be executed at the moment t_g, and $R(t_g) \leq \frac{1}{2}$. At the same moment, according to Proposition 1(b), we had $R_m \left(\mathcal{J}_{\text{light}} \setminus \mathcal{J}_{\text{scheduled}} \right) < \frac{1}{3}$ after Step (2). Based on Lemma 2, we obtain $R_m \left(\mathcal{J}(t_g) \cup (\mathcal{J} \setminus \mathcal{J}_{\text{scheduled}}) \right) < \frac{1}{2} + \frac{1}{3} = \frac{5}{6}$. $\qquad\square$

Proposition 3. *It holds that $t_3 \leq \frac{3}{2}\text{OPT}$.*

Proof. It holds that $t_3 \geq t_1$. If $t_1 = t_3$, then $t_3 \leq OPT \leq \frac{3}{2}OPT$, so assume that $t_3 > t_1$. First, consider a case when $t_3 > t_1 = t_2$. It means that all medium jobs (if they exist) were scheduled starting from moment t_1. As for any medium job $i \in \mathcal{J}_{\text{medium}}$ we have $\frac{1}{3} < r_i \leq \frac{1}{2}$, any two medium jobs can be executed in parallel, and if it is so, more than $\frac{2}{3}$ of the resource is used. In such a case, just after medium jobs are scheduled, we have $t_g = \sup\{t : R(t) \geq \frac{2}{3}\}$, and after Step (3) is finished, one has $R(t) \geq \frac{2}{3}$ for all $t \in [t_2, t_3)$. Now, be reminded about the ignored jobs from the $\mathcal{J}(t_2) \cap \mathcal{J}_{\text{light}}$ set. If we reconsider them, even at the cost of exceeding the available amount of resources or the number of machines, we have $R(t) \geq \frac{2}{3}$ for all $t \in [0, t_3)$. This is enough to state that, based on Lemma 1, $t_3 \leq \frac{3}{2}OPT$, although some of the jobs scheduled before t_3 are ignored and will be rescheduled later.

Now, consider a case when $t_3 > t_1 > t_2$. As $t_1 > t_2$, no light jobs are scheduled in Step (3). This inequality implicates that at least one medium job could have been scheduled together with a heavy job in the $[t_2, t_1)$ interval. As heavy jobs are scheduled in a weakly decreasing order of the resource requirements, and medium jobs are scheduled in a weakly increasing order of the resource requirements, there are two possibilities.

If a medium job is being executed at every moment $t \in [t_2, t_1)$, then $t_g = \sup\{t : R(t) \geq \frac{2}{3}\}$ and—based on the same reasoning as in the previous case—we have $R(t) \geq \frac{2}{3}$ for all $t \in [0, t_g)$. As $t_3 = t_g$, based on Lemma 1 we obtain $t_3 \leq \frac{3}{2}OPT$.

In the second possibility, there exists a point t in the $[t_2, t_1)$ interval, for which $R(t) < \frac{2}{3}$. Consider the latest such point, i.e. $t := \sup\left\{t \in [t_2, t_1) : R(t) < \frac{2}{3}\right\}$. The t value is either equal to t_1, or to a starting time of a medium job. In both cases, no medium job i for which $S_i \geq t$ could have been scheduled earlier. Thus, in the $[t, t_g)$ interval (if non-empty) all jobs are either heavy or medium, and are scheduled on exactly 2 machines at the same time. Moreover, it would be not possible to execute three such jobs in parallel due to their resource requirements, so in the optimal schedule not more than two machines would be busy starting from point t due to the resource requirements of the medium jobs. In our case, both machines are busy in the $[t, t_g)$ interval, so it must hold that $t_g \leq OPT$. If so, then $t_3 = \max\{t_g, t_1\} \leq OPT \leq \frac{3}{2} OPT$. □

After Step (3) is finished, we unschedule ignored jobs from the $\mathcal{J}(t_2) \cap \mathcal{J}_{\text{light}}$ set and all the jobs from the $\mathcal{J}(t_g)$ set, and then we schedule all jobs that are in the updated $\mathcal{J} \setminus \mathcal{J}_{\text{scheduled}}$ set. As we now know that $t_3 \leq \frac{3}{2} OPT$ and that $t_3 \geq t_g$, all the machines are free starting from the t_3 moment. This intuition is shown in Algorithm 1D. It can be now shown that all the jobs to be scheduled are satisfied with a single unit of the resource. As it is so, all the machines can execute m jobs in parallel, whichever m jobs we choose. Thus, a schedule provided by the LPT list strategy is a $\frac{4}{3}$-approximation solution for the $\mathcal{J} \setminus \mathcal{J}_{\text{scheduled}}$ set.

Proposition 4. *After Step (3) is finished, it holds that*

$$R_m((\mathcal{J}(t_2) \cap \mathcal{J}_{\text{light}}) \cup \mathcal{J}(t_g) \cup (\mathcal{J} \setminus \mathcal{J}_{\text{scheduled}})) < 1.$$

Proof. The proof follows directly from Proposition 1–2 and Lemma 2.

Algorithm 1D. Approximation algorithm—Step 4 out of 4

UNSCHEDULE all the ignored jobs from the $\mathcal{J}(t_2) \cap \mathcal{J}_{\text{light}}$ set
UNSCHEDULE all the jobs from the $\mathcal{J}(t_g)$ set
Use an LPT list scheduling approach to SCHEDULE all the jobs from the $\mathcal{J} \setminus \mathcal{J}_{\text{scheduled}}$ set (including just unscheduled ones), starting from moment t_3
$t_4 \leftarrow \max\{t_3, C_{\max}\}$

Theorem 1. *Algorithm 1A–1D is a log-linear $2\frac{5}{6}$-approximation algorithm for the $P|res1 \cdots|C_{max}$ problem.*

Notice that the $2\frac{5}{6}$-approximation ratio leaves us room for immediate improvement. In fact, based on the result by Graham [9], as we can apply the LPT strategy in Step (4) without any concerns about the orthogonal resource, it must hold that $t_4 - t_3 \leq \left(\frac{4}{3} - \frac{1}{3m}\right) \cdot OPT$. Thus, Algorithm 1A–1D is $\left(2\frac{5}{6} - \frac{1}{3m}\right)$-approximation.

4   Simulations and Extensions

The log-linear algorithm presented in Sect. 3 provides a schedule that is not more than $2\frac{5}{6}$ times longer than the optimal one. This is so for arbitrary independent jobs and arbitrary resource requirements. While our principal contribution is in theory, our log-linear algorithm is also easily-implementable, so in this section we evaluate our algorithm and compare its average-case performance to standard heuristics.

4.1   Compared Algorithms

We will compare three variants of our algorithm against a number of greedy heuristics based on list scheduling algorithms. All the algorithms were implemented in PYTHON; we performed our experiments on an Intel Core i7-4500U CPU @ 3.00 GHz with 8 GB RAM.

The theoretical algorithm from Sect. 3 will be denoted by *ApAlg*. Its first extension, denoted by *ApAlg-S*, introduces an additional step of backfilling. Namely, after the *ApAlg* algorithm is finished, we iterate over all the jobs in order of their starting times, and reschedule them so they start at the earliest moment possible. Note that this additional step never increases the starting time of any job, and thus *ApAlg-S* is also a $2\frac{5}{6}$-approximation algorithm. The second extension, denoted by *ApAlg-H* is a heuristic algorithm based on *ApAlg*. In this case, the SCHEDULE-2/3 subroutine (see Algorithm 2) is replaced. In *ApAlg-H*, it schedules jobs in a strict weakly decreasing order of r_i (so no job j such that $r_j < r_i$ is started before job i), regardless of whether the total resource consumption at t has exceeded $\frac{2}{3}$.

We compare the *ApAlg*, *ApAlg-S* and *ApAlg-H* algorithms against four list scheduling algorithms: *LPT* (Longest Processing Time), *HRR* (Highest Resource Requirement), *LRR* (Lowest Resource Requirement), and *RAND* (Random Order). Any list scheduler starts by sorting jobs according to the chosen criterion. Then, when making a scheduling decision, it seeks for the first job on the list that can be successfully scheduled, i.e. has its resource requirements not greater than what is left given jobs being currently executed (if no such job exists, or all processors are busy, the algorithm moves to the next time moment when any job completes). Thus, the worst-case running time of the *ApAlg-S*, *LPT* and *RAND* algorithms is $O(n^2)$. The worst-case running time of the *LRR* and *HRR* algorithms is $O(n \log n)$ – these algorithms can use binary search to find the first job from the list having resource requirement not exceeding the currently available resources.

4.2   Instances

Our simulations are based on the dataset provided by the MetaCentrum Czech National Grid [16,19]. In order to avoid normalizing data from different clusters, we arbitrarily chose the cluster with the largest number of nodes (*Zapat*). The *Zapat* cluster consisted of 112 nodes, each equipped with 16 CPU cores and 134 GB of RAM. This cluster was monitored between January 2013 and April 2015, which resulted in 299 628 log entries.

Each entry provides information about job processing times (p_i) and their main memory requirements (r_i). We limit ourselves to entries for which both p_i and r_i are less or equal to their respective 99th percentiles, so the data can be safely normalized. As different jobs may be executed in parallel on each node, we consider the main memory to be a single orthogonal resource. We assume that the total memory size (total amount of the resource) is equal to the maximum memory requirement in the set of all the considered job entries. Thus, we normalize all the resource requirements so $r_i \in [0,1]$ (where 1 is the resource capacity of the simulated system). As we study the problem with sequential jobs, we also assume that each job from the trace requires a single CPU. In Fig. 2, we present how the job processing times and normalized memory requirements were distributed within the log. Most of the jobs have rather low resource requirements. In fact, the 25th, 50th and 75th percentiles of the resource requirements distribution are equal to 0.0165, 0.0169, and 0.068, respectively. We have also analysed how the values of p_i and r_i correlate to each other. As the distributions of p_i and r_i clearly are not Gaussian-like, we calculated the Spearman's correlation coefficient. This requires an additional assumption that the relation between p_i and r_i is monotonic. The calculated value is 0.14207 which suggests positive, yet not very significant correlation. This result was verified visually.

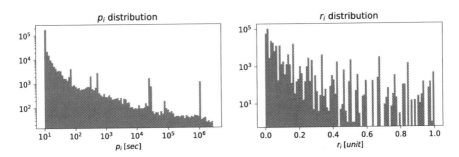

Fig. 2. Job processing time and resource requirement distribution in cluster *Zapat* (both axes limited to the 99th percentile).

For each combination of the number of jobs $n \in \{500, 1000, 5000, 10000\}$ and the number of machines $m \in \{10, 20, 50, 100\}$, we generated 30 problem instances. The processing time and resource requirement of each job were set to the processing time and memory requirement of a job randomly chosen from the log. As the lower bound on the optimal schedule length is $L = \max\{\sum_{i \in \mathcal{J}} p_i/m, \sum_{i \in \mathcal{J}} p_i \cdot r_i\}$, we only considered instances in which $\max_{i \in \mathcal{J}} p_i < L$. This way, we omitted (trivial) instances for which the length of the optimal schedule is determined by a single job.

4.3   Simulation Results

In Fig. 3, we present the results obtained for all the algorithms and all the (n, m) combinations. We report the returned $C_{\max}$ values as normalized by the lower-bound of the optimal schedule length, i.e. $\max\{\sum_{i \in \mathcal{J}} p_i/m, \sum_{i \in \mathcal{J}} p_i \cdot r_i\}$. For lower numbers of machines (left part of the figure) the results of *ApAlg*, *ApAlg-S*, and *ApAlg-H* algorithms are comparable. However, when the number of machines increases, the original approximation algorithm is significantly outperformed by the *ApAlg-S* and *ApAlg-H* variants. In the considered job log, the

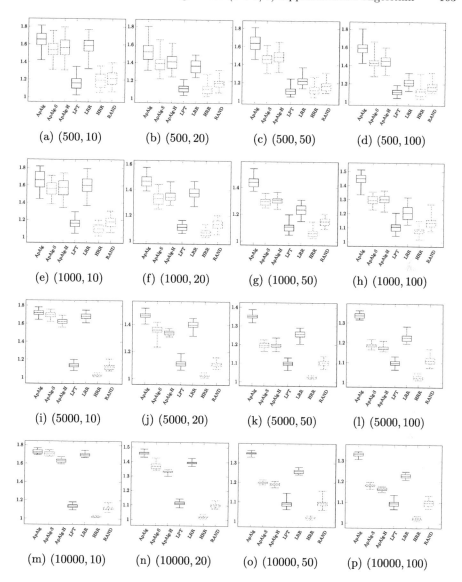

Fig. 3. The $C_{\max}$ values normalized by the lower-bounds on the optimal schedule lengths. Captions (n, m) describe the number of jobs n and the number of machines m.

50th percentile on the normalized resource requirement was 0.0169. We would thus expect that usually not more than 50 machines are busy in the initial part of a schedule provided by the *ApAlg* variant (due to the threshold of $\frac{2}{3}$ on a total resource consumption). In such cases, the *ApAlg-S* and *ApAlg-H* variants gain a clear advantage, as they can potentially make use of all the machines, if possible.

When the numbers of jobs and machines increase (right-bottom part of the figure), the normalized C_{max} values decrease for all the algorithms. In such cases, a greedy heuristic, HRR, provides almost optimal schedules, with a maximum normalized C_{max} value of 1.03. There might be two reasons for that. First, when the number of jobs increases and their processing times come from the same distribution, it is easier for greedy algorithms to provide better results (as the normalized C_{max} value is relative). Second, if job resource requirements are not too small compared to the number of machines, the HRR produces a schedule with the resource being almost fully-utilized most of the time, compared to LPT which makes decisions solely based on the job length.

We also compared the runtime of the algorithms on large instances with 10000 jobs and 100 machines. As expected, log-linear $ApAlg$, $ApAlg\text{-}H$, LRR and HRR algorithms were significantly faster: their runtimes (median over 30 instances) were equal to 2.83 s, 3.29 s, 0.74 s and 0.83 s, respectively—in contrast to $ApAlg\text{-}S$, LPT and $RAND$ algorithms with runtimes of 88.39 s, 88.58 s and 92.94 s.

5   Conclusions

In this paper, we presented a log-linear $2\frac{5}{6}$-approximation algorithm for the parallel-machine scheduling problem with a single orthogonal resource and makespan as the objective function. Our algorithm improves the $\left(3 - \frac{3}{m}\right)$-approximation ratio of Garey and Graham [6]. It is also considerably easier to implement than the approximation algorithms proposed by Niemeier and Wiese [21] and Jansen, Maack and Rau [14].

In the computational experiments, we compared three variants of our algorithm to four list scheduling heuristics. We used the real-life data provided by the MetaCentrum Czech National Grid. The results provided by the HRR (Highest Resource Requirement) list heuristic significantly outperformed all other algorithms for the considered dataset. Although the results provided by the HRR algorithm are promising, the approximation ratio can be improved in general. Thus, in order to provide the best results, one can combine the HRR algorithm with our algorithms and thus obtain good schedules with a better guarantee on their approximation ratio.

Acknowledgements and Data Availability Statement. This research is supported by a Polish National Science Center grant Opus (UMO-2017/25/B/ST6/00116). The authors would like to thank anonymous reviewers for their in-depth comments that helped to significantly improve the quality of the paper.

The datasets and code generated during and/or analyzed during the current study are available in the Figshare repository: https://doi.org/10.6084/m9.figshare.14748267 [20].

References

1. Blazewicz, J.: Complexity of computer scheduling algorithms under resource constraints. In: Proceedings of the First Meeting AFCET-SMF on Applied Mathematics, pp. 169–178 (1978)
2. Blazewicz, J., Cellary, W., Slowinski, R., Weglarz, J.: Scheduling under resource constraints-deterministic models. JC Baltzer AG (1986)
3. Blazewicz, J., Lenstra, J., Kan, A.R.: Scheduling subject to resource constraints: classification and complexity. Discret. Appl. Math. **5**(1), 11–24 (1983). https://doi.org/10.1016/0166-218X(83)90012-4
4. Edis, E.B., Oguz, C., Ozkarahan, I.: Parallel machine scheduling with additional resources: notation, classification, models and solution methods. Eur. J. Oper. Res. **230**(3), 449–463 (2013). https://doi.org/10.1016/j.ejor.2013.02.042
5. Feitelson, D.G.: Job scheduling in multiprogrammed parallel systems (1997)
6. Garey, M., Graham, R.: Bounds for multiprocessor scheduling with resource constraints. SIAM J. Comput. **4**, 187–200 (1975). https://doi.org/10.1137/0204015
7. Garey, M., Johnson, D.: Strong NP-completeness results: motivation, examples, and implications. J. Assoc. Comput. Mach. **25**(3), 499–508 (1978). https://doi.org/10.1145/322077.322090
8. Graham, R.: Bounds for certain multiprocessing anomalies. Bell Syst. Tech. J. **45**(9), 1563–1581 (1966). https://doi.org/10.1002/j.1538-7305.1966.tb01709.x
9. Graham, R.: Bounds on multiprocessing timing anomalies. SIAM J. Appl. Math. **17**(2), 416–429 (1969)
10. Graham, R., Lawler, E., Lenstra, J., Kan, A.R.: Optimization and approximation in deterministic sequencing and scheduling: a survey. In: Hammer, P., Johnson, E., Korte, B. (eds.) Discrete Optimization II, Annals of Discrete Mathematics, vol. 5, pp. 287–326. Elsevier (1979). https://doi.org/10.1016/S0167-5060(08)70356-X
11. Hochbaum, D.S., Shmoys, D.B.: Using dual approximation algorithms for scheduling problems theoretical and practical results. J. ACM **34**(1), 144–162 (1987). https://doi.org/10.1145/7531.7535
12. Jansen, K.: An EPTAS for scheduling jobs on uniform processors: using an MILP relaxation with a constant number of integral variables. SIAM J. Discrete Math. **24**(2), 457–485 (2010). https://doi.org/10.1137/090749451
13. Jansen, K., Klein, K.M., Verschae, J.: Closing the gap for makespan scheduling via sparsification techniques. Math. Oper. Res. **45**(4), 1371–1392 (2020). https://doi.org/10.1287/moor.2019.1036
14. Jansen, K., Maack, M., Rau, M.: Approximation schemes for machine scheduling with resource (in-)dependent processing times **15**(3) (2019). https://doi.org/10.1145/3302250
15. Kellerer, H.: An approximation algorithm for identical parallel machine scheduling with resource dependent processing times. Oper. Res. Lett. **36**(2), 157–159 (2008). https://doi.org/10.1016/j.orl.2007.08.001
16. Klusáček, D., Tóth, Š, Podolníková, G.: Real-life experience with major reconfiguration of job scheduling system. In: Desai, N., Cirne, W. (eds.) JSSPP 2015-2016. LNCS, vol. 10353, pp. 83–101. Springer, Cham (2017). https://doi.org/10.1007/978-3-319-61756-5_5
17. Kovalyov, M.Y., Shafransky, Y.M.: Uniform machine scheduling of unit-time jobs subject to resource constraints. Discrete Appl. Math. **84**(1), 253–257 (1998). https://doi.org/10.1016/S0166-218X(97)00138-8

18. Krause, K.L., Shen, V.Y., Schwetman, H.D.: A task-scheduling algorithm for a multiprogramming computer system. SIGOPS Oper. Syst. Rev. **7**(4), 112–118 (1973).
https://doi.org/10.1145/957195.808058
19. MetaCentrum Czech National Grid: MetaCentrum workload logs (2015). https://
www.cs.huji.ac.il/labs/parallel/workload/l_metacentrum2/index.html
20. Naruszko, A., Przybylski, B., Rzadca, K.: Artifact and instructions to generate experimental results for the Euro-Par 2021 paper: A log-linear $(2 + 5/6)$-
approximation algorithm for parallel machine scheduling with a single orthogonal
resource, August 2021. https://doi.org/10.6084/m9.figshare.14748267
21. Niemeier, M., Wiese, A.: Scheduling with an orthogonal resource constraint. In:
Erlebach, T., Persiano, G. (eds.) WAOA 2012. LNCS, vol. 7846, pp. 242–256.
Springer, Heidelberg (2013). https://doi.org/10.1007/978-3-642-38016-7_20

An MPI-based Algorithm for Mapping Complex Networks onto Hierarchical Architectures

Maria Predari[1]([✉]), Charilaos Tzovas[1], Christian Schulz[2],
and Henning Meyerhenke[1]

[1] Humboldt-Universität zu Berlin, Berlin, Germany
{predarim,charilat,meyerhenke}@hu-berlin.de
[2] Universität Heidelberg, Heidelberg, Germany
christian.schulz@informatik.uni-heidelberg.de

Abstract. Processing massive application graphs on distributed memory systems requires to map the graphs onto the system's processing elements (PEs). This task becomes all the more important when PEs have non-uniform communication costs or the input is highly irregular. Typically, mapping is addressed using partitioning, in a two-step approach or an integrated one. Parallel partitioning tools do exist; yet, corresponding mapping algorithms or their public implementations all have major sequential parts or other severe scaling limitations.

In this paper, we propose a parallel algorithm that maps graphs onto the PEs of a hierarchical system. Our solution integrates partitioning and mapping; it models the system hierarchy in a concise way as an implicit labeled tree. The vertices of the application graph are labeled as well, and these vertex labels induce the mapping. The mapping optimization follows the basic idea of parallel label propagation, but we tailor the gain computations of label changes to quickly account for the induced communication costs. Our MPI-based code is the first public implementation of a parallel graph mapping algorithm; to this end, we extend the partitioning library PARHIP. To evaluate our algorithm's implementation, we perform comparative experiments with complex networks in the million- and billion-scale range. In general our mapping tool shows good scalability on up to a few thousand PEs. Compared to other MPI-based competitors, our algorithm achieves the best speed to quality trade-off and our quality results are even better than non-parallel mapping tools.

Keywords: Load balancing · Process mapping · Hierarchical architectures · Parallel label propagation

This work is partially supported by German Research Foundation (DFG) grant ME 3619/3-2 (FINCA) within Priority Programme 1736 and by DFG grant ME 3619/4-1 (ALMACOM) as well as by the Austrian Science Fund (FWF, project P 31763-N31).

© Springer Nature Switzerland AG 2021
L. Sousa et al. (Eds.): Euro-Par 2021, LNCS 12820, pp. 167–182, 2021.
https://doi.org/10.1007/978-3-030-85665-6_11

1 Introduction

Task mapping is the process of assigning tasks of a parallel application onto a number of available processing elements (PEs) and is an important step in high-performance computing. One reason for the importance of mapping is non-uniform memory access (NUMA), common in many modern architectures, where PEs close to each other communicate faster than PEs further away. The importance stems from the fact that communication is orders of magnitude slower than computation. To alleviate those issues, task mapping is often used as a preprocessing step. Successful mapping solutions assign pairs of heavily-communicating tasks "close to each other" in the parallel system, so that their communication overhead is reduced. Moreover, the network topologies of parallel architectures exhibit special properties that can be exploited during mapping. A common property is that PEs are hierarchically organized into, e.g., islands, racks, nodes, processors, cores with corresponding communication links of similar quality.

Furthermore, mapping becomes even more important when the application's structure and communication pattern are highly irregular. While partitioning the application may work well for mesh-based numerical simulations, large graphs derived from social and other complex networks pose additional challenges [34]. Typical examples are power-law [3] and small-world graphs [21]. The former are characterized by highly skewed vertex degree distribution, the latter exhibit a particularly low graph diameter. Distributed graph processing systems, such as Apache Giraph and GraphLab [23], are made to run analytics on such graphs. For some algorithms, in particular those with local data access, they report good scaling results [23]. For non-local or otherwise complex analytics and highly irregular inputs, running times and scalability of these systems can become unsatisfactory [30]. Consequently, designing MPI-based graph processing applications is necessary to scale to massive instances with high performance. Considering the above and the number of PEs in modern architectures (a number expected to increase in the future), task mapping can have significant impact in the overall application performance [1,4]. Good mapping algorithms should be able to improve the quality of the final mapping, and additionally, they need to be fast in order not to degrade the overall performance of the application. Thus, developing MPI-based mapping algorithms with good scaling behavior becomes all the more crucial. Since finding optimal topology mappings is NP-hard [14], heuristics are often used to obtain fairly good solutions within reasonable time [5,35].

Our contribution is an MPI-based, integrated mapping algorithm for hierarchically organized architectures, implemented within PARHIP. To model the system hierarchy and the corresponding communication costs, we use an implicit bit-label representation, which is very concise and effective. Our algorithm, called PARHIP_MAP, uses parallel label propagation to stir the mapping optimization. As far as we know PARHIP_MAP is currently the only available implementation for parallel mapping. Experiments show that it offers the best speed to quality trade-off; having on average 62% higher quality than the second best competitor (PARHIP), and being only 18% slower than the fastest competitor (XTRAPULP), which favors speed over quality. Moreover, our algorithm scales well up to 3072

PEs and is able to handle graphs of billion edges, with the least failing rate among other MPI-based tools due to memory or timeout issues on massive complex networks. Moreover, compared to a sequential baseline mapping algorithm, PARHIP_MAP has on average 10% better quality results.

2   Background

We model the underlying parallel application with a graph $G_a = (V_a, E_a, \omega_a)$, where vertex u_a represents a computational task of the application and an edge e_a indicates data exchanges between tasks. The amount of exchanged data is quantified by the edge weight $\omega_a(e_a)$. Network information for hierarchically organized systems is often modeled with trees[1] [13,19]; we do so as well, but implicitly (see Sect. 3). The bottom-up input description of the topology follows KAHIP: $H = \{h_0, h_1, \ldots, h_{l-1}\}$ denotes the number of children of a node per level, where l is the number of hierarchy levels; i. e., each processor has h_0 cores, each node h_1 processors, and so on. We also define the set of PEs as V_p of size $k = \prod_{i=0}^{l-1} h_i$. Communication costs are defined via $D = \{d_0, d_1, \ldots, d_{l-1}\}$ such that PEs with a common ancestor in level i of the hierarchy communicate with cost d_i; i. e., two cores in the same processor communicate with d_0 cost, two cores in the same node but in different processors with d_1, and so on. We use $d(u_p, v_p)$ to indicate the time for one data unit exchange between PEs u_p and v_p (i. e., their distance).

A k-way partition of G divides V into k blocks $V_1, \ldots, V_k$, such that $V_1 \cup \ldots \cup V_k = V$, $V_i \neq \emptyset$ for $i = 1, \ldots, k$ and $V_i \cap V_j = \emptyset$ for $i \neq j$. Graph partitioning aims at finding a k-way partition of G that optimizes an objective function while adhering to a balance constraint. The balance constraint demands that the sum of node weights in each block does not exceed a given imbalance threshold ϵ. Moreover, the objective function is often taken to be the edge-cut of the partition $\sum_{i<j} w(E_{ij})$, where $E_{ij} := \{\{u, v\} \in E : u \in V_i, v \in V_j\}$.

A mapping, $\mu : V_a \mapsto V_p$, is defined as a nearly balanced assignment of computational tasks onto PEs such that, for some imbalance parameter $\varepsilon \geq 0$, $|\mu^{-1}(v_p)| \leq (1 + \varepsilon) \cdot \lceil |V_a|/|\mu(V_a)| \rceil$ for all $v_p \in \mu(V_a)$. Hence, $\mu(\cdot)$ induces a balanced partition of G_a with blocks $\mu^{-1}(v_p)$, $v_p \in V_p$. Or inversely, a mapping μ defines a one-to-one mapping from k balanced blocks of V_a to k PEs of V_p. To steer an optimization process for obtaining good mappings, different objective functions have been proposed [14].[2] A widely used [27] mapping objective is Coco$(\cdot)$ (also referred to as *hop-byte* or *qap*), defined as:

$$\text{Coco}(\mu) := \sum_{\substack{e_a \in E_a \\ e_a = \{u_a, v_a\}}} \omega_a(e_a) \, d(\mu(u_a), \mu(v_a)) \tag{1}$$

---

[1] In a tree topology, leaf vertices correspond to PEs, internal nodes to switches.

[2] Most theoretical metrics can only approximate the communication overhead of the application since communication during real-time execution can be affected by many external factors (e.g., network traffic and overhead from competing jobs).

Intuitively speaking, placing pairs of highly communicating tasks in nearby PEs minimizes Coco($\cdot$).

2.1 Related Work

In this section we focus on related techniques for parallel graph partitioning and sequential and parallel task mapping. For more details we refer the reader to the overview articles for task mapping [15,27] and for graph partitioning [7].

Parallel Graph Partitioning. Graph partitioning is closely related to task mapping. First, because it is often used as a building block for mapping and second, because it substitutes mapping when no network information is available. A trivial mapping can be computed from the solution of a graph partitioner, simply by assigning block i to PE i (identity mapping). To this end, a graph-based metric, such as the edgecut, *i. e.*, the total weight of edges between blocks, is minimized. Some popular parallel partitioners are PARMETIS [33], PARHIP [24], and PT-SCOTCH [28]. These tools all follow the multilevel framework, performing one or more cycles of the following procedure: they construct a hierarchy of successively coarser graphs, find an initial solution on the coarsest graph and project the solution successively to the original graph, while refining it on every level. Graph coarsening is often based on edge matching [33] or label propagation [29], while initial partitioning uses recursive bisection, local heuristics or evolutionary algorithms. The main bottleneck for high scalability in these tools seems to be the high memory usage due to successive coarsening and the poor scaling of the initial partitioning phase. XTRAPULP [34], a single-level parallel partitioning tool that uses label propagation, avoids the scalability issue. This advantage comes with the price of reduced quality, though.

Mapping Tools. Existing mapping algorithms are grouped into two categories: integrated approaches and two-phase ones. Integrated approaches address the mapping problem using the network information directly, without decomposing the problem into independent sub-problems. Examples of integrated approaches are included in SCOTCH [26] and KAHIP [32]. SCOTCH uses dual recursive bisection (DRB) [25] to partition both the application graph and the network topology into two blocks recursively. Embedded sectioning [20] and Recursive multisection [8,16] follow a similar technique. Recently, Faraj *et al.* [10] proposed an integrated mapping approach that uses fast label propagation and a more localized local search to achieve mapping solutions of high quality. LIBTOPOMAP [14], TOPOMATCH [17] and MPIPP [9] are typical examples of the two-phase approach, where mapping is solved in two steps. The first step usually involves an established partitioner that obtains a balanced partition. The second step then assigns the resulting blocks to the PEs while minimizing a mapping objective, *e. g.* using a greedy approach [6,14] or metaheuristics [6,19].

To the best of our knowledge, all current mapping algorithms or their public implementations have major sequential parts. LIBTOPOMAP and TOPOMATCH use parallel partitioning, but the mapping step is completely sequential. Regarding integrated approaches, PT-SCOTCH offers parallel mapping only for the trivial case where the underlying network topology corresponds to a complete graph, which is simply partitioning.[3] Moreover, the JOSTLE authors briefly discuss a parallel mapping extension of their sequential approach but do not provide enough details nor an implementation [36].

2.2   Parallel Label Propagation with Size Constraints

Our mapping approach uses the parallel label propagation algorithm (LPA) with size constraints [24], as implemented in PARHIP. We discuss the algorithm and its implementation here for self-containment reasons. In its sequential form, LPA starts with some partition (depending on the algorithm's purpose) and iterates over all vertices. At each vertex v, the block number (= label) of v is set to the dominant one in the neighborhood of v (= block with highest total edge weight incident to v). If a size constraint is imposed, then the dominant block that can still host v is chosen. The loop over all vertices vertices is repeated, *e. g.* a fixed number of times or until no more changes occur.

The parallel version is implemented as follows. First, each PE gets a subgraph of the input graph consisting of a contiguous range of nodes in the interval $I := [a \ldots b]$, the edges incident to the nodes of those blocks, as well as the end points of edges which are not in I (so-called ghost or halo nodes). In any case, the graph data structure only stores edges incident to local vertices. To parallelize the label propagation algorithm, each PE visits all local vertices in a random order. A vertex v is moved to the block that has the strongest eligible connection such that the block will not be overloaded. During the course of the algorithm, local vertices can change their block and hence the blocks in which halo vertices are contained can change as well. Communication is expensive, so instead of updating labels of halo vertices every time they change, the algorithm follows an overlapping scheme, organized in phases. A node is called interface node if it is adjacent to at least one ghost node. The PE associated with the ghost node is called adjacent PE. Each PE stores a separate send buffer for all adjacent PEs. During each phase, the algorithm stores the block label of interface nodes that have changed into the send buffer of each adjacent PE of this node. Communication is then implemented asynchronously. In phase i, the current updates are sent to the adjacent PEs and each PE receives the updates of the adjacent PEs from round $i - 1$, for $i > 1$.

For maintaining the weight of blocks, the algorithm uses two different approaches, one for coarsening and another for uncoarsening. During coarsening, the algorithm uses a localized approach for keeping up with the block weight since the number of blocks is high and the balance constraint is not tight. Roughly speaking, a PE maintains and updates only the local amount of node weight of the blocks of its local and ghost nodes. Due to the way the label propagation

---

algorithm is initialized, each PE knows the exact weights of the blocks of local nodes and ghost nodes in the beginning. Label propagation then uses the local information to bound the block weights. Once a node changes its block, the local block weight is updated. This does not involve additional communication.

During uncoarsening a different approach is taken compared to coarsening since the number of blocks is much smaller. This bookkeeping approach is similar to the one in PARMETIS [33]. Initially, the exact block weights of all k blocks are computed locally. The local block weights are then aggregated and broadcast to all PEs. Both can be done using one allreduce operation. Now each PE knows the global block weights of all k blocks. The label propagation algorithm then uses this information and locally updates the weights. For each block, a PE maintains and updates the total amount of node weight that local nodes contribute to the block weights. Using this information, one can restore the exact block weights with one allreduce operation which is done at the end of each computation phase.

3   Parallel Mapping Algorithm

In this section, we present the main technical contributions of the paper. This includes an integrated mapping algorithm for distributed memory systems based on a concise representation of the hierarchical network topology via bit-labels. Our algorithm uses a parallel local search refinement process, where gain computations for label changes account for communication in the network topology. The bit-label network representation allows a quick gain evaluation. As far as we know, this is the first (implemented and publicly available) parallel mapping algorithm for distributed-memory systems.

3.1   Network Topology Representation

To encode a tree network topology, most representations typically store l numbers for each PE, one for each tree hierarchy level. However, in our work we use a concise bit-label representation that has very low space requirement. For each vertex $v \in V_p$ (*i.e.*, each PE), we only store a single number as a bit-label. This number is also hidden within the labels of vertices in V_a as a bit-prefix. This enables us to use label propagation on G_a for the refinement process and quickly evaluate distances between PEs.

The bit-label of a given vertex $v_p \in V_p$ encodes the full ancestry of v_p in the tree. The ancestor of v_p in level i can be viewed as a block of an implicit partition in that level (see Fig. 1). The local numberings of all ancestors/blocks of v_p are encoded in the bit-label of v_p and indicate ownership of the vertex in the tree hierarchy (in which rack, processor, node etc.., it belongs to). The red vertex in Fig. 1 has a label of 131 (10|000|0|11 in binary). Reading the bit-label from left to right, we have that v belongs to block 2 of the first level partition, block 0 of the second level and so on. For the network topology this means that PE v belongs to rack 2, local processor 0, local node 0 and has local core number 3. To construct the labels for the available PEs we use Algorithm 1. The bit-label

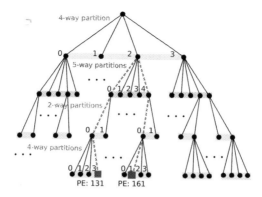

Fig. 1. Example of implicit tree topology. The system has 160 PEs in one island with four racks (first level), five nodes per rack (second), two processors per node (third) and four cores per processor (forth). PEs take labels from 0 to 231 but not all labels are used due to different number of children per level. (Color figure online)

of each PE is divided into l sections, each containing $s[i]$ bits with $0 \leq i < l$, as in Line 5. Each subsection r_i gives the local numbering of the ancestor node of the current PE in level i. For each PE p we loop through the levels of the tree hierarchy and encode the local numbering of each ancestor node in the bit-label of p (see Lines 9 to 13).

To retrieve the distance between two PEs, one needs to find their common ancestor in the tree topology. To achieve this in our representation, we apply the bit-wise operation $xor(\cdot, \cdot)$ on the two bit-labels. We find the level of the common ancestor by finding the section r_i which contains the leftmost non-zero bit on the result of $xor(\cdot, \cdot)$. In the example of Fig. 1, the leftmost non-zero bit of the squared vertices is in the second section. This corresponds to the second level in the tree (illustrated with the blue dashed line). The time complexity of finding the section of the leftmost non-zero bit is $\mathcal{O}(\log l)$. Note that modern processors often have hardware implementation of a count leading zeros operation. This makes the identification of the leftmost non-zero bit a constant time operation.[4]

3.2   Refinement and Gain Computation

Our parallel mapping approach is an integrated solution method that performs one cycle of the multilevel framework. More precisely, we coarsen the graph, compute an initial partition and uncoarsen the solution while refining with local search based on a mapping objective such as Eq. 1. In a parallel setting, each graph vertex v_a has a local vertex label, within the PE, and a global one. The global vertex labels can be used to induce a mapping $\mu(\cdot)$ onto PEs via their prefixes. For instance, in Fig. 2 all vertices of the shaded block of G_a have labels

---

[4]   This holds under the realistic assumption that for any bit-label v_p, the size $\log v_p = \mathcal{O}(\log k)$ of the binary numbers is smaller than the size of a machine word.

Algorithm 1. Algorithm for building the bit-label representation for PEs.

```
 1: function BUILDLABEL(H)
 2:     Input: H, i. e., number of children per node for each hierarchy level
 3:     Output: x, i. e., array of bit-label representation for PEs
 4:     l ← size(H)                                    ▷ number of hierarchies in the tree topology
 5:     s[i] ← ⌈log₂ hᵢ⌉                                              ▷ array of size l
 6:     k ← ∏ᵢ₌₁ˡ hᵢ
 7:     for p ← 0 to k − 1 do
 8:         t ← p
 9:         for i ← 0 to l − 1 do
10:             r[i] ← t mod hᵢ
11:             t ← t/hᵢ
12:             x[i] ← r[i] << (i ∗ s[i])
13:         end for
14:     end for
15:     return x
16: end function
```

with prefix 00|01|01, implying a mapping to PE 5. Using the concise network representation, retrieving communication costs and evaluating Coco can be performed quickly for all edges of G_a. For an edge $e_a = (u_a, v_a) \in E_a$, the prefixes of u_a and v_a are used to compute the communication costs between $\mu(u_a)$ and $\mu(v_a)$, by returning the leftmost non-zero bit on the result of $xor(u_a, v_a)$. Overall, through the bit-label information, we can quickly refine an initial mapping using parallel label propagation. We use the size-constrained version of the algorithm and tailor the gain computations of a potential vertex move to account for the induced communication costs.

The optimization process works as follows: all PEs visit their local vertices in random order and consider moving a given vertex v into another block from the set of candidates $R(v) = \{\mu(u) : u \in N(v)\} \subseteq V_p$ ($N(v)$ is the neighborhood of v). The algorithm performs the move that induces the maximum improvement in Coco as long as the size constraint is respected. To compute the best block assignment, we temporarily move v to each block in $R(v)$ and calculate the communication cost for all possible block assignments; finally, we set $\mu(v) := \text{argmin}_{b \in R(v)} \left(\sum_{u \in N(v)} w(v, u) \, d_{G_p}(b, \mu(u)) \right)$. If the maximum reduction is induced by keeping the vertex in the current block, we do not perform any move. In Fig. 2a and for an implicit tree distance of $D = \{2, 4, 10\}$, the maximum reduction for vertex v, with label 00|01|01| ∗ ∗∗. After a certain number of moves, we do a global communication step to update the labels of the halo nodes of each PE. To handle overloaded blocks, we keep the same modifications to the block selection rule that was proposed in [24]. The process is repeated for a user-defined number of rounds. This is repeated for each refinement level and on the original graph.

3.3   Overall Approach

Here we present a more detailed description of the fully parallel mapping algorithm designed for distributed-memory systems. We implement our algorithm in PARHIP. For the coarsening step we use the parallel size-constrained label

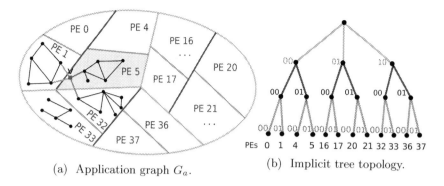

(a) Application graph G_a.

(b) Implicit tree topology.

Fig. 2. Mapping from G_a to the (implicit) tree topology: colored lines in (a) indicate the cuts induced by the tree levels in (b). The decimal PE numbers in (a) correspond to the combined bit-labels on a path from the root to the PE leaf in (b).

propagation as implemented in PARHIP, without any modifications. Each PE computes clusters of its local graph and aggregates them in super-vertices in parallel until the coarsened graph becomes small enough. The distributed coarse graph is then collected on each PE and is partitioned using a min-cut/max-flow algorithm within an evolutionary framework [31]. The best solution among all PEs is kept and broadcast back to them. For the uncoarsening step each PE performs a local search using the parallel size-constrained label propagation on their local part of the coarse graph. This step is repeated for each level of the hierarchy to refine the solution. At this point, we adapt the parallel label propagation to account for the communication overhead among PEs. More precisely, we modify the block selection step during vertex moving and we use the implicit topology representation to quickly retrieve the distance costs among PEs. During gain computation we change the objective from edgecut to Coco($\cdot$).

Avoiding Memory Issues. As already mentioned in Sect. 2.1, classic multilevel algorithms have high memory usage caused by multiple cycles of successive coarsening. Our algorithm performs only one cycle of the multilevel framework, but successive coarsening (even in one cycle) can still damage the scalability of our approach. Moreover, the previous implementation of PARHIP (without our contributions for parallel mapping) uses block partitioning for the initial data distribution.[5] Block partitioning of the input graph often leads to many inter-PE edges even before coarsening, in particular for complex networks. One reason for that is the high-degree nodes of complex networks, also known as hubs, when they become halo vertices. When the number of hubs being halo vertices becomes large enough, the scalability of PARHIP is negatively affected.

In our implementation we propose a simple correction for such instances to avoid high memory usage: first, all PEs globally identify halo nodes of high

---

[5] The initial data distribution is not a mapping solution, only an initial assignment of the input data to the PEs.

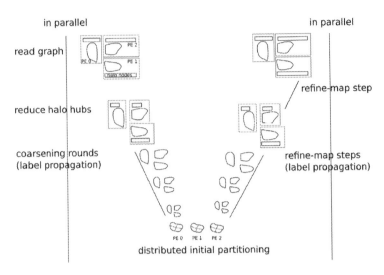

Fig. 3. Schematic interpretation of the parallel mapping for an example with three PEs and a partition in four blocks. The algorithm performs one multi-level cycle with additional pre- and post-processing steps to avoid memory issues.

degree (halo hubs) and then each PE temporarily removes edges connecting halo hubs with non-local nodes, creating a reduced local graph. Then each PE runs PARHIP_MAP on its reduced graph and after completion each PE re-introduces the removed edges. Once the one multilevel cycle is complete, we perform a few extra rounds of parallel label propagation on the original graph to compensate for quality losses due to the re-introduction of the removed edges. This way we avoid the high memory consumption and save communication during coarsening and initial partition steps without sacrificing much of the quality. A schematic interpretation of the overall parallel algorithm is given in Fig. 3.

4   Experiments

We perform experiments to evaluate the behavior of PARHIP_MAP on several graphs (see Table 1) downloaded from SNAP [22] or generated via KaGen [11] and ParMAT [18]. For disconnected graphs (in practice only some R-mat graphs) we extract the largest connected component. We implement PARHIP_MAP in C++, using the PARHIP graph API. For performance experiments, we compare against MPI-based partitioning tools, PARMETIS 4.0.3, PARHIP 3.10 (vanilla version configured to fastsocial) and XTRAPULP 0.3. As mentioned in Sect. 2.1, there are no direct competitors for MPI-based mapping solutions so we use partitioning with identity mapping. Often, identity mapping yields surprisingly good solutions, since it benefits from spatial locality [12]. Experiments were conducted on our local cluster[6] or the HLRN[7] cluster, Lise, in Berlin. Our local cluster contains 16 Linux machines, each equipped with an Intel Xeon X7460 CPU (2 sockets, 12 cores each), and 192 GB RAM. In Lise, each compute node has two Intel Cascade Lake Platinum 9242 CPUs with 384 GB RAM and 96 cores. Unless otherwise specified, we use one MPI process per compute node. We use the default settings for the competing algorithms, and similar build settings among all codes.[8] For all experiments, we report geometric mean results relative to PARHIP_MAP over all graphs (of Table 1). For each graph we repeat the experiment three times and we set the imbalance tolerance to 3%, one of the values used in [36] and in PARMETIS. To ensure reproducibility, all experiments were managed by SimexPal [2]. Our code and the experimental pipeline can be found at https://github.com/hu-macsy/KaHIP.

Table 1. 16 (undirected) graphs used in our experiments. Columns correspond to: name, type, number of vertices, number of edges, degree (average and max).

Network	Type	$|V|$	$|E|$	d_{avg}	d_{max}
coPapersCiteseer	REAL	434 102	16 036 720	73,8	1 188
eu-2005		862 664	16 138 468	37,4	68 963
as-skitter		1 696 415	11 095 298	13	35 455
orkut		3 072 441	117 184 899	76,2	33 313
dbpedia		18 265 512	136 535 446	14,9	612 308
friendster		65 608 366	1 806 067 135	55	612 308
twitter		52 515 193	1 963 197 641	74,7	3 691 240
r-mat (×3)	RMAT	$2^{22} - 2^{24}$	$2^{27} - 2^{29}$	40	18 484–63 345
barabasi-albert (×3)	BA	$2^{23} - 2^{27}$	$2^{26} - 2^{32}$	32	19 905–40 509
random-hyperbolic (×3)	RHG	$2^{25} - 2^{29}$	$2^{29} - 2^{33}$	16	83 645–200 165

4.1 Parallel Performance

We first evaluate the scalability behavior of PARHIP_MAP in a massively parallel setting of up to 3 072 PEs on Lise. In Fig. 4a we report running times for all parallel tools relative to PARHIP_MAP. The results indicate that PARHIP_MAP exhibits a good scaling behavior. Compared to the fastest tools i. e., XTRAPULP and PARMETIS, PARHIP_MAP is on average only 18% and 9% slower, respectively. The high speed of XTRAPULP is not surprising since it is designed to explicitly favor speed over quality. It is important to note that Fig. 4a depicts

---

[6] https://www2.hu-berlin.de/macsy/technical-overview.html.

[7] https://www.hlrn.de/.

[8] On our local cluster: g++ 8.3.1 compiler with -O2 flags and the mpich 3.2 MPI library. On Lise: g++ 9.2 compiler with -O2 flags and openmpi 3.1.5.

aggregated results that may hide out-of-memory or timeout issues. After examining the failing rates, we observed that PARHIP_MAP has the smallest failing rate (17%), followed by XTRAPULP, PARHIP and PARMETIS with failing rates of 42%, 62% and 65% respectively. To reflect a fairer comparison, we also include scalability experiments on our local cluster[9], where we observe a slightly better scaling behavior for PARHIP_MAP and similar trends for the other competitors (see Fig. 4b). It is noteworthy to report that PARHIP_MAP is the only tool that runs successfully for the twitter graph. Precisely, our algorithm maps the twitter graph (a graph in the billion-scale range) into 384 blocks on 48 PEs of our local cluster in less than 6 min. PARMETIS and PARHIP failed for almost all Barabasi-Albert and R-mat graphs, probably due to the highly irregular degree distribution of these graphs, leading to memory issues. Moreover, in

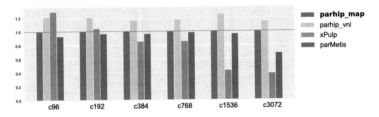

(a) Results for scaling PEs and constant number of blocks= 1536 on Lise.

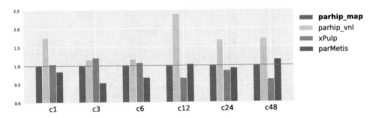

(b) Results for scaling PEs and constant number of blocks= 384 on our local cluster.

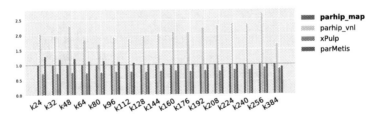

(c) Results for scaling number of blocks and constant number of PEs= 24 on our local cluster.

Fig. 4. Relative running times for different scaling experiments on various clusters.

---

[9] Here, we use one MPI process per core.

Fig. 4c we report scaling results for an increasing number of blocks. We clearly see that PARHIP_MAP is on average 2× faster than PARHIP, slightly faster than PARMETIS and only about 0.7× slower than XTRAPULP.

We also perform weak scaling experiments on Lise, for R-mat and random hyperbolic graphs of different sizes, for up to 768 and 1 536 PEs, respectively. For the experiment, we double the number of vertices as PEs double. The number of blocks is equal to the number of PEs used in the run and missing inputs are due to failing runs. In Fig. 5, we see that PARHIP_MAP has a similar scaling behavior as XTRAPULP while the latter is faster as already observed from strong scaling.

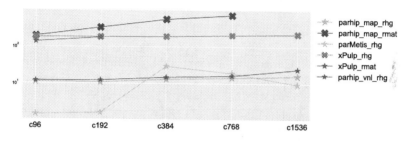

Fig. 5. Absolute running times for weak scaling experiments on Lise (logarithmic scale).

4.2 Quality Results

To evaluate the solution quality, we use the objectives Coco and edgecut and run all parallel competitors as well as a sequential mapping approach from KAHIP, named here KAHIP_MAP[10], known to produce mapping results of high quality [10]. In Fig. 6, we present relative Coco results for a constant number of PEs and an increasing number of blocks, since the latter often affects quality. For edgecut, we report results directly in the text, due to space limitations. Figure 6 shows that PARHIP_MAP achieves consistently the best Coco results compared to all other parallel approaches. More precisely, we are, on average, at least 4× better than XTRAPULP, 62% better than PARHIP, and 70% better than PARMETIS. Regarding edgecut, we are only 10% worse than the best competitor (PARHIP), 5% than PARMETIS, but 2.5× better than XTRAPULP. Those results are surprisingly good for our algorithm – given the fact that we do not optimize for edgecut, as the competitors do. Regarding the sequential baseline, KAHIP_MAP, we even achieve better quality (PARHIP_MAP is 10% better) and we are 30× faster using 24 PEs (as to 1 for KAHIP_MAP). Note that KAHIP_MAP, also fails to finish in time or has memory issues in many cases. Finally we should report that all tools occasionally fail to adhere to the balance constraint of 3% but do not largely overpass it either.

---

[10] Here, we set KAHIP_MAP to the fastsocial configuration.

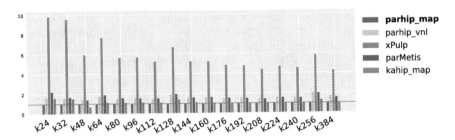

Fig. 6. Relative Coco results for 24 PEs (for the parallel tools). Lower is better.

5   Conclusions

In this work we propose a fully parallel mapping algorithm for distributed-memory systems. Our algorithm is an integrated solution *i. e.*, it addresses the partitioning and mapping problems simultaneously. We target hierachical systems and encode the hierarchy with a concise representation using bit-labels. Our approach exploits the above representation and uses parallel label propagation to devise a fast refinement process. As far as we know, this is the first parallel mapping algorithm for distributed-memory systems with a publicly available implementation (within PARHIP). Given the experimental results, our algorithm offers the best trade-off between mapping quality and speed compared to other MPI-based approaches. For future work we would like to integrate more scalable initial partitioning techniques (like the one proposed in [10]) to improve the performance of our current implementation.

Acknowledgements. This work was partially supported by the North-German Supercomputing Alliance (HLRN). We also thank our colleague Fabian Brandt-Tumescheit for his technical support regarding our group's cluster.

References

1. Aktulga, H.M., Yang, C., Ng, E.G., Maris, P., Vary, J.P.: Topology-aware mappings for large-scale eigenvalue problems. In: Kaklamanis, C., Papatheodorou, T., Spirakis, P.G. (eds.) Euro-Par 2012. LNCS, vol. 7484, pp. 830–842. Springer, Heidelberg (2012). https://doi.org/10.1007/978-3-642-32820-6_82
2. Angriman, E., et al.: Guidelines for experimental algorithmics: a case study in network analysis. Algorithms **12**(7), 127 (2019)
3. Barabási, A.L., Albert, R.: Emergence of scaling in random networks. Science **286**(5439), 509–512 (1999)
4. Bhatelé, A., Kalé, L.V., Kumar, S.: Dynamic topology aware load balancing algorithms for molecular dynamics applications. In: Proceedings of the 23rd International Conference on Supercomputing, pp. 110–116. ICS 2009. Association for Computing Machinery, New York, NY, USA (2009)

5. Bhatelé, A., Gupta, G.R., Kalé, L.V., Chung, I.: Automated mapping of regular communication graphs on mesh interconnects. In: 2010 International Conference on High Performance Computing, pp. 1–10 (2010)
6. Brandfass, B., Alrutz, T., Gerhold, T.: Rank reordering for MPI communication optimization. Comput. Fluids **80**, 372–380 (2013). https://doi.org/10.1016/j.compfluid.2012.01.019
7. Buluç, A., Meyerhenke, H., Safro, I., Sanders, P., Schulz, C.: Recent advances in graph partitioning. In: Algorithm Engineering - Selected Results and Surveys. Lecture Notes in Computer Science, vol. 9220, pp. 117–158 (2016)
8. Chan, S.Y., Ling, T.C., Aubanel, E.: The Impact of heterogeneous multi-core clusters on graph partitioning: an empirical study. Cluster Comput. **15**(3), 281–302 (2012)
9. Chen, H., Chen, W., Huang, J., Robert, B., Kuhn, H.: MPIPP: an automatic profile-guided parallel process placement toolset for SMP clusters and multiclusters. In: Proceedings of the 20th Annual International Conference on Supercomputing, pp. 353–360. ICS 2006. Association for Computing Machinery, New York, NY, USA
10. Faraj, M.F., van der Grinten, A., Meyerhenke, H., Träff, J.L., Schulz, C.: High-Quality Hierarchical Process Mapping. In: 18th International Symposium on Experimental Algorithms (SEA 2020), vol. 160, pp. 4:1–4:15. Dagstuhl, Germany (2020)
11. Funke, D., Lamm, S., Sanders, P., Schulz, C., Strash, D., von Looz, M.: Communication-free massively distributed graph generation. In: 2018 IEEE International Parallel and Distributed Processing Symposium, IPDPS 2018, May 21–May 25 2018, Vancouver, BC, Canada (2018)
12. Glantz, R., Meyerhenke, H., Noe, A.: Algorithms for mapping parallel processes onto grid and torus architectures. In: 23rd Euromicro International Conference on Parallel, Distributed and Network-Based Processing, PDP 2015, Turku, Finland, pp. 236–243 (2015)
13. Glantz, R., Predari, M., Meyerhenke, H.: Topology-induced enhancement of mappings. CoRR abs/1804.07131 (2018). http://arxiv.org/abs/1804.07131
14. Hoefler, T., Snir, M.: Generic topology mapping strategies for large-scale parallel architectures. In: ACM International Conference on Supercomputing (ICS 2011), pp. 75–85. ACM (2011)
15. Hoefler, T., Jeannot, E., Mercier, G.: An overview of process mapping techniques and algorithms in high-performance computing. In: High Performance Computing on Complex Environments, pp. 75–94. Wiley, June 2014
16. Jeannot, E., Mercier, G., Tessier, F.: Process placement in multicore clusters: algorithmic issues and practical techniques. IEEE Trans. Parallel Distrib. Syst. (99), p. 1 (2013). https://doi.org/10.1109/TPDS.2013.104
17. Jeannot, E., Mercier, G., Tessier, F.: Process placement in multicore clusters: algorithmic issues and practical techniques. IEEE Trans. Parallel Distrib. Syst. **25**(4), 993–1002 (2014)
18. Khorasani, F., Gupta, R., Bhuyan, L.N.: Scalable SIMD-efficient graph processing on GPUs. In: Proceedings of the 24th International Conference on Parallel Architectures and Compilation Techniques, pp. 39–50. PACT 2015 (2015)
19. Kirchbach, K.V., Schulz, C., Träff, J.L.: Better process mapping and sparse quadratic assignment. ACM J. Exp. Algorithmics **25**, 1–19 (2020)
20. Kirmani, S., Park, J., Raghavan, P.: An embedded sectioning scheme for multiprocessor topology-aware mapping of irregular applications. IJHPCA **31**(1), 91–103 (2017)

21. Kleinberg, J.: The small-world phenomenon: an algorithmic perspective. In: Proceedings of the Thirty-Second Annual ACM Symposium on Theory of Computing, pp. 163–170. STOC 2000. Association for Computing Machinery, New York, NY, USA (2000)

22. Leskovec, J.: Stanford Network Analysis Package (SNAP). http://snap.stanford.edu/index.html

23. Low, Y., Bickson, D., Gonzalez, J., Guestrin, C., Kyrola, A., Hellerstein, J.M.: Distributed graphlab: a framework for machine learning and data mining in the cloud. Proc. VLDB Endow. **5**(8), 716–727 (2012)

24. Meyerhenke, H., Sanders, P., Schulz, C.: Parallel graph partitioning for complex networks. IEEE Trans. Parallel Distributed Syst. **28**(9), 2625–2638 (2017)

25. Pellegrini, F.: Static mapping by dual recursive bipartitioning of process and architecture graphs. In: Scalable High-Performance Computing Conference (SHPCC), pp. 486–493. IEEE, May 1994

26. Pellegrini, F.: Scotch and libscotch 5.0 user's guide. Technical report, LaBRI, Université Bordeaux I, December 2007

27. Pellegrini, F.: Static mapping of process graphs. In: Graph Partitioning, chap. 5, pp. 115–136. John Wiley & Sons (2011)

28. Pellegrini, F.: Scotch and PT-scotch graph partitioning software: an overview. In: Naumann, U., Schenk, O. (eds.) Combinatorial Scientific Computing, pp. 373–406. CRC Press (2012)

29. Raghavan, U.N., Albert, R., Kumara, S.: Near linear time algorithm to detect community structures in large-scale networks. Phys. Rev. E **76**(3), 036106 (2007)

30. Salihoglu, S., Widom, J.: GPS: a graph processing system. In: Scientific and Statistical Database Management. Stanford InfoLab, July 2013

31. Sanders, P., Schulz, C.: Distributed evolutionary graph partitioning. In: Proceedings of the Meeting on Algorithm Engineering and Expermiments, pp. 16–29. ALENEX 2012, Society for Industrial and Applied Mathematics, USA (2012)

32. Sanders, P., Schulz, C.: Kahip v0.53 - karlsruhe high quality partitioning - user guide. CoRR abs/1311.1714 (2013)

33. Schloegel, K., Karypis, G., Kumar, V.: Parallel static and dynamic multi-constraint graph partitioning. Concurrency Comput. Pract. Experience **14**(3), 219–240 (2002)

34. Slota, G.M., Rajamanickam, S., Devine, K., Madduri, K.: Partitioning trillion-edge graphs in minutes. In: 2017 IEEE International Parallel and Distributed Processing Symposium (IPDPS), pp. 646–655 (2017)

35. Lee, S.-Y., Aggarwal: A mapping strategy for parallel processing. IEEE Trans. Comput. C-**36**(4), 433–442 (1987)

36. Walshaw, C., Cross, M.: JOSTLE: parallel multilevel graph-partitioning software - an overview. In: Magoules, F. (ed.) Mesh Partitioning Techniques and Domain Decomposition Techniques, pp. 27–58. Civil-Comp Ltd. (2007). (Invited chapter)

Pipelined Model Parallelism: Complexity Results and Memory Considerations

Olivier Beaumont, Lionel Eyraud-Dubois[✉], and Alena Shilova

Inria Bordeaux – Sud-Ouest, Université de Bordeaux, Bordeaux, France
`lionel.eyraud-dubois@inria.fr`

Abstract. The training phase in Deep Neural Networks has become an important source of computing resource usage and the resulting volume of computation makes it crucial to perform efficiently on parallel architectures. Data parallelism is the most widely used method, but it requires to replicate the network weights on all processors, and to perform collective communications of the network weights. In this context, model parallelism is an attractive alternative, in which the different layers of the network are distributed over the computing processors. Indeed, it is expected to better distribute weights (to cope with memory problems) and it eliminates the need for large collective communications since only forward activations are communicated. However, to be efficient, it must be combined with pipelining, which in turn induces new memory costs. In this paper, our goal is to formalize pipelined model parallelism as a scheduling problem, to establish its complexity, and to analyze the importance of the assumptions of contiguity and 1-periodicity, implicitly made in practical solutions such as PipeDream.

1 Introduction

Deep Neural Network (DNN) training is a long and memory-intensive operation. Indeed, DNN training requires performing numerous forward and backward computations, each on a subset of input data called a *batch*. In turn, each forward and backward phases involve complex data dependences and induce memory issues. In practice, parallel training is performed both on small groups of GPU machines and on large HPC infrastructures [19], especially because HPC machines offer high-bandwidth and low-latency networks [5,14].

The first approach to use parallelism at the level of the node is to make the best use of the available multi-core by optimizing the individual compute kernels, which usually consist of tensor computations. This approach has been widely used in the context of GPUs and TPUs and has made the success of frameworks such as TensorFlow [1] or PyTorch [17]. At a larger scale, the best known approach to parallel DNN training is the so-called data parallel approach. Using data parallelism [21], the model weights are replicated on all participating nodes. Then, different mini-batches are trained in parallel on different nodes: all participating nodes execute forward and backward phases in parallel, and thus

© Springer Nature Switzerland AG 2021
L. Sousa et al. (Eds.): Euro-Par 2021, LNCS 12820, pp. 183–198, 2021.
https://doi.org/10.1007/978-3-030-85665-6_12

all compute gradients for all weights in the network. Synchronization between the nodes takes place at the end of the backward step, and all gradients are collected and aggregated through collective communications. The above approach is possible as long as two conditions are fulfilled: (i) the communication network infrastructure must be able to support the collective communications of the weights without inducing too much idle time and (ii) each participating node must be able to store all network (model) weights and activations corresponding to the processing of a mini-batch.

In many cases deep and heavy models bring better prediction quality, but they may induce memory issues, which makes the training impossible. Several approaches were proposed to deal with this problem. In general, the memory consumption during the training phase is composed of two main parts [10]: the storage of forward activations (i.e. the outputs of all internal operations of the neural network) until the associated backward operation is performed and the storage of the network parameters (weights). To limit the memory requirements resulting from the storage of network weights, a natural approach, known as model parallelism is to distribute the different layers of the network onto different processors. Model parallelism has been recently advocated in many papers [6,11,15,20]. Each batch is then processed by a sequence of processors, and only activations are communicated between processors. This approach is orthogonal to data parallelism and can naturally be combined with it. Unfortunately, if batches are processed in sequence, model parallelism actually reduces memory requirements, but does not accelerate computations because of the data dependencies imposed by back-propagation, as shown in [11,15]. To obtain some speedup using this approach, it is necessary to process several batches in parallel, using a pipelined approach. As we will see, in turn, processing several mini-batches simultaneously induces extra memory requirements.

All known solutions for pipelined model parallelism [15,16] rely on a certain number of assumptions which make the problem tractable. In particular, they only consider (i) *contiguous* allocations, where each processor is assigned a contiguous set of layers of the network and (ii) 1-*periodic* greedy schedules, where all processors alternate between forward and backward computations. In this paper, our goal is to establish the complexity of both the resource allocation and the scheduling problem and to show that from a theoretical perspective, allowing more general solutions (non-contiguous allocations and k-periodic complex schedules with $k > 1$) can provide significant improvement in terms of throughput. The rest of the document is organized as follows. The related work is presented in Sect. 2. We introduce the notations and the computational model we use in Sect. 3. We establish several complexity results for the search of the optimal allocation of layers to resources in Sect. 4 and consider general periodic patterns in Sect. 5 and non-contiguous allocations in Sect. 6. Finally, conclusions and perspectives of this work are proposed in Sect. 7.

2   Related Works

To reduce the memory requirements related to the storage of forward activations, several approaches have been proposed: re-materialization, based on discarding and recomputing activations on demand [12,13] or offloading [3], based on moving some of the activations from the GPU memory to the CPU memory during the forward phase and then to bring them back in GPU memory when needed. Re-materialization is being increasingly employed to reduce memory usage and or practical use, an implementation[1] of re-materialization based on [2] has been proposed for PyTorch.

Another way of saving memory is to distribute memory load over multiple processors. In this way the authors of [18] managed to implement data parallelism using a distributed cache mechanism. Domain decomposition or spatial parallelism techniques can be used to limit the memory needed to store the forward activations. In [7], dividing large images into smaller ones makes it possible to train the network in parallel on the smaller images and a similar strategy has been proposed for channel and filter parallelism in [8].

Many papers [11,16] have recently explored the use of model parallelism, following the seminal contributions of [11] and [15]. In [20], the authors observe that the scheduling strategy proposed in PipeDream is not satisfactory to take communication costs into account and the number of models to be kept in memory has been improved in [16]. Performing pipelined model parallelism efficiently requires to solve two issues: an efficient allocation of layers of the network to the processors, and a schedule describing how to perform the corresponding operations over time. Most of the papers [11,15,16,20] solve these problems separately, and mostly focus on the first one. However, the actual memory usage strongly depends on the actual schedule, so that these solutions typically require to reduce the throughput at runtime to make sure that the data fits in the processor memory.

3   Model and Notations

3.1   Notations

Like in the papers mentioned above [15,16,20], we consider linear (or linearized) DNNs, in which each forward operation only depends on the result of the previous operation, so that the network is a chain of L layers (see Fig. 1). Each layer l, $1 \leq l \leq L$ is associated to both a forward operation F_l and a backward operation B_l (see Fig. 1). During one iteration of the training process, the input activation $a^{(0)}$ goes through all forward operations to compute a prediction, the quality of which is estimated by a *loss* value $\mathcal{L}$. Then, the parameter weights of all layers have to be updated according to their effect on the loss, given by the partial derivative $\frac{\partial \mathcal{L}}{\partial a^{(l)}}$, where the updates are performed by an *optimizer*, following some predefined strategy. Overall, data dependencies are depicted in

---

[1] https://gitlab.inria.fr/hiepacs/rotor.

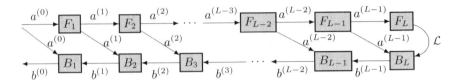

Fig. 1. Dependency DAG for forward-backward propagation

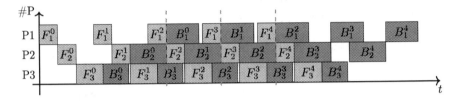

Fig. 2. Pipelined schedule for 3 layers, 3 processors, and 4 iterations. The superscripts indicate iteration numbers. Period is highlighted with dashed lines.

Fig. 1. The training phase consists in many successive iterations of this process, until convergence.

We denote by $a^{(l)}$ the activation tensor output of $F_l, l \leq L$ and by $b^{(l)} = \frac{\partial \mathcal{L}}{\partial a^{(l)}}$ the back-propagated intermediate value provided as input of the backward operation B_l. In the following, we use the following notations:

- u_{F_l} denotes the duration of the forward task on the layer l; u_{B_l} denotes the duration of the backward task on the layer l;
- W_l denotes the memory occupation of the parameter weights for layer l;
- a_l denotes the memory occupation of the activation $a^{(l)}$ produced by F_l;
- a_l also corresponds to the memory occupation of the gradient $b^{(l)}$ produced by B_{l+1}, as each gradient has the same size as the activation with respect to which it is calculated.

The goal of model parallelism is to distribute the layers of the DNN onto P computing resources (typically GPUs denoted as processors in the rest of the paper) with limited memory M, so that each processor is in charge of a subset of the layers. The input activation thus goes through all processors to compute the loss $\mathcal{L}$, and is then back-propagated through all layers in reverse order to compute the corresponding gradients and update the weights. To avoid idle times, these computations are performed in a *pipelined* way (see Fig. 2): the GPU in charge of layer l may compute several forward operations F_l before processing the first backward B_l, so that it could stay busy even while waiting for $b^{(l)}$ to be computed by the other GPUs.

Throughout this paper, we are interested in finding efficient task allocations and schedules. To help navigate the different concepts that we use, we introduce some terminology. We define the input DNN as a chain of *layers* (typically convolutional or dense layers), which are the basic operations that need to be

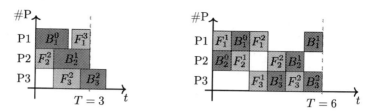

(a) 1-periodic pattern for the schedule (b) 2-periodic pattern for 3 layers where of Figure 2. $u_F = u_B = 1$.

Fig. 3. Examples of periodic patterns. The superscripts indicate shift values.

computed, and a *partitioning* $\mathcal{P}$ of this chain is a collection of *stages*, where each stage contains a contiguous set of layers. An *allocation* is an assignment of stages to the processors. An allocation is said to be *contiguous* if each processor is assigned a single stage, and by extension a partitioning is contiguous if it contains at most P stages. To estimate memory requirements we also introduce *groups* of stages, where each group is a set of stages which are contiguous with respect to the ordering of the network chain.

The model described above assumes that communication times are negligible, but we can remark that all our results can be generalized to the case where communications are taken into account (the same observation was made in [20]). Indeed, for a fixed allocation, each communication between layer l on processor p and layer $l+1$ on processor p' can be represented as an additional computation layer. It involves sending some activation $a^{(l)}$ between F_l on p and F_{l+1} on p', and a gradient $b^{(l)}$ between B_{l+1} on p' and B_l on p, for a total time of $\frac{2a_l}{\beta}$, where β is the bandwidth of the corresponding link. Therefore, an allocation on P processors with communication costs is equivalent to an allocation on $2P - 1$ resources, without communication costs.

A *schedule* $\mathcal{S}$ of a given allocation specifies the timings of all compute operations. In order to keep the description of schedules compact, we actually only focus on periodic schedules. A schedule is periodic if it consists in the repetition of a pattern, and more precisely k-periodic if the pattern contains each computation layer (forward and backward) exactly k times. We consider k-periodic patterns of period T, which specify for each operation (forward and backward): the processor in charge of it, a starting time t, and an index shift h. This pattern is to be repeated indefinitely: in the j-th period, this operation starts at time $jT + t$ and processes the batch number $jk + h$. By convention the shift of the first B_1 operation of the pattern is always 0, so that if in some period this B_1 processes batch index i, an operation with shift h processes batch index $i + h$. A pattern is valid if the schedule obtained in this way is valid, *i.e.* fulfills the dependencies of Fig. 1. Figure 3a shows an example of the 1-periodic pattern associated with the schedule of Figs. 2 and 3b shows a 2-periodic pattern. Figure 3b exhibits a case where idle time is introduced in the schedule for memory-related reasons, as explained below.

3.2   Memory Constraints

In addition to enforcing data dependencies, we need to ensure that the schedules fit into the memory capacity M of the processors. As already noted, during the training phase, there are two main sources of memory usage: parameter weights, and forward activations. As discussed in [16], it is sufficient to keep two versions of the parameter weights. Moreover, as discussed in [18], a certain number of additional copies of the model, for gradients and optimizer states, are required. Their number only depends on the choice of the optimizer and not on the allocation or on the schedule. Overall, we denote with W_l the overall memory load induced by assigning layer l to a processor. On the other hand, with pipelined executions, several forward activations of a given layer l need to be stored in memory at the same time, and this depends on the particular schedule. For instance, in the case of Fig. 2, F_1^2, F_1^3 and F_1^4 simultaneously reside in memory before B_1^2 releases F_1^2.

For a schedule $\mathcal{S}$, we define the *number of concurrent activations* (NCA) of layer l as the maximum number of activations $a^{(l)}$ that are stored at any time. For a general schedule, it can be expressed as $\text{NCA}_l = \max_t \#F_l(t' < t) - \#B_l(t' < t)$, where $\#F_l(t' < t)$ denotes the number of F_l operations performed until time t. For a k-periodic schedule $\mathcal{S}$, NCA_l can be computed from the values of the shifts: for any F_l whose shift is h, if the preceding B_l has shift h', then the number of concurrent activations just after this forward operation is $h - h'$. The value of NCA_l for $\mathcal{S}$ is thus the maximum value of $h - h'$ over all forward operations F_l. As an example, in the pattern of Fig. 3a, $\text{NCA}_1 = 3$ and $\text{NCA}_2 = 2$ (here it is necessary to duplicate the pattern to find the preceding B_2), while for the pattern of Fig. 3b, $\text{NCA}_1 = \text{NCA}_2 = 2$. Given a schedule $\mathcal{S}$, if a processor p processes a set of layers L_p, its maximal memory usage is given by $M^{\mathcal{S}}(p) = \sum_{l \in L_p} W_l + \text{NCA}_l a_l$.

Formal Optimization Problem. We can now formally define the scheduling problem for model parallelism. We are given P homogeneous processors with memory M and L layers with forward and backward computation times u_{F_l} and u_{B_l}, parameter occupation W_l and activation sizes a_l. A solution is represented by an allocation and a corresponding valid k-periodic schedule $\mathcal{S}$ with a period T, so that for all processors p, $M^{\mathcal{S}}(p) \leq M$, and our objective is to find a solution which minimizes the normalized period T/k.

4   Complexity Results

In this section, we analyze the complexity of above problem. We first show that even without memory constraints, finding an optimal allocation is a hard problem. Then we consider the problem of finding a pattern for a fixed allocation, and show that this problem is also NP-hard. In both cases, we use a reduction from the **3-partition problem** [9]: given a set of integers $\{x_1, x_2, \ldots, x_{3m}\}$ such that $\sum_i x_i = mV$, is it possible to partition it into m parts $\{S_1, \ldots, S_m\}$ so that for any $j \leq m$, $|S_j| = 3$ and $\sum_{i \in S_j} x_i = V$. This problem is known to be NP-hard in the strong sense.

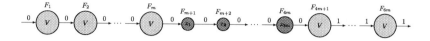

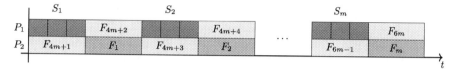

Fig. 4. Network instance for the proof of Theorem 2

Fig. 5. Valid pattern for the proof of Theorem 2

Theorem 1. *The decision problem of determining if there exists an allocation and a periodic pattern whose normalized period is at most T is strongly NP-Complete.*

Proof. Given an instance of 3-partition, we consider the following instance of our problem:

- $L = 3m$, $P = m$;
- $\forall l$, $a_l = W_l = 0$, so that memory constraints are not a concern;
- $\forall l \leq L$, $u_{F_l} = x_l$ and $u_{B_l} = 0$ (actually we can use any choice of values such that $u_{F_l} + u_{B_l} = x_l$).

and the decision problem is to determine if there exists a periodic schedule with period $T = V$.

Let us assume that there exists a solution to the 3-Partition instance. Then, we build a pattern where each group S_i is scheduled (in any order) on a different processor. There always exists a shift assignment such that the schedule is valid. Since there is no memory issues (all sizes are set to 0), we obtain a valid 1-periodic schedule.

Let us now assume that there exists a pattern of normalized period T. Then, since one layer cannot be split between two processors, each processor is allocated to different layers for a total duration at most T. Since the overall load is mT, the load on each GPU must be exactly T. □

In what follows, we prove that even when the allocation is given, *i.e.* if we know which layer is assigned to which processor, the problem remains strongly NP-Complete, so that both the allocation (Theorem 1) and the scheduling (Theorem 2) problems are hard. In this case, given a memory limit M and a task allocation on P processors, the goal is to schedule tasks in periodical manner so that the resulting period is minimal.

Theorem 2. *The allocation of layers being fixed, the decision problem of determining if there exists a periodic schedule of normalized period at most T is NP-Complete in the strong sense.*

Proof. Given an instance of 3-partition, we consider the following instance of our problem, where the network is depicted in Fig. 4 and the processing resources are defined as follows:

- $L = 6m$, $P = 2$, $M = m$, the target period is $T = 2mV$ and $\forall l, W_l = 0$;
- $u_{B_l} = 0$ for all l; $a_l = 0$ if $l \leq 4m$ and $a_l = 1$ otherwise;
- $u_{F_l} = V$ for $l \leq m$ or $l \geq 4m + 1$, and $u_{F_l} = x_{l-m}$ for $m + 1 \leq l \leq 4m$;
- P_1 is assigned to all layers l for $m + 1 \leq l \leq 4m$, and to even layers $4m + 2, 4m + 4, \ldots, 6m$; P_2 is assigned to all layers l for $l \leq m$, and to odd layers $4m + 1, 4m + 3, \ldots, 6m - 1$.

Let us assume that there exists a solution to the 3-Partition instance. Then, we build a pattern where each group S_i is scheduled as depicted in Fig. 5. Since $W_l = 0$ for all l, the memory costs come from storing the activations. Moreover, all operations $F_l, l \geq 4m + 1$ can use the same shift value. Since activation sizes a_l are zero for $l \leq 4m$, the shift values of the other forward operations have no effect on the memory usage and can thus be chosen in a way that makes the pattern valid. Therefore, each layer $l \geq 4m + 1$ has $\text{NCA}_l = 1$, so the memory usage on each processor is exactly m. This shows that there exists a valid pattern of throughput T where all constraints are satisfied.

Let us now assume that there exists a valid schedule S of period T. For simplicity, we assume that S is 1-periodic; however all the arguments can be generalized to a k-periodic schedule. We first prove that operation $F_{4m+1}, \ldots, F_{6m}$ are scheduled as depicted in Fig. 5. Since NCA values are at least 1 and the memory capacity is m, the pattern must satisfy $\text{NCA}_l = 1$ for these layers. Denote by h the shift of F_{6m}; it is easy to see that it is best for all B_l operations (whose durations are negligible) to be performed just after F_{6m} with the same shift h. Hence, the only way to obtain $\text{NCA}_l = 1$ for $l \geq 4m + 1$ is to process F_j just before F_{j+1} with the same shift value h. Since S has period $T = 2mV$, there can be no idle time between these operations. Therefore, operations $F_{4m+1}, \ldots, F_{6m}$ are scheduled as depicted in Fig. 5.

Then, the operations $F_{m+1}, \ldots, F_{4m}$ with durations x_i need to be scheduled on P_1, where there are exactly m holes of size V. Hence, the packing on these tasks into the holes creates a solution to the initial 3-partition instance, what completes the NP-Completeness proof.   □

5   General Periodic Schedules for Contiguous Allocations

In this section, we analyze in more details the scheduling aspect of our problem. In the following, we thus consider that the allocation is fixed and contiguous and scheduling is done at the stage level (sets of consecutive layers), as scheduling inside stages is straightforward, which is equivalent to the special case of a network of length P to be processed on P processors. We present two results in this context: we first show how to compute, for a given period T, a 1-periodic pattern which minimizes the memory usage; then we provide examples showing the benefit of using k-periodic schedules for $k > 1$. To simplify the presentation, we use the notations bound to stages. For example, for stage s_i we compose all forward operations and backward operations inside a stage into one forward step F_{s_i} and one backward step B_{s_i}. We also denote $U(s_i)$ as the total sum of all computational costs of some stage s_i.

5.1 Optimal 1-Periodic Schedules

The authors of [15] propose a 1F1B schedule, which is a particular case of greedy, 1-periodic schedule where the number of concurrent activations of the first stage is $\text{NCA}_1 = P$. For unbalanced allocations, especially when taking communications into account, this can be too conservative. To reduce the number of concurrent activations, we propose the $1F1B^*(T)$ algorithm to compute a pattern for some fixed contiguous allocation $\mathcal{P}$ and a given period T. This algorithm works in three phases, described in Algorithm 1.

Algorithm 1. Summary of Algorithm $1F1B^*$ for a given period T.

Build G groups greedily such that $\sum_{s \in g} U(s) \leq T$, starting from s_P
Schedule operations within group g as an Equal Shift Pattern
Connect the groups with no idle time between the forward operations

---

Phase 1: Groups are built such that each group g satisfies the condition $\sum_{s \in g} U(s) \leq T$. This is done iteratively: start from the last stage s_P, add stages $s_{P-1}, s_{P-2}, \ldots$ as long as the condition is fulfilled, then start a new group with the last stage that was not added. This leads to G groups; for simplicity, groups are numbered in the order of their creation, so that group 1 contains s_P and group G contains s_1.

Phase 2: Operations inside a given group g are scheduled with an Equal Shift Pattern where backward operations have a fixed shift h, and forward operations have shift $h + g - 1$.

Definition 1 (Equal Shift Pattern). *An Equal Shift Pattern (V-shape) is a part of a schedule in which consecutive forward operations are performed one after the other on their respective processors with the same shift h, followed by the sequence of corresponding backward operations, all having the same index shift h'. On each processor, the time between the forward operation and the corresponding backward is idle (as in Fig. 6a).*

Phase 3: All these group schedules are then connected: to connect group $g = (s_i, \ldots, s_j)$ and group $g - 1 = (s_{j+1}, \ldots, s_k)$, the schedule starts $F_{s_{j+1}}$ just after F_{s_j}, with the same index shift. After this connection, if any operation starts later than T, its starting time is lowered by T and its index shift decreased by 1 (see Fig. 6b).

It is easy to see that this algorithm produces a valid pattern. In the following, we prove that for a given period T, the $1F1B^*$ pattern minimizes the NCA of

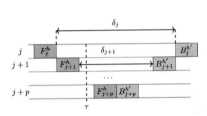

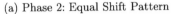

(a) Phase 2: Equal Shift Pattern

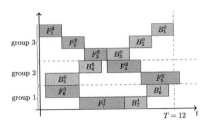

(b) Phase 3: Example of a 1F1B* schedule with 3 groups.

Fig. 6. Scheduling groups in 1F1B*

all layers, among all 1-periodic patterns. For this purpose, we start by showing that the Equal Shift Pattern is necessary to avoid increasing the NCA between two stages[2].

Lemma 1. *Consider any schedule $\mathcal{S}$ for a contiguous partitioning $\mathcal{P}$. If successive stages verify $\mathrm{NCA}_{s_j} = \cdots = \mathrm{NCA}_{s_{j+p}}$, then $\mathcal{S}$ contains a Equal Shift Pattern for these stages.*

Proof. Since $\mathcal{S}$ fulfills the dependencies described in Fig. 1, then

$$\forall s, \forall t, (\#F_s(t' < t) - \#F_{s-1}(t' < t)) \leq 0 \leq (\#B_s(t' < t) - \#B_{s-1}(t' < t)),$$

so that $\forall t, (\#F_s(t' < t) - \#B_s(t' < t)) \leq (\#F_{s-1}(t' < t) - \#B_{s-1}(t' < t))$ and $\mathrm{NCA}_s^{\mathcal{S}} \leq \mathrm{NCA}_{s-1}^{\mathcal{S}}$. Let us consider stage j, we have $\mathrm{NCA}_{s_j} = \mathrm{NCA}_{s_{j+1}}$. Therefore, there exists a time τ in $\mathcal{S}$ when the memory peak is reached for both stage s_{j+1} and stage s_j, which is only possible if $\#F_{s_{j+1}}(t' < \tau) = \#F_{s_j}(t' < \tau)$ and $\#B_{s_{j+1}}(t' < \tau) = \#B_{s_j}(t' < \tau)$. This shows that F_{s_j} and $F_{s_{j+1}}$ process the same batch (and similarly for B_{s_j} and $B_{s_{j+1}}$). Furthermore, since memory peaks always take place after forward operations, no operation can take place for stage s_j between the end of F_{s_j} and the start of B_{s_j}: the input data for B_{s_j} needs to be produced by $B_{s_{j+1}}$, and processing another forward operation F_{s_j} would increase NCA_{s_j}. Recursively, for any $k \leq p$, all forward operations $F_{s_{j+k}}$ process the same batch, and no operation can take place for stage s_{j+k} between the end of $F_{s_{j+k}}$ and the start of $B_{s_{j+k}}$, which concludes the proof. □

Theorem 3. *Consider a contiguous partitioning $\mathcal{P}$ and any 1-periodic schedule $\mathcal{S}$ of period T. For any layer l, the schedule $\mathcal{S}$ does not use fewer concurrent activations than the schedule $1F1B^*(T)$, i.e. $\forall l, \mathrm{NCA}_l^{1F1B^*} \leq \mathrm{NCA}_l^{\mathcal{S}}$.*

Proof. It is easy to see that in $1F1B^*$, a layer l of group g has $\mathrm{NCA}_l^{1F1B^*} = g$. Assume that in $\mathcal{S}$, $\mathrm{NCA}_{s_j} = \mathrm{NCA}_{s_{j+1}} = \cdots = \mathrm{NCA}_{s_{j+p}}$ for some j and p. By Lemma 1, there is an Equal Shift Pattern for stages s_j to s_{j+p}, so if we denote by δ_j the delay between F_{s_j} and the next B_{s_j} (see Fig. 6a), we have $\delta_j \geq \delta_{j+1} +$

---

[2] all layers of the same stage have the same NCA.

$U(s_{j+1})$, and recursively, $\delta_j \geq \sum_{k=j+1}^{j+p} U(s_k)$. Since the period T is the time between two executions of F_{s_j} in $\mathcal{S}$, it is clear that $T \geq U(s_j) + \delta_j$, which yields: if $\mathrm{NCA}_{s_j} = \cdots = \mathrm{NCA}_{s_{j+p}}$, then $T \geq \sum_{k=j}^{j+p} U(s_k)$. By contradiction, assume now that for some stage s_i, the schedule $\mathcal{S}$ uses fewer concurrent activations than the 1F1B* schedule, i.e. $\mathrm{NCA}_{s_i} < g_i$, where g_i is the group number of stage s_i, and consider the largest such index i (for larger indices $j > i$, we thus have $\mathrm{NCA}_{s_j} = g_j$). Denote by $s_{i+1}, \ldots, s_{i+p}$ the group of stage s_{i+1}, so that $\mathrm{NCA}_{s_i} = \mathrm{NCA}_{s_{i+1}} = \cdots = \mathrm{NCA}_{s_{i+p}} = g_{i+1} < g_i$. By the previous result, $T \geq \sum_{k=i}^{i+p} U(s_k)$. However, according to the 1F1B* procedure, $g_i > g_{i+1}$ means that stage s_i could not fit in the group of s_{i+1}, which can only happen if $T < \sum_{k=i}^{i+p} U(s_k)$. This results in a contradiction and completes the proof.   □

For a fixed partitioning, all other memory requirements are constant and do not depend on the schedule, so that 1F1B* schedule is optimal with respect to memory usage among all valid 1-periodic patterns. Note that in case when each group consists of only one stage, 1F1B* behaves as 1F1B schedule used in [15].

5.2 k-Periodic Schedules

Theorem 4. $\forall k$, k-periodic schedules are sometimes necessary to reach optimal throughput, i.e. there are examples where no j-periodic schedule with $j < k$ is able to provide the same throughput as a k-periodic schedule.

Proof. For a given k, let us consider an instance where $P = L = k + 1$, and $M = k + 1$. All layers have the same durations[3] $u_{F_l} = u_{B_l} = 1$ and activation sizes $a_l = 1$, and different weights: $W_1 = 1$, $W_{l+1} = l$ for $l \geq 1$. For such an instance, the memory constraints imply that any valid schedule should satisfy $\mathrm{NCA}_1 \leq k$, and $\mathrm{NCA}_{l+1} \leq k + 1 - l$ for $1 \leq l \leq k$.

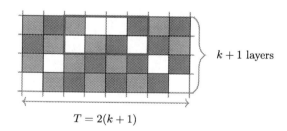

$$T = 2(k+1)$$

Fig. 7. k-periodic pattern for an homogeneous instance. The Equal Shift Pattern is highlighted in thick red. (Color figure online)

Let us consider the k-periodic schedule obtained by unrolling the standard 1-periodic pattern with no idle times, and removing all operations related to every

---

[3] Our arguments actually apply to any homogeneous case where $u_{F_l} + u_{B_l}$ is constant over all layers l.

$(k+1)$-th batch. The resulting pattern has period $2(k+1)$ and normalized period $2(1 + \frac{1}{k})$. It is depicted on Fig. 7 for $k = 3$. The highlighted Equal Shift Pattern shows how this pattern ensures $\text{NCA}_1 = k$. On the other hand, consider any j-periodic schedule S which satisfies the memory constraints. Since $\text{NCA}_1^S \leq k$, and since NCA_l values are non-increasing with l, there must exist a layer l such that $\text{NCA}_l^S = \text{NCA}_{l+1}^S$. From Lemma 1, there is necessarily a Equal Shift Pattern between these layers, during which layer l is idle for at least $u_F + u_B = 2$ units of time. The period T^S of S is thus at least $2j + 2$, leading to a normalized period at least $2(1 + \frac{1}{j})$. If $j < k$, this is always higher than the normalized period of the k-periodic pattern described above.   □

This example shows the benefit of considering more general schedules than the 1-periodic patterns usually explored in the literature [15]. Furthermore, the simple k-periodic pattern used in this proof can easily be applied to many practical cases where memory capacity is limited. Indeed, for a given contiguous allocation with P stages, all such k-periodic patterns for $k < P$ explore a tradeoff between throughput and memory usage: lower values of k have higher normalized period, but lower values of NCA_l.

6   Contiguous Vs General Allocations

Despite being widely used in practice, contiguous allocations can impose significant limitations on the performance. In this section we compare the non-contiguous allocations with the contiguous ones, and we show that in general non-contiguous allocations can reach a throughput which can be up to two times greater than the one of contiguous allocations, when memory is not a bottleneck. While under memory constraints, the improvement in the performance can be arbitrarily high. At the same time, as the non-contiguous allocations are more flexible, they could be the only possible option to execute some large models. Unlike the previous section, any resource can now accommodate an arbitrary set of layers (that can be non-consecutive), thus we do not use the notions of stages and groups anymore. Moreover, we talk about processing costs of layers as their combined computing times of forward and backward operations.

6.1   Without Memory Constraints

As a simple starting example, a chain with 3 layers should be processed on 2 processors, where the processing costs of each layer are 1, 2 and 1 respectively. It is clear that the smallest period achievable by a contiguous allocation is 3: the second layer is sharing resource either with the first or the last layers. On the other hand, a non-contiguous allocation allows to run the first and last layers on one processor, and the layer of cost 2 on the other processor, resulting in a period of 2 and no idle time on any processor. The overhead of the contiguous constraint is thus $\frac{3}{2}$ in this case. The following theorem shows that the exact ratio is actually 2 in the worst case.

Theorem 5. *On any chain, the period of the best contiguous allocation is at most twice the period of the best non contiguous allocation. Furthermore, for any $k \geq 1$, there exists a chain for which the period of the best contiguous allocation is $2 - \frac{1}{k}$ times larger than the best allocation.*

Proof. To prove the first result, consider any chain C, and denote by T^* the period of the best non constrained allocation for this chain. Clearly $T^* \geq \frac{\sum_l u_{F_l} + u_{B_l}}{P}$, and $T^* \geq \max_l(u_{F_l} + u_{B_l})$. We can build a contiguous allocation with period at most $2T^*$ with a greedy Next Fit procedure: add layers to the first processor as long as the total load is below $2T^*$, move to the next processor and repeat. Since no layer has cost more than T^*, each processor except maybe the last one has load at least T^*. This shows that this procedure ends before running out of processors.

Let us now prove the second statement, with an example inspired from [4]. For any $k \geq 1$, let us set $\epsilon = \frac{1}{2k+1}$. Let $P = 2k + 1$, and let us build the chain C_k with $k + 1$ parts: the first k parts contain 4 layers with computation costs $(k, \epsilon, k - 1, \epsilon)$; the last part contains one layer of cost k, $(k - 2)(2k + 1) + 1$ layers of cost ϵ, and one layer of cost 1. Note that the total number of layers of cost ϵ is $2k + (k - 2)(2k + 1) + 1 = (k - 1)(2k + 1)$.

There exists an allocation with period $T^* = k$ for chain C_k: $k + 1$ processors process a layer of cost k, 1 processor processes a layer of cost $k - 1$ and the layer of cost 1, and $k - 1$ processors process a layer of cost $k - 1$ and $2k + 1$ layers of cost ϵ. In this allocation, no processor has any idle time.

Chain C_k contains $2k + 2$ layers with cost at least 1. On any contiguous allocation on $2k + 1$ processors, at least one processor p processes two such layers. If it processes one layer of cost k and one of cost $k - 1$, it also processes the layer of cost ϵ between them, and thus its load is at least as $2k - 1 + \epsilon$. If it processes the layer of cost 1 and the last layer of cost k, it also processes all layers of cost ϵ in between, for a total load at least $k + ((k - 2)(2k + 1) + 1)\epsilon + 1 = 2k - 1 + \epsilon$. This shows that there is no contiguous allocation with period $2k - 1$ or less, which concludes the proof.   □

6.2   With Memory Constraints

The situation is worse when we explicitly take memory into account. Further, for the sake of simplicity, we do not consider activation sizes but model weights only.

Lemma 2. *Non contiguous allocations are sometimes required in order to process training under memory constraints.*

Proof. It is easy to see on the following example: the chain with 3 layers, whose weights W_l are respectively 1, 2 and 1, and it should be executed on 2 processors with memory limit M equal to 2. In such case, contiguous allocations are not possible, as they demand at least a memory of size 3. On the other hand, with non-contiguous allocations allowed, first and the third layers can be placed on

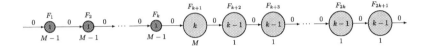

Fig. 8. Bad ratio configuration for contiguous allocations under memory constraint

one device, leaving the second layer alone on the other device, which provides a valid allocation.   □

Theorem 6. *If there exist both a valid contiguous allocation and a valid non-contiguous allocation given a memory constraint, then the ratio between achieved throughputs in the non contiguous and contiguous settings can be arbitrarily large.*

Proof. Let us consider the chain depicted in Fig. 8. For an arbitrarily chosen k, this chain consists of a sequence of k layers with processing cost 1 and model weight $M - 1$, followed by a layer with processing cost k and model weight M and followed by k layers with processing cost $k - 1$ and model weight 1. We want to execute this chain on $P = k + 2$ resources with memory limit $M \geq k$.

Then, a valid solution consists in grouping, $\forall i \leq P$ layer i and layer $k + i + 1$ on processor i, to dedicate processor $k + 1$ to layer $k + 1$ and to leave processor $k + 2$ idle. The required memory $M - 1 + 1$ can fit into the memory and the processing time on each resource is $k + 1$. This gives us a final period $T^* = k$.

If we use contiguous allocation, the first $k + 1$ layers must be on separate processors, because of the memory constraint. Then, the last k layers must be on the last remaining processor, that should be feasible due to $M \geq k$. In such scenario, the period is at least as $k(k - 1)$, which is $k - 1$ times larger than the one of non-contiguous allocation, which concludes the proof.   □

7   Conclusion

In this paper, we consider the possibility of applying model parallelism, which is an attractive parallelization strategy that allows in particular not to replicate all the weights of the network on all the computation resources. Following the ideas proposed in PipeDream [15] we consider the combination of pipelining and model parallelism, which allows to obtain a better resource utilization. Then, model parallelism can be enhanced with data parallelism to improve scalability.

Nevertheless, the combination of pipelining and model parallelism requires to store more activations at the nodes, which in turn causes memory consumption problems. The practical solutions proposed in the literature rely on a number of hypotheses, and limit the search to greedy 1-periodic schedules and contiguous allocations. On the contrary, we analyze in detail the complexity of the underlying scheduling and resource allocation problems, and prove that these hypotheses prevent, in the general case, to find optimal solutions. This work therefore opens up many perspectives, exposing the limits of current practical solutions and formalizing a scheduling problem that is difficult and very useful in practice.

References

1. Abadi, M., et al.: TensorFlow: a system for large-scale machine learning. In: 12th USENIX Symposium on Operating Systems Design and Implementation, OSDI 2016, pp. 265–283 (2016)
2. Beaumont, O., Eyraud-Dubois, L., Herrmann, J., Joly, A., Shilova, A.: Optimal checkpointing for heterogeneous chains: how to train deep neural networks with limited memory. Research Report RR-9302, Inria Bordeaux Sud-Ouest, November 2019
3. Beaumont, O., Eyraud-Dubois, L., Shilova, A.: Optimal GPU-CPU offloading strategies for deep neural network training. In: Proceeding of EuroPar 2020 (2020)
4. Boyar, J., Epstein, L., Levin, A.: Tight results for next fit and worst fit with resource augmentation. Theor. Comput. Sci. **411**(26), 2572–2580 (2010)
5. Chu, C.-H., Kousha, P., Awan, A.A., Khorassani, K.S., Subramoni, H., Panda, D.K.: NV-group: link-efficient reduction for distributed deep learning on modern dense GPU systems. In: Proceedings of the 34th ACM International Conference on Supercomputing, pp. 1–12 (2020)
6. Dean, J., et al.: Large scale distributed deep networks. In: Advances in Neural Information Processing Systems, pp. 1223–1231 (2012)
7. Dryden, N., Maruyama, N., Benson, T., Moon, T., Snir, M., Van Essen, B.: Improving strong-scaling of CNN training by exploiting finer-grained parallelism. In: IEEE International Parallel and Distributed Processing Symposium. IEEE Press (2019)
8. Dryden, N., Maruyama, N., Moon, T., Benson, T., Snir, M., Van Essen, B.: Channel and filter parallelism for large-scale CNN training. In: Proceedings of the International Conference for High Performance Computing, Networking, Storage and Analysis, p. 10. ACM (2019)
9. Garey, M.R., Johnson, D.S.: Computers and Intractability, vol. 174. Freeman, San Francisco (1979)
10. Glorot, X., Bengio, Y.: Understanding the difficulty of training deep feedforward neural networks. In: Proceedings of the 13th International Conference on Artificial Intelligence and Statistics, pp. 249–256 (2010)
11. Huang, Y., et al.: GPipe: efficient training of giant neural networks using pipeline parallelism. In: Advances in Neural Information Processing Systems, pp. 103–112 (2019)
12. Jain, P., et al.: Checkmate: breaking the memory wall with optimal tensor rematerialization (2019)
13. Kusumoto, M., Inoue, T., Watanabe, G., Akiba, T., Koyama, M.: A graph theoretic framework of recomputation algorithms for memory-efficient backpropagation. arXiv preprint arXiv:1905.11722 (2019)
14. Liu, J., Yu, W., Wu, J., Buntinas, D., Panda, D.K., Wyckoff, P.: Microbenchmark performance comparison of high-speed cluster interconnects. IEEE Micro **24**(1), 42–51 (2004)
15. Narayanan, D., et al.: PipeDream: generalized pipeline parallelism for DNN training. In: Proceedings of SOSP 2019, pp. 1–15 (2019)
16. Narayanan, D., Phanishayee, A., Shi, K., Chen, X., Zaharia, M.: Memory-efficient pipeline-parallel DNN training. arXiv preprint arXiv:2006.09503 (2020)

17. Paszke, A., et al.: Automatic differentiation in PyTorch (2017)
18. Rajbhandari, S., Rasley, J., Ruwase, O., He, Y.: ZeRO: memory optimizations toward training trillion parameter models. In: Proceedings of the International Conference for High Performance Computing, Networking, Storage and Analysis, SC 2020. IEEE Press (2020)
19. You, Y., Zhang, Z., Hsieh, C.-J., Demmel, J., Keutzer, K.: ImageNet training in minutes. In: Proceedings of the 47th International Conference on Parallel Processing (New York, NY, USA, 2018), ICPP 2018. Association for Computing Machinery (2018)
20. Zhan, J., Zhang, J.: Pipe-torch: pipeline-based distributed deep learning in a GPU cluster with heterogeneous networking. In: 2019 Seventh International Conference on Advanced Cloud and Big Data, pp. 55–60. IEEE (2019)
21. Zinkevich, M., Weimer, M., Li, L., Smola, A.J.: Parallelized stochastic gradient descent. In: Advances in Neural Information Processing Systems, pp. 2595–2603 (2010)

Data Management, Analytics and Machine Learning

Efficient and Systematic Partitioning of Large and Deep Neural Networks for Parallelization

Haoran Wang[1,2]([⊠]) [iD], Chong Li[1], Thibaut Tachon[1], Hongxing Wang[1],
Sheng Yang[1], Sébastien Limet[2], and Sophie Robert[2]

[1] Huawei Technologies, Paris, France
{wanghaoran19,ch.l,thibaut.tachon,hongxingwang,
sheng.yang1}@huawei.com
[2] Université d'Orléans, Orléans, France
{sebastien.limet,sophie.robert}@univ-orleans.fr

Abstract. Deep neural networks (DNNs) are playing an increasingly important role in our daily life. Since the size of DNNs is continuously growing up, it is highly important to train them effectively by distributing computation on multiple connected devices. The efficiency of training depends on the quality of chosen parallelization strategy. Being able to find a good parallelization strategy for a DNN in a reasonable amount of time is not trivial. Previous research demonstrated the possibility to systematically generate good parallelization strategies. However, systematic partitioning still suffers from either a heavy preprocessing or poor quality of parallelization. In this paper, we take a purely symbolic analysis approach by leveraging the features of DNNs like dense tensor balanced computation. We propose the Flex-Edge Recursive Graph and the Double Recursive Algorithm, successfully limiting our parallelization strategy generation to a linear complexity with a good quality of parallelization strategy. The experiments show that our solution significantly reduces the parallelization strategy generation time from hours to seconds while maintaining the parallelization quality.

Keywords: Distributed algorithm · Distributed machine learning · Neural network partitioning

1 Introduction

The past decade has witnessed the dramatic development of deep learning in almost every domain in our daily ife. On one hand, DNN fra meworks like [1–3] increase the efficiency of DNN development by automating DNN training based on the user's description of the network. On the other hand, the increase of computing power, driven by the availability of new accelerators, enables the design of larger and more complex deep neural networks (DNNs) [4,5]. Deeper and wider DNNs enable new applications but require efficient distribution of computation on connected devices for accelerating the training process.

© Springer Nature Switzerland AG 2021
L. Sousa et al. (Eds.): Euro-Par 2021, LNCS 12820, pp. 201–216, 2021.
https://doi.org/10.1007/978-3-030-85665-6_13

A DNN consists of hundreds or even thousands of operators whose inputs and outputs are tensors (i.e., multidimensional arrays). A DNN can be represented as a *computation graph* whose vertices are the operators and whose edges are the tensors. A *parallelization strategy* defines how to partition the data and the operators of a DNN into multiple devices. The most commonly used parallelization strategy approach is *Data Parallelism* [6]. In data parallelism, each device holds a replica of the entire network and trains it with a subset of training data. This approach is efficient because the subsets of training data are independent, hence there is no communication during the computation of the operators. Data parallelism is not suitable for the layers with large parameter tensors (e.g., *fully connected layers*) due to a long parameter synchronization time. Another widely used approach is *Model Parallelism* [7] where the DNN operators and tensors are distributed over the computing devices. For a given operator, there exist different model parallelisms that introduce different extra communications.

The *Hybrid Parallelism* approach [8,9] has been recently proposed to overcome the disadvantages of data and model parallelism. The hybrid parallelism implements either data or model parallelism on different operators to achieve better performance. By using hybrid parallelism, communication overhead caused by inconvenient parallelization strategies is reduced. Meanwhile, hybrid parallelism introduces data redistribution between operators if two connected operators are assigned different parallelization strategies. Based on the preceding information, the efficiency of hybrid parallelism depends on the parallelization strategy of each operator. Searching for an optimal parallelization strategy for a DNN is a combinatorial problem: the number of strategies grows exponentially with the number of operators and polynomially with the number of devices. Therefore, it is difficult to find the optimal parallelization strategy within an acceptable time regarding the size of the search space. Directly comparing all the possible parallelization strategies of a DNN by profiling is not realistic. For instance, profiling a 21-layer VGG16 [10] network already takes more than 24 h [11].

Many DNN frameworks provide good functionalities on data loading, computational graph execution, and fault tolerance. Some of the frameworks support hybrid parallelism with a manually configured parallelization strategy. However, automatically offering the optimal hybrid parallelization strategy is still one of the biggest challenges for these frameworks. In this paper, we thus focus on how to choose efficient hybrid parallelization strategies for DNNs.

FlexFlow [12] uses a randomized Markov Chain Monte Carlo algorithm to circumvent the parallelization strategy complexity. However, these approaches cannot guarantee the searching time nor the optimality of the result. OptCNN [11] proposes a dynamic programming searching algorithm that reduces the complexity w.r.t. the number of operators from exponential to polynomial. Analyzing a large DNN like ResNet [4] only takes few hours. The algorithm mixes profiling and cost model to estimate the global execution time of the training. The cost model is composed of the profiled execution time of each operator and the estimated communication time. However, the execution time of an operator may vary with DNN configuration changes as well as dataset changes. As a result, new profiling and searching need to be processed after each modification of the model or dataset. Moreover, extra profiling and searching time may offset the gain of DNN training time by using more devices. The estimated communication time in OptCNN is the product of the communication bandwidth and data quantity. However, the communication capacity of a parallel machine is not only dominated by the bandwidth but also other factors such as latency, network topology, etc. A unique bandwidth used in OptCNN may induce substantial errors in the evaluation of a strategy and lead to a wrong decision in the choice. Another drawback of OptCNN solution is that the dynamic programming algorithm is designed for handling *fork-join* graphs, which are suitable for convolution neural networks used in computer vision classification. But the algorithm cannot handle multi-input or multi-output graphs used in other areas like natural language processing, recommendation systems, and image segmentation.

To avoid profiling issues, we introduce a purely symbolic cost model based on the semantics of each operator in Sect. 2. We observed that tensors in DNNs are dense multi-dimension arrays and the operators are typically balanced. Inspired by SGL [13], we proposed a 2-part recursive partitioning to eliminate the influence of a machine's communication capacity. Besides, we introduce a Flex-Edge Recursive Graph (FER Graph) to reduce the searching complexity in Sect. 3. We leverage DNN features to let the traversing of FER Graph be topology-independent. We intend to visit the vertices according to their *importance*. In this way, we can guarantee the quality of the generated strategies. Double Recursive Algorithm (D-Rec), presented in Sect. 4, includes Inner Recursion and Outer Recursion. Inner Recursion is designed to partition the computation graph into two parts. Outer Recursion recursively applies Inner Recursion p times to partition the neural network into 2^p parts.

2 Symbolic Cost Model

The cost of a distributed parallel program is the summation of local computation cost and the communication cost: $Cost = Cost_{comp} + Cost_{comm}$. The local computation is the process executed locally on each device without external data. The communication denotes data communicating between devices. Tensors in DNNs are dense multi-dimensional arrays. The operators (e.g., *Matmul*, *Conv*, *Add*, etc.) are massively parallelizable computations which are evenly computed among the devices. Therefore, the number of operations to perform is constant for any distributed strategy and a fixed number of devices. DNN platforms allow load-balancing of the computation operations among the devices such that $Cost_{comp}$ is equal for any chosen algorithm on a given number of devices. Therefore, our asymptotic analysis can focus only on $Cost_{comm}$.

The communication cost is determined by two factors: the communication capacity of the chosen machines, denoted by g, and the quantity of data needed to be transferred denoted by q. To achieve better performance, modern computer clusters, like supercomputers [14,15] and AI accelerator clusters [16,17], have a hierarchical architecture. A unique g cannot describe precisely the communication capacity of modern machines. Valiant [18] proposed to use different g for each hierarchical level. The communication cost can be calculated by the summation of each level contribution: $Cost_{comm} = \sum_i(g_i \times q_i)$, where i is the hierarchical level. We noticed that the hierarchical architectures are also typically symmetric [19]. Inspired by SGL [13], a hierarchical and symmetric machine can be abstracted in a recursive way. For example, a typical GPU architecture shown on the left of Fig. 1, can be described by an abstract machine on the right. The abstract machine has a tree structure, where the leaves are the computing devices and the branch nodes model the hierarchical structure. The communication is analyzed by a recursion. Each recursion step is a level of the tree whose communication capacity is shared as g_i. For each level, g_i does not affect the choice of the parallelization strategy. Therefore, the communication can be recursively analyzed with only the quantity of communicated data q_i, where i becomes the recursion step.

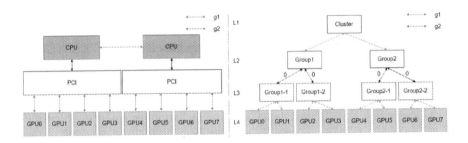

Fig. 1. A typical GPU architecture described by a recursive tree

Parallelization strategy determines how tensors are distributed into devices. We formalize our analysis by logically setting that input and output tensors of operators are evenly distributed among the devices (e.g., GPU0-7 in Fig. 1). The analysis of parallelization strategy is thus equivalent to the analysis of communication quantity. In other words, less communication quantity leads to a better parallelization strategy. Communication and computing overlap techniques [20,21] are orthogonal to our cost analysis: our goal is to find the minimized communication cost regardless of whether overlap techniques are applied.

For each level of the recursive tree, the number of branches depends on the architecture. A specific number of branches acquires a specific set of cost functions. Designing so many cost functions is not realistic. However, each level of the recursive tree is homogeneous, like GPU0-3 in Fig. 1. It can be transformed again into a multi-level tree. Besides, in real academic and industrial practice, the number of devices is usually a power of 2 to achieve the best performance. Therefore, the recursive tree can be transformed into a full binary tree and the partitioning of the symmetric architectures can be realized by recursively dichotomy. As a result, we choose 2-part cost functions to model the cost of partitioning an operator into two parts. Our goal is to find the optimal parallelism policy, so we assume that all devices operate normally and ignore small performance differences between the same devices. In addition, the heterogeneity of symmetric architecture can be decomposed. Based on the above assumptions, homogeneity is applied to all the 2-part analyses in this paper.

It is obvious that partitioning an operator evenly into 2^p part can be done by dichotomy with p recursions. Take a matrix as an example of a tensor, a matrix partitioned into four parts along columns can be the result of partitioning into two parts along column recursively twice; a matrix can be partitioned into 2×2 grid by firstly partitioning along column and then recursively along row. Therefore the recursive 2-part partitioning can be well mapped to the symmetric architecture.

In order to realize the 2-part partitioning, tensors are partitioned along one of the tensor's dimensions at each recursion step. An operator has several input/output tensors, but only a few combinations of tensors' 2-part partitions may lead to optimal communication. For example, partitioning the two input tensors of *MatMul* along column dimension will never lead to optimal communication: all the data need to be communicated. These combinations of tensors' 2-part partitions are defined as *Possible Partition Dimensions (PPDs)*. For each PPD, a cost function is defined to return the communication data quantity. The training of DNN is an iterative process that consists of forward and backward propagation. *Forward Propagation* computes the operators with the intermediate *parameters* from input to output and gets a *loss* that estimates the distance between the output and the expected value. *Backward Propagation* will update the intermediate parameters from output to input based on the loss using an optimizer like Adam [22].

There exist two kinds of data communication during the DNN training:

- Q_{op} is the quantity of data needed to be transferred inside an operator. It is composed of Q_f and Q_b. Q_f is the communication quantity between two groups of devices during the forward propagation. Q_b denotes the communication for updating the parameters during the backward propagation process.
- Q_{redist} is the communication quantity between two connected operators. In fact, the output tensor of the previous operator is the same as the input tensor of the second operator. However, as this tensor may have different parallelization strategies for the two connected operators, the data may need to be redistributed. Q_{redist} models this specific communication.

2.1 Communication Inside Operators: Q_{op}

An operator is defined by a type that describes its computational task (e.g., *Type = Add, Conv, MatMul, Relu*, etc.). It takes tensors as input and produces tensors as output. We denote $Type.\mathcal{D}_P = \{D_0, D_1, \ldots D_k\}$ the set of PPDs for each type of operator. Each PPD can be converted to the partition dimensions of all the tensors in an operator. We denote $d_0, d_1, \ldots$ the dimensions of a tensor. For example for the *MatMul* (Matrix Multiplication) operator $MatMul.\mathcal{D}_P = \{i, k, j\}$. The two input tensors are respectively of $i \times k$ and $k \times j$ dimensions and the output tensor is of $i \times j$ dimension. As shown in Fig. 2 (bottom), PPD i corresponds to partition the first input tensor and output tensor along d_0 and the second input tensor along either d_0 or d_1.

We define the following notions:

- $shape(tensor)$ denotes the shape of a tensor (e.g., $shape(t) = [4;4]$).
- $shape(D)$ denotes the shape of a PPD of an operator (e.g., $shape(i) = 4$).
- $shape(d)$ denotes the shape of a dimension of a tensor (e.g., $shape(d_0) = 4$).
- $input_n$ denotes an input tensor according to its index.
- $Q_{op}(D)$ denotes the Q_{op} of a PPD where $Q_{op}(D) = Q_f(D) + Q_b(D)$.
- $Q_{redist}(d, d')$ denotes the operator's Q_{redist} from the partition dimension d of its tensor and another dimension d' of the its connected operators' tensor.

Q_f Communication occurs when an operator is executed on multiple devices. Each device possesses only a part of data. Therefore, data need to be moved between devices to perform the whole computation. We detail here the most representative operators.

MatMul OP is the operator for Matrix Multiplication, described as:

$$output[i][j] \rightarrow \sum_k input_0[i][k] \times input_1[k][j].$$

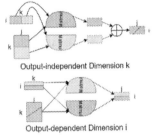

Output-independent Dimension k

Output-dependent Dimension i

Fig. 2. MatMul semantics (Color figure online)

If we cut according to the output-independent dimension, a reduction still needs to occur to combine the partial results. The dimension cut is not specified for the output (represented with a diagonal dashed line on purple in Fig. 2) but still exists. Hence, for any dimension cut, each device is responsible for computing half of the output tensor. To this end, each device preserves half of its data and communicates the other half to the other device. As we assume both communications can happen simultaneously, the communication cost will be proportional to the amount of data communicated by one of them. The 2-part cost function is as follows:

$$Q_f(k) = \frac{shape(i) \times shape(j)}{2}.$$

If we cut according to an output-dependent dimension, partial results simply have to be concatenated. However, one input is wholly needed by each device to compute their partial result. As this input will be cut eventually, each device must receive the half that it does not possess. The 2-part cost functions are presented below:

$$Q_f(i) = \frac{shape(j) \times shape(k)}{2},$$

$$Q_f(j) = \frac{shape(i) \times shape(k)}{2}.$$

Conv OP represents N-dimension convolutions operators. We name one of the inputs as $kernel$. b, c_i, c_o are batch, input channel, output channel dimensions respectively. x and z are computing dimensions. s is stride and d is dilation rate. Bold italic refers to vector. The description is as follows:

$$output[b][\boldsymbol{x}][c_o] \rightarrow \sum_{z\,c_i}(kernel[\boldsymbol{z}][c_i][c_o]$$

$$\times\ input_0[b][x_0 s_0 + d_0 z_0]...[x_{n-1} s_{n-1} + d_{n-1} z_{n-1}][c_i]).$$

If we cut according to an output-dependent dimension:

$$Q_f(b) = \frac{\prod shape(kernel)}{2}, \quad Q_f(k) = \frac{\prod shape(input_0)}{2},$$

$$\forall i \in \boldsymbol{x}, \ Q_f(i) = \frac{\prod shape(kernel)}{2} + \frac{\prod shape(input_0)}{2}.$$

If we cut according to a output-independent dimension:

$$\forall i \in \boldsymbol{z}, \ Q_f(i) = \frac{\prod shape(input_0)}{2} + \frac{\prod shape(output)}{2},$$

$$Q_f(q) = \frac{\prod shape(output)}{2}.$$

Elementwise OP computes each element independently without any communication, for example, *Add, Sub, Mul, ReLU, Log*, etc. The description of *Add* is: $output[\boldsymbol{\mu}] \rightarrow input_0[\boldsymbol{\mu}] + input_1[\boldsymbol{\mu}]$ and the cost will be $\forall i \in \boldsymbol{\mu}, \ Q_f(i) = 0$.

Q_b is the communication quantity at the end of each backward propagation. Certain operators' need to update one of its tensors during the training. These tensors are referred as *Parameters*. When the *batch* dimension is chosen, parameters hosted by each device need to be communicated to compute the average value. We group the parameter tensors as *param*. The communication quantity of a 2-part partitioning is defined $Q_b = \frac{\prod shape(param)}{2}$.

2.2 Communication Between Operators: Q_{redist}

For two connected operators, the output tensor of the first one is the same tensor as the input tensor of the second one. If the two operators choose different partition dimensions for this tensor, it needs to be redistributed which induces communication cost named Q_{redist}. Figure 3 shows two simple situations of redistribution cost.

If the partition strategy of an operator's input tensor and its connected output tensor of the previous operator are equal, $Q_{redist}(d_0, d_0) = 0$. Otherwise, $Q_{redist}(d_0, d_1) = (shape(d_0) \times shape(d_1))/4$. As shown in the second part of Fig. 3, the blue part and red part respectively represent the data stored in the first and second devices. In this situation, a half of the blue part needs to be transferred to the second device while a half of the red part needs to be transferred to the first device. The cost equals

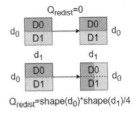

Fig. 3. Redistribution cost (Color figure online)

to the max value between them because both transfers happen simultaneously. More generally for the typical operators in DNNs, Q_{redist} is computed from the shape of the tensor.

3   Flex-Edge Recursive Graph

Choosing the optimal strategy for a DNN necessitates to consider all the operators together. For each operator, the redistribution cost depends on the parallelization strategies of its connected operators. It leads to an exponential searching complexity with regard to the number of operators. We propose a topology-independent graph structure named Flex-Edge Recursive Graph (FER Graph) and a traversal order to avoid backtracking on the graph traversal in this section.

3.1   Preliminary Definitions

An operator in the computation graph is defined as Op. Each Op has its type $Op.Type$. The shape of Op is defined by $Op.Shape = [(d_i \in Op.Type.\mathcal{D}_P : int) \mid 0 \le i \le m - 1]$ where m is the number of dimension names. Also taking $MatMul$ as an example, if its shape is $[(i : 10), (k : 20), (j : 30)]$, the operator computes the product of a 10×20 matrix by a 20×30 matrix.

Definition 1. *The partition strategy of an operator is defined by*

$$Op.Strategy = [d_j \mid d_j \in Op.Type.\mathcal{D}_P]$$

$Op.Strategy$ is a sequence of dimension names that indicates that the operator is partitioned firstly in its d_0 dimension, secondly in the d_1 dimension, and so on. The dimension names in $Op.Strategy$ are not necessarily different.

Definition 2. *A computation graph is defined as $G = (V, E)$ where V is a set of Vertices and E is a set of Edges. A vertex $v \in V$ is a tuple $(Op.Type, Op.Shape, Op.Strategy)$. An edge e is defined as a tuple (v_1, v_2, i_1, i_2) where $v_1, v_2 \in V$ and $i_1, i_2 \in \mathbb{N}$. It means that the i_2 input tensor of the operator of v_2 corresponds to the i_1 output tensor of the operator of v_1.*

As an example, *MatMul* with two input matrices whose shapes are respectively *e.g.*, 20×30 and 30×40. It can be represented as such vertex in the computation graph: $(Op.Type : MatMul, Op.Shape : [(i : 20)(k : 40)(j : 30)], Op.Strategy : \emptyset)$. Note that the MatMul operator has three PPDs $\{i, k, j\}$. *Op.Strategy* is empty at the beginning of the algorithm and will be filled with chosen parallelization strategies by the double recursive algorithm discussed in Sect. 4. A *Strategy* $= [i, i, i, k]$ indicates that the strategies chosen for this operator are along i dimension three times first and then along k dimension once.

3.2 FER Graph

Suppose $G = (V, E)$ a computation graph of a DNN to be partitioned.

Definition 3. *Let σ denote an order on the vertices $v \in V$ such that $\sigma_i(V) \in V$ is the ith visited vertex. From σ order, the Flex-Edge Recursive Graph (FER Graph) G_f can be redefined as*

$$G_f = (\sigma(V), E)$$

Associated with the FER graph G_f a list of sub-graphs is defined in order to establish a traversal rule. This list is built thanks to a concatenation operator denoted $+\!+$.

Definition 4. *Let the FER graph $G_f = (\sigma(V), E)$, the list of sub-graphs $\mathcal{G} = [G_f^i = (\sigma(V_i), E_i)]$ is defined as $G_f^0 = (<>, \{\})$ and $G_f^i = G_f^{i-1} +\!+ \sigma_i(V)$ with*

$$\left|
\begin{aligned}
V_i &= V_{i-1} \cup \sigma_i(V) \\
E_i &= E_{i-1} \cup \bar{E}_i \\
\bar{E}_i = \{e_j \in E \mid j < i, e_j &= (\sigma_i(V), \sigma_j(V), k_1, k_2)\} \\
\cup \{e_j \in E \mid j < i, e_j &= (\sigma_j(V), \sigma_i(V), k_1, k_2)\}
\end{aligned}
\right.$$

Figure 4 illustrates an example where the upper left corner is a FER Graph with ordered vertices $< v_1, v_4, v_2, v_3 >$. The traversal is a process of reconstructing the original FER Graph from an empty one. The vertex v_1 is added first. None of the other vertices connected to $v1$ is added, so no edge is added to G_f^1, then vertex v_4 is added. Similarly, no edge is together visited with v_4. When v_2 is added, their neighbors v_1 and v_4 are already in the graph. Therefore, e_1, e_3 are added with v_2. After all the concatenations, $\mathcal{G} = [(<>, \{\}), (< v_1 >, \{\}), (< v_1, v_4 >, \{\}), (< v_1, v_4, v_2 >, \{e_1, e_3\}), (G)]$.

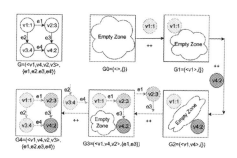

Fig. 4. Traversal of Flex-Edge graph (the number after the colon denotes the order of the vertex. $v2 : 3$ means $v2$ is ordered at the third place).

3.3 Traversing Order

Before discussing the traversal order, we first define the $minCost$ function to compare the quality of strategies and to choose the optimal one. The function takes a vertex and its together visiting edges as inputs, then searches the possible partition dimensions and finds the optimal strategy which minimizes the communication cost.

Let $G_f^{i-1}, G_f^i \in \mathcal{G}$ such that $G_f^i = G_f^{i-1} + \sigma_i(V) = (\sigma(V_i), E_i)$, let op the operator associated to $\sigma_i(V)$. We defined the cost function for an operator: $Cost(d, \sigma_i(V), \bar{E}_i) = Q_{op}(d) + \sum_{e \in \bar{E}_i} Q_{redist}(e, d)$.

Function $minCost(\sigma_i(V), \bar{E}_i)$ returns the chosen strategy d_r which minimizes the cost function s.t. $Cost(d_r, \sigma_i(V), \bar{E}_i) = \text{MIN}_{d \in \sigma_i(V).Type.\mathcal{D}_P} Cost(d, \sigma_i(V), \bar{E}_i)$.

The idea of our traversal order is to find the optimal strategy for the new sub-graph G_f^i when concatenating a vertex $\sigma_i(V)$ to a sub-graph G_f^{i-1}. So that by finding the optimal strategy for every sub-Graph recursively, we can ensure the optimal strategy for the whole graph.

For a vertex, d_{opmin} denotes a dimension in $\mathcal{D}_P$, such that $Q_{op}(d_{opmin}) = \text{MIN}_{d' \in \mathcal{D}_P} Q_{op}(d')$. If there is no Q_{redist} cost between $\sigma_i(V)$ and G_f^i, the optimal strategy of G_f^i is the union of the optimal strategy of G_f^{i-1} and the d_{opmin} of $\sigma_i(V)$. However, if Q_{redist} is large, either $\sigma_i(V)$ or G_f^{i-1} needs to change its strategy. In order to avoid backtracking, we define the order $\sigma(V)$ to ensure that it is always the strategy of $\sigma_i(V)$ that needs to be changed. This change of strategy is referred as a *compromise*. Recall that Q_{redist} is either 0 or a fixed positive value. The *compromise* consists in changing the d_{opmin} to a strategy d_{redist} s.t. $Q_{redist} = 0$. In this way, the price of reducing an operator's Q_{redist} to zero is the increment of its Q_{op}. Therefore, the *compromise price* of an operator (i.e., the price to change the strategy of an operator) is defined as $\gamma_{\sigma_i(V)} = Q_{op}(d_{redist}) - Q_{op}(d_{opmin})$. The order $\sigma(V)$ of the operators is in descending order of their *compromise price* γ_{op}.

Definition 5. *Let $G_f = (\sigma(V), E)$ a FER graph such that the number of V is n, such that*

$$\forall\, 0 \le j < k \le n,\ \sigma_j(V) \text{ is ordered before } \sigma_k(V) \text{ if } \gamma_{\sigma_j(V)} < \gamma_{\sigma_k(V)}$$

The list of sub-graphs of G_f is referred as $\mathcal{G} = [G_f^i = (\sigma(V_i), E_i)]$.

We define *compromise price* of the sub-graph G_f^{i-1} as $\gamma_{G_f^{i-1}}$. It is obvious that $\gamma_{G_f^{i-1}} \ge \gamma_{\sigma_{i-1}(V)} \ge \gamma_{\sigma_i(V)}$. As a result, if we can order the vertices in descending order according to its *compromise price*, the minimized communication cost can be guaranteed.

However, it is not trivial to find the d_{redist} because Q_{redist} relies on the connected vertices. It seems that we return back to the original complexity problem, but the features of DNN help us to handle it. Actually, what we really need is the value of $Q_{op}(d_{redist})$ instead of d_{redist}. For typical operators, we can find their *compromise price* γ because of the characteristics of their semantics.

MatMul OP. MatMul has three PPDs $\{i, j, k\}$. It needs to *compromise* when its d_{opmin} leads to a large Q_{redist}. However, no matter d_{opmin} is i, j or k, when it *compromises* to the other two dimensions, Q_{redist} becomes 0.

The *compromise price* of MatMul is defined as $\gamma = min(Q_{op}(d_0), Q_{op}(d_1)) - Q_{op}(d_{opmin})$. d_0,d_1 are defined as the other two PPDs except d_{opmin}.

Conv OP. Although Conv has many possible partition dimensions, in current real Convolution Neural Networks (e.g., VGG [10], ResNet [4]), only batch dimension b and input channel dimension k will be chosen to cut. The reason is that in a DNN, the size of the kernels is very small so that partitioning kernel tensor usually leads to a super large communication cost. Besides, the channel number increases from input to output of DNN, so that the size of the output tensor is always much bigger than the input.

As there remain only two possible partition dimensions, let d_0 denotes the other dimension except d_{opmin}. The *compromise price* is defined as $\gamma = Q_{op}(d_0) - Q_{op}(d_{opmin})$.

Elementwise OP. Q_{op} of Elementwise OP is always 0, it is evident they do not have *compromise price*. When an Elementwise OP is located between two operators who have Q_{redist} between them, it will hide Q_{redist} between the two neighbors. However, it is not true since the Elementwise OP cannot be adapted to both neighbor operators. To avoid this problem, Elementwise OP are eliminated before the strategy searching. They will reuse one of neighbor's strategy.

Other OP. Except MatMul, Conv, and Elementwise OP, all the other operators (MaxPool, ReduceMean, ReduceSum, ReduceMax, Squeeze... etc.), we noticed in the real DNNs, may have multiple dimensions but they only have two values of Q_{op}. In other words, Q_{op} of several dimensions has the same value. Let d_0 denotes the dimension which has a different Q_{op} as d_{opmin}. The *compromise price* is defined as $\gamma = Q_{op}(d_0) - Q_{op}(d_{opmin})$.

4   Double Recursive Algorithm

Algorithm 1 describes D-Rec composed of Inner Recursion and Outer Recursion. The traversing of FER Graph is called Inner Recursion which takes charge of choosing a dimension in each vertex to partition it into two parts while Outer Recursion is responsible for extending this 2-part partitioning to all devices.

Outer Recursion takes a FER Graph G_f with an empty strategy and the number of partition times N as inputs and returns the strategy assigned Graph as the output. The initial N is obtained from the number of devices. The function *Reorder* sorts the vertex in FER Graph G_f according to the *compromise price* (see Sect. 3.3). At each Outer Recursion step, all the operators in the graph are partitioned into two parts with Inner Recursion. The function *ShapeUpdate* updates the *Shape* of each *Vertex* in G_f according to the chosen *Strategy*. N is decreased by one at each recursion step. Outer Recursion ends when $N = 0$.

Inner Recursion takes the sub-graph list $\mathcal{G}$ and an empty FER Graph G_{f_in} as inputs at each Outer Recursion step. $pop\_end()$ denotes the operation on $\mathcal{G}$

that pops the last graph in the list: $G = pop\_end(\mathcal{G}), \mathcal{G} \leftarrow \mathcal{G} - G$. In Algorithm 1, v_G denotes the visited vertex to construct G from its predecessor and $\bar{E}_G$ denotes the added new edges. At each step of Inner Recursion, a sub-graph G is popped, and the strategy of its vertices will be chosen by $minCost(v_G, \bar{E}_G)$ according to the symbolic cost model. The reconstructed Graph G'_{f_in} is composed by concatenating the strategy updated vertex v_G. The process is recursively applied on the sub-graph list $\mathcal{G}$. The recursion ends when all vertices have been visited.

Algorithm 1. Double-Recursive Algorithm

Input: FER Graph G_f whose Strategy is empty. The number of partition times N.
Output: FER Graph G_f with chosen strategy.
1: **function** OUTERRECURSION(G_f, N)
2:      **if** $N = 0$ **then**
3:          return G_f
4:      **else**
5:          $(\sigma, \mathcal{G}) = Reorder(G_f)$
6:          $G_{f_in} = $ INNERRECURSION($\mathcal{G}, (\varnothing, \varnothing)$)
7:          $G'_f = ShapeUpdate(G_{f\_in})$
8:          return OUTERRECURSION($G'_f, N - 1$)
9:      **end if**
10: **end function**
11:
12: **function** INNERRECURSION($\mathcal{G}, G_{f\_in}$)
13:      **if** $\mathcal{G} = \varnothing$ **then**
14:          return G_{f_in}
15:      **else**
16:          $G = pop\_end(\mathcal{G})$
17:          $d_r = minCost(v_G, \bar{E}_G)$
18:          $v_G.OP.Strategy + [d_r]$
19:          $G'_{f\_in} = G_{f\_in} + v_G$
20:          return INNERRECURSION($\mathcal{G}, G'_{f\_in}$)
21:      **end if**
22: **end function**

---

5   Experiments

This section aims at evaluating the searching efficiency of D-Rec and the quality of the found strategy. The accuracy and training loss of the DNN are not discussed because our approach does not change the semantics of the DNN. These two metrics remain the same as training on a single node.

5.1   Environment Setup

The experiments in this section were run on either an Atlas 900 AI cluster [23] or a GPU cluster. Each node of the Atlas cluster is composed of two ARM CPUs and eight Huawei Ascend910 accelerators. Each Ascend 910 accelerator is equipped with a network module, and all Ascend 910 accelerators are inter-connected directly even from a different node. Each node of the GPU cluster is composed of two Intel Xeon E5-2680 CPUs and eight NVIDIA V100 GPUs. All GPUs of a node communicate with each other via the PCIe (e.g., Fig. 1). Our D-Rec was run on CPU, and the DNN training was run on accelerators. We used MindSpore[1] as the DNN training platform to implement our proposal[2]. We also implemented a dynamic programming (DP) algorithm of OptCNN [11] to compare with. The Imagenet dataset[3] was used to train image classification DNNs like ResNet and VGG.

5.2   Searching Efficiency

We took ResNet101 [4] and BERT [5], two representative DNNs, to validate the strategy searching speed of D-Rec. The computation graph of ResNet101 was fixed, and we varied the number of devices from 2 to 1024 (Fig. 5(a)). The searching time of D-Rec on ResNet101 increases linearly from 0.383 s to 0.825 s. DP took nearly 2 h to find a strategy for 16 devices, 3.5 h for 32 devices and failed to find any strategy for 64 devices after hours.

We then fixed the number of devices to 8 and varied the number of hidden layers of BERT from 4 to 24 (Fig. 5(b)) since the number of operators in pro-portion to the number of hidden layers. The searching time of D-Rec on the variants of BERT is between 4.5 s and 27.7 s. DP does not work on these multi-input graph networks. The experiments showed that D-Rec could handle general large computation graphs in few seconds with a linear growth trend.

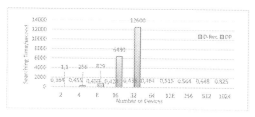

(a) Searching Time of ResNet101

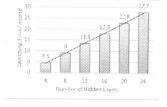

(b) Searching Time of BERT

Fig. 5. Training efficiency

5.3   Strategy Quality

Training throughput, often defined as the capacity of processing *Images Per Second* (IPS), is used to evaluate the quality of a parallelization strategy. DP is

---

[1] https://www.mindspore.cn/en.

[2] https://github.com/mindspore-ai/mindspore/tree/master/mindspore/ccsrc/ frontend/parallel/auto_parallel/rec_core.

[3] http://image-net.org/.

used as the benchmark because with sufficient profiling its result can be regarded
as the state of the art.

The IPS of VGG16, VGG19, ResNet50, ResNet101, and ResNet152 were similar between the parallelization strategies generated by D-Rec and by sufficient-
profiled DP (Fig. 6(a)). It validates the quality of the parallelization strategy
generated by D-Rec for different DNNs. However, the strategies generated by
insufficient-profiled DP on VGG led worse IPS (blue bars in Fig. 6(a)). Thanks
to our symbolic approach, D-Rec does not rely on such time-consuming profiling
that DP requires.

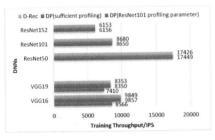 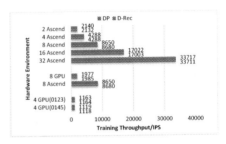

(a) on Different DNNs   (b) on Different Hardware

Fig. 6. Strategy quality (Color figure online)

We then fixed the DNN model as ResNet101 and varied the architecture of
the training machine. We first varied the number of Ascend 910 accelerators
from 2 to 32. Then we used the GPU cluster to compare with the Atlas cluster.
Lastly we varied the communication topology on the GPU cluster (Fig. 6(b)).
In all the above cases, D-Rec obtained a similar IPS as DP. The experiments
consistently validate the strategy quality of D-Rec. It shows that our 2-part
partitioning recursion on symmetric architectures could eliminate the communication capacity g without impact on the strategy quality.

We observed from Fig. 6(b) that by increasing the number of devices, IPS
increases while the training time decreases. However, Fig. 5 shows that using
more training devices makes strategy searching slower. The searching time may
thus overcome the training time. Thanks to the efficiency of D-Rec, DNNs can
be trained on large clusters without such issues.

6   Conclusion

We presented a symbolic cost analysis with FER Graph and D-Rec to generate a
parallelization strategy of DNN training. The FER Graph data structure and its
traversal ordering successfully guarantee the quality of generated parallelization
strategy. Meanwhile, D-Rec reduces the searching complexity dramatically from
exponential (i.e., OptCNN [11]) down to linear while preserving the parallelization strategy quality with FER Graph. Our experiments validate our claims and

show that the optimal parallelization strategies can be generated in seconds. Not only CNNs but also general large DNNs can now be trained efficiently in parallel.

Our symbolic cost analysis could be used to discover better parallel algorithms for DNN training. The main limitation of our approach is that we do not consider inter-layer partitioning (e.g., pipeline parallelism). So we may obtain sub-optimal strategies for very large natural language processing networks like GPT-3 [24]. Extending our symbolic cost analysis for pipeline parallelism is planned for future work. It could also be extended to exploit new possibilities to accelerate DNN computing such as operator fusion in the future. Further studies to find out the way to cover heterogeneous architectures are desirable too.

References

1. Abadi, M., Barham, P., Chen, J., et al.: Tensorflow: a system for large-scale machine learning. In: 12th USENIX Symposium on Operating Systems Design and Implementation (OSDI 2016), Savannah, GA, November 2016, pp. 265–283. USENIX Association (2016)
2. Paszke, A., et al.: Pytorch: an imperative style, high-performance deep learning library. In: Advances in Neural Information Processing Systems, pp. 8026–8037 (2019)
3. MindSpore. https://www.mindspore.cn/
4. He, K., Zhang, X., Ren, S., Sun, J.: Deep residual learning for image recognition. In 2016 IEEE Conference on Computer Vision and Pattern Recognition (CVPR), pp. 770–778 (2016)
5. Devlin, J., Chang, M.-W., Lee, K., Toutanova, K.: BERT: pre-training of deep bidirectional transformers for language understanding. In: Proceedings of the 2019 Conference of the North American Chapter of the Association for Computational Linguistics: Human Language Technologies, Minneapolis, Minnesota, June 2019, vol. 1 (Long and Short Papers), pp. 4171–4186. Association for Computational Linguistics (2019)
6. Krizhevsky, A., Sutskever, I., Hinton, G.E.: Imagenet classification with deep convolutional neural networks. In: Advances in Neural Information Processing Systems, pp. 1097–1105 (2012)
7. Dean, J., Corrado, G.S., Monga, R., et al.: Large scale distributed deep networks. In: Proceedings of the 25th International Conference on Neural Information Processing Systems - vol. 1, NIPS 2012, pp. 1223–1231, Red Hook, NY, USA. Curran Associates Inc (2012)
8. Krizhevsky, A.: One weird trick for parallelizing convolutional neural networks. arXiv preprint arXiv:1404.5997, 2014
9. Shazeer, N., Cheng, Y., Parmar, N., et al.: Mesh-tensorflow: deep learning for supercomputers. In: Advances in Neural Information Processing Systems, pp. 10414–10423 (2018)
10. Simonyan, K., Zisserman, A.: Very deep convolutional networks for large-scale image recognition. In: Bengio, Y., LeCun, Y. (eds.), 3rd International Conference on Learning Representations, ICLR 2015, San Diego, CA, USA, 7–9 May 2015, Conference Track Proceedings (2015)

11. Jia, Z., Lin, S., Qi, C.R., Aiken, A.: Exploring hidden dimensions in accelerating convolutional neural networks. In: Volume 80 of Proceedings of Machine Learning Research, PMLR, 10–15 Jul 2018, pp. 2274–2283 (2018)

12. Jia, Z., Zaharia, M., Aiken, A.: Beyond data and model parallelism for deep neural networks. In: Talwalkar, A., Smith, V., Zaharia, M. (eds.) Proceedings of Machine Learning and Systems, vol. 1, pp. 1–13 (2019)

13. Li, C., Hains, G.: SGL: towards a bridging model for heterogeneous hierarchical platforms. Int. J. High Perform. Comput. Netw. **7**(2), 139–151 (2012)

14. Dongarra, J.: Report on the Fujitsu Fugaku system. University of Tennessee-Knoxville Innovative Computing Laboratory, Tech. Rep. ICLUT-20-06-2020 (2020)

15. Yuksel, A., et al.: Thermal and mechanical design of the fastest supercomputer of the world in cognitive systems: IBM POWER AC 922. In: ASME 2019 InterPACK (2019)

16. Liao, H., Tu, J., Xia, J., Zhou, X.: Davinci: a scalable architecture for neural network computing. In: 2019 IEEE Hot Chips 31 Symposium (HCS), pp. 1–44. IEEE (2019)

17. Nvidia. NVIDIA DGX-1 System Architecture White Paper (2017)

18. Valiant, L.G.: A bridging model for multi-core computing. J. Comput. Syst. Sci. **77**(1), 154–166 (2011)

19. Li, A., et al.: Evaluating modern GPU interconnect: PCIe, NVLink, NV-SLI, NVSwitch and GPUDirect. IEEE TPDS **31**(1), 94–110 (2019)

20. Zhang, H., Zheng, Z., Xu, S., et al.: Poseidon: an efficient communication architecture for distributed deep learning on GPU clusters. In: 2017 USENIX Annual Technical Conference (USENIX ATC 17), pp. 181–193 (2017)

21. Sergeev, A., Balso, M.D.: Horovod: fast and easy distributed deep learning in tensorflow. arXiv preprint arXiv:1802.05799 (2018)

22. Chilimbi, T., Suzue, Y., Apacible, J., Kalyanaraman, K.: Project adam: building an efficient and scalable deep learning training system. In Proceedings of the 11th USENIX Conference on Operating Systems Design and Implementation, OSDI 2014, USA, pp. 571–582. USENIX Association (2014)

23. Atlas900.   https://e.huawei.com/en/products/cloud-computing-dc/atlas/atlas-900-ai

24. Brown, T., Mann, B., Ryder, N.: et al.: Language models are few-shot learners. In: Advances in Neural Information Processing Systems, vol. 33, pp. 1877–1901. Curran Associates Inc (2020)

A GPU Architecture Aware Fine-Grain Pruning Technique for Deep Neural Networks

Kyusik Choi[ID] and Hoeseok Yang[(✉)][ID]

Department of ECE, Ajou University, Suwon, Gyeonggi 16499, Republic of Korea
{chlrbtlr30,hyang}@ajou.ac.kr

Abstract. The model size and computation requirement of Deep Convolutional Neural Networks (DNNs) have ever increased as their applications to various real-life use-cases, e.g., autonomous driving, are getting more pervasive and popular. While DNN workloads are executed on Graphics Processing Units (GPUs) in many cases, it is not trivial to improve the inference speed through the conventional DNN weight pruning techniques, due to the parallel architecture of GPUs. On the other hand, the coarse-grain pruning, also known as structured sparsity or structured pruning, can speedup the inference, but cause significant losses of accuracy. In this paper, we propose two fine-grain DNN pruning techniques that are aware of the underlying GPU architecture. For that, we analyze the hierarchical architecture of parallel processing elements and memory of GPU to identify the finest possible pruning where the removed weights can be safely skipped during the inference. The effectiveness of the proposed techniques has been evaluated with VGG16. Compared to the existing pruning techniques, the proposed methods result in significantly improved inference speed with less accuracy drop.

Keywords: DNN · Architecture-aware pruning · GPU

1 Introduction

The recent breakthrough of Convolutional Neural Networks (CNNs) is largely attributed to the huge compute capability of modern parallel architectures such as Graphics Processing Units (GPUs) that enabled cascading many convolutional layers in a single neural network, so-called Deep Neural Network (DNN) [10]. The accelerated advance of DNNs, in turn, increasingly requires more compute capability and memory capacity [4]. Given the limited compute capability and

This work was supported by Institute of Information & communications Technology Planning & Evaluation (IITP) grant funded by the Korea government (MSIT) (No. 2018-0-00769, Neuromorphic Computing Software Platform for Artificial Intelligence Systems).

© Springer Nature Switzerland AG 2021
L. Sousa et al. (Eds.): Euro-Par 2021, LNCS 12820, pp. 217–231, 2021.
https://doi.org/10.1007/978-3-030-85665-6_14

memory capacity of the underlying hardware architecture, it is crucial to optimize the overhead of convolutional layers to achieve meaningful throughput or latency gains in DNNs.

A number of approaches have been proposed in order to alleviate the overhead of DNNs. Among them, the weight pruning approach [8,11,22] tries to get rid of less important weights in a given DNN in favor of the reduced number of operations and parameters. While the network size, i.e., the number of parameters, could be effectively reduced by this, such pruning approaches at the weight level do not necessarily optimize the inference speed or throughput as they result in irregular sparsity in DNNs. Due to the fact that most underlying processing elements, like SIMD (Single Instruction Multiple Data) CPU or GPU, compute the DNN's convolutional layers in inherently parallel ways, it is not trivial to effectively skip the removed weights in the resultant irregular sparsity pattern. In order to achieve speed gain from the sparsity caused by the weight removals, inferences should be either assisted by special hardware accelerators [7,22] or performed based on the sparse-matrix multiplication [12,18], which shows gain only at a high degree of sparsity [21].

On the other hand, the computational gain can be achieved by removing the consecutive weights in a coarser unit, which is referred to as structured sparsity [11,20]. In this approach, the underlying parallel processing element can skip a chunk of removed weights as a whole effectively, resulting in substantial improvement in latency or throughput. However, this gain comes at the cost of a greater accuracy degradation due to the coarse-grained weight removals. Moreover, it has been reported that such structured sparsity may even result in increased inference times if the pruning is oblivious to the architecture of the underlying parallel processing elements [15].

In this paper, we propose an architecture-aware pruning technique tailored to GPU, which can effectively enhance the latency or throughput of DNN inferences while reducing the accuracy loss. The proposed technique is generally applicable to any GPU architecture as it is based on General Matrix Multiply (GEMM). The granularity and location of pruning are judiciously determined, with respect to the architecture of the target GPU, in a way that memory copies and computations are minimized and balanced over the multiple parallel processing elements. The effectiveness of the proposed technique is verified with *VGG16* [17] in comparison with other existing pruning techniques.

The remainder of this paper is organized as follows. In the next section, we review the existing DNN pruning techniques and how the proposed technique differs from them. Section 3 presents the GEMM-based computation of convolutional layers in GPUs and existing pruning techniques as background. In Sect. 4, the hierarchical GPU architecture is reviewed and how the GEMM operation is restructured with blocking to take advantage of the architectural characteristics of GPU. The proposed GPU architecture aware pruning techniques are illustrated in Sect. 5, followed by the experimental evaluations in Sect. 6. Finally, Sect. 7 presents the conclusion of this paper.

2 Related Work

Han et al. [8] proposed a weight pruning technique where a set of less important weights are forced to be zero to reduce the storage/memory requirement for deploying DNNs. However, in order to obtain a gain in the inference time by this weight pruning, they had to rely on a customized hardware accelerator, called Efficient Inference Engine (EIE) [7], that was designed to effectively skip the computations of the zero (pruned) weights. Similarly, Zhu et al. [22] proposed a non-zero detector that can identify the non-zero weights at runtime and safely exclude the weights that can only result in zero in multiplication. In general processing elements such as CPU or GPU, it has been reported that the computational gain obtained from the weight pruning approach is very limited due to its irregular sparsity pattern [11,15,20–22].

Another approach to achieving computational gain with weight pruning is to use a special sparse matrix multiplication algorithm, in which only non-zero elements in the matrices are used in the computation. Sparse matrix multiplication algorithms are readily available to be used for GPUs in the form of libraries, e.g., clSparse [5] or cuSparse [12]. However, such sparse matrix multiplication algorithms are known to be only beneficial if the degree of sparsity is considerably high. Yao et al. [21] reported that the performance improvement of the sparse matrix multiplication was observed only when the matrices have the sparsity degree of 55% or more, compared to GEMM. Moreover, when considering the end-to-end time for convolutional layers, even in the case that 91.8% of the weights were pruned out, the inference speed based on the sparse matrix multiplication resulted in 4.9× slowdown. This implies that the matrix format conversion imposes substantial computation overhead during the inference. While Chen [3] proposed a direct sparse convolution operation in order to avoid this conversion overhead, this special sparse matrix multiplication approach still suffers from its limitations: lack of generic applicability and limited gain for low sparsity degrees.

In order to avoid irregular sparsity patterns that jeopardize efficient inference in the above mentioned works, Wen et al. [20] proposed to apply pruning at the coarser, thus more structured, granularity. They considered various pruning units, including filter-wise, channel-wise, shape-wise, and depth-wise ones, and proved that such structured pruning can result in meaningful speedups on top of general processing elements like CPUs and GPUs. However, this structured pruning is known to cause larger accuracy losses as it is likely that some important weights could be removed together with unimportant ones [4]. Furthermore, Radu et al. [15] showed that this structured pruning can be a source of the inference speed degradation on GPUs when the pruning decision is made without considering the underlying architecture. Thus, they empirically modeled the performance improvement per the number of removed channels and searched the most desirable number of channels to be pruned based on this model.

The proposed pruning techniques can be seen as a kind of structured sparsity; but they differ from the above mentioned works in that the granularity of pruning is chosen to be as fine-grained as possible, tailored to the architectural characteristics of the given GPU. Also, the load balancing between multiple

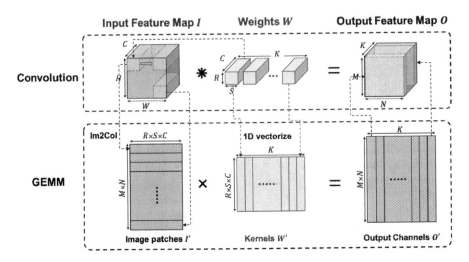

Fig. 1. Processing of convolutional layer in DNN and its conversion (through Im2Col) to GEMM operation.

processing elements in the GPU architecture is considered during the pruning decision. As a result, the pruned chunks of weights could be easily skipped at runtime for memory transfer and calculations during inference.

3   Preliminaries

3.1   Convolutional Layer Operation Using GEMM

The operation of convolutional layer is defined as computing a 3D output feature map ($O \in \mathbb{R}^{K \times M \times N}$) out of a 3D input feature map ($I \in \mathbb{R}^{C \times H \times W}$) and 4D weights ($W \in \mathbb{R}^{K \times C \times R \times S}$) as follows:

$$O[k][m][n] = \sum_{c=0}^{C-1} \sum_{r=0}^{R-1} \sum_{s=0}^{S-1} W[k][c][r][s] \times I[c][m+r][n+s] \quad (1)$$

for all $0 \leq k < K$, $0 \leq m < M$, and $0 \leq n < N$, as illustrated in the upper half of Fig. 1.

Typically, the operation of convolutional layer is converted to the multiplication of two 2D matrices [1,6,14] (GEMM) as illustrated in the lower half of Fig. 1 in order to take advantage of the existing highly optimized matrix multiplication libraries [2]. For that, the 3D input feature map I is rearranged in a $(M \cdot N) \times (R \cdot S \cdot C)$ matrix I' by means of the Image to Column (Im2Col) transformation. Likewise, each of K 3D kernels (W) is vectorized in a column vector of the transformed matrix W'; the transformed weights forms a $(R \cdot S \cdot C) \times K$ matrix. The GEMM operation of $I' \times W'$ produces an output matrix of $(M \cdot N) \times K$, and this should be converted back to the original form of 3D output feature map ($K \times M \times N$).

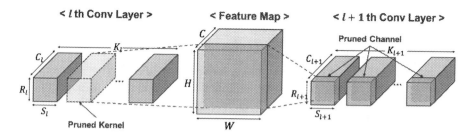

Fig. 2. A kernel-channel pruning example.

3.2 Kernel-Channel Pruning (Existing Structured Pruning)

The kernel-channel pruning is a typical structured pruning approach, where a single 3D tensor (each of the K filters in Fig. 1) is the unit of pruning decision [11,20]. In this approach, if a filter is pruned out, the kernel matrix W' and output channel O' in GEMM are reshaped to $(R \times S \times C) \times (K-1)$ and $(M \times N) \times (K-1)$, respectively. Thus, the conventional GEMM library optimally parallelized for GPUs can be used without any internal modifications. As illustrated in Fig. 2, pruning out a kernel from the ith convolutional layer results in one channel size reduction in the next convolutional layer. Like this, the kernel-channel pruning can achieve a reduction in both model size and computation requirement. However, due to its coarse granularity of pruning, it suffers from significant accuracy losses.

4   GEMM Blocking/Tiling for GPU

GPUs have a hierarchically parallel architecture as shown on the right-hand side of Fig. 3. A GPU device in OpenCL [18] is composed of a number of Compute Units (CUs, referred to as Streaming Multiprocessors in CUDA), each of which, in turn, has multiple Processing Elements (PEs, referred to as Streaming Processors in CUDA) that can execute in parallel. Also, a memory hierarchy of DRAM, SRAM, and, Register File (RF) is associated with this hierarchical architecture. The global memory (in external DRAM) can be accessed by any PEs in the device. Each CU is associated with an on-chip SRAM, called *local memory*, which can be used as shared memory between the constituent PEs within the CU. At last, each PE has a dedicated RF, called *private memory*, that can be accessed by ALU in PE very quickly.

In order to utilize this hierarchically parallel architecture as efficiently as possible, the ordinary GEMM calculation of Eq. (1) is restructured as shown in Fig. 3. Firstly, the output feature map O' is divided into multiple rectangular sections, indexed in 2D, each of which is handled by a single CU. In the OpenCL programming model, each of these rectangular sections is computed by a *work-group* (*thread block* in CUDA). In turn, a *work-group* consists of a 2D $WG_x \times WG_y$ array of *work-items* (*threads* in CUDA) and each *work-item* is running on a

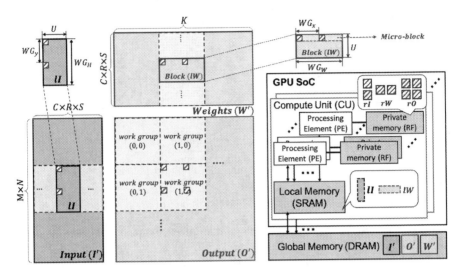

Fig. 3. Blocking/tiling process for GEMM operation in GPU architecture.

single PE. As illustrated in Fig. 3, all work-groups are independent of each other in computation and each of them handles the multiplication of $WG_H \times (C \cdot R \cdot S)$ and $(C \cdot R \cdot S) \times WG_W$ matrices where WG_H and WG_W denote the height and width of each of the rectangular sections of O' that a single work-group calculates, respectively. A single work-item (within a work-group) calculates a *tile* of $T_x \times T_y$ scalar values interleaved by a constant distance as highlighted in the purple grid in the figure. (Note that both T_x and T_y are 2 in this particular example illustrated in Fig. 3.) Therefore, we have $WG_H = T_y \cdot WG_y$ and $WG_W = T_x \cdot WG_x$. To perform the GEMM in an efficient way, the operands (I' and W') and output (O') of the multiply-accumulate (MAC) operations should be maintained in the local memory. For that, the MAC operations are not performed for the entire row and column vectors at once, but iteratively performed on divided portions, called *blocks*, that can fit into the local memory.

Algorithm 1 delineates the GEMM with blocking/tiling for work-item (wi_x, wi_y) in work-group (wg_x, wg_y) in a pseudo code. While it operates on sub-regions of input feature map ($WG_H \times (C \cdot R \cdot S)$) and weights ($(C \cdot R \cdot S) \times WG_W$), it is not feasible to load them all in the local memory due to the limited SRAM capacity. Thus, the input feature map (I') and weights (W') in the DRAM are divided into several 2D *blocks* (lI and lW) and handled one by one iteratively (lines 2–22). At each iteration, a pair of blocks in DRAM are loaded into 1D arrays, lW and lI, in the local memory cooperatively by multiple work-items in the work-group (lines 3–8). Once the loading to the local memory is completed (line 9), each work-item copies the corresponding input feature map and weight values to its private memory (lines 11–16) and perform the MAC operations for the $T_x \times T_y$ tile (lines 17–21). These are iteratively performed by U times to complete the matrix multiplication for the work-group. Note that these MAC operations are performed on operands in private memory (RF), thus results should be written back afterwards to global memory (DRAM) (lines 26–30).

Algorithm 1: GEMM with blocking/tiling for work-item (wi_x, wi_y) in work-group (wg_x, wg_y)

---

1   off $\leftarrow 0$;

2   **for** $i \leftarrow 0$ **to** $B - 1$ **do**

3   **for** $j \leftarrow 0$ **to** $T_x - 1$ **do**

4         $lW[WG_x \cdot j + WG_W \cdot wi_y + wi_x] \leftarrow$
        $W'[\text{off} + wi_y][WG_W \cdot wg_x + WG_x \cdot j + wi_x]$ ▷ DRAM→SRAM

5   **end**

6   **for** $j \leftarrow 0$ **to** $T_y - 1$ **do**

7         $lI[WG_y \cdot j + WG_H \cdot wi_x + wi_y] \leftarrow I'[WG_H \cdot wg_y + WG_y \cdot j + wi_y][\text{off} + wi_x]$
        ▷ DRAM→SRAM

8   **end**

9   Memory Barrier Synchronization;

10   **for** $j \leftarrow 0$ **to** $U - 1$ **do**

11   **for** $k \leftarrow 0$ **to** $T_x - 1$ **do**

12          $rW[k] = lW[j \cdot k \cdot WG_x + wi_x]$ ▷ SRAM→RF

13   **end**

14   **for** $k \leftarrow 0$ **to** $T_y - 1$ **do**

15          $rI[k] = lI[(k + wi_y) \cdot U + j \cdot WG_y \cdot t_y]$ ▷ SRAM→RF

16   **end**

17   **for** $k \leftarrow 0$ **to** $T_y - 1$ **do**

18   **for** $h \leftarrow 0$ **to** $T_x - 1$ **do**

19             $rO[k][h] \mathrel{+}= rI[k] \times rW[h]$ ▷ MAC operations

20   **end**

21   **end**

22   **end**

23   off $\mathrel{+}= U$;

24   Memory Barrier Synchronization;

25 **end**

26 **for** $i \leftarrow 0$ **to** $T_y - 1$ **do**

27   **for** $j \leftarrow 0$ **to** $T_x - 1$ **do**

28         $O'[wg_y \cdot i \cdot WG_y + wi_y][wg_x \cdot j \cdot WG_x + wi_x] = rO[i][j]$ ▷ RF→DRAM

29   **end**

30 **end**

Work-group partitioning and tile sizes are optimized empirically at compile-time using a GPU kernel customizing tool, AutoGEMM [19]. Then, the block size should be properly determined to fit into the limited capacity of the local memory in CU. As illustrated in Fig. 3, the $U \times WG_W$ weight block and the $WG_H \times U$ input feature map block are loaded into the local memory at a time. Therefore, U is determined among multiples of WG_y to satisfy $(WG_H + WG_W) \cdot U \leq$ size of local memory. For simplicy of presentation, hereafter, we assume that U is equal to WG_y. Once the block size is fixed, the number of blocks to be iteratively calculated by an work-item can be calculated as $B = \lceil C \times R \times S/U \rceil$.

5   Proposed GPU-Aware Pruning Technique

In this section, we propose two novel pruning techniques for GPUs, in which the pruning granularity and targets are judiciously determined considering the GPU architecture presented in the previous section.

5.1   Block Pruning

The first approach is called *block pruning* as we propose to perform pruning in the unit of *blocks*. By excluding some blocks, the time taken for GEMM can be effectively reduced by having a smaller for loop iterations (lines 2–25) in Algorithm 1.

Note that a number of work-groups are executed on top of multiple CUs at the same time in the GPU architecture. In order to effectively reduce the end-to-end latency of GEMM, it is undesirable that some work-groups remain idle waiting for the completion of others. Therefore, it is important to make all work-groups have balanced computational workloads in making the pruning decision; the same amount of blocks should be pruned for every work-group. To be more specific, when pruning is performed by a portion of p, the number of blocks that every work-group handles is reduced to $B' = \lceil B \times (1 - p) \rceil$.

The decision on which blocks are to be removed is made based on the l2 norm value of weights within the block. That is, the importance of the kth block that work-group (wg_x, wg_y) handles is quantified by $l2_k = \sqrt{\sum_{i,j} W'[i][j]^2}$ for all $U \cdot k \leq i < U \cdot (k + 1)$ and $WG_W \cdot wg_x \leq j < WG_W \cdot (wg_x + 1)$. Given the pruning ratio of p, only the top $\lceil B \times (1 - p) \rceil$ blocks with the highest l2 values keep the original weight values and, for all other blocks, weights are forced to become zero. Like other pruning approaches, after pruning, we perform re-training on the non-pruned weights. Algorithm 1 can be modified to work for the block pruning approach with trivial offset changes. However, due to space limitation, we omit the GEMM pseudo code for block pruning.

5.2   Micro-Block Pruning

In the second approach, we use an even finer-grain pruning, called *micro-block*, which is actually a row of the blocks. As shown in Algorithm 1, a work-group iteratively handles B consecutive blocks one by one and a single block is composed of U micro-blocks. Thus, there are $B \cdot U$ pruning candidates exist within a single work-group. As in the block pruning approach, we propose to keep the same pruning ratio for all work-groups, in favor of the balanced computational overheads, i.e., for each work-group, $p \cdot B \cdot U$ micro-blocks are to be removed.

Now that all work-groups have the same workloads, the computational burdens distributed to a number of work-items in a work-group should also be balanced. Figure 4 illustrates how the proposed approach performs pruning in a way that the work-items are equally loaded with an example with $T_x = 2$. As can be seen in lines 3–5 of Algorithm 1, each work-item should transfer its

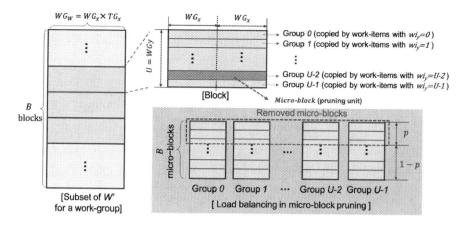

Fig. 4. Proposed load-balanced pruning of micro-blocks.

corresponding W' weights by iterating the for loop by $T_x = 2$ times. (As illustrated in Fig. 4, $U \times WG_x$ weights are copied from the global memory to the local memory per each iteration.) Note that the ith micro-block (row) of a block is copied by the work-items whose wi_y is equal to i.

In order to keep the amounts of data copy that all work-items individually perform uniform, the number of pruned micro-blocks belonging to the area each work-item copies should remain the same. For that, $U \cdot B$ micro-blocks that a single work-group handles are rearranged into U groups as illustrated in Fig. 4 and the same portion of micro-blocks are removed from each group. To be more specific, all micro-blocks that are copied by the work-items with $wi_y = i$ compose group i. As shown in Fig. 4, each group has B micro-blocks in it. Then, the importance of the micro-blocks is again quantified by the l2 norm value of the constituent weights of the micro-block, i.e., the importance of the jth micro-block in the ith block is $l2_{i,j} = \sqrt{\sum_k W'[i \cdot U + j][k]^2}$ for all $WG_W \cdot wg_x \leq k < WG_W \cdot (wg_x + 1)$. Based on this, $p \cdot B$ micro-blocks with the lowest l2 norm value are removed from each group. As well, in the micro-block pruning approach, the re-training should be performed on the non-pruned weights afterwards.

Algorithm 2 illustrates how a DNN compressed by the proposed micro-block pruning technique can actually skip the calculations of pruned weights during inference. Note in line 2 that the number of block processing is reduced to $B' = B \cdot (1 - p)$ as the total number of micro-blocks to be calculated is reduced. However, unlike the block pruning approach, a single for loop iteration now does not deal with a consecutive region of $U \times WG_W$ weights, but U micro-blocks that can now be possibly separate from each other. It is shown in lines 3–4 how the index of the non-pruned micro-block that a work-item should copy is calculated. As a result of pruning, the remaining micro-blocks in the ith group (shown in Fig. 4) is encoded in a U-bit binary string, $map[i]$. For instance, $map[2] = (0, 1, 1, 1, 0, 0, 1, 0, ...)$ indicates that, four (0th, 4th, 5th, and 7th) among the first eight micro-blocks that belong to group 2 are pruned out. The nearest index of non-pruned micro-blocks can be obtained by function $nearest\_one(map, \text{curr})$, which returns the first index i such that $map[i] = 1$ and $i \geq$ curr. For instance, $nearest\_one(map[2], 0)$, $nearest\_one(map[2], 2)$, and $nearest\_one(map[2], 4)$ return 1, 2, and 6, respectively.

Once the corresponding non-pruned micro-blocks are loaded to the local memory (lines 5–10), the same MAC operations can be performed by a set of work-items (line 13). It is worthwhile to mention that these interleaved loading and the changed order of MAC operations between micro-blocks do not make any changes in the results of GEMM as long as the indices (off) are consistently maintained for W' and I'. In other words, the order of MAC operations between a $1 \times (R \cdot S \cdot C)$ row vector and a $(R \cdot S \cdot C) \times 1$ column vector in Fig. 1 can be switched without making any difference in the matrix multiplication result.

Algorithm 2: Micro-block pruned GEMM operation for work-item (wi_x, wi_y) in work-group (wg_x, wg_y)

---

1 curr ← 0;
2 **for** $i \leftarrow 0$ **to** $B' - 1$ **do**
3   curr ← $nearest\_one(map[wi_y], \text{curr})$;
4   off ← $U \cdot$ curr;
5   **for** $j \leftarrow 0$ **to** $T_x - 1$ **do**
6           $lW[WG_x \cdot j + WG_W \cdot wi_y + wi_x] \leftarrow W'[\text{off} + wi_y][WG_W \cdot wg_x + WG_x \cdot j + wi_x]$
         ▷ DRAM→SRAM
7   **end**
8   **for** $j \leftarrow 0$ **to** $T_y - 1$ **do**
9           $lI[WG_y \cdot j + WG_H \cdot wi_y + wi_x] \leftarrow I'[WG_H \cdot wg_y + WG_y \cdot j + wi_x][\text{off} + wi_y]$
         ▷ DRAM→SRAM
10   **end**
11   curr ← curr $+ 1$;
12   Memory Barrier Synchronization;
13   **MAC operations for tile** (lines 10-22 of Algorithm 1)
14   Memory Barrier Synchronization;
15 **end**
16 **Write-back to** O' (lines 26-30 of Algorithm 1)

---

6   Experiments

This section presents the effectiveness of the proposed pruning techniques, in terms of inference speed and accuracy, in comparison with other existing pruning methods. The pruning/re-training procedures have been implemented using the PyTorch framework [13] while the inference engine has been implemented by modifying DarkNet-OpenCL [16]. For evaluations, the proposed pruning techniques were applied to VGG16 [17] that is trained with two different datasets, CIFAR100 [9] and ILSVRC2012 [10]. The target GPU used in the evaluation was NVIDIA Titan XP and we measured the time taken for inference of 10,000 input images.

Figure 5 shows the inference accuracy and speed obtained by the existing and proposed pruning techniques in comparison. In the *Weight pruning* approach [8],

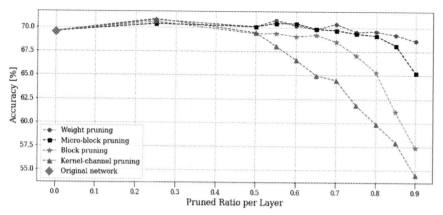

(a) Accuracy-pruning ratio of different pruning techniques

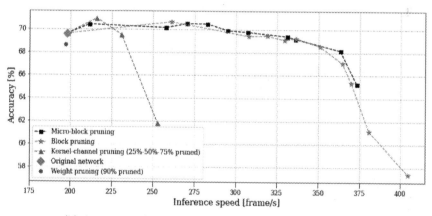

(b) Accuracy-inference speed of different pruning techniques

Fig. 5. Comparisons of the pruning techniques in accuracy and inference speed.

the loss of accuracy was the lowest as the degree of pruning (the X-axis of Fig. 5(a)) increased. However, in terms of inference speed, it showed no gain even in the case of the largest pruning degree ($p = 0.9$) as shown in Fig. 5(b). In the *Kernel-Channel (KC) pruning* case [11, 20], the accuracy drops were much more significant than weight pruning as shown in Fig. 5(a) due to its coarse-grain pruning unit. On the other hand, unlike weight pruning, it could achieve the inference speed improvement up to 252.77 fps at the cost of significantly reduced accuracy when the pruning ratio was 0.75.

Both of the proposed pruning methods, *block pruning* and *micro-block pruning*, outperformed the existing pruning methods in terms of inference speed. It is noteworthy that the proposed techniques could achieve the inference speed improvement even if the pruning degree was as low as 0.25. This indicates that the proposed technique could also be useful when the degree of sparsity is not big, unlike the sparse matrix multiplication approaches [21]. Like other structured pruning approaches, block pruning also showed a steep accuracy drop as the pruning degree grew over 0.7. However, in micro-block pruning, the accuracy drop was kept comparable to that of the weight pruning approach as shown in Fig. 5(a). When the pruning ratio was 0.9, micro-block pruning could improve the inference speed by 1.88X, while keeping the accuracy drop as small as 4.34%.

Table 1. Inference times for 10K images (ILSVRC2012 dataset, $p = 0.75$)

Layer	Dense model	Weight pruning	Kernel-channel pruning	Block pruning	Micro-block pruning
CONV 1	7.299	7.2871	7.0415	4.4303	4.4389
CONV 2	16.4858	16.4467	8.6576	6.7373	9.0847
CONV 3	8.5782	8.5300	8.3145	3.2881	3.9726
CONV 4	13.2603	13.2111	6.0507	4.9525	6.1137
CONV 5	7.4322	7.3871	7.3415	2.8608	3.5273
CONV 6	12.7729	12.7183	4.8682	4.5343	5.6079
CONV 7	12.7752	12.7171	12.6178	4.4829	5.8945
CONV 8	17.2179	17.1750	5.4845	4.8694	5.6872
CONV 9	32.8858	32.8668	30.1641	8.3196	9.8863
CONV 10	32.8714	32.8587	9.0034	8.3439	9.8456
CONV 11	9.3954	9.3596	8.1469	3.0852	3.4741
CONV 12	9.3799	9.3467	3.3546	3.0728	3.4602
CONV 13	9.3775	9.3478	8.2401	3.0808	3.4604
FC 1	51.0578	51.1064	13.3335	50.3217	50.4551
FC 2	9.0312	9.0347	9.0724	8.9573	8.9951
FC 3	4.9850	4.9882	5.1253	4.9764	4.9929
Total (s)	254.8366	254.3816	146.8170	126.3137	138.8966
Speed (fps)	39.2408	39.3110	68.1120	79.1680	71.9960
Accuracy (%)	73.370	70.520	60.654	64.840	67.954

Table 1 reports the inference times taken to perform inference of 10,000 images using VGG16 trained with ILSVRC2012 dataset and pruned by different techniques with the pruning ratio of 0.75. Basically, the same tendency as the previous experiment has also been observed in this experiment. The weight pruning approach showed the lowest accuracy loss, but no inference speed gain achieved from the original one (*Dense*). Kernel-channel pruning showed considerable inference time improvement in every other convolutional layer (denoted as CONV n in the table), i.e., CONV 2, CONV 4, CONV 6, and so forth. This is because that the removed kernels in CONV 1, CONV 3, CONV 5, ..., cannot actually reduce the number of MAC operations in a work-group, but only the number of columns in W' (K in Fig. 1). (See Fig. 2 for this difference between the odd and even convolutional layers.) On the other hand, the proposed techniques constantly showed inference time improvements in all layers. In total, 2.01× and 1.83× speedups have been achieved by block pruning and micro-block pruning, respectively. Compared with the kernel-channel pruning approach, the proposed techniques have been better in terms of both speed and accuracy. Also, unlike the special sparse matrix multiplication approach, the proposed techniques could gain speedups when the pruning degree is low.

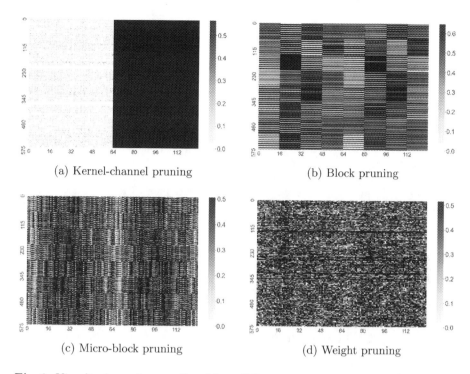

(a) Kernel-channel pruning   (b) Block pruning

(c) Micro-block pruning   (d) Weight pruning

Fig. 6. Visualized pruning results of four different pruning approaches (for the 3rd convolutional layer of *VGG16* with $p = 0.5$) - removed weights are colored in black.

The gain of the proposed technique, i.e., achieving significant speedups while keeping accuracy drops small, comes from the fact that the pruning unit is as fine-grained as the underlying GPU architecture allows. Figure 6 visualize the granularity of pruning in various pruning approaches by showing the weight values of the 3rd convolutional layer after pruning with $p = 0.5$, where the pruned weights are colored in black. As can be seen in the figure, the proposed block and micro-block pruning approaches choose the weight segments to be zeroed out in more fine-grained ways than the kernel-channel pruning approach. While weight pruning offers the most fine-grained pruning, it cannot exploit the parallel GPU architecture during inference as proven in the experiments.

7 Conclusion

In this paper, we propose two GPU architecture-aware pruning techniques: block pruning and micro-block pruning. In both, we aim at effectively skipping the memory copy and MAC operations associated with the pruned weight segments. While the traditional weight pruning requires special hardware skipping unit for the inference speed improvement, we could successfully speed up the inference on top of Commercial Off-The-Shelf (COTS) GPU by applying the proposed technique. Compared to the existing structured pruning methods, the proposed methods enable more efficient pruning in terms of both accuracy and speed.

References

1. Bottleson, J., Kim, S., Andrews, J., Bindu, P., Murthy, D.N., Jin, J.: clCaffe: OpenCL accelerated Caffe for convolutional neural networks. In: 2016 IEEE International Parallel and Distributed Processing Symposium Workshops (IPDPSW), pp. 50–57. IEEE (2016)
2. Chellapilla, K., Puri, S., Simard, P.: High performance convolutional neural networks for document processing. In: Tenth International Workshop on Frontiers in Handwriting Recognition. Suvisoft (2006)
3. Chen, X.: Escort: efficient sparse convolutional neural networks on GPUs. arXiv preprint arXiv:1802.10280 (2018)
4. Cheng, Y., Wang, D., Zhou, P., Zhang, T.: A survey of model compression and acceleration for deep neural networks. arXiv preprint arXiv:1710.09282 (2017)
5. Greathouse, J.L., Knox, K., Poła, J., Varaganti, K., Daga, M.: clSPARSE: a vendor-optimized open-source sparse BLAS library. In: Proceedings of the 4th International Workshop on OpenCL, pp. 1–4 (2016)
6. Gu, J., Liu, Y., Gao, Y., Zhu, M.: OpenCL caffe: accelerating and enabling a cross platform machine learning framework. In: Proceedings of the 4th International Workshop on OpenCL, pp. 1–5 (2016)
7. Han, S., et al.: EIE: efficient inference engine on compressed deep neural network. In: 2016 ACM/IEEE 43rd Annual International Symposium on Computer Architecture (ISCA), pp. 243–254. IEEE (2016)
8. Han, S., Pool, J., Tran, J., Dally, W.: Learning both weights and connections for efficient neural network. In: Advances in Neural Information Processing Systems, pp. 1135–1143 (2015)
9. Krizhevsky, A., Hinton, G., et al.: Learning multiple layers of features from tiny images (2009)
10. Krizhevsky, A., Sutskever, I., Hinton, G.E.: ImageNet classification with deep convolutional neural networks. In: Advances in Neural Information Processing Systems, pp. 1097–1105 (2012)
11. Li, H., Kadav, A., Durdanovic, I., Samet, H., Graf, H.P.: Pruning filters for efficient convnets. arXiv preprint arXiv:1608.08710 (2016)
12. Naumov, M., Chien, L., Vandermersch, P., Kapasi, U.: cuSPARSE library. In: GPU Technology Conference (2010)
13. Paszke, A., et al.: PyTorch: an imperative style, high-performance deep learning library. In: Wallach, H., Larochelle, H., Beygelzimer, A., d'Alché-Buc, F., Fox, E., Garnett, R. (eds.) Advances in Neural Information Processing Systems 32, pp. 8024–8035. Curran Associates, Inc. (2019). http://papers.neurips.cc/paper/9015-pytorch-an-imperative-style-high-performance-deep-learning-library.pdf
14. Perkins, H.: cltorch: a hardware-agnostic backend for the torch deep neural network library, based on OpenCL. arXiv preprint arXiv:1606.04884 (2016)
15. Radu, V., et al.: Performance aware convolutional neural network channel pruning for embedded GPUs. In: 2019 IEEE International Symposium on Workload Characterization (IISWC), pp. 24–34. IEEE (2019)
16. Redmon, J.: Darknet: Open source neural networks in C (2013)

17. Simonyan, K., Zisserman, A.: Very deep convolutional networks for large-scale image recognition. arXiv e-prints arXiv:1409.1556, September 2014
18. Stone, J.E., Gohara, D., Shi, G.: OpenCL: a parallel programming standard for heterogeneous computing systems. Comput. Sci. Eng. **12**(3), 66 (2010)
19. Tanner, D.: Autogemm, October 2015. https://github.com/clMathLibraries/clBLAS/wiki/AutoGemm
20. Wen, W., Wu, C., Wang, Y., Chen, Y., Li, H.: Learning structured sparsity in deep neural networks. In: Advances in Neural Information Processing Systems, pp. 2074–2082 (2016)
21. Yao, Z., Cao, S., Xiao, W., Zhang, C., Nie, L.: Balanced sparsity for efficient DNN inference on GPU. In: Proceedings of the AAAI Conference on Artificial Intelligence, vol. 33, pp. 5676–5683 (2019)
22. Zhu, J., Jiang, J., Chen, X., Tsui, C.Y.: SparseNN: an energy-efficient neural network accelerator exploiting input and output sparsity. In: 2018 Design, Automation & Test in Europe Conference & Exhibition (DATE), pp. 241–244. IEEE (2018)

Towards Flexible and Compiler-Friendly Layer Fusion for CNNs on Multicore CPUs

Zhongyi Lin[1][(✉)], Evangelos Georganas[2], and John D. Owens[1]

[1] University of California, Davis, USA
zhylin@ucdavis.edu
[2] Parallel Computing Laboratory, Intel Corporation, Santa Clara, USA

Abstract. In deep learning pipelines, we demonstrate the performance benefits and tradeoffs of combining two convolution layers into a single layer on multicore CPUs. We analyze when and why fusion may result in runtime speedups, and study three types of layer fusion: (a) 3-by-3 depthwise convolution with 1-by-1 convolution, (b) 3-by-3 convolution with 1-by-1 convolution, and (c) two 3-by-3 convolutions. We show that whether fusion is beneficial is dependent on numerous factors, including arithmetic intensity, machine balance, memory footprints, memory access pattern, and the way the output tensor is tiled. We devise a schedule for all these fusion types to automatically generate fused kernels for multicore CPUs through auto-tuning. With more than 30 layers extracted from five CNNs, we achieve a 1.04x geomean with 1.44x max speedup against separate kernels from MKLDNN, and a 1.24x geomean with 2.73x max speed up against AutoTVM-tuned separate kernels in standalone kernel benchmarks. We also show a 1.09x geomean with 1.29x max speedup against TVM, and a 2.09x geomean with 3.35x max speedup against MKLDNN-backed PyTorch, in end-to-end inference tests.

Keywords: Layer fusion · CNN · Multicore CPUs · Auto-tuning

1 Introduction

Convolutional neural networks (CNNs) have played an increasingly important role in research and industry for the past decade. CNNs are constructed with a series of layers/operators (*ops*). In the vast majority of CNN implementations, ops have a one-to-one correspondence with compute kernels. For reduced memory requirements and/or better producer-consumer locality, production CNNs perform *fusion* for certain ops, i.e., combining two or more neighboring ops into one and computing it with one single kernel. At its core, the fusion problem is a balancing problem between computation and communication, or between the communication of different memory hierarchies, with the hope that reducing mainmemory communication will result in only modest amounts of extra computation

Supported by Intel Labs.

L. Sousa et al. (Eds.): Euro-Par 2021, LNCS 12820, pp. 232–248, 2021.
https://doi.org/10.1007/978-3-030-85665-6_15

or data movement in high-level memory and hence an overall speedup. In particular, today's deep learning (DL) frameworks and compilers (e.g., TVM [5], Tensorflow [1], PyTorch [18], and MXNet [4]), and proprietary kernel libraries like cuDNN [7] and MKLDNN often trivially fuse a convolution layer with the following element-wise layers to save the cost of data movement. Other fusion opportunities such as parallel convolution branch fusion for structures in models like Inception-V3 [22] can be realized by methods like relaxed graph substitution, as proposed by Jia et al. [13].

More complex is the fusion of neighboring *complex ops*, e.g., convolution (conv) and depthwise convolution (dw-conv). As these ops often appear as the hotspot of CNNs, which are compute and/or memory bandwidth intensive, fusing them is a potential way to further enhance compute performance. Showing performance improvements for this fusion type is a significant challenge for three reasons. First, unlike the aforementioned fusion types, simple techniques like inlining or data concatenation and split (to reuse existing proprietary libraries) would not work due to the memory access pattern of these ops. Instead, new compute kernels are necessary, and the optimization space of a fused op is so complex, with so many parameters, that a straightforward search would be impractical. Second, the standalone kernels used as a performance baseline are already highly optimized. Finally, integrating a fused kernel into current DL frameworks is also difficult, as modern frameworks are primarily designed at the granularity of one-op that maps typically to one-kernel.

In this paper, we focus on three opportunities for the fusion of two consecutive complex ops: (1) 3-by-3 dw-conv with 1-by-1 conv, (2) 3-by-3 conv with 1-by-1 conv, and (3) two 3-by-3 convs, all of which are commonly seen in CNNs. The challenge we address in this paper is to show not just *where* we can show performance improvements from complex op fusion but also *why*. We first propose a set of tiling and scheduling principles to intelligently reduce the otherwise intractable parameter space and search for the combination that leads to the best performance. These principles can also be extended to problems with complex loop structures, including other fusion types. Based on these principles, we devise a schedule template for auto-tuning these fused kernels on multicore CPUs, and propose an approach of integrating the fused kernels/ops into DL compiler pipelines. Both of these ideas can be adopted by production DL compilers. We implement the fused kernels by incorporating LIBXSMM's [11] batch-reduce GEMM [9] micro-kernels and extending AutoTVM, TVM's auto-tuning tool, to search for the best schedule. We also integrate these kernels into TVM's compiler infrastructure for end-to-end tests by creating a new fused op.

We make the following contributions:

- We analyze the fusion of two complex ops and answer the question when and why such fusion is beneficial.
- We propose a methodology with tiling and scheduling principles of composing fused kernels for multicore CPUs, and implement kernels for three types of two complex-op fusion.
- We achieve 1.24X and 1.04X geomean speedup in a standalone kernel-level benchmark against TVM and MKLDNN respectively, and 1.09X and 2.09X

geomean speedup in end-to-end tests, by testing with more than 30 workloads extracted from five real CNN models on three multicore CPU platforms.

2   Related Work

Kernel Optimizations and Auto Tuning. Convolutions are the ops that take the largest runtime in current CNNs. They can be implemented in many styles, e.g., direct convolution, im2col + GEMM [7], FFT-based [16], and Winograd-based [14], etc., on different types of compute devices. For direct convolution on CPUs, Georganas et al. [8,9] proposed batch-reduce GEMM (BRGEMM) as a basic building block for tensor contractions and convolution and claimed to achieve better runtime performance than MKLDNN (now renamed to oneDNN). In our work, we adopt the BRGEMM micro-kernel implementation provided in the LIBXSMM [11] library as a building block for our fused kernels.

Autotuning is a common approach for optimizing kernel implementations and has benefited from continuous development through the years. Autotuning can be employed together with the idea of decoupling compute and schedule central to Ragan-Kelley et al. [19,20] and developed by Mullapudi et al. [17] in Halide as well as Chen et al. [5,6] in TVM, easing the process of developing high-performance implementations for DL workloads. Recently, the idea of autoscheduling [2,26] breaks through auto-tuning's limit of relying on a well-composed schedule template by automatically searching for schedules. In this research we adopt AutoTVM as our tool for auto-tuning; in future work, we plan to also port our approach to autoscheduling tools.

Layer Fusion. The fusion of multiple consecutive convolutions first appears in Alwani et al. [3]. Their kernel implementation is completely hand-tuned on FPGAs and the fusion space is explored with a dynamic programming approach. Wang el al. [24] improved inference time on GPUs using a designated subset of fused convolutional layers. However, these works neither explore the large space of code optimization nor show a clear way how the fused kernels can be handily integrated into production end-to-end tests. Our work is the first that focuses on multicore CPUs and addresses the above issues.

3   Principles of Effective Layer Fusion

Consider a CNN model that runs on a multicore system, e.g., a multicore CPU. A well-optimized single-op kernel on this system will take advantage of all cores. Typically such a kernel will output a tensor and that tensor is divided into multi-dimensional *tiles*, with an equal number of tiles computed on each core in parallel. This tiling may be a spatial tiling (e.g., across one or more axes among N, H, W in a typical 4D activation tensor) and/or a tiling across channels (e.g., the C axis). At the end of the kernel, all data is written back to memory before the next kernel begins. The next kernel will then read its input from memory assuming the input is large enough and does not to fit in any level of cache.

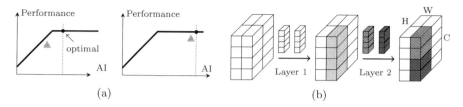

Fig. 1. (a) Roofline model examples. Dotted lines are theoretical fused kernel AI. Orange triangles are empirical fused AI (efAI) derived from separate kernel stats. Fusion is likely: (left) beneficial, as efAI is not close to optimal; or (right) not beneficial as efAI is very close to optimal. (b) Tiling across the channel axis (C) of the second layer results in recomputation on different cores: the blue and red tensors reside on different cores, while both cores need to compute the green tensor. (Color figure online)

In this paper, we show performance gains from fusing kernels of two complex ops. The important contribution of this paper, however, is not the performance gains but instead why and how we achieve these performance gains. What kind of kernels should be fused, and how should we fuse them?

One of our key tools for analysis and verification is the roofline model [25], with which we can determine if a kernel's performance is bound by memory or compute. We characterize the combination of the two separate kernels in the roofline model, with the total compute equal to the sum of the compute in the two kernels, and the memory requirements equal to the sum of the reads and writes for both kernels. If the fused-kernel result is memory-bound, the two kernels are *usually* good candidates for fusion, because fusion's primary benefit is saving the memory writes and reads between the two kernels, with the hope to replace slow (main memory) accesses with fast (cache) accesses. However, this is trickier in practice, since many successful fusions we perform tend to be compute-bound. We also see successful fusion for two compute-bound kernels (as we show in a later example) as well as failure for fusion involving extremely memory-bound kernels like 5-by-5 dw-conv. Nevertheless, the results from the roofline model are generally predictive. We can also refer to the empirical results of proprietary separate kernels to select workloads that might benefit from fusion. As shown in Fig. 1a, fusion is likely beneficial if the derived empirical fused roofline is not too close to the peak throughput at the theoretical fused AI, as fusion moves the roofline towards the *upper right* if it speeds up. In contrast, fusion is likely not beneficial if the derived empirical fused roofline is almost optimal.

We begin by looking at the per-core output of the first kernel and the per-core input of the second kernel. For some pairs of kernels, these are identical, and we can simply concatenate these into one kernel in a straightforward fashion. More often, though, these two do not match. In these cases, writing to memory at the end of the first kernel serves two purposes. The first is to allow a reshuffling of data through the memory system (essentially, a permutation of the intermediate output tensor, distributed across cores). The second is to allow a broadcast so that the output of one core in the first kernel can serve as the input for multiple cores in the second kernel. If we implement a fused kernel, our implementation must either perform a significant amount of intra-core communication for data reuse or perform redundant recompute. Notice that the memory footprint of fused workloads might fit in any level of cache or none of them. For the extreme case that the footprint fits in L1, there is no data movement cost of the intermediate output to reduce, as it always stays in this fastest cache. We discover that this almost never happens with real CNN workloads, and therefore, from this point of view, fusion is always worth trying.

We employ *tiling* and *scheduling* to find the balance between fusion and speedup. Tiling expresses the subdivision of tensor input/intermediate/output data in a way that allows effective and scalable parallel execution. The computation of each part of the output tensor is typically expressed as a series of nested loops, and we also have the freedom to schedule (i.e., reorder, split, merge, parallelize, etc.) these loops to optimize for locality and execution. Because the two unfused kernels are almost certainly highly optimized for the target architecture when using proprietary libraries, we must make near-optimal decisions for tiling and scheduling to achieve competitive performance with our fused kernel.

Tiling Principles. One of the most important decisions in tiling is choosing along which axis to tile. In our fastest kernels on CPUs, we prefer tiling the second layer along spatial axes to tiling along channel axes, because the latter requires (redundant) recomputation of layer-one entries that are inputs to multiple different tiles along layer-two's channel axis, as shown in Fig. 1b. This rules out some compute-heavy kernels like the last few layers of ResNets (i.e., $res\_4x/5x$ as examples), which typically tile along a (relatively long) channel axis.

The spatial axes of the second layer also need to offer sufficient parallelism for a full tiling; without enough parallelism here, fusion does not make sense. In general, CNN kernel implementations on CPUs tend to pack tensors so that the channel axis is packed as vectors in the last dimension, so CPUs with longer vector length, e.g., AVX-512, are better candidates for fusion, since they exploit the parallelism along the channel axis and compensate for our reluctance to tile/parallelize that axis across cores. Also, more cores make fusion more attractive if batch size goes up and/or the spatial dimension is large, since either of these cases expose more potential parallelism.

Finally, for effective fusion, the tiles for the first and second kernels in the separate case should be comparable in size. Given a fixed-size cache, a significant mismatch in size between the two tiles reduces the opportunity for capturing producer-consumer locality, as it leverages the cache poorly. The *mnb1* workloads shown later in Table 2 are examples of such a failure.

Scheduling Principles. Once we have determined our tiling, we turn to the problem of scheduling. A typical fused kernel in our pipelines of interest has on the order of a dozen loops as well as the option to split these loops. Any sort of exhaustive search over valid reorderings of these loops is virtually intractable. Yet our experience is that some search is necessary; the performance landscape of the many possible implementations is complex enough that auto-tuning is necessary to find the fastest fused kernel.

Our approach is to restrict the search space down to a manageable level by only searching over a subset of the loops. In particular, we do not attempt to change the order of the outermost and innermost loops as they either do not affect data locality or are fixed for optimal register usage within a micro-kernel. In contrast, we do search the remaining loops, whose reordering can have a significant impact on data locality. This will be discussed in the next section.

4   Implementation

We mainly focus on three types of 2-layer fusion: (1) 3-by-3 depthwise convolution (dw-conv) followed by 1-by-1 convolution (conv); (2) 3-by-3 conv followed by 1-by-1 conv; (3) two 3-by-3 convs. The first type occurs commonly in computationally lightweight CNN models, e.g., MobileNet-V1 [12], MobileNet-V2 [21], MNasNet-A1 [23], etc. The second and third types occur in computationally heavyweight CNN models like ResNets [10], etc. In this section, we first introduce how we compose schedules to generate kernels for these fusion types, followed by how these kernels are integrated into the TVM inference pipeline.

Kernel-Level Optimization. Often a part of a domain-specific compiler, modern autotuners usually input the *schedule* that we described above, which describes how the mathematical expression of an op is mapped to the hardware (e.g., loop orderings and manipulations, as well as the search for the split loop lengths and ordering combinations that lead to the best performance) to tune the kernel. This may result in many possible mappings and hence a large search space. For example, two axes of length 4 being split and reordered has a search space size of 3 (split of first axis) × 3 (split of second axis) × 2 (reordering) = 18. If two layers are naively fused, the search space size grows exponentially and becomes intractable, even without considering the extra possibility of loop unrolling in the innermost loops. As an aside, though they do not affect the search space, an autotuned fuser must also efficiently integrate element-wise post ops like batch-normalization, ReLU, etc. that follow all complex ops except for the last one.

Our goal is to achieve high performance on the fused kernel and meanwhile limit the search space to make searching tractable. We accomplish this by classifying loops into three categories: parallel loops, micro-kernel loops, and tunable loops. We determined robust, fixed strategies for the first two categories and thus reduce our search space to only searching for the optimal configuration of the third.

We choose to fix the ordering of the first two categories of loops, because reordering parallel loops is trivial for batch size 1, while micro-kernel loops are mapped to ready-to-use micro-kernels with fixed loop order. In our schedules, we place the parallel loops at the outermost location, micro-kernel loops at the innermost location, and tunable loops in between. The skeleton of our implementation structure is shown in Algorithm 1 and Fig. 2. We implement our kernel with the BRGEMM micro-kernels from LIBXSMM. Instead of using the common $NCHW$ or $NHWC$ formats for convolution, we use a packed format, e.g.,

---

Algorithm 1. Fused kernel schedule template with BRGEMM micro-kernels.

1: **Inputs:** $input \in \mathbb{R}^{N \times IC_1 \times IH \times IW \times ic_1}$, $weights_1 \in \mathbb{R}^{OC_1 \times IC_1 \times FH_1 \times FW_1 \times ic_1 \times oc_1}$, $weights_2 \in \mathbb{R}^{OC_2 \times IC_2 \times FH_2 \times FW_2 \times ic_2 \times oc_2}$, optional post ops parameters, e.g., $bias_1 \in \mathbb{R}^{OC_1 \times oc_1}, bias_2 \in \mathbb{R}^{OC_2 \times oc_2}$

2: **Outputs:** $output \in \mathbb{R}^{N \times OC_2 \times OH \times OW \times oc_2}$

3: **Split** OH into H_t, H_o, and H

4: **Split** OW into W_t, W_o, and W

5: **Split** IC_2 into IC_o and IC_i

6: **for** fused($n = 0 \ldots N - 1$, $ht = 0 \ldots H_t - 1$, $wt = 0 \ldots W_t - 1$) **do**

7:     **Exhaustively search** the order of OC_2, IC_o, H_o, and W_o, and mark them as loop 1, 2, 3, 4, and the parallel loop as loop 0 {e.g., IC_o is loop 2.}

8:     **Arbitrarily pick** a loop x from loop 0, 1, 2, 3, 4 {e.g., x is 3.}

9:     **for** loop 1 **do**

10:        **for** loop 2 **do**

11:            **for** loop 3 **do** {Sub-tensors compute here.}

12:                **for** loop 4 **do**

13:                    BRGEMM micro-kernel for layer 1 sub-tensor

14:                **end for**

15:                Compute post ops of layer 1 if necessary

16:                **for** loop 4 **do**

17:                    BRGEMM micro-kernel for layer 2 sub-tensor

18:                **end for**

19:            **end for**

20:        **end for** {IC_o finishes.}

21:        Compute post ops of layer 2 if necessary

22:    **end for**

23: **end for**

$NCHW[x]c$ for feature maps, and $(OC)(IC)H_f W_f[x]ic[y]oc$ for weights, where $x, y = 8, 16, 32, 64 \ldots$, for better data locality on CPUs [9]. At line 3 to 5 of the algorithm, OH, OW, and the reduce loop IC_2 of the *output* tensor are split into 10 loops including the unsplit N. Each loop is split so that the lengths of each sub-loop are factors of its length. We do not split OC_2 as tiling across it brings recomputation as we discuss above. The parallel loops, i.e., N, H_t, and W_t, are fused and parallelized across multiple CPU cores at line 7. Loops H, W, and $oc_{1/2}$ and reduce loops, including FH, FW, IC_i, and $ic_{1/2}$, are all micro-kernel loops expressed within BRGEMM micro-kernels. The remaining four loops, i.e. OC_2, IC_o, H_o, and W_o, are left as the tunable loops to be searched by the auto-tuner.

In our implementation, we exhaustively search for all the orderings of these four loops and at which loop layer we place the computation, i.e., *compute_at*. The sub-tensors of both layers are computed at a loop that is picked among any of these four loops or the fused parallel loop. From a cache point of view, the input feature map sub-tensor of layer one is distributed to different cores on the CPUs, while the weights of each layer are streamed to cache. The sub-tensor output of layer one is computed with vanilla loop ordering if layer one is a dw-conv, or by calling the BRGEMM micro-kernel if layer one is a conv. Its size is

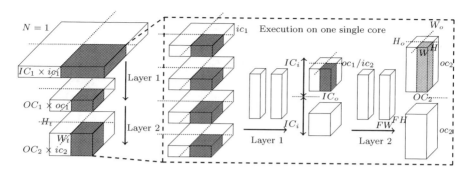

Fig. 2. Algorithm visualization. (**Left**) Tensors are tiled for parallel multicore execution. (**Right**) A light blue (incomplete, as loop IC_o is not fully contracted) sub-tensor of size (H, W, oc_2) is computed from all blue (complete) sub-tensors. Red/green/orange mark the parallel/tunable/micro-kernel loops, respectively. (Color figure online)

inferred by the compiler given the output size of its consumer, i.e., (H, W, oc_2) is known. This sub-tensor is always complete, i.e., all its reduce loops are fully contracted, before it is consumed by layer two, because otherwise it incurs extra computation for each of the incomplete slices. Therefore, it is safe to insert any post ops computation directly after it. Subsequently, this sub-tensor always stays in cache and is consumed by layer two to produce a slice with size (H, W, oc_2). This slice is not necessarily complete as the loop x it computes could be inside the outermost reduce loop of all, IC_o. We insert the post ops right after IC_o because they can only be computed when IC_o is fully contracted. Therefore, the sub-tensor of layer two always stays in cache for proper tiling factors until it is complete and no longer needs access.

We found that grouping the loops in this way greatly limits the search space, making auto-tuning feasible, but still results in high-performance fusion. It can also be extended more generally to polyhedral problems including fusing other types of layers. In this case, a performant micro-kernel is necessary to serve as the core of the output schedule.

AutoTVM Implementation of Fused Kernel. We realize this implementation as an AutoTVM schedule. We first define TE compute functions for the fused layer workloads, then we create AutoTVM tuning tasks with these compute functions and schedules so that AutoTVM can auto-tune them using the XGBoost algorithm. For fast convergence, the schedule is tuned without post ops being added since they do not affect the results, while when the tuning config is produced, we apply it to a new inference schedule where post ops are added as necessary. The methodology can be handily extended to multiple layers with the (straightforward) addition of compiler support, as we can simply follow the same rule by only blocking the last layer being fused and stacking all previous layers at loop x. In fact, this methodology resembles the (manual) 'pyramid' method proposed by Alwani et al. [3], but we generate the fused kernel code automatically via auto-tuning. We also notice that at the cost of searching a much bigger

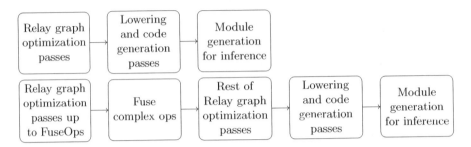

Fig. 3. Top: TVM pipeline without complex-op fusion; **Bottom:** TVM pipeline with complex-op fusion.

space by further splitting the second loop group into eight loops and reordering them, higher fused kernel performance could potentially be achieved with better cache blocking options. However, the advantage of this schedule against ours is marginal, which also requires both smartly designed heuristics and a more powerful autotuner. Hence, we leave the exploration of this idea as future work.

Compiler Integration of Fusion for End-to-End Test. To integrate the fused kernel into end-to-end (full-CNN) tests, we need (1) a new op that defines the compute of the fused conv layers in a compute graph and (2) a compiler pass that is inserted into the pipeline to rewrite the graph for fusion. Both of these are missing in all DL frameworks. Also, post ops like batch-normalization (BN) of the layers being fused need to be properly handled. Since BN ops are usually simplified to *bias-adds* with parameters such as *mean* and *gamma* folded into *weights* for inference, we do not keep them in the compute function for our *fused-conv2D* op. We simply keep the *bias* tensors of each layer together with the input and weights as the inputs to the *fused-conv2D* op, such that the new op is equivalent to a sub-graph of two fused layers and their post ops, e.g., dw-conv/conv+bias-add+relu+conv+bias-add+relu. As currently most DL frameworks fuse only element-wise ops, we must ensure that the complex-op-fusion pass is inserted *after inference simplification* where ops like BN are simplified, and *before element-wise op fusion* where all element-wise ops are fused.

Figure 3 presents how we leverage TVM's existing compiler pipeline to integrate our design into it. Following the above principles, we create a new Relay op for the fused conv layers, as well as a new compiler pass to detect the fusable patterns and rewrite them with the *fused-conv2D* ops. In the TVM pipeline, a Relay compute graph is passed through passes that optimize the graph structure, and then passes for code generation, and finally module generation. We insert the new *fuse-conv* pass right before the *fuse-ops* pass such that post ops like *bias-add* ops are properly handled for the *fused-conv2D*, while post ops are still normally handled for other unfused complex ops in the following *fuse-ops* pass. Our *fused-conv2D* op is also compatible with TVM's graph tuning [15] for layout optimization for CPU inference.

5   Results and Analysis

We extract 33 eligible layers with batch size 1 from five CNN models, including MobileNet-V1, MobileNet-V2, MNasNet-A1, ResNet-18, and ResNet-50. The full list of layers can be found in Table 2. We auto-tune each kernel for 4000 iterations using AutoTVM with XGBoost as the searching algorithm. We conduct both throughput and roofline analysis on these workloads, and integrate them into the end-to-end tests of the five models. The experiments are conducted on one Intel Core(TM) i7_7700K CPU @ 4.2 GHz, one Intel Xeon quad-core Google Cloud Platform (GCP) server (unknown model with Cascade Lake microarchitecture) @ 3.1 GHz, and one AMD EPYC 7B12 quad-core GCP server @ 2.25 GHz, all with Linux Ubuntu 18.04, Python 3.8, and PyTorch 1.8.1. We run our kernel-level experiments for fused kernels against separate kernels shipped by MKLDNN and those generated by AutoTVM as baselines, and model-level experiments against the baselines of AutoTVM + graph tuner as well as MKLDNN-backed PyTorch. For roofline analysis, we measure the DRAM bytes with PCM, and measure the cache bytes and FLOP counts of the kernels with SDE.

Kernel-Level Experiments. In Fig. 4, we show the throughput of all the kernels on three platforms normalized with respect to MKLDNN in the standalone kernel benchmark. Overall, we achieve {geomean, maximum, and minimum} speed-ups of fused-kernel against MKLDNN-separate-kernels of {1.04X, 1.44X, and 0.53X}, and against TVM-separate-kernels of {1.24X, 2.73X, and 0.63X}. As expected, we see that workloads with big activations in their first layer such as $mv1\_1$, $mv2\_1$, $mv2\_2\_1$, etc. have higher speed-ups. Comparing all the MobileNet-V1 and MobileNet-V2 workloads, i.e., $mv1\_x$ and $mv2\_x$, we can see that although the spatial size of the activation changes almost the same way throughout the model, e.g., $112 \rightarrow 56 \rightarrow 28 \rightarrow 14 \rightarrow 7$, we see a higher overall fusion speed-up on $mv2\_x$ than on $mv1\_x$. This is because $mv2\_x$ tends to scale *down* the channel axis between its fused layers, e.g., $mv2\_1$ has 32 channels for its 3-by-3 dw-conv and only 16 channels for its 1-by-1 conv, while $mv1\_x$ tends to scale *up*. Therefore, generally $mv2\_x$ is less compute-bound than $mv1\_x$ and in these cases, closer to the machine balance, as we will show later. We can thus suggest to model designers that without sacrificing accuracy, models can benefit more from fusion if the sizes of adjacent layers are designed to have more balanced AI. In addition, we still see a few examples where considerably compute-bound ResNet workloads are sped up by fusion, which suggests that even compute-bound kernels could also benefit from our methods.

Across platforms we observe that GCP Intel, the only AVX-512 CPU with the highest peak throughput in our evaluation, achieves the highest geomean speed-up (1.13X) on fused kernels against MKLDNN, versus (1.01X) and (0.99X) on the other two platforms. This implies the fact that fusion works better on platforms with higher peak throughput (making workloads 'less compute-bound').

We also plot the roofline model of all the fused and separate kernels we test on the i7_7700K CPU in Fig. 5. We treat each pair of TVM separate kernels and MKLDNN kernels as one standalone kernel and derive its AI as

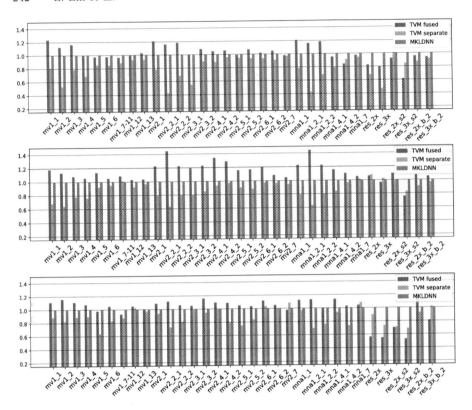

Fig. 4. Throughput comparison between fused and separate kernels without post ops, normalized with respect to MKLDNN. A "TVM fused" result of greater than one indicates our fusion delivers better performance than MKLDNN. **Top:** Intel i7-7700K (511 GFLOPS); **middle:** GCP Intel (711 GFLOPS); **bottom:** GCP AMD (413 GFLOPS).

$AI_s = (\text{flop}_1 + \text{flop}_2)/(\text{bytes}_1 + \text{bytes}_2)$, where bytes_1 and bytes_2 are measured memory traffic for either DRAM or cache. We observe a trend that the roofline of the fused kernel gets closer and closer to that of the separate kernels for both DRAM and L2, especially in workloads from $mv1\_1$ to $mv1\_13$ in MobileNet-V1. This again verifies that fusion tends to get less benefit at later layers than earlier ones. Typically, for workloads in MobileNet-V2 and MNasNet-A1 such as $mv2\_2\_1$, $mv2\_3\_1$, etc., the fused kernels have a smaller advantage on AI compared to their predecessor or successor workloads that have either similar input or output feature sizes. This is because the bottleneck of these workloads is the stride-2 access of their input feature maps that reduces the data reuse; this bottleneck is not relieved by fusion. We also verify that overall the theoretical peaks DRAM AI for $mv2\_x$ tend to be closer to the machine balance than $mv1\_x$ so that they benefit more from fusion. We see that most of the fused kernels still do not reach the theoretical peak DRAM AI and incur extra DRAM accesses, which means there is still room for optimization by extending the schedule's

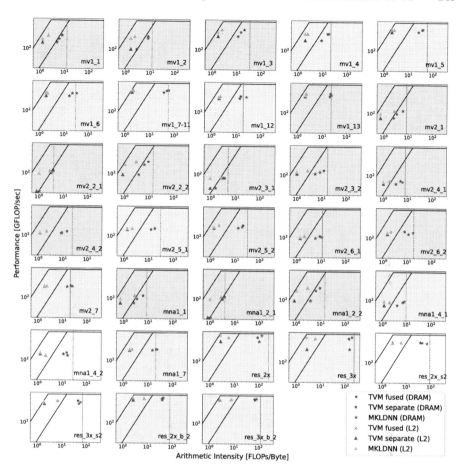

Fig. 5. Standalone kernel rooflines of all the fused and separate kernels without post ops on the Intel i7_7700K CPU. In most cases, both DRAM and L2 AI of the fused kernel moves towards the *upper-right* as fusion delivers better performance. The left and right slopes represent the L2 bandwidth (198.9 GB/s) and DRAM bandwidth (34.7 GB/s). The vertical blue dotted line represents the theoretical peak DRAM AI for the fused kernel. The red and grey background mark layers in which our fused kernel beats both and at least one, respectively. (Color figure online)

search space. Notice that in all cases the L2 AI moves to the *right*, indicating that fusion increases data reuse in L2 cache. For workloads being sped up, the L2 AI moves towards the *upper-right*, which matches our expectation. Among those not sped up, the rooflines of ResNet workloads are very close to the peak throughput and theoretical peak fused AI intersection, matching our previous synthetic examples that project such workloads are less likely to benefit from fusion.

Table 1. End-to-end inference time (in millisecond) of five models on three CPUs. Shortest inference time across tools are shown in bold. Fusion doesn't apply to ResNet-18 on GCP AMD, since the fusion performance of two 3-by-3 convs is inferior to that of both TVM separate and MKLDNN.

CPU types	Models	TVM fused	TVM separate	PyTorch
Intel i7_7700K	MobileNet-V1	**3.38**	3.58	6.11
	MobileNet-V2	**2.44**	2.92	7.28
	MNasNet-A1	**3.31**	3.73	6.53
	ResNet-18	9.69	**9.35**	10.58
	ResNet-50	**20.42**	20.66	26.80
GCP Intel	MobileNet-V1	**2.77**	3.00	5.97
	MobileNet-V2	**2.35**	2.89	7.88
	MNasNet-A1	**3.42**	3.66	7.62
	ResNet-18	**7.17**	7.24	9.79
	ResNet-50	**16.18**	16.19	24.96
GCP AMD	MobileNet-V1	**7.72**	8.42	8.83
	MobileNet-V2	**4.65**	6.01	10.23
	MNasNet-A1	**6.79**	7.35	9.83
	ResNet-18	–	**15.38**	15.47
	ResNet-50	**38.86**	39.82	39.60

End-to-End Experiments. We present the results of the end-to-end inference tests for the five models on three CPU platforms in Table 1. For each model, we tune variants of the compute graph that use a fused form of kernel pairs where we have seen a kernel-level advantage, and for layers that fusion does not have an advantage, e.g., *mv2_7*, *mna1_7*, etc., both fused and not fused, as the fused version might still perform better if layout transformations are needed for the unfused versions. Then we select the instance with the shortest inference time. In practice, we see only a few variants per model and this tuning step is short.

In all test cases except for ResNet-18 on i7_7700K and GCP AMD, fusion speeds up inference, with up to 3.35X against PyTorch for MobileNet-V2 on GCP Intel and 1.29X against TVM-separate for MobileNet-V2 on GCP AMD. We observe that the end-to-end speed-up is not exactly aligned with the aggregation of individual kernel speed-ups. In the standalone kernel benchmark, the cache is flushed for each iteration and the input data of layer one is always read from DRAM. But in end-to-end tests, the output data of a layer stays in cache and may allow the next layer to benefit from producer-consumer locality. Also, the framework itself might also affect the end-to-end results.

We see that the speedups of ResNets are marginal (up to 1.02X) on all three CPU platforms, matching our expectation that fusion for compute-bound layers has limited benefit. We only fuse *res_2x* for ResNet-18, and *res_2x* and/or *res_3x* for ResNet-50, while it is the number of *res_4x* that primarily drives the depth

Table 2. Layer table. Input sizes are in (N,H,W,C) format, while layer configs are (filter HW, output channel or multiplier, stride HW, layer type, post op). Layers that do not benefit from fusion are crossed out and not shown in the result section.

Models	Name	Input	Layer 1	Layer 2
MobileNet-V1	mv1_1	(1, 112, 112, 32)	(3, 1, 1, dw-conv, relu)	(1, 64, 1, conv, relu)
	mv1_2	(1, 112, 112, 64)	(3, 1, 2, dw-conv, relu)	(1, 128, 1, conv, relu)
	mv1_3	(1, 56, 56, 128)	(3, 1, 1, dw-conv, relu)	(1, 128, 1, conv, relu)
	mv1_4	(1, 56, 56, 128)	(3, 1, 2, dw-conv, relu)	(1, 256, 1, conv, relu)
	mv1_5	(1, 28, 28, 256)	(3, 1, 1, dw-conv, relu)	(1, 256, 1, conv, relu)
	mv1_6	(1, 28, 28, 256)	(3, 1, 2, dw-conv, relu)	(1, 512, 1, conv, relu)
	mv1_7-11	(1, 14, 14, 512)	(3, 1, 1, dw-conv, relu)	(1, 512, 1, conv, relu)
	mv1_12	(1, 14, 14, 512)	(3, 1, 2, dw-conv, relu)	(1, 1024, 1, conv, relu)
	mv1_13	(1, 7, 7, 1024)	(3, 1, 1, dw-conv, relu)	(1, 1024, 1, conv, relu)
MobileNet-V2	mv1_1	(1, 112, 112, 32)	(3, 1, 1, dw-conv, relu6)	(1, 16, 1, conv, bias)
	mv2_2_1	(1, 112, 112, 96)	(3, 1, 2, dw-conv, relu6)	(1, 24, 1, conv, bias)
	mv2_2_2	(1, 56, 56, 144)	(3, 1, 1, dw-conv, relu6)	(1, 24, 1, conv, bias)
	mv2_3_1	(1, 56, 56, 144)	(3, 1, 2, dw-conv, relu6)	(1, 32, 1, conv, bias)
	mv2_3_2	(1, 28, 28, 192)	(3, 1, 1, dw-conv, relu6)	(1, 32, 1, conv, bias)
	mv2_4_1	(1, 28, 28, 192)	(3, 1, 2, dw-conv, relu6)	(1, 64, 1, conv, bias)
	mv2_4_2	(1, 14, 14, 384)	(3, 1, 1, dw-conv, relu6)	(1, 64, 1, conv, bias)
	mv2_5_1	(1, 14, 14, 384)	(3, 1, 1, dw-conv, relu6)	(1, 96, 1, conv, bias)
	mv2_5_2	(1, 14, 14, 576)	(3, 1, 1, dw-conv, relu6)	(1, 96, 1, conv, bias)
	mv2_6_1	(1, 14, 14, 576)	(3, 1, 2, dw-conv, relu6)	(1, 160, 1, conv, bias)
	mv2_6_2	(1, 7, 7, 960)	(3, 1, 1, dw-conv, relu6)	(1, 160, 1, conv, bias)
	mv2_7	(1, 7, 7, 960)	(3, 1, 1, dw-conv, relu6)	(1, 320, 1, conv, bias)
MNasNet-A1	mna1_1	(1, 112, 112, 32)	(3, 1, 1, dw-conv, relu)	(1, 16, 1, conv, bias)
	mna1_2_1	(1, 112, 112, 96)	(3, 1, 2, dw-conv, relu)	(1, 24, 1, conv, bias)
	mna1_2_2	(1, 56, 56, 144)	(3, 1, 1, dw-conv, relu)	(1, 24, 1, conv, bias)
	mna1_4_1	(1, 28, 28, 240)	(3, 1, 2, dw-conv, relu)	(1, 80, 1, conv, bias)
	mna1_4_2	(1, 14, 14, 480)	(3, 1, 1, dw-conv, relu)	(1, 80, 1, conv, bias)
	mna1_7	(1, 7, 7, 960)	(3, 1, 1, dw-conv, relu)	(1, 320, 1, conv, bias)
~~MNasNet-B1~~	~~mnb1_3_1~~	(1, 56, 56, 72)	(5, 1, 2, conv, relu)	(1, 40, 1, conv, bias)
	~~mnb1_3_2~~	(1, 28, 28, 240)	(5, 1, 1, conv, relu)	(1, 40, 1, conv, bias)
	~~mnb1_5_1~~	(1, 14, 14, 480)	(3, 1, 1, conv, relu)	(1, 112, 1, conv, bias)
	~~mnb1_5_2~~	(1, 14, 14, 672)	(3, 1, 1, conv, relu)	(1, 112, 1, conv, bias)
	~~mnb1_6_1~~	(1, 14, 14, 672)	(5, 1, 2, conv, relu)	(1, 160, 1, conv, bias)
	~~mnb1_6_2~~	(1, 7, 7, 960)	(5, 1, 1, conv, relu)	(1, 160, 1, conv, bias)
ResNet-18	res_2x	(1, 56, 56, 64)	(3, 64, 1, conv, relu)	(3, 64, 1, conv, bias)
	res_3x	(1, 28, 28, 128)	(3, 128, 1, conv, relu)	(3, 128, 1, conv, bias)
	~~res_4x~~	(1, 14, 14, 256)	(3, 256, 1, conv, relu)	(3, 256, 1, conv, bias)
	~~res_5x~~	(1, 7, 7, 512)	(3, 512, 1, conv, relu)	(3, 512, 1, conv, bias)
	res_2x_s2	(1, 56, 56, 64)	(3, 64, 2, conv, relu)	(3, 64, 1, conv, bias)
	res_3x_s2	(1, 28, 28, 128)	(3, 128, 2, conv, relu)	(3, 128, 1, conv, bias)
	~~res_4x_s2~~	(1, 14, 14, 256)	(3, 256, 2, conv, relu)	(3, 256, 1, conv, bias)
	~~res_5x_s2~~	(1, 7, 7, 512)	(3, 512, 2, conv, relu)	(3, 512, 1, conv, bias)
ResNet-50	res_2x_b_2	(1, 56, 56, 64)	(3, 64, 1, conv, relu)	(1, 256, 1, conv, relu)
	res_3x_b_2	(1, 28, 28, 128)	(3, 128, 1, conv, relu)	(1, 512, 1, conv, relu)
	~~res_4x_b_2~~	(1, 14, 14, 256)	(3, 256, 1, conv, relu)	(1, 1024, 1, conv, relu)
	~~res_5x_b_2~~	(1, 7, 7, 512)	(3, 512, 1, conv, relu)	(1, 2048, 1, conv, relu)

of ResNets; thus we expect to see marginal benefit from kernel fusion on ResNets that have more than 50 layers.

6 Conclusion and Future Works

Individual kernels, such as those inside MKLDNN or NVIDIA's cuDNN, are highly optimized. They set a high bar for the implementation of fused kernels. One conclusion we draw is that the benefits of fusion are dependent on both the characteristics of the workloads and the CPU on which they are run, and the benefits of fusion are difficult to predict and, at this point, require actually implementing and running the kernels.

In future work, we hope to integrate the idea of fusion with TVM's autoscheduler [26] so as to leverage its power to search for high-performance schedules for fused layers. Next, we plan to target the compiler level to enable intermediate padding so that fusion can be extended to more layer types. Finally, we would also like to study fusion for the cases when batch size is greater than 1.

References

1. Abadi, M., et al.: TensorFlow: a system for large-scale machine learning. In: Proceedings of the 12th USENIX Conference on Operating Systems Design and Implementation, pp. 265–283. OSDI 2016, USA (2016). https://doi.org/10.5555/3026877.3026899
2. Adams, A., et al.: Learning to optimize Halide with tree search and random programs. ACM Trans. Graph. **38**(4), 1–12 (2019). https://doi.org/10.1145/3306346.3322967
3. Alwani, M., Chen, H., Ferdman, M., Milder, P.: Fused-layer CNN accelerators. In: 2016 49th Annual IEEE/ACM International Symposium on Microarchitecture (MICRO), October 2016. https://doi.org/10.1109/micro.2016.7783725
4. Chen, T., et al.: MXNet: a flexible and efficient machine learning library for heterogeneous distributed systems. CoRR arXiv:1512.01274, December 2015
5. Chen, T., et al.: TVM: end-to-end optimization stack for deep learning. CoRR arXiv:1802.04799, February 2018
6. Chen, T., et al.: Learning to optimize tensor programs. In: Proceedings of the 32nd International Conference on Neural Information Processing Systems, pp. 3393–3404. NIPS 2018, Red Hook, NY, USA (2018). https://doi.org/10.5555/3327144.3327258
7. Chetlur, S., et al.: cuDNN: efficient primitives for deep learning. CoRR arXiv:1410.0759 (Oct 2014)
8. Georganas, E., et al.: Anatomy of high-performance deep learning convolutions on SIMD architectures. In: SC18: International Conference for High Performance Computing, Networking, Storage and Analysis, pp. 830–841, November 2018. https://doi.org/10.1109/sc.2018.00069
9. Georganas, E., et al.: Harnessing deep learning via a single building block. In: 2020 IEEE International Parallel and Distributed Processing Symposium (IPDPS), pp. 222–233 (2020). https://doi.org/10.1109/IPDPS47924.2020.00032

10. He, K., Zhang, X., Ren, S., Sun, J.: Deep residual learning for image recognition. In: 2016 IEEE Conference on Computer Vision and Pattern Recognition (CVPR), pp. 770–778 (2016). https://doi.org/10.1109/CVPR.2016.90

11. Heinecke, A., Henry, G., Hutchinson, M., Pabst, H.: LIBXSMM: accelerating small matrix multiplications by runtime code generation. In: SC16: Proceedings of the International Conference for High Performance Computing, Networking, Storage and Analysis, pp. 981–991 (2016). https://doi.org/10.1109/SC.2016.83

12. Howard, A.G., et al.: MobileNets: efficient convolutional neural networks for mobile vision applications. CoRR arXiv:1704.04861, April 2017

13. Jia, Z., Thomas, J., Warszawski, T., Gao, M., Zaharia, M., Aiken, A.: Optimizing DNN computation with relaxed graph substitutions. In: Talwalkar, A., Smith, V., Zaharia, M. (eds.) Proceedings of Machine Learning and Systems, pp. 27–39 (2019)

14. Lavin, A.: Fast algorithms for convolutional neural networks. CoRR arXiv:1509.09308, September 2015

15. Liu, Y., Wang, Y., Yu, R., Li, M., Sharma, V., Wang, Y.: Optimizing CNN model inference on CPUs, pp. 1025–1040. USENIX ATC 2019, USA (2019). https://doi.org/10.5555/3358807.3358895

16. Mathieu, M., Henaff, M., LeCun, Y.: Fast training of convolutional networks through FFTs. In: Bengio, Y., LeCun, Y. (eds.) 2nd International Conference on Learning Representations, ICLR 2014, 14–16 April 2014, Banff, AB, Canada, Conference Track Proceedings (2014)

17. Mullapudi, R.T., Adams, A., Sharlet, D., Ragan-Kelley, J., Fatahalian, K.: Automatically scheduling halide image processing pipelines 35(4), July 2016. https://doi.org/10.1145/2897824.2925952

18. Paszke, A., et al.: Pytorch: an imperative style, high-performance deep learning library. In: Wallach, H., Larochelle, H., Beygelzimer, A., d'Alché-Buc, F., Fox, E., Garnett, R. (eds.) Advances in Neural Information Processing Systems 32, pp. 8024–8035 (2019)

19. Ragan-Kelley, J., Adams, A., Paris, S., Levoy, M., Amarasinghe, S., Durand, F.: Decoupling algorithms from schedules for easy optimization of image processing pipelines. ACM Trans. Graph. 31(4), 32:1–32:12, July 2012. https://doi.org/10.1145/2185520.2185528

20. Ragan-Kelley, J., Barnes, C., Adams, A., Paris, S., Durand, F., Amarasinghe, S.: Halide: a language and compiler for optimizing parallelism, locality, and recomputation in image processing pipelines. In: Proceedings of the 34th ACM SIGPLAN Conference on Programming Language Design and Implementation, pp. 519–530. PLDI 2013, Jun 2013. https://doi.org/10.1145/2491956.2462176

21. Sandler, M., Howard, A., Zhu, M., Zhmoginov, A., Chen, L.C.: Mobilenetv 2: inverted residuals and linear bottlenecks. In: 2018 IEEE/CVF Conference on Computer Vision and Pattern Recognition, pp. 4510–4520 (2018). https://doi.org/10.1109/CVPR.2018.00474

22. Szegedy, C., Vanhoucke, V., Ioffe, S., Shlens, J., Wojna, Z.: Rethinking the inception architecture for computer vision. In: 2016 IEEE Conference on Computer Vision and Pattern Recognition (CVPR), June 2016. https://doi.org/10.1109/cvpr.2016.308

23. Tan, M., et al.: MnasNet: platform-aware neural architecture search for mobile. In: 2019 IEEE/CVF Conference on Computer Vision and Pattern Recognition (CVPR), pp. 2815–2823. Los Alamitos, CA, USA, June 2019. https://doi.org/10.1109/CVPR.2019.00293

24. Wang, X., Li, G., Dong, X., Li, J., Liu, L., Feng, X.: Accelerating deep learning inference with cross-layer data reuse on GPUs. In: Euro-Par 2020: Parallel Processing, pp. 219–233 (2020). https://doi.org/10.1007/978-3-030-57675-2_14

25. Williams, S., Waterman, A., Patterson, D.: Roofline: an insightful visual performance model for multicore architectures. Commun. ACM **52**, 65–76 (2009). https://doi.org/10.1145/1498765.1498785

26. Zheng, L., et al.: Ansor: generating high-performance tensor programs for deep learning. In: 14th USENIX Symposium on Operating Systems Design and Implementation, pp. 863–879. OSDI 2020, November 2020

Smart Distributed DataSets for Stream Processing

Tiago Lopes[1,2], Miguel Coimbra[1,2], and Luís Veiga[1,2(✉)]

[1] INESC-ID Lisboa, Lisbon, Portugal
[2] Instituto Superior Técnico, Universidade de Lisboa, Lisbon, Portugal
{tiago.mourao,miguel.e.coimbra}@tecnico.ulisboa.pt,
luis.veiga@inesc-id.pt

Abstract. There is an ever-increasing amount of devices getting connected to the internet, and so is the volume of data that needs to be processed - the Internet-of-Things (IoT) is a good example of this. Stream processing was created for the sole purpose of dealing with high volumes of data, and it has proven itself time and time again as a successful approach. However, there is still a necessity to further improve scalability and performance on this type of system. This work presents SDD4STREAMING, a solution aimed at solving these specific issues of stream processing engines. Although current engines already implement scalability solutions, time has shown those are not enough and that further improvements are needed. SDD4STREAMING employs an extension of a system to improve resource usage, so that applications use the resources they need to process data in a timely manner, thus increasing performance and helping other applications that are running in parallel in the same system.

1 Introduction

The increasing amount of devices connected with each other created a big demand for systems that can cope with the high volume that needs to be processed and analyzed according to certain criteria. Great examples of this are smart cities [6], operational monitoring of large infrastructures, and the Internet-of-Things (IoT) [13]. Since most of this data is most valuable closest to the time it was generated, we need systems that can, in real-time, process and analyze all of the data as quickly as possible. To enable this, the concept of stream processing and its solutions were created.

First, we should explain what the stream processing paradigm is. It is equivalent to dataflow programming [12], event stream processing [4] and reactive programming [2], but simplifying software and hardware parallelization by restricting the parallel computation that can be performed. For a given sequence of data elements (a stream), this is achieved by applying a series of operators to each element in the stream.

Even though this paradigm simplifies the processing of variable volumes of data through a limited form of parallel processing, it still has quite some issues that need to be tackled in order to have a resilient and performant system. Since

© Springer Nature Switzerland AG 2021
L. Sousa et al. (Eds.): Euro-Par 2021, LNCS 12820, pp. 249–265, 2021.
https://doi.org/10.1007/978-3-030-85665-6_16

the volume of data is ever-changing, the system needs to be able to adapt in order to accommodate and process this data accordingly in a timely manner, while also being resilient so that no data is lost while any stream is being processed.

We present SDD4STREAMING as an extension to `Flink` to improve resource usage efficiency, so that applications use only the resources needed to process data in a timely manner, therefore increasing overall performance by freeing resources for other applications running in parallel in the same system.

The rest of this document is structured as follows. Section 2 briefly describes the fundamentals and state-of-the-art works on stream processing, resource management and input/processing management. Section 3 describes the architecture and the resource management algorithm that compose SDD4STREAMING. Section 4 presents the evaluation of our SDD4STREAMING solution, showing its performance on applications. Finally, Sect. 5 wraps up the paper with our main conclusions.

2   Related Work

We present related work first giving insight on what stream processing is and how it works. After that we explain how one relevant stream processing system works, namely `Apache Flink` which is the system we have developed our solution against. We then provide a brief explanation of two different solutions that solve specific issues inherent to stream processing.

Stream Processing. Taking into account that stream processing systems are parallel and distributed data processing systems, stream processing can be decomposed in various dimensions/aspects which need to be addressed to create a functional system offering good Quality-of-Service (QoS). For our solution, the most important dimension that we focus on solving is scalability, which we address next.

For a system that is constantly dealing with data and with clients that are expecting a certain Quality-of-Service[1] from the system, we need to have a degree of scalability to be prepared for any type of situation that might happen. Scalability is thus an important property that a system must have - to be elastic [10] (the ability to adapt) to accommodate its requirements and the ever-changing amount of work it receives. This involves a change in the number of resources available, consisting of either growing whenever there is more work than resources available, or shrinking when the amount of work decreases over time and we have more resources than the ones needed.

As an example, we can imagine an API that internally has a load-balancer that redirects the requests to the worker machines which will then process them. Suppose such a system supports 1000 requests per second at a certain point in time. Three situations can then occur: *a)* receiving fewer requests than the limit supported by the system, and thus wasting resources (e.g. incurring unnecessary

---

[1] https://www.networkcomputing.com/networking/basics-qos.

billing, etc.); *b)* having the exact supported amount of requests, which would be the perfect situation for the system (although it is not a real scenario that we should take into account as it usually only happens for a really small amount of time); *c)* receiving a number of requests exceeding the limit of what the system supports and so a bottleneck shall occur and the QoS will decrease while latency increases.

For examples of other systems, we note `Aurora` [1] and `Medusa` [3] which, despite aiming for scalability as stream processing engines, still have some issues for which there are explanations and solution proposals in the literature [7].

2.1 Apache Flink

`Apache Flink`[2] [5] offers a common runtime for data streaming and batch processing applications. Applications are structured as arbitrary directed acyclic graph DAGs, where special cycles are enabled via iteration constructs. `Flink` works with the notion of streams onto which transformations are performed. A stream is an intermediate result, whereas a transformation is an operation that takes one or more streams as input, and computes one or multiple streams. During execution, a `Flink` application is mapped to a streaming dataflow that starts with one or more sources, comprises transformation operators, and ends with one or multiple sinks (entities in the dataflow which represent outputs). Although there is often a mapping of one transformation to one dataflow operator, under certain cases, a transformation can result in multiple operators. `Flink` also provides APIs for iterative graph processing, such as `Gelly`.

The parallelism of `Flink` applications is determined by the degree of parallelism of streams and individual operators. Streams can be divided into stream partitions whereas operators are split into sub-tasks. Operator sub-tasks are executed independently from one another in different threads that may be allocated to different containers or machines.

The state of the streaming applications is stored at a configurable place (such as the master node, or HDFS). In case of a program failure, `Flink` stops the distributed streaming dataflow. The system then restarts the operators and resets them to the latest successful checkpoint. The input streams are reset to the point of the state snapshot. Any records that are processed as part of the restarted parallel dataflow are guaranteed to not have been part of the previously checkpointed state.

SpinStreams for Resource Management. When developing a stream processing application/job, the programmer will define a DAG with all the operations that will be performed on received inputs. The right choice for this topology can make a system go from very performant with high throughput to very slow with high latency and bottlenecks. Due to this, the literature has seen proposals such as `SpinStreams` [11], a static optimization tool able to leverage cost models

---

[2] https://flink.apache.org/.

that programmers can use to detect and understand the potential inefficiencies of an initial application design. SpinStreams suggests optimizations for restructuring applications by generating code to be run on a stream processing system. For the testing purposes of SpinStreams, the streaming processing system Akka [9] was used.

There are two basic types of restructuring and optimization strategies applied to streaming topologies:

- **Operator fission.** Pipelining is the simplest form of parallelism. It consists of a chain (or pipeline) of operators. In a pipeline, every distinct operator processes, in parallel, a distinct item; when an operator completes a computation of an item, the result is passed ahead to the following operator. By construction, the throughput of a pipeline is equal to the throughput of its slowest operator, which represents the bottleneck. A technique to eliminate bottlenecks applies the so-called pipelined fission, which creates as many replicas of the operator as needed to match the throughput of faster operators (possibly adopting proper approaches for item scheduling and collection, to preserve the sequential ordering).
- **Operator fusion.** A streaming application could be characterized by a topology aimed at expressing as much parallelism as possible. In principle, this strategy maximizes the chances for its execution in parallel, however, sometimes it can lead to a misuse of operators. In fact, on the one hand, the operator processing logic can be very fine-grained, i.e. much faster than the frequency at which new items arrive for processing. On the other hand, an operator can spend a significant portion of time in trying to dispatch output items to downstream operators, which may be too slow and could not temporarily accept further items (their input buffers are full). This phenomenon is called *back pressure* and recursively propagates to upstream operators up to the sources.

The SpinStreams workflow [11] is summarized as follows. The first step is to start the GUI by providing the application topology as input. It is expected that the user knows some profiling measures, like the processing time spent on average by the operators to consume input items, the probabilities associated with the edges of the topology, and the operator selectivity parameters. This information can be obtained by executing the application as is for a sufficient amount of time, so that metrics stabilize, and by instrumenting the code to collect profiling measures.

SmartFlux for Input and Processing Management. A stream processing application will usually be used for a certain type of data (e.g. data being generated by sensors in a smart city) and not for a range of applications. So with this, we can create an application that depends on the input it receives and, based on previous training (machine learning), it decides whether or not it should process them or just simply return the last results. For certain applications where the workflow output changes slowly and without great significance in a short time window, resources are inefficiently used, making the whole process take a lot longer than it needs to while the output remains moderately accurate.

To overcome these inefficiencies, `SmartFlux` [8] presents a solution that involves looking at the input the system receives, training a model using machine learning and using the model to check and analyze (with a good confidence level) if the received input needs to be processed all over or not. This is done through a middleware framework called `SmartFlux` which affects a component (the workflow management system) of a stream processing engine in order to intercept the way the workflows are being processed.

3 Architecture

SDD4STREAMING[3] was designed as a stream processing engine extension, focused on improving scalability and overall performance. We seek to accomplish these improvements while trying to minimize the loss of output accuracy which is usually inherent to adaption during the run-time of complex stateful systems.

Stream processing involves processing a variable volume of time-sensitive data and the system needs to be prepared to handle the issues stemming from it. We can take as guaranteed from the underlying system many things such as reliability and low-level resource management (at the task level), so we do not need to further address these specific aspects.

Since `Flink` already handles these issues, it is not necessary to focus on low-level aspects related to resource usage and system alterations, which would otherwise be needed. Overall, we adapt the execution of jobs by changing the used level of parallelism. On these systems, multiple jobs can be executed at the same time, each taking a percentage of the total resources and the number of resources needed to process the input changes through time. We propose two ways to handle these two aspects.

When creating, a job we can define the level of parallelism we want, changing how `Flink` handles tasks (transformations/operators, data sources, and sinks). The higher parallelism we have, the higher amount of data that can be processed at a time on a job. However, this also creates an overhead on overall memory usage due to more data needing to be stored for savepoints/checkpoints.

Before acting on the system, it is necessary for the client application to provide information to base decisions on, and this is defined in our Service Level Agreement (SLA). The SLA is comprised of:

- **Maximum number of task slots**. What is the maximum amount of parallelism or number of task slots allowed for the job in order to avoid a job scaling up indefinitely?
- **Resource Usage**. What is the maximum resource usage allowed in the system?
- **Input coverage**. What is the minimum amount of inputs that should be processed?

---

[3] https://github.com/PsychoSnake/SDD4Streaming.

This SLA will allow us to make decisions according to the type of performance the client needs from the system. This is essential because every client has an idea of how the system should behave, which our proposed extension, as an external element, is not aware of. This is the basis of our resource management component that on these values will check against the metrics obtained from the system and decide what to do in order to improve performance and scalability. To try and mitigate overhead caused by our solution, a decision was made to separate responsibilities into the two following parts:

- SDD4STREAMING library. Responsible for communicating with our server and overriding `Flink` operator functions;
- Resource management server. Responsible for handling all metric-related information as well as deciding the state of known jobs and their adaptation;

With these, the system where the client application runs will be able to use its resources in a more efficient manner, focusing solely on the computation it was designed to do. Most of our contribution is structured on the server, where our major features are located.

Regarding the two parts explained above, they can further be divided into the following components:

- **SDD4Streaming library**
  - Middleware. Responsible for extending the `Flink` programming model in order to override the operator functions;
- **Resource Management Server**
  - `Metric Manager`. Component responsible for handling all metric related information, from fetching it from `Flink` to storing it in our data structure for later use;
  - `Resource Manager`. Component responsible for making decisions based on the system state through the use of stored metrics and altering the system based on them;

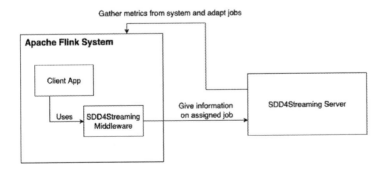

Fig. 1. Relation between client application and our components.

Figure 1 depicts the relation between the client application and the two components above. Explaining each of these components entails going over the employed data structures.

Data Structure. SDD4STREAMING has two major sets of data structures necessary for its execution. These consist of data that the client application provides about the overall system where execution will take place, as well as metrics fetched from said system.

Initialization Data. To be able to achieve anything at all in the system, some initialization data is first necessary, and it comes directly from the client application using our solution. These will provide the means to query the system about its resources as well as enable dynamically changing it. This structure has the following elements:

- **Service Level Agreement (SLA).** Details the optimal performance the clients want the system to have;
- **Job name.** Used to identify a running job;
- **Server base URL.** The base URL for where our web server is running;
- **Client base URL.** The base URL for the JobManager where the job shall be executed;
- **JAR archive name.** Name of the JAR used to create the job;

System Metrics. Apache Flink provides an extensive REST API that can be used to query or modify the system in various ways. We make use of this API to fetch metrics about the resources being used in the system. To accomplish this, it is necessary to map the necessary endpoints from the API, according to the data that must be sent and received for each one. On some elements this is not so simple and so, instead of directly determining the relation between components, it is necessary to gather this information ourselves.

A job in Apache Flink has multiple levels and we are able to gather different information on each one of them. The levels important for our solution are as follows:

- JobManager. Orchestrator of a Flink Cluster;
- Job. The runtime representation of a logical graph (also often called dataflow graph);
- TaskManager. Supervises all tasks assigned to it and interchanges data between then;
- Task: Node of a Physical Graph. Its the basic unit of work.
- SubTask. A Task responsible for processing a partition of the data stream;

For our solution, we will use and store data about the JobManager, TaskManagers and the tasks still running from the known jobs. While on Flink's API these elements are not directly related to each other, they are connected in our data structure to enable easily checking all elements required of the job in order to make decisions.

Regarding the kinds of data obtainable from these elements, the `Flink` API provides a valuable degree of information with different representations. Information can be gathered either on a collection of items (e.g. the metrics for all task managers in the system) or for a specific element, which may then be used to store in our internal structure.

Our data structure will be comprised of these elements with the following relation: `JobManager` $< - >$ `TaskManager` $< - >$ `Task`.

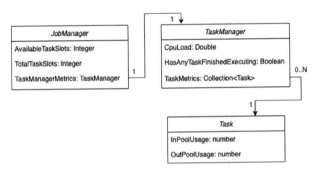

Fig. 2. SDD4STREAMING metric data structure.

As shown in Fig. 2, each structure is visible, as well as relations between each other. For the `JobManager`, we will store the available and total amount of task slots it has available. This is necessary to know if a job can be scaled up or not, because on `Flink`, whenever a job does not have enough slots available for its parallelism level, it will stay waiting until any slot frees up to achieve the required level.

We then have the `TaskManager` which will store the CPU load on the system. This load represents the average load between all the `TaskManagers` the job is affecting, meaning all those where tasks are being executing.

Finally we have the `Task`, which the `TaskManager` will store a collection of, with each one having the buffer usage for input and output, which are then used to identify back pressure issues (e.g. possible bottlenecks).

Middleware. To work as expected, our solution requires that the user specifies (intended to be simple) modifications to its application. These will involve using our components instead of the ones `Flink` offers, as well as providing initialization data with information about the overall system the client created.

For the middleware component of the solution, we can create our own versions of the operators `Flink` provides so we can override their functionality. We do this so we can verify how the system is behaving and act upon it and to seamlessly handle resource management without our solution having to make any extra communication with the client application.

Besides this, SDD4STREAMING also has internal metric management with the information obtained from an API Flink provides. This API not only provides metrics about each component running in the system (e.g. Jobs, Tasks and others), it also allows the system to be adapted. This allows for the creation of an internal data structure that supports decision-making, and then it is also possible to act on the system with the same API.

Metric Manager. SDD4STREAMING's decisions and actions are based on information gathered from the system through our Metric Manager. This component is responsible for getting metrics on the current system from Flink and organizing them according to our data structure.

Flink allows its clients to fetch system metrics through various means. For SDD4STREAMING, we find that the provided REST API is the best way to achieve this. This API supplies details on every level and component of the system without requiring extra work to identify these. Another way of getting this information from the system is through the Java Management Extensions (JMX) but for this to work it is necessary to know the port for each running component, and there is no easy way to find out programmatically, so this solution was not adopted.

For the API, each of the endpoints deemed to be useful were internally mapped to obtain the needed information. These are ones corresponding to the components the system has running at any point in time. We are able to gather information from the highest level (the job itself) to the lowest one (the sub-tasks generated by Flink from the operators the client is using).

Resource Manager. For SDD4STREAMING, the Resource Manager component is the most important one and where all the decisions on the system will happen. This component will make use of the metrics received from the Metric Manager and make decisions depending on the system's compliance with the SLA.

To avoid performance issues, the system must make the best of the resources it has available. Whenever needed, the system will undergo changes to accommodate the ever-changing needs for processing the incoming data. The system can be affected in two different ways. Either by re-scaling the assigned job or by suppressing inputs for the sake of performance at the cost of result accuracy.

Algorithm 1 presents the pseudo-code for checking the job-related metrics and adapting the system accordingly. For every input received, the state of the job will be analyzed. First, the Metric Manager is checked to find what are the current metrics for the job. If there are no metrics available or the job is getting re-scaled, true is returned (line 1) since there is nothing that can be done at that point. If there are metrics currently available and the job is not getting re-scaled, then our solution checks the job state and also if it is compliant with the defined SLA.

This allows SDD4STREAMING to make the decision of simply passing the control back to the user code and processing the input or to satisfy the need to

---

Algorithm 1. Decision Algorithm

Input: taskInfo
Output: shouldProcessInput

1 **if** *!JobGettingRescaled(taskInfo) OR !areMetricsAvailable()* **then**
2 | return true

3 **if** *isJobDegraded(taskInfo)* **then**
4 | **if** *shouldUpScaleJob()* **then**
5 | | upscaleJob() return true

6 | **if** *shouldSuppressInput()* **then**
7 | | return false

8 **if** *shouldDownScaleJob()* **then**
9 | downscaleJob()

10 return true

---

act upon the system first. If the system is running smoothly, before control is passed to the user code, it checks if the job can be scaled down (lines 9–10). If the system is running abnormally, it means changes must be made, but before a decision may be made in that direction, the appropriate corrections must be determined. Three possible actions may take place at this point, depending on the decision undertaken:

- Process Input
- Suppress Input
- Re-scale Job

If enough resources are available in the system, it is possible to simply re-scale the job (lines 4–6). This will help solve bottlenecks and decrease the load on each task, thus helping to reduce performance degradation. But the current job is re-scaled only if no other re-scaling operation is happening on the job. If not enough resources are available for this operation, then a different approach must take place. The other approach is suppressing the input partially and not processing it (lines 7–8). This will decrease the load and help reduce performance degradation. But this comes with the cost of reducing the accuracy of the output data, which is why there is a rule for it the SLA, where the user may declare what is the minimum accuracy (i.e. the percentage of the input subject to processing/reflected in the output) required at all times. Lastly, if all of the other approaches are not possible, then the control will have to be passed to the user code and allow it to process the input as normal (line 12). Even though this will increase the load in the system, there is nothing more that can be done without breaking the SLA with the user.

4   Evaluation

To evaluate SDD4STREAMING system, we want to look at its core focus, the increase in performance while decreasing possible bottlenecks and a dynamic resource usage depending on the needs of the system at any point in time. Our tests are based on how applications behave with our solution, comparing them with the scenario of exclusively using what `Flink` provides to see how much improvement is achieved.

We start by looking into the used workloads, then we document the dataset we used as well as the transformations necessary to make the data viable. We then move on to an analysis of the metrics we intended to gather, and present and analyse the results.

Workloads. For the workload we have an application that is able to demonstrate how our solution behaves. This workload involves sending a variable volume of data to the job and checking how our solution will scale the job and the overall performance of the system.

The producer of data will be `Kafka` [14], an open-source stream-processing software platform developed by the Apache Software Foundation that aims to provide a unified, high-throughput, low-latency platform for handling real-time data feeds.

Initially, `Kafka` is prepared with a big volume of data which the application will read from upon starting. Since the volume of data is so high, after the application finishes processing it, there is a waiting period after which we check if our solution down-scales the job since its load at the time will be very low. Finally after the waiting period, another large volume of data will be sent over to `Kafka` to see if our solution is able to adapt the system to support the new load.

Dataset. For the explained workload, we will use a dataset provided by the University of Illinois System. This dataset represents the taxi trips (116 GB of data) and fare data (75 GB of data) from the year 2010 to 2013 in New York.

Filtering and Data Cleanup. The dataset of the taxi rides/fares is extensive, totalling 116 GB, of which we need not use everything in order to cause a heavy load on the system. For this reason, we decided to use the latest available data which is for the year 2013. Before the data can be used by the application, it requires cleanup.

The data must be analyzed to remove rows that are missing essential information since these will provide nothing for our results, and to map the columns which are necessary for our execution.

Metrics. For each execution, we look to extract two key groups of data: system performance and overhead caused by our solution. The following lists (performance and overhead) describe these in more detail:

System Performance:

- **Resource utilization**. This metric assesses whether or not the solution is scaling the system accordingly. The resources used by tasks scale to keep up with the input rate;
- **Latency**. If the input is taking too long to be processed;
- **Throughput**. How much data is being processed per period of time;
- **Accuracy**. Observes variation of application accuracy over time to assess Quality-of-Service fulfillment.
- **CPU usage**. Checks percentage of CPU being used by tasks in the cluster as well as CPU that is reserved but not used (assesses resource waste and costs).

Solution Overhead:

- **CPU load**. This metric assesses how much of the CPU is affected by the execution of our solution;
- **Memory load**. This metric assesses how much of the memory is affected by storing our data structures by our solution.

Testbed Configuration. We designed the test runs to be executed in managed infrastructure (commonly known as cloud services). The cloud service used for this was the Google Cloud Platform (GCP). This service provides 300 credits in a free trial per account, which for our use case is enough to perform the necessary tests.

The setup consisted of 3 VMs each with two vCPUs, 4 GiB of RAM and 20 GiB of storage. Each of these machines will be responsible for each part necessary for testing. One will host the `Flink` cluster where the job will run, the other will host the data that the job will read from and the third one will host our web server.

Besides this, we also needed a way to gather the metrics from the system while our jobs were running. To accomplish this we decided to use a metric reporter[4], having chosen `Prometheus`[5]. `Prometheus` is a time series database (TSDB) combined with a monitoring and alerting toolkit. The TSDB of `Prometheus` is a non-relational database optimized for storing and querying of metrics as time series and therefore can be classified as NoSQL. `Prometheus` mainly uses the pull method where every application that should be monitored has to expose a metrics endpoint in the form of a REST API either by the application itself or by a metrics exporter application running alongside the monitored application. The monitoring toolkit then pulls the metrics data from those endpoints in a specified interval. This tool was executed in the authors' personal computers to avoid using more credits on GCP than were needed.

---

[4] https://ci.apache.org/projects/flink/flink-docs-release-1.9/monitoring/metrics.html#reporter.

[5] https://prometheus.io/.

Results. For both tests `Apache Flink` was configured to have one `JobManager` and one `TaskManager`. The `JobManager` was configured to 1024 MiB memory while the `TaskManager` which is responsible for managing all the tasks (the units of work) has double that amount at 2048 MiB. The amount of available tasks are 50 and each of the tests are started with a parallel level of 20, therefore using 20 of the 50 total slots.

First we go over the metrics resulting from the test where the application is running without using SDD4STREAMING. All figures below for this test belong to the same time interval and have a duration of 23 min.

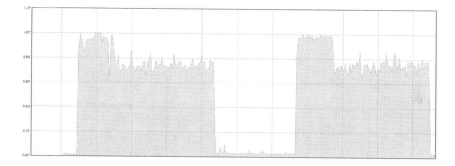

Fig. 3. CPU load on the `TaskManager`.

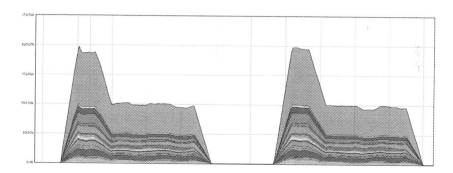

Fig. 4. Amount of records getting processed by each sub-task per second (throughput).

Figure 3 showcases high CPU usage for the tested workload. Besides the first minutes where data is fetched from `Kafka`, the load is mostly constant overall, with occasional fluctuations. For throughput in Fig. 4, behavior similar to the CPU load graph is shown, which is to be expected because higher throughput means that more data is being processed, and for that to happen, higher CPU load is expected. These figures depict an initial very high throughput which then decreases after a few minutes but remains constant. Also when comparing the first volume of data sent and the second one, it can be observed that the CPU load and throughput are fairly similar.

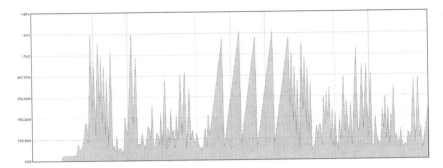

Fig. 5. Heap memory usage.

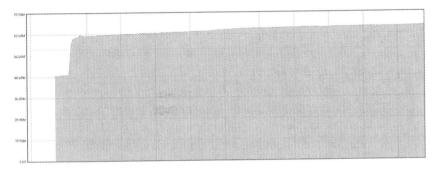

Fig. 6. Non-heap memory usage.

Memory usage by the `TaskManager/Tasks` for heap and non-heap memory is shown in Figs. 5 and 6 respectively.

For the test where the application runs incorporated with our solution, the configurations are the same as the other test but there is an extra configuration of SDD4STREAMING. The important part needed before showing the results is the SLA used for this test:

– Max number of task slots: 22;
– Resource usage: 50%
– Input coverage: 80%;

All figures below for this test belong to the same time interval and have a duration of 30 min.

CPU load and throughput are shown in Figs. 7 and 8 respectively. The graphs show that the execution was very different from the one without our solution. For example, there are visible drops in both of them that mostly represent when the job was getting re-scaled, since at that point no input will be processed and so throughput will drop to 0 and CPU will be mostly used by the `TaskManager` that is adapting the job.

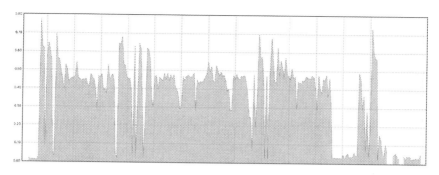

Fig. 7. CPU load on the `TaskManager`.

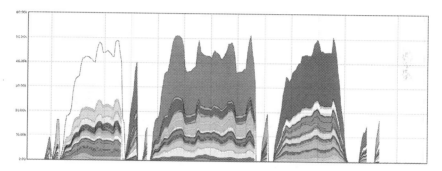

Fig. 8. Amount of records getting processed by each sub-task per second (throughput).

Figures 9 and 10 show the memory usage for the heap and non-heap respectively. From these it can be seen that the non-heap memory is very similar to the previous test, but for the heap memory quite different results are obtained. Since our solution will adapt the system in runtime, the `TaskManager` will need to use more memory in order to do the re-scaling of the jobs. And due to this

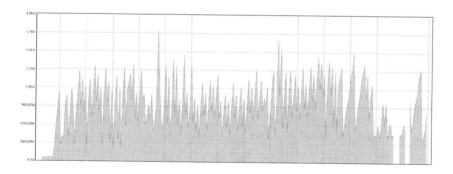

Fig. 9. Heap memory usage.

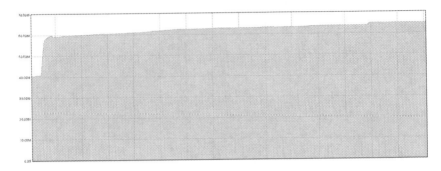

Fig. 10. Non-heap memory usage.

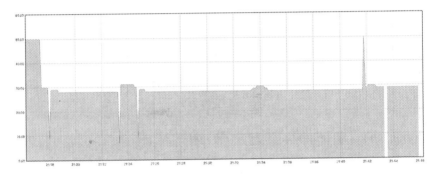

Fig. 11. Number of available task slots.

we observe a higher average use of memory as well as the maximum amount of memory used overall.

Finally, specifically for the test with our solution we have in Fig. 11 the number of available slots throughout the execution of the job.

5   Conclusion

SDD4STREAMING was devised to serve as an extension of the scalability and performance capabilities of a stream processing engine such as `Flink`. Results show it is able to adapt, in run-time, to current application requirements, supporting current load and improving efficiency. Through the separation of responsibilities between the library and the server we are able to mitigate most of the overhead that our solution causes on the system. In future work, we intend to address similar issues in the `Gelly` graph library and also in the `Spark` [15] engine.

Acknowledgements. This work was supported by national funds through FCT, Fundação para a Ciência e a Tecnologia, under projects UIDB/50021/2020 and PTDC/EEI-COM/30644/2017.

References

1. Abadi, D., et al.: Aurora: a data stream management system. In: SIGMOD Conference, p. 666. Citeseer (2003)
2. Bainomugisha, E., Carreton, A.L., van Cutsem, T., Mostinckx, S., de Meuter, W.: A survey on reactive programming. ACM Comput. Surv. (CSUR) **45**(4), 1–34 (2013)
3. Balazinska, M., Balakrishnan, H., Stonebraker, M.: Load management and high availability in the medusa distributed stream processing system. In: Proceedings of the 2004 ACM SIGMOD International Conference on Management of Data, pp. 929–930. ACM (2004)
4. Barga, R.S., Goldstein, J., Ali, M., Hong, M.: Consistent streaming through time: a vision for event stream processing. arXiv preprint cs/0612115 (2006)
5. Carbone, P., Katsifodimos, A., Ewen, S., Markl, V., Haridi, S., Tzoumas, K.: Apache flink: stream and batch processing in a single engine. Bull. IEEE Comput. Soc. Tech. Committee Data Eng. **36**(4), 28–38 (2015)
6. Cheng, B., Longo, S., Cirillo, F., Bauer, M., Kovacs, E.: Building a big data platform for smart cities: experience and lessons from santander. In: 2015 IEEE International Congress on Big Data, pp. 592–599. IEEE (2015)
7. Cherniack, M., Balakrishnan, H., Balazinska, M., Carney, D., Cetintemel, U., Xing, Y., Zdonik, S.B.: Scalable distributed stream processing. CIDR **3**, 257–268 (2003)
8. Esteves, S., Galhardas, H., Veiga, L.: Adaptive execution of continuous and data-intensive workflows with machine learning (2018)
9. Gupta, M.: Akka Essentials. Packt Publishing Ltd., Birmingham (2012)
10. Heinze, T., Jerzak, Z., Hackenbroich, G., Fetzer, C.: Latency-aware elastic scaling for distributed data stream processing systems. In: Proceedings of the 8th ACM International Conference on Distributed Event-Based Systems, pp. 13–22. ACM (2014)
11. Mencagli, G., Dazzi, P., Tonci, N.: SpinStreams: a static optimization tool for data stream processing applications (2017)
12. Sousa, T.B.: Dataflow programming concept, languages and applications. In: Doctoral Symposium on Informatics Engineering, vol. 130 (2012)
13. Tönjes, R., et al.: Real time IOT stream processing and large-scale data analytics for smart city applications. In: Poster Session, European Conference on Networks and Communications (2014)
14. Wang, G., et al.: Building a replicated logging system with Apache Kafka. Proc. VLDB Endow. **8**(12), 1654–1655 (2015)
15. Zaharia, M., et al.: Apache spark: a unified engine for big data processing. Commun. ACM **59**(11), 56–65 (2016)

Cluster, Cloud and Edge Computing

Colony: Parallel Functions as a Service on the Cloud-Edge Continuum

Francesc Lordan$^{(\boxtimes)}$ ⓘ, Daniele Lezzi ⓘ, and Rosa M. Badia ⓘ

Department of Computer Sciences, Barcelona Supercomputing Center (BSC),
Barcelona, Spain
{francesc.lordan,daniele.lezzi,rosa.m.badia}@bsc.es

Abstract. Although smart devices markets are increasing their sales figures, their computing capabilities are not sufficient to provide good-enough-quality services. This paper proposes a solution to organize the devices within the Cloud-Edge Continuum in such a way that each one, as an autonomous individual −*Agent*−, processes events/data on its embedded compute resources while offering its computing capacity to the rest of the infrastructure in a Function-as-a-Service manner. Unlike other FaaS solutions, the described approach proposes to transparently convert the logic of such functions into task-based workflows backing on task-based programming models; thus, agents hosting the execution of the method generate the corresponding workflow and offloading part of the workload onto other agents to improve the overall service performance. On our prototype, the function-to-workflow transformation is performed by COMPSs; thus, developers can efficiently code applications of any of the three envisaged computing scenarios – sense-process-actuate, streaming and batch processing – throughout the whole Cloud-Edge Continuum without struggling with different frameworks specifically designed for each of them.

Keywords: Edge · Fog · Cloud · Compute Continuum · Distributed systems · Programming model · Runtime system · Serverless · Function-as-a-Service · Stream-processing · Task-based workflow

1 Introduction

Embedding computing and networking capabilities into everyday objects is a growing trend; smart devices markets – e.g., phones, cameras, cars or speakers – are rapidly increasing their sales. Since the computing power available on them is often not sufficient to process the information they collect and provide a good-enough-quality service, such devices must cooperate in distributed infrastructures to share the hosting and processing of data.

In recent years, the Fog has raised as a complement to the established Cloud model by bringing down the compute and storage capabilities to the Edge. This mitigates the economic expenses and the network-related issues – high latency and low bandwidth – associated with the Cloud and enables new service opportunities relying only on on-premise, commodity devices. Mobile devices are a

© Springer Nature Switzerland AG 2021
L. Sousa et al. (Eds.): Euro-Par 2021, LNCS 12820, pp. 269–284, 2021.
https://doi.org/10.1007/978-3-030-85665-6_17

non-negligible source of resources; involving them in such platforms leads to an increase of the available computing power. However, mobility introduces dynamism to the infrastructure but also unreliability requiring to change the computational model to stateless and serverless.

Major Cloud providers relegate the Edge to be a serf of the Cloud neglecting all the intermediate devices within the network infrastructure. We envisage infrastructures not exclusively building on the Fog or the Cloud but exploiting the whole Cloud-Edge continuum by combining both paradigms. This work elevates the Fog as an autonomous peer of the Cloud functioning even when disconnected from it. This paper describes Colony, a framework for organizing the devices within the Cloud-Edge continuum resembling organic colonies: communities of several individuals closely associated to achieve a higher purpose. Each member of the colony – *Agent* – is an autonomous individual capable of processing information independently that can establish relations with other agents to create new colonies or to participate into already-existing ones. Agents offer the colony their embedded resources to execute functions in a serverless, stateless manner; in exchange, they receive a platform where to offload their computing workload achieving lower response times and power consumption.

In such environments, we identify three possible scenarios that require computation. On the first one, known as *sense-process-actuate*, the infrastructure provides a proper response to an event detected on one of its sensors. A second scenario is *stream processing*: sensors continuously produce data to be processed in real-time. Besides computations triggered by data or infrastructure changes, users can also request synchronous executions directly to the platform or submit jobs to a workload manager; this third scenario, named *batch processing*, is generally used for launching data analytics applications to generate new knowledge out of the information collected by or stored in the infrastructure. As discussed in detail in Sect. 6, developers must use different state-of-the-art frameworks to tackle each of these scenarios. To contribute to the current state-of-the art, we propose a single solution that tackles the three scenarios by taking a task-based approach. Converting the complex logic of the computation into an hybrid workflow – supporting both atomic and continuous-processing tasks – allows to parallelize and distribute the workload across the whole platform. For testing purposes and without loss of generality, our prototype leverages on COMPSs [27,30] to make this conversion, and we modified the COMPSs runtime to delegate the execution of the nested tasks onto Colony. Nevertheless, other programming models following a task-based approach, such as Swift [34] or Kepler [15], could also be integrated in the framework with the appropriate glue software.

In summary, the contribution of this work is to bring together parallel programming, Function-as-a-Service (FaaS) and the Compute Continuum. For doing so, this paper describes Colony: a framework to create compute infrastructures following the recommendations of the OpenFog Consortium [19]. In it, each device offers its embedded computing resources to host the execution of functions in a service manner; however, by converting the logic of such functions into hybrid workflows – composed of atomic and persistent tasks –, the device can share the workload with the rest of the platform to achieve an efficient, parallel, distributed execution on any of the three computing scenarios. To validate the viability of the described design, a prototype leveraging on the COMPSs programming model is evaluated on two use cases.

The article continues by casting a glance over the components involved in our solution, and Sects. 3 and 4 respectively discuss the internals of an agent and how colonies are organized. Section 5 evaluates two use cases to validate the solution. Finally, Sect. 6 introduces related work and Sect. 7 presents the conclusions and identifies potential research lines to complete it.

2   Problem Statement and Solution Overview

The Cloud-Edge continuum is a distributed computing environment composed of a wide variety of devices going from resource-scarce single-board computers – e.g., Raspberry Pi – to the powerful servers that compose the datacenters supporting a cloud. Applications cannot assume any feature from the device where they run. Those devices closer to the application end user – within a PAN or LAN range – are often purpose-specific and dedicated to a single user. However, the further the device gets from the user, the more likely it is to be shared among multiple users and applications. For dealing with software heterogeneity and resource multi-tenancy, Colony proposes **virtualizing** the software **environment** either as a virtual machine or a container. Such environments would ensure that the necessary software is available on the devices running the application, and provide isolation from other applications running on the device.

For the sake of performance, applications can exploit **hardware heterogeneity** by running part of their logic on GPUs, FPGAs or other accelerators embedded on the devices. The underlying infrastructure might be composed of a large number of nodes, and centralizing the hardware-awareness of a dynamically-changing infrastructure on a single device might become a significant burden at computational and networking level. Therefore, each node must be able to work in a standalone manner and run the computation efficiently using all the computing devices embedded in it. For that purpose, each node of the infrastructure hosts a persistent service or agent that provides a Functions as a Service (FaaS) interface to **execute serverless functions** using the computational resources available on the device.

To overcome resource scarcity on edge devices, agent interaction is enabled to **offload task executions onto other agents** either on other edge devices, the Cloud or at any other device from an intermediate tier of the infrastructure. A typical feature of edge devices worth highlighting is mobility; mobile devices are likely to join and leave the infrastructure at any time with or without prior notice. Thus, agents should be aware of that and take appropriate measures to exploit all the computing resources at their best while preventing any failure due to the departure of any device. Both, functions and tasks, are computations totally independent of the state of the agent. All the necessary data bound to the computation is shipped along with the request – or at least a source from where to fetch the value –; thus, tasks can run on any agent of the infrastructure in a **serverless** manner. When new nodes join in the infrastructure, agents previously composing the infrastructure can offload onto them part of their computation, and vice versa. Conversely, when nodes leave the infrastructure, the **fault-tolerance mechanisms** must ensure the ongoing operations completion by resubmitting to still-available resources those tasks offloaded onto the no-longer-available agents.

Unlike traditional distributed computing, applications no longer have a single entry point – the main method –; events may arise anywhere in the infrastructure and invoke a handler function to provide the appropriate response. When a node triggers a new execution, it contacts its local agent which orchestrates the effective completion of the operation. By leveraging on task-based parallel programming models, the logic of such functions can be automatically converted into workflows composed of several other isolated compute units (tasks) whose parallel execution can exploit the whole infrastructure when delegated onto other agents through Colony. Thus, if the programming model supports both atomic tasks and persistent tasks with continuous input/output, Colony can handle applications requiring any of the three aforementioned computing patterns: **sense-process-actuate**, **stream processing**, **batch processing**.

3   Agent Architecture

Agents are the cornerstone of the Colony platform. The purpose of an agent is to offer an interface where to request the execution of functions that will run either on the computing resources embedded on the host device or transparently offloaded onto other nodes on the Cloud-Edge Continuum. The entry-point to the agent is its API which offers methods for requesting the execution of a function with a certain parameter values and performing resource pool modifications.

Users or applications request a function execution detailing the logic to execute, the resource requirements to run the task, the dependencies with previously submitted tasks and the sources where to fetch the data involved in the operation. Upon the reception of a request, the API directly invokes the Colony runtime system. The goal of this runtime is to handle the asynchronous execution of tasks on a pool of resources. To achieve its purpose, the runtime has four main components. The first one, the Resource Manager (RM), keeps track of the computing resources – either embedded on the device or on remote nodes – currently available. Upon the detection of a change in the resource pool, the RM notifies all the other components so they react to the change. If dynamic resource provisioning is enabled, this component should also adapt dynamically the reserved resources to the current workload. The second component is the Task Scheduler (TS), which picks the resources and time lapse to host the execution of each tasks while meeting dependencies among them and guaranteeing the exclusivity of the assigned resources. For that purpose, it keeps track of the available resources in each computing device and a statistical analysis of previous executions of each function. The default policy pursues exploiting the data locality; it assigns new ready (with no pending dependencies) tasks to the idle resource having more data values on its local storage; if all the resources are busy, it will pick the ready task with more data values on the node at the moment of the resources release. However, TS policies are designed in a plug-in style to allow the extension of the runtime with application/infrastructure-specific policies; the policy used by the TS is selected at agent boot time. The Data Manager (DM), the third piece of the runtime, establishes a data sharing mechanism across the whole infrastructure to fetch the necessary input data to run the task locally and publish the results. For guaranteeing that the involved data values remain available even on network disruption situations, the DM leverages on distributed persistent storage solutions like dataClay [28]. The last component, the Execution Engine (EE), handles the execution of tasks on the resources. When the TS decides to offload a task to a remote agent, the EE forwards the function execution request to the API of the remote agent. Conversely, if the TS determines that the local computing devices will host the execution of a task, the EE fetches from the DM all the necessary data missing in the node, launches the execution according to its description and the assigned resources, and publishes the task results on the DM. It is during the task execution when the task-based programming models take the scene and convert the logic of the method into a workflow. When the selected PM detects a task, instead of invoking the corresponding runtime, it refers to the TS of the local Agent to create a new task indicating the operation, the involved data and the dependencies that the new task has with previously submitted tasks. The Colony runtime will handle the execution of such task in the same manner as if it were an external request and the TS will guarantee that dependencies with previous tasks are considered. Thus, the expressiveness limitations to convert a function into a workflow depend on the specific programming model selection rather of being a limitation of Colony on its own. Figure 1 depicts the control flow followed by a function throughout the runtime components when the TS decides to host the execution locally (leftmost part of the figure) and to offload the execution onto a remote agent (rightmost part of the figure).

To control the pool of resources, the Agent API offers three methods which notify the desired change to the RM. To increase the pool with more resources, the Agent API offers a method to indicate the name of the new node and its computing capabilities. If the node is already a part of the pool, the agent expands it with the provided resources. To remove resources from the pool, the API offers two methods. The immediate removal method aims to support the disconnection of a remote device, the agent assumes that all the non-completed tasks offloaded onto the node have failed and resubmits them onto other nodes of the infrastructure. On the contrary, the gentle removal method backs the case when the system administrator wants to reduce the usage of a remote node. In this case, the agent does not submit more tasks to the to-be-removed device until there are enough idle resources to satisfy the removal request; then, it releases the resources and continues to use the remaining ones, if any.

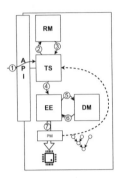
(a) Execution on local resources

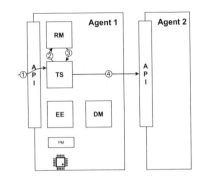
(b) Execution offloaded onto remote agent

Fig. 1. Function/Task flow throughout the Colony's runtime components

4   Colony Organization

For infrastructures with a small number of devices, a single Colony agent can individually orchestrate the execution of the tasks on any of the other agents composing the infrastructure. However, the bigger the infrastructure is, the higher the complexity of the scheduling problem becomes and its computational burden is more likely to grow bigger than the actual computational load of the application and simply not fit in resource-scarce devices.

To overcome such problem, this article proposes to reduce the amount of scheduling options by gathering resources under the concept of a colony. Colonies are disjoint groups of agents that share their workload; one of the colony members acts as the interaction gateway and orchestrates the workload execution within the colony. Thus, agents no longer consider all the other agents to run the task; it only picks a gateway agent to whom delegate the problem. This gateway agent organizes the agents within the colony in sub-colonies and considers the rest of the infrastructure as a new colony where the first agent acts as the gateway. Thus, a computation triggered by an agent could run on any node of the infrastructure without adding a significant overhead due to the scheduling.

Combining this serverless capability of Colony with the ability to decompose the logic of the computation into several tasks allows any request to use as many resources as needed. If the tablet at home colony of the example illustrated in Fig. 2 requires some computation, its local agent could use the embedded processor to host the function execution. After converting it into a workflow, it offloads part of the execution of its inner tasks onto the agent on the fog-enabled – with compute capabilities – Wi-Fi router. In turn, the Wi-Fi router agent decides which part of the computation hosts, which part it offloads onto the laptop, and which part submits to the remote parts of the platform – through the agent on a cluster server. As with the previous agent, the server can host part of the execution, forward it to the other nodes of the cluster or send it to the smartphone or the server in the office. Regardless the device being the

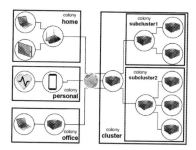

Fig. 2. Colony deployment example connecting devices from four different environments: those at user's home (laptop, tablet, and other devices connected to the Wi-Fi), those at user's office (the laptop and an on-premise server), those moving with the user (smartphone and wearables) and a remote cluster with large computing power. Each of these environments becomes a colony hierarchically organized and the gateway in the cluster acts as nexus among colonies.

source of computation requests, the computing load can be distributed across the entire infrastructure and thus executed by any node. The decisions taken by each agent will depend on the scheduling policy configured by the device owner.

Mobile devices may join or leave the infrastructure unexpectedly. When a device – e.g., a smartphone –, which might be part of a colony – the *personal* colony of the example –, joins the infrastructure, it attaches to an already-member device – for instance, the Wi-Fi router of the *home* colony. From the smartphone point of view, the whole infrastructure becomes a colony where to offload tasks through the agent on the router; for those devices already part of the infrastructure, the incoming device/colony becomes a new subcolony also available through the router. Likewise, when a device disconnects, the communication link between two agents breaks and they both lose the corresponding colonies. To ensure that ongoing computations finish, the involved agents need to re-schedule the execution of the unfinished tasks already offloaded onto the lost colony and assign them to still-available agents.

Currently, the platform topology is manually set up by the platform administrator and can be changed dynamically using the resource management operations of the Agent API. Good criteria to build the topology are the stability and latency of the network; this ensures that agents will always try to offload tasks onto nearby resources, on the fog, rather than submitting them to the Cloud achieving a higher performance. Besides, the system remains usable even when the cloud is unavailable because of network disruptions.

5   Usage Scenarios and Evaluation

This section presents the results of the tests conducted to evaluate the viability of the described proposal. For that purpose, a prototype leveraging on the COMPSs programming model – whose runtime has been adapted to delegate the task execution onto Colony – has been developed. The implemented tests are based on two use cases aiming two different platforms. The first use case, a service running a classification model, aims to test the whole Cloud-Edge Continuum. The training of the model (batch processing scenario) runs on the Cloud part and allows to evaluate the performance and scalability of the solution; by submitting simultaneous user requests simulating readings from multiple sensors (sense-process-actuate scenario), we evaluate the workload balancing. The second use case, a real-time video analysis, demonstrates the streaming support within Fog environment without support from the Cloud.

5.1   Baseline Technology - COMP Superscalar (COMPSs)

COMP Superscalar (COMPSs) is a framework to ease the development of parallel, distributed applications. The core of the framework is its programming model with which developers write their code in a sequential, infrastructure-unaware manner. At execution time, a runtime system decomposes the application into computing units (tasks) and orchestrates their executions on a distributed platform guaranteeing the sequential consistency of the code.

COMPSs' main characteristic is that developers code applications using plain Java/Python/C++ as if the code was to be run on a single-core computer. For the runtime system to detect the inherent tasks, application developers need to select, using annotations or decorators depending on the language, a set of methods whose invocations become tasks to be executed asynchronously and, potentially, in an out-of-order manner.

To guarantee the sequential consistency of the code, the runtime system monitors the data values accessed by each task – the arguments, callee object and results of the method invocation – to find dependencies among them. For the runtime to better-exploit the application parallelism, developers need to describe how the method operates (reads, generates or updates) on each data value by indicating its directionality (IN, OUT, INOUT, respectively). Such data values can be either files, primitive types, objects or even streams.

Upon the arrival of a new task execution request, the COMPSs runtime analyses which data values are being accessed and which operations the task performs on them. With that information, it detects the dependencies with other tasks accessing the same values and constructs a task dependency graph. Once all the accesses of the task have been registered, the runtime schedules its execution on the available resources guaranteeing the sequential consistency of the original code. Thus, COMPSs is able to convert the logic of any function into an hybrid task-based workflow - data-flow and support the three compute scenarios identified in Sect. 1.

Conceptually, COMPSs tasks and Colony function execution requests are similar; both refer to serverless, stateless executions; Thus, native support for the COMPSs programming model within Colony is straightforward modifying the COMPSs runtime system to delegate task executions onto the Colony runtime. Upon the detection of a task and the registration of all the data accesses to find dependencies with previous tasks, the COMPSs runtime calls the Colony runtime to handle the execution of the tasks on the underlying platform as if it were a regular invocation of a function. Colony's TaskScheduler runtime will consider the detected dependencies and guarantee the sequential consistency of the tasks and, therefore, of the user code following the COMPSs model.

5.2 Classification Service

This first use case deploys a classification service on the Cloud-Edge continuum. On the one hand, the training of such model allows us to validate the system running compute-heavy applications on a batch-processing scenario; usually, the service administrator or a periodic task triggers the training of the model on the Cloud. On the other hand, having nodes on the infrastructure acting as sensors allows us to validate the behaviour of the system on sense-process-actuate scenarios. These sensors submit their lectures to classify them and react to it.

The algorithm supporting the model, RandomForest, constructs a set of individual decision-trees, also known as estimators, each classifying a given input into classes based on decisions taken in a random order. The final classification of the model is the aggregate of the classification of all the estimators; thus, the accuracy of the model depends on the number of estimators composing it. The training of the estimators are independent from each other, each one consisting of two tasks: a first one that selects a combination of 30,000 random samples from the training set, and a second one that builds the decision tree.

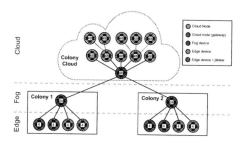

Fig. 3. Testbed for the sense-process-actuate experiment (Color figure online)

To conduct the experiment, we deployed a 3-level infrastructure – depicted in Fig. 3 – on Marenostrum, a 3,456-node (48 servers of 72 nodes) supercomputer where each node has two 24-core Intel Xeon Platinum 8160 and 98 GB of main memory. Each node hosts the execution of an agent managing its 48 cores. All the agents within the same server join together as a colony and one of them acts as the gateway; in turn, one of these gateway nodes becomes the interconnection point among all the server colonies (darker gray on the figure). Two of these colonies are configured to act as the Fog parts of the deployment: one resource-rich node with 24 CPU cores (green) and four Edge nodes with 4 CPUs each. While four edge devices (depicted in blue) play a passive role and only provide computing power to their respective colony, two edge devices of each colony (depicted in red) act as sensors submitting compute requests to its local agent. To produce the workload, these nodes run an instance of jMeter [5].

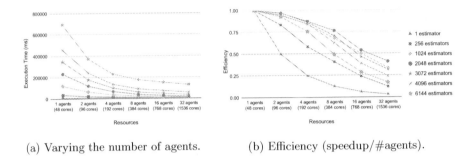

(a) Varying the number of agents.   (b) Efficiency (speedup/#agents).

Fig. 4. RandomForest's training time

Charts in Fig. 4 depict the results of the scalability tests for the training of the model varying to the number of agents on the Cloud. Figure 4a illustrates the evolution of the training time when changing the number of resources to train a fixed-size model demonstrating the benefits of parallelization: the larger the infrastructure grows, the shorter the execution time becomes. Figure 4b presents the efficiency (ratio between the speedup compared to the 1-agent execution of the same-size problem and the size of the infrastructure) of the execution revealing some scalability problems. Up to 2048 estimators, the performance loss can be explained mainly by the load imbalance. The larger the infrastructure is, the more resources remain idle waiting for others to complete the training. A second cause is the overhead of COMPSs when detecting new tasks. COMPSs sequentially detects tasks as the main code runs; the task creation delays build up. Training one estimator requires about 7 s (running both tasks). To keep the whole infrastructure busy on the 1,536 cores scenario, COMPSs must generate a task every 2.25 ms. The granularity of the tasks is too fine given the size of the infrastructure.

Beyond 2048 estimators, the performance loss is explained by the implementation of the Task Scheduler; it has a single thread that handles in a FIFO basis both new task requests and end of task notifications. Hence, several end of task notifications may stack up before a new task request leaving several nodes idle waiting for a new task. Likewise, many new task request might accumulate in front of the task end notification; thus, despite the resources are idle, the scheduler is not aware of that and does not offload more work to the node.

For the second experiment, regarding the processing submitted by the sensors, the cloud part of the infrastructure has 6 nodes on the same server. Figures 5a, 5b and 5c depict the evolution of the number of requests being handled by each device when 10, 100 and 300 users submit requests at an average pace of 1 request per second (with a random deviation of ± 500 ms following Gaussian distribution) during 15 min.

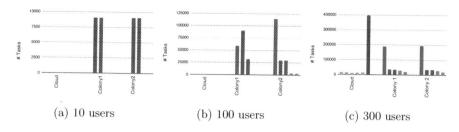

Fig. 5. Number of tasks executed on each node. The colors of the bars match the color from the respective node as depicted in Fig. 3 (Color figure online).

On the 10-user case, the Edge nodes receiving the request are able to host all the workload; only 3 requests out of 36,000 were offloaded to the Fog nodes on peak-load moments. The average response time was 104 ms. On the 100-user case, the nodes cannot assume the whole workload and offload onto their respective Fog colony which handles most of the requests. On Colony1, one of the edge nodes receives the requests at a periodic pace; thus, it is able to assume the whole workload (90,000 requests) by itself. On the other edge node, the requests arrive in bursts, and the scheduler decides to offload tasks to the Fog node (58,432). On Colony2, both edge nodes also receive the request in bursts, and both offload tasks to the Fog node which actually processes up to 116,041 requests. This Fog node cannot assume the whole workload and decides to offload part of it to the idle edge nodes (3,738 and 3,142 requests, respectively). The average response time is also 104 ms. Finally, on the last case, with 300 users, both colonies cannot assume the workload locally and a large portion of the requests (464,999/1,080,000) are offloaded onto the Cloud. The average response time slightly increases to 109 ms.

5.3   Real-Time Video Processing

On the real-time video processing use case, the application obtains a video-stream directly from a camera, processes each of the frames to identify the people in it, and maintains an updated report with stats of their possible identifications.

Figure 6 depicts the workflow of the use case deployed on a 2-device testbed composed of a Raspberry Pi (rPi) equipped with a camera and a laptop. The *watch* task is a persistent task that obtains the input from a webcam and publishes frames onto a stream. By defining constraints for the task, the agent ensures that the task runs on a camera-enabled device (rPi). For each frame, a *detectPeople* task finds the areas in the picture containing a person using a pre-trained Caffe implementation of Google's MobileNet Single-Shot Detector DNN[1]. Each detection triggers the execution of an *IdentifyPerson* task. *IdentifyPerson* detects the face of the person – using a DNN provided by OpenCV [18] –, aligns the image by recognizing 68 landmarks on the face, and extracts 128

---

[1] https://github.com/chuanqi305/MobileNet-SSD.

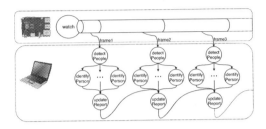

Fig. 6. Testbed and workflow of the video-processing use case

features – using OpenFace's [16] nn4.small2 DNN. Finally, a SVM classification [2] – identifies the person. Finally, the *update_report* task relates the people detected on the current frame with people appearing on the previous ones – tracking – and the individual information is aggregated into a *Report* object that can be queried in parallel.

The average time to process a frame containing one person on the rPi is 41,293 ms – *detectPeople* lasts 18,920 ms and *IdentifyPerson*, 22,339 ms – providing a framerate of 0.024 fps. As baseline for the comparison on distributed systems, we implemented the service as two different applications communicating through a TCP Socket. The application running on the rPi obtains the images from the webcam, serializes the frame and ships it through the socket; thus, the rPi produces a frame every 453 ms. The second application, running on the laptop, reads from the socket and processes the frame (132 ms). Thus, hand-tuned code is able to process 2.14 fps. Finally, we conducted the test running the service taskified with COMPSs obtaining a processing rate of 2.79 fps. The analysis of the time elapsed on each part of the application revealed that the performance difference between both versions lies in the frame serialization, which shrinks from 120 ms to 20 ms. Both tests run with the same JVM and they use the same code to perform the operation; therefore, we attribute this difference to the JVM internal behavior – probably, JNI verifications – or to OS memory management.

6   Related Work

This papers aims to bring together Function-as-a-Service (FaaS) with the Computing Continuum. Regarding FaaS, Zimki was the first framework to offer serverless computing in 2005; in 2014, Amazon introduced Lambda [3], becoming the first large cloud service provider to offer FaaS, followed by Google and Microsoft that respectively launched Cloud Functions [8] and Azure Functions [6]. In 2016, IBM announced an open-source FaaS project, OpenWhisk [13], that allowed FaaS deployments on private clouds; Microsoft adapted its solution to support the execution on on-premise cloud. OpenWhisk broke the vendor lock-in by supporting the execution on container managers and IBM branched

---

[2] model trained with 10,000 images of 125 people from CASIA-WebFace facial dataset.

the project to release Cloud Functions [10]. Two other open-source alternatives to OpenWhisk are OpenFaaS [12], supported by VMWare, and Fn [14], backed by Oracle.

For economic reasons – it is cheaper to provision the resources directly as cloud instances –, all major FaaS solutions limit the execution time for each function inhibiting long-lasting (batch-processing) computations. To develop such computations, cloud vendors usually offer programming solutions perfectly integrated in their platforms; otherwise, developers manually set up the cluster to use a myriad of distributed programming models. For instance, to develop workflows and scientific computing, they can turn to Swift [34], COMPSs [27], Kepler [15], Taverna [23] or Pegasus [21]; on the data analytics field, MapReduce [20] and other solutions building on it – such as Twister [22] or Apache Spark [35]. Likewise, major cloud providers also offer their own stream-processing alternatives such as Amazon Data Pipeline [1]. However, developers frequently use the stream-oriented low-level frameworks, such as Apache Kafka [25], or dataflow models like Apache Storm [32], Apache Spark-Streaming [36] or Heron [26]. Apache Beam [4], COMPSs [30] and Twister2 [24] have gone a step further aiming to merge both workflows and dataflows in one single solution.

Towards exploiting the Compute Continuum, all the solutions from the major cloud vendors (Amazon IoT Greengrass [2], Microsoft Azure IOT Edge [7] and Google Cloud IOT [9]) maintain the cloud as a necessary part but allow the manual deployment of function executions on Edge devices. The Osmosis framework [33] also follows this top-down approach. The developer defines microElements (MELs) and describes how these MELs relate to each other. From the cloud, Osmosis orchestrates MEL deployments and migrations taking into account resource availability, each MEL's QoS and the infrastructure topology.

As of today, for all major Cloud providers the Edge is totally reliant on the Cloud; it should become autonomous and function even disconnected from the Cloud, and, in that direction, a lot of research is being done. Selimi et al. [31] attack the problem from a bottom-up approach and propose a framework for placing cloud services in Community Networks. Ramachandran et al. identified the challenges to provide a peer-to-peer standing for the Edge to the Cloud [29]. Departing from a real-world case of study, Beckman et al. [17] diagnose the technical shortcomings to implement a solution; they consider Twister2 for data analytics and indicate the necessary implementations.

The novelty of the work presented in this paper is to bring together programmability, FaaS and Compute Continuum. Unlike other frameworks targetting the Continuum, Colony offers a FaaS approach to submit computations. Compared to FaaS solutions on the Cloud, able to delegate tasks on Edge devices, Colony allows to automatically convert the logic of the function into a workflow; thus, being able to parallelize and distribute its execution to achieve lower response times and better infrastructure exploitation. By leveraging on the COMPSs programming model, the overall solution is able to tackle the three described computing scenarios: batch processing, stream-processing and sense-process-actuate.

7   Conclusion and Future Work

This manuscript introduces Colony: a framework to develop applications running throughout the whole Cloud-Edge Continuum. This framework proposes a hierarchic organization of the computational resources building on the concept of an Agent: an autonomous process running on each device that allows executing software in a Function-as-a-Service manner. By automatically transforming these functions into task-based workflows, an Agent is able not only to parallelize the execution; it can also distribute the workload offloading part of the execution onto other Agents. Thus, the workload is balanced across the whole platform while taking advantage of the low-latency network interconnecting nearby resources. COMPSs is a task-based programming model that supports not only atomic tasks, but also persistent tasks producing/consuming a stream of data. By natively supporting COMPSs, Colony offers a common programming interface to deal with the three computing patterns necessary on Cloud-Edge services.

Section 5 suggests some shortcomings of the proposal. The current prototype only allows the detection of tasks on the main function, enabling the detection during the execution of any task would allow to parallelize the task generation, and thus, improve the application performance. The default scheduling policy problem aims to keep the resources busy unnecessarily offloading tasks as shown on the 100-user test on Sect. 5.2. Other scheduling policies – maybe based on QoS and SLA with time-constrains – would distribute the workload differently.

Other Cloud-Edge-related issues remain open for further investigation, for instance, the automatic resource discovery and configuration of the resources. Regarding data, privacy/IP-sensitive data should never abandon the device or on-premise resources, extending the model with data-access/movement control policies is also a future research line. As Sect. 3 explains, Colony delegates the data management; significant infrastructure divisions may entail misbehaviours in the used solution and some data values become unavailable. We aim to enable a fault-tolerance mechanism – e.g., lineage – to recompute missing values.

Automatically triggering executions based on events related to stored data or external webservices (Eventing) is supported by most of the framework named in Sect. 6. Colony does not include such component; applications need to run a persistent task monitoring a state/value/stream that triggers the computation when certain condition is met or relay on external services like IFTTT [11].

Finally, as discussed in the related work section, large cloud providers enforce users to follow their own software. To overcome this vendor lock-in while using their cloud platforms, Colony must use their IaaS solution and deploy an agent there. Another line of research to delve into is Interoperability; implementing software to let Colony offload tasks onto these large clouds through their FaaS software would entail a significant improvement in terms of cost efficiency.

Acknowledgements. This work has been supported by the Spanish Government (PID2019-107255GB), by Generalitat de Catalunya (contract 2014-SGR-1051), and by the European Commission through the Horizon 2020 Research and Innovation program under Grant Agreement No. 101016577 (AI-SPRINT project).

References

1. Amazon Data Pipeline. https://aws.amazon.com/datapipeline/
2. Amazon Greengrass. https://aws.amazon.com/greengrass/
3. Amazon Lambda. https://aws.amazon.com/lambda/
4. Apache Beam. https://beam.apache.org/
5. Apache JMeter. https://jmeter.apache.org/
6. Azure Functions. https://azure.microsoft.com/services/functions/
7. Azure IoT-Edge. https://azure.microsoft.com/en-us/services/iot-edge/
8. Google Cloud Functions. https://cloud.google.com/functions
9. Google IoT Cloud. https://cloud.google.com/solutions/iot/
10. IBM Cloud Functions. https://www.ibm.com/cloud/functions
11. IFTTT. https://ifttt.com/
12. OpenFaas. https://www.openfaas.com/
13. OpenWhisk. https://openwhisk.apache.org/
14. The FN project. https://fnproject.io/
15. Altintas, I., Berkley, C., Jaeger, E., Jones, M., Ludascher, B., Mock, S.: Kepler: an extensible system for design and execution of scientific workflows. In: Proceedings. 16th International Conference on Scientific and Statistical Database Management, pp. 423–424. IEEE (2004)
16. Amos, B., Ludwiczuk, B., Satyanarayanan, M.: Openface: a general-purpose face recognition library with mobile applications. Technical report, CMU-CS-16-118, CMU School of Computer Science (2016)
17. Beckman, P., et al.: Harnessing the computing continuum for programming our world. In: Fog Computing: Theory and Practice, pp. 215–230 (2020)
18. Bradski, G.: The OpenCV library. Dr. Dobb's J. Softw. Tools **120**, 122–125 (2000)
19. Consortium, O., et al.: OpenFog reference architecture for fog computing. Architecture Working Group, pp. 1–162 (2017)
20. Dean, J., Ghemawat, S.: MapReduce: simplified data processing on large clusters. In: Proceedings of the 6th Conference on Symposium on Opearting Systems Design & Implementation, Berkeley, CA, USA, OSDI 2004, vol. 6, p. 10. USENIX Association (2004). http://dl.acm.org/citation.cfm?id=1251254.1251264
21. Deelman, E., et al.: Pegasus, a workflow management system for science automation. Future Gener. Comput. Syst. **46**, 17–35 (2015). https://doi.org/10.1016/j.future.2014.10.008
22. Gunarathne, T., Zhang, B., Wu, T.L., Qiu, J.: Scalable parallel computing on clouds using Twister4Azure iterative MapReduce. Future Gener. Comput. Syst. **29**(4), 1035–1048 (2013). https://doi.org/10.1016/j.future.2012.05.027, http://www.sciencedirect.com/science/article/pii/S0167739X12001379
23. Hull, D., et al.: Taverna: a tool for building and running workflows of services. Nucl. Acids Res. **34**, W729–W732 (2006). https://doi.org/10.1093/nar/gkl320
24. Kamburugamuve, S., Govindarajan, K., Wickramasinghe, P., Abeykoon, V., Fox, G.: Twister2: design of a big data toolkit. Concurrency Comput. Pract. Experience **32**(3), e5189 (2020). https://doi.org/10.1002/cpe.5189, https://onlinelibrary.wiley.com/doi/abs/10.1002/cpe.5189, e5189 cpe.5189

25. Kreps, J., Narkhede, N., Rao, J.: Kafka: a distributed messaging system for log processing. In: ACM SIGMOD Workshop on Networking Meets Databases (2011)
26. Kulkarni, S., et al.: Twitter heron: stream processing at scale. In: Proceedings of the ACM SIGMOD International Conference on Management of Data, vol. 2015-May, pp. 239–250 (2015). https://doi.org/10.1145/2723372.2723374
27. Lordan, F., et al.: ServiceSs: an interoperable programming framework for the cloud. J. Grid Comput. **12**(1), 67–91 (2014). https://doi.org/10.1007/s10723-013-9272-5
28. Martí, J., Queralt, A., Gasull, D., Barceló, A., José Costa, J., Cortes, T.: Dataclay: a distributed data store for effective inter-player data sharing. J. Syst. Softw. **131**, 129–145 (2017). https://doi.org/10.1016/j.jss.2017.05.080
29. Ramachandran, U., Gupta, H., Hall, A., Saurez, E., Xu, Z.: Elevating the edge to be a peer of the cloud. In: 2019 IEEE 12th International Conference on Cloud Computing (CLOUD), pp. 17–24. IEEE (2019)
30. Ramon-Cortes, C., Lordan, F., Ejarque, J., Badia, R.M.: A programming model for hybrid workflows: combining task-based workflows and dataflows all-in-one. Future Gener. Comput. Syst. **113**, 281–297 (2020). https://doi.org/10.1016/j.future.2020.07.007
31. Selimi, M., Cerdà-Alabern, L., Freitag, F., Veiga, L., Sathiaseelan, A., Crowcroft, J.: A lightweight service placement approach for community network micro-clouds. J. Grid Comput. **17**(1), 169–189 (2018). https://doi.org/10.1007/s10723-018-9437-3
32. Toshniwal, A., et al.: Storm @Twitter. In: Proceedings of the ACM SIGMOD International Conference on Management of Data, pp. 147–156 (2014). https://doi.org/10.1145/2588555.2595641
33. Villari, M., Fazio, M., Dustdar, S., Rana, O., Jha, D.N., Ranjan, R.: Osmosis: the osmotic computing platform for microelements in the cloud, edge, and internet of things. Computer **52**(8), 14–26 (2019)
34. Wilde, M., Hategan, M., Wozniak, J.M., Clifford, B., Katz, D.S., Fos-ter, I.: Swift: a language for distributed parallel scripting. Parallel Comput. **37**(9), 633–652 (2011). https://doi.org/10.1016/j.parco.2011.05.005
35. Zaharia, M., Chowdhury, M., Franklin, M.J., Shenker, S., Stoica, I.: Spark: cluster computing with working sets. In: HotCloud 2010 Proceedings of the 2nd USENIX Conference on Hot Topics in Cloud Computing (2010). https://doi.org/10.1007/s00256-009-0861-0
36. Zaharia, M., Das, T., Li, H., Shenker, S., Stoica, I.: Discretized streams: an efficient and fault-tolerant model for stream processing on large clusters (2012)

Horizontal Scaling in Cloud Using Contextual Bandits

David Delande[1,2]([✉]) [ID], Patricia Stolf[2] [ID], Raphaël Feraud[1] [ID],
Jean-Marc Pierson[2] [ID], and André Bottaro[1] [ID]

[1] Orange Labs, Lannion, France
{david.delande,raphael.feraud,andre.bottaro}@orange.com
[2] IRIT, Université de Toulouse, 31062 Toulouse, France
{patricia.stolf,jean-marc.pierson}@irit.fr

Abstract. One characteristic of the Cloud is elasticity: it provides the ability to adapt resources allocated to applications as needed at runtime. This capacity relies on scaling and scheduling. In this article online horizontal scaling is studied. The aim is to determine dynamically applications deployment parameters and to adjust them in order to respect a Quality of Service level without any human parameters tuning. This work focuses on CaaS (container-based) environments and proposes an algorithm based on contextual bandits (HSLinUCB). Our proposal has been evaluated on a simulated platform and on a real Kubernetes's platform. The comparison has been done with several baselines: threshold based auto-scaler, Q-Learning, and Deep Q-Learning. The results show that HSLinUCB gives very good results compared to other baselines, even when used without any training period.

Keywords: Cloud scaling · Reinforcement learning · Contextual bandits

1 Introduction

Cloud hosted services need agile, automated and dynamic elasticity techniques. The Cloud elasticity can be decomposed in two sub-problems [9]: scaling and scheduling. The former consists in determining and adjusting the appropriate number of resources and the second consists in assigning workflow jobs on resources for execution. Automatic scaling techniques help to guarantee SLA (Service Level Agreement) to applications while optimizing the resources allocation of the Cloud provider [22]. An auto-scaler is defined as a system that autonomously takes decisions to optimize the latency, i.e., the response time, under the constraint of minimizing the number of allocated resources. Depending on the workflow, scheduling has to be taken into account or not. For parallel and distributed computing, the scheduling has to find the most efficient allocation between jobs and resources, while in Web application the scheduling is implicitly done by the load balancer. This paper focuses on the auto-scaling problem for Web application in the Cloud, and hence the scheduling problem is not considered.

© Springer Nature Switzerland AG 2021
L. Sousa et al. (Eds.): Euro-Par 2021, LNCS 12820, pp. 285–300, 2021.
https://doi.org/10.1007/978-3-030-85665-6_18

Two different elasticity techniques can be achieved depending on the used Cloud technology [7]. Horizontal elasticity is a technique allowing to create or delete a complete Cloud resource (container for a CaaS technology and virtual machine for the IaaS technology). These resources have predefined size (number of CPU, ram size, storage size...) at creation time and a dedicated pricing model. Any desired change in the Cloud resource type implies the complete deletion/recreation of a Cloud resource. The second technology is the vertical elasticity technique. The vertical elasticity can be used in two different modes: resizing or replacement [10]. The resizing mode allows to modify an existing Cloud resource size without the constraint to completely delete/recreate the resource. The replacement mode consists in creating a new more powerful resource and deleting the old one. This paper focuses on the horizontal scaling as it is the most widely used method to provide elasticity.

Resource creation time, service stabilization time and the adaptation capacity to dynamically create a new resource in face of a workload change is an important constraint in horizontal resource elasticity [18]. Indeed in a IaaS environment a virtual machine creation time is in the range of the minute [2]. Container in a CaaS Cloud computing environment is said to not suffer from these constraints as the creation time is considered to be in the range of the second under the assumptions that the container image does not need to be downloaded and that the container manager does not suffer from resource constraints. Hence, CaaS environment has been chosen in this work.

When a new application is hosted in the Cloud, the auto-scaler has no knowledge about its hosting requirements nor its specific workload. Furthermore, nowadays the DevOps process has been adopted by many companies. This process implements some automatic delivery procedures which dramatically reduce the delivery time and increase the delivery frequency. This introduces some minor to major changes in both the hosting requirements and the workload. The hot-start or cold-start mode define respectively an auto-scaler, starting to operate, with or without environment knowledge. An auto-scaler, which can quickly perform from a cold-start, can be used for a new hosted application or for a major change in an existing application. An auto-scaler which can only work from a hot-start can only handle minor changes.

In this paper, the cold-start processing capability is sought, and thus, the minimization of the interactions number needed to adapt the resources to the current workload. That is why the use of contextual bandits is considered among the relevant learning techniques towards the best horizontal scaling policy in CaaS environments. The contributions in this article are the following: i) a mathematical formulation of the horizontal scaling problem in Cloud is provided, ii) a new scaling algorithm called Horizontal Scaling LinUCB (HSLinUCB) is proposed, iii) a complete experimental environment is made publicly available through a GitHub repository, iv) extensive simulations and real experiments have been conducted to exhibit the benefits of HSLinUCB over approaches from the literature. In the next section the state of the art on auto-scaling is presented. Then, the problem of Cloud elasticity is described and formalized as a contextual bandit problem. Then, the proposed algorithm HSLinUCB is detailed. The experimental section presents the Cloud platform used for comparing the approach with different baselines. The real platform is used to generate and store datasets which are then used to simulate, with different workload, the behaviour of our proposal. Then, real online experiments are presented in a real CaaS environment. The last section is devoted to the conclusion and future works.

2 Related Work

The surveys in [3, 9, 14, 19] show the active research topics on automatic scaling for Cloud infrastructure and applications. Threshold-based auto-scaling is the most popular technique. Basically, most Cloud computing environments[1][2] offer to application providers a threshold based auto-scaler. In their turn, application providers have to configure thresholds on Cloud resources e.g., CPU, memory, network throughput, consumed by their application deployment units to be used, e.g., virtual machines and containers. This configuration task is complex: setting the thresholds is dependent on each application and requires a deep understanding of workload trends.

Time-series analysis is essentially used for resource requirement forecasting [12, 16, 17, 21]. Various prediction techniques are firstly used to extrapolate future values, e.g., moving average, auto-regression, exponential smoothing and various machine learning techniques like neural networks. Prediction adds pieces of information to the auto-scaler to take decisions. It is worth noting that Amazon combined the Threshold techniques with Time-series analysis to bring pro-activity to their auto-scaler.[3] This paper does not focus on time series analysis, but this approach could be used in combination of reinforcement learning for predicting the future states of the environment.

Another approach consists in modeling the system with queuing theory [24], and control theory in order to shape specific controllers [3, 14]. These approaches are efficient but necessitate a deep understanding of the system (Cloud, workload and applications). These model-based approaches are effective for specific applications, for which the model has been well tuned. However, to be resilient in case of change of the environment, they require to be tuned over time. Authors in [11] showed that model-free reinforcement learning is better suited to adapt in case of varying workload than model-based systems.

In reinforcement learning, an agent interacts with an environment. The agent observes the state of the environment, and then plays an action. The played action changes the state of the environment, and depending on the reached state the environment can generate a reward. The goal of the agent is to maximize its cumulative rewards. When the agent has a model of the environment, i.e., model-based reinforcement learning, this problem is reduced to the planning problem.

---

[1] https://aws.amazon.com/ec2/autoscaling/.

[2] https://docs.openstack.org/senlin/latest/tutorial/autoscaling.html.

[3] https://aws.amazon.com/blogs/aws/new-predictive-scaling-for-ec2-powered-by-machine-learning/.

When the agent does not know the environment, i.e., model-free reinforcement learning, it has to interact with the environment to learn an efficient policy. Reinforcement Learning has been widely studied in the Cloud Elasticity research field for both scaling and scheduling aspects [9]. Q-learning has been used for horizontal scaling of IaaS Cloud environment in [4,5,8,27] and for horizontal scaling of CaaS Cloud environment in [20]. Despite the fact that Q-learning based auto-scalers have proved their ability to learn the intrinsic dynamic of the environment, as it will be shown in our experiments, Q-Learning auto-scaler needs a lot of interactions (trials/errors) with the environment before starting to provide an efficient decision. If the learning is done online, the high number of interactions needed to explore the space of policies would increase hosting cost by over-provisioning, and would degrade the latency by under-provisioning. That is why Q-Learning auto-scalers are limited to hot start with an offline learning in a simulated environment. A particular case of reinforcement learning is used in this paper: Multi-Armed Bandits. The main difference with standard reinforcement learning is that the received reward only depends on the played action and not on the past sequence of actions. This simplification allows significant gain in terms of exploration costs, and hence allows to learn a model from cold start.

The use of Multi-Armed Bandits for Cloud elasticity is not as widespread as the use of standard reinforcement learning. However, Combinatorial Bandits has been used for task scheduling in [28]. [25] uses a service mesh combined with a Multi-armed Bandits based on a Thompson sampling algorithm. The Multi-armed Bandits is not used for the scaling nor the scheduling parts of the elasticity but for identifying the best communication path between CaaS components. In [6], the authors propose a resource controller dedicated to IaaS environment for adjusting vCPU and memory on a fixed number of virtual machines. As a contextual bandit is pre-trained on a simulated environment and then transferred on a real system, authors tackle only the hot-start stage and not the cold-start stage. In this paper, authors demonstrate the good behavior of a contextual bandit for vertical scaling.

In contrast, in the present work the horizontal scaling problem in CaaS environment is formalized as a contextual bandit problem in cold-start that could be also applied to IaaS environment.

3   Optimization of Container Allocation

3.1   Optimization of Container Allocation as a Reinforcement Learning Problem

Our objective is to find and set the smallest number of containers required to satisfy SLA (Service Level Agreement) of a single client application under varying workloads. Here the SLA is expressed in term of response latency. Let $l_t \in \mathbb{R}_+$ be the observed latency at time t, and $l^* \in \mathbb{R}_+$ be the maximum latency corresponding to SLA. Let $w_t \in \mathbb{R}_+$ be the observed workload of the considered application at time t. Let $c_t \in \mathbb{N}_+$ be the number of containers of the application at time t. Let f be the function that given the number of containers allocated at time t c_t, and the workload at the next time step w_{t+1} returns the latency at the next time step l_{t+1}:

$$f : \mathbb{R}_+ \times \mathbb{N}_+ \to \mathbb{R}_+, \quad l_{t+1} \leftarrow f(w_{t+1}, c_t). \tag{1}$$

The optimal allocation of containers of the application is defined as:

$$c_t^* = \arg \min_{c_t \in \mathbb{N}_+} \{c_t \text{ such that } f(w_{t+1}, c_t) \leq l^*\}. \tag{2}$$

In the following, this optimal allocation of containers of the application is denoted Oracle.

f is a complex function that depends on the Cloud environment, and that in the general case is unknown to the application. Moreover, the number of containers of the application is allocated at time t, while the latency at time $t + 1$ depends on the workload at time $t + 1$. As a consequence, the latency at time $t + 1$ cannot be evaluated with the only knowledge of f at time t. Let w_{t+1} be the observed value at time $t + 1$ of the random variable w sampled from an unknown distribution v_w. Hence, the latency l_{t+1} is also the observed value at time $t + 1$ of a random variable l sampled from an unknown distribution v_l.

Algorithm 1. Optimization of Container Allocation.

1: **for** $t \leftarrow 1, ..., T$
2: The agent observes the workload $w_t \sim v_w$
3: The agent chooses a number of containers c_t
4: The latency $l_{t+1} \sim v_l$ is revealed
5: **End For**

Algorithm 1 provides a summary of the problem of optimization of container allocation in Cloud environments. Observing the latency at time $t + 1$, a reward can be evaluated. Hence, this problem can be formalized as a reinforcement learning problem, where an agent interacts with an unknown environment.

3.2 Reward Function

A set of three actions available to the agent is considered: $\mathcal{A} = \{u, s, d\}$, where:

- u is the choice of increasing the number of containers by one,
- s is the choice of staying with the same number of containers,
- d is the choice of decreasing the number of containers by one.

In practice, the Oracle is not available to the agent or the Cloud platform. The only feedback that the agent can obtain is the observed latency. For handling the optimization problem stated in Eq. 2 as a reinforcement learning problem, a reward function based on the latency has to be built. Under the assumption that the workload does not change every time step, but every two time steps, the reward of the action $a \in \mathcal{A}$ is defined as:

$$r_{a,t} \equiv \begin{cases} r_{u,t} = 1 - \mathbb{1}\left\{l_t < l^*\right\}, \\ r_{s,t} = \mathbb{1}\left\{l_t \leq l^*\right\}, \\ r_{d,t} = \mathbb{1}\left\{l_{t+1} \leq l^*\right\}. \end{cases} \tag{3}$$

If the observed latency at time t is higher than the maximum latency, the agent has to increase the number of container: $r_{u,t} = 1$. Else the agent has to choose between the action stay s and the action down d. The choice of the action up is automatic when $l_t > l^*$, while the choice of the action stay s or down d is a 2-armed bandits. The agent is facing the explore/exploit dilemma: The agent can explore a loosely estimated action, or exploit the action with the higher estimated reward. Note that for evaluating the reward of the action down d, one time step has to be spent for evaluating the latency at time $t + 1$ when the number of containers has been decreased.

3.3 Optimization of Container Allocation as a Contextual Linear Bandit Problem

In Algorithm 1, the reward at time t does not depend on the sequence of choices of the agent, but only of the choice of the agent at time t. That is why this reinforcement learning problem can be reduced as a contextual bandit problem. Before choosing an action, the agent observes the state of environment. The state of environment corresponds to a vector of observed variables, which depend on the workload w_t: the number of requests per second, the CPU occupancy rate, the RAM occupancy rate, and the latency l_t. The agent also knows the current number of containers c_t. Using these variables as a basis in a sliding time window, a context vector $\mathbf{x_t} \in \mathbb{R}^D$ describing the state of the environment is built, where D is the number of contextual variables, and $\|\mathbf{x}_t\|_2 \leq 1$. For all actions $a \in \{s, d\}$, it is assumed that, there exists unknown weight vectors $\theta_a^* \in \mathbb{R}^D$ with $\|\theta_a^*\|_2 \leq 1$ so that $\forall t$:

$$\mathbb{E}[r_{a,t}|\mathbf{x}_t] = \theta_a^{*\top} \mathbf{x}_t. \tag{4}$$

Using this linear assumption, the goal of the player is to minimize the pseudo-regret between the optimal linear policy and the linear policy played by the player:

$$R(2T) = \sum_{t=1;t=t+2}^{2T} \left(\theta_{a_t^*}^{*\top} \mathbf{x}_t - \theta_{a_t}(t)^\top \mathbf{x_t}\right), \tag{5}$$

where $\theta_{a_t^*}^*$ is the optimal parameter for the optimal action at time t, and $\theta_{a_t}(t)$ is the parameter at time t for the action a_t chosen by the player. To be consistent with the evaluation of the reward, which necessitates one additional time step after the choice of the action, the regret is evaluated at time $2T$ for T choices of actions.

3.4   Horizontal Scaling LINUCB

The proposed HSLINUCB algorithm (See Algorithm 2) is an extension of the LinUCB algorithm proposed in [13]; it includes a reactive action to increase the number of containers (line 8). LinUCB has a regret bound in the order of $O\left(D\sqrt{T\log T}\right)$ [1], and hence HSLINUCB benefits of the same theoretical guarantee. The key idea of LinUCB algorithm is to apply online ridge regression to incoming data to obtain an estimate of the coefficients θ_a for $a = \{s,d\}$. At each time step the arm with the highest upper confidence bound of the reward $a_t = \arg\max_a(\theta_a^\top \mathbf{x}_t + b_a)$ is selected, where $b_a = \beta\sqrt{\mathbf{x}_t^\top \mathbf{A}_a^{-1}\mathbf{x}_t}$ is the standard deviation, β is a constant that depends on the probability of failure δ of the estimation done by the ridge regression, and $\mathbf{A}_a$ is the covariance matrix of the a-th arm context.

Algorithm 2. HSLINUCB for Optimization of Container Allocation

---

1: **Input:** $\delta \in (0,1)$
2: $\beta \leftarrow 1 + \sqrt{\log(2/\delta)/2}$, $\forall a \in \{s,d\}$, $\mathbf{A}_a \leftarrow \mathbf{I}_D$, $v_a \leftarrow \mathbf{0}_D$, $\theta_a \leftarrow \mathbf{0}_D$
3: **for** $t \leftarrow 1, 2, ..., 2T$ **do**
4:     observe $\mathbf{x}_t, l_t$
5:     **for** $a \in \{s,d\}$ **do**
6:         $\theta_a \leftarrow \mathbf{A}_a^{-1}\mathbf{v}_a$, $b_a \leftarrow \beta\sqrt{\mathbf{x}_t^\top \mathbf{A}_k^{-1}\mathbf{x}_t}$,
7:     **end for**
8:     **if** $l_t > l^*$ **then** play $a_t \leftarrow u$
9:     **else**   play arm $a_t \leftarrow \arg\max_a(\theta_a^\top \mathbf{x}_t + b_a)$
10:    **end if**
11:    l_{t+1} is revealed and $r_{a_t,t}$ is evaluated according to Equation 3
12:    **if** $a_t \neq u$ **then**
13:        $\mathbf{A}_{a_t} \leftarrow \mathbf{A}_{a_t} + \mathbf{x}_t\mathbf{x}_t^\top$,
14:        $\mathbf{v}_a \leftarrow \mathbf{v}_a + r_{a_t,t}\mathbf{x}_t$
15:    **end if**
16: **end for**

---

4   Experimentation

Cloud scaling has been extensively studied on simulated environments or on few private real implementations. Evaluation on a real environment is necessary to capture all the system dynamics. To provide reproducible results and make experiments, the complete installed environment and the implemented algorithms have been shared on a GitHub repository[4]. The following section provides a general overview but a more in-depth environment description is available on the GitHub repository.

---

[4] https://github.com/Orange-OpenSource/HSLinUCB.

4.1 Experimental Environment

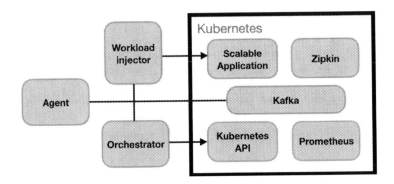

Fig. 1. Overall architecture view

The environment (Fig. 1) is running inside virtual machines hosted on an Openstack Cloud. The agent server (4 VCPU/4 GB RAM) handles the reinforcement learning agent algorithm. It makes Cloud resource adaptation and drives the workload injector server. The workload injector is based on the Locust software, it allows to change the injected user number. The Kafka message bus allows the components to inter-operate with each other. The Kubernetes platform is composed of 5 servers each with 8 VCPU/16 GB RAM. A service MESH has been implemented inside the Kubernetes platform with the ISTIO framework. It implements by default a system monitoring with Prometheus and a latency monitoring with Zipkin. The orchestrator component collects metrics, computes contexts for the agent and executes scaling operation on Kubernetes. The orchestrator supports the raised context storage into an HDF5 file allowing to create a dataset. When a change on the container number is requested, the orchestrator realizes the modification on the Kubernetes API and waits until the monitored metrics reflect the change. This waiting time allows for system stabilization accounting. During real experiments, the contexts and actions are respectively retrieved and executed on the platform. During simulation, the contexts are retrieved from real stored datasets and actions are simulated through changes in a variable which describes the number of containers.

Evaluated Web Application. The scalable application is an Apache server running a python script with the Kubernetes configuration (the units correspond to resource units in Kubernetes) set to Requests, Limits : $[CPU : 500m, RAM : 512Mi]$. The python code simply performs some array computation by adding and removing elements a number of times specified in the client request. In our experiments, an injected user always asks the component to perform 200 cycles of array manipulation and waits for a randomly chosen time between 0 and 2 s before sending another request. With these settings a new container is needed approximately every 10 new users injected. As the maximum number of injected user is around 50, these settings allow to provide a reasonable elasticity while avoiding an important number of injection servers.

Context, Actions, Reward Function and Common Experimentation Settings. The orchestrator component permanently collects the observed latency and system metrics and keeps them inside an history buffer. The system metrics are collected every 5 s. For each request sent to the Web application, the history buffer contains the response latency with its timestamp. For the system metrics, each entry in the history buffer contains the mean of the CPU and RAM requests and limits[5] over all currently allocated containers. When a context is requested by the agent, the orchestrator is computing, from the history buffer, the 95th percentile latency and the number of requests per second within a 10 s time window. For the system metrics the mean of the CPU and RAM requests and limits are computed on the last 10 entries of the history buffer. The following context vector is used by all algorithms:

$\mathbf{x}_t = $ [number of containers, 95th percentile latency, requests per second, cpu request mean, cpu limit mean, ram request mean, ram limit mean].

As defined in Sect. 3.2, three actions are used: the up action is automatically handled, while stay and down are handled by the reinforcement algorithms. All experiments have been repeated 10 times to capture means and confidence intervals. The latency l^* is set to 600 ms.

Baselines. Different algorithms have been implemented as baselines for the simulated and/or the real experiments. All the algorithms parameters have been experimentaly tuned with a grid-search.

Q-Learning. To reduce the state-action space, Q-Learning [23] uses the following context information: [number of containers, 95th percentile latency rounded to the hundred, requests per second rounded to the ten, mean cpu request rounded to the decimal, mean ram request rounded to the decimal]. The learning rate α is set to 0.1 and the discount factor γ is set to 0.9. ϵ-greedy starts in pure exploration and increases to pure exploitation by 0.000166 at each step.

Deep-Q-Learning. Deep-Q-Learning [15] uses DQN architecture with experience replay memory. The neural network is composed of 2 hidden layers with 24 and 12 neurons using Relu activation function and Huber loss function. The context variables are scaled between $[0, 1]$ for neural network compliance. The learning rate α is set to 0.01, the discount factor γ is set to 0.9 and the batch size is set to 50. For the simulated experiments the target network is updated every 100 steps. ϵ-greedy starts in pure exploration and increases to pure exploitation by 0.000333 at each step. For the experiments on the real environment, as there are less experimentation steps, the target network is updated every 50 steps, and the increase of ϵ is set to 0.00125.

---

[5] https://kubernetes.io/docs/concepts/configuration/manage-resources-containers/.

Kubernetes Threshold Algorithm. To evaluate a threshold algorithm, the Kubernetes horizontal pod auto-scaler algorithm has been implemented[6]. The threshold auto-scaler uses the metrics context directly from Kubernetes and the threshold level was set to the average CPU = 470 m. With this value, experimentally tuned, a new container is created approximately every 10 new users injected allowing the algorithm to stick with the environment setting.

Oracle. A simulated optimal policy (see Sect. 3.1) is also used as a baseline for the simulated experiments. This policy can only be computed for a known dataset generated by a real platform and then used for simulation. To compute this policy from a dataset: for a given workload (number of users), the minimal number of containers that satisfies $l_t \leq l^*$ is searched in the dataset.

4.2   Experiments in Simulated Environment

The simulated environment is not using classical Cloud simulator. It is based on Python code which simulates a Cloud environment by reading metrics from a dataset and changing the virtual number of containers regarding the action chosen by the evaluated algorithm.

Dataset Description. For all experiments done in simulation, a dataset has been used for providing to algorithms the contexts (see Sect. 4.1) and the corresponding latencies. The dataset is a set of records of different contexts, and latencies built on variations of the injected user numbers in the real platform. Users varied from 5 to 50 with a step of 5 users. For each number of users, the number of containers varied from 1 to 10. As expected, for the same injected user number and number of containers there are different values in the captured contexts since a random waiting time is implemented at the injected user side (see Sect. 4.1). This allows us to collect a set of metrics to build the dataset. To analyse the algorithm behavior when learning on data and acting on unseen ones, two different datasets D_1, D_2 have been captured on the same real environment. For each tuple [user number; container number], 20 and 40 contexts have been stored respectively in the dataset D_1 and D_2.

Workload Pattern. In simulated experiments the workload pattern used is depicted in Fig. 2(a). This synthetic pattern is a 9000 steps repetitive triangular pattern with the number of users increasing/decreasing by 5 users every 50 steps.

Cold-Start and Hot-Start Evaluation Protocol. In this section the behavior of baselines and HSLinUCB are evaluated with different starting points. First, each algorithm is evaluated from a cold-start where the agent has no knowledge about the environment with context information extracted from the dataset

---

[6] https://github.com/kubernetes/kubernetes/tree/master/pkg/controller/podautoscaler.

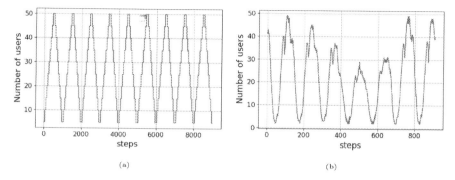

Fig. 2. (a): 9000 steps workload pattern for simulated experiments. (b): 900 steps workload pattern extracted from a week of Wikibench traces from 9/18/2007 to 09/24/2007 for real experiments.

D_1. Then, the experiment is restarted on the same dataset D_1 but with a hot-start where the agent uses the knowledge learnt from the cold-start experiment. Finally, the experiment is restarted with a hot-start using a new dataset D_2 and using the knowledge from the cold-start experiment on dataset D_1. ϵ-greedy exploration is activated for Q-learning and Deep Q-learning only for the first cold-start experiment. Pure exploitation is used for the second and the third experiments. The first experiment will demonstrate how the agent performs on cold-start while learning a new environment. The second, how the agent performs on an already learnt environment. The last, if the agent can perform self-adaptation on un-learnt contexts.

Cold-Start and Hot-Start Evaluation Results. In the case of cold start, HSLinUCB outperforms the other algorithms by quickly converging to the Oracle policy in around 500 steps (Fig. 3). DQN requires less steps than Q-Learning thanks to the Neural Network that captures the model. HSLinUCB realizes 183 times less errors than Q-Learning and 92 times less than Deep Q-Learning while allocating a quite similar mean number of containers (Table 1). This is due to the efficient exploration, and to the robust ridge regression used in LinUCB.

In the case of hot start, for seen and unseen contexts HSLinUCB obtains quite similar results than DQN, which benefits for the high learning performances of Deep Neural Networks. Q-learning obtains worse results than other baselines on unseen contexts while it obtains similar results on seen contexts. This is due to the fact that for unseen contexts, Q-learning faces new contexts and does not know what is the optimal action to perform.

To conclude on simulated experiments, HSLinUCB provides better results in cold-start, performs almost as good as the Oracle with just a few over container allocation in hot-start with seen contexts. It is also quite as good as DQN in hot start with unseen contexts.

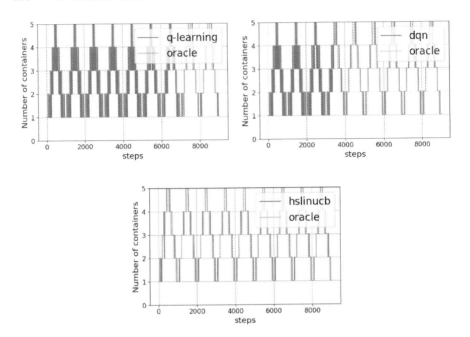

Fig. 3. Number of containers on Cold-start for Q-Learning, Deep Q-Learning and HSLinUCB.

Table 1. Numerical results for different algorithms in simulator.

Mode	Algorithm	Mean l	Mean errors l	Mean c
	Oracle	286 ± 1.95	0 ± 0	3 ± 0.0248
Cold-start	HSLinUCB	$\mathbf{291 \pm 1.64}$	$\mathbf{6.1 \pm 0.584}$	2.97 ± 0.025
	DQN	345 ± 3.72	560 ± 14.7	3 ± 0.026
	Q-learning	438 ± 4.16	1118 ± 13.1	$\mathbf{2.72 \pm 0.025}$
Hot-start seen contexts	HSLinUCB	281 ± 1.83	$\mathbf{0 \pm 0}$	3.02 ± 0.024
	DQN	$\mathbf{266 \pm 1.57}$	0.1 ± 0.186	3.12 ± 0.0265
	Q-learning	304 ± 1.74	0.6 ± 0.303	$\mathbf{2.93 \pm 0.0265}$
Hot-start unseen contexts	HSLinUCB	255 ± 1.65	2.0 ± 0	3.23 ± 0.023
	DQN	$\mathbf{252 \pm 1.47}$	$\mathbf{0 \pm 0}$	3.24 ± 0.026
	Q-learning	324 ± 1.77	226 ± 30.4	$\mathbf{2.91 \pm 0.026}$

4.3 Experimental Results on a Real Platform

Workload Pattern. A real pattern of traffic containing HTTP requests traces is extracted from one week of Wikipedia website [26]. In order to obtain a reasonable computational time, the seven days of traffic have been reproduced and translated in 900 steps load variation (Fig. 2(b)). Then, the load variation of the Wikipedia servers has been reproduced on the real platform with users injections.

Real Environment Evaluation Protocol. In this section the best algorithms from the previous simulated experiments are compared in cold-start to the standard threshold based auto-scaler. Moreover, in order to illustrate the expected performance of DQN trained in a simulated environment and deployed in a real environment, hot-start DQN trained in simulation (Sect. 4.2) is deployed in the real environment. Finally, notice that contrary to the simulated experiments the Oracle can not be estimated in real environment. Indeed, in a simulated environment, the Oracle is computed from datasets and the experiments use the same datasets. This allows a stable baseline for algorithm policy comparison. In a real environment it is impossible to perfectly estimate the future, hence it is impossible to build a stable baseline and to accurately compare an algorithm policy to an unknown perfect one.

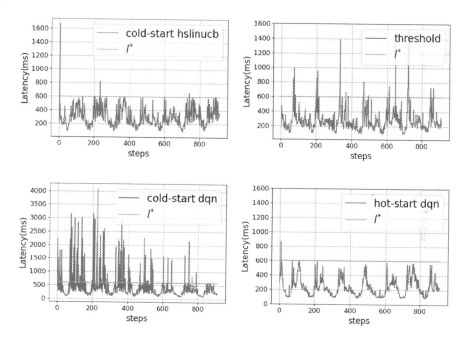

Fig. 4. Latency captured on a real platform for HSLinUCB, threshold, Deep Q-Learning (vertical scale is different) in cold-start, and Deep Q-Learning trained in simulations, then used in hot-start.

Real Environment Evaluation Results. The experiments duration on a real environment is around 15 h for the threshold algorithm, 16 h for HSLinUCB and 37 h for DQN. These differences are explained by the number of changes on the Cloud performed by each algorithm mainly during the exploration stages. While our solution is designed for a unlimited number of containers, the workload has been scaled in the experiments to limit the running time with a maximum of about 5 containers. Figure 4 depicts the latency results for the evaluated algorithms and the Table 2 presents some numerical results. Cold-start HSLinUCB

Table 2. Numerical results for different algorithms on a real platform.

Algorithm	Mean l	Mean errors l	Mean c
Cold-start HSLinUCB	285 ± 6.55	4.4 ± 0.495	2.56 ± 0.0768
Cold-start DQN	428 ± 15.9	109 ± 6.89	$\mathbf{2.39 \pm 0.07}$
Threshold	279 ± 7.45	31.9 ± 2.75	2.6 ± 0.086
Hot-start DQN	$\mathbf{237 \pm 7}$	$\mathbf{1.1 \pm 0.51}$	3 ± 0.057

achieves to maintain the latency under l^* with 4.4 SLA violations on average which is 7.25 times less than the threshold algorithm and 26.3 times less than Cold-start DQN. In cold-start, HSLinUCB outperforms the other algorithms while allocating fewer containers than the threshold algorithm. Even optimally tuned and configured to react as quickly as possible, the threshold auto-scaler reacts later on workload increase which leads to SLA violation. It also reacts later on workload decrease which drives to over allocation. In the case of cold start, DQN is still penalized by its exploration strategy as it explores more the down action than HSLinUCB which results in less number of containers on average and more SLA violations on average. In the case of hot start, despite the fact that the synthetic workload pattern and the real load pattern look alike (Fig. 2), hot-start DQN over-allocates (20% more containers than HSLinUCB), which explains its low mean latency and mean number of errors (Table 2).

To conclude on real experiments, HSLinUCB provides better results in cold-start without the complex and costly parameters tuning of the threshold algorithm. The HSLinUCB internal exploration strategy allows to quickly follow the workload with few SLA violations while optimizing the container usage (less over-provisioning). DQN, thanks to its neural network is a good performer but is penalized by its random exploration strategy.

5   Conclusion

In this paper, the horizontal scaling problem in container-based environments has been solved using contextual bandits. A mathematical formulation has been presented. A new algorithm HSLinUCB based on LinUCB has been proposed. A simulated environment with synthetic workload pattern and a real platform with the Wikipedia workload pattern has been used to evaluate the approach. The complete experimental environment has been made publicly available through a GitHub repository. An intensive comparison between HSLinUCB and state of the art algorithms has been made with different starting points. All the experiments conclude that the proposed algorithm HSLinUCB performs very well compared to other state of the art algorithms and is close to the optimal policy in simulation. On a real platform, HSLinUCB is able to quickly learn from a cold start allowing it to be used for a new Web application deployment or for a minor and major changes in existing application. In this work the container resource configuration and the Kubernetes node computation power are always the same during an experiment. The workload, even issued from a production trace, is regular and does not contain some extreme or sudden changes. As future works, we plan to study these workload and Cloud stationarity changes. Although HSLinUCB continue to work with more injected users and more managed containers, the current environment settings allows HSLinUCB to satisfy the SLA by adding or removing a container one by one. Hence we also plan to evaluate the HSLinUCB performance with more actions and explore how this approach could be applied to vertical scaling.

References

1. Abbasi-Yadkori, Y., Pal, D., Szepesvari, C.: Improved algorithms for linearstochastic bandits. In: NIPS (2011)
2. Abdullah, M., Iqbal, W., Bukhari, F.: Containers vs virtual machines for autoscaling multi-tier applications under dynamically increasing workloads. In: Intelligent Technologies and Applications (2019)
3. Al-Dhuraibi, Y., Paraiso, F., Djarallah, N., Merle, P.: Elasticity in cloud computing: State of the art and research challenges. IEEE Trans. Serv, Comput. 11(2), 430–447 (2018). https://doi.org/10.1109/TSC.2017.2711009
4. Ayimba, C., Casari, P., Mancuso, V.: SQLR: short term memory q-learning for elastic provisioning. CoRR (2019)
5. Barrett, E., Howley, E., Duggan, J.: Applying reinforcement learning towards automating resource allocation and application scalability in the cloud. Concurr. Comput. Pract, Exp 25(12), 1656–1674 (2013)
6. Cano, I., et al.: ADARES: Adaptive resource management for virtual machines. arXiv (2018)
7. Coutinho, E.F., de Carvalho Sousa, F.R., Rego, P.A.L., Gomes, D.G., de Souza, J.N.: Elasticity in cloud computing: a survey. annals of telecommunications - annales des télécommunications, pp. 289–309 (2014). https://doi.org/10.1007/s12243-014-0450-7
8. Dutreilh, X., Kirgizov, S., Melekhova, O., Malenfant, J., Rivierre, N., Truck, I.: Using reinforcement learning for autonomic resource allocation in clouds: Towards a fully automated workflow. In: ICAS (2011)
9. Gari, Y., Monge, D.A., Pacini, E., Mateos, C., Garino, C.G.: Reinforcement learning-based autoscaling of workflows in the cloud: A survey. CoRR (2020)
10. Hwang, K., Bai, X., Shi, Y., Li, M., Chen, W., Wu, Y.: Cloud performance modeling with benchmark evaluation of elastic scaling strategies. IEEE Trans. Parallel Distrib. Syst. 27(1), 130–143 (2016)
11. Jin, Y., Bouzid, M., Kostadinov, D., Aghasaryan, A.: Model-free resource management of cloud-based applications using reinforcement learning. In: ICIN (2018)
12. Khatua, S., Ghosh, A., Mukherjee, N.: Optimizing the utilization of virtual resources in cloud environment. In: VECIMS (2010)
13. Li, L., Chu, W., Langford, J., Schapire, R.E.: A contextual-bandit approach to personalized news article recommendation. In: WWW (2010)
14. Lorido-Botran, T., Miguel-Alonso, J., Lozano, J.A.: A review of auto-scaling techniques for elastic applications in cloud environments. J. Grid Comput. 1–34 (2014). https://doi.org/10.1007/s10723-014-9314-7
15. Mnih, V., et al.: Human-level control through deep reinforcement learning. Nature 518(7540), 529–533 (2015)

16. Nguyen, H., Shen, Z., Gu, X., Subbiah, S., Wilkes, J.: AGILE: Elastic distributed resource scaling for infrastructure-as-a-service. In: ICAC (2013)

17. Nikravesh, A.Y., Ajila, S.A., Lung, C.: Towards an autonomic auto-scaling prediction system for cloud resource provisioning. In: SEAMS (2015)

18. Pascual, J.A., Lozano, J.A., Miguel-Alonso, J.: Effects of reducing VMs management times on elastic applications. J. Grid Comput. **518**(7540), 529–533 (2018)

19. Qu, C., Calheiros, R.N., Buyya, R.: Auto-scaling web applications in clouds: a taxonomy and survey. ACM Comput. Surv. **51**(4), 1–33 (2018)

20. Schuler, L., Jamil, S., Kühl, N.: AI-based resource allocation: Reinforcement learning for adaptive auto-scaling in serverless environments. arXiv (2020)

21. Shariffdeen, R.S., Munasinghe, D.T.S.P., Bhathiya, H.S., Bandara, U.K.J.U., Bandara, H.M.N.D.: Adaptive workload prediction for proactive auto scaling in PaaS systems. In: CloudTech (2016)

22. Singh, P., Gupta, P., Jyoti, K., Nayyar, A.: Research on auto-scaling of web applications in cloud: Survey, trends and future directions. Pract. Experience Scalable Comput. **20**(2), 399–432 (2019)

23. Sutton, R.S., Barto, A.G.: Introduction to Reinforcement Learning. MIT Press, Cambridge (1998)

24. Tadakamalla, V., Menasce, D.A.: Model-driven elasticity control for multi-server queues under traffic surges in cloud environments. In: ICAC (2018)

25. Toslali, M., Parthasarathy, S., Oliveira, F., Coskun, A.K.: JACKPOT: Online experimentation of cloud microservices. In: HotCloud (2020)

26. Urdaneta, G., Pierre, G., van Steen, M.: Wikipedia workload analysis for decentralized hosting. Comput. Netw. **53**(11), 1830–1845 (2009)

27. Wei, Y., Kudenko, D., Liu, S., Pan, L., Wu, L., Meng, X.: A reinforcement learning based auto-scaling approach for SaaS providers in dynamic cloud environment. Math. Prob. Eng. **2019**, 11 p. (2019). Article ID 5080647. https://doi.org/10.1155/2019/5080647

28. Xu, H., Liu, Y., Lau, W.C., Zeng, T., Guo, J., Liu, A.X.: Online resource allocation with machine variability: a bandit perspective. IEEE/ACM Trans. Networking **28**(5), 2243–2256 (2020). https://doi.org/10.1109/TNET.2020.3006906

Geo-distribute Cloud Applications at the Edge

Ronan-Alexandre Cherrueau, Marie Delavergne$^{(\boxtimes)}$, and Adrien Lèbre

Inria, LS2N Laboratory, Nantes, France
marie.delavergne@inria.fr

Abstract. With the arrival of the edge computing a new challenge arises for cloud applications: How to benefit from geo-distribution (locality) while dealing with inherent constraints of wide-area network links? The admitted approach consists in modifying cloud applications by entangling geo-distribution aspects in the business logic using distributed data stores. However, this makes the code intricate and contradicts the software engineering principle of externalizing concerns. We propose a different approach that relies on the modularity property of microservices applications: (i) one instance of an application is deployed at each edge location, making the system more robust to network partitions (local requests can still be satisfied), and (ii) collaboration between instances can be programmed outside of the application in a generic manner thanks to a service mesh. We validate the relevance of our proposal on a real use-case: geo-distributing OpenStack, a modular application composed of 13 million of lines of code and more than 150 services.

Keywords: Edge computing · Resource sharing · DSL · Service composition · Service mesh · Modularity

1 Introduction

The deployment of multiple micro and nano Data Centers (DCs) at the edge of the network is taking off. Unfortunately, our community is lacking tools to make applications benefit from the geo-distribution while dealing with high latency and frequent disconnections inherent to wide-area networks (WAN) [12].

The current accepted research direction for developing geo-distributed applications consists in using globally distributed data stores [1]. Roughly, distributed data stores emulate a shared memory space among DCs to make the development of geo-distributed application easier [13]. This approach however implies to *entangle* the geo-distribution concern in the business logic of the application. This contradicts the software engineering principle of externalizing concerns. A principle widely adopted in the cloud computing where a strict separation between development and operational (abbreviated as *DevOps*) teams exists [6,8]: Programmers focus on the development and support of the business logic

© Springer Nature Switzerland AG 2021
L. Sousa et al. (Eds.): Euro-Par 2021, LNCS 12820, pp. 301–316, 2021.
https://doi.org/10.1007/978-3-030-85665-6_19

of the application (i.e., the services), whereas DevOps are in charge of the execution of the application on the infrastructure (e.g., deployment, monitoring, scaling).

The lack of separation between the business logic and the geo-distribution concern is not the only problem when using distributed data stores. Data stores distribute resources across DCs in a pervasive manner. In most cases, resources are distributed across the infrastructure identically. However, all resources do not have the same scope in a geo-distributed context. Some are useful in one DC, whereas others need to be shared across multiple locations to control the latency, scalability and availability [3,4]. And scopes may change as time passes. It is therefore tedious for programmers to envision all scenarios in advance, and a fine-grained control per resource is mandatory.

Based on these two observations, we propose to deal with the geo-distribution as an independent concern using the service mesh concept widely adopted in the cloud. A service mesh is a layer over microservices that intercepts requests in order to decouple concerns such as monitoring or auto-scaling [8]. The code of the Netflix Zuul[1] load balancer for example is independent of the domain and generic to any modular application by only considering their requests. In this paper, we explore the same idea for the geo-distribution concern. By default, one instance of the cloud application is deployed on each DC, and a dedicated service mesh *forwards* requests between the different DCs. The forwarding operation is programmed using a domain specific language (DSL) that enables two kinds of collaboration. First, the access of resources available at another DC. Second, the replication of resources on a set of DCs. The DSL reifies the resource location. This makes it clear how far a resource is and where its replicas are. It gives a glimpse of requests probable latencies and a control on resources availability.

The contributions of this paper are as follows:

- We state what it means to geo-distribute an application and illustrate why using a distributed data store is problematic, discussing a real use-case: OpenStack[2] for the edge. OpenStack is the defacto application for managing cloud infrastructures (Sect. 2).
- We present our DSL to program the forwarding of requests and our service mesh that interprets expressions of our language to implement the geo-distribution of a cloud application. Our DSL lets clients specify for each request, in which DC a resource should be manipulated. Our service mesh relies on guarantees provided by modularity to be independent of the domain of the application and generic to any microservices application (Sect. 3).
- We present a proof of concept of our service mesh to geo-distribute OpenStack.[3] With its 13 million of lines of code and more than 150 services,

---

[1] https://netflixtechblog.com/open-sourcing-zuul-2-82ea476cb2b3. Accessed 2021-02-15. Zuul defines itself as an API gateway. In this paper, we do not make any difference with a service mesh. They both intercept and control requests on top of microservices.

[2] https://www.openstack.org/software. Accessed 2021-02-15.

[3] https://github.com/BeyondTheClouds/openstackid/tree/stable/rocky. Accessed 2021-02-15.

OpenStack is a complex cloud application, making it the perfect candidate to validate the independent geo-distribution mechanism that we advocate for. Thanks to our proposal, DevOps can make multiple independent instances of OpenStack collaborative to use a geo-distributed infrastructure (Sect. 4).

We finally conclude and discuss about limitations and future work to push the collaboration between application instances further (Sect. 5).

2   Geo-distributing Applications

In this section, we state what it means to geo-distribute a cloud application and illustrate the invasive aspect of using a distributed data store when geo-distributing the OpenStack application.

2.1   Geo-distribution Principles

We consider an edge infrastructure composed of several geo-distributed micro DCs, up to thousands. Each DC is in charge of delivering cloud capabilities to an edge location (i.e., an airport, a large city, a region ...) and is composed of up to one hundred servers, nearly two racks. The expected latency between DCs can range from 10 to 300 ms round trip time according to the radius of the edge infrastructure (metropolitan, national ...) with throughput constraints (i.e., LAN vs WAN links). Finally, disconnections between DCs are the norm rather than the exception, which leads to network split-brain situations [10]. We underline we do not consider network constraints within a DC (i.e., an edge location) since the edge objective is to bring resources as close as possible to its end use.

Cloud applications of the edge have to reckon with these edge specifics in addition to the geo-distribution of the resources themselves [14]. We hence suggest that geo-distributing an application implies adhering to the following principles:

Local-first. A geo-distributed cloud application should minimize communications between DCs and be able to deal with network partitioning issues by continuing to serve local requests at least (i.e., requests delivered by users in the vicinity of the isolated DC).

Collaborative-then. A geo-distributed cloud application should be able to share resources across DCs on demand and replicate them to minimize user perceived latency and increase robustness when needed.

Unfortunately, implementing these principles produces a code that is hard to reason about and thus rarely addressed [2]. This is for instance the case of OpenStack that we discuss in the following section.

2.2   The Issue of Geo-distributing with a Distributed Data Store

OpenStack is a resource management application to operate one DC. It is responsible for booting Virtual Machines (VMs), assigning VMs in networks, storing operating system images, administrating users, or any operation related to the management of a DC.

A Complex but Modular Application. Similarly to other cloud applications such as Netflix or Uber, OpenStack follows a modular design with many services. The compute service for example manages the compute resources of a DC to boot VMs. The image service controls operating system BLOBs like Debian. Figure 1 depicts this modular design in the context of a boot of a VM. The DevOp starts by addressing a boot request to the compute service of the DC (Step 1). The compute service handles the request and contacts the image service to get the Debian BLOB in return (Step 2). Finally, the compute does a bunch of internal calls – schedules VM, setups the network, mounts the drive with the BLOB – before booting the new VM on one of its compute nodes (Step 3).[4]

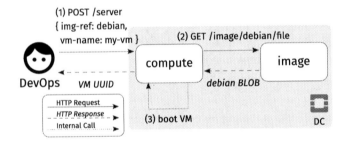

Fig. 1. Boot of a Debian VM in OpenStack

Geo-distributing Openstack. Following the local-first and collaborative-then principles implies two important considerations for OpenStack. First, each DC should behave like a usual cloud infrastructure where DevOps can make requests and use resources belonging to one site without any external communication to other sites. This minimizes the latency and satisfies the robustness criteria for local requests. Second, DevOps should be able to manipulate resources between DCs if needed [3]. For instance, Fig. 11 illustrates an hypothetical sharing with the "boot of a VM at one DC using the Debian image available in a second one".

---

[4] For clarity, this paper simplifies the boot workflow. In a real OpenStack, the boot also requires at least the network and identity service. Many other service may also be involved. See https://www.openstack.org/software/project-navigator/openstack-components. Accessed 2021-02-15.

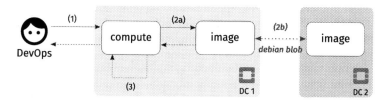

Fig. 2. Boot of a VM using a remote BLOB

Code 1.1. Retrieval of a BLOB in the image service

```
1 @app.get('/image/{name}/file')
2 def get_image(name: String) -> BLOB:
3   # Lookup the image path in the data store: `path = proto://path/debian.qcow`
4   path = ds.query(f'''SELECT path FROM images WHERE id IS "{name}";''')
5
6   # Read path to get the image BLOB
7   image_blob = image_collection.get(path)
8   return image_blob
```

To provide this resource sharing between DC 1 and DC 2, the image service has to implement an additional dedicated means (Step 2b). Moreover, it should be configurable as it might be relevant to replicate the resource if the sharing is supposed to be done multiple times over a WAN link. Implementing such a mechanism is a tedious task for programmers of the application, who prefer to rely on a distributed data store [4] (Fig. 2).

Distributed Data Store Tangles the Geo-distribution Concern. The OpenStack image service team currently studies several solutions to implement the "booting a VM at DC 1 that benefits from images in DC 2" scenario. All are based on a distributed data store that provides resource sharing between multiple image services: a pull mode where DC 1 instance gets BLOBs from DC 2 using a message passing middleware, a system that replicates BLOBs around instances using a shared database, etc.[5] The bottom line is that they all require to *tangle* the geo-distribution concern with the logic of the application. This can be illustrated by the code that retrieves a BLOB when a request is issued on the image service (code at Step 2 from Fig. 11).

Code 1.1 gives a coarse-grained description of that code. It first queries the data store to find the path of the BLOB (l. 3,4). It then retrieves that BLOB in the `image_collection` and returns it to the caller using the `get` method (l. 6–8). Particularly, this method resolves the protocol of the `/path/` and calls the proper library to get the image. Most of the time, that path refers to a BLOB on the local disk (e.g., `file:///path/debian.qcow`). In such a case, the

---

[5] https://wiki.openstack.org/wiki/Image_handling_in_edge_environment.   Accessed 2021-02-15.

method `image_collection.get` relies on the local `open` python function to get the BLOB.

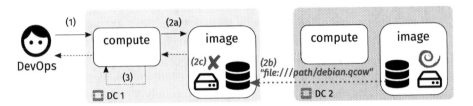

Fig. 3. Booting a VM at DC 1 with a BLOB in DC 2 using a distributed data store (does not work)

The code executes properly as long as only one OpenStack is involved. But things go wrong when multiple are unified through a data store. If Code 1.1 remains unchanged, then the sole difference in the workflow of "booting a VM at DC 1 using an image in DC 2" is the distributed data store that federates all image paths (including those in DC 2—see Fig. 3). Unfortunately, because DC 2 hosts the Debian image, the file path of that image returned at Step 2b is local to DC 2 and *does not exist* on the disk of DC 1. An *error* results in the `image_collection.get` (2c).

The execution of the method `image_collection.get` takes place in a specific environment called its *execution context*. This context contains explicit data such as the method parameters. In our case, the image `path` found from the data store. It also contains implicit assumptions made by the programmer: "A path with the `file:` prototype must refer to an image stored on the local disk". Alas, such kind of assumptions are wrong with a distributed data store. They have to be fixed. For this scenario of "booting a VM at DC 1 using an image in DC 2", it means changing the `image_collection.get` method in order to allow the access of the disk of DC 2 from DC 1. More generally, a distributed data store constrains programmers to take the distribution into account (and the struggle to achieved it) in the application. And besides this entanglement, a distributed data store also strongly limits the collaborative-then principle. In the code above, there is no way to specify whether a particular BLOB should be replicated or not.

Our position is that the geo-distribution must be handled outside of the logic and in a fine-grained manner due to its complexity.

3   Geo-distribute Applications with a Service Mesh

In this section, we first introduce the foundations and notations for our proposal. We then build upon this to present our service mesh that decouples the geo-distribution concern from the business logic of an application.

3.1 Microservices and Service Mesh Basics

An application that follows a microservices architecture combines several services [7]. Each service defines endpoints (operations) for managing one or various resources [5]. The combination of several services endpoints forms a series of calls called a workflow. Deploying all services of an application constitutes one application instance (often shortened instance in the rest). The services running in an application instance are called service instances. Each application instance achieves the application intent by exposing all of its workflows which enables the manipulation of resource values.

Figure 4 illustrates such an architecture. Figure 4a depicts an application *App* made of two services *s*, *t* that expose endpoints *e*, *f*, *g*, *h* and one example of a workflow *s.e → t.h*. *App* could be for example the OpenStack application. In this context, service *s* is the compute service that manages VMs. Its endpoint *e* creates VMs and *f* lists them. Service *t* is the image service that controls operating system BLOBs. Its endpoint *g* stores an image and *h* downloads one. The composition *s.e → t.h* models the boot workflow (as seen in Fig. 1). Figure 4b shows two application instances of *App* and their corresponding service instances: s_1 and t_1 for App_1; s_2 and t_2 for App_2. A client (•) triggers the execution of the workflow *s.e → t.h* on App_2. It addresses a request to the endpoint *e* of s_2 which handles it and, in turn, contacts the endpoint *h* of t_2.

Microservices architectures are the keystone of DevOps practices. They promote a modular decomposition of services for their independent instantiation and maintenance. A service mesh takes benefit of this situation to implement communication related features such as authentication, message routing or load balancing outside of the application. In its most basic form, a service mesh consists in a set of reverse proxies around service instances that encapsulate a specific code to control communications between services [8]. This encapsulation in each proxy *decouples* the code managed by DevOps from the application business logic maintained by programmers. It also makes the service mesh *generic* to all services by considering them as black boxes and only taking into account their communication requests.

Figure 5 illustrates the service mesh approach with the monitoring of requests to have insight about the application. It shows reverse proxies mon_s and mon_t

(a) Application *App* made of two services *s* and *t* and four endpoints *e*, *f*, *g*, *h*. The *s.e → t.h* represents an example of a workflow.

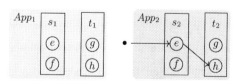

(b) Two independent instances App_1 and App_2 of the *App* application. The • represents a client that executes the *s.e → t.h* workflow in App_2.

Fig. 4. Microservices architecture of a cloud application

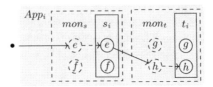

Fig. 5. Service mesh *mon* for the monitoring of requests

that collect metrics on requests toward service instances s_i and t_i during the execution of the workflow $s.e \rightarrow t.h$ on App_i. The encapsulated code in mon_s and mon_t collects for example requests latency and success/error rates. It may send metrics to a time series database as InfluxDB and could be changed by anything else without touching the *App* code.

3.2   A Tour of Scope-lang and the Service Mesh for Geo-distributing

Interestingly, running one instance of a microservices application *automatically* honors the local-first principle. In Fig. 4b, the two instances are independent. They can be deployed on two different DCs. This obviously cancels communications between DCs as well as the impact of DCs' disconnections. However for the global system, it results in plenty of concurrent values of the same resource distributed but isolated among all instances (e.g., *s1* and *s2* manage the same kind of resources but their values differ as time passes). Manipulating any concurrent value of any instance requires now on to code the collaboration in the service mesh and let clients to specify it at will.

App_i, App_j ::= application instance
s, t ::= service
s_i, t_j ::= service instance
Loc ::= App_i single location
               | $Loc \& Loc$ multiple locations
σ ::= $s : Loc, \sigma$ scope
               | $s : Loc$

$$\mathcal{R}[\![s : App_i]\!] = s_i$$
$$\mathcal{R}[\![s : Loc \& Loc']\!] = \mathcal{R}[\![s : Loc]\!] \text{ and } \mathcal{R}[\![s : Loc']\!]$$

(a) scope-lang expressions σ and the function that resolves service instance from elements of the scope $\mathcal{R}$.

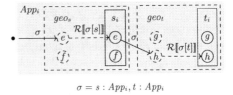

$\sigma = s : App_i, t : App_i$

(b) Scope σ interpreted by the geo-distribution service mesh *geo* during the execution of the $s.e \xrightarrow{\sigma} t.h$ workflow in App_i. Reverse proxies perform requests forwarding based on the scope and the $\mathcal{R}$ function.

Fig. 6. A service mesh to geo-distribute a cloud application

In that regard, we developed a domain specific language called scope-lang. A scope-lang expression (referred to as the *scope* or σ in Fig. 6a) contains location information that defines, for each service involved in a workflow, in which instance the execution takes place. The scope "$s : App_1, t : App_2$" intuitively tells to use the service s from App_1 and t from App_2. The scope "$t : App_1 \& App_2$" specifies to use the service t from App_1 and App_2.

Clients set the scope of a request to specify the collaboration between instances they want for a specific execution. The scope is then *interpreted* by our service mesh during the execution of the workflow to fulfill that collaboration. The main operation it performs is *request forwarding*. Broadly speaking, reverse proxies in front of service instances (geo_s and geo_t in Fig. 6b) intercept the request and interpret its scope to forward the request somewhere. "Where" exactly depends on locations in the scope. However, the interpretation of the scope always occurs in the following stages:

1. A request is addressed to the endpoint of a service of one application instance. The request piggybacks a scope, typically as an HTTP header in a RESTful application. For example in Fig. 6b: $\bullet \xrightarrow{s:App_i,t:App_i} s.e$.
2. The reverse proxy in front of the service instance intercepts the request and reads the scope. In Fig. 6b: geo_s intercepts the request and reads σ which is equal to $s : App_i, t : App_i$.
3. The reverse proxy extracts the location assigned to its service from the scope. In Fig. 6b: geo_s extracts the location assigned to s from σ. This operation, notated $\sigma[s]$, returns App_i.
4. The reverse proxy uses a specific function $\mathcal{R}$ (see Fig. 6a) to resolve the service instance at the assigned location. $\mathcal{R}$ uses an internal registry. Building the registry is a common pattern in service mesh using a *service discovery* [8] and therefore is not presented here. In Fig. 6b: $\mathcal{R}[\![s : \sigma[s]]\!]$ reduces to $\mathcal{R}[\![s : App_i]\!]$ and is resolved to service instance s_i.
5. The reverse proxy *forwards* the request to the endpoint of the resolved service instance. In Fig. 6b: geo_s forwards the request to $s_i.e$.

In this example of executing the workflow $s.e \xrightarrow{\sigma} t.h$, the endpoint $s_i.e$ has in turn to contact the endpoint h of service t. The reverse proxy geo_s propagates the scope on the outgoing request towards the service t. The request then goes through stages 2 to 5 on behalf of the reverse proxy geo_t. It results in a forwarding to the endpoint $\mathcal{R}[\![t : \sigma[t]]\!].h$ that is resolved to $t_i.h$.

Here, the scope only refers to one location (i.e., App_i). Thus the execution of the workflow remains *local* to that location. The next sections detail the use of forwarding in order to perform collaboration between instances.

3.3 Forwarding for Resource Sharing

A modular decomposition of the code is popular for programmers of microservices architecture. It divides the functionality of the application into *independent and interchangeable* services [9]. This brings well-known benefits including ease of reasoning. More importantly, modularity also gives the ability to *change* a service with a certain API by any service exposing the same API and logic [11].

A load balancer, such a Netflix Zuul mentioned in the introduction, makes a good use of this property to distribute the load between multiple instances of the

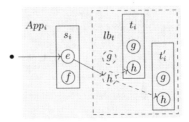

Fig. 7. Load balancing principle

same modular service [5]. Figure 7 shows this process with the reverse proxy for load balancing lb_t of the service t. lb_t intercepts and balances incoming requests within two service instances t_i and t'_i during the execution of the workflow $s.e \rightarrow t.h$ in App_i. From one execution to another, the endpoint $s_i.e$ gets result from $t_i.h$ or $t'_i.h$ in a safe and transparent manner thanks to modularity.

We generalize this mechanism to share resources. In contrast to the load balancer that changes the composition between multiple instances of the same service *inside* a single application instance. Here, we change the composition between multiple instances of the same service *across* application instances. As a consequence, the different service instances share their resources during the execution of a workflow.

Figure 8 depicts this cross dynamic composition mechanism during the execution of the workflow $s.e \xrightarrow{s:App_1,t:App_2} t.h$. The service instance s_1 of App_1 is dynamically composed thanks to the forwarding operation of the service mesh with the service instance t_2 of App_2. This forwarding is safe relying on the guaranty provided by modularity. (If t is modular, then we can swap t_1 by t_2 since they obviously have the same API and logic.) As a result, the endpoint $s_1.e$ benefits from resource values of $t_2.h$ instead of its usual $t_1.h$.

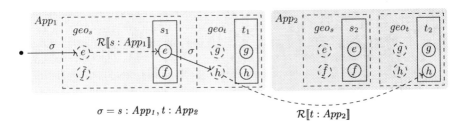

Fig. 8. Resource sharing by forwarding across instances

3.4 Forwarding for Resource Replication

Replication is the ability to create and maintain identical resources on different DCs: an operation on one replica should be propagated to the other ones according to a certain consistency policy. In our context, it is used to deal with latency and availability.

In terms of implementation, microservices often follow a RESTful HTTP API and so generate an identifier for each resource. This identifier is later used to retrieve, update or delete resources. Since each application instance is independent, our service mesh requires a meta-identifier to manipulate replicas across the different DCs as a unique resource.

For example, the image service t exposes an endpoint g to create an image. When using a scope for replication, such as $t : App_1 \& App_2$, the service mesh generates a meta-identifier and maps it $\{metaId : [App_1 : localID_{t_1}, App_2 : localID_{t_2}]\}$. In Fig. 9, if t_1 creates a replica with the identifier 42 and t_2 6, and our meta-identifier was generated as 72, the mapping is: $\{72 : [App_1 : 42, App_2 : 6]\}$. Mappings are stored in an independent database alongside each application instance.

The replication process is as follows:

1. A request for replication is addressed to the endpoint of a service of one application instance. For example in Fig. 9: $\bullet \xrightarrow{t:App_1 \& App_2} t.g$.
2. Similarly to the sharing, the $\mathcal{R}$ function is used to resolve the endpoints that will store replicas. $\mathcal{R}[\![s : Loc\&Loc']\!] = \mathcal{R}[\![s : Loc]\!]$ and $\mathcal{R}[\![s : Loc']\!]$. In Fig. 9: $\mathcal{R}[\![t : App_1 \& App_2]\!]$ is equivalent to $\mathcal{R}[\![t : App_1]\!]$ and $\mathcal{R}[\![t : App_2]\!]$. Consequently, t_1 and t_2.
3. The meta-identifier is generated along with the mapping and added in the database. In Fig. 9: $\{ 72 : [App_1 : none, App_2 : none]\}$.
4. Each request is forwarded to the corresponding endpoints on involved DCs and a copy of the mapping is stored in those DCs' database simultaneously. In Fig. 9: geo_t forwards the request to $t_1.g$ and $t_2.g$ and stores the mapping $\{72 : [App_1 : none, App_2 : none]\}$ in App_1 and App_2 databases.
5. Each contacted service instance executes the request and returns the results (including the local identifier) to the service mesh. In Fig. 9: t_1 and t_2 returns respectively the local identifier 42 and 6.
6. The service mesh completes the mapping and populates the involved DCs' databases. In Fig. 9: the mapping now is $\{72 : [App_1 : 6, App_2 : 42]\}$ and added to databases of App_1 and App_2.

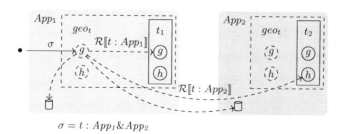

$\sigma = t : App_1 \& App_2$

Fig. 9. Replication by forwarding on multiple instances

7. By default, the meta identifier is returned as the final response. If a response other than an identifier is expected, the first received response is transferred (since others are replicas with similar values).

This process ensures that only interactions with the involved DCs occur, avoiding wasteful communications. Each operation that would later modify or delete one of the replicas will be applied to every others using the mapping available on each site. To prevent any direct manipulation, local identifiers of replicas are hidden.

This replication control perfectly suits our collaborative-then principle. It allows a client to choose "when" and "where" to replicate. Regarding the "how", our current process for forwarding replica requests, maintaining mappings and ensuring that operations done on one replica are applied on others, is naive. Implementing advanced strategies is left as future work. However, we underline that it does not change the foundations of our proposal. Ultimately, choosing the strategy should be made possible at the scope-lang level (e.g., weak, eventual or strong consistency).

3.5   Towards a Generalized Control System

The code of scope-lang is independent of cloud applications and can easily be extended with new features in it. Scope-lang is thus a great place to implement additional operators that would give more control during the manipulation of resources although it has been initially designed for resources sharing and replication. Choosing between different levels of consistency, as highlighted in the previous section, is one example of new operators. Here, we give two other ones to stress the generality of our approach.

The new *otherwise* operator ("$Loc_1; Loc_2$" in Fig. 10a) informally tells to use the first location or fallback on the second one if there is a problem. This operator comes in handy when a client wants to deal with DCs' disconnections. Adding it to the service mesh implies to implement in the reverse proxy what to do when it interprets a scope with a (;). The implementation is straightforward: Make the reverse proxy forward the request to the first location and proceed if it succeeds, or forward the request to the second location otherwise.

Ultimately, we can built new operators upon existing ones. This is the case of the `around` function that considers all locations reachable in a certain amount of time, e.g., `around(`App_1`, 10ms)`. To achieve this, the function combines the available locations with the otherwise operator (;), as shown in Fig. 10b. Thus it does not require to change the code of the interpreter in the service mesh.

$Loc ::= \dots$ see Fig. 6a
$\quad | \quad Loc; Loc$ otherwise location

$\mathcal{R}[\![s : Loc_1; Loc_2]\!] =$
$\quad \mathcal{R}[\![s : Loc_1]\!]$ otherwise $\mathcal{R}[\![s : Loc_2]\!]$

```
def around(loc: Loc, radius: timedelta) -> Loc:
  # Find all Locs in the `radius` of `loc`
  # >  locs = [App1, App2, ..., Appn]
  locs = _find_locs(loc, radius)

  # Combine all `locs` with `;`
  # >  App1;App2;...;Appn
  return foldr(;, locs, loc)
```

(a) The otherwise (;) operator. It requires to update the code of the interpreter in the service mesh.

(b) The **around** operator build upon (;). It does not need to update the code of the interpreter in the service mesh.

Fig. 10. New operators for scope-lang

4   Validation on OpenStack

We demonstrate the feasibility of our approach with a prototype for OpenStack.[6] In this proof of concept, we set up an HAProxy[7] in front of OpenStack services. HAProxy is a reverse proxy that intercepts HTTP requests and forwards them to specific backends. In particular, HAProxy enables to dynamically choose a backend using a dedicated Lua code that reads information from HTTP headers. In our proof of concept, we have developed a specific Lua code that extracts the scope from HTTP headers and interprets it as described in Sect. 3.2 to 3.4.

In a normal OpenStack, the booting of a VM with a Debian image (as presented in Fig. 1) is done by issuing the following command:

```
$ openstack server create my-vm --image debian          (Cmd. 1)
```

We have extended the OpenStack command-line client with an extra argument called --scope. This argument takes the scope and adds it as a specific header on the HTTP request. Thus it can latter be interpreted by our HAProxy. With it, a DevOps can execute the previous Cmd. 1 in a specific location by adding a --scope that, for instance, specifies to use the compute and image service instance of DC 1:

```
$ openstack server create my-vm --image debian\
            --scope { compute: DC 1, image: DC 1 }     (Cmd. 2)
```

In the case where the DevOps is in DC 1, the request is entirely local and thus will be satisfied even during network disconnections between DCs. Actually, all locally scoped requests are always satisfied because each DC executes one particular instance of OpenStack. This ensures the local-first principle.

The next command (Cmd. 3) mixes locations to do a resource sharing as explained in Sect. 3.3. It should be read as "boot a VM with a Debian image using the compute service instance of DC 1 and the image service instance of DC 2":

---

[6] https://github.com/BeyondTheClouds/openstackoid/tree/stable/rocky.   Accessed 2021-02-15.

[7] https://www.haproxy.org/. Accessed 2021-02-15.

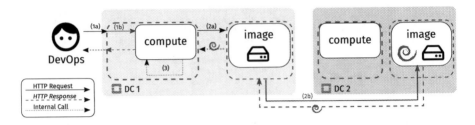

Fig. 11. Boot of a VM at DC 1 with a BLOB in DC 2 using scope-lang

```
$ openstack server create my-vm --image debian\
            --scope { compute: DC 1, image: DC 2 }        (Cmd. 3)
```

Figure 11 shows the execution. Dotted red squares represent HAProxy instances. Step 1b and 2b correspond to the forwarding of the request according to the scope. The execution results in the sharing of the Debian image at DC 2 to boot a VM at DC 1. That collaboration is taken over by the service mesh. No change to the OpenStack code has been required.

Mixing locations in the scope makes it explicit to the DevOps that the request may be impacted by the latency. If DC 1 and DC 2 are far for from each other, then it should be clear to the DevOps that Cmd. 3 is going to last a certain amount of time. To mitigate this, the DevOps may choose to replicate the image:

```
$ openstack image create debian --file ./debian.qcow2\
            --scope { image: DC 1 & DC 2 }                (Cmd. 4)
```

This command (Cmd. 4) creates an identical image on both DC 1 and DC 2 using the protocol seen in Sect. 3.4. It reduces the cost of fetching the image each time it is needed (as in Cmd. 3). Moreover, in case of partitioning, it is still possible to create a VM from this image on each site where the replicas are located. This fine-grained control ensures to replicate (and pay the cost of replication) only when and where it is needed to provide a collaborative-then application.

Our proof of concept has been presented twice at the OpenStack Summit and is mentioned as an interesting approach to geo-distribute OpenStack in the second white paper published by the Edge Computing Working Group of the OpenStack foundation in 2020.[8]

5   Conclusion

We propose a new approach to geo-distribute microservices applications without meddling in their code. By default, one instance of the application is deployed on each edge location and collaborations between the different instances are achieved through a generic service mesh. A DSL, called scope-lang, allows

---

[8] https://www.openstack.org/use-cases/edge-computing/edge-computing-next-steps-in-architecture-design-and-testing Accessed 2021-02-18.

the configuration of the service mesh on demand and on a per request basis, enabling the manipulation of resources at different levels: locally to one instance (by default) and across distinct instances (sharing) and multiple (replication). Expliciting the location of services in each request makes the user aware of the number of sites that are involved (to control the scalability), the distance to these sites (to control the network latency/disconnections), and the number of replicas to maintain (to control the availability/network partitions).

We demonstrated the relevance of our approach with a proof of concept that enables to geo-distribute OpenStack, the defacto cloud manager. Thanks to it, DevOps can make multiple independent instances of OpenStack collaborative. This proof of concept is among the first concrete solutions to manage a geo-distributed edge infrastructure as an usual IaaS platform. Interestingly, by using our proposal over our proof of concept, DevOps can now envision to geo-distribute cloud applications.

This separation between the business logic and the geo-distribution concern is a major change with respect to the state of the art. It is important however to underline that our proposal is built on the modularity property of cloud applications. In other words, an application that does not respect this property cannot benefit from our service mesh. Regarding our future work, we have already identified additional collaboration mechanisms that can be relevant. For instance, we are investigating how a resource that has been created on one instance can be extended or even reassigned to another one.

We believe that a generic and non invasive approach for geo-distributing cloud applications, such as the one we propose, is an interesting direction that should be investigated by our community.

References

1. Abadi, D.: Consistency tradeoffs in modern distributed database system design: CAP is only part of the story. Computer **45**(2), 37–42 (2012)
2. Alvaro, P., et al.: Consistency analysis in bloom: a CALM and collected approach. In: 5th Biennial Conference on Innovative Data Systems Research, CIDR 2011, Online Proceedings, Asilomar, CA, USA, 9–12 January 2011, pp. 249–260 (2011)
3. Cherrueau, R., et al.: Edge computing resource management system: a critical building block! initiating the debate via openstack. In: USENIX Workshop on Hot Topics in Edge Computing, HotEdge 2018, Boston, MA, 10 July. USENIX Association (2018)
4. Corbett, J.C., et al.: Spanner: Google's globally-distributed database. In: 10th USENIX Symposium on Operating Systems Design and Implementation, OSDI 2012, Hollywood, CA, USA, 8–10 October 2012, pp. 261–264 (2012)
5. Fielding, R.T.: Architectural styles and the design of network-based software architectures. Ph.D. thesis, University of California, Irvine (2000)
6. Herbst, N.R., et al.: Elasticity in cloud computing: what it is, and what it is not. In: 10th International Conference on Autonomic Computing, ICAC 2013, San Jose, CA, June 2013, pp. 23–27. USENIX Association (2013)
7. Jamshidi, P., et al.: Microservices: the journey so far and challenges ahead. IEEE Softw. **35**(3), 24–35 (2018)

8. Li, W., et al.: Service mesh: challenges, state of the art, and future research opportunities. In: 2019 IEEE International Conference on Service-Oriented System Engineering (SOSE), pp. 122–1225 (2019)

9. Liskov, B.: A design methodology for reliable software systems. In: Proceedings of the AFIPS 1972 Fall Joint Computer Conference, USA, 5–7 December, pp. 191–199. American Federation of Information Processing Societies (1972)

10. Markopoulou, A., et al.: Characterization of failures in an operational IP backbone network. IEEE/ACM Trans. Netw. **16**(4), 749–762 (2008)

11. Parnas, D.L.: On the criteria to be used in decomposing systems into modules. Commun. ACM **15**(12), 1053–1058 (1972)

12. Satyanarayanan, M.: The emergence of edge computing. Computer **50**(1), 30–39 (2017)

13. Shapiro, M., et al.: Just-right consistency: reconciling availability and safety. CoRR abs/1801.06340 (2018). http://arxiv.org/abs/1801.06340

14. Tato, G., et al.: Split and migrate: resource-driven placement and discovery of microservices at the edge. In: 23rd International Conference on Principles of Distributed Systems, OPODIS 2019, 17–19 December, Neuchâtel, Switzerland. LIPIcs, vol. 153, pp. 9:1–9:16. Schloss Dagstuhl - Leibniz-Zentrum für Informatik (2019)

A Fault Tolerant and Deadline Constrained Sequence Alignment Application on Cloud-Based Spot GPU Instances

Rafaela C. Brum[1]([✉]), Walisson P. Sousa[2], Alba C. M. A. Melo[3],
Cristiana Bentes[2], Maria Clicia S. de Castro[2],
and Lúcia Maria de A. Drummond[1]

[1] Fluminense Federal University, Niterói, Brazil
`rafaelabrum@id.uff.br, lucia@ic.uff.br`
[2] State University of Rio de Janeiro, Rio de Janeiro, Brazil
`walisson.sousa@pos.ime.uerj.br, cris@eng.uerj.br, clicia@ime.uerj.br`
[3] University of Brasilia, Brasilia, Brazil
`alves@unb.br`

Abstract. Pairwise sequence alignment is an important application to identify regions of similarity that may indicate the relationship between two biological sequences. This is a computationally intensive task that usually requires parallel processing to provide realistic execution times. This work introduces a new framework for a deadline constrained application of sequence alignment, called MASA-CUDAlign, that exploits cloud computing with Spot GPU instances. Although much cheaper than On-Demand instances, Spot GPUs can be revoked at any time, so the framework is also able to restart MASA-CUDAlign from a checkpoint in a new instance when a revocation occurs. We evaluate the proposed framework considering five pairs of DNA sequences and different AWS instances. Our results show that the framework reduces financial costs when compared to On-Demand GPU instances while meeting the deadlines even in scenarios with several instances revocations.

Keywords: Cloud computing · Spot GPU · Sequence alignment

1 Introduction

Biological sequence alignment is an important and extensively used computational procedure that arranges sequences of DNA, RNA, or proteins to identify regions of similarities and differences. However, this procedure presents quadratic complexity in terms of execution time. Many parallel versions of the sequence alignment algorithm were proposed in the literature exploiting different types of architectures focusing on providing realistic execution times [3,7,15,18]. Among these solutions, MASA-CUDAlign [18] stands out for the comparison of huge

© Springer Nature Switzerland AG 2021
L. Sousa et al. (Eds.): Euro-Par 2021, LNCS 12820, pp. 317–333, 2021.
https://doi.org/10.1007/978-3-030-85665-6_20

biological sequences using GPUs. It achieved 10,370 GCUPS (Billions of Cells Updated per Second) on a cluster with 128 compute nodes and 384 GPUs. The impressive results were obtained on a very expensive platform, usually unattainable for scientists.

Cloud platforms are an attractive option to execute parallel applications at low cost, presenting well-known potential advantages such as availability and scalability on a pay-as-you-go basis. There are many cloud service providers, such as Amazon Web Services (AWS), Microsoft Azure, or Google Cloud Platform, that offer On-Demand powerful parallel resources, including clusters of GPUs, with minimal management effort. In November 2010, AWS announced the first GPU instance type in the Amazon Elastic Compute Cloud (EC2), the *cg1.4xlarge* instance [2], which included 2 Fermi GPUs attached to it. Nowadays, EC2 offers many GPU instance types, from Kepler to Volta architectures.

Cloud providers offer several types of Virtual Machines (VMs) in different markets with different availability guarantees. EC2 presents two main markets to deploy a VM: the On-Demand and the Spot markets. The On-Demand market allocates VMs for a fixed cost per time unit, and its availability is ensured during the whole execution. The Spot market offers VMs with an up to 90% price discount, but instances' price and availability fluctuate according to an auction model and the cloud's current demand, which can terminate a Spot VM at any time. In December 2017, AWS adopted a new price model for the EC2 VMs in the Spot market. Since then, spot prices have less variations and the instances' availability is defined mostly by the supply and demand of spare capacity disregarding the bids of the previous auction model [14].

In this scenario, Spot GPU instances provide a low-cost alternative to execute sequence alignment applications. However, the application must be fault-tolerant to deal with revocations. In this work, we propose a framework to run a deadline constrained and fault-tolerant version of MASA-CUDAlign on the cloud using Spot and On-Demand GPU instances to minimize the total execution cost. We used a fault-tolerant version of MASA-CUDAlign that runs on a single GPU [18] and we assess the framework performance when compared to On-Demand single-GPU executions.

This paper is organized as follows: Sect. 2 describes related works. Section 3 gives a brief description of the Sequence Alignment Problem. Section 4 explains the proposed framework for Spot GPUs. Section 5 presents the experimental results. Finally, Sect. 6 concludes and presents ideas for future work.

2   Related Works

The Spot market has received a lot of attention in the last years [5,11,22,25]. All works consider Spot VMs containing only CPUs and only a few papers exploit Spot GPU VMs. Some works use Spot VMs to train Machine Learning (ML) models. Lee and Son [8] proposed DeepSpotCloud that searches the cheapest AWS Spot instances available in different countries to train Deep Learning tasks. The authors used checkpoints of intermediate training results to recover revoked VMs. Also, the authors implemented a live migration heuristic to reduce execution costs. DeepSpotCloud is specific for ML applications. To deal with revocations in distributed ML training, Wagenländer *et al.* [26] proposed the Spotnik, which deals with the VMs revocations by synchronizing the communication phase of each isolated model and ignoring the changes in the iterations when the provider revokes any VM. With this synchronization, Spotnik avoids the overhead incurred by checkpoints. This technique cannot handle revocations of all VMs. If all preemptive VMs are revoked, the ML training restarts from the beginning. Zhou *et al.* [27] implemented a fault-tolerant stencil computation (SC) on the AWS Spot GPU instances. The proposed framework takes advantage of pipelining to overcome the communication overhead and to increase the processing speed. It uses a low-cost checkpointing mechanism to handle the possible termination of the spot instances. The checkpointing mechanism periodically copies the memory block from the GPU to a buffer on the host memory using CUDA memcopy and sends it to the backup server using a non-blocking MPI send. The results were obtained in two different environments, a 4-node cluster and Amazon's GPU instances (*g2.2xlarge*). Our work focuses on minimizing the monetary cost using Spot VMs to execute a Smith-Waterman (SW) [21] based sequence alignment algorithm while observing a deadline constraint. Table 1 summarizes the main characteristics of these three works and our work: target application; objective; constraint; and how the proposal is evaluated. All of them use fault-tolerance mechanisms at the application level.

Table 1. Main characteristics of works related to the use of Spot GPUs in clouds.

Paper	Application	Objective	Constraint (minimize)	Evaluation approach
Lee e Son [2017] [8]	ML	Monetary cost	-	Real cloud
Wagenländer et al. [2020] [26]	ML	Execution time	-	Real cloud
Zhou et al. [2019] [27]	SC	Execution time	-	Real cloud
Our work	SW	Monetary cost	Deadline	Real cloud

Concerning the use of GPU on clouds to solve the sequence alignment problem, to the best of our knowledge, there are very few papers in the literature. Lee et al. [9, 10] present the Smith-Waterman algorithm (SW) with a frequency-based filtration method on GPUs and a user-friendly interface for potential cloud server applications with GPUs. The proposed method focuses on the intra-task parallelization to calculate the frequency distance and perform Smith-Waterman comparisons on a single GPU. The results consider small protein sequences and were run only in a local cluster.

Our proposal considers a sequence alignment algorithm with deadline constraints executing in real cloud GPU instances, focusing on the Spot VMs, wherein the revocations impose some new challenges.

3   Sequence Alignment Problem

Biological sequence alignment is one of the most used operations in Bioinformatics. Its goal is to retrieve a score, which provides the similarity between the sequences, and an alignment, which shows clearly the parts of the sequences with high similarity. Three cases are considered: (a) matches, where the characters are identical; (b) mismatches, where the characters are distinct and (c) the additions of the character $-$ (gap) in one of the sequences. Figure 1 illustrates an alignment and score, for $match = +1$, $mismatch = -1$, $gap = -2$.

$$
\begin{array}{c}
C\ G\ A\ T\ C\ T\ -\ A\ C \\
C\ G\ T\ T\ C\ T\ G\ A\ C \\
\hline
+1+1-1+1+1+1-2+1+1 \\
\underbrace{\qquad\qquad\qquad\qquad\qquad} \\
score = 4
\end{array}
$$

Fig. 1. Example of alignment and score.

3.1   DP Algorithms for Sequence Comparison

The Smith-Waterman (SW) [21] algorithm retrieves the optimal local alignment between two sequences S_0 and S_1, with time and space complexity $O(mn)$, where m and n are the lengths of the sequences. The SW algorithm executes in two steps: (1) compute the DP matrix and (2) traceback. In step 1, a DP matrix of size $(m + 1) * (n + 1)$ is computed, with data dependencies on $(i - 1, j)$, $(i, j - 1)$ and $(i - 1, j - 1)$ for each DP cell (i, j). At the end of step 1, we have the DP matrix, the value for the maximum score, and the position (a, b) in the DP matrix where the maximum score occurs. The traceback step begins after the matrix computation finishes, and it starts from (a, b), following the traceback path until a zero-valued cell is reached. Figure 2 illustrates the SW matrix.

The SW algorithm was modified by Gotoh [4] to use the affine gap model, where the first gap of a sequence of gaps (G_{first}) has a higher penalty than the subsequent gaps (G_{extend}). Gotoh uses 3 DP matrices, instead of one, to retrieve the optimal alignment. The time and space complexities remain $O(mn)$. Myers and Miller [12] modified Gotoh's algorithm to retrieve the alignments in linear space, using a divide-and-conquer approach that retrieves the points that belong to the optimal alignment (crosspoints) recursively.

The performance metric commonly used to compare Smith-Waterman tools is Giga Cells Updated per Second (GCUPS), which is computed as the product of the sequences lengths ($m*n$) divided by ($execution\_time\_in\_seconds * 10^9$).

	*	A	C	G	A	T	T	T	C	T	G
*	0	0	0	0	0	0	0	0	0	0	0
T	0	0	0	0	0	1	1	1	0	1	0
C	0	0	1	0	0	0	0	0	2	0	0
G	0	0	0	2	0	0	0	0	0	1	1
A	0	1	0	0	3	1	0	0	0	0	0
G	0	0	0	1	1	2	0	0	0	0	1
T	0	0	0	0	0	2	3	1	0	1	0
T	0	0	0	0	0	1	3	4	2	1	0
A	0	1	0	0	1	0	1	2	3	1	0
C	0	0	2	0	0	0	0	0	3	2	0
C	0	0	1	1	0	0	0	0	1	2	1

Fig. 2. SW matrix for $S_0 = ACGATTTCTG$ and $S_1 = TCGAGTTACC$. Values for match, mismatch and gap are $+1$, -1 and -2. DP cells in bold show the traceback path.

3.2 MASA-CUDAlign

CUDAlign 4.0 [18] is a Smith-Waterman based tool for GPUs that retrieves optimal alignments with variants of the Gotoh and Myers-Miller algorithms (Sect. 3.1). It employs highly optimized parallelization techniques, such as parallelogram processing and speculative traceback (in the case of multiple GPUs), as well as sophisticated algorithmic variants, like orthogonal execution and balanced partitions. CUDAlign 4.0 achieved 10,370 GCUPS [18], and this is, to our knowledge, the best performance among the Smith-Waterman tools for GPUs.

In 2014, CUDAlign's code was re-organized in platform-dependent and independent parts, generating a platform-independent architecture called MASA (Multiple Sequence Aligner Architecture) [17]. For this reason, since 2016, CUDAlign 4.0 is called MASA-CUDAlign. Nowadays, MASA supports implementations for CPU, Intel Phi, and GPU.

Although MASA-CUDAlign achieves 10,370 GCUPS at a multi-node platform (384 GPUs running in 128 nodes), its application-level checkpoint is only suitable for single-node platforms. Due to this limitation, we used the single GPU version of MASA-CUDAlign [16]. Figure 3 gives an overview of the MASA-CUDAlign execution in one GPU.

It executes in 5 stages, where stage 1 executes step 1 of the algorithm (compute the DP matrices) and stages 2 to 5 execute step 2 (traceback). Stage 1 computes the DP matrices with Gotoh's algorithm and gives as output the optimal score and its position. Some rows are stored in a special rows area (SRA), on memory+disk or disk, and some blocks are pruned (gray blocks). Traceback is executed in a divide-and-conquer manner. Stage 2 finds crosspoints that belong to the optimal alignment using the special rows and saves special columns. Stage 3 finds more crosspoints over special columns stored in the previous stage. Stage

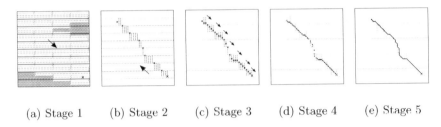

(a) Stage 1   (b) Stage 2   (c) Stage 3   (d) Stage 4   (e) Stage 5

Fig. 3. General overview of the MASA-CUDAlign execution in one GPU [16]

4 executes Myers and Miller's algorithm between successive crosspoints. Finally, stage 5 obtains the complete alignment between each successive crosspoints.

When comparing Megabase sequences in one GPU, stage 1 is the most compute-intensive and it corresponds, on average, to more than 85% of the total execution time [16]. In stage 1, special rows are stored in the SRA with two main purposes: accelerate the traceback stages and implement an application-specific checkpoint. If MASA-CUDAlign's execution is interrupted in the middle of stage 1 execution, the user can instruct MASA-CUDAlign to restart from the last saved row, by providing the path to the file that contains the SRA. These saved rows are evenly distributed over the matrix and the distance between two consecutive rows is proportional to the size of the SRA, determined by the user.

4   Proposed Framework

The proposed framework is inspired by HADS [23], a scheduler of Bag-of-Tasks applications on Spot and On-Demand CPUs. HADS minimizes the execution costs while respecting a deadline constraint in the presence of Spot interruptions. It also takes advantage of the possibility of Spot VMs resuming. Unfortunately, when we consider Spot GPUs, once revoked, they are permanently inactive. Moreover, checkpointing and recovering GPU applications is much more challenging than in CPUs [6].

The proposed framework contains two parts: a Controller and a Worker. The Controller is responsible for choosing the Spot GPU VM, deploying it in the EC2, and eventually migrating the application to a new VM when the previously selected one is revoked. The Worker monitors the deployed VM and communicates with the Controller informing an eventual change in the VM status, from *active* to *revoked*. In case of revocation, the Controller manages the application migration to another GPU VM (Spot or On-Demand).

Let I_{spot} be the set of Spot GPU instance types and $I_{ondemand}$ be the set of On-Demand GPU instance types that can execute MASA-CUDAlign on AWS. Initially, both sets contain the same instance types. Let e_i be the expected execution time of MASA-CUDAlign in an instance type it_i, both in I_{spot} and in $I_{ondemand}$. We assume that e_i is the same for both markets, if no Spot revocation occurs. We will use a slowdown index to represent the computational power of an instance type. To clarify the concept of the slowdown index, suppose that MASA-CUDAlign takes 30 min in an instance type it_j, considered as the baseline, and takes 60 min to execute in an instance type it_k, the slowdown index of instance type it_k, named $slowdown_k$, is equal to 2. In other words, let re_k and re_j be the execution times of MASA-CUDAlign in instance types it_k and it_j, the slowdown of an instance type it_k is defined as $slowdown_k = re_k/re_j$. Note that the higher the slowdown, the worse the performance.

In case of revocation, the framework spends some time to select a new VM, deploy it, and recover the interrupted application from the last checkpoint. As previously explained, MASA-CUDAlign adopts an application-level checkpoint (Sect. 3.2). In the worst scenario, the application is interrupted while performing the checkpointing, which means that MASA-CUDAlign needs to restart the execution from the previous special row fully stored. In that scenario, the application has to re-execute the whole block between these two consecutive special rows. The number of cells inside this block is named here as $worst\_size$.

We have to guarantee that even in that worst scenario, there will be enough time to recover the application and execute it, respecting the given deadline, called here M^D. Although the spare time is necessary only if a revocation occurs, it has to be considered in the initial allocation, which, consequently, has to adopt a new deadline, earlier than the user-provided one. To calculate that new deadline, named M^{DSpot}, the maximum required time to restart the application in the worst scenario has to be estimated. Considering that $GCUPS_i$ is the number of billions of cells updated per second by MASA-CUDAlign on each instance type it_i, the ratio $worst\_size/GCUPS_i$ gives the amount of time that it_i requires to execute a $worst\_size$ block. Thus, the time spent to recover the application on instance it_i in the worst scenario can be calculated by Eq. 1, where α is the overhead to deploy a new VM.

$$restart\_overhead_i = worst\_size/GCUPS_i + \alpha \tag{1}$$

Considering that I is the set of all instance types that can be used for recovering, the maximum restart time that MASA-CUDAlign will spend is defined by Eq. 2.

$$max\_restart\_time = \max_{i \in I}(restart\_overhead_i) \tag{2}$$

The new deadline is calculated as presented in Eq. 3.

$$M^{DSpot} = M^D - max\_restart\_time \tag{3}$$

The Controller executes a greedy algorithm to select the initial Spot GPU VM. The algorithm searches for the instance type that meets the deadline M^{DSpot} and executes the application with minimum cost. If no Spot VM is able to meet the deadline, the user is warned to choose another deadline.

4.1 Migrating the Application to a New GPU Virtual Machine

When a revocation occurs, to minimize the financial costs, our framework tries to allocate the application on a different instance type of the Spot market. The framework does not use the same type, because, in our experiments, we realized that once an instance type is revoked, the cloud provider often revokes it again in a short time. If no suitable Spot instance is available, the framework migrates the application to an On-Demand instance.

Before migrating the application, the Controller calculates the percentage of processing that MASA-CUDAlign has already performed, named p_{total}. Due to eventual instance revocations, the application may have executed in several instance types, which have different computational power. Thus, the percentage of the performed processing is calculated at each revocation.

Let $time_f$ be the elapsed execution time of the application including the framework overhead and $time_{app}$ be the total elapsed time of MASA-CUDAlign execution (without that overhead). The framework overhead includes the time spent to choose and deploy the VM to execute the application and the time spent to monitor the application over its execution. Let $time_{last}$ be the application execution time when the last revocation occurred. At the end of each migration process, $time_{last}$ is updated with $time_{app}$. When the instance type it_i is revoked, the percentage of execution performed in this instance, named $p_{current}$, is calculated as presented in Eq. 4, where $time_{app} - time_{last}$ gives the execution time in the current instance type it_i.

$$p_{current} = \frac{time_{app} - time_{last}}{e_i} \tag{4}$$

Now, p_{total} can be updated as shown in Eq. 5.

$$p_{total} = p_{total} + p_{current} \tag{5}$$

Thus, once the application migrates to instance it_i, the remaining execution time, ret_i, is calculated as the sum of $e_i * (1 - p_{total})$ and the restart overhead $restart\_overhead_i$ (Eq. 1), as presented in Eq. 6.

$$ret_i = restart\_overhead_i + e_i * (1 - p_{total}) \tag{6}$$

Algorithm 1 shows the Controller steps to choose the next GPU instance type after a revocation. The algorithm receives as input the revoked instance type, $it_{current}$, both sets of GPU instance types, I_{spot} and $I_{ondemand}$, the M^D deadline, the M^{DSpot} Spot deadline and the framework elapsed time $time_f$.

Initially, the algorithm updates the percentage of processing p_{total} using Eqs. 4 and 5 (line 1) and removes the revoked instance type from I_{spot} (line 2). The variables it_{min} and $cost_{min}$ are defined as the cheapest instance type that can execute within the deadline and its corresponding cost. Then, the Controller searches for the Spot instance type $it_i \in I_{spot}$ with the cheapest estimated cost capable of meeting the deadline (lines 5 to 13). For each Spot instance type $it_i \in I_{spot}$, the Controller computes the remaining execution time ret_i from Eq. 6 (line 6). Then, it checks if this instance type can finish within the M^{DSpot} deadline, considering the elapsed time $time_f$ (line 7). If the instance type it_i can meet the M^{DSpot} deadline, the Controller checks if the estimated cost is lower than

---

Algorithm 1. *Selecting a new GPU VM for Migration*

Input: $it_{current}$, I_{spot}, $I_{ondemand}$, M^D, M^{DSpot} and $time_f$
1: $p_{total} \leftarrow$ update_ptotal() {Equations 4 and 5}
2: $I_{spot} \leftarrow I_{spot} - it_{current}$
3: $it_{min} \leftarrow None$
4: $cost_{min} \leftarrow \infty$
5: **for all** $it_i \in I_{spot}$ **do**
6:     $ret_i \leftarrow$ compute_remaining_execution_time(it_i, p_{total}) {Equation 6}
7:     **if** $(time_f + ret_i) \leq M^{DSpot}$ **then**
8:         **if** $ret_i * price_i^{spot} < cost_{min}$ **then**
9:             $cost_{min} \leftarrow ret_i * price_i^{spot}$
10:             $it_{min} \leftarrow it_i$
11:         **end if**
12:     **end if**
13: **end for**
14: **if** it_{min} is $None$ **then**
15:     **for all** $it_i \in I_{ondemand}$ **do**
16:         $ret_i \leftarrow$ compute_remaining_execution_time(it_i, p_{total}) {Equation 6}
17:         **if** $(time_f + ret_i) \leq M^D$ **then**
18:             **if** $ret_i * price_i^{ondemand} < cost_{min}$ **then**
19:                 $cost_{min} \leftarrow ret_i * price_i^{ondemand}$
20:                 $it_{min} \leftarrow it_i$
21:             **end if**
22:         **end if**
23:     **end for**
24: **end if**
25: **return** it_{min}

---

the current minimum cost (line 8). If no suitable Spot VM is found (line 14), the Controller searches for the On-Demand instance type $it_i \in I_{ondemand}$ capable of meeting the deadline M^D with the lowest estimated cost, where $price_i^{ondemand}$ is the current On-Demand price of it_i (lines 15 to 23). For each On-Demand instance type $it_i \in I_{ondemand}$, the Controller computes the remaining execution time ret_i from Eq. 6 (line 16) and executes the same steps already described for the case of Spot instances (line 17 and line 18). At the end, the algorithm returns the instance type with minimum cost it_{min} that meets the deadline (line 25).

AWS usually sends a two-minute notice to a Spot instance that will be revoked, by updating an instance metadata [20]. In the proposed framework, the Worker monitors that instance metadata every five seconds, as recommended by AWS. So, when the Worker gets aware of this change, it sends a signal to the Controller to begin the migration process. However, AWS also suggests that applications running on Spot instances handle themselves sudden interruptions as AWS may not send this two-minute notice before the interruption in some cases [20]. Therefore, the Worker also monitors the VM state by using the AWS SDK for Python, boto3 [19]. Moreover, if the communication between the Controller and the Worker, which is performed via SSH, fails three times in a row, the Controller assumes that a revocation has occurred and it initiates the migration process.

5   Experimental Results

Experiments were performed on real DNA sequences, with millions of base pairs.
Sequences were obtained from the NCBI website [13]. In our experiments, we
saved the SRA only in disk and used the same sequences as [16]. Table 2 shows
the accession number of each sequence, their sizes, the SRA size used (|SRA|),
and the score obtained by each pair.

Table 2. DNA sequences used in our evaluation.

Seq.	Human		Chimpanzee		|SRA|	Score
	Accession number	Real size	Accession number	Real size		
chr19	NC_000019.10	58,617,616	NC_006486.4	61,309,027	24 GB	24,326,407
chr20	NC_000020.11	64,444,167	NC_006487.4	66,533,130	24 GB	36,230,870
chr21	NC_000021.9	46,709,983	NC_006488.4	33,445,071	10 GB	25,131,337
chr22	NC_000022.11	50,818,468	NC_006489.4	37,823,149	10 GB	20,426,645
chrY	NC_000024.10	57,227,415	NC_006492.4	26,350,515	10 GB	1,448,250

Amazon EC2 offers five instance families that are classified into: general purpose, compute optimized, memory optimized, storage optimized, and accelerated
computing. We used the accelerated computing family, and some instance types,
as shown in Table 3. The instances were chosen considering their cost (less than
1 USD/hour) and different GPU architectures, Kepler (K520 and K80), Maxwell
(M60), and Turing (T4). K520, M60, and K80 combine two graphics processors,
but only one processor was used for the tests. The tests were performed on the
us-east-1 availability zone (Northern Virginia) with the Amazon Elastic Block
Store (EBS) for storage service.

Table 3. Selected Instances.

Name	CPU	RAM (GiB)	GPU
g2.2xlarge	Intel Xeon E5-2670 2.6 GHz	15	Nvidia K520
g3s.xlarge	Intel Xeon E5-2686 v4 2.3 GHz	30.5	Nvidia M60
g4dn.xlarge	Intel Xeon 24C 2.5 GHz	16	Nvidia T4 Tensor Core
g4dn.2xlarge	Intel Xeon 24C 2.5 GHz	32	Nvidia T4 Tensor Core
p2.xlarge	Intel Xeon E5-2686 v4 2.3 GHz	61	Nvidia K80

5.1   Execution Times and Costs Without the Framework

Table 4 shows the execution time and the financial cost of MASA-CUDAlign
execution for each pair of sequences on each AWS instance using On-Demand
and Spot. We observe that MASA-CUDAlign runs faster on instances with T4

Table 4. Execution time and cost for MASA-CUDAlign without the framework.

Seq.	Instance	On-Demand		Spot	
		Exec. time	Cost	Exec. time	Cost
chr19	g2.2xlarge	21:58:33	$14.28	Revoked	-
	g3s.xlarge	10:43:04	$8.04	10:46:08	$2.42
	g4dn.xlarge	04:56:49	$2.60	05:01:55	$0.79
	g4dn.2xlarge	04:49:27	$3.63	05:14:24	$1.18
	p2.xlarge	15:52:57	$14.29	Revoked	-
chr20	g2.2xlarge	23:33:58	$15.32	Revoked	-
	g3s.xlarge	12:12:16	$9.15	12:12:37	$2.75
	g4dn.xlarge	05:57:15	$3.13	05:44:30	$0.91
	g4dn.2xlarge	05:51:01	$4.40	05:48:14	$1.31
	p2.xlarge	17:48:38	$16.03	Revoked	-
chr21	g2.2xlarge	10:06:57	$6.58	Revoked	-
	g3s.xlarge	05:09:29	$3.87	05:11:01	$1.17
	g4dn.xlarge	02:31:39	$1.33	02:26:04	$0.38
	g4dn.2xlarge	02:27:40	$1.85	02:26:10	$0.55
	p2.xlarge	07:11:25	$6.47	Revoked	-
chr22	g2.2xlarge	12:10:45	$7.92	Revoked	-
	g3s.xlarge	05:38:00	$4.23	05:38:38	$1.33
	g4dn.xlarge	02:38:30	$1.39	02:40:54	$0.42
	g4dn.2xlarge	02:51:23	$2.15	02:53:37	$0.65
	p2.xlarge	09:24:26	$8.47	Revoked	-
chrY	g2.2xlarge	12:28:35	$8.11	Revoked	-
	g3s.xlarge	05:53:08	$4.41	05:54:34	$1.33
	g4dn.xlarge	02:45:52	$1.45	02:26:37	$0.39
	g4dn.2xlarge	02:43:55	$2.05	02:42:35	$0.55
	p2.xlarge	09:02:06	$8.13	Revoked	-

and M60 GPUs, as presented in Fig. 4, which are the most recent ones and provide more memory space and bandwidth. We can also observe that, although the execution times are almost the same for On-Demand and Spot instances (Figs. 4(a) and (c)), On-Demand executions are much more expensive than the Spot ones. The financial cost increases from 2x to 4x on the On-Demand instances (Figs. 4(b) and (d)). However, on the Spot instances *g2.2xlarge* and *p2.xlarge* MASA-CUDAlign was not able to finish the sequence alignment, due to revocation. On average, *g2.2xlarge* and *p2.xlarge* were revoked after 3 and 15 h, respectively. Therefore, to take advantage of the reduced cost of Spot instances, MASA-CUDAlign requires a fault-tolerant approach.

5.2   Evaluation of the Overhead of the Framework in a Scenario Without Revocations

The goal of this experiment is to measure the impact on the financial cost and execution time of the proposed framework. This experiment was run on *g4dn.xlarge*, the instance selected by our greedy algorithm in all tested cases. Based on previous experiments, we considered the VM deployment overhead, α, equal to 180 s. The MASA-CUDAlign checkpoint, which might be accessed by different VMs, was saved in a 100 GB disk of the Amazon EBS service. That EBS disk can be attached to a new VM in case of revocation and presented the best financial costs and performance results in cases similar to ours, as presented in a previous work [24].

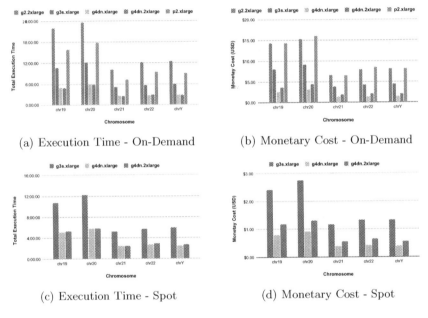

(a) Execution Time - On-Demand   (b) Monetary Cost - On-Demand

(c) Execution Time - Spot   (d) Monetary Cost - Spot

Fig. 4. Execution times and monetary costs for both On-Demand and Spot markets. The results of the *g2.xlarge* and *p2.xlarge* instances are not shown on the Spot market due to the revocation.

We used the highest execution time of each sequence comparison (Sect. 5.1) as its deadline M^D. This allows the framework to have more options to decide about the most suitable VM (considering time and cost) to execute the application. Table 5 presents the used deadline M^D, and the average execution times and financial costs for each sequence with and without the framework in a Spot *g4dn.xlarge* instance. The averages were obtained by three executions with a standard deviation below 1%. These results show that the proposed framework presents a low overhead of less than 3% on average.

Table 5. Average execution times and costs with and without the framework on a single Spot VM.

Seq.	With framework			Without framework	
	M^D	Exec. time	Cost	Exec. time	Cost
chr19	22:00:00 (79,200 s)	05:10:05	$0.81	05:01:55	$0.79
chr20	24:00:00 (86,400 s)	05:45:07	$0.90	05:44:30	$0.91
chr21	10:00:00 (36,000 s)	02:28:12	$0.39	02:26:04	$0.38
chr22	12:00:00 (43,200 s)	02:45:58	$0.43	02:40:54	$0.42
chrY	10:00:00 (36,000 s)	02:33:11	$0.40	02:26:37	$0.39

5.3 Evaluation of the Proposed Framework in a Scenario with Simulated Revocations

As Amazon EC2 revokes Spot VMs due to internal factors, which are transparent to the cloud user, we have emulated different patterns of Spot revocations by using a Poisson distribution [1] with $\lambda = 1/k_r$, where k_r is the average time between failures in seconds. For our experiments, we used three different values for k_r, based on the real events of revocations observed in our previous experiments (Sect. 5.1). So we created three scenarios of revocations: (i) S1 with $k_r = 7200$ and $\lambda = 1/7200$, (ii) S2 with $k_r = 14400$ and $\lambda = 1/14400$; and (iii) S3 with $k_r = 21600$ and $\lambda = 1/21600$.

For this experiment, both I_{spot} and $I_{ondemand}$ sets were initialized with five instance types: g2.2xlarge, g3s.xlarge, g4dn.xlarge, g4dn.2xlarge, p2.xlarge. To calculate the expected execution times, the following slowdown indexes were used: 1.02 for g4dn.2xlarge instance, 1.95 for g3s.xlarge instance, 3.33 for p2.xlarge instance and 4.16 for g2.2xlarge instance, having the g4dn.xlarge instance as baseline, since it presented the lowest execution times in the previous tests.

Table 6 shows the average results of three executions in each of the evaluated scenarios. It shows the average numbers of used Spot and On-Demand VMs, average execution times (Exec. time), and average monetary costs (Cost) of each tested scenario. Besides, it also shows the execution time (Exec. time) and monetary cost (Cost) using only the g4dn.xlarge On-Demand instance. The comparison of execution time and monetary cost among all simulated scenarios and the On-Demand only execution can be seen in Fig. 5.

Our framework used the same instance types to compare the different sequences. It started with instance g4dn.xlarge, then migrated the application to g4dn.2xlarge, when the first revocation occurred, and to g3s.xlarge, when the next revocation occurred. When the third revocation occurred, it migrated to g2.2xlarge and to p2.xlarge when the next revocation occurred. The On-Demand instance g4dn.xlarge was used when the fifth revocation occurred, in scenario S1 of chromosome 20. Even with revocations, the framework reduced the monetary cost significantly, 60% on average, compared to the On-Demand execution, without increasing the execution time sharply, 13% on average. We observed

Table 6. Average number of used Spot and On-Demand VMs, average execution times, and average costs with simulated revocations, versus the On-Demand results

Seq.	Simulated revocations					On-Demand VM	
	Scenario	Spot VMs	On-Demand VMs	Exec. time	Cost	Exec. time	Cost
chr19	S1	4	0	07:18:45	$1.39	04:56:49	$2.60
	S2	2	0	05:58:34	$1.18		
	S3	2.67	0	06:17:53	$1.31		
chr20	S1	4.33	0.67	08:35:08	$2.34	05:57:15	$3.13
	S2	2.67	0	07:35:34	$1.44		
	S3	2	0	06:02:27	$1.14		
chr21	S1	2	0	02:31:51	$0.46	02:31:39	$1.33
	S2	1.67	0	02:25:24	$0.43		
	S3	1	0	02:29:27	$0.39		
chr22	S1	2	0	03:19:12	$0.61	02:38:30	$1.39
	S2	1.33	0	02:50:13	$0.49		
	S3	1.33	0	02:47:40	$0.49		
chrY	S1	1.33	0	02:40:29	$0.44	02:45:52	$1.45
	S2	1	0	02:38:34	$0.41		
	S3	1.67	0	02:42:41	$0.49		

that each revocation is handled within four minutes, which is minimal considering the number of hours required to execute the application. The worst case scenario, considering monetary cost, occurred in scenario S1 of chromosome 20, with five revocations, forcing the framework to migrate the application several times. In this scenario, all Spot instance types and the On-Demand instance were used. Even in this case, the framework was able to reduce the monetary cost by 25%. The worst case scenario, considering execution time, occurred in S1 of chromosome 19, where four revocations occurred. In this scenario, the framework migrated the application to the slowest Spot instance, *g2.2xlarge*, which increased the execution time by almost 48%, but even so it reduced the monetary cost by 46%.

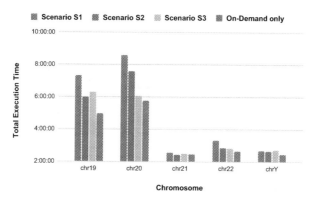

(a) Execution time of simulated scenarios vs. On-Demand only execution

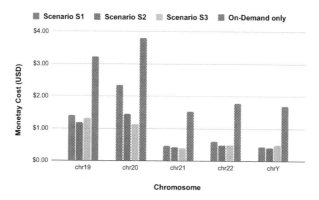

(b) Monetary cost of simulated scenarios vs. On-Demand only execution

Fig. 5. Comparison of execution time and monetary cost between each scenario of simulated revocations and On-Demand only execution

6   Concluding Remarks

This paper investigated the viability of running a deadline constrained application (MASA-CUDAlign) on Spot GPU instances, aiming to minimize the financial cost. The proposed framework executes a MASA-CUDAlign's fault-tolerant version and restarts the application on a new VM when the previously used is revoked. Our results showed that the framework reduces financial costs when compared to executions on On-Demand GPU instances while meeting the deadline even in presence of several revocations.

For future work, we intend to investigate the impact of the value of the deadline (M^D) on the monetary cost and execution time of applications running in our framework. We also intend to use more VM types in our experiments.

Moreover, we intend to extend the framework to support parallel execution on several Spot GPUs, applying also a generic GPU checkpoint, such as CRAC [6].

Acknowledgments. This research is supported by project CNPq/AWS 440014/2020-4, Brazil, by the *Programa Institucional de Internacionalização* (PrInt) from CAPES (process number 88887.310261/2018-00) and by *Conselho Nacional de Desenvolvimento Científico e Tecnológico* (CNPq) (process 145088/2019-7).

References

1. Ahrens, J.H., Dieter, U.: Computer methods for sampling from gamma, beta, poisson and bionomial distributions. Computing **12**(3), 223–246 (1974)
2. Barr, J.: New EC2 instance type - the cluster GPU instance (2010). https://aws.amazon.com/pt/blogs/aws/new-ec2-instance-type-the-cluster-gpu-instance/. Accessed 01 Feb 2021
3. Batista, R.B., Boukerche, A., de Melo, A.C.M.A.: A parallel strategy for biological sequence alignment in restricted memory space. J. Parallel Distrib. Comput. **68**(4), 548–561 (2008)
4. Gotoh, O.: An improved algorithm for matching biological sequences. J. Mol. Biol. **162**(3), 705–708 (1982)
5. Huang, X., Li, C., Chen, H., An, D.: Task scheduling in cloud computing using particle swarm optimization with time varying inertia weight strategies. Cluster Comput. **23**(2), 1137–1147 (2019). https://doi.org/10.1007/s10586-019-02983-5
6. Jain, T., Cooperman, G.: CRAC: checkpoint-restart architecture for CUDA with streams and UVM. In: Proceedings of the International Conference for High Performance Computing, Networking, Storage and Analysis, SC 2020. IEEE Press (2020)
7. Jiang, X., Liu, X., Xu, L., Zhang, P., Sun, N.: A reconfigurable accelerator for Smith-Waterman algorithm. IEEE Trans. Circ. Syst. II Exp. Brief. **54**(12), 1077–1081 (2007)
8. Lee, K., Son, M.: DeepSpotCloud: leveraging cross-region GPU spot instances for deep learning. In: 2017 IEEE 10th International Conference on Cloud Computing (CLOUD), pp. 98–105 (2017)
9. Lee, S., Lin, C., Hung, C.L., Huang, H.Y.: Using frequency distance filteration for reducing database search workload on GPU-based cloud service. In: 4th IEEE International Conference on Cloud Computing Technology and Science Proceedings, pp. 735–740 (2012)
10. Lee, S.T., Lin, C.Y., Hung, C.L.: GPU-based cloud service for Smith-Waterman Algorithm using frequency distance filtration scheme. BioMed Res. Int. **2013**, 721738 (2013)
11. Lu, Y., Sun, N.: An effective task scheduling algorithm based on dynamic energy management and efficient resource utilization in green cloud computing environment. Clust. Comput. **22**(1), 513–520 (2019)
12. Myers, E.W., Miller, W.: Optimal alignments in linear space. Comp. App. in Biosci. **4**(1), 11–17 (1988)
13. National Center for Biotechnological Information. https://www.ncbi.nlm.nih.gov/
14. Pary, R.: New Amazon EC2 spot pricing model: simplified purchasing without bidding and fewer interruptions (2017). https://aws.amazon.com/pt/blogs/compute/new-amazon-ec2-spot-pricing/. Accessed 01 Feb 2021

15. Sánchez, F., Cabarcas, F., Ramirez, A., Valero, M.: Long DNA sequence comparison on multicore architectures. In: D'Ambra, P., Guarracino, M., Talia, D. (eds.) Euro-Par 2010. LNCS, vol. 6272, pp. 247–259. Springer, Heidelberg (2010). https://doi.org/10.1007/978-3-642-15291-7_24

16. Sandes, E.F.O., Melo, A.C.M.A.: Retrieving Smith-Waterman alignments with optimizations for megabase biological sequences using GPU. IEEE Trans Parallel Dist. Syst. **24**(5), 1009–1021 (2013)

17. Sandes, E.F.O., Miranda, G., Martorell, X., Ayguade, E., Teodoro, G., Melo, A.C.M.A.: MASA: a multiplatform architecture for sequence aligners with block pruning. ACM Trans. Parallel Comput. **2**(4), 1–31 (2016)

18. Sandes, E.F.O., et al.: CUDAlign 4.0: incremental speculative traceback for exact chromosome-wide alignment in GPU clusters. IEEE Trans. Parallel Dist. Syst. **27**(10), 2838–2850 (2016)

19. Services, A.W.: Boto 3 Documentation (2021). https://boto3.readthedocs.io/. Accessed 03 Feb 2021

20. Services, A.W.: User Guide for Linux Instances - spot instance interruptions (2021). https://docs.aws.amazon.com/AWSEC2/latest/UserGuide/spot-interruptions.html. Accessed 03 Feb 2021

21. Smith, T.F., Waterman, M.S.: Identification of common molecular subsequences. J. Mol. Biol. **147**(1), 195–197 (1981)

22. Teylo, L., Arantes, L., Sens, P., Drummond, L.M.A.: A bag-of-tasks scheduler tolerant to temporal failures in clouds. In: 31st International Symposium on Computer Architecture and High Performance Computing, pp. 144–151 (2019)

23. Teylo, L., Arantes, L., Sens, P., Drummond, L.M.: A dynamic task scheduler tolerant to multiple hibernations in cloud environments. Cluster Comput. **27**, 1–23 (2020)

24. Teylo, L., Brum, R.C., Arantes, L., Sens, P., Drummond, L.M.A.: Developing checkpointing and recovery procedures with the storage services of Amazon web services. In: Proceedings of the 49th International Conference on Parallel Processing: Workshops (2020)

25. Varshney, P., Simmhan, Y.: AutoBoT: resilient and cost-effective scheduling of a bag of tasks on spot VMs. IEEE Trans. Parallel Distrib. Syst. **30**(7), 1512–1527 (2019)

26. Wagenländer, M., Mai, L., Li, G., Pietzuch, P.: Spotnik: designing distributed machine learning for transient cloud resources. In: 12th USENIX Workshop on Hot Topics in Cloud Computing, HotCloud 2020. USENIX Association (July 2020)

27. Zhou, J., Zhang, Y., Wong, W.: Fault tolerant stencil computation on cloud-based GPU spot instances. IEEE Trans. Cloud Comput. **7**(4), 1013–1024 (2019)

Sustaining Performance While Reducing Energy Consumption: A Control Theory Approach

Sophie Cerf[1]([✉]) , Raphaël Bleuse[1] ,
Valentin Reis[2], Swann Perarnau[2] ,
and Éric Rutten[1]

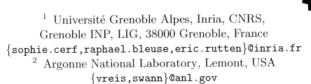

[1] Université Grenoble Alpes, Inria, CNRS,
Grenoble INP, LIG, 38000 Grenoble, France
{sophie.cerf,raphael.bleuse,eric.rutten}@inria.fr
[2] Argonne National Laboratory, Lemont, USA
{vreis,swann}@anl.gov

Abstract. Production high-performance computing systems continue to grow in complexity and size. As applications struggle to make use of increasingly heterogeneous compute nodes, maintaining high efficiency (performance per watt) for the whole platform becomes a challenge. Alongside the growing complexity of scientific workloads, this extreme heterogeneity is also an opportunity: as applications dynamically undergo variations in workload, due to phases or data/compute movement between devices, one can dynamically adjust power across compute elements to save energy without impacting performance. With an aim toward an autonomous and dynamic power management strategy for current and future HPC architectures, this paper explores the use of control theory for the design of a dynamic power regulation method. Structured as a feedback loop, our approach—which is novel in computing resource management—consists of periodically monitoring application progress and choosing at runtime a suitable power cap for processors. Thanks to a preliminary offline identification process, we derive a model of the dynamics of the system and a proportional-integral (PI) controller. We evaluate our approach on top of an existing resource management framework, the Argo Node Resource Manager, deployed on several clusters of Grid'5000, using a standard memory-bound HPC benchmark.

Keywords: Power regulation · HPC systems · Control theory

1 Introduction

Energy efficiency is an ongoing and major concern of production HPC systems. As we approach exascale, the complexity of these systems increases, leading to inefficiencies in power allocation schemes across hardware components. Furthermore, this issue is becoming dynamic in nature: power-performance variability

© Springer Nature Switzerland AG 2021
L. Sousa et al. (Eds.): Euro-Par 2021, LNCS 12820, pp. 334–349, 2021.
https://doi.org/10.1007/978-3-030-85665-6_21

across identical components in different parts of the system leads to applications performance issues that must be monitored at runtime in order to balance power across components. Similarly, application phases can result in energy inefficiencies. For example, during an application's I/O phase for which performance is limited by current network capacity, the power allocated to the processor could be reduced without impact on the application performance.

In this paper we focus on the design of a controller that can dynamically measure application performance during runtime and reallocate power accordingly. Our goal is to improve the efficiency of the overall system, with limited and controllable impact on application performance. How to design such a controller is a challenge: while several mechanisms have appeared to regulate the power consumption of various components (processors, memories, accelerators), there is no consensus on the most appropriate means to measure application performance at runtime (as an estimator of total execution time).

At the hardware level, multiple runtime mechanisms have been demonstrated for regulating power usage. Some of them rely on DVFS (dynamic voltage and frequency scaling) [2], a frequency and voltage actuator, and build up a power regulation algorithm [13,14]. Another approach involves using DDCM (dynamic duty cycle modulation) as a power handle [4]. More recently, Intel introduced in the Sandy Bridge microarchitecture RAPL (running average power limit) [6,23]. It is an autonomous hardware solution (i.e., a control loop); and while the base mechanism behind it remains not public, RAPL has the benefit of being stable and widespread across current production systems. On the application side, the characterization of its behavior, including phases, or its compute- or memory-boundedness is more challenging. Indeed, heavy instrumentation can have an impact on the system itself and result in a change in behavior, while few mechanisms are available to monitor an application from the outside. The most versatile such mechanisms, hardware performance counters, require careful selection of which counters to sample and are not necessarily good predictors of an application's total execution time (e.g. , instructions per seconds are not enough in memory-bound applications). Furthermore, existing online solutions rely on simple control loop designs with limited verifiable properties in terms of stability of the control or adaptability to application behavior.

In this paper we advocate the use of control theory as a means to formalize the problem of power regulation under a performance bound, using well-defined models and solutions to design an autonomous, online control loop with mathematical guaranties with respect to its robustness. Based on the work of RAMESH et al. [21] for an online application performance estimator (a lightweight heartbeat advertising the amount of progress towards an internal figure of merit), we design a closed control loop that acts on the RAPL power cap on recent processors. The next section provides background on measurement and tuning and feedback loop control. Section 3 presents the workflow of control theory adapted to HPC systems. Section 4 details our modeling and control design , validated and discussed in Sect. 5. In Sect. 6 we discuss related works and conclude in Sect. 7 with a brief summary.

2   Background

2.1   Application Measurement and Tuning

Measuring Progress with Heartbeats. We follow the work of RAMESH et al. [21] in using a lightweight instrumentation library that sends a type of application heartbeat. Based on discussions with application developers and performance characterization experts, a few places in the application code are identified as representing significant progress toward the *science* of the application (or its *figure of merit*). The resulting instrumentation sends a message on a socket local to the node indicating the amount of progress performed since the last message. We then derive a *heartrate* from these messages.

RAPL. RAPL is a mechanism available on recent Intel processors that allows users to specify a power cap on available hardware domains, using model-specific registers or the associated Linux sysfs subsystem. Typically, the processors make two domains available: the CPU package and a DRAM domain. The RAPL interface uses two knobs: the power limit and a time window. The internal controller then guarantees that the average power over the time window is maintained. This mechanism offers a *sensor* to measure the energy consumed since the processor was turned on. Consequently, RAPL can be used to both measure and limit power usage [24].

NRM. The Argo Node Resource Manager [22] is an infrastructure for the design of node-level resource management policies developed as a part of Argo within the U.S. Department of Energy Exascale Computing Project. It is based on a daemon process that runs alongside applications and provides to users a unified interface (through Unix domain sockets) to the various monitoring and resource controls knobs available on a compute node (RAPL, performance counters). It also includes libraries to gather application progress, either through direct lightweight instrumentation or transparently using PMPI. In this paper all experiments use a Python API that allows users to bypass internal resource optimization algorithms and implement custom synchronous control on top of the NRM's bookkeeping of sensor and actuator data.

2.2   Runtime Self-Adaptation and Feedback Loop Control

Designing feedback loops is the object of control theory, which is widespread in all domains of engineering but only recently has been scarcely applied to regulation in computing systems [12,25]. It provides systems designers with methodologies to conceive and implement feedback loops with well-mastered behavior.

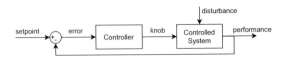

Fig. 1. Block diagram for a simplistic control loop.

In short, the design of control functions is based on an approximated model—since a perfect model is not necessary, nor is it always feasible—of the dynamics of the process to be controlled (*Controlled System* in Fig. 1), in order to derive controllers with properties including convergence, avoidance of oscillations, and mastering of overshoot effects. This process implies the identification of certain variables of interest in the infrastructure: the *performance*, which is a measurable indicator of the state of the system; the *setpoint*, the objective value to which we want to drive the *performance*; the *knob*, the action through which the *performance* can be modified or regulated to match the *setpoint* value; the *error*, the difference between the *setpoint* value and the system's *performance*, as a measure of deviation; and the *disturbance*, an external agent that affects the system's dynamics in an unpredictable way.

Through the knowledge of a system's dynamical model, the approaches of control theory can deliver management strategies that define how to adjust system's knobs to get the desired performance: i.e., to control the state of the system. Traditional control solutions include proportional-integral-derivative controllers [15] where the value of the command to be executed is given by an equation with three terms: P proportional to the *error*, I involving an integration over time of the error past values (i.e., a memory-like effect), and D based on its current "speed" or rate of change, which takes into account possible future trends.

3   Control Methodology for Runtime Adaptation of Power

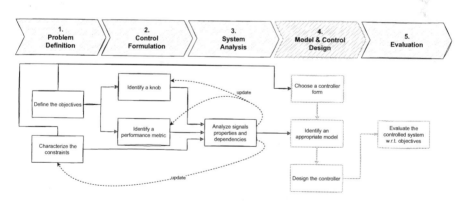

Fig. 2. Methodological steps in using control theory for HPC systems. Step 4 (highlighted in pink) can be done independently by control experts. (Color figure online)

The use of control theory tooling for computing systems is recent, especially in HPC [27]. The community still lacks well-defined and accepted models. Needed, therefore, is a methodology to identify and construct models upon which controllers can be designed. Figure 2 depicts the method used for this work. It adapts the traditional workflow of control theory [11], by explicitly considering the upstream work of defining the problem and translating it to a control-friendly formulation in five main steps:

(1) Problem definition. First, the objectives have to be settled and the challenging characteristics and constraints identified. Here the problem definition naturally results from Sects. 1 and 2. It consists of sustaining the application execution time while reducing energy usage as much as possible. This is challenging given the following constraints: applications have unpredictable phases with exogenous limits on progress, progress metrics are application-specific, processor characteristics and performance are various, power actuators have a limited accuracy and are distributed on all packages, and thermal considerations induce nonlinearities.

(2) Control formulation. The objectives are then translated into suitable control signals: these are knobs that enable one to act on the system at runtime and performance metric(s) to monitor the system's behavior. They need to be measurable or computable on the fly. For example, the RAPL powercap value and the application progress are such signals.

(3) System analysis. The knobs are then analyzed to assess the impact of both their levels and the change of their levels on the performance signals during the execution time (cf. Sect. 4.3). The control formulation may be updated after this analysis to ease the control development (select adequate sampling time, modify signals with logarithmic scales, offsets). New constraints may be highlighted, such as the number of packages in a node.

(4) Model and control design. Once the relationships between signals and the system's behavior have been identified, the control theory toolbox may be used [15]. According to the objectives and the identified system characteristics challenging them, a controller form is chosen, a PI controller in this case. An adequate model is identified from experimental data, such as a first-order dynamical model (see Sect. 4.4), and then used to design and tune the controller, following the pole placement method here (see Sect. 4.5).

(5) Evaluation. Eventually, the controlled system is evaluated with respect to the objectives (cf. Sect. 5). In this paper we are interested in evaluating the energy reduction and execution time increase according to the maximal allowed degradation given to the controller.

4   Model and Controller Development

We defined the problem under study in Sects. 1 and 2. Following the method described in Sect. 3, we now focus on formulating it as a control problem, analyzing the system to derive a model and design a controller (Steps 2 to 4). As depicted in Fig. 2, the early steps are refined in an iterative process with respect to the analysis results. Since the analysis of the system requires observing the behavior of the system, we first describe the experimental setup.

Table 1. Hardware characteristics of Grid'5000 clusters used for the experiments.

Cluster	CPU	Cores/CPU	Sockets	RAM [GiB]
gros	Xeon Gold 5220	18	1	96
dahu	Xeon Gold 6130	16	2	192
yeti	Xeon Gold 6130	16	4	768

4.1 Experimental Setup

Platform. All experiments were conducted on the Grid'5000 testbed. We ran the experiments on nodes of three different clusters: gros, dahu, and yeti. These clusters were chosen because their nodes have modern Intel CPUs and a varying number of sockets. We list in Table 1 the main characteristics of the clusters. The exact specifications of the clusters are available on the Grid'5000 wiki.[1]

Software Stack. All experiments ran on a deployed environment with a custom image. The deployed environment is a minimal GNU/Linux Debian 10.7 "buster" with kernel 4.19.0-13-amd64. The management of applications and resources was implemented within the Argo NRM, a resource management framework developed at Argonne National Laboratory. We used the version tagged as expe-0.6 for this work.[2] NRM and benchmarks are packaged with the Nix functional package manager [8]: we rely on a multiuser installation of Nix version 2.3.10.

Benchmark. All experiments involved execution of the STREAM benchmark [17]. STREAM is chosen as it is representative of memory-bound phases of applications and shows a stable behavior. STREAM is also easy to modify into an iterative application, which allows computation of the progress metric by reporting heartbeats. We used version 5.10 with a problem size set to 33,554,432 and 10,000 iterations, further adapted to run in a way that progress can be tracked: its 4 kernels ran a configurable number of times in a loop, with a heartbeat being reported to the NRM each time the loop completed (after one run of the four kernels).

Characterization vs. Evaluation Setup. Although the hardware and software stack remain the same, we need to distinguish characterization and evaluation experiments. For the analysis of the system (characterization), we observe the behavior of the system, and the resource manager follows a predefined plan. This contrasts with the evaluation setup, where the resource manager reacts to the system's behavior. From the control theory perspective, the former setup is an open-loop system while the latter is a closed-loop system.

---

[1] https://www.grid5000.fr/w/Hardware with reference API version 9925e0598.
[2] Available at https://xgitlab.cels.anl.gov/argo/hnrm.

4.2   Control Formulation

The power actuator is RAPL's power limit denoted $\text{pcap}(t_i)$. To define a progress metric, we aggregate the heartbeats that the application generates at times t_k (see Sect. 2.1) into a signal synchronized with the power actuator. The progress metric at t_i is formally defined as the median of the heartbeats arrival frequencies since the last sampling time t_{i-1}:

$$\text{progress}(t_i) = \underset{\forall k,\, t_k \in [t_{i-1}, t_i[}{\text{median}} \left(\frac{1}{t_k - t_{k-1}} \right) \tag{1}$$

A central tendency indicator, in particular the median, was selected to be robust to extreme values so as to provide the controller with a smooth signal. The primary performance objective is based on the application's execution time, while for control purposes a runtime metric is needed.

Before further control development, let us ensure the correlation between the two. We compute the Pearson correlation coefficient [18] between the progress metric and execution time. The Pearson value is respectively 0.97, 0.80, and 0.80 on gros, dahu, and yeti clusters when computed by using static characterization data (constant powercap over the whole benchmark duration; see Sect. 4.4). The high correlation results validate the progress definition choice, with a notably strong correlation on the 1-socket cluster.

4.3   System Analysis

The analysis phase assesses the trustworthiness of the power actuator and progress sensor and measures how powercap levels impact progress.

During the benchmark execution, the powercap is gradually increased by steps of 20 W on the clusters' reasonable power range (i.e., from 40 W to 120 W), and the progress is measured; see Fig. 3. First, we see that the measured power never corresponds to the requested level and that the error increases with the powercap value. The RAPL powercap actuator accuracy is poor [7] and will have to be taken into account. The progress variations follow the power ones, whereas the higher the power level, the less a power increase impacts the progress. This highlights the nonlinearity of the power-to-progress dynamical system, with a saturation effect at high power values. The saturation results from the memory-boundedness of the application: at high power levels, the processor power is not limiting performance as memory is. The power level at which the saturation appears is related to the processors' thermal design power. We also note that the more packages there are in the cluster, the noisier the progress. Additionally, Fig. 3c illustrates that the progress is impacted by external factors, since in this run the power signal in itself does not explain the progress plateau from 20 s to 60 s and the drop to 10 Hz at 80 s. This behavior is further discussed in Sect. 5.2.

In summary, this analysis shows that soundly tuning the power level enables application progress to be maintained while reducing the energy footprint. This highlights the need for runtime feedback to cope with external factors. Since all clusters show similar behavior, a common controller can be designed. Cluster-specific modeling will further enable leveraging of its parameters.

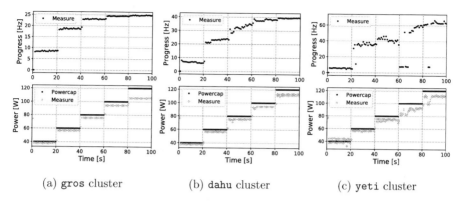

(a) gros cluster   (b) dahu cluster   (c) yeti cluster

Fig. 3. Impact of power changes on progress: the time perspective. Each sub-figure depicts a single representative execution.

4.4 Modeling

A system model—namely, a set of equations linking the power and progress—is a first step toward a controller taking sound actions. This step needs to be performed only once per cluster to measure model parameters to tune the controller.

Static Characteristic: Averaged Behavior. The time-averaged relation between power and progress is first modeled in a so-called static characterization, in the sense that it considers stabilized situations. In Fig. 4a, each data point corresponds to an entire benchmark execution where a constant powercap is applied (at the level reported on x-axis) and for which the progress signal is averaged (y-axis). We depict with different colors and markers the measures for the three clusters we use in this work. For each cluster, at least 68 experiments were run. Note that the curves are flattening, indicating the nonlinear behavior and saturation at large power previously identified.

Based on those experiments, a static model, linking the *time-stabilized* powercap to the progress is: progress $= K_L \left(1 - e^{-\alpha(a \cdot \mathrm{pcap} + b - \beta)}\right)$ where a and b parameters represent RAPL actuator accuracy on the cluster (slope and offset, resp.: power $= a \cdot \mathrm{pcap} + b$), α and β characterize the benchmark-dependent power-to-progress profile, and K_L is the *linear gain* being both benchmark and cluster specific. The effective values of these parameters can be automatically found by using nonlinear least squares; they are reported in Table 2. The solid lines in Fig. 4a illustrate our model, which shows good accuracy ($0.83 < R^2 < 0.95$).

Control Formulation Update. Given the nonlinearity of Sect. 4.4, we simplify the control by linearizing the powercap and progress signals; see Fig. 4b. The linearized version of a signal $\star$ is denoted by $\star_L$:

$$\mathrm{pcap}_L = -e^{-\alpha(a \cdot \mathrm{pcap} + b - \beta)} \quad ; \quad \mathrm{progress}_L = \mathrm{progress} - K_L \qquad (2)$$

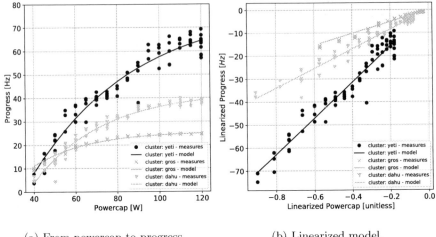

(a) From powercap to progress.

(b) Linearized model.

Fig. 4. Static characteristic: modeling of time-averaged behavior. Each point depicts a single execution.

Dynamic Perspective: Modeling Impact of Power Variations. We now characterize the dynamics, that is, the effects of a change of the power level on the progress signal *over time*. First, the model form is selected. As a compromise between accuracy and simplicity, we opt for a first-order model [12]. It means that the prediction of the progress requires only one previous value of the measured progress and the enforced powercap level: $\mathrm{progress}_L(t_{i+1}) = f\left(\mathrm{progress}_L(t_i), \mathrm{pcap}_L(t_i)\right)$. Control theory provides a first-order model formulation based on the static characteristic gain K_L and on a time constant τ characterizing the transient behavior:

$$\mathrm{progress}_L(t_{i+1}) = \frac{K_L \Delta t_i}{\Delta t_i + \tau} \cdot \mathrm{pcap}_L(t_i) + \frac{\tau}{\Delta t_i + \tau} \cdot \mathrm{progress}_L(t_i) \qquad (3)$$

where $\Delta t_i = t_{i+1} - t_i$. Based on experimental data , $\tau = 1/3\,\mathrm{Hz}$ for all clusters.

4.5 Control Design

The control objective is given as a degradation factor ϵ, that is, the tolerable loss of performance. The controller translates ϵ in a progress setpoint to track using the maximum progress ($\mathrm{progress}_{\max}$) estimated by using Sect. 4.4 with the cluster maximal power. A feedback PI controller is developed (see Sect. 2.2), setting the powercap proportionally to the progress error $e(t_i) = (1-\epsilon) \cdot \mathrm{progress}_{\max} - \mathrm{progress}(t_i)$ and to the integral of this error (see Sect. 2.2):

$$\mathrm{pcap}_L(t_i) = (K_I \Delta t_i + K_P) \cdot e(t_i) - K_P \cdot e(t_{i-1}) + \mathrm{pcap}_L(t_{i-1}) \qquad (4)$$

The parameters K_P and K_I are based both on the model parameters K_L and τ and on a tunable parameter τ_{obj}: $K_P = \tau/(K_L \cdot \tau_{\mathrm{obj}})$ and $K_I = 1/(K_L \cdot \tau_{\mathrm{obj}})$,

Table 2. Model and controller parameters for each cluster.

Description	Notation	Unit	gros	dahu	yeti
RAPL slope	a	[1]	0.83	0.94	0.89
RAPL offset	b	[W]	7.07	0.17	2.91
	α	[W^{-1}]	0.047	0.032	0.023
Power offset	β	[W]	28.5	34.8	33.7
Linear gain	K_L	[Hz]	25.6	42.4	78.5
Time constant	τ	[s]	1/3	1/3	1/3
	τ_{obj}	[s]	10	10	10

with τ_{obj} defining the desired dynamical behavior of the controlled system [3]. The controller is chosen to be nonaggressive, tuned with $\tau_{\mathrm{obj}} = 10\mathrm{s} > 10\tau$. The powercap is computed from its linearized value by using Eq. (2).

5 Evaluation

The experimental setup has been described in Sect. 4.1. We evaluate here the performance of the model and controller designed in the preceding section using the memory-bound STREAM benchmark run on three clusters with varying number of sockets.

We recapitulate in Table 2 the values of the model and controller parameters. The model parameters a, b, α, and β have been fitted for each cluster with the static characterization experiments (cf. Fig. 4). The model parameters K_L and τ and the controller parameter τ_{obj} have been chosen with respect to the system's dynamic (cf. Fig. 3). These values have been used for the evaluation campaign.

5.1 Measure of the Model Accuracy

The presented model is not intended to perform predictions: it is used only for the controller tuning. However, we take a brief look at its accuracy. To do so, a random powercap signal is applied, with varying magnitude (from 40 W to 120 W) and frequency (from 10^{-2} Hz to 1 Hz), and the benchmark progress is measured. For each cluster, at least 20 of such identification experiments were run. Figure 5 illustrates a single execution for each cluster, with the progress measure and its modeled value through time on the top plots and the powercap and power measures on the bottom ones. Visually, the modeling is fairly accurate, and the fewer the sockets, the less noisy the progress metric and the better the modeling. The average error is close to zero for all clusters. Nevertheless, our model performs better on clusters with few sockets (narrow distribution and short extrema).

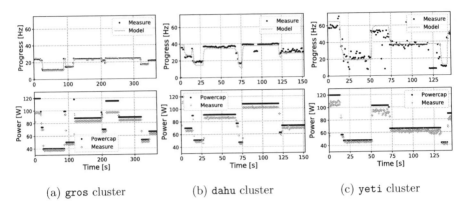

(a) gros cluster   (b) dahu cluster   (c) yeti cluster

Fig. 5. Modeling the time dynamics. Each sub-figure depicts a single representative execution.

5.2   Evaluation of the Controlled System

In this section we evaluate the behavior of the system when the controller reacts to the system's evolution. Results are reported for different clusters with the controller required to reach a set of degradation factors ($\epsilon \in [0, 0.5]$). Experiments are repeated 30 times for each combination of cluster and degradation value.

Figure 6a shows a typical controlled system behavior through time on the gros cluster. The initial powercap is set at its upper limit, and the controller

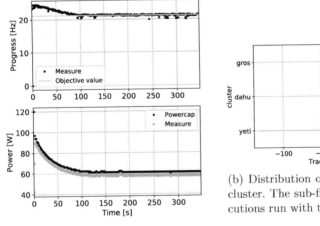

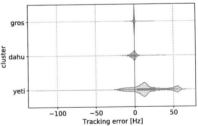

(b) Distribution of the tracking error per cluster. The sub-figure aggregates all executions run with the controller.

(a) Controlled system behavior: Progress and powercap trough time ($\epsilon = 0.15$, gros cluster). Single representative execution.

Fig. 6. Evaluation of the controlled system.

smoothly decreases its value until progress reaches the objective level (15% degradation here). Note that the controlled system behavior shows neither oscillation nor degradation of the progress below the allowed value. We report in Fig. 6b the distribution of the tracking error: the difference between the progress setpoint chosen by the controller and the measured progress. The depicted distributions aggregate all experiments involving the controller. The distributions of the error for the `gros` and `dahu` clusters are unimodal, centered near 0 (-0.21 and -0.60, resp.) with a narrow dispersion (1.8 and 6.1, resp.). On the other hand, the distribution of the error for the `yeti` cluster exhibits two modes: the second mode (located between 50 Hz and 60 Hz) is due to the model limitations. For reasons to be investigated, the progress sometimes drops to about 10 Hz regardless of the requested power cap. This behavior is notably visible in Fig. 3c and is on a par with the observation that the more sockets a system has, the noisier it becomes.

The controller objective is to adapt the benchmark speed by adapting the powercap on the fly, meaning we are exploiting *time-local* behavior of the system. Nevertheless, we are interested in the *global* behavior of the benchmark, in other words, the total execution time and the total energy consumption. To this end, we assessed the performance of the controlled system with a post mortem analysis. We tested a total of twelve degradation levels ranging from 0.01 to 0.5, and ran each configuration a minimum of thirty times. Figure 7 depicts the total execution time and the total energy consumption for each tested degradation level ϵ in the time/energy space. The experiments unveil a Pareto front for the `gros` and `dahu` clusters for degradation levels ranging from 0% to 15% (Figs. 7a and 7b): this indicates the existence of a family of trade-offs to save energy. For example, the $\epsilon = 0.1$ degradation level on the `gros` cluster is interesting because it allows, on average, saving 22% energy at the cost of a 7% execution time increase when compared with the baseline execution ($\epsilon = 0$ degradation level).

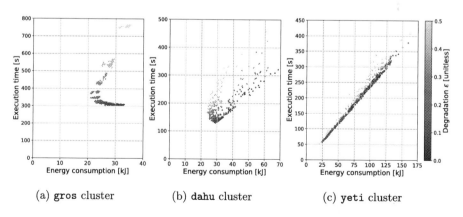

(a) **gros** cluster   (b) **dahu** cluster   (c) **yeti** cluster

Fig. 7. Execution time with respect to energy consumption. Color indicates the requested degradation level ϵ. Each point depicts a single execution. (Color figure online)

Note that degradation levels over 15% are not interesting because the increase in the execution time negates the energy savings. The behavior on the `yeti` cluster is too noisy to identify interesting degradation levels. However, the proposed controller does not negatively impact the performance.

Discussion. The proposed controller has an easily configured behavior: the user has to supply only an acceptable degradation level. The controller relies on a simple model of the system, and it is stable on the `gros` and `dahu` clusters. The approach does, however, show its limits on the `yeti` cluster, since the model is unable to explain the sporadic drops to 10 Hz in the application's progress. This is particularly visible on Fig. 3c between 60 s and 70 s. Nevertheless, we observe that these events can be characterized by the wider gap between the requested powercap and the measured power consumption. We suspect that the number of packages and the NUMA architecture, or exogenous temperature events, are responsible for these deviations. Further investigations are needed to confirm this hypothesis. If it is confirmed, development of control strategies will be considered for integrating distributed actuation or temperature disturbance anticipation.

On the Generalization to Other Benchmarks. The use of STREAM benchmark is motivated by its stable memory-bound profile, and its ability to be instrumented with heartbeats—thanks to its straightforward design. Figures 3 and 5 illustrate this stability: while no powercap change occurs, performance is largely constant. The presented approach extends similarly for memory intensive phases of applications. We expect compute-bound phases to show a different (simpler) power to progress profile (Fig. 4), less amenable to optimization. Indeed, every power increase should improve performance, even for high powercap values. Furthermore, with such linear behavior, modeling will have to be recomputed, and controller parameters updated. Overall, controlling an application with varying resource usage patterns thus requires *adaptation*—a control technique implying automatic tuning of the controller parameters—to handle powercap-to-progress behavior transitions between phases. It is a natural direction of research for future work.

6   Related Work

On Power Regulation in HPC. A large body of related work seeks to optimize performance or control energy consumption on HPC systems using a wide range of control knobs [4,9,19,20]. Most of these methods, however, target a different objective from our work or are based either on static schemes used at the beginning of a job or on simple loops without formal performance guarantees. This is also the case for GeoPM [10], the most prominent available power management infrastructure for HPC systems. An open source framework designed by Intel, GeoPM uses the same actuator than as our infrastructure (RAPL) does but with application-oblivious monitoring (PMPI or OMPT) capabilities.

On Using Control Theory for Power Regulation. Control-theory-based approaches to power regulation focus mainly on web servers [1], clouds [28], and real-time systems [13] applications. They typically leverage DVFS [2] as an actuator and formulate their objectives in terms of latency. Controllers are adaptive, with an update mechanism to cope with unmodeled external disturbances. The present work stands out for two reasons. First, it uses Intel's RAPL mechanism, a unified architecture-agnostic and future-proof solution, to leverage power. Moreover, we do not consider applications with predefined latency objectives but instead focus on the *science* performed by HPC applications, based on a heartrate progress metric. Other works similarly use RAPL in web servers [16] and real-time systems [14] contexts and non-latency-based performance metrics [26]. To the best of our knowledge, however, we present the first control theory approach to power regulation using RAPL for HPC systems.

7   Conclusion

We address the problem of managing energy consumption in complex heterogeneous HPC by focusing on the potential of dynamically adjusting power across compute elements to save energy with limited and controllable impact on performance. Our approach involves using control theory, with a method adapted to HPC systems, and leads to identification and controller design for the targeted system. Experimental validation shows good results for systems with lower numbers of sockets running a memory-bound benchmark. We identify limiting aspects of our method and areas for further study, such as integrating measures of the temperature or extending the control to heterogeneous devices.

Acknowledgments and Data Availability Statement. Experiments presented in this paper were carried out using the Grid'5000 testbed, supported by a scientific interest group hosted by Inria and including CNRS, RENATER and several Universities as well as other organizations (see https://www.grid5000.fr). Argonne National Laboratory's work was supported by the U.S. Department of Energy, Office of Science, Advanced Scientific Computer Research, under Contract DE-AC02-06CH11357. This research was supported by the Exascale Computing Project (17-SC-20-SC), a collaborative effort of the U.S. Department of Energy Office of Science and the National Nuclear Security Administration. This research is partially supported by the NCSA-Inria-ANL-BSC-JSC-Riken-UTK Joint-Laboratory for Extreme Scale Computing (JLESC, https://jlesc.github.io/).

The datasets and code generated and analyzed during the current study are available in the Figshare repository: https://doi.org/10.6084/m9.figshare.14754468 [5].

References

1. Abdelzaher, T., et al.: Introduction to control theory and its application to computing systems. In: Performance Modeling and Engineering, pp. 185–215. Springer (2008). https://doi.org/10.1007/978-0-387-79361-0_7

2. Albers, S.: Algorithms for dynamic speed scaling. In: STACS. LIPIcs, vol. 9, pp. 1–11. Schloss Dagstuhl - Leibniz-Zentrum für Informatik (2011). https://doi.org/10.4230/LIPIcs.STACS.2011.1

3. Åström, K.J., Hägglund, T.: PID Controllers: Theory, Design, and Tuning. International Society of Automation, second edn. (1995)

4. Bhalachandra, S., et al.: Using dynamic duty cycle modulation to improve energy efficiency in high performance computing. In: IPDPS Workshops, pp. 911–918. IEEE, May 2015. https://doi.org/10.1109/IPDPSW.2015.144

5. Cerf, S., et al.: Artifact and instructions to generate experimental results for the Euro-Par 2021 paper: Sustaining Performance While Reducing Energy Consumption: A Control Theory Approach, August 2021. https://doi.org/10.6084/m9.figshare.14754468

6. David, H., et al.: RAPL: memory power estimation and capping. In: ISLPED, pp. 189–194. ACM (2010). https://doi.org/10.1145/1840845.1840883

7. Desrochers, S., et al.: A validation of DRAM RAPL power measurements. In: MEMSYS, pp. 455–470. ACM, October 2016. https://doi.org/10.1145/2989081.2989088

8. Dolstra, E., et al.: Nix: a safe and policy-free system for software deployment. In: LISA, pp. 79–92. USENIX (2004). http://www.usenix.org/publications/library/proceedings/lisa04/tech/dolstra.html

9. Dutot, P., et al.: Towards energy budget control in HPC. In: CCGrid, pp. 381–390. IEEE/ACM, May 2017. https://doi.org/10.1109/CCGRID.2017.16

10. Eastep, J., et al.: Global extensible open power manager: a vehicle for HPC community collaboration on co-designed energy management solutions. In: ISC. Lecture Notes in Computer Science, vol. 10266, pp. 394–412. Springer, June 2017. https://doi.org/10.1007/978-3-319-58667-0_21

11. Filieri, A., et al.: Control strategies for self-adaptive software systems. ACM Trans. Auton. Adapt. Syst. 11(4), 24:1–24:31, February 2017. https://doi.org/10.1145/3024188

12. Hellerstein, J.L., et al.: Feedback control of computing systems. Wiley, Hoboken (2004). https://doi.org/10.1002/047166880X

13. Imes, C., et al.: POET: a portable approach to minimizing energy under soft real-time constraints. In: RTAS, pp. 75–86. IEEE, April 2015. https://doi.org/10.1109/RTAS.2015.7108419

14. Imes, C., et al.: CoPPer: soft real-time application performance using hardware power capping. In: ICAC, pp. 31–41. IEEE, June 2019. https://doi.org/10.1109/ICAC.2019.00015

15. Levine, W.S.: The Control Handbook (three volume set). CRC Press, Boca Raton, second edn. (2011). https://doi.org/10.1201/9781315218694

16. Lo, D., et al.: Towards energy proportionality for large-scale latency-critical workloads. In: ISCA, pp. 301–312. IEEE, June 2014. https://doi.org/10.1109/ISCA.2014.6853237

17. McCalpin, J.D.: Memory bandwidth and machine balance in current high performance computers. IEEE Comput. Soc. Tech. Committee Comput. Archit. (TCCA) Newsl. 2, 19–25 (1995)

18. Montgomery, D.C., Runger, G.C.: Applied Statistics and Probability for Engineers. Wiley, Hoboken, seventh edn. January 2018

19. Orgerie, A., et al.: Save watts in your grid: green strategies for energy-aware framework in large scale distributed systems. In: ICPADS, pp. 171–178. IEEE, December 2008. https://doi.org/10.1109/ICPADS.2008.97

20. Petoumenos, P., et al.: Power capping: what works, what does not. In: ICPADS, pp. 525–534. IEEE, December 2015. https://doi.org/10.1109/ICPADS.2015.72
21. Ramesh, S., et al.: Understanding the impact of dynamic power capping on application progress. In: IPDPS, pp. 793–804. IEEE, May 2019. https://doi.org/10.1109/IPDPS.2019.00088
22. Reis, V., et al.: Argo Node Resource Manager. https://www.mcs.anl.gov/research/projects/argo/overview/nrm/ (2021)
23. Rotem, E., et al.: Power-management architecture of the Intel microarchitecture code-named Sandy Bridge. IEEE Micro **32**(2), 20–27 (2012). https://doi.org/10.1109/MM.2012.12
24. Rountree, B., et al.: Beyond DVFS: a first look at performance under a hardware-enforced power bound. In: IPDPS Workshops, pp. 947–953. IEEE (2012). https://doi.org/10.1109/IPDPSW.2012.116
25. Rutten, É., et al.: Feedback control as MAPE-K loop in autonomic computing. In: Software Engineering for Self-Adaptive Systems. Lecture Notes in Computer Science, vol. 9640, pp. 349–373. Springer (2017). https://doi.org/10.1007/978-3-319-74183-3_12
26. Santriaji, M.H., Hoffmann, H.: GRAPE: minimizing energy for GPU applications with performance requirements. In: MICRO, pp. 16:1–16:13. IEEE, October 2016. https://doi.org/10.1109/MICRO.2016.7783719
27. Stahl, E., et al.: Towards a control-theory approach for minimizing unused grid resources. In: AI-Science@HPDC, pp. 4:1–4:8. ACM (2018). https://doi.org/10.1145/3217197.3217201
28. Zhou, Y., et al.: CASH: supporting IaaS customers with a sub-core configurable architecture. In: ISCA, pp. 682–694. IEEE, June 2016. https://doi.org/10.1109/ISCA.2016.65

Theory and Algorithms for Parallel and Distributed Processing

Algorithm Design for Tensor Units

Rezaul Chowdhury[1], Francesco Silvestri[2]([envelope]) [ORCID], and Flavio Vella[3] [ORCID]

[1] Stony Brook University, New York, USA
rezaul@cs.stonybrook.edu
[2] University of Padova, Padova, Italy
silvestri@dei.unipd.it
[3] Free University of Bozen, Bolzano, Italy
flavio.vella@unibz.it

Abstract. To respond to the intense computational load of deep neural networks, a plethora of domain-specific architectures have been introduced, such as Google Tensor Processing Units and NVIDIA Tensor Cores. A common feature of these architectures is a hardware circuit for efficiently computing a dense matrix multiplication of a given small size. In order to broaden the class of algorithms that exploit these systems, we propose a computational model, named the TCU model, that captures the ability to natively multiply small matrices. We then use the TCU model for designing fast algorithms for several problems, including matrix operations (dense and sparse multiplication, Gaussian Elimination), graph algorithms (transitive closure, all pairs shortest distances), Discrete Fourier Transform, stencil computations, integer multiplication, and polynomial evaluation. We finally highlight a relation between the TCU model and the external memory model.

1 Introduction

Deep neural networks are nowadays used in several application domains where big data are available. The huge size of the data set, although crucial for improving neural network quality, gives rise to performance issues during the training and inference steps. In response to the increasing computational needs, several domain-specific hardware accelerators have been recently introduced, such as Google's Tensor Processing Units (TPUs) [11] and NVIDIA's Tensor Cores (TCs) [16]. These compute units have been specifically designed for accelerating deep learning. Although such accelerators significantly vary in their design, they share circuits for efficiently multiplying small and dense matrices of fixed size, which is one of the most important computational primitives in deep learning.

A preliminary draft appeared as brief announcement at SPAA 2020 [5]. This work was partially supported by NSF grant CNS-1553510, UniPD SID18 grant, PRIN17 20174LF3T8 AHeAd, UniBZ-CRC 2019-IN2091 Project, and INdAM-GNCS Project 2020 NoRMA. Some results are based upon work performed at the AlgoPARC Workshop on Parallel Algorithms and Data Structures, in part supported by NSF Grant CCF-1930579.

© Springer Nature Switzerland AG 2021
L. Sousa et al. (Eds.): Euro-Par 2021, LNCS 12820, pp. 353–367, 2021.
https://doi.org/10.1007/978-3-030-85665-6_22

By using the terminology introduced in [8], we refer to all accelerators supporting hardware-level dense matrix multiplication as *Tensor Core Units (TCUs)* (or
simply tensor units). By focusing on a specific computational problem, namely
matrix multiplication, TCUs exhibit both high performance and low energy consumption which set them apart from traditional CPU or GPU approaches [11].
Although TCUs were developed for deep neural networks, it would be interesting
and profitable to extend their application domain, for instance by targeting linear
algebra and graph analytics. A similar scenario appeared with the introduction
of GPUs for general purpose computations. *Will domain-specific architectures
have the same wide impact as GPUs?* Some recent results are providing insights
in this direction: TCUs have been indeed used for accelerating scans and prefix sums [8], the Discrete Fourier Transform [15,19], linear algebra kernels and
graph analytics on sparse matrices [9,22], dimensionality reduction and similarity join [2].

The goals of this paper are to present a framework for designing and analyzing
algorithms for TCUs, and to further expand the class of algorithms that can
exploit TCUs from a theoretical perspective. We propose a computational model
for tensor core units, named (m, ℓ)-*TCU*, that captures the main features of
tensor units. We then design TCU algorithms for matrix multiplication (sparse
and dense), Gaussian Elimination, graph algorithms (transitive closure, all pairs
shortest distances), Discrete Fourier Transform, stencil computations, integer
multiplication and polynomial evaluation. Finally, we observe that some lower
bounds on the I/O complexity in the external-memory model [21] translate into
lower bounds on TCU time. We refer to the extended version of this paper [6]
for all proofs and more details.

2   The (m, ℓ)-TCU Model

We propose a computational model for tensor core units that captures the following three properties.

(1) Matrix acceleration. The hardware circuits implement a parallel algorithm
to multiply two matrices of a fixed size, and the main cost is dominated by
reading/writing the input and output matrices. For a given hardware parameter
m, the multiplication of two $\sqrt{m} \times \sqrt{m}$ matrices A and B requires $O(m)$ time.
With time, we mean the running time as seen by the CPU clock and it should not
be confused with the total number of operations executed by the unit, which is
always $\Theta(m^{3/2})$ (no existing tensor unit implements fast matrix multiplication
algorithms, e.g. Strassen [20]). The matrix multiplication operation is called by
an instruction specifying the memory addresses of the input and output matrices,
and data will be loaded/stored by the tensor unit.

(2) Latency cost. A call to the tensor unit has a latency cost. As the state of
the art tensor units use systolic algorithms, the first output entry is computed in
$\Omega(\sqrt{m})$ time. There are also initial costs associated with activation, which can
significantly increase when the unit is not connected to the CPU by the internal

system bus. We thus assume that the cost of the multiplication of two matrices of size $\sqrt{m} \times \sqrt{m}$ is $O(m + \ell)$, where $\ell > 0$ is the latency cost.

(3) Asymmetric behavior. As tensor units are designed for improving training and inference in deep networks, the two matrices in the multiplication $A \times B$ are managed differently. Matrix B represents the model (i.e., the weights of the deep neural network), while the rows of matrix A represent the input vectors to be evaluated. As the same model can be applied to n vectors, with $n >> \sqrt{m}$, it is possible to first load the weights in B and then to stream the n rows of A into the tensor unit (possibly in chunks of $\sqrt{m}$ rows), reducing thus latency costs. Thus, we assume in our model that two matrices of size $n \times \sqrt{m}$ and $\sqrt{m} \times \sqrt{m}$ are multiplied in time $O(n\sqrt{m} + \ell)$, where the number n of rows is defined by the algorithm and $n \geq \sqrt{m}$.

More formally, we define the *Tensor Core Unit (TCU) model* as follows. The (m, ℓ)-*TCU* model is a standard RAM model where the CPU contains a circuit, named tensor unit, for performing a matrix multiplication $A \times B$ of size $n \times \sqrt{m}$ and $\sqrt{m} \times \sqrt{m}$ in time $O(n\sqrt{m} + \ell)$, where $m \geq 1$ and $\ell \geq 0$ are two model parameters and $n \geq \sqrt{m}$ is a value (possibly input dependent) specified by the algorithm. The matrix operation is initialized by a constant-size instruction containing the addresses in memory of the two input matrices A and B, of the output matrix C, and the row number n of A. The *running time* of a TCU algorithm is given by the total cost of all operations performed by the CPU, including all calls to the tensor unit. We assume no concurrency between tensor unit, memory and CPU, and hence at most one component is active at any time. Each memory word consists of κ bits and, if not differently stated, we assume $\kappa = \Omega(\log n)$ where n is the input size.

Discussion on the Model. The goal of this work is to understand how to exploit architectures able to multiply matrices of fixed size. We then do not include in the model some characteristics of existing hardware accelerators, like limited numerical precision and parallel tensor units. In particular, the modeling of only a single tensor unit can be seen as a major weakness of our model since existing boards contain a large number of tensor cores (e.g., more than 500 cores in the Nvidia Titan RTX). However, we believe that the first step to exploit tensor accelerators is to investigate which problems can benefit of matrix multiplication circuits; we have then opted for a simple model with only a TCU. Moreover, existing hardware accelerators use different parallel architectures and interconnection networks, while they agree on matrix multiplication as main primitive.

We now make some considerations on how Google TPUs and NVIDIA TCs fit our model. In the Google TPU (in the version described in [11]), the right matrix B has size 256×256 words (i.e., $m = 65536$). The left matrix A is stored in the local unified buffer of $96k \times 256$ words; thus, TPUs can compute the product between two matrices of size $96k \times 256$ and 256×256 in one (tensor) operation. The number of rows of the left matrix in the TCU model is a user defined parameter (potentially a function of the input size); on the other hand, the number of rows of the left matrix in the TPU is user defined but it is upper bounded by a hardware-dependent value (i.e., 96K). Being this bound relatively large, a TPU better exploits a tall left matrix than a short one, as in our TCU model. The systolic array works in low precision with 8 bits per word ($\kappa = 8$). The bandwidth between CPU and TPU was limited in the first version (16 GB/s), but it is significantly higher in more recent versions (up to 600 GB/s). Although TPU has a quick response time, the overall latency is high because the right hand matrix has to be suitably encoded via a TensorFlow function before loading it within the TPU: in fact, the TPU programming model is strongly integrated with TensorFlow, and it does not allow to use bare matrices as inputs. The programming model of NVIDIA TCs (specifically, the Volta architecture) allows one to multiply matrices of size 16×16, although the basic hardware unit works on 4×4 matrices; we thus have $m = 256$. Memory words are of $\kappa = 16$ bits. TCs exhibit high bandwidth and low latency, as data are provided by a high bandwidth memory shared with the GPU processing units. Matrices A and B can be loaded within TCs without a special encoding as in Google TPUs, since the NVIDIA TCs natively provide support for matrix multiplication. Finally we observe that, as TCs are within a GPU, any algorithm for TCs has also to take into account GPU computational bottlenecks [1,13].

3 Algorithms

3.1 Matrix Multiplication

Dense Matrix Multiplication. A Strassen-like algorithm for matrix multiplication is defined in [4] as a recursive algorithm that utilizes as base case an algorithm $\mathcal{A}$ for multiplying two $\sqrt{n_0} \times \sqrt{n_0}$ matrices using p_0 element multiplications and $O(n_0)$ other operations (i.e., additions and subtractions); we assume $n_0 = O(p_0)$. Given two $\sqrt{n} \times \sqrt{n}$ matrices with $n > n_0$, a Strassen-like algorithm envisions the two $\sqrt{n} \times \sqrt{n}$ matrices as two matrices of size $\sqrt{n_0} \times \sqrt{n_0}$ where each entry is a submatrix of size $\sqrt{n/n_0} \times \sqrt{n/n_0}$: then, the algorithm recursively computes p_0 matrix multiplications on the submatrices (i.e., the p_0 element multiplications in $\mathcal{A}$) and then performs $O(n)$ other operations. For given parameters p_0 and n_0, the running time of the algorithm is $T(n) = O(n^{\omega_0})$, where[1] $\omega_0 = \log_{n_0} p_0$. By setting $n_0 = 4$ and $p_0 = 8$, we get the standard matrix multiplication algorithm ($\omega_0 = 3/2$), while with $n_0 = 4$ and $p_0 = 7$ we get the Strassen algorithm ($\omega_0 = \log_4 7 \sim 1.403$). Any fast matrix multiplication algorithm can be converted into a Strassen-like algorithm [17].

The TCU model can be exploited in Strassen-like algorithms by ending the recursion as soon as a subproblem fits the tensor unit: when $n \leq m$, the two input matrices are loaded in the tensor unit and the multiplication is computed in $O(m)$ time. We assume $m \geq n_0$, otherwise the tensor unit would not be used.

Theorem 1. *Given a Strassen-like algorithm with parameters n_0 and p_0, then there exists a TCU algorithm that multiplies two $\sqrt{n} \times \sqrt{n}$ matrices on an (m, ℓ)-TCU model, with $m \geq n_0$, in $O\left(\left(\frac{n}{m}\right)^{\omega_0} (m + \ell)\right)$ time.*

---

[1] We observe that ω_0 corresponds to $\omega/2$, where ω is the traditional symbol used for denoting the exponent in fast matrix multiplication algorithms.

The running times of the standard recursive algorithm and of the Strassen algorithm are $O\left(n^{3/2}/\sqrt{m} + (n/m)^{3/2}\ell\right)$ and $O(n^{1.4037}/m^{0.4037} + (n/m)^{1.4037}\ell)$.

We now show how to decrease the latency cost, i.e., $(n/m)^{3/2}\ell$, in the TCU algorithm based on the standard algorithm. The idea is to keep as much as possible the right matrix B within the tensor unit by using a tall left matrix A. We split the left matrix A and the output matrix C into $\sqrt{n/m}$ blocks A_i and C_i of size $\sqrt{n} \times \sqrt{m}$ (i.e., vertical strips of width $\sqrt{m}$), and the right matrix B into square blocks $B_{i,j}$ of size $\sqrt{m} \times \sqrt{m}$, with $0 \le i, j < \sqrt{n/m}$. Then, we compute $C_{i,j} = A_i \cdot B_{i,j}$ for each $0 \le i, j < \sqrt{n/m}$ using the tensor unit in time $O\left(n\sqrt{m} + \ell\right)$. The final matrix C follows by computing the $\sqrt{n} \times \sqrt{m}$ matrices $C_i = \sum_{j=0}^{\sqrt{n/m}-1} C_{i,j}$.

Theorem 2. *There exists an algorithm that multiplies two $\sqrt{n} \times \sqrt{n}$ matrices in the (m, ℓ)-TCU model in $\Theta\left(\frac{n^{3/2}}{\sqrt{m}} + \frac{n}{m}\ell\right)$ time. The algorithm is optimal when only semiring operations are allowed.*

From the previous Theorem 2, we get the following corollary for rectangular matrices (a similar result holds also when using the algorithm for fast matrix multiplication in Theorem 1).

Corollary 1. *A $\sqrt{n} \times r$ matrix can be multiplied by an $r \times \sqrt{n}$ matrix in the (m, ℓ)-TCU model in $\Theta\left(\frac{rn}{\sqrt{m}} + \frac{r\sqrt{n}}{m}\ell\right)$ time, assuming $n, r^2 \ge m$.*

Sparse Matrix Multiplication. A TCU algorithm to multiply two sparse matrices follows from the work [10] that uses as a black box a fast matrix multiplication algorithm for multiplying two $\sqrt{n} \times \sqrt{n}$ matrices in $O\left(n^{\omega/2}\right)$ time. Let I be the number of non-zero entries in the input matrices A and B, and let Z be the number of non-zero entries in the output $C = A \cdot B$. We consider here the case where the output is balanced, that is there are $\Theta\left(Z/\sqrt{n}\right)$ non-zero entries per row or column in C; the more general case where non-zero entries are not balanced is also studied in [10] and can be adapted to TCU with a similar argument. The algorithm in [10] computes the output in time $\tilde{O}\left(\sqrt{n}Z^{(\omega-1)/2} + I\right)$ with high probability. The idea is to compress the rows of A and the columns of B from $\sqrt{n}$ to $\sqrt{Z}$ using a hash function or another compression algorithm able to build a re-ordering of the matrix A. Then the algorithm computes a dense matrix multiplication between a $\sqrt{Z} \times \sqrt{n}$ matrix and a $\sqrt{n} \times \sqrt{Z}$ matrix using the fast matrix multiplication algorithm. By replacing the fast matrix multiplication with the TCU algorithm of Theorem 1, we get the following claim.

Theorem 3. *Let A and B be two sparse input matrices of size $\sqrt{n} \times \sqrt{n}$ with at most I non-zero entries, and assume that $C = A \cdot B$ has at most Z non-zero entries evenly balanced among rows and columns. Then, there exists an algorithm for the (m, ℓ)-TCU model requiring $O\left(\sqrt{\frac{n}{Z}}\left(\frac{Z}{m}\right)^{\omega_0}(m + \ell) + I\right)$ time, when $Z \ge m$ and where $\omega_0 = \log_{n_0} p_0$ is the exponent given by a Strassen-like algorithm.*

```
GE-FORWARD( X )
(X points to the √n × √n input matrix c. We assume that m
divides n, where √m × √m is the size of the matrix multipli-
cation unit of the TCU.)

1. Split X into √(n/m) × √(n/m) square submatrices of size √m ×
   √m each. The submatrix of X at the i-th position from
   the top and the j-th position from the left is denoted
   by X_ij. X' is a √m × √n matrix split into √m × √m
   submatrices, where the submatrix at j-th position from
   the left is denoted by X'_j.
2. for k ← 1 to √(n/m) do
3.     A( X_kk )
4.     for j ← k + 1 to √(n/m) do
5.         B( X_kj, X_kk, X'_j )
6.     for i ← k + 1 to √(n/m) do
7.         C( X_ik, X_kk )
8.     for j ← k + 1 to √(n/m) do
9.         for i ← k + 1 to √(n/m) do
10.            D( X_ij, X_ik, X'_j )
```

```
A( X )
(X points to a √m × √m matrix, where √m × √m is the size
of the matrix multiplication unit of the TCU.)

1. for k ← 1 to √m − 1 do
2.     for i ← k + 1 to √m do
3.         for j ← k + 1 to √m do
4.             X[i, j] ← X[i, j] − (X[i, k] × X[k, j]) /X[k, k]
```

```
B( X, Y, X' )
(X, Y and X' point to disjoint √m × √m matrices, where
√m × √m is the size of the matrix multiplication unit of the
TCU.)

1. for k ← 1 to √m − 1 do
2.     for i ← k + 1 to √m do
3.         for j ← 1 to √m do
4.             X[i, j] ← X[i, j] − (Y[i, k] × X[k, j]) /Y[k, k]
5.     for i ← 1 to √m do
6.         for j ← 1 to √m do
7.             X'[i, j] ← −X[i, j]/Y[i, i]
```

```
D( X, Y, Z )
(X, Y and Z point to disjoint √m × √m matrices, where √m ×
√m is the size of the matrix multiplication unit of the TCU.)

1. for k ← 1 to √m do
2.     for i ← 1 to √m do
3.         for j ← 1 to √m do
4.             X[i, j] ← X[i, j] + Y[i, k] × Z[k, j]
```

```
C( X, Y )
(X and Y point to disjoint √m × √m matrices, where √m × √m
is the size of the matrix multiplication unit of the TCU.)

1. for k ← 1 to √m do
2.     for i ← 1 to √m do
3.         for j ← k + 1 to √m do
4.             X[i, j] ← X[i, j] − (X[i, k] × Y[k, j]) /Y[k, k]
```

Fig. 1. TCU algorithm for Gaussian elimination without pivoting which is called as GE-FORWARD(c), where c is the $\sqrt{n} \times \sqrt{n}$ matrix representing a system of $\sqrt{n} - 1$ equations with $\sqrt{n} - 1$ unknowns.

3.2 Gaussian Elimination Without Pivoting

Gaussian elimination without pivoting is used in the solution of systems of linear equations and LU decomposition of symmetric positive-definite or diagonally dominant real matrices [7]. We represent a system of $r - 1$ equations in $r - 1$ unknowns $(x_1, x_2, \ldots, x_{r-1})$ using an $r \times r$ matrix c, where the i-th ($1 \leq i < r$) row represents the equation $a_{i,1}x_1 + a_{i,2}x_2 + \ldots + a_{i,r-1}x_{r-1} = b_i$:

$$
c = \begin{pmatrix}
a_{1,1} & a_{1,2} & \cdots & a_{1,r-1} & b_1 \\
a_{2,1} & a_{2,2} & \cdots & a_{2,r-1} & b_2 \\
\vdots & \vdots & \ddots & \vdots & \vdots \\
a_{r-1,1} & a_{r-1,2} & \cdots & a_{r-1,r-1} & b_{r-1} \\
0 & 0 & \cdots & 0 & 0
\end{pmatrix}
$$

The method proceeds in two phases. In the first phase, an upper triangular matrix is constructed from c by successive elimination of variables from the equations. This phase requires $\Theta(r^3)$ time. In the second phase, the values of the unknowns are determined from this matrix by back substitution. It is straightforward to implement this second phase in $\Theta(r^2)$ time, so we will concentrate on the first phase.

Our TCU algorithm for the forward phase of Gaussian elimination without pivoting is shown in Fig. 1. The algorithm is invoked as GE-FORWARD(c), where c is the $\sqrt{n} \times \sqrt{n}$ matrix representing a system of $\sqrt{n} - 1$ equations with $\sqrt{n} - 1$ unknowns (i.e. $r = \sqrt{n}$). In the proposed algorithm only the calls to

TRANSITIVE-CLOSURE(X)

(X points to the $n \times n$ input 0/1 matrix d. We assume that m divides n, where $\sqrt{m} \times \sqrt{m}$ is the size of the matrix multiplication unit of the TCU.)

1. Split X into $\frac{n}{\sqrt{m}} \times \frac{n}{\sqrt{m}}$ square submatrices of size $\sqrt{m} \times \sqrt{m}$ each. The submatrix of X at the i-th position from the top and the j-th position from the left is denoted by X_{ij}.
2. **for** $k \leftarrow 1$ **to** $\frac{n}{\sqrt{m}}$ **do**
3.   A(X_{kk})
4.   **for** $j \leftarrow 1$ **to** $\frac{n}{\sqrt{m}}$ **do**
5.   **if** $j \neq k$ **then** B(X_{kj}, X_{kk})
6.   **for** $i \leftarrow 1$ **to** $\frac{n}{\sqrt{m}}$ **do**
7.   **if** $i \neq k$ **then** C(X_{ik}, X_{kk})
8.   **for** $j \leftarrow 1$ **to** $\frac{n}{\sqrt{m}}$ **do**
9.   **for** $i \leftarrow 1$ **to** $\frac{n}{\sqrt{m}}$ **do**
10.   **if** $i \neq k$ **and** $j \neq k$ **then**
11.   D(X_{ij}, X_{ik}, X_{kj})

A(X)

(X points to a $\sqrt{m} \times \sqrt{m}$ 0/1 matrix, where $\sqrt{m} \times \sqrt{m}$ is the size of the TCU matrix multiplication unit.)

1. **for** $k \leftarrow 1$ **to** $\sqrt{m}$ **do**
2.   **for** $i \leftarrow 1$ **to** $\sqrt{m}$ **do**
3.   **for** $j \leftarrow 1$ **to** $\sqrt{m}$ **do**
4. $X[i,j] \leftarrow X[i,j] \vee (X[i,k] \wedge X[k,j])$

B(X, Y)

(X, Y and X' point to disjoint $\sqrt{m} \times \sqrt{m}$ 0/1 matrices, where $\sqrt{m} \times \sqrt{m}$ is the size of the TCU matrix multiplication unit.)

1. **for** $k \leftarrow 1$ **to** $\sqrt{m}$ **do**
2.   **for** $i \leftarrow 1$ **to** $\sqrt{m}$ **do**
3.   **for** $j \leftarrow 1$ **to** $\sqrt{m}$ **do**
4. $X[i,j] \leftarrow X[i,j] \vee (Y[i,k] \wedge X[k,j])$

C(X, Y)

(X and Y point to disjoint $\sqrt{m} \times \sqrt{m}$ 0/1 matrices, where $\sqrt{m} \times \sqrt{m}$ is the size of the TCU matrix multiplication unit.)

1. **for** $k \leftarrow 1$ **to** $\sqrt{m}$ **do**
2.   **for** $i \leftarrow 1$ **to** $\sqrt{m}$ **do**
3.   **for** $j \leftarrow 1$ **to** $\sqrt{m}$ **do**
4. $X[i,j] \leftarrow X[i,j] \vee (X[i,k] \wedge Y[k,j])$

D(X, Y, Z)

(X, Y and Z point to disjoint $\sqrt{m} \times \sqrt{m}$ 0/1 matrices, where $\sqrt{m} \times \sqrt{m}$ is the size of the TCU matrix multiplication unit.)

1. **for** $k \leftarrow 1$ **to** $\sqrt{m}$ **do**
2.   **for** $i \leftarrow 1$ **to** $\sqrt{m}$ **do**
3.   **for** $j \leftarrow 1$ **to** $\sqrt{m}$ **do**
4. $X[i,j] \leftarrow X[i,j] + (Y[i,k] \times Z[k,j])$
5.   **for** $i \leftarrow 1$ **to** $\sqrt{m}$ **do**
6.   **for** $j \leftarrow 1$ **to** $\sqrt{m}$ **do**
7.   **if** $X[i,j] > 1$ **then** $X[i,j] \leftarrow 1$

Fig. 2. TCU algorithm for computing transitive closure of an n-vertex graph which is called as TRANSITIVE-CLOSURE(d), where d is the $n \times n$ adjacency matrix of the graph with $d[i,j] = 1$ if vertices i and j are adjacent and $d[i,j] = 0$ otherwise.

function D (in line 10), which multiplies $\sqrt{m} \times \sqrt{m}$ matrices, are executed on the TCU. In each iteration of the loop in line 8, X'_j is loaded into the TCU as the weight matrix, and the $\left(\sqrt{n/m} - k\right)\sqrt{m} = \sqrt{n} - k\sqrt{m}$ rows of the $\sqrt{n/m} - k$ submatrices X_{ik} inside the loop in line 9 are streamed through the TCU.

Theorem 4. *The forward phase of Gaussian elimination without pivoting applied on a system of $\sqrt{n} - 1$ equations with $\sqrt{n} - 1$ unknowns can be performed in the (m, ℓ)-TCU model in $\Theta\left(\frac{n^{3/2}}{\sqrt{m}} + \frac{n}{m}\ell + n\sqrt{m}\right)$ time. This complexity reduces to the optimal cost of multiplying two dense $\sqrt{n} \times \sqrt{n}$ matrices (see Theorem 2) when $\sqrt{n} \geq m$.*

3.3 Graph Transitive Closure

For an n-vertex directed graph G, its *transitive closure* is given by an $n \times n$ matrix $c[1..n, 1..n]$, where for all $i, j \in [1, n]$, $c[i,j] = 1$ provided vertex j is reachable from vertex i and $c[i,j] = 0$ otherwise. An algorithm for computing transitive closure is similar to the iterative matrix multiplication algorithm except that bitwise-AND ($\wedge$) and bitwise-OR ($\vee$) replace multiplication ($\times$) and addition ($+$), respectively (Fig. 2). However, we observe that function D which updates block X using data from blocks Y and Z that are disjoint from X can be implemented to use "$\times$" and "$+$" instead of "$\wedge$" and "$\vee$", respectively, provided we set $X[i,j] \leftarrow \min(X[i,j], 1)$ for all i, j after it completes updating X. Function D is invoked in line 11 of TRANSITIVE-CLOSURE almost $\frac{n^2}{m}$ times. We execute lines

1– 4 of function D (which represent standard multiplication of two $\sqrt{m} \times \sqrt{m}$ matrices) on a TCU. In each iteration of the loop in line 8, X_{kj} is loaded into the TCU as the weight matrix, and the $(n/\sqrt{m} - 1)\sqrt{m} = \sqrt{n} - \sqrt{m}$ rows of the $n/\sqrt{m} - 1$ submatrices X_{ik} inside the loop in line 9 are streamed through the TCU.

Theorem 5. *The transitive closure of an n-vertex directed graph can be computed in the (m, ℓ)-TCU model in $\Theta\left(\frac{n^3}{\sqrt{m}} + \frac{n^2}{m}\ell + n^2\sqrt{m}\right)$ time. This complexity reduces to the optimal cost of multiplying two dense $n \times n$ matrices (see Theorem 2) when $n \geq m$.*

3.4   All Pairs Shortest Distances (APSD)

We discuss TCU implementation of Seidel's algorithm [18] for computing APSD in an unweighted undirected graph $G = (V, E)$, where $n = |V|$ and vertices are numbered by unique integers from 1 to n. Let A be the adjacency matrix of G. The adjacency matrix $A^{(2)}$ of the squared graph $G^{(2)} = (V, E^{(2)})$ is obtained by squaring A and replacing all non-zero entries in the square matrix by 1. Indeed, for any given pair of vertices $u, v \in V$, $(u, v) \in E^{(2)}$ (i.e., $A^{(2)}[u, v] = 1$) provided there exists a vertex $w \in V$ such that $(u, w), (w, v) \in E$ (i.e., $A[u, w] = A[w, v] = 1$). Let $\delta(u, v)$ and $\delta^{(2)}(u, v)$ represent the shortest distance from u to v in G and $G^{(2)}$, respectively. Seidel shows that if all $\delta^{(2)}$ values are known one can correctly compute all $\delta(u, v)$ values from them. Let $D^{(2)}$ be the distance matrix of $G^{(2)}$ and let $C = D^{(2)}A$. Then Seidel shows that for any pair $u, v \in V$, $\delta(u, v) = 2\delta^{(2)}(u, v)$ provided $\sum_{(w,v) \in E} D^{(2)}[u, w] = C[u, v] \geq deg(v) \times D^{(2)}[u, v]$, and $\delta(u, v) = 2\delta^{(2)}(u, v) - 1$ otherwise, where $deg(v)$ is the number of neighbors of v in G. Thus the distance matrix D of G can be computed from $D^{(2)}$ by computing $C = D^{(2)}A$. The $D^{(2)}$ matrix is computed recursively. The base case is reached when we encounter $G^{(h)}$ where $h = \lceil \log_2(n) \rceil$. Its adjacency matrix $A^{(h)}$ has all 1's, and it's distance matrix is simply $D^{(h)} = A^{(h)} - I_n$. Clearly, there are h levels of recursion and in each level we compute two products of two $n \times n$ matrices. Hence, using Theorem 1 we obtain the following.

Theorem 6. *All pairs shortest distances of an n-vertex unweighted undirected graph can be computed in the (m, ℓ)-TCU model in $O\left(\left(\frac{n^2}{m}\right)^{\tilde{\omega}_0} (m + \ell) \log n\right)$ time.*

3.5   Discrete Fourier Transform

The Discrete Fourier Transform y of an n-dimensional (column) vector x can be defined as the matrix-vector product $y = x^T \cdot W$, where W is the Fourier matrix (or DFT matrix) and T denotes the transpose of a matrix/vector. The Fourier matrix W is a symmetric $n \times n$ matrix where the entry at row r and column c is defined as: $W_{r,c} = e^{-(2\pi i/n)rc}$. This solution was used in [15] to compute the DFT on a server of Google TPUs: however, a matrix-vector multiplication does not fully exploit tensor cores, which are optimized for matrix multiplication.

Better performance can be reached by computing batches of DFTs since the DFT of n vectors $x_i, \ldots x_n$ can be computed with the matrix multiplication $X^T \cdot W$, where the i-th column of X denotes the i-th vector. We now describe a more efficient hybrid approach based on the algebraic formulation and the Cooley-Tukey algorithm.

The Cooley-Tukey algorithm is an efficient and recursive algorithm for computing the DFT of a vector. The algorithm arranges x as an $n_1 \times n_2$ matrix X (in row-major order) where $n = n_1 \cdot n_2$; each column $X_{*,c}$ is replaced with its DFT and then each entry $X_{r,c}$ is multiplied by the twiddle factor w_n^{rc}; finally, each row $X_{r,*}$ is replaced by its DFT and the DFT of x is given by reading the final matrix X in column-major order. For simplicity, we assume that the TCU model can perform operations (e.g., addition, products) on complex numbers; this assumption can be easily removed with a constant slow down in the running time: for instance, the multiplication between $\sqrt{m} \times \sqrt{m}$ complex matrices can be computed with four matrix multiplications and two sums of real values. To compute the DFT of x using a (m, ℓ)-TCU, we use the Cooley-Tukey algorithm where we set $n_1 = \sqrt{m}$ and $n_2 = n/\sqrt{m}$ (we assume all values to be integers). Then, we use the tensor unit for computing the n_2 DFTs of size $n_1 = \sqrt{m}$ by computing $X^T \cdot W_{\sqrt{m}}$. Then, we multiply each element in X by its twiddle factor and transpose X. Finally, we compute the n_1 DFTs of size n_2: if $n_2 > \sqrt{m}$, the DFTs are recursively computed; otherwise, if $n_2 \leq \sqrt{m}$, the n_1 DFTs are computed with the multiplication $X^T \cdot W_{n_2}$ by using the tensor unit.

Theorem 7. *The DFT of a vector with n entries can be computed in the (m, ℓ)-TCU in $O\left((n + \ell) \log_m n\right)$ time.*

The above algorithm generalizes the approach in [19] for computing a DFT on an NVIDIA Volta architecture: in [19], the vector is decomposed using $n_1 = 4$ and $n_2 = n/4$ and subproblems of size 4 are solved using a tensor core.

3.6   Stencil Computations

Stencil computations are iterative kernels over a d-dimensional array, widely used in scientific computing. Given a d-dimensional matrix A, a stencil computation performs a sequence of sweeps over the input: in a sweep, each cell is updated with a function $f(\cdot)$ of the values of its neighboring cells at previous sweeps. An example of stencil computation is the discretization of the 2D heat equation, where each entry at time t is updated as follows:

$$A_t[x, y] = A_{t-1}[x, y] +$$
$$+ \frac{\alpha \Delta t}{\Delta x^2}\left(A_{t-1}[x-1, y] + A_{t-1}[x+1, y] - 2A_{t-1}[x, y]\right)$$
$$+ \frac{\alpha \Delta t}{\Delta y^2}\left(A_{t-1}[x, y-1] + A_{t-1}[x, y+1] - 2A_{t-1}[x, y]\right)$$

where $\alpha, \Delta t, \Delta x^2, \Delta y^2$ are suitable constant values given by the heat diffusion equations and by the discretization step.

The algorithm given in this section works for periodic stencils, e.g., the stencil obtained by replacing $x-1$, $x+1$, $y-1$, and $y+1$ with $(x-1+N) \mod N$, $(x+1) \mod N$, $(y-1+N) \mod N$, and $(y+1) \mod N$, respectively, where $N \times N$ is the size of the grid. Our algorithm is based on the shared-memory parallel algorithm given in [3]. For the sake of simplicity, we assume $d = 2$ and that each update depends only on the values of the cell and of its eight (vertical/horizontal/diagonal) neighbors at previous sweep. However, the presented techniques extend to any $d = O(1)$ and to any update function that depends on a constant number of neighbors.

Given $n, k \geq 1$, an (n, k)-*stencil computation*, over an input $\sqrt{n} \times \sqrt{n}$ matrix A is the matrix A_k obtained by the following iterative process: let $A_0 = A$ and $1 \leq t \leq k$; matrix A_t is defined by computing, for each $0 \leq i, j < \sqrt{n}$, $A_t[i, j] = f(i, j, A_{t-1})$ where f is a suitable function of cells $A_{t-1}[i+\alpha, j+\beta]$ with $\alpha, \beta \in \{-1, 0, 1\}$. We say that a stencil computation is *linear* if f is a linear, that is $A_t[i, j] = \sum_{\alpha, \beta \in \{-1, 0, 1\}} w_{\alpha, \beta} A_{t-1}[i+\alpha, j+\beta]$ where $w_{\alpha, \beta}$ are suitable real values. The above stencil computation for approximating heat equations is linear. We assume k to be even and that all values are integers.

By unrolling the update function of a linear (n, k)-stencil computation, each entry $A_k[i, j]$ can be represented as a linear combination of $O(k^2)$ entries of A, specifically all entries (i', j') in A where $|i - i'| \leq k$ and $|j - j'| \leq k$. That is, there exists a $(2k+1) \times (2k+1)$ matrix W such that $A_t[i, j] = \sum_{-k \leq \alpha, \beta \leq k} W[k+\alpha, k+\beta] A[i+\alpha, j+\beta]$.

We now show that a linear (n, k)-stencil on a matrix A reduces to $\Theta(n/k^2)$ convolutions of size $O(k^2)$, which are then computed with the TCU algorithm for DFT in Theorem 7. Let matrix A be split into submatrices $A_{r,c}$ of size $k \times k$, with $0 \leq r, c < \sqrt{n}/k$; similarly, let $A_{k,r,c}$ denote the $k \times k$ submatrices of A_k. For each $A_{r,c}$, we define the following matrix $A'_{r,c}$ of size $3k \times 3k$:

$$A'_{r,c} = \begin{bmatrix} A_{r-1,c-1} & A_{r-1,c} & A_{r-1,c+1} \\ A_{r,c-1} & A_{r,c} & A_{r,c+1} \\ A_{r+1,c-1} & A_{r+1,c} & A_{r+1,c+1} \end{bmatrix}.$$

where we assume that a matrix $A_{i,j}$ is a zero matrix when i and j are not in the range $[0, \sqrt{n}/k)$. We then compute the circular discrete convolution $A^*_{r,c} = A'_{r,c} \circledast W'$, where W' is a $3k \times 3k$ matrix obtained by flipping W and by adding $k/2$ (resp., $k/2-1$) rows and columns of zeros on the left and top (resp., right and bottom) sides of W.[2] Finally, we set $A_{k,r,c}$ to be the $k \times k$ matrix obtained from $A^*_{r,c}$ by selecting the i-row and j-th column for all $k \leq i, j < 2k$. By repeating the following procedure for each submatrix $A_{r,c}$, we get the output matrix A_k.

Each convolution can be efficiently computed by exploiting the convolution theorem and the DFT algorithm of Theorem 7. We indeed recall that a 2-dimensional DFT is given by computing a 1-dimensional DFT for each row and for each column. If W is given, we have the following claim:

---

[2] With a slight abuse of notation, given two $n \times n$ matrices A and B with n even, we define $(A \circledast B)[i, j] = \sum_{\alpha, \beta \in [-n/2, n/2)} A[(i+\alpha) \mod n, (j+\beta) \mod n] W[n/2 - \alpha, n/2 - \beta]$. In the paper, we omit the mod operation from the notation.

Lemma 1. *Given a linear (n, k)-stencil computation and its weight matrix W, then the stencil can be computed in the (m, ℓ)-TCU in $O\left((n + \ell) \log_m k\right)$ time.*

The weight matrix W can be trivially computed in $O\left(k^3\right)$ time by recursively unrolling function f. However, as soon as $k \geq (n \log_m k)^{1/3}$, the cost for computing W dominates the cost of the stencil algorithm. A more efficient solution follows by representing W as the powering of a bivariate polynomial and then using the DFT to compute it, with $O\left(k^2 \log_m k + \ell \log k\right)$ total time. Therefore, given Lemma 1 and the computation of W, we get the following result:

Theorem 8. *Given a linear (n, k)-stencil computation with $k \leq n$, then the stencil can be computed in the (m, ℓ)-TCU in $O\left(n \log_m k + \ell \log k\right)$ time.*

3.7 Integer Multiplication

We now study how to multiply two long integers by exploiting tensor cores. The input is given by two integers a and b of n bits each (without loss of generality, we assume both integers to be positive and $n > m$), and the output is the binary representation of $c = a * b$, of size $2n - 1$. For this problem, we introduce in the design a third parameter κ, which is the bit length of a memory word in the TCU model. We assume that $\kappa = \Omega(\log n)$, that is there are enough bits in a word to store the input/output size. It is easy to see that the tensor unit can multiply matrices of (positive) integers of $\kappa' = \kappa/4$ bits without overflow: the largest integer in the output matrix using κ' bits is $2^{2\kappa'}\sqrt{m}$ which requires $2\kappa' + \log \sqrt{m} < \kappa$ (if $n >> m$, then $\kappa' = \kappa/2 - 1$ suffices).

We initially show how to speed up the long integer multiplication algorithm [14], also known as the schoolbook algorithm, by exploiting the tensor unit. Then, we will use this algorithm to improve the recursive Karatsuba algorithm [12]. Let $A(x) = \sum_{i=0}^{n'-1} A_i x^i$ be a polynomial where $n' = n/\kappa'$ and $A_i = (a_{(i+1)\kappa'-1} \dots a_{i\kappa'})_2$ is the integer given by the ith segment of κ' bits of a. Let $B(x)$ be defined similarly for b. We have that $a = A(2^{\kappa'})$ and $b = B(2^{\kappa'})$. We define $C(x) = A(x) \cdot B(x)$ and we observe that c is given by evaluating $C(2^{\kappa'})$. Note that $A(X)$ and $B(X)$ have degree $n' - 1$, while c has degree at most $(2n - 1)/\kappa' \leq 2n' - 1$. The coefficients of $C(x)$ can be computed with the matrix multiplication $C = A \cdot B$ where:

- B is the column vector with the n' coefficients of $B(X)$;
- A is a $(2n' - 1) \times n'$ matrix where $A_{i,j} = A_{n'-i+j-1}$ and we assume that $A_h = 0$ if $h < 0$ or $h \geq n'$.

The product $C = A \cdot B$ cannot exploit TCU since B is a vector. To fully exploit an (m, ℓ)-TCU, we calculate C coefficients via the multiplication $C' = A' \cdot B'$ where A is a $(n' + \sqrt{m} - 1) \times \sqrt{m}$ matrix and B is a $\sqrt{m} \times n'/\sqrt{m}$ matrix.

- Matrix B' follows by considering vector B as the column major representation of a $\sqrt{m} \times n'/\sqrt{m}$ matrix, that is $B'_{i,j} = B_{n'-i-j\sqrt{m}-1}$.

- Matrix A' is given by considering all segments of length $\sqrt{m}$ in the sequence $0_{\sqrt{m}-1}, A_0, A_1, \ldots A_{n'-1}, 0_{\sqrt{m}-1}$, where $0_{\sqrt{m}-1}$ denotes a sequence of $\sqrt{m}-1$ zeros. More formally, the ith row $A'_{i,*}$ is $[A_{n'-i-1}, A_{n'-i-2}, \ldots A_{n'-i-\sqrt{m}}]$, where we assume again that $A_h = 0$ if $h < 0$ or $h \geq n'$.

Then, we compute $C' = A' \cdot B'$ with the algorithm for dense matrix multiplication of Theorem 2 (or equivalently Theorem 1): We decompose B' into into n'/m submatrices of size $\sqrt{m} \times \sqrt{m}$ and then compute n'/m products of a $(n' + \sqrt{m} - 1) \times \sqrt{m}$ matrix with a $\sqrt{m} \times \sqrt{m}$ matrix. The coefficient of the x^h indeterminate in $C(x)$, for each $0 \leq h < 2n' - 1$, follows by summing all entries in $C'_{i,j}$ such that $h = 2(n'-1) - i - j\sqrt{m}$. Finally we compute $c = C(2^{\kappa})$.

Theorem 9. *Two integers of n bits can be multiplied in a (m, ℓ)-TCU with κ-bit operations in $O\left(\frac{n^2}{\kappa^2 \sqrt{m}} + \frac{n}{\kappa m}\ell\right)$ time.*

The Karatsuba algorithm is a well-known algorithm that computes $c = a \cdot b$ by recursively computing three integer multiplications of size $n/2$ and then combining the solution in $O(n/\kappa)$ time. If we stop the recursion as soon as the input size is $n \leq k\sqrt{m}$ and solve the subproblem with the algorithm of Theorem 9, we get the following result.

Theorem 10. *Two integers of n bits can be multiplied in a (m, ℓ)-TCU with κ-bit operations in $O\left(\left(\left(\frac{n}{\kappa\sqrt{m}}\right)^{\log 3}\right)\left(\sqrt{m} + \frac{\ell}{\sqrt{m}}\right)\right)$ time.*

3.8 Batch Polynomial Evaluation

We now show how to exploit tensor cores for evaluating a given polynomial of $A(x) = \sum_{i=0}^{n-1} a_i x^i$ of degree $n-1$ on p points p_i, with $0 \leq i < p$. For simplicity we assume n to be a multiple of $\sqrt{m}$, $p \geq \sqrt{m}$, and that the polynomial can be evaluated without overflow on the memory word available in the TCU. We initially compute for each p_i the powers $p_i^0, p_i^1, \ldots p_i^{\sqrt{m}-1}$ and $p_i^{\sqrt{m}}, p_i^{2\sqrt{m}}, \ldots p_i^{n-\sqrt{m}}$, that is p_i^j for each $j \in \{0, 1, \ldots, \sqrt{m}-1\} \cup \{k\sqrt{m}, \forall k \in \{1, \ldots, n/\sqrt{m}-1\}\}$. We define the following matrices:

- A matrix X of size $p \times \sqrt{m}$ where the ith row is $X_{i,*} = [p_i^0, p_i^1, \ldots, p_i^{\sqrt{m}-1}]$ for each $0 \leq i < p$.
- A matrix A of size $\sqrt{m} \times n/\sqrt{m}$ where $A_{i,j} = a_{i+j\sqrt{m}}$ for each $0 \leq i < \sqrt{m}$ and $0 \leq j < n/\sqrt{m}$. Stated differently, we consider the sequence $a_0, \ldots, a_{n-1}$ as the column major representation of A.

We then compute $C = X \cdot A$ by exploiting the tensor unit: we decompose A into $\sqrt{m} \times \sqrt{m}$ submatrices and then solve n/m multiplications. Then, for each p_i, the values $A(p_i)$ follows by the sum $\sum_{j=0}^{n/\sqrt{m}-1} C_{i,j} p_i^{j\sqrt{m}}$.

Theorem 11. *A polynomial of degree $n-1$ can be evaluated on p points in the (m, ℓ)-TCU in $O\left(\frac{pn}{\sqrt{m}} + p\sqrt{m} + \frac{n}{m}\ell\right)$ time.*

4   Relation with the External Memory Model

In this section we highlight a relation between the external memory model and the TCU model. We recall that the external memory model (also named I/O model and almost equivalent to the ideal cache model) is a model capturing the memory hierarchy and it consists of an external memory of potential unbounded size, of an internal memory of $M \geq 1$ words, and a processor. The processor can only perform operations with data in the internal memory, and moves (input/output) blocks of $B \geq 1$ words between the external memory and the internal memory. The I/O complexity of an algorithm for the external memory model is simply the number of blocks moved between the two memories. We refer to the excellent survey in [21] for a more exhaustive explanation.

The time of some of the previous TCU algorithms recall the I/O complexity of the respective external memory algorithms. For instance, the cost of dense matrix multiplication with only semiring operations (Theorem 2) is $O\left(n^{3/2}/\sqrt{m}\right)$ when $\ell = O(1)$, while the I/O complexity for the same problem in the external memory model is $O\left(n^{3/2}/\sqrt{M}\right)$ when $B = O(1)$ [21].

The multiplication of two matrices of size $\sqrt{m} \times \sqrt{m}$ requires $O(m)$ I/Os to load and storing the input in an internal memory with $M = 3m$ and $B = O(1)$. Therefore any call to the tensor unit in a TCU can be simulated in the external memory of size $M = 3m$ with $\Theta(m)$ I/Os. Leveraging on this claim, we show that a lower bound in the external memory model translates into a lower bound in a weaker version of the TCU model. In the *weak TCU model*, the tensor unit can only multiply matrices of size $\sqrt{m} \times \sqrt{m}$ (i.e., we cannot exploit tall left matrices). Any algorithm for the original TCU model can be simulated in the weak version with a constant slowdown when $\ell = O(m)$: indeed, the multiplication between an $n \times \sqrt{m}$ matrix with a $\sqrt{m} \times \sqrt{m}$ can be executed in the weak model by splitting the $n \times \sqrt{m}$ matrix into $n/\sqrt{m}$ matrices of size $\sqrt{m} \times \sqrt{m}$ and then performing $n/\sqrt{m}$ matrix multiplications with total time $O(n\sqrt{m})$.

Theorem 12. *Consider a computational problem $\mathcal{P}$ with a lower bound $F_{\mathcal{P}}$ on the I/O complexity in an external memory with memory size $M = 3m + O(1)$ and block length $B = 1$. Then, any algorithm for $\mathcal{P}$ in the weak TCU model requires $\Omega(F_{\mathcal{P}})$ time.*

5   Open Questions

The paper leaves several open questions that we plan to investigate in the future. First, the TCU model should be experimentally validated by analyzing the performances of our algorithms on state-of-the-art tensor cores, such as Google TPUs and Nvidia TCs, to understand the gap between the theoretical model and actual accelerators. Second, the class of algorithms that may benefit from such architectures should be further extended by addressing, for instance, computational geometry and data mining. Finally, new tensor accelerators support low numerical precision and structured sparsity (e.g., Nvidia Ampere): including these features in the TCU model in the TCU algorithm design is an open question.

References

1. Afshani, P., Sitchinava, N.: Sorting and permuting without bank conflicts on GPUs. In: Proceedings European Symposium on Algorithms (ESA), pp. 13–24 (2015)
2. Ahle, T.D., Silvestri, F.: Similarity search with tensor core units. In: Proceedings of the 13th International Conference on Similarity Search and Application (SISAP), vol. 12440, pp. 76–84 (2020)
3. Ahmad, Z., Chowdhury, R., Das, R., Ganapathi, P., Gregory, A., Zhu, Y.: Fast stencil computations using fast Fourier transforms. In: Proceedings of the 33rd ACM Symposium on Parallelism in Algorithms and Architectures (SPAA) (2021)
4. Ballard, G., Demmel, J., Holtz, O., Schwartz, O.: Graph expansion and communication costs of fast matrix multiplication. J. ACM **59**(6), 32:1–32:23 (2013)
5. Chowdhury, R., Silvestri, F., Vella, F.: Brief announcement: a computational model for tensor core units. In: Proceedings of the 32nd ACM Symposium on Parallelism in Algorithms and Architectures (SPAA) (2020)
6. Chowdhury, R.A., Silvestri, F., Vella, F.: A computational model for tensor core units arxiv preprint arxiv: 1908.06649 (2020)
7. Cormen, T.H., Leiserson, C.E., Rivest, R.L., Stein, C.: Introduction to Algorithms. The MIT Press, Cambridge (2001)
8. Dakkak, A., Li, C., Xiong, J., Gelado, I., Hwu, W.M.: Accelerating reduction and scan using tensor core units. In: Proceedings of the International Conference on Supercomputing (ICS), pp. 46–57 (2019)
9. Firoz, J.S., Li, A., Li, J., Barker, K.: On the feasibility of using reduced-precision tensor core operations for graph analytics. In: 2020 IEEE High Performance Extreme Computing Conference (HPEC), pp. 1–7 (2020)
10. Jacob, R., Stöckel, M.: Fast output-sensitive matrix multiplication. In: Proceedings of European Symposium on Algorithms (ESA), pp. 766–778 (2015)
11. Jouppi, N.P., et al.: In-datacenter performance analysis of a tensor processing unit. In: Proceedings of the 44th International Symposium on Computer Architecture (ISCA), pp. 1–12 (2017)
12. Karatsuba, A., Ofman, Y.: Multiplication of multidigit numbers on automata. Soviet Physics Doklady **7**, 595 (1963)
13. Karsin, B., Weichert, V., Casanova, H., Iacono, J., Sitchinava, N.: Analysis-driven engineering of comparison-based sorting algorithms on GPUs. In: Proceedings of the 32nd International Conference on Supercomputing (ICS), pp. 86–95 (2018)
14. Kleinberg, J., Tardos, E.: Algorithm Design. Addison Wesley, Boston (2006)
15. Lu, T., Chen, Y., Hechtman, B.A., Wang, T., Anderson, J.R.: Large-scale discrete Fourier transform on TPUs. In: arXiv preprint arXiv: 2002.03260
16. Nvidia Tesla V100 GPU architecture. http://images.nvidia.com/content/volta-architecture/pdf/volta-architecture-whitepaper.pdf
17. Raz, R.: On the complexity of matrix product. SIAM J. Comput. **32**(5), 1356–1369 (2003)
18. Seidel, R.: On the all-pairs-shortest-path problem in unweighted undirected graphs. J. Comput. Syst. Sci. **51**(3), 400–403 (1995)

19. Sorna, A., Cheng, X., D'Azevedo, E., Won, K., Tomov, S.: Optimizing the fast Fourier transform using mixed precision on tensor core hardware. In: Proceedings of the 25th International Conference on High Performance Computing Workshops (HiPCW), pp. 3–7 (2018)
20. Strassen, V.: Gaussian elimination is not optimal. Numer. Math. 13(4), 354–356 (1969). https://doi.org/10.1007/BF02165411
21. Vitter, J.S.: Algorithms and data structures for external memory. Found. Trends Theor. Comput. Sci. 2(4), 305–474 (2006)
22. Zachariadis, O., Satpute, N., Gómez-Luna, J., Olivares, J.: Accelerating sparse matrix–matrix multiplication with GPU tensor cores. Comput. Electr. Eng. 88, 106848 (2020)

A Scalable Approximation Algorithm for Weighted Longest Common Subsequence

Jeremy Buhler[1], Thomas Lavastida[2], Kefu Lu[3(✉)], and Benjamin Moseley[2]

[1] Washington University in St. Louis, St. Louis, MO, USA
jbuhler@wustl.edu
[2] Carnegie Mellon University, Pittsburgh, PA, USA
{tlavasti,moseleyb}@andrew.cmu.edu
[3] Washington and Lee University, Lexington, VA, USA
klu@wlu.edu

Abstract. This work introduces novel parallel methods for weighted longest common subsequence (WLCS) and its generalization, all-substrings WLCS. Previous work developed efficient algorithms for these problems via Monge matrix multiplication, which is a limiting factor for further improvement. Diverging from these approaches, we relax the algorithm's optimality guarantee in a controlled way, using a different, natural dynamic program which can be sketched and solved in a divide-and-conquer manner that is efficient to parallelize.

Additionally, to compute the base case of our algorithm, we develop a novel and efficient method for all-substrings WLCS inspired by previous work on unweighted all-substrings LCS, exploiting the typically small range of weights.

Our method fits in most parallel models of computation, including the PRAM and the BSP model. To the best of our knowledge this is the fastest $(1 - \epsilon)$-approximation algorithm for all-substrings WLCS and WLCS in BSP. Further, this is the asymptotically fastest parallel algorithm for weighted LCS as the number of processors increases.

Keywords: Parallel approximation algorithms · Weighted LCS

1 Introduction

Technologies for sequencing DNA have improved dramatically in cost and speed over the past two decades [15], resulting in an explosion of sequence data that presents new opportunities for analysis. To exploit these new data sets, we must devise scalable algorithms for analyzing them. A fundamental task in analyzing DNA is comparing two sequences to determine their similarity.

A basic similarity measure is weighted longest common subsequence (WLCS). Given two strings x and y over a finite alphabet Σ (e.g. $\{A, C, G, T\}$), a *correspondence* between them is a set of index pairs $(i_1, j_1) \ldots (i_\ell, j_\ell)$ in x and y such that

B. Moseley, K. Lu and T. Lavastida were supported in part by a Google Research Award and NSF Grants CCF-1617724, CCF-1733873, and CCF-1725661.

© Springer Nature Switzerland AG 2021
L. Sousa et al. (Eds.): Euro-Par 2021, LNCS 12820, pp. 368–384, 2021.
https://doi.org/10.1007/978-3-030-85665-6_23

for all $k < \ell$, $i_k < i_{k+1}$ and $j_k < j_{k+1}$. A correspondence need not use all symbols of either string. We are given a non-negative scoring function $f : \Sigma \times \Sigma \to \mathbb{N}$ on pairs of symbols, and the goal is to find a correspondence (the WLCS) that maximizes the total weight $\sum_{k=1}^{\ell} f(x[i_k], y[j_k])$. We assume, consistent with actual bioinformatics practice [23], that the maximum weight σ returned by f for any pair of symbols is a small constant [10], so that the maximum possible weight for a correspondence between sequences is proportional to their length. WLCS is a special case of the weighted edit distance problem [14] in which match and mismatch costs are non-negative and insertion/deletion costs are zero. This problem is sufficient to model similarity scoring with a match bonus and mismatch and gap penalties, provided we can subsequently normalize alignment weights by the lengths of the two sequences [24]. If f scores +1 for matching symbol pairs and 0 for all others, the problem reduces to unweighted LCS.

A generalization of WLCS is the *all-substrings WLCS* or *AWLCS* problem. In this variant, the goal is to compute a matrix H such that $H[i, j]$ is the weight of a WLCS between the entire string x and substring $y[i..j]$. This "spectrum" of weights can be used to infer structure in strings, such as approximate tandem repeats and circular alignments [21]. Of course, H includes the weight of a WLCS between the full strings x and y as an entry.

Throughout the paper, we let $|x| = n$, $|y| = m$ and assume that $n \geq m$.

Sequential Methods. The WLCS problem, like the unweighted version, can be solved by dynamic programming in time $O(nm)$. In particular, the well-known Needleman-Wunsch algorithm [14] for weighted edit distance, which is the basis for many practical biosequence comparison tools [18–20,22], solves the WLCS problem as a special case. Sub-quadratic time algorithms are also known for the WLCS problem based on the "Four Russians" technique [13], which works for integer weights. In addition, there is the work of Crochemore et al. that works for unrestricted weights and also achieves sub-quadratic time [8]. At the same time, the sequential complexity of the LCS and WLCS problem is well understood - results in fine-grained complexity give strong lower bounds assuming the Strong Exponential Time Hypothesis [1,6,7].

Schmidt [21] showed that AWLCS, which naively requires much more computation than WLCS, can be solved in time $O(nm \log m)$ as a special case of all-substrings weighted edit distance. Alves et al. reduced this cost to $O(nm)$ for the special case of unweighted all-substrings LCS (ALCS) [4].

Parallel Methods. One way to solve large WLCS problems more efficiently is to parallelize their solution. Krusche and Tiskin [12] study parallelization of standard dynamic programming algorithms for LCS. However, the straightforward dynamic programming approaches for LCS and WLCS do not easily parallelize because they contain irreducible chains of dependent computations of length $\Theta(n+m)$. The fastest known parallel algorithms for these problems instead take a divide-and-conquer approach (such as [5]), combining the all-substrings generalization of LCS with methods based on max-plus matrix multiplication as we will describe.

Let x_1 and x_2 be two strings, and let H_1 and H_2 be AWLCS matrices on string pairs (x_1, y) and (x_2, y), respectively. Defining matrix multiplication over the ring $(\max, +)$, $H_1 \times H_2$ is the AWLCS matrix for strings $x_1 \cdot x_2$ and y [25]. Hence, we can compute the AWLCS matrix for the pair (x, y) on p processors by subdividing x into p pieces x_k, recursively computing matrices H_k for each x_k with y, and finally multiplying the H_k together. Given a base-case algorithm to compute AWLCS in time $B(m, n)$ and an algorithm to multiply two $m \times m$ AWLCS matrices in time $A(m)$, this approach will run in time $B(m, \frac{n}{p}) + A(m) \log p$.

Fast multiplication algorithms exist that exploit the *Monge property* of AWLCS matrices: for all $1 \leq i < k \leq m$ and $1 \leq j < \ell \leq n$, $H[i,j] + H[k,\ell] \leq H[i,\ell] + H[k,j]$. Tiskin [25] showed that for the special case of unweighted ALCS, $A(m) = O(m \log m)$, yielding an overall time of $O\left(\frac{mn}{p} + m \log m \log p\right)$. Leveraging related strategies yields other fast BSP algorithms for unweighted ALCS with improved per-processor memory and communication costs [3,11].

For AWLCS, $A(m) = O(m^2)$ using an iterated version of the SMAWK algorithm [2,17]. No faster multiplication algorithm is known for the general case. Practically subquadratic multiplication has been demonstrated for specific scoring functions f [17], but the performance of these approaches depend on f in a difficult-to-quantify manner. In [16] a complex divide-and-conquer strategy was used to achieve an optimal running time for the pairwise sequence alignment problem, which is similar but more general than our problem. In our work we use an alternative divide-and-conquer strategy to obtain a fast parallel algorithm.

Results. This paper introduces a new approach to parallelizing AWLCS and therefore WLCS. We introduce algorithms that are $(1 - \epsilon)$ approximate. Our algorithm's running time improves upon the best BSP algorithms for the problems and scales to $o(m^2)$ in the PRAM setting as the number of processors increases.

The new algorithm is our main contribution. Our algorithm sketches a sequential dynamic program and uses a divide-and-conquer strategy which can be parallelized. This sketch comes with a cost of approximating the objective to within a $1 - \epsilon$ factor for any parameter $\epsilon \in (0, 1)$. By relaxing the algorithm's optimality guarantee, we are able to obtain subquadratic-time subproblem composition by building on recent results on parallelizing dynamic programs for other problems [9]. Additionally, we develop and utilize a new base case algorithm for AWLCS that takes advantage of the small range of weights typically used [10]. The following theorem summarizes our main result.

Theorem 1. *Let W be the largest possible correspondence weight and let p be the number of processors. For any $\epsilon \in (0, 1)$, there is a BSP algorithm running in time $O(B(m, \frac{n}{p}) + m \frac{\log^2(W) \log^2(n) \log(p)}{\epsilon^2})$ and using $O(\frac{n}{p} + m \frac{\log^2(W) \log^2(n)}{\epsilon^2})$ local memory per processor that computes a $(1 - \epsilon)$-approximate solution to the WLCS problem.*

In the BSP model with p processors and using Schmidt's algorithm $(B(m,n) = mn \log m)$ for the base case, we obtain a parallel algorithm with running time $O\left(\frac{mn \log m}{p} + m\frac{\log^2 W \log^2 n}{\epsilon^2} \log p\right)$, where W is the largest possible correspondence weight between strings(which, by our assumption of bounded weights, is $O(\min(n,m))$). As mentioned, this is the first parallel algorithm for weighted LCS for which the running time scales as $o(m^2)$, and also the fastest $(1-\epsilon)$-approximation algorithm for weighted LCS in BSP. In contrast, previous methods' running times have a $\Theta(m^2)$ term that does not diminish as the number of processors p increases. Our method uses $O\left(\frac{n}{p} + m\frac{\log^2 \sigma m \log^2 n}{\epsilon^2}\right)$ local memory per processor, where σ is the highest weight produced by the scoring function.

Using Schmidt's algorithm for the base case dominates the running time. We would like to improve the $O(mn \log m)$ running time of the base case to get as close to $O(mn)$ as possible. We develop an interesting alternative base case algorithm by extending Alves's $O(mn)$ algorithm for ALCS [4] to the weighted case of AWLCS. This is our second major contribution. This algorithm, like our overall divide-and-conquer strategy, exploits the small range of weights typically used by scoring functions for DNA comparison.

Theorem 2. *Let σ be the highest weight produced by the scoring function f. There is a sequential algorithm running in time $O(\sigma nm)$ time for computing an implicit representation of the AWLCS matrix using space $O(\sigma m)$.*

Using this algorithm as the base case in Theorem 1, we achieve an overall running time of $O(\frac{\sigma mn}{p} + m\log^2(\sigma m)\log^2(n)\log(p)/\epsilon^2)$.

Algorithmic Techniques. The algorithms developed in this paper leverage two main techniques. The first is *parallelizing a natural dynamic program* for a problem via sketching. Let $C(i,j)$ be the weight of a WLCS between $x[1:n]$ and $y[i:j]$; we want to compute this quantity for all $1 \le i < j \le m$. One may add a third index to specify $C_k(i,j)$, the weight of a WLCS between $x[1:k]$ and $y[i:j]$. C_k can be computed via the following recurrence: $C_k(i,j) = \max\{C_{k-1}(i,j), C_k(i,j-1), C_{k-1}(i,j-1) + f(x[k],y[j])\}$. But this recurrence is both inefficient, requiring time $O(nm^2)$, and difficult to parallelize, with dependent computation chains of size $\Omega(n+m)$.

To improve efficiency, we abandon direct computation of $C(i,j)$ and instead compute some $D(i,w)$ which is subsequently be used to derive the entries of $C(i,j)$. $D(i,w)$ is the least index j s.t. there exists a correspondence of weight at least w between $y[i:j]$ and $x[1:n]$. We compute and store $D(i,w)$ only for values w that are powers of $1+\epsilon'$ for some fixed $\epsilon' > 0$. This sketched version of D effectively represents the $O(m^2)$ sized matrix C using $O(m\log_{1+\epsilon'} m\sigma)$ entries. Although our sketching strategy is not guaranteed to find the optimal values $C(i,j)$, we show that it exhibits bounded error as a function of ϵ'.

A straightforward computation of $D(i,w)$ entails long chains of serial dependencies. Thus, we use a divide-and-conquer approach instead. Let $D_{r_1,r_2}(i,w)$

store the the minimum index j s.t. a correspondence of weight at least w exists between $y[i : j]$ and $x[r_1 : r_2]$. We will show how to compute $D_{r_1,r_3}(i, w)$ given $D_{r_1,r_2}(i, w')$ and $D_{r_2+1,r_3}(i, w')$ for values $w' \leq w$. If we compute D matrices for non-overlapping substrings of x in parallel and double the range of x covered by each D matrix at each step, we can compute $D_{1,n}(i, w)$ in a logarithmic number of steps.

In realistic applications, we seek to compare sequences with millions of DNA bases; the number of available processors is small in comparison, that is, $p \ll \min(n, m)$. Speedup is therefore limited by the base-case work on each processor, which must sequentially solve an AWLCS problem of size roughly $m \times \frac{n}{p}$. Solving these problems using Schmidt's algorithm, which is insensitive to the magnitude of weights, takes time $O(\frac{n}{p}m \log m)$. However, Schmidt's algorithm involves building complex binary trees which proved to have high overhead in practice. Our second main technique is developing a weight-sensitive AWLCS algorithm utilizing an efficient and compact implicit representation.

We show that if the scoring function f assigns weights at most σ to symbol pairs, the matrix $C(i, j)$ can be represented implicitly using only $O(m\sigma)$ storage rather than $O(m^2)$. Moreover, we can compute this representation in sequential time $O(\frac{n}{p}m\sigma)$. The algorithm computes and stores values of the form $h_s(j)$, which is the least index i such that $C(i, j) \geq C(i, j-1) + s$, for $1 \leq s \leq \sigma$. These h values indicate where there is an increase of s in the optimal correspondence weight when the index j increases. The key to the technique is showing that these values contain information for reconstructing C and how to compute them efficiently without complex auxiliary data structures.

Roadmap. Section 3.1 presents the main dynamic program which can be parallelized via a divide-and-conquer strategy, while Sect. 3.2 shows how to use sketching to make this step time and space efficient while retaining $(1 - \epsilon)$-approximate solutions. Section 3.3 presents our new algorithm for AWLCS which we use as an efficient local base case algorithm on each processor. Finally, Sect. 4 completes our analysis.

2   Preliminaries

We denote by $x[i : j]$ the contiguous substring of x that starts at index i and ends at index j. The goal of AWLCS is to find correspondences of maximum weight between $x[1 : n]$ and $y[i : j]$ for all $1 \leq i \leq j \leq m$. We develop a method to obtain the *weights* of the desired correspondences; the alignments can be recovered later by augmenting the recurrence to permit traceback of an optimal solution. However, for AWLCS, the weights alone suffice for many applications [21]. Finally, we denote by W the highest possible weight of a WLCS between x and y, which we assume to be $O(\sigma \min(n, m))$. Here $\sigma = \max_{c,c' \in \Sigma} f(c, c')$ is the maximum possible weight of matching two characters. We note that in practice, σ is a constant and typically less than 20.

We now define two key matrices utilized in the design of our algorithms. $C(i, j)$ will denote the maximum weight of a correspondence between x and

$y[i : j]$. The AWLCS problem seeks to compute $C(i, j)$ for all $1 \leq i < j \leq m$. An alternative way to view these weights is via the matrix D, where we swap the entry stored in the matrix with one of the indices. Let $D(i, w) = \min\{j \mid C(i, j) \geq w\}$. If no such j exists, we define $D(i, w) = \infty$. D stores essentially the same information as C; a single entry of $C(i, j)$ can be queried via the matrix D in time $O(\log W)$ by performing a binary search over possible values of w. However, the matrix D will be a substantially more compact representation than C once we introduce our sketching strategy.

3 All-Substrings Weighted Longest Common Subsequence

Here we present our algorithm for AWLCS. Following the divide-and-conquer strategy of prior work, we initially divide the string x equally among the processors, each of which performs some local computation using a base-case algorithm to solve AWLCS between y and its portion of x, yielding a solution in the form of the D matrix defined above. We then combine pairs of subproblem solutions iteratively to arrive at a global solution. We first describe the algorithm's divide and combine steps while treating the base case as a black box, then discuss the base-case algorithm.

3.1 Divide-and-Conquer Strategy

Let D_{r_1,r_2} be the D matrix resulting from the AWLCS computation between strings $x[r_1 : r_2]$ and y. Our goal is to compute $D_{1,n}$, which encompasses all of x and y.

Our algorithm first divides x into p substrings of length $\frac{n}{p}$, each of which is given to one processor along with the entire string y. We assume that consecutive substrings of x are given to consecutive processors in some global linear processor ordering. If a processor is given a substring $x[r_1 : r_2]$, it computes the subproblem solution D_{r_1,r_2} using our new local, sequential base-case algorithm described in Sect. 3.3. It then remains to combine the p subproblem solutions to recover the desired solution $D_{1,n}$. We compute $D_{1,n}$ in $O(\log p)$ rounds. In the j'th round, the algorithm computes $O(2^{\log(p)/j})$ subproblem solutions, where each solution combines two sub-solutions from adjacent sets of 2^{j-1} consecutive processors.

Let D_{r_1,r_2} and D_{r_2+1,r_3} be adjacent sub-solutions obtained from previous iterations. We combine these solutions to obtain D_{r_1,r_3}. To compute $D_{r_1,r_3}(i, w)$, we consider all possible pairs w_1, w_2 for which $w = w_1 + w_2$. For each possible w_1, we use the solution of the first subproblem to find the least index j' for which there exists a correspondence of weight w_1 between $x[r_1 : r_2]$ and $y[i : j']$. We then use the solution of the second subproblem to find the least j such that a correspondence of weight $w_2 = w - w_1$ exists between $x[r_2 + 1 : r_3]$ and $y[j' + 1 : j]$. (Clearly, $j \geq j'$.) These two correspondences use non-overlapping substrings of x and y and can be combined feasibly. The exact procedure can be found in Algorithm 1.

Algorithm 1. Combining Subproblems

---

  procedure COMBINE($D_{r_1,r_2}, D_{r_2+1,r_3}$)
    for $i = 1$ **to** m **do**
      for $w = 0$ **to** W **do**
        $D_{r_1,r_3}(i, w) \leftarrow \infty$
        for $w_1 = 0$ **to** w **do**
          $w_2 \leftarrow w - w_1$
          $j' \leftarrow D_{r_1,r_2}(i, w_1)$
          $j \leftarrow D_{r_2+1,r_3}(j' + 1, w_2)$
          $D_{r_1,r_3}(i, w) = \min(D_{r_1,r_3}(i, w), j)$

3.2   Approximation via Sketching

Algorithm 1 solves the AWLCS problem exactly; the cost to combine two sub-problems is $O(mW^2)$. For unweighted ALCS, $W = m$; the combine step is $O(m^3)$. To overcome this cost, we *sketch* the values of w. Sketching reduces the number of distinct weights considered from W to $O(\log W)$ and hence reduces the cost to combine two subproblems from $O(mW^2)$ to $O(m \log^2 W)$. We analyze its precise impact on solution quality and overall running time in Sect. 4.

Our sketching strategy fixes a constant $\epsilon > 0$ and sets $\beta = 1 + \frac{\epsilon}{\log n}$. Define $D^*(i, s)$ to be the least j such that there exists a correspondence between x and $y[i : j]$ with weight $w \geq \lfloor \beta^s \rfloor$. Define $D^*_{r_1,r_2}$ analogously to D_{r_1,r_2} for substrings of x. To compute $D^*_{r_1,r_3}$ from $D^*_{r_1,r_2}$ and $D^*_{r_2+1,r_3}$, we modify the algorithm described above as follows. For each power s s.t. $\lfloor \beta^s \rfloor \leq W$, we consider each power $s_1 \leq s$ and compute the least s_2 such that $\lfloor \beta^{s_1} \rfloor + \lfloor \beta^{s_2} \rfloor \geq \lfloor \beta^s \rfloor$. Let $j' = D^*_{r_1,r_2}(i, s_1)$ and $j = D^*_{r_2+1,r_3}(j' + 1, s_2)$. Then there exist non-overlapping correspondences with weights at least β^{s_1} and β^{s_2}, and hence a combined correspondence of weight at least β^s, between $x[r_1 : r_3]$ and $y[i : j]$. We take $D^*_{r_1,r_3}(i, s)$ to be the least j' that results from this procedure. In Sect. 4, we formally show that this sketching strategy preserves $(1 - \epsilon)$-approximate solutions and analyze the runtime and space usage of our algorithm.

3.3   Base Case Local Algorithm

We now describe a sequential algorithm, inspired by the work of [3], to obtain the initial matrices $D_{r_1,r_2}(i, w)$ for each individual processor.

In theory, one could continue the divide and conquer approach on each local machine until the entry to compute is of the form $D_{r_1,r_1+1}(i, w)$, yielding a simple base case to solve. However, this procedure proves computationally inefficient with a fixed number p of processors. Instead, we propose a different base case algorithm for computing $D_{r_1,r_2}(i, w)$ which better fits our setting.

For this section, we will drop the indices r_1 and r_2 and create an algorithm for computing D for strings x and y. Each processor applies this same algorithm, but to different substrings $x[r_1 : r_2]$.

The algorithm works in two steps. First, we calculate two sequences of indices, referred to as the h- and v-indices. Then, we use these indices to compute $D(i, w)$ for all desired i, w. Intuitively, these indices give compact information about the structure of the C matrix (and hence the D matrix), specifically the magnitude of change between weights in adjacent rows and columns of C.

Definition of the Indices. Recall the definition of the AWLCS matrix C, and let C^ℓ be the C matrix corresponding to the strings $x[1 : \ell]$ and y. Before proceeding with the definition of the h- and v-indices, we note a lemma concerning the *Monge* properties of C^ℓ. These properties are well-known; see, e.g., [3].

Lemma 1. *For any triple of indices* i, j, ℓ, $C^\ell(i - 1, j - 1) + C^\ell(i, j) \geq C^\ell(i - 1, j) + C^\ell(i, j - 1)$, *and* $C^\ell(i - 1, j) + C^{\ell-1}(i, j) \geq C^{\ell-1}(i - 1, j) + C^\ell(i, j)$.

The following corollaries result from rearranging terms in the previous lemma.

Corollary 1. *For any* i, j, ℓ, $C^\ell(i, j) - C^\ell(i, j - 1) \geq C^\ell(i - 1, j) - C^\ell(i - 1, j - 1)$.

Corollary 2. *For any* i, j, ℓ, $C^\ell(i, j) - C^{\ell-1}(i, j) \leq C^\ell(i - 1, j) - C^{\ell-1}(i - 1, j)$.

We now consider the implications of Corollary 1. Fix i, j and ℓ with $C^\ell(i, j) - C^\ell(i, j - 1) = s$ for some s. This s is the difference in WLCS weight if the second string is allowed one extra character at its end ($y[j]$), since it is comparing $x[1 : \ell]$ with either $y[i : j]$ or $y[i : j - 1]$. The corollary states that this difference is only greater for a substring of y that starts at $i' > i$ instead of i. Therefore, for each pair of fixed j, ℓ, there exists some minimal i such that $C^\ell(i, j) - C^\ell(i, j - 1)$ is *first* greater than s, as it will be true for all $i' > i$. For different values of s, there are possibly different corresponding i which are minimal. Similar implications can be derived from Corollary 2.

Using this insight, we can define the h-indices and v-indices. These values $h_1, \dots, h_\sigma$ and $v_1, \dots, v_\sigma$ are the key to our improved base case algorithm. For $s \in [\sigma]$, $h_s(\ell, j)$ is the smallest index i such that $C^\ell(i, j) \geq C^\ell(i, j - 1) + s$. That is, each $h_s(\ell, j)$ for a fixed ℓ and j marks the row of C^ℓ where we start to get a horizontal increment of s between columns $j - 1$ and j. The v-indices are slightly different; $v_s(\ell, j)$ is the smallest index i such that $C^\ell(i, j) < C^{\ell-1}(i, j) + s$. The v-indices mark the row where we stop getting a vertical increment of s in column j between $C^{\ell-1}$ and C^ℓ. The entire matrix C^ℓ can be computed recursively as a function of the indices as follows:

$$
C^\ell(i, j) = \begin{cases} C^\ell(i, j - 1) & i < h_1(\ell, j) \\ C^\ell(i, j - 1) + s & h_s(\ell, j) \leq i < h_{s+1}(l, j) \\ C^\ell(i, j - 1) + \sigma & h_\sigma(\ell, j) \leq i \end{cases} \tag{1}
$$

$$
C^\ell(i, j) = \begin{cases} C^{\ell-1}(i, j) + \sigma & i < v_\sigma(\ell, j) \\ C^{\ell-1}(i, j) + s & v_{s+1}(\ell, j) \leq i < v_s(l, j) \\ C^{\ell-1}(i, j) & v_1(\ell, j) \leq i \end{cases} \tag{2}
$$

The h and v-indices provide an efficient way to compute the entries in $D(i, w)$. If we can compute $C^\ell(i, j)$ for all i, j, then $D(i, w)$ is the smallest j for which $C^\ell(i, j) \geq w$. The indices actually correspond to a recursive definition of the values of $C^\ell(i, j)$.

The following intuition may help to interpret the h-indices. consider $h_1(\ell, j)$ for a fixed ℓ and j. This is the smallest value of i for which $C^\ell(i, j)$ exceeds $C^\ell(i, j-1)$ by at least 1. Suppose we compare the best WLCS of x and $y[i : j-1]$ against that of x and $y[i : j]$. There is a gain of one character (the last one) in the second pair of strings, so the second WLCS might have more weight. There is a unique value $h_1(\ell, j)$ of i for which the difference in weight first becomes ≥ 1. The uniqueness of this value can be inferred from Corollary 1.

The increment in the WLCS weight due to adding $y[j]$ may become greater as i increases, i.e., as we allow fewer opportunities to match x to earlier characters in y. However, the increment cannot exceed σ, the greatest possible weight under f of a match to $y[j]$. Note that if $h_s(\ell, j) \geq j$, there is no index fulfilling the condition since the substring $y[h_s(\ell, j) : j]$ has no characters.

Given the h-indices for every ℓ, j, we may compute $C^\ell(i, j)$ for any fixed ℓ as follows. $C^\ell(i, i) = 0$ by definition, and $C^\ell(i, j+1)$ can be computed from $C^\ell(i, j)$ by comparing i against each possible $h_s(\ell, i+1)$. One may then compute $D(i, w)$ from $C^n(i, j)$. However, one may directly compute D from the h-indices more efficiently using an approach described in Sect. 3.3.

The v-indices can be interpreted similarly, though the ordering of $v_1 \ldots v_\sigma$ is reversed. Consider $v_\sigma(\ell, j)$ for some fixed ℓ and j. This is the smallest value of i for which $C^\ell(i, j)$ does *not* exceed $C^{\ell-1}(i, j)$ by at least σ. Here, the comparison is between the WLCS of $x[1 : l]$ and $y[i : j]$ and that of $x[1 : l-1]$ and $y[i : j]$. The first WLCS might have more weight, and so there is unique index where the difference in weight first becomes less than σ. In this case, due to Corollary 2, the difference between $C^\ell(i, j)$ and $C^{\ell-1}(i, j)$ can only be less than the difference between $C^\ell(i-1, j)$ and $C^{\ell-1}(i-1, j)$. Now $v_\sigma(\ell, j)$ is the unique value of i after which the difference can be no more than $\sigma - 1$. Similar intuition applies to all the other v-indices.

We note that the v-indices are not explicitly involved in the procedure for computing entries of D; however, they are necessary in computing the h-indices.

Recursive Computation of the Indices. We now show how to compute the h-indices $h_s(\ell, j)$ for all ℓ, j. We first show a general recursive formula for these indices, then show a more efficient strategy to compute them.

In the formula, h_s will always refer to $h_s(\ell-1, j)$ unless indices are specified. Similarly, v_s will always refer to $v_s(\ell, j-1)$ unless indices are specified.

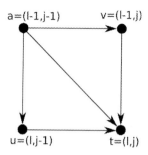

Fig. 1. Relationship between four points.

Let $d = f(x_\ell, y_j)$, where f is the scoring function. For the general case $\ell, j > 0$:

$$h_s(\ell, j) = \begin{cases} \text{if } d < s: \min\limits_{z \in [s,\sigma]} \left(\max(h_z, v_{z-(s-1)}) \right) \\ \text{if } d \geq s: \\ \min \left(\min\limits_{z \in [d+1,\sigma]} \left(\max(h_z, v_{z-(s-1)}) \right), v_{d-(s-1)} \right) \end{cases} \quad (3)$$

$$v_s(\ell, j) = \begin{cases} \text{if } d < s: \max\limits_{z \in [s,\sigma]} \left(\min(h_{z-(s-1)}, v_z) \right) \\ \text{if } d \geq s: \\ \max \left(\max\limits_{z \in [d+1,\sigma]} \left(\min(h_{z-(s-1)}, v_z) \right), h_{d-(s-1)} \right) \end{cases} \quad (4)$$

The base cases are $h_s(0, j) = j$ and $v_s(\ell, 0) = 0$ for all s. The first corresponds to an empty substring of x, which has an empty WLCS with any substring of y. The second corresponds to an empty substring of y, which has an empty WLCS with any substring of x. Recurrences (3) and (4) generalize the recurrences for h and v for unweighted LCS in [3], which can be recovered as a special case of our recurrence for $\sigma = 1$.

We now describe the calculations for these indices, beginning with the $h_s(\ell, j)$ calculations. To calculate $h_s(\ell, j)$, we use the entries $v_s(\ell, j - 1)$ and $h_s(\ell - 1, j)$ (for all possible s) in addition to the value of d. It is useful to visualize the situation using Fig. 1. In the figure, a represents the weight of the WLCS between $x[1 : l - 1]$ and $y[i : j - 1]$ for some i. Similarly, u represents the weight of the WLCS between $x[1 : l]$ and $y[i : j - 1]$, and v is the WLCS between $x[1 : l - 1]$ and $y[i : j]$. Finally, t represents the WLCS between $x[1 : l]$ and $y[i : j]$. The edges represent the relationship between the WLCS weights. First, u and v are both at least a. Further, one possible value for t could be $a + d$, since one may take the WLCS which corresponds to a and add in the match between $x[l]$ and $y[j]$, which has weight d. Alternatively, t could also be the same value as either u or v. If $t = u$, then $y[j]$ is unused in the WLCS; similarly, if $t = v$, the character $x[l]$ is unused.

The value of $h_s(\ell, j)$ has a natural interpretation: it is the first value of i for which the difference between t and u is at least s. Recall h_s will always refer to $h_s(\ell - 1, j)$ unless indices are specified; similarly, v_s will always refer to $v_s(\ell, j - 1)$ unless indices are specified. Thus, h_s is exactly the minimum i where there is a difference of at least s between v and a. Similarly, v_s is the minimum i where there is a difference less than s between u and a. We will relate t and u by comparing both to a. Then we can determine the correct $h_s(\ell, j)$ where $t \geq u + s$ for any $i \geq h_s(\ell, j)$.

Suppose we seek to calculate $h_s(\ell, j)$ for a fixed $s > d$. One possible weight for t is $a + d$, but this edge cannot determine h_s as $u \geq a$, and hence $a + d$ is not greater than u by at least s. The WLCS which involves a never yields any information about the minimum i where $t \geq u + s$. However, consider an i such that $i \geq h_s(\ell - 1, j)$. The edge weight t can have value $a + s$. In this case, if $i \geq v_1(\ell, j - 1)$, then we know that $u = a$ and hence $t \geq u + s$. Therefore, if i is greater than both h_s and v_1, then the difference between t and u is at least s. Hence, it would seem that $h_s(\ell, j)$ is just equal to $\max(h_s, v_1)$. However, there are many other *pairs* which also fulfill this condition, e.g. if i is greater than both h_{s+1} and v_2. In general, if i is greater than any h_x and $v_{x-(s-1)}$ for some positive integer $\sigma \geq x > s$, then the difference between t and u is at least s. Therefore, in the case where $s > d$ the expression for $h_s(\ell, j)$ is the minimum of the pairwise maximum of such pairs. This is formalized in Eq. (3).

The other case is when we seek to compute h_s for a fixed $s \leq d$. Here, the weight $a + d$ is always possible for t. The expression in Eq. (3) is essentially a truncated version of the expression for $s > d$. Namely, we need not consider the pairs involving h_s where $s \leq d$. (If $i \geq v_{d-(s-1)}$ then immediately we already know that $t \geq u + s$ regardless of whether i is also greater than some h value.)

The $v_s(\ell, j)$ computations are similar. We are interested in the difference between t and v, so we will relate both t and v to a. First, consider computing $v_s(\ell, j)$ where $s > d$. In this case we can again ignore the case where $t = a + d$. Recall that $v_s(\ell, j)$ defines the value of i where if $i > v_s(\ell, j)$, then the $t < v + s$. Consider the case where only a single important pair of values exist, h_1 and v_s. If i is greater than v_s then $t = u < a + s$. A similar property holds if $i > h_1$. Hence, $v_s(\ell, j)$ is the value of the minimum of v_s and h_1 if that is the only pair. Once again, when there are multiple pairs of v_s, h_1 and v_{s+1}, h_2 and so on, the expression becomes more complex as it becomes the maximum of the minima of these pairs.

The case for computing $v_s(\ell, j)$ when $s \leq d$ is similar to the case for the $h_s(\ell, j)$ computations in Eq. (3) except where the formula is truncated; no pairs which involve v_s for $s \leq d$ are used. Since a weight of $a + d$ can always be attained, only $h_{d-(s-1)}$ needs to be checked for any of the lesser v_s pairs.

Equations (3) and (4) give a recursive computation for all of the h-indices and v-indices. There are $O(mn\sigma)$ total entries to compute, and following the two equations above yield a $O(mn\sigma^2)$ time algorithm for computing the h- and v-indices. However, using a clever observation, it is possible to compute these entries in $O(mn\sigma)$ time, which we show next.

Faster Computation of h- and v-Indices. Naively computing the recurrences 3 and 4 for each $1 \leq s \leq \sigma$ takes $O(\sigma^2)$ time. We show how to improve this to $O(\sigma)$ now.

We start with the following definitions. For $1 \leq s \leq \sigma$ define $z^*(s)$ to be the value such that the following holds: (1) $z < z^*(s) \implies v_{z-s+1} > h_z$ and (2) $z \geq z^*(s) \implies v_{z-s+1} \leq h_z$. Similarly, define $z^\#(s)$ to be the value such that (1) $z < z^\#(s) \implies h_{z-s+1} < v_z$ and (2) $z \geq z^\#(s) \implies h_{z-s+1} \geq v_z$. These values are well defined since the sequences h and v are respectively non-decreasing and non-increasing, so either the inequalities above trivially hold, or there is a point where the sequences cross. The existence of a crossing point is not affected by applying an offset to one of the sequences. We will simultaneously compute $z^*(s)$ and $z^\#(s)$ while computing new values of h_s and v_s.

To see why the above definitions are useful, consider substituting them into (3) and (4). First, consider the calculation of h_s when $d < s$:

$$h_s(\ell, j) = \min_{z=s}^{\sigma} \left(\max(h_z, v_{z-s+1}) \right)$$

$$= \min \left(\min_{z<z^*(s)} \max \left(h_z, v_{z-s+1} \right), \ \min_{z \geq z^*(s)} \max \left(h_z, v_{z-s+1} \right) \right)$$

$$= \min \left(\min_{z<z^*(s)} v_{z-s+1}, \ \min_{z \geq z^*(s)} h_z \right) = \min \left(v_{z^*(s)-s}, h_{z^*(s)} \right)$$

where we again use the property that h and v are respectively non-decreasing and non-increasing. Similar calculations can be done with $z^\#(s)$ for computing $v_s(\ell, j)$ and for the case when $d \geq s$. This shows that given $z^*(s)$ and $z^\#(s)$, it is possible to compute $h_s(\ell, j)$ and $v_s(\ell, j)$ in constant time.

The only remaining task is to compute $z^*(s)$ and $z^\#(s)$ for each weight s. This can be done by sweeping through h and v in $O(\sigma)$ time. We may then compute $h_s(\ell, j)$ and $v_s(\ell, j)$ for each s in $O(\sigma)$ time.

Computing the D Matrix. We now show how to compute the entries $D(i, w)$ directly from the h-indices. The computation requires only the indices $h_s(n, j)$; in this section, we drop the n and refer to these indices simply as $h_s(j)$. We compute the entries of $D(i, w)$ row by row, iterating through one value of i at a time. At each iteration, we will keep T, a data structure storing pairs of the form $(j, h_s(j))$. During iteration i, we may insert pairs into T or delete pairs from T, maintaining the following invariant:

$$(j, h_s(j)) \in T \iff j > i \text{ and } h_s(j) \leq i. \tag{5}$$

The invariant guarantees two useful properties. First, all pairs in T have $h_s(j) \leq i$, the existence of such a pair in T means that the difference between $C(i, j)$ and $C(i, j-1)$ is s. Note that if $(j, h_s(j)) \in T$, then clearly $(j, h_{s'}(j)) \in T$ for all $s' < s$ since $h_{s'}(j) \leq h_s(j)$. Thus, one can think of each pair in T as representing an increase of 1.

Algorithm 2. Construct D matrix using the h-indices

$T \leftarrow \emptyset$
$j \leftarrow 1,\ s \leftarrow 1$
for $i = 1, \ldots, m$ **do**
    while $h_s(j) \leq i$ **do**
        if $j > i$ **then**   ▷ Insert pairs w/ $j > i$.
            $T.\text{insert}((j, s, h_s(j)))$
        end if
        $s \leftarrow s + 1$
        if $s > \sigma$ **then**
            $s \leftarrow 1$
            $j \leftarrow j + 1$
        end if
        for $k \in K$ **do**   ▷ Compute $D(i, k)\ \forall k$
            $(j', s', h') \leftarrow T.\text{search\_by\_rank}(k)$
            $D(i, k) = j'$
    Remove from T all (j, s, h) where $j = i$

Second, if the pairs in T are sorted increasingly by j, then $D(i, k)$ is exactly the j_k which corresponds to the pair of rank k within T. This can be shown as follows: Let $j_1, j_2, \ldots j_k$ denote the pairs of rank 1 through k (represented by say $(j_k, h_s(j_k))$ within T. Each fixed j_x among these means that there is a difference of 1 between $C(i, j_x - 1)$ and $C(i, j_x)$. There are k pairs here, each denoting a difference of 1 between some $C(i, j_x)$ and $C(i, j_x - 1)$ and there are a total of k such differences. Note by the invariant, $j_1 > i$. Furthermore, clearly $j_1 \leq j_k$. Thus, between $C(i, i)$ and $C(i, j_k)$ there are a total of k differences of 1 each. Since $C(i, i) = 0$ the difference between $C(i, i)$ and $C(i, j_k)$ is exactly k. Hence, j_k is exactly the value of $D(i, k)$.

This analysis yields Algorithm 2, where T is a balanced tree data structure.

4   Analysis of Approximation and Runtime

We now formally describe the sketching strategy for the D matrix and prove the claims about the performance of Algorithm 1 under our sketching procedure.

Recall that our sketching strategy fixes a constant $\epsilon > 0$ and sets $\beta = 1 + \frac{\epsilon}{\log n}$. Define $D^*(i, s)$ to be the least j such that there exists a correspondence between x and $y[i : j]$ with weight $w \geq \lfloor \beta^s \rfloor$. Define $D^*_{r_1, r_2}$ analogously to D_{r_1, r_2} for substrings of x. To compute $D^*_{r_1, r_3}$ from $D^*_{r_1, r_2}$ and $D^*_{r_2+1, r_3}$, we modify Algorithm 1 as follows. For each power s s.t. $\lfloor \beta^s \rfloor \leq W$, we consider each power $s_1 \leq s$ and compute the least s_2 such that $\lfloor \beta^{s_1} \rfloor + \lfloor \beta^{s_2} \rfloor \geq \lfloor \beta^s \rfloor$. Let $j' = D^*_{r_1, r_2}(i, s_1)$ and $j = D^*_{r_2+1, r_3}(j' + 1, s_2)$. Then there exist non-overlapping correspondences of weights at least β^{s_1} and β^{s_2}, and hence a combined correspondence of weight at least β^s, between $x[r_1 : r_3]$ and $y[i : j]$. We take $D^*_{r_1, r_3}(i, s)$ to be the least j' that results from this procedure.

4.1   Quality of the Solution

In Sect. 3.2, we showed how to reduce the space and time requirement of computing the D matrix using Algorithm 1 via sketching. We consider only weights of the form $\lfloor \beta^s \rfloor$ for $\beta = 1 + \epsilon/\log n$ and so will not obtain the exact optimum. However, we show that we can recover a $(1 - \epsilon)$ approximation to the optimum.

Computationally, we only need to construct the matrix D^* in order to extract solutions to the AWLCS and WLCS problems. However, for analysis purposes it is useful to define C^*, an approximate version of the matrix C. Let $C_{r_1,r_2}(i,j)$ be the optimal weight of a WLCS between $x[r_1 : r_2]$ and $y[i : j]$. Equivalently, we have $C_{r_1,r_2}(i,j) = \max\{w \mid D_{r_1,r_2}(i,w) \leq j\}$. This motivates defining C^* as follows. Let $C^*_{r_1,r_2}(i,j) = \max_s\{\lfloor \beta^s \rfloor \mid D^*_{r_1,r_2}(i,s) \leq j\}$.

We prove the following lemma which shows that the C^* matrices approximate the C matrices well, and hence the matrices D^* implicitly encode good solutions.

Lemma 2. *Let $x[r_1, r_2]$ be a substring of x considered by our algorithm in some step. Then for all i, j we have*

$$C^*_{r_1,r_2}(i,j) \geq (1 - \epsilon)\, C_{r_1,r_2}(i,j)$$

Proof. We prove the following stronger claim by induction. Let ℓ be the level at which we combined substrings to arrive at $x[r_1 : r_2]$ in our algorithm. Then for all i, j we have

$$C^*_{r_1,r_2}(i,j) \geq \left(1 - \frac{\epsilon}{\log n}\right)^{\ell} C_{r_1,r_2}(i,j)$$

In particular this implies the lemma since we can use the inequality $(1 - z)^{\ell} \geq 1 - \ell z$ for all $z \leq 1$ and $\ell \geq 0$.

$$C^*_{r_1,r_2}(i,j) \geq \left(1 - \frac{\epsilon}{\log n}\right)^{\ell} C_{r_1,r_2}(i,j)$$
$$\geq \left(1 - \frac{\epsilon\ell}{\log n}\right) C_{r_1,r_2}(i,j) \geq (1 - \epsilon) C_{r_1,r_2}(i,j)$$

Now to prove the claim by induction on the levels ℓ. Fix a pair of indices i, j in y. If $x[r_1, r_2]$ was considered at the first level, then we computed the exact matrix D_{r_1,r_2} using our base case algorithm, so the base case follows trivially. Now suppose that we considered $x[r_1, r_2]$ at some level ℓ after the first. Our algorithm combines the subproblems corresponding to $x[r_1, r']$ and $x[r' + 1, r_2]$ that occur at level $\ell - 1$. where $r' = \lfloor (r_1 + r_2)/2 \rfloor$. To compute the solution for r_1, r_2 and i, j we concatenate solutions corresponding to $x[r_1, r']$ and $y[i : j']$ and $x[r' + 1, r_2]$ and $y[j' + 1 : j]$, for some j'. We get the sum of their weights, but rounded down due to sketching. Thus we have:

$$C^*_{r_1,r_2}(i,j) \geq \frac{C^*_{r_1,r'}(i,j') + C^*_{r'+1,r_2}(j',j)}{(1 + \epsilon/\log n)}. \tag{6}$$

Now $C_{r_1,r_2}(i,j) = C_{r_1,r'}(i,j'') + C_{r'+1,r_2}(j''+1,j)$ for some j'', since the solution corresponding to $C_{r_1,r_2}(i,j)$ can be written as the concatenation of two sub-solutions between $x[r_1 : r']$, $y[i : j'']$ and $x[r'+1 : r_2]$, $y[j''+1 : j]$. Note that our algorithm chooses j' such that $C^*_{r_1,r'}(i,j') + C^*_{r'+1,r_2}(j',j) \geq C^*_{r_1,r'}(i,j'') + C^*_{r'+1,r_2}(j''+1,j)$. Now applying the induction hypothesis to $C^*_{r_1,r'}(i,j'')$ and $C^*_{r'+1,r_2}(j''+1,j)$ we have:

$$C^*_{r_1,r'}(i,j') + C^*_{r'+1,r_2}(j',j) \geq C^*_{r_1,r'}(i,j'') + C^*_{r'+1,r_2}(j''+1,j)$$

$$\geq \left(1 - \frac{\epsilon}{\log n}\right)^{\ell-1} \left(C_{r_1,r'}(i,j'') + C_{r'+1,r_2}(j''+1,j)\right)$$

$$= \left(1 - \frac{\epsilon}{\log n}\right)^{\ell-1} C_{r_1,r_2}(i,j)$$

Now combining this with (6) we have:

$$C^*_{r_1,r_2}(i,j) \geq \frac{\left(1 - \frac{\epsilon}{\log n}\right)^{\ell-1} C_{r_1,r_2}(i,j)}{1 + \frac{\epsilon}{\log n}} \geq \left(1 - \frac{\epsilon}{\log n}\right)^{\ell} C_{r_1,r_2}(i,j),$$

which completes the proof of the general case.

4.2   Running Time

We now analyze the running time of our algorithm, starting with the combining procedure in Algorithm 1.

Lemma 3. *Let* $n' = r_3 - r_1 + 1$ *be the number of characters of the string* x *assigned to one call to Algorithm 1. Let* $\epsilon' = \epsilon/2\log(n)$ *and* $t = \log_{1+\epsilon'}(\sigma \min(n', m))$. *Then the procedure described in Algorithm 1 uses* $O(mt)$ *space and runs in* $O(mt^2)$ *time.*

Proof. First note that $\sigma \min(n', m)$ is an upper bound on the maximum weight for the instance passed to Algorithm 1. The matrix D contains an entry for each pair of starting indices and each weight. There are m starting indices. To prove the space bound, it suffices to show that the number of possible weights is $O(t)$. Recall that sketching the weights yields an entry for each weight of the form $(1 + \epsilon/2\log_2 n)^{\ell} = (1 + \epsilon')^{\ell}$ for integer ℓ, up to some upper bound on the weight. Hence, taking t as in the statement of the lemma implies that $(1 + \epsilon')^t \geq \sigma \min(n', m)$, so $O(t)$ different weights suffices.

The bound on the running time follows by noting that each of the $O(m)$ iterations of the algorithm iterates through all pairs of weights, yielding total time $O(mt^2)$.

$O(\log(p))$ rounds of combining are required to merge the p base-case results into the final D matrix, since each round reduces the number of remaining sub-problems by half. To analyze the entire algorithm, we separately consider the two steps.

Lemma 4. *Let $B(m, n)$ be the running time of a base-case algorithm computing D. Then our algorithm runs in time $B(m, n/p) + O(m \log_{1+\epsilon'}^2 (\sigma m) \log(p))$ on p processors.*

Proof. The base case algorithm is run on subproblems of size $n/p \times m$. Each of the $O(\log(p))$ rounds of merging has cost $O(m \log_{1+\epsilon'}^2 (\sigma m))$ by the previous lemma.

Finally, since $\log_{1+\epsilon'}(\sigma m) = O(\log(\sigma m)/\epsilon') = O(\log_2(n) \log(\sigma m)/\epsilon)$, our algorithm achieves the claimed runtime and local memory per processor.

References

1. Abboud, A., Backurs, A., Williams, V.V.: Quadratic-time hardness of LCS and other sequence similarity measures. CoRR abs/1501.07053 (2015). http://arxiv.org/abs/1501.07053
2. Aggarwal, A., Klawe, M., Moran, S., Shor, P., Wilber, R.: Geometric applications of a matrix-searching algorithm. Algorithmica **2**, 195–208 (1987)
3. Alves, C., Cáceres, E., Song, S.: A coarse-grained parallel algorithm for the all-substrings longest common subsequence problem. Algorithmica **45**, 301–335 (2006). https://doi.org/10.1007/s00453-006-1216-z
4. Alves, C., Cáceres, E., Song, S.: An all-substrings common subsequence algorithm. Discrete Appl. Math. **156**(7), 1025–1035 (2008). https://doi.org/10.1016/j.dam.2007.05.056. http://www.sciencedirect.com/science/article/pii/S0166218X07002727
5. Apostolico, A., Atallah, M.J., Larmore, L.L., McFaddin, S.: Efficient parallel algorithms for string editing and related problems. SIAM J. Comput. **19**(5), 968–988 (1990). https://doi.org/10.1137/0219066
6. Bringmann, K., Chaudhury, B.R.: Sketching, streaming, and fine-grained complexity of (weighted) LCS. In: 38th IARCS Annual Conference on Foundations of Software Technology and Theoretical Computer Science, FSTTCS 2018, Ahmedabad, India, 11–13 December 2018, pp. 40:1–40:16 (2018). https://doi.org/10.4230/LIPIcs.FSTTCS.2018.40
7. Bringmann, K., Künnemann, M.: Multivariate fine-grained complexity of longest common subsequence. In: Proceedings of the 29th Annual ACM-SIAM Symposium on Discrete Algorithms, SODA 2018, New Orleans, LA, USA, 7–10 January 2018, pp. 1216–1235 (2018). https://doi.org/10.1137/1.9781611975031.79
8. Crochemore, M.M., Landau, G., Ziv-Ukelson, M.: A subquadratic sequence alignment algorithm for unrestricted scoring matrices. SIAM J. Comput. **32**, 1654–1673 (2003). https://doi.org/10.1137/S0097539702402007
9. Im, S., Moseley, B., Sun, X.: Efficient massively parallel methods for dynamic programming. In: Proceedings of the 49th Annual ACM SIGACT Symposium on Theory of Computing (STOC), Montreal, Canada, pp. 798–811 (2017)
10. Jones, N.: An Introduction to Bioinformatics Algorithms. MIT Press, Cambridge (2004)
11. Krusche, P., Tiskin, A.: New algorithms for efficient parallel string comparison. In: Proceedings of the 22nd Annual ACM Symposium on Parallelism in Algorithms and Architectures (SPAA), Thira, Santorini, Greece, pp. 209–216 (2010)

12. Krusche, P., Tiskin, A.: Efficient longest common subsequence computation using bulk-synchronous parallelism. In: International Conference on Computational Science and its Applications (Proceedings, Part V), ICCSA 2006, Glasgow, UK, 8–11 May 2006, pp. 165–174 (2006). https://doi.org/10.1007/11751649_18

13. Masek, W.J., Paterson, M.: A faster algorithm computing string edit distances. J. Comput. Syst. Sci. **20**(1), 18–31 (1980). https://doi.org/10.1016/0022-0000(80)90002-1

14. Needleman, S., Wunsch, C.: A general method applicable to the search for similarities in the amino acid sequence of two proteins. J. Mol. Biol. **48**, 443–453 (1970)

15. Program, N.G.S.: DNA sequencing costs: Data (2017). https://www.genome.gov/sequencingcostsdata/

16. Rajko, S., Aluru, S.: Space and time optimal parallel sequence alignments. IEEE Trans. Parallel Distrib. Syst. **15**(12), 1070–1081 (2004). https://doi.org/10.1109/TPDS.2004.86

17. Russo, L.: Monge properties of sequence alignment. Theor. Comput. Sci. **423**, 30–49 (2012). https://doi.org/10.1016/j.tcs.2011.12.068

18. http://jaligner.sourceforge.net/

19. https://github.com/mengyao/Complete-Striped-Smith-Waterman-Library

20. https://github.com/Martinsos/opal

21. Schmidt, J.: All highest scoring paths in weighted graphs and their applications to finding all approximate repeats in strings. SIAM J. Comput. **27**, 972–992 (1998)

22. Smith, T., Waterman, M.: Identification of common molecular subsequences. J. Mol. Biol. **147**(1), 195–197 (1981)

23. States, D., Gish, W., Altschul, S.: Improved sensitivity of nucleic acid database searches using application-specific scoring matrices. METHODS Companion Meth. Enzymol. **3**, 66–70 (1991)

24. Tiskin, A.: Semi-local string comparison: algorithmic techniques and applications, ch 6.1 (2013). https://arxiv.org/abs/0707.3619, v21

25. Tiskin, A.: Fast distance multiplication of unit-monge matrices. Algorithmica **71**(4), 859–888 (2015). https://doi.org/10.1007/s00453-013-9830-z

TSLQueue: An Efficient Lock-Free Design for Priority Queues

Adones Rukundo[✉] and Philippas Tsigas

Chalmers University of Technology,
Gothenburg, Sweden
{adones,tsigas}@chalmers.se

Abstract. Priority queues are fundamental abstract data types, often used to manage limited resources in parallel systems. Typical proposed parallel priority queue implementations are based on heaps or skip lists. In recent literature, skip lists have been shown to be the most efficient design choice for implementing priority queues. Though numerous intricate implementations of skip list based queues have been proposed in the literature, their performance is constrained by the high number of global atomic updates per operation and the high memory consumption, which are proportional to the number of sub-lists in the queue.

In this paper, we propose an alternative approach for designing lock-free linearizable priority queues, that significantly improves memory efficiency and throughput performance, by reducing the number of global atomic updates and memory consumption as compared to skip-list based queues. To achieve this, our new design combines two structures; a search tree and a linked list, forming what we call a Tree Search List Queue (*TSLQueue*). The leaves of the tree are linked together to form a linked list of leaves with a head as an access point. Analytically, a skip-list based queue insert or delete operation has at worst case $O(\log n)$ global atomic updates, where n is the size of the queue. While the *TSLQueue* insert or delete operations require only 2 or 3 global atomic updates respectively. When it comes to memory consumption, *TSLQueue* exhibits $O(n)$ memory consumption, compared to $O(n \log n)$ worst case for a skip-list based queue, making the *TSLQueue* more memory efficient than a skip-list based queue of the same size. We experimentally show, that *TSLQueue* significantly outperforms the best previous proposed skip-list based queues, with respect to throughput performance.

Keywords: Shared data-structures · Concurrency · Lock-freedom · Performance scalability · Priority queues · External trees · Skip lists · Linked lists

1 Introduction

A priority queue is an abstract data type that stores a set of items and serves them according to their given priorities (*keys*). There are two typical operations

© Springer Nature Switzerland AG 2021
L. Sousa et al. (Eds.): Euro-Par 2021, LNCS 12820, pp. 385–401, 2021.
https://doi.org/10.1007/978-3-030-85665-6_24

supported by a priority queue: *Insert()* to insert a new item with a given priority in the priority queue, and *DeleteMin()* to remove a minimum item from the priority queue. Priority queues are of fundamental importance and are essential to designing components of many applications ranging from numerical algorithms, discrete event simulations, and operating systems. Though there is a wide body of literature addressing the design of concurrent priority queue algorithms, the problem of designing linearizable lock-free, scalable, priority queues is still of high interest and importance in the research and application communities. While early efforts have focused mostly on parallelising Heap structures [12], recent priority queues, based on Pugh's skip lists [16], arguably have higher throughput performance [13,18,19].

Skip lists are increasingly popular for designing priority queues due to their performance behaviour, mentioned above. A major reason being that skip lists allow concurrent accesses to different parts of the data structure and are probabilistically balanced. Skip lists achieve probabilistic balance through having a logarithmic number of sub-list layers that route search operations [16]. Although this is good for the search cost, it penalises the *Insert()* and *DeleteMin()* performance due to the high number of atomic instructions required to update multiple nodes belonging to different sub-lists per operation (*global atomic updates*). This also leads to high memory utilisation/consumption to accommodate the sub-lists. Trying to address this problem, a *quiescently consistent*[1] [10] multi-dimensional linked list priority queue [22], was proposed to localise the multiple global atomic updates to a few consecutive nodes in the queue. However, similar to the skip list, the multi-dimensional queue also suffers from a high number of global atomic updates and high memory consumption, which are proportional to the number of queue dimensions. A high number of global atomic updates typically increases the latency of an operation, and can also lead to high contention which limits scalability. Optimisation techniques such as lock-free chunks [2], flat combining [9], elimination [3], batch deleting [13] and back-off [19], and semantic relaxation [1] have been proposed to improve the performance of priority queues. However, these techniques mostly target to reduce the scalability challenges associated with the *DeleteMin()* sequential bottleneck. Although numerous skip list queue designs and optimisation techniques have been proposed in the literature, the underlying skip list design behaviour that generates a high number of atomic updates and memory consumption persists.

In this paper, we propose an alternative approach for designing efficient, lock-free, lineraizable priority queues with a minimal number of global atomic updates per operation. Our design is based on a combination of a binary external search tree [7,15] and an ordered linked list [8,21]. Typically, an external tree is composed of a sentinel node (*root*), internal-nodes and leaf-nodes. We modify the tree to add a link between the leaf-nodes, forming a linked list of leaf-nodes with a sentinel node (*head*). We also combine the internal-node and leaf-node into one physical *node*. Within the tree, the *node* is accessed as an internal-node,

---

[1] Quiescent consistency semantics allow weaker object behaviour than strong consistency models like linearizability to allow for better performance.

whereas at the list level, the *node* is accessed as a leaf-node. We maintain only two levels in which a *node* can be accessed, that is, tree level and list level. Our combination of a tree and a linked list forms what we refer to as a tree-search-list priority queue (*TSLQueue*). *TSLQueue* is not guaranteed to be balanced due to the underlying binary external search tree structure.

Similar to a balanced skip list, a balanced *TSLQueue* has a search cost of $O(\log n)$. However, *TSLQueue* has a minimal number of global atomic updates. *TSLQueue Insert()* performs one or two global atomic updates on one or two consecutive *nodes*. *TSLQueue DeleteMin()* performs two or three global atomic updates on two or three *nodes*. The tree design requires only one internal-node update for either *Insert()* or *DeleteMin()*, a property that we leverage to achieve low global atomic updates and consequently better performance. Having a single *node* to represent both the tree and the list level, gives *TSLQueue* minimal memory consumption of $O(n)$. Reducing the memory consumption significantly improves cache behaviour and lowers memory latency, especially for larger priority queues as we discuss later in Sect. 5. Optimisation techniques such as batch deleting, frequently used in concurrent data structure designs are limited by memory availability. However, *TSLQueue* can efficiently execute batch deletes due to its low memory consumption.

We experimentally compare our implementation of *TSLQueue* to two state-of-the-art skip list based priority queues, one that is linearizable [13] and one that is quiescently consistent [18]. Overall *TSLQueue* outperforms the two algorithms in all the tested benchmarks, with a throughput performance improvement of up to more than 400% in the case of *DeleteMin()* and up to more than 65% in the case of *Insert()*.

The rest of the paper is organised as follows. In Sect. 2 we discuss the literature related to this work. We present our proposed *TSLQueue* design together with its implementation details in Sect. 3, and prove its correctness in Sect. 4. We experimentally evaluate our implementation in comparison to skip list based priority queues in Sect. 5 and conclude in Sect. 6.

2   Related Work

Concurrent priority queues have been extensively studied in the literature, with most proposed designs based on three paradigms: heaps [5,6,12,14,20], skip lists [13,18,19] and multi-dimensional linked lists [22]. However, empirical results in the literature show that heap based priority queues do not scale past a few numbers of threads. Therefore, we leave out the details of heap priority queues due to space constraints.

Skip lists are search structures based on hierarchically ordered linked lists, with a probabilistic guarantee of being balanced [16]. The basic idea behind skip lists is to keep items in an ordered list, but have each record in the list be part of up to a logarithmic number of sub-lists. These sub-lists play the same role as the routing nodes (internal-nodes) of a binary search tree structure. To search a list of n items, $O(\log n)$ sub-list levels are traversed, and a constant number of items is traversed per sub-list level, making the expected overall complexity of $O(\log n)$.

Maintaining sub-lists penalizes the *Insert()* and *DeleteMin()* performance, due to the high number of global atomic memory updates required to update multiple nodes belonging to different sub-lists. This also leads to high memory consumption to accommodate the sub-lists. In the worst case, the number of global atomic updates of a balanced skip list based queue can go up to $O(\log n)$ for each operation, whereas memory consumption can go up to $O(n \log n)$, where n is the number of items in the queue. Several skip list based priority queues have been proposed in the literature, including; quiescently consistent ones [18,22] and linerizable ones [13,19]. Linerizabilty [11] is the typical expected behaviour of a concurrent data structure. Quiescent consistency [10] is a form of relaxed linearizability that allows weaker data structure behaviour to achieve better performance.

A quiescently consistent multi-dimensional linked list priority queue [22] has been proposed to avoid distant updates by localising the queue operations to a few consecutive nodes. The multi-dimensional queue is composed of nodes that contain multiple links to child nodes arranged by their dimensionality. Nodes are ordered by their coordinate prefixes through which they can be searched. The insertion operation maps a scalar key to a high-dimensional vector, then uniquely locates the insertion point by using the vector as coordinates. Generally, the *Insert()* and *DeleteMin()* operations update pointers in consecutive nodes, but the number of global atomic updates is proportional to the number of dimensions, similar to the skip list. Just like the skip list, multi-dimensional queues also exhibit high memory consumption, proportional to the number of dimensions.

Like other concurrent priority queues, skip list based priority queues have an inherent sequential bottleneck when accessing the minimum item, especially when performing a *DeleteMin()*. Building on [19], a skip list based priority queue with batch deleting has been proposed with the aim of addressing the sequential bottleneck challenge [13]. The algorithm achieves batch deleting, by not physically deleting nodes after performing a logical delete. Instead, the algorithm performs physical deletion in batches for a given number of logically deleted nodes. Each batch deletion is performed by simply moving the queue *head* pointers, so that they point past the logically deleted nodes, thus making them unreachable. Batch deleting achieves high performance by reducing the number of global atomic updates associated with physical deletes. However, this does not reduce the number of global atomic updates associated with the *Insert()*. Also, the batch deleting technique used is limited by the memory latency generated from traversing logically deleted nodes.

3   Algorithm

3.1   Structure Overview

In this section, we give an overview of our *TSLQueue* design structure depicted in Fig. 1. Our *TSLQueue* is a combination of two structures; a binary external

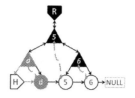

(a) *TSLQueue node* structure

(b) *TSLQueue* with three *nodes* (5, 6 and a *dummy*)

Fig. 1. The triangle represents the *internal*, the circle represents the *leaf*. *internal* and *leaf* physical connection is represented by the blue dashed diamond pointed line. (H) represents the *head* while (R) represents the *root* and (d) for *dummy*. (Color figure online)

search tree and an ordered linked list. The *TSLQueue* is comprised of *nodes* in which queue items are stored and can be accessed through the *root* or the *head*. Each physical *node* has two logical forms; internal-node (*internal*) and leaf-node (*leaf*), and can either be active or deleted. At the tree level, the *node* is accessed as an *internal* to facilitate binary search operations. Whereas at the list level, the *node* is accessed as a *leaf* to facilitate linear search operations. A *node* has four pointers as shown in Fig. 1a: left child, right child, parent and next. A list of *leaves* is created using the next-pointer while the other pointers are used to create the tree. To identify a *leaf*, we reserve one least significant bit (leaf-flag) on each child-pointer, a common method used in the literature [8]. If the leaf-flag is set to true, then the given child is a *leaf*. To simplify linearizability and also to avoid the ABA[2] problem at the *head*, we keep an empty node (*dummy*) between the *head* and the rest of the active *nodes* as shown in Fig. 1b. *DeleteMin()* always deletes the *dummy* and returns the value of the next *leaf*. The *node* whose value has been returned becomes a *dummy*. In other words, a *leaf* preceded by a deleted *leaf* is always a *dummy*. *TSLQueue* supports the two typical priority queue operations; insert an item and delete a minimum item, plus search for an item. Just like for the leaf-flag, we reserve one least significant bit (delete-flag) on the next-pointer. A *node* is logically deleted if the delete-flag is set to true, and physically deleted if it cannot be reached through the *head* or the *root*.

Search: For simplicity, we design two types of tree search operations; *Insert-Search()* and *CleanTree()*. *InsertSearch()* searches for an active *leaf* preceding a given search key, whereas *CleanTree()* searches for an active *dummy* while physically deleting logically deleted nodes from the tree. Both search operations start from the *root*, traversing *internals* until the desired *leaf* is reached. Partial search operations are also supported, as we describe later.

---

[2] The ABA problem occurs when multiple processors access a shared location without noticing each others' changes.

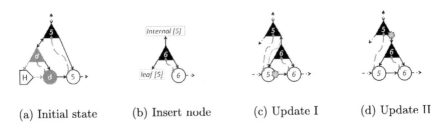

(a) Initial state   (b) Insert node   (c) Update I   (d) Update II

Fig. 2. An illustration of inserting node (key = 6). The starred areas indicate the atomic operation execution point.

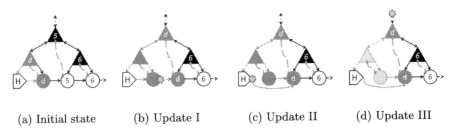

(a) Initial state   (b) Update I   (c) Update II   (d) Update III

Fig. 3. An illustration of *DeleteMin()* that returns minimum node (key = 5). The starred areas indicate the atomic operation execution points.

Insert: Inserting a queue item starts with an *InsertSearch()* operation. *InsertSearch()* locates an active preceding *leaf* (*precLeaf*) to the item key, together with the *precLeaf parent* and succeeding *leaf* (*succLeaf*). Using the search information, a new-node is allocated with its next-pointer pointing to the *succLeaf*, left child-pointer pointing to the *precLeaf* and parent-pointer pointing to the *parent* as shown in Fig. 2b. Both left and right child-pointers are marked as *leaves* since insertion happens at the list level. *Insert()* performs two global atomic updates as illustrated in Fig. 2 in the following order:

I Atomically adds the new-node to the list, by updating the *precLeaf* next-pointer from *succLeaf* to new-node, see Fig. 2c. On the success of this atomic operation, *Insert()* linearizes and the new-node becomes active.

II Atomically adds the new-node to the tree, by updating the given *parent* child-pointer from *precLeaf* to the new-node with the leaf-flag set to false, see Fig. 2d. *Insert()* completes and returns success.

Delete Minimum: For retrieving a minimum queue item, the operation starts from the *head*. A linear search on the list is performed until an active *dummy* is located. *DeleteMin()* performs three atomic global updates as shown in Fig. 3 and in the following order:

I Atomically, logically deletes the *dummy* by setting the next-pointer delete-flag to true. On the success of this atomic operation, *DeleteMin()* linearizes and reads the succeeding *leaf* as the minimum item to be returned. The succeeding *leaf* becomes a *dummy* as shown Fig. 3b.

II Atomically, physically deletes the logically deleted *dummy* from the list, by updating the *head* next-pointer from the deleted *dummy* to the new active *dummy* as shown in Fig. 3c.

III Atomically, physically deletes the logically deleted *dummy* from the tree, by updating the closest active ancestor's left child-pointer to point to the active *dummy*. It is likely that the closest active ancestor is already pointing to the active *dummy* as illustrated in Fig. 3d, in that case, *DeleteMin()* ignores the update. *DeleteMin()* completes and returns the value read at the linearization point (update I). We note that there can be different methods of locating the closest active ancestor. However for simplicity reasons, in this paper, we use the earlier discussed *CleanTree()* to locate the closest active ancestor to the *dummy*, as detailed in Sect. 3.2.

3.2   Implementation

Algorithm 1: TSLQueue

```
1.1  Struct node
1.2  │ key; val;
1.3  │ *parent; *left; *next; *right; ins; ptrp;

1.4  Struct head
1.5  │ *next;

1.6  Struct root
1.7  │ *child;

1.8  Struct seek
1.9  │ *sucNode; *pNode; *preNode; dup; ptrp;

1.10 Function insert(key,val)
1.11 │ while true do
1.12 │ │ seek←InsertSearch(key);
1.13 │ │ if seek.dup then
1.14 │ │ │ return dup;
1.15 │ │ pNode←seek.pNode;
     │ │ nextLeaf←seek.sucNode;
     │ │ leaf←seek.preNode; ptrp←seek.ptrp;
1.16 │ │ newNode←allocNode(key,val);
1.17 │ │ newNode.right←MRKLEAF(newNode);
     │ │ newNode.left←MRKLEAF(leaf);
     │ │ newNode.next←nextLeaf;
     │ │ newNode.parent←pNode;
     │ │ newNode.ptrp←ptrp; newNode.ins←1;
1.18 │ │ if CAS(leaf.next,nextLeaf,newNode) then
1.19 │ │ │ if ptrp=RIGHT then
1.20 │ │ │ │ CAS(pNode.right,leaf,newNode);
1.21 │ │ │ else if ptrp=LEFT then
1.22 │ │ │ │ CAS(pNode.left,leaf,newNode);
1.23 │ │ │ newNode.ins←0; return success;
```

```
1.24 Function delete()
1.25 │ hNode←head.next;
1.26 │ if prHead=hNode then
1.27 │ │ dummy←prDummy;
1.28 │ else
1.29 │ │ GarbageCollector(timestamp);
     │ │ dummy←prHead←hNode;
1.30 │ while true do
1.31 │ │ nextLeaf←dummy.next;
1.32 │ │ if nextLeaf=null then
1.33 │ │ │ return null;
1.34 │ │ else
1.35 │ │ │ if DEL(nextLeaf) then
1.36 │ │ │ │ dummy←nextLeaf; continue;
1.37 │ │ │ xorLeaf←FAXOR(dummy.next,1);
1.38 │ │ │ if !DEL(xorLeaf) then
1.39 │ │ │ │ value←xorLeaf.val; prDummy←xorLeaf;
1.40 │ │ │ │ if !randPhysicalDel() then
1.41 │ │ │ │ │ return value;
1.42 │ │ │ │ if CAS(head.next,hNode,xorLeaf) then
1.43 │ │ │ │ │ CleanTree(xorLeaf);
1.44 │ │ │ │ │ nextLeaf←hNode;
1.45 │ │ │ │ │ while nextLeaf≠xorLeaf do
1.46 │ │ │ │ │ │ cur←nextLeaf;
     │ │ │ │ │ │ nextLeaf←nextLeaf.next; FREE(cur);
1.47 │ │ │ │ return value;
1.48 │ │ │ dummy←xorLeaf;
```

Algorithm 2: Search Functions

2.1 **Macro** $GORIGHT(pNode)$
2.2 $\quad$ ptrp←RIGHT; cNode←pNode.right;

2.3 **Macro** $GOLEFT(pNode)$
2.4 $\quad$ ptrp←LEFT; cNode←pNode.left;

2.10 **Function** $InsertSearch(sKey)$
2.11 $\quad$ pNode←root; cNode←root.child;
2.12 $\quad$ **while** *true* **do**
2.13 $\quad\quad$ **if** $DEL(pNode)$ **then**
2.14 $\quad\quad\quad$ GORIGHT(pNode); mNode←pNode;
2.15 $\quad\quad\quad$ **while** *True* **do**
2.16 $\quad\quad\quad\quad$ **if** $DEL(pNode)$ **then**
2.17 $\quad\quad\quad\quad\quad$ **if** $!LEAF(cNode)$ **then**
2.18 $\quad\quad\quad\quad\quad\quad$ pNode←cNode; GORIGHT(pNode); continue;
2.19 $\quad\quad\quad\quad\quad$ **else**
2.20 $\quad\quad\quad\quad\quad\quad$ pNode←cNode.next; GORIGHT(pNode); break;
2.21 $\quad\quad\quad\quad$ **else**
2.22 $\quad\quad\quad\quad\quad$ **if** $randInsClean()$ **then**
2.23 $\quad\quad\quad\quad\quad\quad$ CAS(gNode.left,mNode,pNode);
2.24 $\quad\quad\quad\quad\quad$ TREVERSE(); break;
2.25 $\quad\quad\quad$ continue;
2.26 $\quad\quad$ **if** $!LEAF(cNode)$ **then**
2.27 $\quad\quad\quad$ gNode←pNode; pNode←cNode;
2.28 $\quad\quad\quad$ TRAVERSE();
2.29 $\quad\quad$ **else**
2.30 $\quad\quad\quad$ next←cNode.next;
2.31 $\quad\quad\quad$ **if** $DEL(cNode)$ **then**
2.32 $\quad\quad\quad\quad$ pNode←next;
2.33 $\quad\quad\quad\quad$ GORIGHT(pNode);
2.34 $\quad\quad\quad$ **else if** $next \wedge next.ins$ **then**
2.35 $\quad\quad\quad\quad$ HelpInsert(next);
2.36 $\quad\quad\quad\quad$ pNode←next; TRAVERSE();
2.37 $\quad\quad\quad$ **else if** $next \wedge next=sKey$ **then**
2.38 $\quad\quad\quad\quad$ seek.dup←True; return seek;
2.39 $\quad\quad\quad$ **else if** $ptrp=LEFT \wedge pNode.left!=cNode$ **then**
2.40 $\quad\quad\quad\quad$ TRAVERSE();
2.41 $\quad\quad\quad$ **else if** $ptrp=RIGHT \wedge pNode.right!=cNode$ **then**
2.42 $\quad\quad\quad\quad$ TRAVERSE();
2.43 $\quad\quad\quad$ **else**
2.44 $\quad\quad\quad\quad$ seek.preNode←cNode;
2.45 $\quad\quad\quad\quad$ seek.pNode←pNode;
2.46 $\quad\quad\quad\quad$ seek.sucNode←next;
2.47 $\quad\quad\quad\quad$ seek.ptrp←ptrp;
2.48 $\quad\quad\quad\quad$ return seek;

2.5 **Macro** $TRAVERSE()$
2.6 $\quad$ **if** $sKey \leq pNode.key \wedge !DEL(pNode)$ **then**
2.7 $\quad\quad$ GOLEFT(pNode);
2.8 $\quad$ **else**
2.9 $\quad\quad$ GORIGHT(pNode);

2.49 **Function** $CleanTree(dummy)$
2.50 $\quad$ pNode←root; cNode←root.child;
2.51 $\quad$ **while** *True* **do**
2.52 $\quad\quad$ **if** $DEL(pNode)$ **then**
2.53 $\quad\quad\quad$ GORIGHT(pNode); mNode←pNode;
2.54 $\quad\quad\quad$ **while** *True* **do**
2.55 $\quad\quad\quad\quad$ **if** $DEL(pNode)$ **then**
2.56 $\quad\quad\quad\quad\quad$ **if** $!LEAF(cNode)$ **then**
2.57 $\quad\quad\quad\quad\quad\quad$ pNode←cNode;
2.58 $\quad\quad\quad\quad\quad\quad$ GORIGHT(pNode); continue;
2.59 $\quad\quad\quad\quad\quad$ **else**
2.60 $\quad\quad\quad\quad\quad\quad$ next←cNode.next;
2.61 $\quad\quad\quad\quad\quad\quad$ **if** $next.ins$ **then**
2.62 $\quad\quad\quad\quad\quad\quad\quad$ HelpInsert(next);
2.63 $\quad\quad\quad\quad\quad\quad$ **else if** $pNode.right=cNode$ **then**
2.64 $\quad\quad\quad\quad\quad\quad\quad$ gNode.key←0; goto FINISH;
2.65 $\quad\quad\quad\quad\quad\quad$ GORIGHT(pNode); continue;
2.66 $\quad\quad\quad\quad$ **else**
2.67 $\quad\quad\quad\quad\quad$ **if** $!DEL(gNode)$ **then**
2.68 $\quad\quad\quad\quad\quad\quad$ **if** $CAS(gNode.left,mNode,pNode)$ **then**
2.69 $\quad\quad\quad\quad\quad\quad\quad$ GOLEFT(pNode); break;
2.70 $\quad\quad\quad\quad\quad\quad$ pNode=gNode; GOLEFT(pNode); break;
2.71 $\quad\quad\quad\quad\quad$ goto FINISH;
2.72 $\quad\quad$ **else**
2.73 $\quad\quad\quad$ **if** $!LEAF(cNode)$ **then**
2.74 $\quad\quad\quad\quad$ **if** $!pNode.key \vee pNode=dummy$ **then**
2.75 $\quad\quad\quad\quad\quad$ pNode.key←0; goto FINISH;
2.76 $\quad\quad\quad\quad$ gNode←pNode; pNode←cNode; GOLEFT(pNode); continue;
2.77 $\quad\quad\quad$ **else**
2.78 $\quad\quad\quad\quad$ next←cNode.next;
2.79 $\quad\quad\quad\quad$ **if** $DEL(cNode)$ **then**
2.80 $\quad\quad\quad\quad\quad$ **if** $next.ins$ **then**
2.81 $\quad\quad\quad\quad\quad\quad$ HelpInsert(next);
2.82 $\quad\quad\quad\quad\quad$ **else if** $pNode.left=cNode$ **then**
2.83 $\quad\quad\quad\quad\quad\quad$ next.key←0; goto FINISH;
2.84 $\quad\quad\quad\quad$ GOLEFT(pNode); continue;
2.85 $\quad$ FINISH: break;

In this section, we present the implementation of our *TSLQueue* design. *TSLQueue Insert()* and *DeleteMin()* are presented in Algorithm 1, while *InsertSearch()* and *CleanTree()* are presented in Algorithm 2.

Insert() (Line 1.10) takes two parameters, the key and value of the item to be inserted into the queue. Using the item key as the search key, an insertion point is located by performing the *InsertSearch()* operation (Line 1.12). *Insert-Search()* returns a *precLeaf* (`preNode`) together with its *parent* (`pNode`), *succLeaf* (`sucNode`) and its pointer position (`ptrp`) on the *parent* (left or right). However, if the search key is a duplicate *Insert()* terminates (Line 1.13), otherwise a new-node is allocated (Line 1.16). The new-node is then prepared for insertion using the search information (Line 1.17). *Insert()* occurs at the *leaves* level, and therefore, the left child-pointer of the new-node always points to the *precLeaf* as a *leaf* while the right child-pointer points to the new-node self as a *leaf*. The new-node next-pointer points to the *succLeaf* to maintain a link between the *leaves*. Using a CAS[3] instruction, insert first adds the new-node to the list, by atomically updating the next-pointer of the *precLeaf* from *succLeaf* to new-node (Line 1.18). If the CAS fails, insert retries with another *InsertSearch()* operation. If the CAS succeeds, insert proceeds to add the new-node to the tree, by atomically updating the given *parent* child-pointer from *precLeaf* to the new-node using a CAS instruction (Line 1.20 or 1.22). The CAS adding a new-node to the tree can only fail if another concurrent thread performing a search operation has helped to complete the process (Line 2.35 or 2.62). Therefore, the inserting thread does not need to retry the tree update, but rather continues and sets the new-node insert label to complete and returns success (Line 1.23).

DeleteMin() (Line 1.24) does not take any parameter. A thread trying to retrieve a minimum item, accesses the list through the *head dummy* (Line 1.25) or a *dummy* (Line 1.27) whose value was last returned by the thread (*prevDummy*). If the *dummy* is the last node in the list, the queue is empty and the thread returns the empty state (Line 1.32). Otherwise, if the *dummy* is deleted, the thread hops to the next *dummy* (Line 1.36). The thread linearly hops from one deleted *dummy* to another until an active *dummy* is reached, and tries to logically delete the *dummy* using a fetch-and-xor[4] instruction (Line 1.37). If the *dummy* is already deleted (Line 1.48), the thread hops to the next *dummy* (Line 1.48) in the list and retries. Otherwise, if the thread successfully marks an unmarked *dummy* (Line 1.38), it randomly decides whether to physically delete the logically deleted *dummy* (or *dummies*) or return (Line 1.40). We randomise physical deletes to reduce possible contention that might arise from multiple concurrent threads attempting to perform the physical delete procedure at the same time. To physically delete *dummies* from the queue, the thread starts by updating first the *head* to point to an active *dummy* (Line 1.42). Consequently, a *CleanTree()* is performed to update active ancestors pointing to logically deleted children to point to active children (Line 1.43). By updating the *head* and the ancestors, the thread physically deletes *dummies* (batch physical delete) from

---

[3] CAS atomically compares the contents of a memory location with a given value and, only if they are the same, modifies the contents of that memory location.

[4] Fetch and xor atomically replaces the current value of a memory location with the result of bit-wise XOR of the memory location value, and returns the previous memory location value before the XOR.

the list and the tree respectively. Only the thread that physically deleted a given set of logically deleted *dummies* from the list can free their memory for reclamation (Line 1.45). The thread always returns the value of the *dummy* next to the *dummy* it logically deleted (Line 1.39).

As discussed earlier, a thread inserting a queue item has to perform an *Insert-Search()* operation to get the insertion point of the given item. Using the item key as the search key, *InsertSearch()* starts from the *root* (Line 2.11) and traverses the tree *nodes* (*internals*) until an active *internal* with a *leaf* child is reached (Line 2.29). While searching, if the search key is less than or equal to that of an active *internal*, the left of the *internal* is traversed (Line 2.6), whereas if the search key is higher than that of an active *internal*, the right of the *internal* is traversed (Line 2.8). On the other hand, if the *internal* is deleted (Line 2.13), the search traverses the right of the *internal* until an active *internal* (Line 2.21) or *leaf* child is reached (Line 2.19). If the search reaches an active *internal* preceded by a logically deleted *internal*, the thread randomly decides whether to physically delete the preceding logically deleted *internal* (or *internals*) from the tree (Line 2.22) or not. The thread can then proceed with the traversal at the given active *internal* (Line 2.24). The physical delete is accomplished by updating the left of the last traversed active ancestor (Line 2.27) to point to the active *internal* using a CAS instruction (Line 2.23). This operation facilitates batch physical deleting of logically deleted *nodes* from the tree. Randomising physical deletes for the *InsertSearch()* operation, reduces possible contention between concurrent threads trying to physically delete the same *internal* (or *internals*).

If *InsertSearch()* reaches a deleted *leaf* (Line 2.19 or 2.31), the thread proceeds to the next *leaf* as the *dummy* and performs a partial tree search starting with a right traverse on the *dummy* (Line 2.33). If *InsertSearch()* reaches an active *leaf*, the parent to child edge must be checked for incomplete *Insert()* before the search operation returns the *leaf* as the point for insertion. An incomplete *Insert()* operation on the edge must be helped to complete (Line 2.34), and for that, a partial search is performed starting from the helped *internal* (Line 2.35 to 2.36). Our implementation does not consider duplicate keys, if the search key is equal to an active *node* that is not a *dummy*, duplicate is returned (Line 2.37) and *Insert()* returns. To know if an active *internal* is not a *dummy*, the thread has to traverse until a *leaf* is reached. A thread with a search key equal to the *internal* key always traverses the left of the *internal* (Line 2.6), therefore, if the *internal* is not a *dummy* it will be a *succLeaf* to the search key (Line 2.37).

The *CleanTree()* operation physically deletes logically deleted *internals* from the tree. Only a thread that has physically deleted a set of logically deleted *leaves* from the list (Line 1.42) can perform a *CleanTree()* operation (Line 1.43). This is to make sure that the logically deleted *nodes* are completely physically deleted from the queue (Line 1.43) before their memory can be reclaimed. *CleanTree()* searches for an active *dummy* following the same basic steps as the *InsertSearch()* operation with a few differences. *CleanTree()* always traverses the left of an active *internal* and only traverses the right if the *internal* is deleted. If *CleanTree()* encounters an active *internal* after traversing a logically deleted *internal* or a series of logically deleted *internals* (Line 2.66), the thread must try to physically delete the *internal* (or *internals*) by updating the left of the last traversed active ancestor to point to the active *internal* using a CAS instruction (Line 2.68). The update can fail if another concurrent thread performing a *CleanTree()* or *InsertSearch()* has updated the ancestor. In this case, unlike *InsertSearch()* that proceeds to traverse the *internal*, the thread performing the *CleanTree()* has to retry with a partial search starting from the ancestor (Line 2.70). This facilitates batch physical deleting of logically deleted *nodes* and allows memory for the given *nodes* to be freed for reclamation.

Unlike *InsertSearch()*, if *CleanTree()* reaches an active *leaf*, it terminates. However, if the *leaf* is logically deleted, the parent to child edge must be checked for incomplete *Insert()* before *CleanTree()* terminates (Line 2.64 or 2.83). An incomplete insert on the given edge must be helped to complete, and for that, a partial search retry is performed starting from the previous *internal*. Since logical deleting (Line 1.37) does not check for incomplete inserts, there can be deleted *leaves* pending to be added to the tree. Completing insert updates on edges leading to a deleted *leaf* helps search traverse all possible deleted *internals* leading to a *dummy*. Helping inserts during the *CleanTree()* operation is more efficient than blocking *DeleteMin()* operations from marking *nodes* with pending insert updates on their edges.

The information used to help an incomplete insert is stored in the *node* by the inserting thread that allocated the *node* (Line 1.17).

3.3 Memory Management

We manage memory allocation and reclamation using, but not limited to, a generic epoch-based garbage collection library (ssmem) from the ASCYLIB framework [4]. The freed memory is not reclaimed until when it is certain that no other threads can access that memory. Using timestamps, each thread holds a garbage collector version number (*gc-version*) that it timestamps every time it performs a fresh access to the *TSLQueue* list through the *head* (Line 1.29). Accessing the list through the *head* means that the thread cannot access previously freed *nodes*. The garbage collector will only reclaim the memory of *nodes* that were freed before all the threads performed a fresh access to the list through the *head*. Note that a thread that accesses the list using a previous-*dummy* (Line 1.27) does not update its *gc-version*, implying that, *nodes* accessed through the previous-*dummy* will still be un-reclaimed even if they are freed, and thus can route the thread to an active *dummy*.

4   Correctness

In this section, we prove correctness and progress guarantees for our proposed *TSLQueue*. Line numbers in this section refer to the algorithmic functions presented in Sect. 3. The *TSLQueue* is composed of *nodes* that can be accessed through the *head* or *root*. Queue items are stored within the *nodes*, each *node* having an item priority (*key*) k, where $0 < k$.

Linearizability [11] is widely accepted as the strongest correctness condition of concurrent data structures. Informally, linearizability states that in every execution of the data structure implementation, each supporting operation appears to take effect instantaneously at some point (*linearization point*) between the operation's invocation and response. *TSLQueue Insert()* linearizes on the success of the CAS operation that adds the new-node to the list, by updating the next-pointer of the preceding *leaf* to point to the new-node (Line 1.18). The new-node becomes active (visible to other threads) after the *Insert()* has been linearized. If the queue is not empty, *TSLQueue DeleteMin()* linearizes on the success of the fetch-and-xor operation that logically deletes an active *dummy* by setting the delete-flag of the active *dummy* from false to true (Line 1.37). If the queue is empty, *TSLQueue DeleteMin()* linearizes on the reading of the NULL next-pointer of the *dummy* (Line 1.32).

The proofs of the following Lemmas and Theorems have been omitted because of space constraints. They can be found in the extended version of the paper.

Lemma 1. *An active node key is the maximum key of its left-descendant(s) and the minimum key of its right-descendant(s). Also implying, that an active leaf key is the maximum key of all its preceding active leaves and the minimum of all its succeeding active leaves in the list.*

Lemma 2. *An active node can only be logically deleted once and after all its left-descendants have been deleted. Also implying, that an active leaf can only be logically deleted once and after all its preceding leaves have been logically deleted. Further implying that* DeleteMin() *cannot linearize on a logically deleted node.*

Lemma 3. *An inserted node is always pointed to by an active node next-pointer. Also implying, that* Insert() *cannot linearize on a logically deleted node.*

Theorem 1. TSLQueue *is a linearizable priority queue.*

Theorem 2. TSLQueue *is lock-free.*

5   Evaluation

To evaluate our queue design, we compare it with two state-of-the-art queue designs based on the skip list; *Lotan* [18] and *Linden* [13]. As we mentioned earlier, skip list based concurrent priority queues arguably have better throughput performance [13,18,19] compared to other previously proposed designs. These two algorithms are performance wise the best representatives of the skip list based queues designs. *Lotan* is a quiescently consistent lock-free adaptation of [18] and maintains most of the skip list operation routines. *Linden* on the other hand customises the skip list to optimise the queue *DeleteMin()* operation through batch deleting. *Linden* is an adaptation of [19], and is accepted by the community, to be one of the fastest skip list based priority queue in the literature.

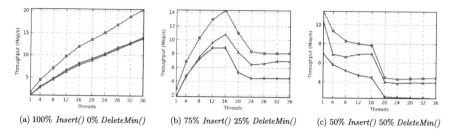

(a) 100% *Insert()* 0% *DeleteMin()*   (b) 75% *Insert()* 25% *DeleteMin()*   (c) 50% *Insert()* 50% *DeleteMin()*

Fig. 4. Throughput results for intra-socket (1 to 18 threads) and inter-socket (20 to 36 threads) with an initial queue size of $12 * 10^3$ items.

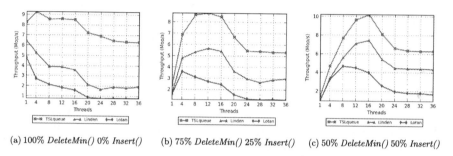

(a) 100% *DeleteMin()* 0% *Insert()*   (b) 75% *DeleteMin()* 25% *Insert()*   (c) 50% *DeleteMin()* 50% *Insert()*

Fig. 5. Throughput results for intra-socket (1 to 18 threads) and inter-socket (20 to 36 threads) with an initial queue size of $12 * 10^6$ items.

Our benchmark methodology is a variation of a commonly used synthetic benchmark [4], in which Threads randomly choose whether to perform an *Insert()* or a *DeleteMin()*. The priorities of inserted items are chosen uniformly at random, attempting to capture a common priority queue access pattern. To maintain fairness, the algorithms are run using the same framework and the same memory management scheme [4]. Both *Lotan* and *Linden* use the same method to determine node height based on the distribution of the skip list. To demonstrate the effect of the queue size on the throughput performance, we consider first a queue of small size with $12 * 10^3$ items Fig. 4, and one of a larger size with $12 * 10^6$ items Fig. 5. The queue size is an important evaluation parameter that helps us to also evaluate the memory latency effects for the three algorithms. All three algorithms do not consider duplicates, in their original designs, an insert with a duplicate completes without changing the state of the queue. To avoid duplicates that could skew our results, we use a key range of 2^{30} which is big enough to accommodate the queue sizes experimented with.

We conduct our experiments on a dual-processor machine with two Intel Xeon E5-2695 v4 @ 2.10 GHz. Each processor has 18 physical cores with three cache levels; 32 KB L1 and 256 KB L2 private to each core and 46 MB L3 shared among the 18 cores. Threads were pinned one per physical core filling one socket at a time. Throughput is measured as an average of the number of million operations performed per second out of five runs per benchmark. We observed similar trends

on two other hardware platforms; a single processor Intel Xeon Phi CPU 7290
@ 1.50 GHz with 72 cores and dual-processor Intel Xeon CPU E5-2687W v2 @
3.40 GHz with 16 cores; results are shown in the extended version of this paper
due to space constraints.

5.1   Results

First, we evaluate the performance of the *Insert()* operation running without
any concurrent *DeleteMin()* operation, the results are presented in Fig. 4a. We
observe that *Linden* and *Lotan* have similar *Insert()* throughput performance
due to their similar *Insert()* design that is based on the skip list structure. The
Insert() operation can achieve high parallelism through concurrent distributed
accesses of different parts of the queue. However, for *Linden* and *Lotan*, the
Insert() performance is limited by the high number of global atomic updates,
proportional to the number of list levels (*node* height), that the *Insert()* performs to several distant *nodes*. Concurrent threads inserting *nodes* at different
points within the queue can still contend while updating the different sub-list
level *nodes*, shared by the given inserted *nodes*. Unlike *Linden* and *Lotan*, the
TSLQueue scales better by leveraging on the lower number of required global
atomic updates. *TSLQueue* updates only one or two consecutive *nodes* for each
Insert(). *TSLQueue* supports single *node* update by storing both the right-child
pointer and the next-pointer in the same physical node. When inserting a right
child to a *node*, the two atomic updates will operate on the same physical *node*.
Having one tree update per insert operation reduces the possible contention
between concurrent threads inserting *nodes* at different points within the queue
list. For this part of the valuation, *TSLQueue* achieves from 40% to more than
65% better throughput performance compared to both *Lotan* and *Linden*.

   Then we evaluate the performance of the *DeleteMin()* operation running
without any concurrent *Insert()*, the results are presented in Fig. 5a. The three
algorithms use a similar marking method to logically delete a *node*. For *Linden*
and *TSLQueue*, a single *node* can be marked at a time, turning the logical delete
into a sequential bottleneck. *Lotan* is quiescently consistent and it is possible for
more than one *node* to be marked at a time. However, *TSLQueue* and *Linden*
batch physical deletes to reduce contention at *nodes* that have to be updated for
each physical delete, especially the *head*. *Linden* batch performance is limited
by the fact that threads have to linearly transverse all logically deleted *nodes*
to reach an active *node*. *TSLQueue* on the other hand uses a randomised approach to avoid contention, and partial linear search to reduce operation latency.
TSLQueue combines the advantages of partial linear search, batched physical
deletes and reduced number of atomic updates per physical delete, to achieve,
for this part of the evaluation, from 25% to more than 400% throughput performance compared to both *Linden* and *Lotan* as observed in Fig. 5a. For the
three algorithms, *DeleteMin()* scalability is generally limited by the sequential
bottleneck at the queue *head* and the minimum queue item.

   Lastly, we evaluate the algorithms on workloads that include concurrent
Insert() and *DeleteMin()* operations. In Fig. 4c and 5c we observe a significant

drop in throughput under inter-socket executions for all three algorithms. This drop is attributed to the expensive communication between sockets. *TSLQueue* can efficiently execute batch operations and overall keep a low number of global atomic updates reducing inter-socket communication, thus the observed better performance. Unlike *Lotan* and *Linden*, *TSLQueue* can perform partial searches further reducing the inter-socket communication, especially for the larger queue size as observed in Fig. 5. In Fig. 4c, we observe limited or no scalability as the number of threads increase. This is because for smaller queue sizes, there are few items on which threads can spread their operations leading to contention. However, *TSLQueue* still has better throughput due to the same structural advantages discussed above. We also observe that *TSLQueue* has a significant performance advantage over *Linden* and *Lotan* for the larger queue size compared to the smaller one. Apart from the above structural advantages, this can also be attributed to low memory usage which reduces memory latency.

6   Conclusion

In this paper, we have introduced a new design approach for designing efficient priority queues. We have demonstrated the design with a linearizable lock-free priority queue implementation. Our implementation has outperformed the previously proposed state-of-the-art skip list based priority queues. In the case of *DeleteMin()* we have achieved a performance improvement of up to more than 400% and up to more than 65% in the case of *Insert()*. Though numerous optimisation techniques such as flat combining, elimination and back-off can be applied to further enhance the performance of *TSLQueue*, they are beyond the scope of this paper and are considered for future research.

Acknowledgements and Data Availability Statement. The data sets and code generated and/or analysed during the current study are available in the Figshare repository: https://doi.org/10.6084/m9.figshare.14748420 [17]. This work has been supported by SIDA/Bright Project (317) under the Makerere-Sweden bilateral research programme 2015–2020, Mbarara University of Science and Technology and Swedish Research Council (Vetenskapsrådet) Under Contract No.: 2016-05360.

References

1. Alistarh, D., Kopinsky, J., Li, J., Shavit, N.: The SprayList: a scalable relaxed priority queue. ACM SIGPLAN Not. **50**(8), 11–20 (2015). https://doi.org/10.1145/2858788.2688523
2. Braginsky, A., Cohen, N., Petrank, E.: CBPQ: high performance lock-free priority queue. In: Dutot, P.-F., Trystram, D. (eds.) Euro-Par 2016. LNCS, vol. 9833, pp. 460–474. Springer, Cham (2016). https://doi.org/10.1007/978-3-319-43659-3_34
3. Calciu, I., Mendes, H., Herlihy, M.: The adaptive priority queue with elimination and combining. In: Kuhn, F. (ed.) DISC 2014. LNCS, vol. 8784, pp. 406–420. Springer, Heidelberg (2014). https://doi.org/10.1007/978-3-662-45174-8_28

4. David, T., Guerraoui, R., Trigonakis, V.: Asynchronized concurrency: the secret to scaling concurrent search data structures. SIGARCH Comput. Archit. News **43**(1), 631–644 (2015). https://doi.org/10.1145/2786763.2694359

5. Deo, N., Prasad, S.: Parallel heap: an optimal parallel priority queue. J. Supercomput. **6**(1), 87–98 (1992). https://doi.org/10.1007/BF00128644

6. Dragicevic, K., Bauer, D.: Optimization techniques for concurrent STM-based implementations: a concurrent binary heap as a case study. In: 2009 IEEE International Symposium on Parallel Distributed Processing, pp. 1–8 (2009). https://doi.org/10.1109/IPDPS.2009.5161153

7. Ellen, F., Fatourou, P., Helga, J., Ruppert, E.: The amortized complexity of non-blocking binary search trees. In: Proceedings of the 2014 ACM Symposium on Principles of Distributed Computing, PODC 2014, New York, NY, USA, pp. 332–340. Association for Computing Machinery (2014). https://doi.org/10.1145/2611462.2611486

8. Harris, T.L.: A pragmatic implementation of non-blocking linked-lists. In: Welch, J. (ed.) DISC 2001. LNCS, vol. 2180, pp. 300–314. Springer, Heidelberg (2001). https://doi.org/10.1007/3-540-45414-4_21

9. Hendler, D., Incze, I., Shavit, N., Tzafrir, M.: Flat combining and the synchronization-parallelism tradeoff. In: Proceedings of the Twenty-Second Annual ACM Symposium on Parallelism in Algorithms and Architectures, SPAA 2010, New York, NY, USA, pp. 355–364. Association for Computing Machinery (2010). https://doi.org/10.1145/1810479.1810540

10. Herlihy, M., Shavit, N.: The Art of Multiprocessor Programming. Morgan Kaufmann Publishers Inc., San Francisco (2008)

11. Herlihy, M.P., Wing, J.M.: Linearizability: a correctness condition for concurrent objects. ACM Trans. Program. Lang. Syst. **12**(3), 463–492 (1990). https://doi.org/10.1145/78969.78972

12. Hunt, G.C., Michael, M.M., Parthasarathy, S., Scott, M.L.: An efficient algorithm for concurrent priority queue heaps. Inf. Process. Lett. **60**(3), 151–157 (1996). https://doi.org/10.1016/S0020-0190(96)00148-2

13. Lindén, J., Jonsson, B.: A skiplist-based concurrent priority queue with minimal memory contention. In: Baldoni, R., Nisse, N., van Steen, M. (eds.) OPODIS 2013. LNCS, vol. 8304, pp. 206–220. Springer, Cham (2013). https://doi.org/10.1007/978-3-319-03850-6_15

14. Liu, Y., Spear, M.: Mounds: array-based concurrent priority queues. In: Proceedings of the 2012 41st International Conference on Parallel Processing, ICPP 2012, USA, pp. 1–10. IEEE Computer Society (2012). https://doi.org/10.1109/ICPP.2012.42

15. Natarajan, A., Ramachandran, A., Mittal, N.: FEAST: a lightweight lock-free concurrent binary search tree. ACM Trans. Parallel Comput. **7**(2), 1–64 (2020). https://doi.org/10.1145/3391438

16. Pugh, W.: Skip lists: a probabilistic alternative to balanced trees. Commun. ACM **33**(6), 668–676 (1990). https://doi.org/10.1145/78973.78977

17. Rukundo, A., Tsigas, P.: Artifact and instructions to generate experimental results for the euro-par 2021 paper: Tslqueue: An efficient lock-free design for priority queues, August 2021. https://doi.org/10.6084/m9.figshare.14748420

18. Shavit, N., Lotan, I.: Skiplist-based concurrent priority queues. In: Proceedings 14th International Parallel and Distributed Processing Symposium. IPDPS 2000, pp. 263–268 (2000). https://doi.org/10.1109/IPDPS.2000.845994

19. Sundell, H., Tsigas, P.: Fast and lock-free concurrent priority queues for multi-thread systems. J. Parallel Distrib. Comput. **65**(5), 609–627 (2005). https://doi.org/10.1016/j.jpdc.2004.12.005

20. Tamir, O., Morrison, A., Rinetzky, N.: A heap-based concurrent priority queue with mutable priorities for faster parallel algorithms. In: 19th International Conference on Principles of Distributed Systems (OPODIS 2015), volume 46 of Leibniz International Proceedings in Informatics (LIPIcs), Dagstuhl, Germany, pp. 1–16. Schloss Dagstuhl-Leibniz-Zentrum fuer Informatik (2016). https://doi.org/10.4230/LIPIcs.OPODIS.2015.15

21. Valois, J.D.: Lock-free linked lists using compare-and-swap. In: Proceedings of the Fourteenth Annual ACM Symposium on Principles of Distributed Computing, PODC 1995, New York, NY, USA, pp. 214–222. ACM (1995). https://doi.org/10.1145/224964.224988

22. Zhang, D., Dechev, D.: A lock-free priority queue design based on multi-dimensional linked lists. IEEE Trans. Parallel Distrib. Syst. **27**(3), 613–626 (2016). https://doi.org/10.1109/TPDS.2015.2419651

G-Morph: Induced Subgraph Isomorphism Search of Labeled Graphs on a GPU

Bryan Rowe and Rajiv Gupta[✉]

CSE Department, University of California, Riverside, Riverside, USA
{roweb,gupta}@cs.ucr.edu

Abstract. Induced subgraph isomorphism search finds the occurrences of embedded subgraphs within a single large data graph that are strictly isomorphic to a given query graph. Labeled graphs contain object types and are a primary input source to this core search problem, which applies to systems like graph databases for answering queries. In recent years, researchers have employed GPU parallel solutions to this problem to help accelerate runtimes by utilizing the filtering-and-joining framework, which first filters vertices that cannot be part of the solution then joins partial solutions with candidate edges until full iso-morphisms are determined. However, the performance of current GPU-based solutions is hindered by limited filtering effectiveness and presence of extrane-ous computations. This paper presents G-Morph, a fast GPU-based induced sub-graph isomorphism search system for labeled graphs. Our filtering-and-joining system parallelizes both phases by upfront eliminating irrelevant vertices via a novel space-efficient vertex signature hashing strategy and efficiently joining par-tial solutions through use of a novel sliding window algorithm (slide-join) that provides overflow protection for larger input. Together these techniques greatly reduce extraneous computations by reducing Cartesian products and improving edge verification while supporting large scan operations (split-scan). G-Morph outperforms the state-of-the-art GPU-based GSI and CPU-based VF3 systems on labeled real-world graphs achieving speedups of up to 15.78× and 43.56× respectively.

Keywords: Graph databases · Subgraph isomorphism · Breadth-first search · GPU programming · Parallel computing

1 Introduction

Labeled real-world graphs are ubiquitous and naturally arise as social networks [9], knowledge graphs [23], information networks [22], and various other types. These schemaless graphs are processed to extract insightful analytics in real time. Designing efficient, cost-effective graph analysis systems that process structurally diverse graphs has become an important research problem that is receiving considerable attention.

Given a query graph G_q and data graph G_d, one such graph analysis problem *sub-graph isomorphism search* is deployed when one is interested in finding subgraphs of G_d that are isomorphic (i.e. same structure with labels) to G_q. Chemical sub-structure search [18], protein-protein interaction network search [5], and RDF graph databases [28] are select applications that benefit from subgraph search systems.

© Springer Nature Switzerland AG 2021
L. Sousa et al. (Eds.): Euro-Par 2021, LNCS 12820, pp. 402–417, 2021.
https://doi.org/10.1007/978-3-030-85665-6_25

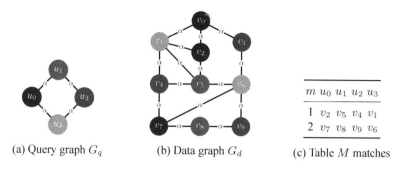

(a) Query graph G_q (b) Data graph G_d (c) Table M matches

m	u_0	u_1	u_2	u_3
1	v_2	v_5	v_4	v_1
2	v_7	v_8	v_9	v_6

Fig. 1. Example with vertex labels (colors) & edge labels and results table M.

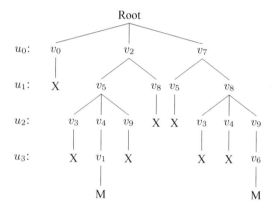

Fig. 2. Search tree for Fig. 1 graph with filtering based on vertex label per level. **X** is a pruned endpoint and **M** is a valid match.

Consider Fig. 1 with G_q, the query graph, and G_d, the data graph. The subgraph search system finds isomorphic subgraph matches M where rows are matches m with corresponding label-preserving vertex mappings $u \mapsto v$. This work handles both induced and non-induced versions of this search problem. In Fig. 1(c), the system would only return $m = 2$ if only *induced* matches are allowed since $m = 2$ does not contain extra edges between mapped data vertices. The match at $m = 1$ would be omitted because the non-edge (u_3, u_1) in G_q is not a valid match to the edge (v_1, v_5) in G_d.

Traditional subgraph isomorphism search algorithms [7,8,11,25,30] are generally based on a 2-phase *filtering-and-verifying* design [15]. The *filtering* phase performs vertex elimination to filter out initial nonsolution vertices. The *verifying* phase performs recursive backtracking to traverse a search tree (Fig. 2) such that each level of the tree represents a query vertex map and each path from the root to leaf in the tree represents a possible match. Existing algorithms explore novel methods of pruning the search tree.

Subgraph isomorphism search is NP-hard [21] and considered a computationally demanding problem to solve. In recent years, progress has been made to accelerate runtimes via deployment on distributed [20] and multithreaded platforms [6,17,19].

Table 1. Comparison of filtering-and-joining strategies.

System	Filter	Join (edges)	Join (M table)
GpSM [24]	Initialize-recurse	Verify-write	Verify-write
GSI [29]	Local indexing	N/A	Prealloc-combine
G-Morph	Local+cycle indexing	Slide-join	Verify-write

Specifically, the graphics processing unit (GPU) has shown to be an efficient and cost-effective platform to implement parallel graph algorithms [14,27]. With design principles of avoiding warp divergence [10] and favoring coalesced memory accesses, subgraph search on GPUs that run in single-instruction multiple data (SIMD) fashion has seen promising results with systems including GpSM [24], GunrockSM [26], and GSI [29].

GPU-accelerated systems are based on a 2-phase *filtering-and-joining* strategy where the *joining* phase is a parallelism friendly form of *verifying*. The *filtering* phase analyzes each vertex in G_d and determines via filtering strategies if data vertex v_i is a member of the query candidate set $C(u_j)$, that is, if $v_i \in C(u_j)$, and adds only relevant data vertex candidates to each query candidate set. The *joining* phase takes as input the candidate vertices and performs a parallel set join operation between adjacent candidate vertices to incrementally build valid partial matches until final matches M are realized.

Problems. Existing GPU-based systems propose different parallel strategies that handle both filtering and joining phases, but are prone to contribute to *extraneous computations* in both phases. Effective filtering of irrelevant vertices as well as efficient filtering in terms of time and space are key to eliminate extraneous search paths. The joining phase is prone to extraneous edge verification depending on algorithms used.

Current filtering strategies employed by GpSM and GSI (Table 1) present a tradeoff between filtering time and space required. GpSM's *initalize-recurse* suffers from multiple execution rounds but benefits from no metadata overhead. GSI's *local indexing* uses precomputed signatures to perform faster filtering but signatures used are prone to higher storage costs and only index immediate neighbors.

Joining consists of candidate edge and M table construction. The duplication of *edge verification*, the determination of adjacency between candidate vertices, when constructing candidate edges is a performance issue. GpSM's *verify-write* (Table 1) is employed in both joining parts, which involves duplicate verification by counting the join size before writing results to an allocated array. GSI's vertex-centric *prealloc-combine* avoids duplicate joins via preallocation, but lacks candidate edges for fast lookups.

Our Approach. In this paper we present **G-Morph**, an efficient GPU-based, filtering-and-joining subgraph isomorphism search system of labeled graphs, the first to support both *induced* and *non-induced* matches. Our design goal is to exploit labels to quickly eliminate irrelevant vertices and to improve edge verification, both of which limit extraneous computations. We propose *joining* phase algorithms that complement our *filtering* strategy while utilizing GPU parallelism and coalesced memory accesses.

We propose a novel space-efficient vertex signature *local+cycle indexing* strategy (Table 1) that leverages vertex properties of labeled graphs and stores them as hash codes used for fast membership decisions. Compared with GpSM, *local+cycle indexing* quickly filters in one round. Comprised *local* (LOC) and triangle *cycle* (TRI) hash codes facilitate fast filtering with integer-wise metadata (a compact alternative of GSI).

We propose a novel sliding window algorithm *slide-join* for efficient joining, which builds candidate edges without duplicate edge verification (an improvement of GpSM) and offers overflow protection by segmenting the Cartesian product space. Utilizing efficient candidate edges with *slide-join* can lead to speedups over the GSI vertex-centric strategy. Additionally, *split-scan* is employed to support large *scans* [2].

Experiments show that our system achieves significant speedups over current state-of-the-art CPU- and GPU- based systems on labeled graphs. On labeled real-world graphs, G-Morph handily outperforms the best available GPU-based GSI and CPU-based VF3 algorithms delivering speedups of up to 15.78× and 43.56× respectively.

2   Preliminaries: Subgraph Isomorphism Search

Our goal is to find all subgraph isomorphisms, i.e. matches, of a single large data graph G_d such that each instance is *subgraph isomorphic* to a given query graph G_q. This paper considers *undirected labeled* graphs supporting both vertex and edge labels.

Definition 1 (Labeled Graph). A labeled graph is defined as 4-tuple $G = (V, E, L, l)$, where V is a set of vertices, $E \subseteq V \times V$ is a set of edges, L is a vertex labeling function, and l is an edge labeling function.

Definition 2 (Graph Isomorphism). Given two labeled graphs $G_a = (V_a, E_a, L_a, l_a)$ and $G_b = (V_b, E_b, L_b, l_b)$, G_a is *graph isomorphic* to G_b iff a *bijective* function $f : G_a \mapsto G_b$ exists such that:

(i) $\forall\, u \in V_a, \quad L_a(u) = L_b(\, f(u)\,)$
(ii) $\forall\, (u, v) \in E_a, \; (f(u), f(v)) \in E_b \;\land\; l_a(\,(u,v)\,) = l_b(\,(f(u), f(v))\,)$
(iii) $\forall\, (f(u), f(v)) \in E_b, \; (u, v) \in E_a \;\land\; l_b((f(u), f(v))) = l_a((u,v))$

Definition 3 (Subgraph Isomorphism). Given two labeled graphs $G_q = (V_q, E_q, L_q, l_q)$ and $G_d = (V_d, E_d, L_d, l_d)$, G_q is *subgraph isomorphic* to G_d if an *injective* function $f : G_q \mapsto G_d$ exists such that:

(i) $\forall\, v \in V_q, \; f(v) \in G_d \land L_q(v) = L_d(f(v))$
(ii) $\forall\, (u, v) \in E_q, \; (f(u), f(v)) \in E_d \land l_q(u,v) = l_d(f(u), f(v))$

Graph and subgraph isomorphism are decision problems. However, practical real-world applications benefit more from listing the *matches* of subgraphs found via subgraph isomorphism *search*, which is the problem studied here.

Definition 4 (Subgraph Isomorphism Search). Given two labeled graphs $G_q = (V_q, E_q, L_q, l_q)$ and $G_d = (V_d, E_d, L_d, l_d)$, subgraph isomorphism search finds all matches, $m \in M$, of G_d, where a *match* is a representative subgraph of G_d that is *subgraph isomorphic* to G_q.

Table 2. Notation.

Symbol	Definition
$C\_Set(V_q)$	Total candidate set of all data vertices $\forall u \in V_q$
$C(u)$	Candidate set of data vertices for query vertex u
$N(u)$	Neighbor set of $u \in V$
$deg(u)$	Degree of vertex u
M', M	Partial matches table, Final matches table
$m \in M$	Subgraph isomorphism match instance
$freq(L(u))$	Count of unique vertices labeled by L
$\mathcal{L}, \|\mathcal{L}\|$	Set of vertex labels, Count of distinct vertex labels
$\ell, \|\ell\|$	Set of edge labels, Count of distinct edge labels
$VS\_List(V)$	Total vertex signature list $\forall u \in V$
$VS(u)$	Vertex signature of $u \in V$
$\vee, \oplus$	Bitwise OR, Bitwise XOR
$<< (n, m)$	Rotational left shift n by m bits
$\mathcal{E}$	Hash code in definitions

Definition 5 (Induced Subgraph Isomorphism Search). Given labeled graphs $G_q = (V_q, E_q, L_q, l_q)$ and $G_d = (V_d, E_d, L_d, l_d)$, induced subgraph isomorphism search finds all matches, $m \in M$, of G_d, where a *match* is a representative subgraph of G_d that is *graph isomorphic* to G_q.

The stricter *induced* version of the search problem prohibits extra edges between mapped vertices $\forall m \in M$ that do not appear in the G_q, i.e. $\forall m \in M$, there is a valid match of both edges and non-edges between G_q and m. Table 2 contains key notations.

3 Vertex Signature Hashing

We define our space-efficient vertex signature $VS(u)$ used as our *local+cycle indexing* strategy, which comprises of two hash codes for high filtering power to help reduce extraneous computations in joining. We later discuss & evaluate our implementation.

3.1 Vertex Signature

The vertex signature encodes *local* and *cycle* properties of v, exploits surrounding $N(v)$ information for *local* filtering to extract data that is specific to $v \in V_d$, and is used for filtering purposes w.r.t. $u \in V_q$. Additionally, *cycle* properties are utilized to express refined filtering with triangles that *local* properties would not be able to exploit.

Definition 6 (Local Label Encoding - LOC). Given a vertex $u \in V$ and hash function f, a *local label encoding* (LOC) is an n-length bit-vector hash code $\mathcal{E}_{loc}$ that incorporates neighboring edge/vertex label pairs $\forall v \in N(u), l((u, v))$ and $L(v)$, s.t. $\mathcal{E}_{loc}$ is the bitwise $\vee$ result computed as:

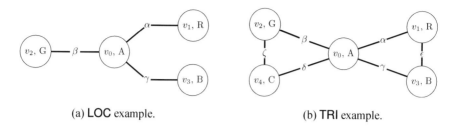

(a) **LOC** example.   (b) **TRI** example.

Fig. 3. Example depictions of LOC and TRI.

$$\mathcal{E}_{loc} = f(\ l(\ (u, v_0)\ ), L(v_0)\ ) \vee f(\ l(\ (u, v_1)\ ), L(v_1)\ ) \cdots \vee$$
$$f(\ l(\ (u, v_{|N(u)|-1})\ ), L(v_{|N(u)|-1})\ ).$$

Example 1 (Local Label Encoding). Given Fig. 3(a), where $L(v_0) = A$, $L(v_1) = R$, $L(v_2) = G$, $L(v_3) = B$, $l(\ (v_0, v_1)\ ) = \alpha$, $l(\ (v_0, v_2)\ ) = \beta$, and $l(\ (v_0, v_3)\ ) = \gamma$, assume $n = 8$, vertex and edge labels map to integers, and hash function $f(x, y) = <<$ $(1, y * |\ell| + x)$, the $\mathcal{E}_{loc}$ at vertex v_0 is:

$$\mathcal{E}_{loc} = f(\ \alpha, R\ ) \vee f(\ \beta, G\ ) \vee f(\ \gamma, B\ )$$
$$= [0,0,0,0,1,0,0,0] \vee [0,1,0,0,0,0,0,0] \vee [0,0,0,0,0,0,1,0]$$
$$= [0,1,0,0,1,0,1,0]$$

Definition 7 (Triangle Edge Encoding - TRI). Given a vertex $u \in V$ and hash function g, $\forall\ v \in N(v)$, a *triangle edge encoding* (TRI) is an n-length bit-vector hash code $\mathcal{E}_{tri}$ that encapsulates vertex and edge labels of immediate *triangles* of u such that u, a, and b form a *triangle*, which is a subgraph $\triangle$ where $a \in N(u)$, $b \in N(u)$, and there exists an edge, i.e. triangle edge, between a and b. $\forall \triangle \in N(u)$, $\mathcal{E}_{tri}$ is the bitwise $\vee$ result computed as:

$$\mathcal{E}_{tri} = g(\ L(a_0), L(b_0), l(\ (a_0, b_0)\ )\ ) \vee g(\ L(a_1), L(b_1), l(\ (a_1, b_1)\ )\ ) \cdots \vee$$
$$g(\ L(a_{|\triangle|-1}), L(b_{|\triangle|-1}), l(\ (a_{|\triangle|-1}, b_{|\triangle|-1})\ )\ ).$$

Example 2 (Triangle Edge Encoding). Given Fig. 3(b), assume $n = 8$, vertex and edge labels map to integers, and hash function $g(x, y, z) = <<$ $(1, (\ (x \oplus y)$ mod $|\mathcal{L}|\ ) * |\ell| + z)$, the $\mathcal{E}_{tri}$ at vertex v_0 is:

$$\mathcal{E}_{tri} = g(G, C, \varsigma) \vee g(R, B, \epsilon)$$
$$= [1,0,0,0,0,0,0,0] \vee [0,0,0,0,0,0,0,1]$$
$$= [1,0,0,0,0,0,0,1]$$

Definition 8 (Vertex Signature). Given a vertex $u \in V$, a vertex signature is a 2-tuple $VS(u) = (\mathcal{E}_{loc}, \mathcal{E}_{tri})$ that represents a $|\mathcal{E}_{loc}| + |\mathcal{E}_{tri}|$-length bit-vector encoding of u.

3.2   Implementation and Evaluation

We store hash codes $\mathcal{E}_{loc}$ and $\mathcal{E}_{tri}$ as 64-bit unsigned integers regardless of $|\mathcal{L}|$ and $|\ell|$ as a general-purpose, space-efficient strategy using f and g previously defined. Data signatures $\forall v \in V_d$ are generated offline while query signatures $\forall u \in V_q$ are generated at runtime, which are compared against each other to determine $C(u)$ membership:

```
1  typedef unsigned long long ull64;
2  bool dvertex_is_candidate(ull64 online, ull64 offline) {
3      return online & offline == online;
4  }
```

Our filtering in G-Morph (GM) differs from GSI [29] with size flexibility since GSI stores 2-bit counts per vertex sized $2|\mathcal{L}| * |\ell|$, which may become large if directly implemented with large unique label counts. GM guarantees matching vertex labels, which saves space, differs from [29,31], and is used to optimize joining. Our TRI filtering strategy is based on triangles rather than connecting edges [31] and utilizes the XOR operator, $|\mathcal{L}|$, and $|\ell|$ to evenly distribute possible input combinations.

We compared GM filtering against the filtering described in GSI. We used graphs identified in Table 4 (later in the paper) with 64-bit unsigned integers for both LOC and TRI, sized $|\mathcal{E}_{loc}| + |\mathcal{E}_{tri}| = 128$ bits, which equaled GSI's signature $2|\mathcal{L}| * |\ell| = 128$ bits with dataset $|\mathcal{L}| = 8$ & $|\ell| = 8$. Exact label and max degree filtering were applied with a uniquely labeled triangle query. Minimum candidate sizes (Table 3) were obtained.

Table 3. GM vs. GSI: comparing filtering effectiveness.

Graph	$|V_d|$	GM $(min(|C(u)|))$	GSI $(min(|C(u)|))$
CM	23k	37	59
AM	335k	132	392
DB	317k	442	695
EN	37k	139	167
BK	58k	98	164
GO	197k	570	745
FB	22k	158	181

GM filters more candidates in this scenario due to the distinct pair labeling of the query graph when signature sizes match. We see the addition of TRI is effective and helps filter additional candidates that would otherwise be unfiltered. We acknowledge that GSI may filter more vertices in other scenarios but with a space penalty of larger signature sizes.

4   G-Morph

In this section, we describe G-Morph, an efficient GPU-based induced subgraph isomorphism search system. We begin with a high-level overview then transition to

```
1   void SubgraphSearch(graph q_graph, graph d_graph,
2               siglist offline_vertex) {
3       /* Generate Signatures */
4       siglist online_vertex(q_graph);
5       /* Filtering */
6       set c_set[q_graph.size][d_graph.size];
7       c_set.filter( q_graph, d_graph,
8               offline_vertex, online_vertex );
9       c_set.compact(d_graph);
10      /* Joining */
11      join_order order(q_graph);
12      list c_edges;
13      c_edges = vertex_join( d_graph,
14              c_set, order );
15      matches m;
16      m = edge_join(c_edges, order);
17  }
```

Fig. 4. Subgraph isomorphism search with G-Morph.

describe the specific algorithms used within each stage. **G-Morph** uses the *filtering-and-joining* framework with control flow in Fig. 4. Inputs of a query graph $G_q = (V_q, E_q, L_q, l_q)$ and a larger data graph $G_d = (V_d, E_d, L_d, l_d)$, which are compressed sparse row (CSR) undirected graphs, are used to output M containing matches.

The *filtering* phase utilizes additional inputs, the offline & online vertex signature lists $VS\_List(V_d)$ & $VS\_List(V_q)$, respectively. $VS\_List(V_d)$ is generated if null. The 2D array sized $O(|V_q||V_d|)$ stores *true* at index (i, j) if $V_d(j)$ is a candidate of $V_q(i)$ (*false* otherwise). After elimination, this phase generates the *compacted* $C\_Set(V_q)$ (line 9) that stores numerical data for vertex candidates $\forall u \in V_q$.

The *joining* phase first computes a *join order* via BFS of G_q. The first node and subsequent branches are selected according to adopted function $Rank(u) = \frac{freq(L_d(u))}{deg(u)}$ [11], which favors higher degree query vertices with less frequently occurring G_d labels. $C\_Set(V_q)$ is the input in vertex joining that joins adjacent candidate vertices together to form the label-compliant candidate edges (line 13). Lastly, using join order, the candidate edges are *connected* together to build partial M' and final M matches.

4.1 Parallel Filtering

The filtering procedure accepts inputs $VS\_List(V_q)$ and $VS\_List(V_d)$, which are the online and offline vertex signatures, respectively, with the goal of populating $C\_Set(V_q)$, the 2D array that stores candidate vertices. Our vertex signature strategy utilizes **LOC** and **TRI** bit-vector encodings described in Sect. 3, which offer fast, branchless, vertex elimination in parallel on the GPU.

A host procedure launches a kernel (see Fig. 5) $\forall u \in V_q$ with $|V_d|$ threads per launch. $C(u) \in C\_Set(V_q)$ is passed to the kernel to set $C(u)$ elements to *true* or *false* (i.e. filtered). Vertices $v \in V_d$ must pass a vertex label filter (line 6) to proceed to

```
1   __device__
2   void kernel_filter (vertex u,
3               graph q_graph, graph d_graph,
4               siglist offline_vertex,
5               siglist online_vertex, set c_set) {
6       if (u.label != d_graph[threadIdx].label
7          || !compare_loc (online_vertex.LOC[u],
8               offline_vertex.LOC[threadIdx])
9          || !compare_tri (online_vertex.TRI[u],
10              offline_vertex.TRI[threadIdx]),
11         || u.degree < d_graph[threadIdx].degree) {
12             c_set[threadIdx] = false;
13      }
14      else {
15             c_set[threadIdx] = true;
16      }
17  }
```

Fig. 5. Parallel filtering kernel.

encoding comparisons (see Sect. 3) to reduce signature memory accesses; comparisons occur in the order of LOC then TRI. Line 11 guarantees that $deg(v)$ is greater than or equal to $deg(u)$, otherwise, v is filtered. A barrier synchronizes kernel launches per u.

4.2 Split-Scan Compaction

The compaction procedure converts the Boolean arrays of $C\_Set(V_q)$ to newly allocated compacted numerical arrays, i.e., each *true* at i is replaced by v_i and each *false* no longer occupies space between numerical values. The algorithm used to generate the output indices array to compact $C\_Set(V_q)$ is *split-scan*, a wrapper for an ordinary GPU-based *scan*. The advantage of split-scan is that it bypasses thread limits per scan.

The split-scan algorithm works as follows on the example in Fig. 6. It first finds the size of each split by dividing the input array size by 2 until the size is less than or equal to a threshold value (e.g. max thread count). The first row of Fig. 6 is the input array, middle rows are intermediate values, and the last row has the output. The split size is 4 (by color); X is a value yet to be accessed. An exclusive *scan* is run on each split iteratively with *adjustments* from each last value (e.g. $0 + 2$, $1 + 4$, and $1 + 5$).

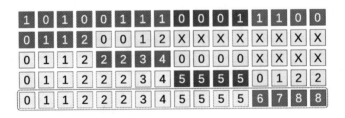

Fig. 6. Example of split-scan with intermediate values shown.

Compaction iterates each $C(u) \in C\_Set(V_q)$ and uses split-scan to generate the array of indices necessary to compact $C\_Set(V_q)$ sized as the last value of split-scan. Kernels are launched with original and split-scan arrays to populate compacted arrays.

4.3 Slide-Join

Given compacted $C\_Set(V_q)$ and edge-based *join order*, the vertex joining step performs adjacency checks in $C(u_1) \times C(u_2)$ for each edge (u_1, u_2) in the join order. Our sliding window algorithm *slide-join* performs edge verification once and provides overflow protection for larger input via segmentation.

Candidate edges adopt a CSR-like data structure [24]. The candidate edges of a given (u_1, u_2) comprise of arrays: row offsets (abbr. *ver*), column indices (abbr. *edg*), and destination values (abbr. *val*). The last panel (Fig. 7) depicts a final structure.

Slide-join builds CSR-like structures per *join order* edge (u_1, u_2) that represents candidate edges $(v_i, v_j) \in C(u_1) \times C(u_2)$. The Cartesian product size is compared against a max threshold to determine segment usage. It creates the adjacency (abbr. *adj*) array in parallel where the value at $i * |C(u_2)| + j$ is 1 if $v_i \in C(u_1)$ is adjacent to $v_j \in C(u_2)$ s.t. $l_q((u_1, u_2)) = l_d((v_i, v_j))$ (0 otherwise) then compacts *adj* via split-scan. We launch additional kernels to populate each CSR-like array. If the threshold value is exceeded, this process is performed by segment of the $C(u_1)$ against all of $C(u_2)$ with the window size calculated s.t. its value by $|C(u_2)|$ cannot exceed the threshold to build partial structures. Finally, kernels coalesce partials together and reindex *ver* in parallel.

Figure 7 illustrates slide-join with segmented candidate edge building. The window size is 2 and each partial structure is built iteratively. The first panel depicts (v_0, v_1),

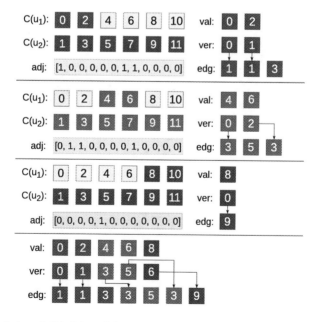

Fig. 7. Depiction of slide-join to join vertices and build candidate edges of a query edge.

(v_2, v_1) and (v_2, v_3) as valid candidate edges from *adj* array using the indexing rules. The last panel depicts the final coalesced structure with reindexed *ver* values.

4.4 Edge Joining

Lastly, we build M from built candidate edges. Iteratively using the *join order*, partial matches M' are built until final matches M are realized. Our adopted edge joining [12,24] strategy counts the number of matches per row in M' then allocates enough memory to write out the matches to M; split-scan determines the write address.

Specifically, this step first builds M' with initially two columns representing the first candidate edge. Subsequent candidate edges are iteratively joined to M', growing column width size, using joining rules between existing M' and the next connecting $C(u_i)$ of the join order, which is done via edge verification kernels with binary search of potential extensions and split-scan for write addresses in M'. Processing continues until partial solutions grow to the final M table after iterating all join order edges.

Furthermore, our system supports both *induced* and *non-induced* matching logic determined by the user and offers split-scan to exploit the sorted candidate edges of slide-join for edge verification. We avoid duplicate checks with guaranteed label matches and use a strided memory layout of M for coalesced memory accesses since each row is accessed by a contiguous thread index.

5 Experimental Evaluation

We evaluate G-Morph with real-world and synthetic graphs by measuring runtimes; scalability is measured by varying query and data sizes. We used some graphs from the Stanford Large Network Dataset Collection (SNAP) [16] repository. Synthetic graphs were generated with PaRMAT [13]. All graphs are undirected with self-loops removed. G-Morph outputs correct, exact solutions and was extensively compared against the output of Boost VF2 [1] and tested systems.

The experiments were performed on a machine with one GPU and one CPU – NVIDIA GeForce RTX 2080 Ti with 68 SMs and 11 GB of GDDR6 RAM, 8-core Intel Core i7-9700K running Ubuntu 18.04, kernel 4.15.0-106-generic, with 32 GB DDR4 RAM and solid-state storage, and CUDA Toolkit 10.2. All runtimes presented are averages over five repetitions of the same experiment. Graph load times and offline metadata generation times on all systems were not factored in and runtimes were calculated when the final solution was stored into memory.

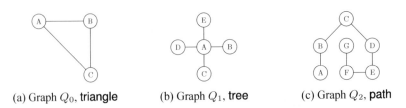

(a) Graph Q_0, **triangle**   (b) Graph Q_1, **tree**   (c) Graph Q_2, **path**

Fig. 8. Query graphs: Q_0 is needed to evaluate TRI while Q_1 and Q_2 are generic pattern types previously used in other similar evaluations [19].

Table 4. SNAP graph datasets used in evaluation.

	ca-CondMat	com-Amazon	com-DBLP	email-Enron	loc-Brightkite
ID	CM	AM	DB	EN	BK
$|V_d|$	23k	335k	317k	37k	58k
$|E_d|$	93k	926k	1.05M	184k	214k

	loc-Gowalla	musae-Facebook	web-Google	web-NotreDame	web-Stanford
ID	GO	FB	WG	WN	WS
$|V_d|$	197k	22k	876k	326k	282k
$|E_d|$	950k	171k	5.11M	1.50M	2.31M

Table 5. Comparison on real-world graphs as runtimes (ms).

Graph	GM-TL	GM-L	GSI	VF3	VF3P
CM	1.04	1.10	8.47	1.35	80
AM	2.80	3.20	44.17	43.16	10,668
DB	3.46	3.82	40.31	41.31	9,491
EN	0.954	0.952	10.39	4.00	132
BK	0.980	0.983	11.74	4.12	269
GO	2.88	3.33	31.65	47.41	3,602
FB	0.89	0.90	9.13	3.45	79.9
WG	19.71	19.93	115.10	385.80	180,628
WN	3.57	3.93	36.60	33.37	6,254
WS	5.38	5.56	54.86	168.17	8,515
WG5	102.27	170.25	118.91	1,633	400,946
WN5	10.85	15.62	38.5	109.21	18,210
WS5	42.46	42.61	71.55	1,827	29,288
EN1	N/A	542.19*	163.32	23,620	N/A
GO1	N/A	9,961*	1,802	167,743	N/A

*LOC off due to unlabeled graph.

5.1   Real-World Graphs

The experiments in this section were designed to measure the effectiveness of our overall strategy for real-world graphs. We obtain runtimes to measure the performance of G-Morph against a variety of real-world SNAP datasets (Table 4). All graphs were undirected; web-type graphs were converted for evaluation. Data graph labeling: $|\mathcal{L}| = 10$ & $|\ell| = 5$ for graphs with no suffix number (e.g. EN), $|\mathcal{L}| = |\ell| = 5$ for graphs suffixed with "5" (e.g. WG5), and $|\mathcal{L}| = |\ell| = 1$ for graphs suffixed with "1" (e.g. EN1). Query graph: Q_0 (Fig. 8(a)) with distinct edge labels (unlabeled in "1" suffixed graphs).

We measure G-Morph (GM) under two modes: (1) GM-TL (LOC & TRI on) and (2) GM-L (LOC on, TRI off). GM is compared against the best existing systems – GPU-based GSI [4] and CPU-based VF3 [3]. The multithreaded version of VF3, VF3P, was used with 8 threads. Table 5 shows that GM outperforms GSI, VF3, and VF3P for most graphs. GM-TL achieved a max speedup of 15.78× vs. GSI, AM. It obtained speedups of 43.56× vs. VF3, EN1 and 9165× vs. VF3P, WG.

GM-TL outperforms GM-L due to indexing triangles. WG5 experienced the greatest benefit from TRI usage, which proves the effectiveness of TRI especially in larger graphs (WG is the largest tested w.r.t. $|V_d|$). GM-L alone outperforms GSI in most cases, suggesting TRI is optional for smaller graphs if more space is needed since LOC with slide-join often produce ample speedups.

Although this paper's focus is labeled graphs, two unlabeled experiments (EN1 & GO1) were run for completeness with LOC & TRI off. GM easily outperformed VF3 in these unlabeled experiments, but GSI outperformed GM in this case. VF3P crashed with no results here and VF3P also experienced relatively slow runtimes throughout.

5.2 Scalability

This subsection measures G-Morph performance against other systems by increasing the data graph and query graph size, respectively. All experiments have LOC enabled while the experiment using Q_0 also has TRI enabled.

Data Graph Size: We study the scalability of G-Morph with varying *data graph* size. Five input RMAT graphs started at size $|V_d| = 50k$ and $|E_d| = 200k$ and doubly scaled $|V_d|$ & $|E_d|$ (largest $|V_d| = 250k$ and $|E_d| = 1M$). The same datasets were run vs. three query patterns (Fig. 8). The labeling scheme was: Q_0 as $|\mathcal{L}| = |\ell| = 3$, Q_1 as $|\mathcal{L}| = |\ell| = 5$, and Q_2 as $|\mathcal{L}| = 7$ & $|\ell| = 3$. G_d used the same labeling counts per query graph. G-Morph (GM) is compared against GSI and VF3 with induced matches.

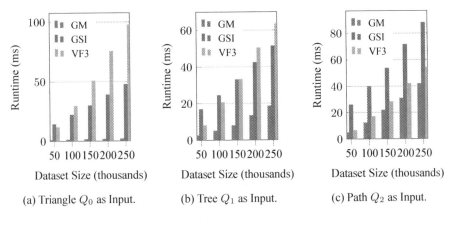

(a) Triangle Q_0 as Input.   (b) Tree Q_1 as Input.   (c) Path Q_2 as Input.

Fig. 9. Scalability with increasing data size.

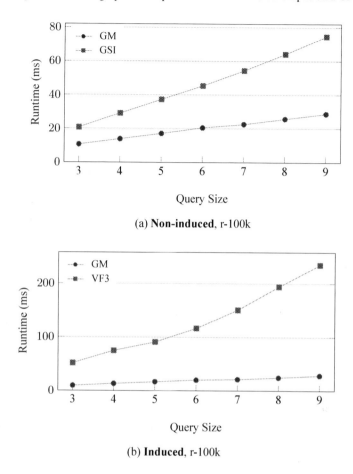

(a) **Non-induced**, r-100k

(b) **Induced**, r-100k

Fig. 10. Scalability with increasing query size.

Figure 9 shows results across all query graphs from Fig. 8 with runtimes (ms) against dataset sizes. GM outperforms the best existing systems with promising scalability. GM speedups are significant against smaller datasets but level out as they scale. GM achieves speedups up to 23.15×, 6.47×, and 5.34× vs. GSI on respective patterns. Speedups vs. VF3 were around 47.39×, 4.14×, and 1.39× on respective patterns.

Query Graph Size: We measure GM scalability with varying *query* size. Path queries with an incrementing size were used against an RMAT dataset ($|V_d| = 100k$, $|E_d| = 2M$, $|\mathcal{L}| = 10$, $|\ell| = 5$). V_q were distinctly labeled; E_q labeled with incrementing value mod $|\ell|$. Experimental configuration: *induced* mode *off* vs. GSI and *on* vs. VF3.

GM outperformed both GSI and VF3 in these experiments too. Figure 10 shows promising scalability of GM against GSI and especially VF3. GM's runtime increases very slowly with query size, especially against VF3 with *induced* matches. GM's speedups against GSI and VF3 were 2.6× and 8.19×, respectively, for the query size of 9.

6 Conclusions

We presented G-Morph, an efficient GPU-based subgraph isomorphism search system on labeled graphs. We proposed a novel space-efficient vertex signature strategy that can be implemented as integers with good filtering power of proposed LOC and TRI codes implementing *local+cycle indexing*. By reducing downstream Cartesian products and improving edge verification, extraneous computations are limited. We also proposed a novel joining procedure *slide-join*, a sliding window algorithm that avoids duplicate edge verification and offers overflow protection; *split-scan* handles large scans. Experiments on labeled real-world graphs show G-Morph outperforming both GSI and VF3.

Acknowledgement. This work is supported in part by National Science Foundation grants CCF-1813173, CCF-2002554, and CCF-2028714 to the University of California Riverside.

References

1. Boost Graph Library: VF2 (Sub)Graph Isomorphism - master (2020). https://www.boost.org/doc/libs/master/libs/graph/doc/vf2_sub_graph_iso.html. Accessed July 2020
2. Chapter 39. Parallel Prefix Sum (Scan) with CUDA (2020). https://developer.nvidia.com/gpugems/gpugems3/part-vi-gpu-computing/chapter-39-parallel-prefix-sum-scan-cuda. Accessed July 2020
3. MiviaLab/vf3lib: VF3 Algorithm - The fastest algorithm to solve subgraph isomorphism on large and dense graphs (2020). https://github.com/MiviaLab/vf3lib. Accessed July 2020
4. bookug/GSI: GPU-friendly subgraph isomorphism (2020). https://github.com/bookug/GSI. Accessed Oct 2020
5. Bonnici, V., Giugno, R., Pulvirenti, A., Shasha, D., Ferro, A.: A subgraph isomorphism algorithm and its application to biochemical data. BMC Bioinformatics **14**(S7), S13 (2013)
6. Carletti, V., Foggia, P., Saggese, A., Vento, M.: Introducing VF3: a new algorithm for subgraph isomorphism. In: Foggia, P., Liu, C.-L., Vento, M. (eds.) GbRPR 2017. LNCS, vol. 10310, pp. 128–139. Springer, Cham (2017). https://doi.org/10.1007/978-3-319-58961-9_12
7. Cordella, L.P., Foggia, P., Sansone, C., Vento, M.: A (sub) graph isomorphism algorithm for matching large graphs. IEEE Trans. Pattern Anal. Mach. Intell. **26**(10), 1367–1372 (2004)
8. Cordella, L.P., Foggia, P., Sansone, C., Vento, M.: An improved algorithm for matching large graphs. In: Workshop on Graph-Based Representations in Pattern Recognition, pp. 149–159 (2001)
9. Fan, W., Wang, X., Wu, Y.: Diversified top-k graph pattern matching. Proc. VLDB Endowment **6**(13), 1510–1521 (2013)
10. Han, T.D., Abdelrahman, T.S.: Reducing branch divergence in GPU programs. In: Workshop on General Purpose Processing on Graphics Processing Units, pp. 1–8 (2011)
11. Han, W.S., Lee, J., Lee, J.H.: TurboISO: towards ultrafast and robust subgraph isomorphism search in large graph databases. In: ACM SIGMOD International Conference on Management of Data, pp. 337–348 (2013)
12. He, B., et al.: Relational joins on graphics processors. In: ACM SIGMOD International Conference on Management of Data, pp. 511–524 (2008)
13. Khorasani, F., Gupta, R., Bhuyan, L.N.: Scalable SIMD-efficient graph processing on GPUs. In: International Conference on Parallel Architectures and Compilation Techniques, pp. 39–50 (2015)

14. Khorasani, F., Vora, K., Gupta, R., Bhuyan, L.N.: CuSha: vertex-centric graph processing on GPUs. In: International Symposium on High-performance Parallel and Distributed Computing, pp. 239–252 (2014)
15. Lee, J., Han, W.S., Kasperovics, R., Lee, J.H.: An in-depth comparison of subgraph isomorphism algorithms in graph databases. Proc. VLDB Endowment **6**(2), 133–144 (2012)
16. Leskovec, J., Krevl, A.: SNAP Datasets: Stanford large network dataset collection (2014). http://snap.stanford.edu/data
17. McCreesh, C., Prosser, P., Solnon, C., Trimble, J.: When subgraph isomorphism is really hard, and why this matters for graph databases. J. Artif. Intell. Res. **61**, 723–759 (2018)
18. Raymond, J.W., Willett, P.: Maximum common subgraph isomorphism algorithms for the matching of chemical structures. J. Comput. Aided Mol. Des. **16**(7), 521–533 (2002)
19. Reza, T., Ripeanu, M., Tripoul, N., Sanders, G., Pearce, R.: PruneJuice: pruning trillion-edge graphs to a precise pattern-matching solution. In: International Conference for High Performance Computing, Networking, Storage and Analysis, pp. 265–281 (2018)
20. Serafini, M., De Francisci Morales, G., Siganos, G.: QFrag: distributed graph search via subgraph isomorphism. In: Symposium on Cloud Computing, pp. 214–228 (2017)
21. Shamir, R., Tsur, D.: Faster subtree isomorphism. In: Israeli Symposium on Theory of Computing and Systems, pp. 126–131 (1997)
22. Shi, C., Li, Y., Zhang, J., Sun, Y., Philip, S.Y.: A survey of heterogeneous information network analysis. IEEE Trans. Knowl. Data Eng. **29**(1), 17–37 (2016)
23. Song, Q., Wu, Y., Lin, P., Dong, L.X., Sun, H.: Mining summaries for knowledge graph search. IEEE Trans. Knowl. Data Eng. **30**(10), 1887–1900 (2018)
24. Tran, H.-N., Kim, J., He, B.: Fast subgraph matching on large graphs using graphics processors. In: Renz, M., Shahabi, C., Zhou, X., Cheema, M.A. (eds.) DASFAA 2015. LNCS, vol. 9049, pp. 299–315. Springer, Cham (2015). https://doi.org/10.1007/978-3-319-18120-2_18
25. Ullmann, J.R.: An algorithm for subgraph isomorphism. JACM **23**(1), 31–42 (1976)
26. Wang, L., Wang, Y., Owens, J.D.: Fast parallel subgraph matching on the GPU. In: High Performance Parallel and Dist. Computing (2016)
27. Wang, Y., Davidson, A., Pan, Y., Wu, Y., Riffel, A., Owens, J.D.: Gunrock: a high-performance graph processing library on the GPU. In: Symposium on Principles and Practice of Parallel Programming, pp. 1–12 (2016)
28. Webber, J.: A programmatic introduction to Neo4j. In: Conference on Systems, Programming, and Apps: Software for Humanity, pp. 217–218 (2012)
29. Zeng, L., Zou, L., Özsu, M.T., Hu, L., Zhang, F.: GSI: GPU-friendly subgraph isomorphism. In: International Conference on Data Engineering, pp. 1249–1260 (2020)
30. Zhang, S., Li, S., Yang, J.: GADDI: distance index based subgraph matching in biological networks. In: International Conference on Extending Database Technology: Advances in Database Technology, pp. 192–203 (2009)
31. Zheng, W., Zou, L., Lian, X., Hong, L., Zhao, D.: Efficient subgraph skyline search over large graphs. In: ACM International Conference on Information and Knowledge Management, pp. 1529–1538 (2014)

Parallel and Distributed Programming, Interfaces, and Languages

Accelerating Graph Applications Using Phased Transactional Memory

Catalina Munoz Morales[1(✉)], Rafael Murari[2], Joao P. L. de Carvalho[1],
Bruno Chinelato Honorio[1], Alexandro Baldassin[2], and Guido Araujo[1]

[1] Institute of Computing, UNICAMP, Campinas, Brazil
{catalina.morales,joao.carvalho,bruno.honorio,guido}@ic.unicamp.br
[2] Universidade Estadual Paulista (UNESP), Rio Claro, Brazil
{rafael.murari,alexandro.baldassin}@unesp.br

Abstract. Due to their fine-grained operations and low conflict rates, graph processing algorithms expose a large amount of parallelism that has been extensively exploited by various parallelization frameworks. Transactional Memory (TM) is a programming model that uses an optimistic concurrency control mechanism to improve the performance of irregular applications, making it a perfect candidate to extract parallelism from graph-based programs. Although fast Hardware TM (HTM) instructions are now available in the ISA extensions of some major processor architectures (e.g., Intel and ARM), balancing the usage of Software TM (STM) and HTM to compensate for capacity and conflict aborts is still a challenging task. This paper presents a Phased TM implementation for graph applications, called Graph-Oriented Transactional Memory (GoTM). It uses a three-state (HTM, STM, GLOCK) concurrency control automaton that leverages both HTM and STM implementations to speed-up graph applications. Experimental results using seven well-known graph programs and real-life workloads show that GoTM can outperform other Phased TM systems and lock-based concurrency mechanisms such as the one present in Galois, a state-of-the-art framework for graph computations.

Keywords: Hardware transactional memory · Software transactional memory · Graph processing · Large-scale graphs

1 Introduction

Graphs are data structures that can model complex relationships between information data points. As graph-based applications have become pervasive in many areas like social sciences, biology [2], and networking [21], graph sizes have rapidly grown, thus increasing application execution time. To address that, specialized parallel programming models have been developed aiming at extracting performance from graph-based application frameworks [12]. For example,

---

C.M. Morales—This work was supported by FAPESP (grant 2017/15236-0) under the CEPID Center for Computational Engineering and Sciences project.

L. Sousa et al. (Eds.): Euro-Par 2021, LNCS 12820, pp. 421–434, 2021.
https://doi.org/10.1007/978-3-030-85665-6_26

Vertex/edge-centric and block-centric models [12] have been designed to expose different granularity levels and shape coordination within tasks. The popular vertex-centric model was first proposed in [20] to motivate programmers to write programs that operate on a single vertex at a time using the information propagated by other vertices in its neighborhood. A typical parallel data-driven vertex-centric program processes one vertex at a time, schedules vertices from a list, and assigns them to a set of parallel threads. As a result, two or more vertices inside the same neighborhood can be simultaneously processed, thus creating a potential conflict. Hence, the programmer must foresee any potential data dependencies that can occur in the program and use some synchronization mechanism to deal with the conflicts. However, due to the irregular nature of graph applications, optimal handling of such synchronization can become a challenging task in modern multi-core architectures.

This paper introduces Graph-Oriented Transactional Memory (GoTM), an approach that tailors TM [15] to the needs of a high-level synchronization mechanism for graph programming. By relying on transactions, the burden of devising complex lock-based synchronization is removed from programmers and left to the underlying runtime system. In particular, GoTM is a phased TM implementation, which leverages Hardware TM (HTM), available in modern architectures [16,17], and Software TM (STM) implementations [10,13] to optimize the execution of transactions under software and hardware (e.g., size of speculative storage) limitations. The motivation for using a Phased TM implementation in graph programs comes from the fact that the size of a vertex neighborhood can vary considerably. Processing a vertex-centric function inside a transaction may demand different speculative storage sizes causing some executions to exceed the speculative storage capacity of the underlying HTM hardware, in which case switching to STM execution is required. Hence, the TM runtime needs to handle not only the conflicting accesses between neighboring vertices but also the transactions that exceed the machine's speculative storage, as discussed in [14]. To address this issue, GoTM gathers runtime information to chose among three execution modes: (a) Hardware (HW), (b) Software (SW), and (c) Global Locking (GLOCK).

1.1 Motivating Example

To illustrate the relevance of GoTM, consider the pseudocode in Fig. 1a of Single Source Shortest Path (SSSP), an algorithm that finds the values of the subpaths of all the vertices from a source vertex. SSSP starts with a worklist W containing only the source vertex. Vertex u is then removed from a thread-local worklist (line 1), and passed to the vertex function (line 2). The vertex function iterates through its neighborhood $N(u)$ propagating the minimum path value in a push-style computation (line 5), by comparing the current path value $v.p$ of v with the path value $u.p$ of u plus the connecting edge (u, v) weight $e.w$ (line 6). If a vertex path $v.p$ is changed, it must be pushed into the global worklist (line 8) to schedule it for a new computation.

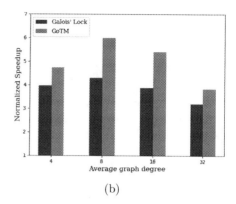

```
1  for all vertex u in W
2      execute SSSP(u)
3
4  SSSP(vertex u)
5    for all e(u,v) in N(u)
6        if (v.p > e.w+u.p) {
7            v.p = e.w+u.p
8            push_to_W(v)
9        }
```

(a)   (b)

Fig. 1. (a) Pseudocode for a Vertex-Centric SSSP program. (b) GoTM and Galois'
Lock speedup for graphs with different graph degrees.

Notice that the iterations of the *for* loop (the vertex function) in line 1 can
be executed in parallel. To create such implementation, a domain-specific programming model such as Galois [22] can be used. Galois is a C++ library for
shared-memory architectures that implements specific-purpose graphs, queues,
and other specialized data structures for concurrent irregular computation. A
performance comparison is carried with the SSSP algorithm implemented in
Galois. The speedup was measured for Galois' original lock-based mechanism
(Galois' Lock) and GoTM with respect to Galois' execution with 1 thread (no
concurrency control), using Rmat workloads with 10 million vertices and variable average degree. As shown in Fig. 1b, GoTM delivers improved performance
over the lock-based mechanism for graphs of all graphs. In this example, capacity abort rate of GoTM varies from 1.5% to 13.5% as the average degree and
graph size increase. To handle such variation the GoTM runtime needs to decide
whether to execute transactions in either HW or SW mode.

Most graph-based applications have a set of common features. First, similarly
to SSSP, many graph applications such as Kcore and Connected Components
(CC), can be written using the same asynchronous data-driven programming
style. Second, many real-life graphs follow a power degree distribution, in which
the majority of the vertices have a small degree, but a smaller portion of vertices
have a much larger degree [8]. As a result, to enable an efficient execution, graph
programs need to dynamically adjust its computation to the degree variability
happening at run time. Hence, any TM approach that aims at improving the
performance of graph applications needs to take the above mentioned points
into consideration. This insight was the central motivation for the proposal of
GoTM.

1.2   Contributions

This paper makes the following contributions:

- A Phase TM implementation called Graph-Oriented TM (GoTM) that executes parallel graph programs. GoTM uses committed transactions throughput as a metric to dynamically decide the best execution mode between HW, SW, or GLOCK (Sect. 3);
- A thorough analysis of the execution modes of graph programs that shows both the merits and limitations of GoTM for some workloads (Sect. 4);
- Experimental results that show speedup improvements when using GoTM in comparison to a lock-based approach and a TM implementation. The performance was evaluated for seven graph programs and five graph workloads including two real-life datasets and three randomly generated graphs with power-law degree distribution (Sect. 4).

The rest of this paper is organized as follows. Section 2 presents background on TM and describes the graph programming model used for writing the graph applications that were evaluated. Section 3 describes the proposed Phased TM automaton for graph programs (GoTM). Section 4 reports the experimental results for various graph applications and workloads. Section 5 describes the related work, and finally, Sect. 6 concludes the paper.

2   Background

2.1   TM Background

Synchronization mechanisms are required to avoid data inconsistencies due to concurrent accesses in shared-memory architectures. They can be roughly classified into blocking and non-blocking.

Transactional Memory (TM) is a non-blocking concurrency control mechanism for parallel programming in shared-memory architectures [15]. It facilitates software development by providing the user with a high-level abstraction where concurrency control issues are hidden from the programmer. In TM, the programmer delimits the portion of code corresponding to the transaction and the runtime system assures that transactions will satisfy the *atomicity, isolation* and *consistency* properties [15]. Such properties guarantee that the effects of a transaction are only visible outside its scope if the conflict detection mechanism indicates no conflict, in which case the transaction will *commit*. On the other hand, if a conflict with another concurrent transaction occurs, one of the transactions will *abort*.

Several runtime implementations of TM have been designed in both Hardware (HTM) [16,24] and Software (STM) [10,13]. However, both HTM and STM runtimes have their drawbacks. HTM offers excellent performance but has limitations when the transaction overflows its local storage capacity, thus increasing the abort rate. On the other hand, although STM runtimes have no capacity limitations, its conflict detection, commit, and abort mechanisms are slower than HTM. For these reasons, some approaches attempt to benefit from both STM and HTM by implementing hybrid systems [4,9,11], where transactions can be concurrently executed in both hardware and software, depending on the availability of HTM and the requirement of a software-based fallback path. However, hybrid TM systems need additional work to coordinate conflict detection within transactions running in hardware and software. This coordination might generate unnecessary overhead when hardware transactions are executed, which may hurt the overall performance [11]. An alternative solution to leverage both STM and HTM is to execute all transactions in a single HW or SW mode of execution according to the program phase. This idea leads to a TM implementation called phased TM (PhTM), first designed by Lev et al. in [19]. This design was then revised and implemented in a new version called PhTM* [5]. In those phased TM systems, the execution mode controller decides when to switch between modes, based on gathered runtime information such as transaction execution cycle count and number of HW retries. If transactions consistently abort due to the lack of speculative storage capacity, the controller generates a transition to SW mode. Moreover, if after a maximum number of retries conflict-related aborts still occur, the execution mode switches to Global Locking (GLOCK) mode. Although PhTM techniques improve the performance of TM code, they do not specifically target graph programs, and thus do not take into consideration the large execution time fluctuations found in these programs due to the unbalanced vertex degree distribution. The GoTM approach proposed in this paper aims to address this problem.

2.2 Programming Model for Graph Applications

Graph programs require at least one data structure representing the graph itself and other auxiliary data structures, such as queues, to track the order of tasks to be executed. For parallel programming of irregular applications, the Galois C++ library [22] provides the user with concurrent data structures, along with a series of loop constructs such as the for_each function that receives as arguments: (a) a worklist of items to be operated in parallel; (b) a function or function pointer; and (c) a series of optional parameter settings for custom execution of such loop.

For applications prone to conflict, the default Galois system uses a lock-based access control mechanism (Galois' Lock), in which all read operations of a conflicting vertex performed inside the vertex function should happen before any write operation occurs. In this paper, the Galois' Locking mechanism was replaced by the GoTM model proposed in Sect. 3, thus relieving the vertex functions from using locks. Instead, the vertex function is speculatively executed inside a transaction. To facilitate the use of the GoTM runtime and free the programmer from the task of performing manual instrumentation, the proposed approach uses constructs available in the GNU Compiler Collection (GCC) since version 4.7, which allow creating a transactional region by enclosing the operator code between two braces preceded by the __transaction_atomic annotation.

3   Graph Oriented Phased TM (GoTM)

The execution of transactions in the GoTM automaton presented in Fig. 2 starts in HW mode by default. In any mode, the throughput of the committed transactions (HW/SW_THRU) is measured during a window of time called mode threshold (MODE_THRSD). During this time window, the abort rates due to conflict and capacity are also measured. When the measured execution cycles (mode_cycles) in a mode (state) reaches the MODE_THRSD limit, the automaton is forced to switch to the other mode (HW → SW or SW → HW) to collect new commit throughput numbers and decide the best current execution mode. While in the HW or SW modes (states) of the automaton (Fig. 2), the transitions occur as follows:

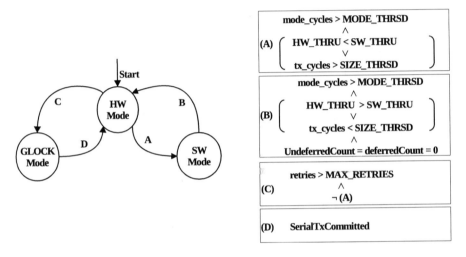

Fig. 2. Graph-oriented TM automaton (GoTM).

HW Mode. The system executes in HW mode until reaching MODE_THRSD time. After this, the throughput (HW_THRU) is compared with the last commit throughput seen in SW mode (SW_THRU). If SW_THRU > HW_THRU, the SW mode is more beneficial to the system, and the automaton switches to SW mode (transition A in Fig. 2). Moreover, the automaton will also switch to SW mode (A) if, after reaching MODE_THRSD, the average cycle count (tx_cycles) of the transactions executed in HW mode is greater than a certain time threshold (SIZE_THRSD). The tx_cycles count acts here as a proxy to the size of a transaction that can lead to capacity aborts. Another transition out of HW mode is to the GLOCK mode (transition C). This transition takes place when persistent conflict aborts occur, and the HW transaction exceeds a maximum number of retries (MAX_RETRIES). The HW → GLOCK transition serves as an escape route for conflict-related aborts to avoid unwanted HW → SW transitions that would add extra overheads.

SW Mode. In SW mode, the throughput of the SW committed transactions (SW_THRU) is measured during the MODE_THRSD time window. In this case, to trigger an SW → HW transition (transition B), one of the following two conditions must be met after reaching MODE_THRSD: SW_THRU < HW_THRU, which indicates that HW mode may be more beneficial than SW mode; or that tx_cycles is less than SIZE_THRSD, to ensure that transactions are small enough and that there is a lower chance of capacity aborts once in HW mode. Additionally, two variables called deferred_counter and undeferred_counter keep count of the number of transactions that, while in HW mode triggered a transition to SW mode (deferred_counter), and the number of transactions that are executing in SW but did not increment the deferred counter (undeferred_counter). When executing in SW mode, all transactions that incremented these counters must be executed before a new transition to HW mode occurs. Therefore, the automaton triggers transition B once the counters are verified to have a zero value, thus ensuring that the transactions that caused a transition have committed before a new transition occurs and that there are no transactions currently running.

GLOCK Mode. When in GLOCK mode, transactions start execution by acquiring a global lock and keep it while running, thus serializing execution. Once the transaction that triggered the transition to GLOCK mode finishes, the automaton makes an immediate transition back to HW mode (transition D).

The transaction throughput metric proposed in GoTM is particularly beneficial to the types of computation typically found in data-driven graph programs, in which work is scheduled as new data is available, and there is no way to foresee the behavior of future transactions. Moreover, a careful look at the power-degree graphs used for the experiments (Sect. 4) shows that it is possible to predict that transactions operating on vertices with a higher degree, which are fewer, have larger tx_cycle count that triggers a transition to SW mode. Therefore, these transactions have a greater chance of being executed and committed in SW mode. Moreover, vertices with a lower degree have less chance of suffering capacity related aborts, making those transactions better suited for execution in HW mode.

4 Experimental Results

This section shows how GoTM can leverage HTM/STM to improve graph applications performance, even in the face of persistent capacity and conflict aborts. Our results with 18 threads of execution show that, when using GoTM, graph programs with large workloads do not only scale but also show performance improvements over Galois' lock-based approach (Galois' Lock), and PhTM*, a state-of-the-art phased TM implementation that has shown to outperform other related TM runtimes. The experiments reveal that GoTM can improve performance for various graph applications and different workload characteristics.

Experimental Setup. Experiments were carried out in an Intel(R) Xeon(R) Gold 5220 CPU @ 2.20 GHz machine with 18 cores. Each application was run 10 times for each input graph. Average and a 95% confidence interval are reported in the graphs. Applications were compiled with g++ (GCC) version 7.4.0 and -O3 compiler optimization. Parameters MODE_THRSD (100 ms) and SIZE_THRSD (100000 cycles) were empirically chosen based on the results of the experiments, similarly as in other related works [23,26].

Table 1. Input graphs characteristics.

Name	$|V|$	$|E|$	Mean degree
Rmat8	30M	240M	8
Rmat16	30M	480M	16
Rmat32	30M	960M	32
Soc-lv	4M	68M	14
Friendster	65M	1806M	28

The experiments were carried out with seven graph applications and two types of commonly used workloads. To study the performance variation with respect to the graph degree, graphs with different vertex degrees were generated, namely three Rmat input graphs with power-law degree distribution and average in-degree of 8, 16, and 32 from the Chakrabarti [6] recursive matrix model. Two real-life graph datasets from the Stanford Large Network Dataset Collection [18] were also used for evaluation: (a) Friendster, an online gaming network where a user is represented by a vertex and the outgoing edges of the vertex are his/her friendship connections; and (b) Soc-lv, a ground-truth based directed graph representing an online community of bloggers. A description of all graph inputs is presented in Table 1.

4.1   Applications

All applications were constructed using the Galois framework. The transactional versions of the applications replace the lock-based mechanism of Galois with transactions. All applications are push-style and data-driven. All tests for Galois's Lock, PhTM*, and GoTM were performed with the same application implementation.

- **Single Source Shortest Path (SSSP).** In SSSP, at each execution of the vertex function, neighboring vertices are updated with the minimum available value and added to the worklist in a push programming style.
- **Breadth-First Search (BFS).** Similar to SSSP, the BFS algorithm updates to the minimum level each vertex in a push style.
- **Spanning tree (ST).** This application traverses an unweighted graph from a source vertex and constructs a tree subgraph with edges selected greedily.
- **Kcore.** In this application, the worklist is initialized with the vertices that have a degree lower than k. The edges connected to these vertices are logically removed and the degree of the adjacent vertices is subtracted by 1.
- **Betweeness Centrality (BC).** A parallel version of the Brandes algorithm [3] was implemented. First, for each vertex u in graph G a shortest path is computed starting at source vertex v, and each edge on the path is stored. Second, a back-propagation is executed to count the number of times each vertex appears on the path between u and v.

- **Page Rank (PR).** PR is an algorithm used by search engines to rank webpages by order of importance. An asynchronous push-style version was selected, based on the residual value. In this case, the active vertex updates its value and pushes an updated residual value to its neighbors as in [25].
- **Weakly Connected Components (WCC).** WCC finds (possibly) undirected paths between any pair of vertices in the connected component. This algorithm propagates, in a data-driven manner, the minimum label value over the connected components until no further changes occur.

4.2   GoTM Performance

The performance of GoTM was compared to Galois's Lock and PhTM* by calculating the normalized speedup of the three approaches over Galois' execution with 1 thread (no concurrency control). Performance results are shown in Fig. 3 for both Rmat and real-life workloads. Table 2 shows the SW and HW execution mode percentage (remaining percentage belongs to GLOCK mode), Capacity abort rate, and conflict abort rate of GoTM for all workloads with 18 threads. All applications running with GoTM scale with respect to the baseline.

Performance for Rmat Workloads. For all Rmat workloads, SSSP, BFS, ST, BC, and WCC scale up to 18 threads, and Kcore scales up to 12 threads due to its lower number of iterations. For applications SSSP, BFS, ST, and WCC, GoTM outperforms both lock Galois and PhTM* when running with 12 and 18 threads on all inputs graphs. These applications show an abort rate of up to 28% (see Table 2), and are able to leverage the HW mode (HTM) during a larger portion of the execution time. Since the GoTM automaton is based on commit throughput measurements, aborted transactions are handled either by SW or GLOCK modes to deal with capacity or conflict aborts, respectively. In that sense, applications that are not able to execute more than 60% of the time in either HW or SW modes are outperformed by Galois' Lock. This is the case of the PR application for which GoTM has its worse performance. As shown in Table 2, PR has a total abort rate between 20% and 70% when running with 18 threads. Specifically, for the Rmat32 workload, only 5% of the execution time is spent in HW mode, thus resulting in very poor performance when compared to Galois' Lock execution with the same number of threads. This is due to a high capacity-related abort rate that decreases throughput in HW mode, and over-instrumentation of the vertex-function in SW mode. Similar behavior is also observed in the BC application, where GoTM presents an inferior performance for a higher degree input (Rmat32), running 54% of the execution time in HW mode, but shows speedup for the other lower degree Rmat workloads. PhTM* shows lower performances compared to GoTM in most cases because execution is unnecessarily maintained for longer periods in SW and GLOCK modes. For example, for SSSP with the Rmat32 workload, execution in HW mode is over 12% with PhTM*, while with GoTM is 47%. However, for Kcore, PhTM* is able to maintain a performance improvement over both Galois' Lock and GoTM, as it executes over 90% in HW mode.

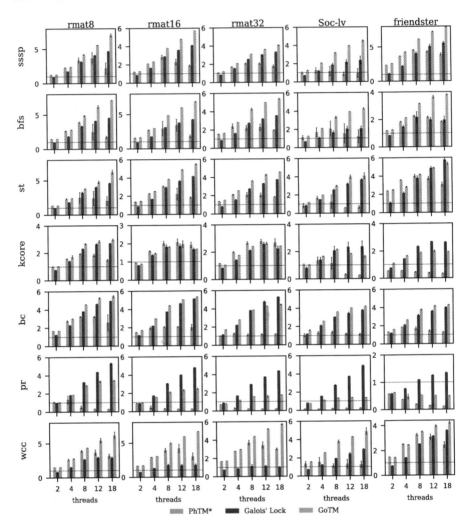

Fig. 3. GoTM, PhTM* and Galois' lock normalized speedup for the applications described in Sect. 4.1.

The best performance of GoTM with the Rmat workloads is shown by the WCC application, with a speedup between 3.56x and 7.59x over the single-thread baseline, outperforming Galois' Lock which produced a speedup between 1.0x and 1.3x. In this application, Galois' Lock shows a very poor scalability, decreasing its performance as the average degree of the input graph increases due to a larger number of iterations. For the WCC application, an increase in the number of iterations occurs when the propagation of vertex labels with the lowest values are delayed, which is consistent with the abort handling strategy of Galois'

Lock that postpones the execution of aborted transactions to avoid persistent conflicts. The most representative example of the three-mode execution of GoTM is the ST application. Even though this application shows an abort rate between 10.6% and 28% (mostly capacity-related) (see Table 2), and execution in HW mode as low as 42%, GoTM ST is still able to outperform Galois' Lock by executing between 4.6% and 21.85% of the time in SW mode.

Performance for Real-Life Workloads. With GoTM, SSSP, BFS, BC and WCC scale from 2 to 18 threads and outperform Galois' Lock and PhTM* with both Soc-lv and friendster, which is the largest workload of this experiment. On the other hand, when running ST with Soc-lv, GoTM shows a performance improvement over both Galois' Lock and PhTM* for all threads, but with Friendster it only outperforms Galois' Lock up to 8 threads, and is outperformed by PhTM* for 2 and 4 threads. As shown in Table 2, when ST runs the Friendster workload, performance improvement over Galois' Lock decreases with increased thread count, reaching 51% in HW mode execution for 18 threads. PR shows poor scalability for GoTM with both real-life workload. This is due to a total abort rate of over 45% for Friendster (mostly capacity-related), and 51.8% for Soc-lv (mostly conflict-related). For Kcore, GoTM is also outperformed by Galois' Lock with Friendster as only 38% of execution time is spent in HW mode. Finally, GoTM delivers an overall better performance in the WCC application.

Both capacity and conflict-related aborts have a direct impact on the throughput of an execution mode, which dictates the transition between SW and HW. However, a particular drawback in phased TM systems is the number of phase transitions that may cause an overhead. GoTM seeks to avoid a continuous mode switching by using the mode threshold parameter ($MODE\_THRDS$), only issuing a transition every certain amount of time spent in the same mode if the commit throughput drops. For example, as the average degree and size of the graphs increase, the total abort rate increases significantly, thus reducing the HW mode commit throughput, making it necessary to perform a mode transition to SW to recover the commit throughput.

5   Related Work

TM systems have had great advances in recent years, both in software (STM) runtimes [10,13] and in hardware (HTM) support [16,24]. However, few studies have shown performance improvements for large applications beyond the traditional benchmarks (e.g., STAMP [7]). The use of TM in specific graph processing applications was first proposed by M. Besta in [1]. That work does not propose a runtime for graph applications, but an alternative for fine-grained atomic operations, such as accumulate and compare-and-swap, showing how to combine inter-process communication with HTM to accelerate commonly used atomic operations called activities. The most similar work to ours in terms of TM runtime implementation is the TuFast TM library presented in [23]. It proposes a TM library to develop graph applications with a hybrid approach that schedules

Table 2. Execution statistics for Rmat and real-life workloads (Conf.: conflict abort rate. Cap.: capacity abort rate).

	Input	SW (%)	HW (%)	Conf. (%)	Cap. (%)	Input	SW (%)	HW (%)	Conf. (%)	Cap. (%)
SSSP	Rmat8	1.7	80.1	0.37	3.25	Soc-lv	5.9	64.5	5.23	4.14
	Rmat16	1.0	66.0	0.58	8.80	friendster	2.4	46.2	1.15	11.74
	Rmat32	0.1	47.0	0.80	22.20					
ST	Rmat8	4.6	74.3	1.57	11.95	Soc-lv	16.0	58.8	11.09	1.56
	Rmat16	21.3	43.0	0.80	15.20	friendster	2.7	51.5	2.54	16.84
	Rmat32	20.9	42.0	0.96	27.10					
KCORE	Rmat8	10.0	80.1	1.12	1.40	Soc-lv	31.1	58.7	9.39	5.97
	Rmat16	10.4	66.0	0.60	3.20	friendster	1.2	38.4	3.70	25.82
	Rmat32	6.9	47.0	0.24	7.05					
BC	Rmat8	2.1	86.0	0.80	18.06	Soc-lv	7.7	75.0	7.28	9.70
	Rmat16	1.3	72.0	1.11	24.65	friendster	1.3	73.9	1.54	17.10
	Rmat32	0.5	54.0	1.72	45.07					
PR	Rmat8	0.3	72.3	3.28	31.14	Soc-lv	1.2	33.8	33.12	18.79
	Rmat16	0.2	19.2	3.20	50.93	friendster	0.7	29.1	2.99	42.47
	Rmat32	0.1	5.0	3.59	66.37					
WCC	Rmat8	3.4	87.0	0.56	1.14	Soc-lv	12.6	66.5	1.85	2.02
	Rmat16	2.1	75.0	2.46	3.75	friendster	2.8	52.8	0.24	9.09
	Rmat32	4.0	56.0	1.72	13.02					
BFS	Rmat8	6.2	78.8	0.22	3.52	Soc-lv	18.7	63.0	1.71	3.09
	Rmat16	6.1	65.0	0.45	9.76	friendster	5.9	55.1	0.65	8.51
	Rmat32	8.1	48.9	0.64	21.07					

transactions according to a user-provided shared-data size estimate. The workflow of the scheduler initializes by reading the vertex degree as a hint for the shared-memory contention level. Although the applications in which TuFast was tested are not detailed in the paper, the suggested vertex degree hint may not be useful in data-driven algorithms, since transaction duration tends to decrease as the algorithm converges making the latter transactions more likely to fit in hardware. In their approach, aside from the shared-data size hint, the user is required to manually annotate all data reads and writes making the coding process relatively cumbersome. We argue that our approach is more suited for the general case of graph applications, based on the premise that Phased TM runtimes show better performance than other hybrid approaches as discussed in [5]. GoTM does not require additional shared-data information. Instead, the runtime is capable of adapting the execution mode based on the history of the transaction throughput and abort rate. Another work was proposed by Y. Xia. et al. in [26]. It presents a STM system for deterministic parallel programming, using a modified version of *Deterministic Reservation* and TM support. However, TM adds complexity to the proposed deterministic framework as it requires all transactions to be scheduled in the same order.

6   Conclusion

This paper presents a phased transactional memory implementation for vertex-centric graph programs called GoTM. GoTM was tested using a set of programs built in Galois, a well-known C++ library for irregular computation such as graph algorithms, revealing improved performance for different graph applications. The experimental results show a speedup between 2x and 7x for randomly generated workloads with power-law distribution and publicly available datasets over a lock transactional model and a well-known phased TM implementation. GoTM also demonstrates how a programming model with a high-level abstraction such as TM can facilitate program writing and still provide performance improvements. The core of GoTM is an automaton that uses a committed transaction throughput metric to decide between three execution modes based on efficient hardware and software implementations. The throughput measurement is particularly useful in graph programs as it avoids early or permanent transitions from hardware to software mode.

References

1. Besta, M., Hoefler, T.: Accelerating irregular computations with hardware transactional memory and active messages. In: Proceedings of the 24th International Symposium on High-Performance Parallel and Distributed Computing, HPDC 2015, pp. 161–172. Association for Computing Machinery, New York (2015)
2. Bolt, T.S., Hampton, R.S., Furr, R.M.: Chapter 3-integrating personality/character neuroscience with network analysis. In: Absher, J.R., Cloutier, J. (eds.) Neuroimaging Personality, Social Cognition, and Character, pp. 51–69. Academic Press, San Diego (2016)
3. Brandes, U.: A faster algorithm for betweenness centrality. J. Math. Sociol. **25**(2), 163–177 (2001)
4. Calciu, I., Gottschlich, J., Shpeisman, T., Herlihy, M., Pokam, G.: Invyswell: a hybrid transactional memory for Haswell's restricted transactional memory. In: 2014 23rd International Conference on Parallel Architecture and Compilation Techniques (PACT), pp. 187–199 (2014)
5. de Carvalho, J.P.L., Araujo, G., Baldassin, A.: Revisiting phased transactional memory. In: Proceedings of the International Conference on Supercomputing, ICS 2017. Association for Computing Machinery, New York (2017)
6. Chakrabarti, D., Zhan, Y., Faloutsos, C.: R-MAT: a recursive model for graph mining, vol. 6 (April 2004). https://doi.org/10.1137/1.9781611972740.43
7. Minh, C.C., Chung, J.W., Kozyrakis, C., Olukotun, K.: STAMP: stanford transactional applications for multi-processing. In: 2008 IEEE International Symposium on Workload Characterization, pp. 35–46 (2008)
8. Clauset, A., Shalizi, C.R., Newman, M.E.: Power-law distributions in empirical data. SIAM Rev. **51**(4), 661–703 (2009). https://doi.org/10.1137/070710111
9. Dalessandro, L., et al.: Hybrid NOrec: a case study in the effectiveness of best effort hardware transactional memory. SIGARCH Comput. Archit. News **39**(1), 39–52 (2011)

10. Dalessandro, L., Spear, M.F., Scott, M.L.: NOrec: streamlining STM by abolishing ownership records. In: Proceedings of the 15th ACM SIGPLAN Symposium on Principles and Practice of Parallel Programming, PPoPP 2010, pp. 67–78. Association for Computing Machinery, New York (2010)

11. Damron, P., Fedorova, A., Lev, Y., Luchangco, V., Moir, M., Nussbaum, D.: Hybrid transactional memory. SIGOPS Oper. Syst. Rev. **40**(5), 336–346 (2006)

12. Diaz-Perez, A., Garcia-Robledo, A., Gonzalez-Compean, J.L.: Graph processing frameworks. In: Sakr, S., Zomaya, A. (eds.) Encyclopedia of Big Data Technologies (2018). Springer, Cham. https://doi.org/10.1007/978-3-319-63962-8_283-1

13. Felber, P., Fetzer, C., Riegel, T.: Time-based software transactional memory. IEEE Trans. Parallel Distrib. Syst. **21**(12), 1793–1807 (2010)

14. Hasenplaugh, W.: Quantifying the capacity limitations of hardware transactional memory. In: WTTM, pp. 1–6 (2015)

15. Herlihy, M., Moss, J.E.B.: Transactional memory: architectural support for lock-free data structures. ACM SIGARCH Comput. Archit. News **21**(2), 289–300 (1993)

16. Intel: Architecture instruction set extensions programming reference (2012). https://www.intel.com/content/dam/www/public/us/en/documents/manuals/64-ia-32-architectures-optimization-manual.pdf

17. Le, H.Q., et al.: Transactional memory support in the IBM POWER8 processor. IBM J. Res. Dev. **59**(1), 8:1–8:14 (2015)

18. Leskovec, J., Krevl, A.: SNAP datasets: Stanford large network dataset collection (June 2014). http://snap.stanford.edu/data

19. Lev, Y., Moir, M., Nussbaum, D.: PhTM: phased transactional memory. In: 2nd ACM SIGPLAN Workshop on Transactional Computing (2007). http://anon.cs.rochester.edu/meetings/TRANSACT07/papers/lev.pdf

20. Malewicz, G., et al.: Pregel: a system for large-scale graph processing. In: Proceedings of the 2010 ACM SIGMOD International Conference on Management of Data, pp. 135–146. Association for Computing Machinery, New York (2010)

21. Morris, R., Tarassenko, L.: Sensory processing, chap. 4. In: Cognitive Systems - Information Processing Meets Brain Science, pp. 85–104 (2006)

22. Nguyen, D., Lenharth, A., Pingali, K.: A lightweight infrastructure for graph analytics. In: Proceedings of the 24th ACM Symposium on Operating Systems Principles, SOSP 2013, pp. 456–471. Association for Computing Machinery, New York (2013). https://doi.org/10.1145/2517349.2522739

23. Shang, Z., Yu, J.X., Zhang, Z.: TuFast: a lightweight parallelization library for graph analytics. In: IEEE 35th International Con. on Data Engineering, pp. 710–721 (2019)

24. Wang, A., et al.: Evaluation of blue gene/q hardware support for transactional memories. In: Proceedings of the 21st International Conference on Parallel Architectures and Compilation Techniques, PACT 2012, pp. 127–136. Association for Computing Machinery, New York (2012). https://doi.org/10.1145/2370816.2370836

25. Whang, J.J., Lenharth, A., Dhillon, I.S., Pingali, K.: Scalable data-driven pagerank: algorithms, system issues, and lessons learned. In: Träff, J.L., Hunold, S., Versaci, F. (eds.) Euro-Par 2015. LNCS, vol. 9233, pp. 438–450. Springer, Heidelberg (2015). https://doi.org/10.1007/978-3-662-48096-0_34

26. Xia, Y., Yu, X., Moses, W., Shun, J., Devadas, S.: LiTM: a lightweight deterministic software transactional memory system. In: Proceedings of the 10th International Workshop on Programming Models and Applications for Multicores and Many-cores, pp. 1–10. Association for Computing Machinery, New York (2019)

Efficient GPU Computation Using Task Graph Parallelism

Dian-Lun Lin[✉] and Tsung-Wei Huang

University of Utah, Utah, USA
{dian-lun.lin,tsung-wei.huang}@utah.edu

Abstract. Recently, CUDA introduces a new task graph programming model, *CUDA graph*, to enable efficient launch and execution of GPU work. Users describe a GPU workload in a task graph rather than aggregated GPU operations, allowing the CUDA runtime to perform whole-graph optimization and significantly reduce the kernel call overheads. However, programming CUDA graphs is extremely challenging. Users need to explicitly construct a graph with verbose parameter settings or implicitly capture a graph that requires complex dependency and concurrency managements using streams and events. To overcome this challenge, we introduce a lightweight task graph programming framework to enable efficient GPU computation using CUDA graph. Users can focus on high-level development of dependent GPU operations, while leaving all the intricate managements of stream concurrency and event dependency to our optimization algorithm. We have evaluated our framework and demonstrated its promising performance on both micro-benchmarks and a large-scale machine learning workload. The result also shows that our optimization algorithm achieves very comparable performance to an optimally-constructed graph and consumes much less GPU resource.

1 Introduction

The performance of GPU architectures continues to increase with every new generation. Modern GPUs are fast and, in many scenarios, the time taken by each GPU operation (e.g., kernel or memory copy) is now measured in microseconds. The overheads associated with the submission of each operation to the GPU, also at the microsecond scale, are becoming significant and can dominate the performance of a GPU algorithm. For instance, inferencing a large neural network launches many dependent kernels on partitioned data and models. If each of these operations is launched to the GPU separately and repetitively, the overheads can combine to form a significant overall degradation to performance. To address this issue, CUDA has recently introduced a new *CUDA graph* programming model to enable efficient launch and execution of GPU work. CUDA graph enables a define-once-run-repeatedly execution flow that reduces the overhead of kernel launching. Users describe dependent GPU operations in a *task graph* rather than aggregated single operations. The CUDA runtime can perform

© Springer Nature Switzerland AG 2021
L. Sousa et al. (Eds.): Euro-Par 2021, LNCS 12820, pp. 435–450, 2021.
https://doi.org/10.1007/978-3-030-85665-6_27

whole-graph optimization and launch the entire graph in a single CPU operation to reduce overheads [4,5].

However, programming CUDA graphs is extremely challenging. First, users can *explicitly* construct a CUDA graph that maps each vertex to a GPU operation and each edge to a dependency between two GPU operations. Explicit CUDA graph construction is often the most efficient, but it requires all the parameters known upfront, which is impossible for many high-performance third-party libraries, such as cuSparse, cuBLAS, and cuDNN. Also, the CUDA runtime maximally parallelizes the given CUDA graph without limiting the stream usage. In large graphs, the GPU memory can explode. The second option is *implicit* graph construction, which *captures* a CUDA graph using existing stream-based application programming interfaces (APIs). Implicit CUDA graph construction is more flexible and general, allowing users to manually allocate and control streams. However, it requires users to wrangle with concurrency details through events and streams that are known difficult to program correctly.

Consequently, we propose in this paper a lightweight task graph programming framework to enable efficient GPU computation using CUDA graph. Our framework introduces an *expressive* GPU task graph programming model for users to focus on high-level development of dependent GPU operations with relatively ease of programming. A written task graph is then cast to a native CUDA graph through our transformation algorithm optimized for kernel concurrency and graph size. The process is *transparent*. Users need not to handle any intricate concurrency details and dependency controls using streams and events. More importantly, we identify a research problem of optimizing CUDA graphs through stream capturers. The proposed research can assist CUDA developers in improving the performance of existing GPU applications through new CUDA graph parallelism.

2   The Proposed GPU Task Graph Programming Model

Our GPU task graph programming model consists of two parts, *cudaFlow* and *cudaFlowCapturer*, to handle explicit and implicit graph constructions in different use cases.

2.1   cudaFlow: Explicit CUDA Graph Construction

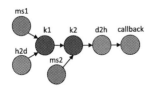

Fig. 1. An example of GPU task graph.

cudaFlow provides methods for users to explicitly construct a GPU task graph that presents a one-to-one mapping to a native CUDA graph. Each node in the task graph represents a GPU operation (copy, kernel, etc.), and each edge represents a dependency between two operations. Figure 1 shows a GPU task graph of seven nodes (two kernels, k1 and k2, two typed copies, h2d and d2h, two untyped copies, ms1 and ms2, and one host callback, callback) and six dependencies (e.g., k1→k2). Listing 1.1 gives the implementation of Fig. 1 using our model. We create a cudaFlow object (cf) and use the four methods, kernel, memset, copy, and host, to create the seven task graph nodes and use the two methods, succeed and precede, to relate dependencies between nodes. The code *explains itself* through an expressive graph description language in just 12 lines of code. The same example but written in the plain CUDA graph model is partially shown in Listing 1.2, which requires more than 150 lines of code.

Listing 1.1. Example code of Fig. 1 using cudaFlow.

```
cudaFlow cf;
cudaTask h2d = cf.copy(inputVec_d, inputVec_h, inputSize);
cudaTask ms1 = cf.memset(outputVec_d, 0, input_size);
cudaTask ms2 = cf.memset(result_d, 0, 1);
cudaTask k1 = cf.kernel(reduce, inputVec_d, outputVec_d, inputSize);
cudaTask k2 = cf.kernel(reduce_final, outputVec_d, result_d);
cudaTask d2h = cf.copy(result_h, result_d, 1);
cudaTask callback = cf.host(fn, &hostFnData);
k1.succeed(h2d, ms1);
k2.succeed(k1, ms2);
k2.precede(d2h);
d2h.precede(callback);
```

Listing 1.2. Example code of Fig. 1 using the plain CUDA graph.

```
cudaStream_t streamForGraph;
cudaGraph_t graph;
std::vector<cudaGraphNode_t> nodeDependencies;
cudaGraphNode_t memcpyNode, kernelNode, memsetNode;
checkCudaErrors(cudaStreamCreate(&streamForGraph));
cudaKernelNodeParams kernelNodeParams = {0};
cudaMemcpy3DParms memcpyParams = {0};
cudaMemsetParams memsetParams = {0};
memcpyParams.srcArray = NULL;
memcpyParams.srcPos = make_cudaPos(0, 0, 0);
memcpyParams.srcPtr =
    make_cudaPitchedPtr(inputVec_h, sizeof(float) * inputSize, inputSize, 1);
memcpyParams.dstArray = NULL;
memcpyParams.dstPos = make_cudaPos(0, 0, 0);
memcpyParams.dstPtr =
    make_cudaPitchedPtr(inputVec_d, sizeof(float) * inputSize, inputSize, 1);
memcpyParams.extent = make_cudaExtent(sizeof(float) * inputSize, 1, 1);
memcpyParams.kind = cudaMemcpyHostToDevice;
checkCudaErrors(cudaGraphCreate(&graph, 0));
checkCudaErrors(
  cudaGraphAddMemcpyNode(&memcpyNode, graph, NULL, 0, &memcpyParams
));
//... more than 100 lines of code to follow
```

2.2   cudaFlowCapturer: Implicit CUDA Graph Construction

cudaFlow allows users to explicitly construct a CUDA graph, but it requires all execution parameters known in advance. This property restricts users from using commercial CUDA libraries, such as cuDNN and cuBLAS, that do not provide details for launching kernels but a public stream-based API. To overcome this restriction, we introduce cudaFlowCapturer with a stream-based method to capture GPU kernels and transform the given task graph into a native CUDA graph using our graph transformation algorithm. Listing 1.3 shows the cudaFlow-Capturer code of Fig. 1, assuming the two kernels, k1 and k2, are only invokable through a stream-based API. The cudaFlowCapture provides a method, on, that passes a stream created by our optimizer to the callable for users to capturer kernels or other asynchronous GPU operations.

Listing 1.3. Example code of Fig. 1 using cudaFlowCapturer.

```
cudaFlowCapturer cap;
cudaTask h2d = cap.copy(inputVec_d, inputVec_h, inputSize);
cudaTask ms1 = cap.memset(outputVec_d, 0, input_size);
cudaTask ms2 = cap.memset(result_d, 0, 1);
cudaTask k1 = cap.on([&](cudaStream_t stream){
  cublas_gemm(stream, my_paremeters...);
});
cudaTask k2 = cap.on([&](cudaStream_t stream){
  cublas_gemv(stream, my_paremeters...);
});
cudaTask d2h = cap.copy(result_h, result_d, 1);
cudaTask callback = cf.host(fn, &hostFnData);
k1.succeed(h2d, ms1);
k2.succeed(k1, ms2);
k2.precede(d2h);
d2h.precede(callback);
```

3   Transform a cudaFlowCapturer to a CUDA Graph

By default, we translate a cudaFlow directly into a native CUDA graph and use a single CPU call to offload the graph. To launch a cudaFlowCapturer, we need to transform the task graph defined in the cudaFlowCapturer into a native CUDA graph using stream capturer.

3.1   Problem Formulation

We describe the transformation problem as follows: Given a task graph G_t and the number of streams ($num\_streams$), discover an order to construct dependencies between nodes, i.e., assign each node $n \in G_t$ to a stream and decide an event for each node such that the execution order of tasks ("transformed CUDA graph") imposed by the streams and events is topologically identical to the original task graph. The objective is to balance the load of each stream and minimize the transformed graph size. For example, using two streams, the task graph in Fig. 2(a) can be transformed into two different CUDA graphs, (b) and (c), both resulting in different critical paths and graph sizes. CUDA stream is in-order. Placing two dependent nodes at two different streams may require creating an event to build a dependency in the CUDA graph, as shown in the red points. Since the optimal number of streams is highly dependent on application level, we leave *num_streams* to users to tune the number of streams based on their applications.

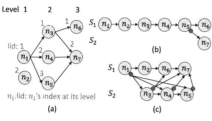

Fig. 2. Transformation of a task graph to a CUDA graph using two streams. (Color figure online)

This transformation problem has two challenges: Firstly, CUDA stream capture is stateful [1]. We can only construct a dependency in *one direction* from an assigned node to the node that is being enqueued to a stream. That is, optimizing the event count and, hence, the graph size, through back-and-forth traversal is not possible. Second, graph size matters. The same task graph can have many feasible transformations (see Fig. 2). Different transformations result in different execution efficiencies.

3.2   Our Algorithm: Round Robin with Dependency Pruning

At a high level, our algorithm assigns each node to a stream in a round-robin fashion and applies a dependency pruning to reduce redundant dependencies. We use Fig. 3 to illustrate our algorithm transforming the task graph of Fig. 2(a) to a CUDA graph using two streams. First, we levelize the task graph, G_t, to a 2D level list. Based on the 2D level list, we assign each node n_i to indicate the index of the topological ordering of G_t, and $n_i.lid$ to indicate the index of its level (see Fig. 2(a)). We assign each node to a stream of id equal to $(n_i.lid + 1)\%num\_streams + 1$ as a result of the round-robin. For example, n_4 is assigned to stream s_2 (i.e., $(2+1)\%2 + 1$). Assigning nodes in a round-robin manner at each level facilitates load balancing because nodes are evenly distributed across streams. The motivation of levelization is to implicitly capture dependencies between levels using the same stream. For instance, the dependency between n_1 and n_3 is implicitly captured by s_1.

We iterate each node level by level to perform three steps: *construct dependencies*, *assign stream*, and *decide an event*. At the first level, since n_1 does not have predecessors, we assign it to s_1 (Fig. 3(a)). We then check if any of n_1's successors (n_3, n_4, n_5) will be assigned to the different stream, s_2. Since n_4 will be assigned to s_2, we need to create an event for n_1 so that the later iteration can wait on it to create a dependency edge (Fig. 3(b)). At the second level, since n_3 is assigned to the same stream as its predecessor, n_1, we do not create a dependency from n_3 to n_1; but, we create an event for n_3 because its successor n_7 will be assigned to s_2, as shown in Fig. 3(c). Figure 3(d) and (e) show the process of n_4. Since n_4 is assigned to the different stream from it's predecessor,

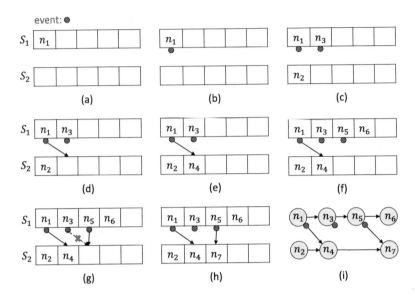

Fig. 3. Illustration of our algorithm on Fig. 2 using two streams.

n_1, we need to create a dependency before assigning n_4 to s_2 by waiting on n_1's event. The same procedure continues until we iterate all nodes. Our dependency pruning happens at assigning n_7 to s_2 (Fig. 3(g) and (h)). n_7's predecessors, n_3 and n_5, are both assigned to s_1. We only construct a dependency from n_5 to n_7 since n_5 is guaranteed to be executed after n_3 in the same stream, s_1. This pruning reduces redundant dependencies. The transformed CUDA graph from this assignment is shown in Fig. 3(i).

Algorithm 1 presents the details of our algorithm. We iterate all nodes at each level to perform the three tasks: *construct dependencies*, *assign stream*, and *decide an event*. For simplicity, $n.idx$ represents n_i's index, i.

Construct Dependencies (Lines 6–19): We construct dependencies from n's predecessor, *pred*, to n. Since n's predecessors may be assigned to the same stream that implicitly capturers sequential order of enqueued nodes, we only need to construct a dependency from the last assigned predecessor, *last_assign*, to n and prune the other dependencies starting from n's predecessors that is assigned to the same stream.

Assign Stream (Line 20) & Decide an Event (Lines 21–30): We assign n to s_{sid}, where sid is the id of the stream assigned to n. We decide an event by checking whether n is assigned to a different stream from one of its successors, *suc*. If true, we create and record an event for n so that *suc* can construct a dependency from n to *suc* at the later iteration. We further assign *suc.sm* to s_{sid} for dependency pruning that happened in the later *construct dependencies* stage.

Algorithm 1: Round Robin with Dependency Pruning.

Input: $num\_streams$: number of streams

Input: $graph$: task graph defined by users

```
/* create streams...                                        */
```

1 $levelized \leftarrow$ levelize($graph$)

2 **for** $each\_level\_graph$ in $levelized$ **do**

3   **for** n in $each\_level\_graph$ **do**

4          $sid \leftarrow (n.lid + 1)\%num\_streams + 1$

5          $last\_assign \leftarrow$ **null**

6   **for** $pred$ in $n.predecessors$ **do**

7              $psid \leftarrow (pred.lid + 1)\%num\_streams + 1$

8   **if** $s_{psid} == n.sm$ **then**

9   **if** $last\_assign ==$ **null** or $last\_assign.idx < pred.idx$ **then**

10                     $last\_assign = pred$

11   **end**

12   **end**

13   **else if** $s_{psid} \mathrel{!=} s_{sid}$ **then**

14   cudaStreamWaitEvent(s_{sid}, $pred.event$)

15   **end**

16   **end**

17   **if** $last\_assign \mathrel{!=}$ **null** **then**

18   cudaStreamWaitEvent(s_{sid}, $last\_assign.event$)

19   **end**

20         $n.assign(s_{sid})$

21   **for** suc in $n.successors$ **do**

22             $ssid = (suc.lid + 1)\%num\_streams + 1$

23   **if** $s_{ssid} \mathrel{!=} s_{sid}$ **then**

24   **if** $n.event ==$ **null** **then**

25   cudaCreateEvent($n.event$)

26   cudaEventRecord($n.event$, s_{sid})

27   **end**

28                 $suc.sm \leftarrow s_{sid}$

29   **end**

30   **end**

31   **end**

32 **end**

4 Experimental Results

We evaluate the performance of cudaFlow and cudaFlowCapturer on (1) five micro-benchmarks[1] that are representative for many GPU algorithm patterns, and (2) a large-scale machine learning workload directly derived from the 2020 champion of the HPEC Sparse Deep Neural Network (DNN) Inference Challenge [24]. Both cudaFlow and cudaFlowCapturer have different use cases that

---

[1] Source code: https://github.com/dian-lun-lin/cudaFlow-benchmarks.

complement each other. The purpose of our experiment is not to demonstrate which one outperforms another but to highlight that our transformation algorithm can achieve comparable performance (or even better) to the optimally-constructed CUDA graph when explicit graph construction is not possible. By default, we transform a cudaFlow into a CUDA graph of the same topology because all kernel execution parameters are known up-front. In cudaFlowCapturer, we use RR1, RR2, RR4, and RR8 to represent our algorithm using 1, 2, 4, and 8 streams in the round-robin loop, respectively. To demonstrate the effectiveness of our dependency pruning, RR4$^-$ and RR8$^-$ represent our algorithm without dependency pruning under 4 and 8 streams. We do not report RR1$^-$ and RR2$^-$ because redundant dependencies only occur between nodes that are assigned to different streams. Using one or two streams creates few redundant dependencies. All experiments ran on a Ubuntu Linux 5.0.0-21-generic x86 64-bit machine with 40 Intel Xeon Gold 6138 CPU cores at 2.00 GHz, one GeForce RTX 2080 Ti GPU with 11 GB memory, and 256 GB RAM. We compiled all programs using Nvidia CUDA nvcc 11.1 on a host compiler of GNU GCC-9.2.1 with C++17 standards and optimization flags -O2 enabled. All data is an average of ten runs.

4.1   Micro-benchmarks

We consider five common GPU task graphs as our micro-benchmarks: linear chain (LC), embarrassing parallelism (EP), map-reduce (MR), divide and conquer (DC), and random DAG. LC task graph defines a sequence of sequentially dependent nodes. EP task graph defines only independent nodes. MR task graph defines several iterations each of 16 mappers and one reducer. DC task graph defines a complete binary tree. Random DAG defines a more generalized task graph; we randomly generate up to 50 nodes at each level and create at most five edges per node between successive levels. For all benchmarks, each node contains three sequential GPU operations: host-to-device (H2D) copy, reduction kernel, and device-to-host (D2H) copy. H2D operation first copies 2^{20} integers from CPU to GPU, the reduction kernel performs parallel sum reduction on all elements, and D2H operation copies the reduced sum from GPU to CPU. We focus on large GPU work where the effect of task graph parallelism is significant.

Performance Comparison. Table 1 compares the native CUDA graph size (#nodes+#edges) of each benchmark among cudaFlow and cudaFlowCapturer of different stream counts. Apparently, all methods have the same CUDA graph size in the LC task graph. cudaFlowCapturer has a larger CUDA graph size than cudaFlow in the EP task graph, since our algorithm assigns independent nodes to streams that implicitly capture the sequential execution order of enqueued nodes. The same situation happens in the DC task graph, where the number of independent nodes grows exponentially over levels. The CUDA graph size of DC, MR, and random DAG task graphs using cudaFlowCapturer become larger as we increase the number of streams. In our algorithm, more streams can have higher concurrency. However, it may result in more events to implicitly capture

Table 1. Comparison of CUDA graph sizes (#nodes+#edges) on linear chain, embarrassing parallelism, divide and conquer, map-reduce, and random DAG task graphs between cudaFlow and cudaFlowCapturer under different stream numbers 1 (RR1), 2 (RR2), 4 (RR4), and 8 (RR8). RR4$^-$ and RR8$^-$ represent our algorithm without the dependency pruning.

Task graph	cudaFlow	cudaFlowCapturer					
		RR1	RR2	RR4	RR4$^-$	RR8	RR8$^-$
Linear chain (65536 nodes)	393215	393215	393215	393215	393215	393215	393215
Embarrassing parallelism (65536 nodes)	327680	393215	393214	393212	393212	393208	393208
Divide and conquer (16 levels)	393209	393209	425975	442356	442356	450543	450543
Map-reduce (1024 iterations)	119813	104453	113668	125954	129026	132094	133118
Random DAG (512 levels)	103316	77893	86981	99217	104084	107822	112182
Random DAG (1024 levels)	207552	155437	169574	201875	214088	217454	226009
Random DAG (2048 levels)	410639	311453	347290	403291	423119	437859	447629
Random DAG (4096 levels)	832298	628715	693860	808276	857334	859342	892507

Table 2. Comparison of the number of streams issued by the CUDA runtime to run each task graph between cudaFlow and cudaFlowCapturer.

Task graph	cudaFlow	cudaFlowCapturer			
		RR1	RR2	RR4	RR8
Linear chain (65536 nodes)	12	12	13	15	19
Embarrassing parallelism (65536 nodes)	65547	12	14	18	26
Divide and conquer (16 levels)	32779	12	14	18	26
Map-reduce (1024 iterations)	15372	12	14	18	26
Random DAG (512 levels)	5318	12	80	244	559
Random DAG (1024 levels)	10547	12	150	440	1106
Random DAG (2048 levels)	21116	12	263	888	2213
Random DAG (4096 levels)	42545	12	522	1757	4348

the dependencies of the original task graph. Our dependency pruning shows a significant effect on reducing the CUDA graph size in MR and random DAG task graphs. For example, the CUDA graph size on Random DAG with 4096 levels using RR8 is 5.7% smaller than RR8$^-$. This is because MR and random DAG task graphs contain nodes that have more dependencies than others.

Table 2 compares the number of streams issued by the CUDA runtime to run each task graph. cudaFlow consumes much larger numbers of streams than cudaFlowCapturer on all benchmarks except the LC graph. By default, cudaFlow keeps a one-to-one mapping between the task graph and the CUDA graph. The CUDA runtime will issue as many streams as possible to maximize the task concurrency, whereas cudaFlowCapturer transforms the task graph into CUDA graph with a limited number of streams.

Figure 4 shows the execution time (including CUDA graph construction time) of each benchmark. Since LC task graph contains only sequential nodes, all

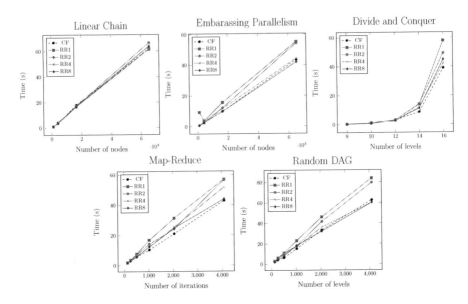

Fig. 4. Execution time of each task graph at different task graph sizes running on cudaFlow and cudaFlowCapturer of RR1, RR2, RR4, and RR8.

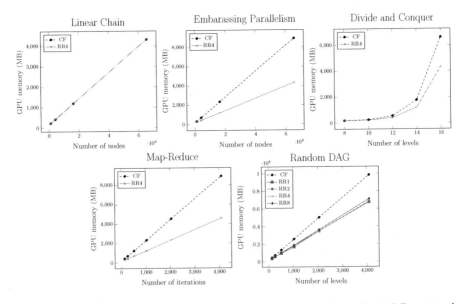

Fig. 5. Comparison of peak GPU memory usage of each task graph at different task graph sizes between cudaFlow and cudaFlowCapturer.

methods have almost the same execution time. RR4, RR8, and cudaFlow are faster than RR1 and RR2 in all other task graphs, because more streams have higher concurrency that leads to faster execution time. Figure 5 compares the

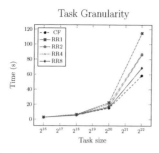

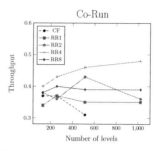

(a) Execution time of random DAG with 1024 levels at different task sizes.

(b) Throughput of corunning random DAG at different task graph sizes.

Fig. 6. (a) Task granularity and (b) co-run of random DAG running on cudaFlow and cudaFlowCapturer.

peak GPU memory usage of each benchmark at different task graph size running on cudaFlow and cudaFlowCapturer. We only compare cudaFlow with RR4 in LC, EP, DC, and MR task graphs since RR1, RR2, RR4, and RR8 have almost the same GPU memory usage in these task graphs. The GPU memory usage of cudaFlow is much higher than cudaFlowCapturer on all benchmarks except the LC task graph. In EP task graph, cudaFlow consumes 2.1× more GPU memory than cudaFlowCapturer. This is because the CUDA runtime does not limit the number of streams to run CUDA graphs. Figure 6(a) compares the execution time under different task sizes. Task size is the number of elements computed at each node. cudaFlow and RR8 become faster than the others when the task size grows. Compared to lightweight tasks with the same stream count, heavy tasks benefit more from higher kernel concurrency.

Next, we study the throughput of co-running multiple GPU graphs. The motivation is to emulate a server-like environment where multiple client GPU programs run concurrently on the same machine. We consider four co-run processes each executing one random DAG with the same number of levels. The throughput is defined as the execution time of running one process over the execution time of running four processes concurrently [16]. A throughput of 1 implies that the co-run's throughput is the same as if the processes were run consecutively. Figure 6(b) compares the throughput of each method. RR4 produces the highest throughput than others, whereas cudaFlow runs out of GPU memory due to unlimited streams.

4.2 Machine Learning: Large Sparse Neural Network Inference

The second experiment compares the performance of our transformation algorithm with an optimally-constructed CUDA graph (i.e., cudaFlow) using a large-scale machine learning workload from the IEEE HPEC Graph Challenge 2020. The challenge is to inference extremely large sparse DNN models. We rearchitect the CUDA graph-based champion solution in [24] using cudaFlow and

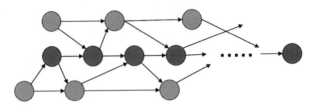

Fig. 7. [24] describes the inference workload in a task graph. A blue node represents a memory copy, and a red node represents a kernel. (Color figure online)

cudaFlowCapturer. We run the experiment on six DNN models composed of different neurons and layers. The statistics of each DNN and its modeled task graph size are summarized in Table 3. Figure 7 shows a partial task graph of the inference workload.

Table 3. The modeled task graph size (#nodes+#edges) and the statistics of each DNN benchmark (model size and image nonzeros).

Neurons/layers	120	480	1920	Model size	Image nonzeros
4096	599	2399	9599	5.40 GB	25,019,051
65536	599	2399	9599	94.70 GB	392,191,985

Table 4. Comparison of the execution time between cudaFlow and cudaFlowCapturer for completing six DNN models.

#Neurons	#Layers	cudaFlow	cudaFlowCapturer			
			RR1	RR2	RR4	RR8
4096	120	1.61	1.34	1.19	1.20	1.19
	480	4.70	4.74	4.19	4.19	4.20
	1920	17.41	19.14	17.08	17.14	17.15
65536	120	14.78	15.99	14.06	14.06	14.05
	480	43.00	50.59	42.92	42.81	42.90
	1920	162.20	193.11	162.12	162.35	162.30

Performance Comparison. Table 4 compares the execution time (in seconds) of each benchmark using cudaFlow and cudaFlowCapturer at different stream numbers. All methods except RR1 have similar execution time across all DNNs. We observe cudaFlowCapturer of two streams finishes the inference workload with comparable performance of cudaFlow. Using four or eight streams does not decrease the runtime. Table 5 compares the number of streams issued by the CUDA runtime. cudaFlow consumes a similar number of streams to cudaFlow-Capturer. This is because the maximum degree of concurrency in this particular

Table 5. Comparison of number of streams issued by the CUDA runtime between cudaFlow and cudaFlowCapturer for completing six DNN models.

#Neurons	#Layers	cudaFlow	cudaFlowCapturer			
			RR1	RR2	RR4	RR8
4096	120	35	23	36	38	42
	480	35	23	36	38	42
	1920	35	23	36	38	42
65536	120	35	23	36	38	42
	480	35	23	36	38	42
	1920	35	23	36	38	42

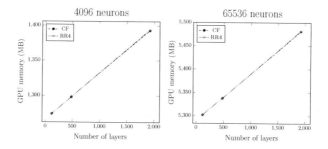

Fig. 8. Comparison of peak GPU memory usage at different number of layers between cudaFlow and cudaFlowCapturer (RR4).

task graph is around two, and the CUDA runtime will not consume too many streams to maximize the parallelism. Figure 8 compares the peak GPU memory usage at different numbers of layers. Both methods have almost the same peak GPU memory usage due to similar stream usage. This experiment demonstrates the efficiency of our transformation algorithm.

5   Related Work

[2,28] presents a compiler transformation method that translates OpenMP code into CUDA graphs. However, their transformation method only considers explicit graph construction. Our work offers users both explicit graph construction APIs (cudaFlow) and implicit graph construction APIs (cudaFlowCapturer) using our scheduling algorithm. [25] proposes a compiler-based approach that combines CUDA graph with an image processing DSL and a source-to-source compiler called Hipacc. Their kernel pipelining approach optimizes the schedule specifically for the scattering-pattern applications. [9] presents the Hybrid Task Graph Scheduler (HTGS) to aid in building hybrid workflows for high performance image processing. This architecture is different from our model that can handle and schedule arbitrary GPU task graphs.

Graph-based model is extensively studied on CPU-parallel architectures. Just name a few: Cpp-Taskflow [15,16,19,20,22,23] develops a simple and powerful task programming model enabling efficient implementations of heterogeneous decomposition strategies. PaRSEC [10] expresses applications as DAG of tasks with labeled edges designating data dependencies. It provides a generic framework for architecture-aware scheduling and management of micro-tasks on distributed many-core heterogeneous architectures. Kokkos [11] uses functional approaches to offer task graph constructions. It enables applications to achieve performance portability on diverse many-core architectures. Legion [8] describes a runtime system that dynamically extracts parallelism from Legion programs, using a distributed, parallel scheduling algorithm that identifies both independent tasks and nested parallelism. These models have their own pros and cons, but they do not target GPU graph parallelism.

Another line of related work to our transformation algorithm is the removal of redundant dependencies in DAGs. A common category is *transitive reduction* in graph theory. Alfred V. Aho et al. [6] propose algorithms for transitive reduction based on matrix multiplication. Other work [7,14,26,27,29,30] focuses on DAG traversal that processes each node separately. However, it is unknown how these algorithms can apply to our problem domain, in which the stateful property of CUDA stream constrains the order of dependency construction.

6   Conclusion

In this paper, we have introduced a lightweight task graph programming framework, cudaFlow and cudaFlowCapturer, to enable efficient GPU computation using CUDA graph in different scenarios. In five micro-benchmarks and a real machine learning workload, our transformation algorithm achieves comparable performance to the optimally-constructed CUDA graph and consumes much less GPU resource. The source of our programming model is available in [3].

7   Future Work

Future work includes applying reinforcement learning to find an optimal (near-optimal) scheduling solution and choose the optimal number of streams. An optimal scheduling solution varies due to not only different applications, but also different hardware specifications (e.g., GPUs) and different software (e.g., CUDA runtime). We plan to deploy a learning-based algorithm to learn from user environments and find optimal (near-optimal) scheduling solutions. Another line of future work is to extend our work to multiple GPUs. For example, we plan to introduce new stream management algorithms for multiple CUDA graphs that can run in parallel. On the application sides, we plan to use the proposed cudaFlow to solve large-scale simulation workloads in VLSI designs [12,13,17,18,21] and machine learning [24].

References

1. NVIDIA CUDA graph example. https://github.com/NVIDIA/cuda-samples/blob/master/Samples/simpleCudaGraphs/simpleCudaGraphs.cu
2. OpenMP. https://www.openmp.org
3. Taskflow. https://taskflow.github.io
4. Cuda graph in tensorflow. In: NVIDIA GPU Technology Conference (GTC) (2021). https://www.nvidia.com/en-us/on-demand/session/gtcspring21-s31312/
5. Effortless CUDA graphs. In: NVIDIA GPU Technology Conference (GTC) (2021). https://www.nvidia.com/en-us/on-demand/session/gtcspring21-s32082/
6. Aho, A.V., Garey, M.R., Ullman, J.D.: The transitive reduction of a directed graph. SIAM J. Comput. **1**(2), 131–137 (1972)
7. Augonnet, C., Thibault, S., Namyst, R., Wacrenier, P.A.: StarPU: a unified platform for task scheduling on heterogeneous multicore architectures. Concurr. Comput. Pract. Exp. **23**(2), 187–198 (2011)
8. Bauer, M., Treichler, S., Slaughter, E., Aiken, A.: Legion: expressing locality and independence with logical regions. In: Proceedings of the International Conference on High Performance Computing, Networking, Storage and Analysis, SC 2012, pp. 1–11. IEEE (2012)
9. Blattner, T., Keyrouz, W., Bhattacharyya, S.S., Halem, M., Brady, M.: A hybrid task graph scheduler for high performance image processing workflows. J. Sig. Process. Syst. **89**(3), 457–467 (2017)
10. Bosilca, G., Bouteiller, A., Danalis, A., Herault, T., Lemariner, P., Dongarra, J.: DAGuE: a generic distributed DAG engine for high performance computing. In: 2011 IEEE International Symposium on Parallel and Distributed Processing Workshops and Phd Forum, Anchorage, Alaska, USA, pp. 1151–1158. IEEE (2011)
11. Edwards, H.C., Trott, C.R., Sunderland, D.: Kokkos: enabling many-core performance portability through polymorphic memory access patterns. J. Parallel Distrib. Comput. **74**(12), 3202–3216 (2014). Domain-Specific Languages and High-Level Frameworks for High-Performance Computing. https://doi.org/10.1016/j.jpdc.2014.07.003. http://www.sciencedirect.com/science/article/pii/S0743731514001257
12. Guo, G., Huang, T.W., Lin, Y., Wong, M.: GPU-accelerated Pash-based timing analysis. In: ACM/IEEE Design Automation Conference (DAC) (2021)
13. Guo, Z., Huang, T.W., Lin, Y.: GPU-accelerated static timing analysis. In: IEEE/ACM International Conference on Computer-Aided Design (ICCAD), pp. 1–8 (2020)
14. Habib, M., Morvan, M., Rampon, J.X.: On the calculation of transitive reduction-closure of orders. Discret. Math. **111**(1–3), 289–303 (1993)
15. Huang, T.W.: A general-purpose parallel and heterogeneous task programming system for VLSI CAD. In: IEEE/ACM International Conference on Computer-aided Design (ICCAD) (2020)
16. Huang, T.W., Lin, C.X., Guo, G., Wong, M.: Cpp-taskflow: fast task-based parallel programming using modern c++. In: 2019 IEEE International Parallel and Distributed Processing Symposium (IPDPS), pp. 974–983. IEEE (2019)
17. Huang, T.W., Lin, C.X., Wong, M.D.F.: OpenTimer v2: a parallel incremental timing analysis engine. IEEE Trans. Comput. Aided Des. Integr. Circ. Syst. (TCAD) **40**(4), 776–789 (2021)
18. Huang, T.W., Lin, C.X., Wong, M.D.F.: OpenTimer v2: a parallel incremental timing analysis engine. IEEE Des. Test **38**(2), 62–68 (2021)

19. Huang, T.W., Lin, D.L., Lin, Y., Lin, C.X.: Taskflow: a general-purpose parallel and heterogeneous task programming system. IEEE Trans. Comput. Aided Des. Integr. Circ. Syst. (TCAD) (2021)
20. Huang, T.W., Lin, Y., Lin, C.X., Guo, G., Wong, M.D.F.: Cpp-Taskflow: a general-purpose parallel task programming system at scale. IEEE Trans. Comput. Aided Des. Integr. Circ. Syst. (TCAD) **40**, 1687–1700 (2021)
21. Huang, T.W., Wong, M.: OpenTimer: a high-performance timing analysis tool. In: IEEE/ACM International Conference on Computer-Aided Design (ICCAD), pp. 895–902 (2015)
22. Lin, C.X., Huang, T.W., Guo, G., Wong, M.: An efficient and composable parallel task programming library. In: IEEE High Performance Extreme Computing (HPEC), pp. 1–7 (2019)
23. Lin, C.X., Huang, T.W., Guo, G., Wong, M.D.F.: A modern c++ parallel task programming library. In: ACM Multimedia Conference, pp. 2284–2287 (2019)
24. Lin, D.L., Huang, T.W.: A novel inference algorithm for large sparse neural network using task graph parallelism. In: IEEE High Performance Extreme Computing Conference (HPEC), pp. 1–7. IEEE (2020)
25. Qiao, B., Akif Özkan, M., Teich, J., Hannig, F.: The best of both worlds: combining CUDA graph with an image processing DSL. In: 2020 57th ACM/IEEE Design Automation Conference (DAC), pp. 1–6 (2020). https://doi.org/10.1109/DAC18072.2020.9218531
26. Simon, K.: An improved algorithm for transitive closure on acyclic digraphs. Theoret. Comput. Sci. **58**(1–3), 325–346 (1988)
27. Valdes, J., Tarjan, R.E., Lawler, E.L.: The recognition of series parallel digraphs. In: Proceedings of the 11th Annual ACM Symposium on Theory of Computing, pp. 1–12 (1979)
28. Yu, C., Royuela, S., Quiñones, E.: OpenMP to CUDA graphs: a compiler-based transformation to enhance the programmability of NVIDIA devices.. In: Proceedings of the 23th International Workshop on Software and Compilers for Embedded Systems, SCOPES 2020, New York, NY, USA, pp. 42–47. Association for Computing Machinery (2020). https://doi.org/10.1145/3378678.3391881
29. Zhou, J., Yu, J.X., Li, N., Wei, H., Chen, Z., Tang, X.: Accelerating reachability query processing based on DAG reduction. VLDB J. **27**(2), 271–296 (2018)
30. Zhou, J., Zhou, S., Yu, J.X., Wei, H., Chen, Z., Tang, X.: DAG reduction: fast answering reachability queries. In: Proceedings of the 2017 ACM International Conference on Management of Data, pp. 375–390 (2017)

Towards High Performance Resilience Using Performance Portable Abstractions

Nicolas Morales[1][✉], Keita Teranishi[1], Bogdan Nicolae[3], Christian Trott[2],
and Franck Cappello[3]

[1] Sandia National Laboratories, Livermore, CA, USA
{nmmoral,knteran}@sandia.gov
[2] Sandia National Laboratories, Albuquerque, NM, USA
crtrott@sandia.gov
[3] Argonne National Laboratory, Chicago, IL, USA
{bnicolae,cappello}@anl.gov

Abstract. In the drive towards Exascale, the extreme heterogeneity of
supercomputers at all levels places a major development burden on HPC
applications. To this end, performance portable abstractions such as
those advocated by *Kokkos*, *RAJA* and *HPX* are becoming increasingly
popular. At the same time, the unprecedented scalability requirements
of such heterogeneous components means higher failure rates, motivat-
ing the need for resilience in systems and applications. Unfortunately,
state-of-art resilience techniques based on checkpoint/restart are lagging
behind performance portability efforts: users still need to capture consistent states manually, which introduces the need for fine-tuning and
customization. In this paper we aim to close this gap by introducing a
set of abstractions that make it easier for the application developers to
reason about resilience. To this end, we extend the existing abstractions
proposed by performance portability efforts towards resilience. By marking critical data structures that need to be checkpointed, one can enable
an optimized runtime to automate checkpoint-restart using high performance and scalable asynchronously techniques. We illustrate the feasibility of our proposal using a prototype that combines the *Kokkos* runtime
(HPC performance portability), with the *VELOC* runtime (large-scale
low overhead checkpoint-restart). Our experimental results show negligible performance overhead compared with a manually tuned implementation of checkpoint-restart while requiring minimal changes in the
application code.

Keywords: Performance portability · Resilience · Fault tolerance ·
Checkpointing · Programming models

1 Introduction

Supercomputing facilities have seen a rapid evolution towards heterogeneous
architectures, both from a computational (many-core CPUs, GPUs, other

L. Sousa et al. (Eds.): Euro-Par 2021, LNCS 12820, pp. 451–465, 2021.
https://doi.org/10.1007/978-3-030-85665-6_28

accelerators) and I/O perspective (deep memory hierarchies, node-local persistent storage, external parallel file systems, key-value stores, etc.). This places a major burden on HPC applications, because they need to interface with a large variety of vendor APIs and/or customize their codes accordingly.

In an effort to address this problem, *performance portability* [8] has been proposed as a potential solution. The key idea of performance portability is the abstraction of hardware heterogeneity behind a unified programming model that eliminates the need for customization on the application side, while shifting the awareness of the intrinsic aspects of different heterogeneous accelerators to the runtimes, which can transparently provide optimized implementations of the high-level abstractions for each type of accelerator. Efforts such as *Kokkos* [8], *RAJA* [13], *DPC++* [20] are just some examples that illustrate this concept.

Unfortunately, the increasing number of heterogeneous components driven by the quest to achieve Exascale also leads to an increasing failure rate, which means resilience is another important challenge that needs to be addressed by the applications. Since most of the applications running on HPC machines are tightly coupled, failures are hard to isolate and quickly propagate from one process to another. In many cases, error detection can be more limited on heterogeneous nodes (such as on a GPU) [5]. Therefore, the main resilience strategy used by these applications is global checkpoint/restart where all processes agree periodically on a globally consistent state that is persisted and used to restart from in case of failures.

While there are many optimized checkpointing frameworks available that combine a variety of techniques (e.g. asynchronous multi-level resilience strategies as illustrated by *VELOC* [19]) to reduce the checkpointing overhead as much as possible, such frameworks typically require the application developers to manually assemble critical data structures and serialize them into node-local files, which are then persisted to resilient storage. On heterogeneous nodes, this is a non-trivial task. First, some data structures may live on GPUs or other accelerators and are not accessible in the host space. Secondly, there may be multiple references to the same data structure that only needs to be checkpointed once. Finally, a data structure may need to be part of the critical state in one location of the code but not in another (e.g., some data structures may be discarded at the end of a main loop). Therefore, there is a need to simplify how application developers reason about resilience in order to address the aforementioned issues without sacrificing the ability to leverage optimized checkpointing frameworks.

To this end, we propose a set of resilience abstractions for heterogeneous architectures that hide the complexity of interacting with checkpoint-restart frameworks, similar to how performance portability approaches hide the complexity of interacting with heterogeneous hardware. By synergizing with such efforts, we leverage the fact that users already define their data structures using constructs such as *memory views*. These can be extended and used together with another construct, the *scoped resilient execution contexts*, allowing the runtime to both capture the critical data structures and checkpoint them at the right moment automatically. This unique combination provides an intuitive and efficient way for performance-portable applications to employ resilience, reducing developer time and cost, while enabling a straightforward integration with optimized checkpointing frameworks.

We summarize our contributions as follows: first, we introduce a novel resilience model specifically designed to take advantage of performance portability to automate both how to capture and when to checkpoint critical data structures. Second, we show how to implement such a model in practice based on the *Kokkos* [8] and *VELOC* projects [19]. Finally, we run extensive experiments to demonstrate the benefits of our proposal, both using synthetic benchmarks and real-life HPC applications.

2   Related Work

The move towards Exascale and heterogeneous computing platforms has increased the complexity of HPC hardware and software systems. Various studies have explored the effects of extreme-scale on application resilience. Di Martino et al. [4,5] analyze the resiliency of 5 million HPC application runs on the Blue Waters supercomputer, considering both CPU compute nodes and CPU nodes with GPUs and recording the hardware and software failure rates over the better part of a year. Hukerikar and Engelmann [14] lay out a set of resilience design patterns for large scales and a literature survey of the field.

Multi-level checkpoint/restart is a popular approach to leverage multiple storage levels in the context of HPC checkpointing. Works representative of this approach include SCR [18] and FTI [2], which introduce support for local storage, partner replication, erasure coding (XOR and Reed-Solomon) and finally external storage (parallel file systems). Recent efforts such as *VELOC* can take advantage of heterogeneous storage for each level and introduce advanced asynchronous techniques that leverage synergies between the levels [19] and predictions of application behavior to mitigate interference [23].

A growing field of user-level software resilience techniques has emerged around the idea of enabling MPI processes to repair the communicators (instead of terminating the whole MPI deployment), which can be leveraged to implement forward recovery techniques. Examples in this direction are the ULFM extension to MPI [15,22] and user-level programming models such as Fenix [9,10,12,24], as well as the Relax transactional framework proposed by De Kruijf et al. [3].

Other areas of software fault tolerance focused on extreme scale and heterogeneous systems include resilience for task-parallel programming models [17,21], GPU snapshotting approaches [1], and the DataSpaces staging service [6] along with resilience strategies for multi-application staging [7]. Additionally, there has been recent focus on local checkpointing and rollback functionality to prevent a global rollback over the entire system [11,16,22].

All the approaches mentioned above require significant development effort either to capture and serialize the global state as checkpoints (rollback recovery) periodically, or to reconstruct consistent states after failures in other ways (forward recovery). To the best of our knowledge, we are the first to explore the idea of leveraging performance portability abstractions as building blocks for a resilience model that bridges the gap between application development productivity and other resilience strategies.

3   Background

The goal of performance portability is to provide HPC applications with a unified programming model that allows code to be written once and reused for a diverse array of architectures with similar performance. Several efforts have been proposed in this space, including *Kokkos* [8], *RAJA* [13] and *DPC++* [20]. These frameworks provide abstractions for parallel/concurrent computation and memory/data representation for heterogeneous computing systems to hide platform specific programming features and complex interactions between the host CPUs and the accelerators. Under these frameworks, individual data objects (e.g. arrays) encapsulate the metadata information such as device location and memory layout. Adding a unique identification to the metadata enables to track the state of individual data objects, facilitating an automation of application-based checkpointing and recovery. For the purpose of this work, we focus on *Kokkos*. However, it is important to remember that our approach does not depend on any particular performance portability framework and can be adapted accordingly.

To achieve this goal, *Kokkos* introduces three abstractions: (1) *execution spaces*, which define how computational kernels can be executed at fine granularity in a data-parallel fashion; (2) *memory views*, which define multi-dimensional arrays that computational kernels operate on; (3) *polymorphic data layout*, which enables memory views to be reinterpreted dynamically.

In terms of execution spaces, simple *Kokkos* patterns look similar to those exposed by OpenMP, the main difference is the focus on a C++-oriented model. Of interest to us is how these patterns interact with the data structures, which are captured as memory views. Specifically, the memory views can be annotated with properties and hints that refer to their layout, location (host or device), and access pattern. This enables the application to fix accessibility and performance relationships. For example, a memory view can be interpreted in different ways when being processed on a CPU or GPU: extra copies can be avoided if it is known to be read-only (*const*) or a computation in the GPU execution space could access data directly from the host memory (e.g. using unified virtual memory) with degraded performance.

4   Performance Portable Resilience Abstractions

Starting from the performance portable abstractions discussed above, this section introduces the core design principles of our proposal.

Scoped Resilient Execution Contexts: As mentioned above, the *Kokkos* execution spaces (e.g., parallel for) require the user to encapsulate the computational kernels into lambda functors. We extend this notion to provide a higher-level resilient execution context. These contexts are encapsulated into lambda functions and can encompass one or more *Kokkos* operations that exist in any execution space. Using this approach, any external memory views used in the body of the lambda function are automatically captured when the context is closed, forming a set of critical data structures that can be checkpointed and used to restart. In turn, the resilient execution context will handle all other aspects automatically: when to checkpoint, how to serialize the critical memory views, and so on. An example of how this works is illustrated in Listing 1. It is important to note that this approach grants high levels of flexibility: users can simply compose multiple scoped resilient execution contexts, each with its own lambda captures and therefore an implicit minimal set of critical memory views. Therefore, users are freed from manually keeping track of what data structures are critical in all alternative paths of their code. This would normally be a cumbersome process that is both prone to errors (for example, if the user forget to checkpoint a critical data structure) and sub-optimal performance (checkpointing a data structure that is not critical).

Optimized Tracking of Critical Memory Views: Our goal is to avoid introducing a new construct that forces the developers to differentiate between "regular" and critical memory views, which is why users are allowed to capture regular memory views in resilient execution contexts. When it is time to checkpoint, a naive approach would be to serialize all captured memory views into a checkpoint file and continue the execution. However, such an approach is inefficient for several reasons. First, memory views may be reinterpreted or copied in multiple execution contexts, but only one instance is enough to reconstruct the state on restart. In this case, we allow memory views to be marked as *transient* (checkpoint not required) or *aliased* by a unique identifier. Aliasing views allow the runtime to track two views with different names as the same. This is primarily useful for adapting codes where a view is replaced by another that is functionally the same but has a different allocation. An example of this would be a double-buffering algorithm, where two views are named differently but are swapped so only one is mutable at a time. While aliasing can be used to ensure correctness of some code, it isn't necessary in most cases. Marking a view as transient does not affect correctness, but can provide some performance benefits by reducing checkpointing size.

All views are reference counted intrinsically; a memory view is checkpointed only once even if it is captured multiple times. The combination of aliasing and reference counting create a de-duplication opportunity that can significantly reduce the checkpoint sizes independently of the checkpoint backend. Furthermore, another optimization opportunity lies in the fact that memory views may be read-only, which means either a different execution context was responsible for generating it or can simply be regenerated on restart. Our approach can detect what views are read-only based on their "*const*-ness". This can be leveraged to take advantage of checkpointing backends that implement incremental checkpointing techniques.

```
const int dim0 = 5, dim1 = 5;
auto view = Kokkos::View< double ** >( "test_view", dim0, dim1 );

for ( int iter = 0; iter < max_iter; ++iter ) {
  KokkosResilience::checkpoint(plugin, "test_checkpoint", iter, [=]() {
    Kokkos::parallel_for( dim0, KOKKOS_LAMBDA( int i ) {
      for ( int j = 0; j < dim1; ++j )
        view( i, j ) = 3.0;
    } );
  } );
}
```

Listing 1: Example usage of scoped resilient execution context.

Dynamic Pluggable Checkpointing Backends: Once the minimal set of critical memory views was determined, our approach can transparently interface with any checkpointing backend that was specifically optimized for a particular scenario and/or machine. The translation from our unified model to the various APIs of the checkpointing backends are implemented as independent plugins that can be flexibly assigned by the users to each resilient execution context. In fact, it is perfectly possible to mix different checkpointing backends in the same application or even dynamically switch between them. Although outside of the scope of this paper, it is important to note that this capability can be leveraged as a building block for more advanced checkpointing approaches, such as dynamic decisions based on the size and/or content (such as applying compression algorithms if the memory views are large and/or sparse).

5   Implementation

The resilience layer functions on two levels. The first level operates at compile time and encompasses the definition of the resilient execution contexts and the detection of views along with their type properties such as *const*-ness. The second level is the runtime component that tracks view usage (as defined in the first layer), aliases, and the interface with the checkpointing backend.

Defining the Resilient Execution Context: In order to specify the actual critical regions of code that must be made resilient through checkpoint/restart, one must define the beginning and the end. In general, code in the resilient region should have no side effects. If code inside the region were to modify global or static variables, these would not be included in the checkpoint and could affect correctness of the program during a restart. Under these assumptions, scoped resilient execution contexts can be defined as lambda captures, as mentioned in Sect. 4.

Listing 1 shows a simple usage scenario, where `plugin` is the resilience plugin, `test_checkpoint` is the label and `iter` is the iteration number to be checkpointed. Finally, the scoped resilient context is specified as a lambda with input and output views part of the lambda capture. Note that the user does not need to

```
Kokkos::View< double * > ping( /*...*/ ), pong( /*...*/ );
for ( int i = 0; i < max_ts; ++i ) {
  Kokkos::View< const double * > read;
  Kokkos::View< double * > write;
  if ( i % 2 )
    read = pong; write = ping;
  else
    read = ping; write = pong;
  KokkosResilience::checkpoint( ctx, "iterate", i, [=]() {
    Kokkos::parallel_for( /*...*/, KOKKOS_LAMBDA( int j ) {
      write( j ) = do_calculation( read );
    } );
  } );
}
```

Listing 2: Example of a ping-pong buffer for which a minimal set of critical memory views is automatically detected by examining *const*-ness of all captured views.

explicitly remember to capture a view; it is automatically captured by value. This incurs a minimal overhead and does not create extra copies, because *Kokkos* views are constructed as references. In the case that existing code makes extensive use of global views, it is possible to explicitly capture the global variable (or make reference counted copies of the global that are implicitly used within the lambda) to bring it under the scope of the resilience tracking algorithms.

Tracking of Critical Memory Views: One of the primary features of our approach, as outlined in the previous section, is the optimization of *const Kokkos* memory views. Normally a view has a datatype associated with it (such as double). If the datatype is instead *const*, such as const double, the view becomes immutable. *Kokkos* already provides conversions from mutable to *const* views that work as expected; similarly these views share the same reference count and control block. We take advantage of this fact in our implementation; when a view is only used in a checkpoint region for reading, marking it as *const* will prevent the runtime from needing to checkpoint the view. This can be determined at compile time, when the lambda capture list is built. This is straightforward with C++ function overloading. List-building is delegated to two functions, one taking a templated *const* view type, and another taking a non-*const* view type. In this way, *const* views can be filtered from the checkpoint list. Of course, this relies on some input by the user in marking *const* views; however this is generally well-accepted practice both in C++ programming in general and *Kokkos* code. We apply the same principle for transient views, while aliased views are de-duplicated at runtime.

To illustrate this point, consider the following example in Listing 2: a buffer that is written to changes every iteration. However, only one buffer should be actually checkpointed, since the other one is redundant. Since the read buffer is not written to and is *const*, it can be ignored. On a restart the write buffer would be loaded and immediately swapped into the new read buffer. This automatic optimization would, in this example, lead to a 50% reduction in checkpoint size as opposed to checkpointing every view.

Checkpointing Backend Integration: Our research prototype implements a plugin for *VELOC* [19], a low overhead checkpointing runtime specifically designed to deliver high performance and scalability for HPC machines thanks to a combination of multi-level resilience strategies that are applied asynchronously. *VELOC* is a particularly well suited candidate for illustrating our proposal because it implements a memory-oriented API that separates the registration of critical memory regions from the actual checkpointing operations, thereby simplifying the integration.

Specifically, we automatically register and unregister the *Kokkos* memory views with *VELOC* as contiguous memory regions defined by pointer and size whenever this is possible, which gives *VELOC* direct memory access and therefore reduces the checkpointing overhead. However, in the case of views with non-contiguous layout or views in inaccessible memory (e.g., GPU memory) that cannot be directly registered/unregistered with *VELOC*, we have implemented a proxy layer that collects all non-contiguous and/or inaccessible memory regions into a host buffer, which in turn is then registered with *VELOC*. At the start of any subsequent checkpoint, the runtime synchronizes with the backend and completes any pending asynchronous operations.

In addition to *VELOC*, we have implemented a simple synchronous approach that writes the checkpoints directly to a parallel file system. Based on this initial set of plugins, we plan to interface with several other backends.

6   Results

6.1   Experimental Setup

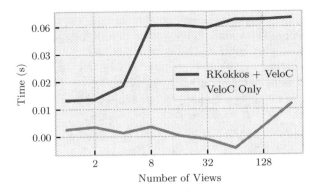

Fig. 1. Stress-test results for a weak scalability experiment that involves an increasing number of checkpointed memory views. The comparison refers to the bookkeeping overhead related to tracking the memory views using our approach vs. manual registration using *VELOC*. Checkpointing is deactivated, but tracking is still active. This timing data includes compute time.

Our experiments were carried out on an experimental testbed at Sandia National Laboratories featuring 1488 compute nodes, each equipped with 2.1 GHz Intel Broadwell CPUs (36 cores, 72 hardware threads). The memory of each node is 128 GB of RAM. Omni-Path interconnect is used between the nodes, which is exposed through OpenMPI v.4.0. All compute nodes have access to a Lustre parallel file system to persist their data.

In terms of software ecosystem, we forked Kokkos v.3.0 and added our scoped resilient execution abstraction on top of it. The *VELOC* checkpoint plugin was written for *VELOC* v.1.4, which features a client library and an encapsulated resilience engine that can be either linked with the application as a synchronous checkpointing library, or as a separate service in an active backend that enables asynchronous support. Our experimental setup leverages the latter to improve the checkpointing efficiency. Furthermore, *VELOC* was configured to use a `tmpfs` in-memory filesystem based on shared memory (`/dev/shm`) in order to minimize the overhead of capturing local checkpoints, which are then flushed asynchronously to Lustre.

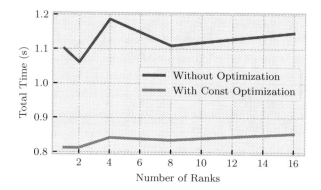

Fig. 2. Weak scaling of the *ping-pong* microbenchmark (Sect. 5) with and without the *const* memory view tracking optimization. The checkpoint size is 50% smaller when the const-tracking is activated, which significantly improves the checkpointing performance.

6.2   Methodology

To evaluate our proposal, we devise a series of experiments that mix both synthetic benchmarks and real-life HPC applications.

Specifically, we designed two micro-benchmarks to evaluate particular aspects of our implementation in order to understand potential limitations and bottlenecks in extreme cases. These will be discussed in the rest of this section along with the results. In addition, we use two scientific mini-apps:

MiniMD: is a parallel molecular dynamics application written using Kokkos abstractions for the Mantevo[1] project. We forked the code and implemented resilience using the abstractions of our proposal, as discussed in Sect. 5.

HeatDis: is a heat distribution solver (HeatDis) that is used as an example by *VELOC*[2]. First, we parallelized HeatDis with *Kokkos*, but kept the original resilience implementation that calls *VELOC* directly. Next, we re-implemented the resilience in the Kokkos-enabled HeatDis using our own abstractions.

We conducted experiments at scale using multiple nodes, each of which leverages the available cores using OpenMP-based *Kokkos*, which was configured to use 70 threads. Although *VELOC* is designed to prevent interference with the applications during asynchronous checkpointing, we decided to eliminate this noise from our experiments by allocating the remaining core (2 hardware threads) on each compute node exclusively to the *VELOC* active backend.

6.3   Results: Microbenchmarks

First, we ran a series of experiments to understand the overheads that are introduced by our approach due to tracking of the memory views. To this end, we compare our approach with a baseline that relies on manual registration of the critical data structures using *VELOC*. To emphasize this overhead as much as possible, we do not perform an actual checkpoint (they are converted to no-ops), which means the runtime directly measures the bookkeeping overhead of tracking overhead vs. manual registration. Since most of our implementation relies on compile-time constructs with some runtime tracking, we expect this overhead to be negligible. This expectation is confirmed by the results in Fig. 1, which show a stable trend for an increasing number of checkpointed views: at the extreme of 128 views, the overhead is less than 0.06 s, compared with the bookkeeping overhead of *VELOC* which is 0.01. s. Given that most applications need to checkpoint few but large data structures, we conclude that our bookkeeping overhead is negligible.

Next, we evaluate the *ping-pong* microbenchmark that was discussed in Sect. 5. This benchmark measures the reduction in checkpointing overhead of using the *const* tracking optimizations versus a baseline case that is not using them. The benchmark exhibits a 50% reduction in checkpointing size due to *const* tracking (i.e., only one out of two equally sized memory views is checkpointed). As observed in Fig. 2, this translates in practice to an almost 30% speedup over the non-optimized version.

6.4   Results: HPC Mini-Apps

In order to analyze the performance of our approach in a holistic manner, we performed several scaling experiments with the two scientific mini-apps mentioned in Sect. 6.2.

---

[1] Original implementation at https://github.com/Mantevo/miniMD.

[2] https://github.com/ECP-VeloC/VELOC.

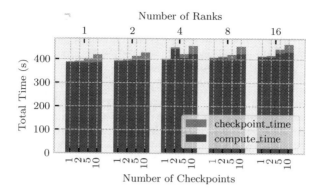

Fig. 3. *MiniMD*: breakdown of checkpointing time vs. compute time for a increasing number of nodes and checkpoints in a weak scalability scenario over 1000 time steps.

Figure 3 shows a broad overview of the performance of our checkpointing scheme on the MiniMD molecular dynamics app with 13 million atoms and 1000 timesteps. We vary both the number of checkpoints executed during the entire simulation run and the number of ranks. MiniMD scales weakly, as we can see by the red bars in the figure. Even at a high number of ranks, the checkpoints do not become more expensive. Furthermore, a large number of checkpoints (one every 40 s) has very little impact on the total execution size for this problem.

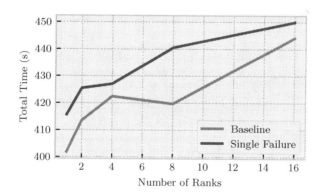

Fig. 4. *MiniMD*: comparison of a baseline checkpoint every 200 iterations and a checkpoint/restart with a failure at iteration 401 in a weak scalability scenario.

Figure 4 gives an overview of performance with a checkpoint every 200 iterations with and without a failure.

In the *MiniMD* we also performed a brief evaluation of the reduction of code complexity for the user. The three main data structures used in the application contained a total of 65 views. Modifying the code for resilience required manual tracking of only the three objects; this represents a significant decrease in code complexity compared to manually tracking all 65 views.

We performed another weak scaling study with the *HeatDis* heat solver mini-app. In this case, we varied the problem size (which directly corresponds to the size of the checkpoints). We compare a run that takes ten checkpoints (one every 100 iterations) without restart (Fig. 5) and a run that does the same but also restarts from the third checkpoint (by simulating a failure at iteration 301). The results are depicted in Fig. 6).

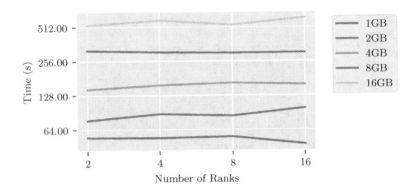

Fig. 5. *HeatDis*: total runtime for an increasing number of ranks and checkpoint size per rank in a weak scalability scenario without restart (1000 iterations, checkpoint every 100 iterations).

As can be observed for both *MiniMD* and *HeatDis*, the evaluated scenarios exhibit minimal overhead due to checkpoint-restart, which is the result of combining optimized memory tracking with the asynchronous techniques introduced by *VELOC*. Based on the bookkeeping experiments discussed in Sect. 6.3, memory tracking has negligible overhead, while enabling automated checkpointing with minimal coding effort. Indeed, for our benchmarks and applications, a single lambda declaration (i.e., a single line of code) to wrap the code into a resilient execution context was enough to take advantage of the advanced checkpointing techniques exposed by VELOC.

From a qualitative perspective our approach solves three important challenges that manual checkpointing faces: (1) difficulty in identifying the critical data structures in complex codes that combine multiple execution contexts; (2) inefficient checkpoints that duplicate critical data structures or include data structures that are not critical; (3) deciding best moment to checkpoint the critical data structures.

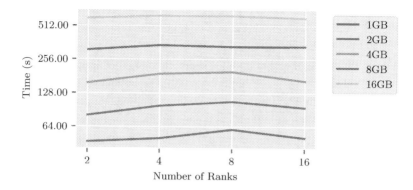

Fig. 6. *HeatDis*: total runtime for an increasing number of ranks and checkpoint size per rank in a weak scalability scenario with restart (1000 iterations, checkpoint every 100 iterations, restart at iteration 301).

7   Conclusion and Future Work

Our contribution is designed to provide convenient and efficient checkpointing for performance portable HPC applications. Our work extends the performance portable abstraction to that of *resilience portability*, allowing existing code to be made resilient with minimal changes. Moreover, we use type information determined at compile time to analyze the usage of resilient data, permitting the use of optimization based on usage patterns. We demonstrate the performance results of our work on various mini-apps and microbenchmarks. We show that compared to manually invoking state-of-the art resilience backends, we introduce negligible overhead.

In the future we would like to extend the idea of compiler analysis. Although compile-time data-flow analysis using C++ lambda introspection provides a useful way to determine inputs and outputs of checkpoint regions, a compiler pass could enable more robust detection, including analyzing any side-effects from references to global variables or static objects. Furthermore, we would like to extend our approach to a greater variety of backends and applications in order to understand better any performance implications and usability issues.

Acknowledgments. This material is based upon work supported by the U.S. Department of Energy (DOE), Office of Science, Office of Advanced Scientific Computing Research, under Contract DE-AC02-06CH11357. Sandia National Laboratories is a multimission laboratory managed and operated by National Technology & Engineering Solutions of Sandia, LLC, a wholly owned subsidiary of Honeywell International Inc., for the U.S. Department of Energy's National Nuclear Security Administration (NNSA) under contract DE-NA0003525. This work was funded by NNSA's Advanced Simulation and Computing (ASC) Program. This paper describes objective technical results and analysis. Any subjective views or opinions that might be expressed in the paper do not necessarily represent the views of the U.S. Department of Energy or the United States Government.

References

1. Baird, M., Fensch, C., Scholz, S.-B., Šinkarovs, A.: A lightweight approach to GPU resilience. In: Mencagli, G., et al. (eds.) Euro-Par 2018. LNCS, vol. 11339, pp. 826–838. Springer, Cham (2019). https://doi.org/10.1007/978-3-030-10549-5_64

2. Bautista-Gomez, L., Tsuboi, S., Komatitsch, D., Cappello, F., Maruyama, N., Matsuoka, S.: FTI: high performance fault tolerance interface for hybrid systems. In: SC 2011: The 2011 ACM/IEEE International Conference for High Performance Computing, Networking, Storage and Analysis, Seattle, USA, pp. 32:1–32:32 (2011)

3. De Kruijf, M., Nomura, S., Sankaralingam, K.: Relax: an architectural framework for software recovery of hardware faults. In: ACM SIGARCH Computer Architecture News, vol. 38, pp. 497–508. ACM (2010)

4. Di Martino, C., Kalbarczyk, Z., Iyer, R.K., Baccanico, F., Fullop, J., Kramer, W.: Lessons learned from the analysis of system failures at petascale: the case of blue waters. In: 2014 44th Annual IEEE/IFIP International Conference on Dependable Systems and Networks, pp. 610–621. IEEE (2014)

5. Di Martino, C., Kramer, W., Kalbarczyk, Z., Iyer, R.: Measuring and understanding extreme-scale application resilience: a field study of 5,000,000 HPC application runs. In: 2015 45th Annual IEEE/IFIP International Conference on Dependable Systems and Networks, pp. 25–36. IEEE (2015)

6. Docan, C., Parashar, M., Klasky, S.: Dataspaces: an interaction and coordination framework for coupled simulation workflows. Cluster Comput. **15**(2), 163–181 (2012)

7. Duan, S., et al.: Scalable data resilience for in-memory data staging. In: 2018 IEEE International Parallel and Distributed Processing Symposium (IPDPS), pp. 105–115. IEEE (2018)

8. Edwards, H.C., Trott, C.R., Sunderland, D.: Kokkos: enabling manycore performance portability through polymorphic memory access patterns. J. Parallel Distrib. Comput. **74**(12), 3202–3216 (2014)

9. Gamell, M., Katz, D.S., Kolla, H., Chen, J., Klasky, S., Parashar, M.: Exploring automatic, online failure recovery for scientific applications at extreme scales. In: SC 2014: Proceedings of the International Conference for High Performance Computing, Networking, Storage and Analysis, pp. 895–906. IEEE (2014)

10. Gamell, M., et al.: Evaluating online global recovery with fenix using application-aware in-memory checkpointing techniques. In: 2016 45th International Conference on Parallel Processing Workshops (ICPPW), pp. 346–355. IEEE (2016)

11. Gamell, M., et al.: Local recovery and failure masking for stencil-based applications at extreme scales. In: SC 2015: Proceedings of the International Conference for High Performance Computing, Networking, Storage and Analysis, pp. 1–12. IEEE (2015)

12. Gamell, M., Van der Wijngaart, R.F., Teranishi, K., Parashar, M.: Specification of fenix MPI fault tolerance library version 1.0. Tech. rep., Technical Report SAND2016-9171, Sandia National Laboratories, Livermore, CA (2016)

13. Hornung, R.D., Keasler, J.A.: The RAJA portability layer: overview and status. Tech. rep., Lawrence Livermore National Lab. (LLNL), Livermore, CA (United States) (2014)

14. Hukerikar, S., Engelmann, C.: Resilience design patterns: a structured approach to resilience at extreme scale. Tech. Rep. ORNL/TM-2016/767, Oak Ridge National Laboratory, Oak Ridge, TN, USA (2016)

15. Laguna, I., et al.: Evaluating and extending user-level fault tolerance in MPI applications. Int. J. High Perform. Comput. Appl. **30**(3), 305–319 (2016)
16. Losada, N., Bosilca, G., Bouteiller, A., González, P., Martín, M.J.: Local rollback for resilient MPI applications with application-level checkpointing and message logging. Future Gener. Comput. Syst. **91**, 450–464 (2019)
17. Martsinkevich, T., Subasi, O., Unsal, O., Cappello, F., Labarta, J.: Fault-tolerant protocol for hybrid task-parallel message-passing applications. In: 2015 IEEE International Conference on Cluster Computing, pp. 563–570. IEEE (2015)
18. Moody, A., Bronevetsky, G., Mohror, K., De Supinski, B.R.: Design, modeling, and evaluation of a scalable multi-level checkpointing system. In: SC 2010: Proceedings of the 2010 ACM/IEEE International Conference for High Performance Computing, Networking, Storage and Analysis, pp. 1–11. IEEE (2010)
19. Nicolae, B., Moody, A., Gonsiorowski, E., Mohror, K., Cappello, F.: VeloC: towards high performance adaptive asynchronous checkpointing at large scale (2019)
20. Silveira, A., Ávila, R.B., Barreto, M.E., Navaux, P.O.A.: DPC++: object-oriented programming applied to cluster computing. In: Arabnia, H.R. (ed.) Proceedings of the International Conference on Parallel and Distributed Processing Techniques and Applications, PDPTA 2000, 24–29 June, 2000, Las Vegas, Nevada, USA. CSREA Press (2000)
21. Subasi, O., Arias, J., Unsal, O., Labarta, J., Cristal, A.: Nanocheckpoints: a task-based asynchronous dataflow framework for efficient and scalable checkpoint/restart. In: 2015 23rd Euromicro International Conference on Parallel, Distributed, and Network-Based Processing, pp. 99–102. IEEE (2015)
22. Teranishi, K., Heroux, M.A.: Toward local failure local recovery resilience model using MPI-ULFM. In: Proceedings of the 21st European Mpi Users' Group Meeting, p. 51. ACM (2014)
23. Tseng, S.-M., Nicolae, B., Bosilca, G., Jeannot, E., Chandramowlishwaran, A., Cappello, F.: Towards portable online prediction of network utilization using MPI-level monitoring. In: Yahyapour, R. (ed.) Euro-Par 2019. LNCS, vol. 11725, pp. 47–60. Springer, Cham (2019). https://doi.org/10.1007/978-3-030-29400-7_4
24. Van Der Wijngaart, R.I., Gamell, M.R.U., Teranishi, K., Valenzuela, E., Heroux, M.A., Parashaar, M.R.U.: Fenix; a portable flexible fault tolerance programming framework for MPI applications. Tech. rep., Sandia National Lab. (SNL-NM), Albuquerque, NM (United States) (2016)

Enhancing Load-Balancing of MPI Applications with Workshare

Thomas Dionisi[1], Stephane Bouhrour[1], Julien Jaeger[1,2,3(✉)], Patrick Carribault[2,3], and Marc Pérache[2,3]

[1] Exascale Computing Research Laboratory, 2 Rue de la Piquetterie, 91680 Bruyères-le-châtel, France
[2] CEA, DAM, DIF, 91297 Arpajon, France
julien.jaeger@cea.fr
[3] Université Paris-Saclay, CEA, Laboratoire en Informatique Haute Performance pour le Calcul et la simulation, 91680 Bruyères-le-châtel, France

Abstract. Some high-performance parallel applications (e.g., simulation codes) are, by nature, prone to computational imbalance. With various elements, such as particles or multiple materials, evolving in a fixed space (with different boundary conditions), an MPI process can easily end up with more operations to perform than its neighbors. This computational imbalance causes performance loss. Load-balancing methods are used to limit such negative impacts. However, most load-balancing schemes rely on shared-memory models, and those handling MPI load-balancing use too much heavy machinery for efficient intra-node load-balancing. In this paper, we present the *MPI Workshare* concept. With *MPI Workshare*, we propose a programming interface based on directives, and the associated implementation, to leverage light MPI intra-node load-balancing. In this work, we focus on loop worksharing. The similarity of our directives with OpenMP ones makes our interface easy to understand and to use. We provide an implementation of both the runtime and compiler directive support. Experimental results on well-known mini-applications (MiniFE, LULESH) show that *MPI Workshare* succeeds in maintaining the same level of performance as well-balanced workloads even with high imbalance parameter values.

1 Introduction

The ever-growing need for computational power by simulation programs led to larger and more complex supercomputer architectures. Simulating natural phenomena can be complex and their evolving natures may lead to imbalanced workloads during execution. For example, considering a set of particles in a 3D space, they will be spread across all computing workers. If the initial distribution of the particles favored similar workloads on all computing workers, the balance may shift once the particles move through the 3D space and lead to some computing workers having to deal with more particles than their neighbors. Such

© Springer Nature Switzerland AG 2021
L. Sousa et al. (Eds.): Euro-Par 2021, LNCS 12820, pp. 466–481, 2021.
https://doi.org/10.1007/978-3-030-85665-6_29

workload imbalance causes performance loss. To circumvent this problem, different work balancing methods emerged, mainly relying on shared-memory capabilities. If mixing MPI with a shared-memory programming model (MPI+X) is now common, hence providing a favorable ground for load-balancing, such hybrid programming is not always ideal regarding performances. First, runtime stacking, i.e., having the runtimes for each programming model running at the same time, is a challenge. Each runtime, often developed as if it will be the only runtime running with the application, might make decisions that would hurt the performance of the other running runtime. Second, the load-balancing will only happen within the scope of the shared-memory models. This means that even if multiple MPI processes are on the same node, no computational load-balancing will ever happen. MPI load-balancing has been proposed in the past, where message passing concepts are frequently used to support both inter-node and intra-node load balancing. Although this methodology is necessary for inter-node, using a distributed-memory mechanism can be heavy to handle intra-node load-balancing.

This paper exposes the *MPI Workshare* concept, which aims at providing the simplicity of OpenMP worksharing constructs to the MPI scope. We propose a set of directives, inspired by OpenMP, with a work stealing runtime system to provide shared-memory load-balancing to legacy MPI codes. Using *pragmas* similar to those of OpenMP, we ensure an easy-to-adopt interface for users, with a minimal impact on the program. In this first implementation, we focus on loop worksharing. The contributions of this paper are: 1) the presentation of the *MPI Workshare* concept, 2) the definition of the *MPI Workshare* programming interface, easy-to-adopt and leveraging incremental evolution of MPI (and MPI+OpenMP) codes to include MPI shared-memory constructs, 3) an implementation of directive compiler support and *MPI Workshare* runtime for loop worksharing, and 4) performance evaluations of MPI load-balancing on intra-node and inter-node benchmarks (pure MPI and MPI+OpenMP).

The paper is organized as follows. Section 2 documents related work to highlight the lack of efficient intra-node MPI load-balancing. The *MPI Workshare* concept is presented in Sect. 3, along with details on the loop workshare focus, and definition of the *MPI Workshare* interface. Section 4 focuses on the runtime and implementation details. Then experimental results are displayed in Sect. 5, before concluding in Sect. 6.

2   Related Work

Work-sharing concepts have long been studied in HPC. The first version of the OpenMP standard exposes such constructs through the `pragma omp for` and `pragma omp sections` directives. The loop worksharing construct distributes the associated loop iterations to all OpenMP threads, either statically or dynamically. Thus OpenMP have seen numerous work trying to improve the balance of its worksharing. [5] introduced a novel loop scheduling option, named *adaptive*. The scheduling strategy is based on the static scheduler by creating a per-worker queue. They enable a work stealing scheduler between the workers to dynamically balance the work along the execution when a thread becomes idle. Contrary to [18] where the number of stolen tasks is statically defined, a worker is allowed to steal the half of its victim's queue. In [19], the authors show that a state-of-the art runtime loop schedule is not efficient enough, and a mixed-approach with polyhedral compiler analysis driving the runtime decision can leverage much better performances. Recently, [2] exposes the state of the art of OpenMP loop scheduling and argues for the need of more scheduling policies. The introduction of tasking in the OpenMP standard led to studies aiming to improve the scheduling of numerous task [3,11,12,20]. These studies mainly advocates for local work-stealing to avoid extra costs.

Work sharing principles have already been integrated in some MPI applications. Most of these studies rely on an MPI+X approach, with the load-balancing enabled for intra-node only through a thread-based programming model [16]. Few studies looked at real MPI load-balancing. In [15], authors use a Divide-and-Conquer algorithm based on MPI dynamic processes to improve performance of an N-Queens problem. FLEX-MPI [9] provides a whole library on top of MPICH-2, to dynamically evaluate the load imbalance with hardware counters and online MPI profiling, and redistributes the data through communications. However, the user needs to register all data use in the computation for the runtime to automatically load-balance the work, which is very cumbersome and can induce some overheads. A more recent approach uses fine grain integration of tasking with MPI [8], using Task-Aware MPI [17]. If this work allows to have better scheduling of task including MPI communications, and tasks depending on these communications, the load-balancing is still confined to the scope of one MPI process. Most papers really targeting MPI load-balancing rely on message passing to exchange redistributed data. Though it is mandatory for inter-node load balancing, intra-node load balancing can be lighter by relying on shared-memory principles directly in the MPI runtime.

For several years, Partitioned Global Address Space (PGAS) programming models extend the shared memory paradigm across a whole cluster. This *unified* view of the memory allows embedding load-balancing concepts more easily in their runtimes. The authors of [4] implements an optimized (lock queue reduction, stealing more than one tasks at a time, ...) work stealing scheduler thanks to the PGAS *ARMCI*, able to scale on a large distributed system. The HabaneroUPC++ [6,7] PGAS model focus on work stealing scheduler thanks to the concatenation of the Habanero task programming model and the UPC++ PGAS tool. In [10], the authors introduce a dynamic tasking library for UPC, with a new Hierarchical Victim Selection (HVS) method to preserve locality. The main problem of PGAS models is the necessity to rewrite the program with their semantics.

Intra-node inter-process load-balancing is either too code intrusive with PGAS, or too heavy-weight with regular MPI load-balancing. However, a recent work presents simple intra-node *communication* load-balancing [13]. So why the same kind of concept is not also applied to intra-node computation load-balancing? Our *MPI Workshare* concept aims at leveraging the simplicity and efficiency of OpenMP worksharing, but between MPI processes on the same node. The proposed programming interface inspired by OpenMP ensures a quick understanding of its use, and limits the efforts and impacts on the source code, compared to a PGAS oriented rewrite. As we focus on intra-node MPI load-balancing, this work is complementary to all inter-node load-balancing schemes, and also with shared-memory model load-balancing such as OpenMP worksharing constructs.

3   MPI Workshare

MPI Workshare offers worksharing features to MPI, to leverage some load balancing in one of the most used parallel programming API. This section first presents the general idea of *MPI Workshare*, before describing our loop workshare implementation and the proposed interface.

3.1   *MPI Workshare* Concept

MPI Workshare exposes to users a way to enable inter-MPI process load-balancing on some specific parts of the program. Thus it is composed of two parts:

1. a programming interface allowing users to identify the parts of the local work that will be exposed to other MPI processes, and
2. a runtime implementation handling these parts and leveraging a stealing mechanism between MPI processes.

Marking the code parts that will be exposed to other MPI processes is left to the user. To ease the adoption of our *MPI Workshare* interface, this step requires to be the less invasive possible in the code, and easy to grasp and to use. To this end, we propose a programming interface inspired by OpenMP and its worksharing mechanism. The code selection for *MPI Workshare* is done through pragmas, with a set of `#pragma ws` directives inspired from OpenMP ones. These directives are detailed in Sect. 3.2. Based on these directives, the *MPI Workshare* runtime will transform the selected work into subtasks that can be executed by other MPI processes.

The second part is the work stealing mechanism, and when to actually steal work from another MPI process. In an MPI program, most performance loss comes from the synchronization induced by the MPI communications. Stealing work means that the local MPI process will have to check is there is some work to steal from another MPI process. This verification induces communications, hence synchronization, which can be harmful to the global performances. To avoid adding extra synchronization, probing for work to steal is done only when the local MPI process is already in a waiting state due to the MPI semantics. Instead of just waiting for the pending communications, the MPI runtime activates the *MPI Workshare* runtime to check if it can help any busy MPI process. With this behavior, the original semantics of the MPI process is kept, and no additional synchronizations are inserted due to the *MPI Workshare*.

Loop Workshare. In this work, we limit the scope of the *MPI Workshare* app-roach to *for* loops. The method used for the *MPI Workshare* on loops is very sim-ilar to the one used in OpenMP for the loop workshare constructs (e.g., `#pragma omp for` directive). Thus the loop iterations are decomposed into chunks. One major difference with the OpenMP construct is that these chunks are not initially spread onto the available MPI processes. Each MPI process is still in charge of executing its own loop, as expected from a usual MPI program. However, these chunks are exposed to the other MPI processes for workshare. If another MPI process finishes its work and ends up in a waiting state, it can steal available chunks. Figure 1 displays this behavior with 3 MPI processes located on the same node. Rank 0 has no loop, whereas ranks 1 and 2 have each one for loop, symbolized with the plain lines. Rank 1 has less iterations than rank 2. All MPI processes synchronize through an MPI call, represented with the dotted lines. With no workshare (left frame), rank 0 just waits for rank 1 and rank 2 to finish their work. Rank 2 has the heavier load, and delays the completion time of all ranks. Thanks to workshare (right frame), rank 0 starts to look for chunks to steal as soon as it enters the synchronizing call. It first steals rank 1, helping to finish its local work sooner. Then, both ranks are in the synchronizing call, and they both steal chunks from rank 2. Thanks to the stealing, rank 2 finishes its local work more quickly. It enters the synchronizing call earlier, thus "freeing" the other ranks from the synchronizing call earlier too.

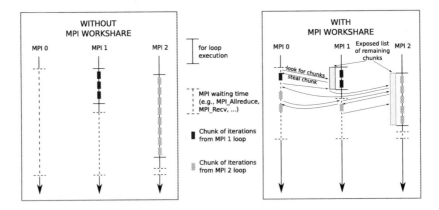

Fig. 1. *MPI Workshare* mechanism on 3 MPI processes, 2 MPI processes having a for loop with a `#pragma ws for` directive.

Like for OpenMP, it is possible as well to provide additional information to influence the sizes and numbers of chunks. It is also possible to define the equivalent of the `guided` and `dynamic` clauses of the `#pragma omp for` directive to have different size of chunks for the same loop, to leverage finer load balancing. All the new directives provided for *MPI Workshare* are detailed in the following Section.

Workshare Workers for Spare Cores. In regular MPI+OpenMP programs, there are less MPI processes than compute resources, as to leave compute resources dedicated to the OpenMP threads that will be spawned during execution. When *MPI workshare* is applied on a loop, it prevents OpenMP to be applied on the same loop. This means: 1) iterations won't be distributed among OpenMP threads and will execute sequentially (from the OpenMP perspective) and, 2) compute resources dedicated to OpenMP threads may remain idle as the corresponding OpenMP threads won't be awake. To avoid this, the *MPI Workshare* spawns *workers* on the idle resources. Each MPI process has its own set of *workers* on its local idle resources. Each *worker* helps performing local chunks (current MPI process) and work stealing (remote MPI process). With this policy, the *workers* behave for the local MPI processes in a fashion similar to OpenMP threads with a `#pragma omp for` directive. It is possible for a compute resource to host both an OpenMP thread and a workshare *worker*. However, they won't be active at the same time.

3.2 *MPI Workshare* Interface

The *MPI Workshare* interface is based on 3 directives, inspired by OpenMP standard, that enable loop worksharing.

Directive `#pragma ws for`. The main directive is `#pragma ws for`.

```
#pragma ws for [clause[ [,] clause] ... ] new-line
loop-nest
```

where loop-nest is a canonical loop nest and clause is one of the following:

```
private(list)
firstprivate(list)
lastprivate([lastprivate-modifier:]list)
reduction([reduction-modifier,]reduction-identifier:list)
schedule([modifier [, modifier]:]kind[, chunk_size])
collapse(n)
steal_schedule([modifier [, modifier]:]kind[, chunk_size])
```

This directive acts as the `#pragma omp for` in the OpenMP specification, but in the MPI scope. This construct specifies that the iterations of the associated loop/loopnest will be exposed to other MPI processes. Thus if an MPI process is in a waiting phase and is allowed to steal work, it will be able to execute some of the exposed iterations in parallel of the local MPI process. If multiple MPI processes are in this position, then the iterations will be distributed across all stealing MPI processes.

Both the `schedule` and `steal_schedule` clauses specify how iterations of the associated loop(s) are divided into chunks, and how these chunks are distributed among the MPI processes. The `schedule` clause drives the chunk choice only on the local MPI process. The `steal_schedule` clause specifies how other MPI processes will steal loop iterations. Both of these clauses accepts the same values as the `schedule` clause in the OpenMP specification: static, dynamic or guided.

All other clauses that can be passed to the `#pragma ws for` directive are similar to those of the `#pragma omp for` construct in the OpenMP specification. For example, it is possible to include a reduction operation in the scope of the `#pragma ws for` directive through the use of `reduction` clause with the right operator and the final variable.

Directive `#pragma ws atomic`. As the `reduction` clause cannot cover all the *reducing* operations that can happen in a loop body, the OpenMP specification offers the possibility to specify atomic instructions through the `#pragma omp atomic` construct. To offer the same level of expressiveness, we also provide the directive `#pragma ws atomic`.

```
#pragma ws atomic [clause[ [,] clause] ... ] new-line
statement
```

For this directive, the clauses, and according statements, supported are the same as for the `#pragma omp atomic` in the OpenMP specification. The behavior is also similar, as it ensures that the specified storage location is atomically updated, to avoid race conditions due to concurrent accesses of multiple MPI processes.

Directive `#pragma ws critical`. The `#pragma ws critical` is a generalization of the `#pragma ws atomic`. The construct applies on a scope defined with a structured block.

```
#pragma ws critical [(name)]  new-line
structured-block
```

This construct ensures that the code in the scope will be executed only by one MPI process at a time. The accepted clauses are similar to the ones accepted by the `#pragma omp critical` in the OpenMP specification.

4   Implementation

We implemented *MPI Workshare* into the MPC runtime [14]. MPC provides both an OpenMP and an MPI implementation, with the MPI runtime having both process-based and thread-based flavors. In the latter, all MPI processes in a node are in fact threads in one encompassing OS process. In this mode, the *MPI Workshare* runtime in MPC is very similar to the OpenMP runtime. Inside a node, all MPI processes are threads able to access the same memory space. An *MPI Workshare* structure is created for each MPI process. To help other

MPI ranks, an MPI process iterates on the *MPI Workshare* structure of each other MPI process until finding one with unfinished exposed work. Such work is symbolized by a *shared index* inside the *MPI Workshare* structure with a value between the lower and upper bound of the shared loop. To steal a chunk, the MPI process has to get the current iteration chunk index, and update its value to the next chunk. Thus this MPI process will be in charge of performing the loop iterations in the selected chunk. These three operations are performed atomically with a *compare_and_swap* operation. State-of-the-art stealing optimizations have been implemented (stealing from the end of the list) along with several victim selection policies (MPI process with the most iterations remaining, or with less thieves, or closest according to hardware topology). The whole stealing method is realized with a lock-free implementation.

MPI Calls in Shared Loops. It is possible that the loop tagged for workshare contains MPI calls. Thus an MPI process stealing iterations should act as if it was indeed the former MPI process performing the call. The MPC runtime provides such features through the `MPIX_Disguise` function [1]. It allows an MPI process to temporarily assume the identity of another MPI process in the same compute nodes. Thanks to this feature, our implementation enables workshare even with MPI calls in the associated loop body.

However, we have the following restrictions for the moment. First, it is forbidden to access/modify the locations of data in the loop with RMA procedures. Second, we apply the same restriction on the loop iterations than OpenMP: there must be no semantic dependencies between iterations (either data dependencies, or ordering dependencies such as with MPI collective initialization procedures). The last restriction could be leveraged. OpenMP proposed the `ordered` directive to enforce that part of the parallel loop should be executed in order according to the iterations. As future plan, we envision to implement such `ordered` directive for *MPI Workshare*. With such addition, it can then be possible to balance loops containing MPI collective initialization procedures, as long as they are protected with the `ordered` directive.

Compilation and OpenMP Compatibility. Directives require compiler support to translate the *MPI Workshare* pragmas into the associated runtime calls. We implement this translation into GCC 7.3.0 (the most-recent supported by MPC at the time the work was performed) for C and C++, based on the existing OpenMP pass. We provide a new flag `-fws`, that enables *MPI workshare* directives. It is possible to have both OpenMP and *MPI workshare* directives in one program, and to use both `-fws` and `-fopenmp` flags. The runtimes are compatible and can work concurrently. However it is not possible to have both OpenMP and *MPI workshare* constructs on the same loop.

5   Experimental Results

To evaluate our *MPI Workshare* concept, we realized several experimentations on
a platform composed of dual-socket Intel Xeon Platinum 8168 (Skylake) nodes,
each with 24 cores at 2.7 GHz, equipped with Mellanox MT27700 (Connect-
IB) InfiniBand boards. Results are grouped into two categories: pure MPI runs,
and hybrid MPI+OpenMP executions. For pure MPI runs, workshare results
are produced without any *workers*, as all compute resources are populated with
MPI processes. For MPI+OpenMP runs, *MPI Workshare* spawns *workers* on
each compute resources originally used by OpenMP.

All results with *MPI Workshare* are realized using MPC 3.4.0. We compare
those results to both MPC 3.4.0 without activating *MPI Workshare* and openmpi
2.0.4. When OpenMP is involved, openmpi uses GCC 7.3.0 OpenMP runtime,
and MPC 3.4.0 without *MPI Workshare* uses its own OpenMP runtime relying
on GCC 7.3.0 for directive translation. For such tests, MPC 3.4.0 with *MPI
Workshare* replaces OpenMP loop pragmas with *MPI Workshare* pragmas, and
OpenMP threads are replaced with workshare *workers*.

5.1   Pure MPI Benchmarks with *MPI Workshare*

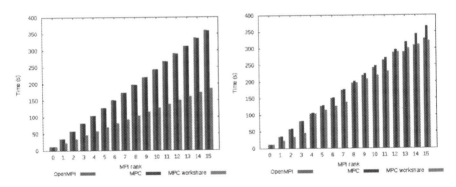

Fig. 2. Timing of each MPI ranks on a microbenchmark with imbalanced workload (see
Listing 1.1), without (`openmpi`, `MPC`) and with *MPI Workshare*. Left: 16 MPI processes
on a single node. Right: 16 MPI processes on 4 nodes (4 MPI processes per node).
(Color figure online)

Double-Loop Microbenchmark. Listing 1.1 shows an example of imbalanced
microbenchmark based on nested loops Iterations of the outer loop have monotonically increasing workload. Thus, the iterations of this loop are distributed
across multiple MPI processes, to expose imbalanced workload across MPI.

Figure 2 (left) displays the execution time for 16 MPI processes located on the
same node. The first two bars are for openmpi and MPC runs without workshare.
The timings convey the monotonically increasing workload on each MPI process.
The last bar (blue) is for MPC with *MPI Workshare*. The timings reported are

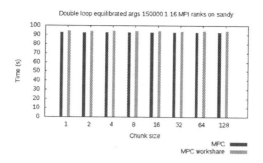

Fig. 3. *MPI Workshare* overhead evaluation on balanced workload, on a single node using 16 cores.

for the local completion of the loop nest on each rank. The timing of the whole benchmark is the same for each rank, and is similar to the local completion time of the slowest rank, due to MPI_Finalize synchronizing effect. As described in Sect. 3.1, *MPI Workshare* runtime is active only when the MPI runtime is idle. Thus, the *MPI Workshare* activates at the call to MPI_Finalize after the loop nest. The difference between the local timing and the global timing (local rank vs slowest rank) is the time spent waiting in the MPI_Finalize call, hence the time the MPI process can help other MPI processes by stealing loop iterations.

Rank 0 is the rank with the least workload. It performs all its iterations without help, hence its local completion time is the same with workshare (blue bar) than without (purple and green bars). Once its work is done, it waits in the barrier, and start looking for iterations to steal. Rank 1 is the first to be stolen, with a local completion timing lower with workshare. One after another, all waiting ranks start stealing the following MPI processes. Ultimately, rank 15, which is the rank with the greater workload, reaches the barrier nearly twice as fast as regular MPI execution, thanks to *MPI Workshare*.

Figure 2 (Left) is the best case for *MPI Workshare*, with all MPI processes on the same compute node. Figure 2 (Right) displays the results of executing the same benchmark on 4 nodes with 4 MPI processes per node. Once again, *MPI Workshare* allows the blue bar to grow slower than usual MPI. This is because *MPI Workshare* works only on intranode. Hence, workload is balanced only between the 4 MPI processes on the same node.

Overhead Study on Balanced Workload. Using the same microbenchmark based on nested loops, we change the inner loop so each iteration will perform the same computation as the other iterations, completely balancing the workload. We kept the same global number of iterations over all the MPI processes. This configuration allows to evaluate the overhead of *MPI Workshare* on a balanced workload. The results are displayed in Fig. 3. We varied the size of the chunk of iterations (1 meaning 1 iteration per chunk, 128 meaning 128 iterations per chunk). As we can see, on a balanced workload, the performance using

MPI Workshare is very close to the pure MPI approach. The observed overhead remains under 2% of the total execution time.

Lulesh and MiniFE Miniapps. Lulesh and miniFE (from the CORAL suite on resp. hydrodynamic and finite elements) both offer a parameter to insert workload imbalance between MPI processes. We ran Lulesh on an Intel KNL processor because of Lulesh restrictions. Indeed, Lulesh can only run with a number of MPI processes which is a cube. We opted for 64 MPI processes, and the KNL architecture was the only one available to us which allowed to have all 64 MPI processes on the same node. MiniFE experimentations are performed on the Skylake platform. Both experimentations display similar performances in intra-node (Fig. 4 for Lulesh and Fig. 5 (Left) for miniFE). For openmpi or standard MPC, the performance progressively drops when increasing the load imbalance parameter. However, with *MPI Workshare*, the performance stays constant regardless of the load imbalance.

```
MPI_Init();
...
#pragma ws loop
for i = MPIid*N/P to (MPIid+1)*N/P
{
  for j = 0 to i
  {
    do_some_work();
  }
}
...
MPI_Finalize();
```

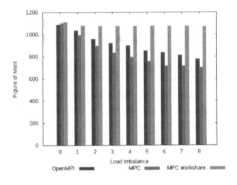

Source Code 1.1: Imbalance loop work-load on MPI processes

Fig. 4. Performance on Lulesh against the load imbalance with size = 100 and 64 MPI processes on KNL processors

Figure 5 (Right) displays miniFE behavior for varying number of nodes, with a load imbalance parameter fixed to 500. We observe that *MPI Workshare* still leverages better performance than usual MPC runs, though the speed-up being less important with a greater number of nodes, due to the intra-node scope limiting the workshare.

5.2   MPI+OpenMP Benchmarks with *MPI Workshare Workers*

We also evaluated *MPI Workshare* on MPI+OpenMP applications by replacing some OpenMP loop directives by the *Workshare* counterpart. *MPI Workshare* will spawn *workers* to populate the compute resources left vacant by the removed OpenMP directive. Hence, in intra-node, all the 48 cores are always used with a fitting combination of MPI processes with either OpenMP threads or *workers* (e.g., 1 MPI process with 48 threads, or 8 MPI processes with 6 threads).

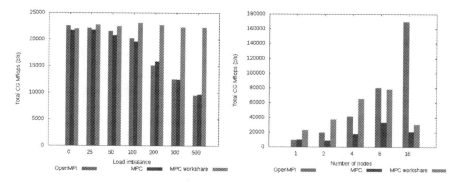

Fig. 5. Performance on miniFE with nx = ny = nz = 200 and 48 MPI processes per node on Skylake processors. Left: results on one node, x-axis is the percentage of imbalance as proposed by miniFE configuration. Right: results for varying number of nodes with a fixed load-imbalance percentage of 500.

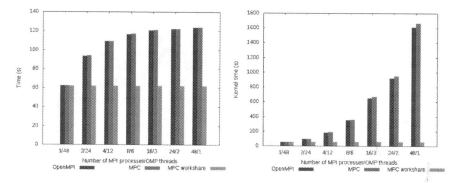

Fig. 6. Comparing MPI+OpenMP with MPI+*MPI Workshare* with *workers*. Second number of x-axis is number of OpenMP threads for `openmpi` and MPC, and number of *MPI Workshare workers* for `MPC+Workshare`. Left: microbenchmark with imbalanced workload (see Listing 1.1). Right: GAP Triangle Counting (TC) benchmark.

Double-Loop and GAP Triangle Count Microbenchmarks. We adapted microbenchmark Listing 1.1 and the Triangle Count benchmark from GAP Suite to run MPI+OpenMP tests. The Triangle Count benchmark is very highly imbalanced parallelized with OpenMP, relying on dynamic scheduling to enable load balancing. Since it does not use MPI, we did a basic MPI implementation distributing the same number of iterations between the MPI processes (similar to our double-loop benchmark). In our microbenchmark, we added OpenMP directives on the outer loop. Thus, for both benchmarks, when running with openmpi and MPC, the loop is parallelized with OpenMP in each MPI process, and for MPC with *MPI Workshare*, loop iterations are exposed to other MPI processes. Both benchmarks display similar behaviors (see Fig. 6). For 1 MPI process on the node, results are similar. With both OpenMP and *MPI Workshare*, the whole workload is balanced on the 48 availables cores. For more than 1 MPI process per node, OpenMP cannot balance the whole workload, as its scope is limited to intra-MPI process. With *MPI Workshare*, the whole workload continues to be perfectly balanced between all the *workers* of all MPI processes, keeping the same performance for every configuration.

miniFE miniapp. Figure 7 (Left) exposes results running MPI+OpenMP version of miniFE (MPI being either openmpi or MPC) compared to MPC+*MPI Workshare* using *workers* with different combinations of MPI processes and threads. Pure OpenMP executions of the miniapp showed that with a number of threads higher than 8, OpenMP scalability is degrading and performances collapse. This can be observed on the MPI+OpenMP version. Up to 4 MPI processes, the number of OpenMP threads are higher than 8, and the performances are driven by the OpenMP poor scalability. Hence, since performance issues do not come from the MPI workload imbalance, *MPI Workshare* do not bring any improvement. However, with more than 4 MPI processes, the OpenMP scalability is good, and the performance is driven by the MPI imbalance. Thus, the *MPI Workshare* brings better performance for such configurations.

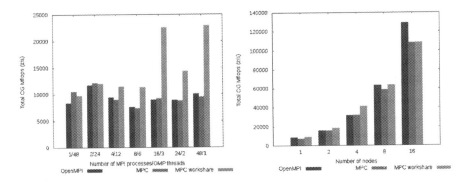

Fig. 7. MiniFE performance with an imbalance of 500. Second number of x-axis is number of OpenMP threads for `openmpi` and `MPC`, and number of *MPI Workshare* *workers* for `MPC+Workshare`. Left: varying the number of MPI processes, and accompanying threads/*workers*, on one node. Right: varying number of nodes, fixed number 8 MPI ranks with 6 threads/*workers* per node.

Figure 7 (Right) displays the internode performance with 8 MPI processes and 6 OpenMP threads, or 6 workshare *workers*. For a large number of nodes, the intra-node scope of *MPI Workshare* prevents it from having much benefit. However, for a small number of nodes, *MPI Workshare* succeeds in improving the performance.

6   Conclusion

MPI load-balancing can be critical to leverage good performance. Though most load-balancing mechanism are available on intra-node for other programming models, MPI load-balancing existing techniques rely on the heavy machinery of message passing. In this paper, we presented the *MPI Workshare* concept, offering the possibility to annotate an MPI program source code to allow inter-MPI processes intra-node load-balancing. The proposed interface is inspired from OpenMP directives to facilitate its adoption. We described our implementation of *MPI Workshare* directives and runtime, targeting loop iteration worksharing.

We tested our implementation on several microbenchmarks and CORAL miniapps. We showed that intra-node load-balancing is very efficient even with heavy load imbalance for pure MPI runs. In inter-node, *MPI Workshare* also provides speed-up, though it is inherently limited by its intra-node scope. With MPI+OpenMP applications, the addition of workshare *workers*, to populate the cores occupied by idle OpenMP threads, enables combining intra-MPI process iterations distribution with inter-MPI process load-balancing.

The *MPI Workshare* concept shows promising results on the tested benchmarks. However, our implementation only applies on regular loops, hence limiting the scope in actual simulation programs. In future work, we aim to extend *MPI Workshare* to other worksharing constructs inspired by OpenMP, such as `sections` and `tasks`. These constructs would allow a user to apply *MPI Workshare* load-balancing to independent parts of the code outside of regular for loops, which is mandatory to be efficient on real-life applications.

Acknowledgments. This work was performed under the Exascale Computing Research collaboration, with the support of CEA and UVSQ.

References

1. Besnard, J.B., et al.: Mixing ranks, tasks, progress and nonblocking collectives. In: Proceedings of the 26th European MPI Users' Group Meeting. EuroMPI 2019, Association for Computing Machinery, New York (2019). https://doi.org/10.1145/3343211.3343221

2. Ciorba, F.M., Iwainsky, C., Buder, P.: OpenMP loop scheduling revisited: making a case for more schedules. In: de Supinski, B.R., Valero-Lara, P., Martorell, X., Mateo Bellido, S., Labarta, J. (eds.) IWOMP 2018. LNCS, vol. 11128, pp. 21–36. Springer, Cham (2018). https://doi.org/10.1007/978-3-319-98521-3_2

3. Clet-Ortega, J., Carribault, P., Pérache, M.: Evaluation of OpenMP task scheduling algorithms for large NUMA architectures. In: Silva, F., Dutra, I., Santos Costa, V. (eds.) Euro-Par 2014. LNCS, vol. 8632, pp. 596–607. Springer, Cham (2014). https://doi.org/10.1007/978-3-319-09873-9_50

4. Dinan, J., Larkins, D.B., Sadayappan, P., Krishnamoorthy, S., Nieplocha, J.: Scalable work stealing. In: Proceedings of the Conference on High Performance Computing Networking, Storage and Analysis, pp. 1–11 (November 2009). https://doi.org/10.1145/1654059.1654113

5. Durand, M., Broquedis, F., Gautier, T., Raffin, B.: An efficient OpenMP loop scheduler for irregular applications on large-scale NUMA machines. In: Rendell, A.P., Chapman, B.M., Müller, M.S. (eds.) IWOMP 2013. LNCS, vol. 8122, pp. 141–155. Springer, Heidelberg (2013). https://doi.org/10.1007/978-3-642-40698-0_11

6. Kumar, V., Murthy, K., Sarkar, V., Zheng, Y.: Optimized distributed work-stealing. In: 2016 6th Workshop on Irregular Applications: Architecture and Algorithms (IA3), pp. 74–77 (November 2016). https://doi.org/10.1109/IA3.2016.019

7. Kumar, V., Zheng, Y., Cavé, V., Budimlić, Z., Sarkar, V.: Habaneroupc++: A compiler-free pgas library. In: Proceedings of the 8th International Conference on Partitioned Global Address Space Programming Models, PGAS 2014, pp. 5:1–5:10. ACM, New York (2014). https://doi.org/10.1145/2676870.2676879

8. Maroas, M., Teruel, X., Bull, J.M., Ayguad, E., Beltran, V.: Evaluating worksharing tasks on distributed environments. In: 2020 IEEE International Conference on Cluster Computing (CLUSTER), pp. 69–80 (2020). https://doi.org/10.1109/CLUSTER49012.2020.00017

9. Martín, G., Marinescu, M.-C., Singh, D.E., Carretero, J.: FLEX-MPI: an MPI extension for supporting dynamic load balancing on heterogeneous non-dedicated systems. In: Wolf, F., Mohr, B., an Mey, D. (eds.) Euro-Par 2013. LNCS, vol. 8097, pp. 138–149. Springer, Heidelberg (2013). https://doi.org/10.1007/978-3-642-40047-6_16

10. Min, S.J., Iancu, C., Yelick, K.: Hierarchical work stealing on manycore clusters. In: 5th Conference on Partitioned Global Address Space Programming Models, p. 35 (2011)

11. Muddukrishna, A., Jonsson, P.A., Vlassov, V., Brorsson, M.: Locality-aware task scheduling and data distribution on NUMA systems. In: Rendell, A.P., Chapman, B.M., Müller, M.S. (eds.) IWOMP 2013. LNCS, vol. 8122, pp. 156–170. Springer, Heidelberg (2013). https://doi.org/10.1007/978-3-642-40698-0_12

12. Olivier, S.L., Porterfield, A.K., Wheeler, K.B., Spiegel, M., Prins, J.F.: Openmp task scheduling strategies for multicore numa systems. Int. J. High Perform. Comput. Appl. **26**(2), 110–124 (2012). https://doi.org/10.1177/1094342011434065

13. Ouyang, K., Si, M., Hori, A., Chen, Z., Balaji, P.: Cab-mpi: Exploring interprocess work-stealing towards balanced mpi communication. In: Proceedings of the International Conference for High Performance Computing, Networking, Storage and Analysis, SC 2020, IEEE Press (2020)

14. Pérache, M., Carribault, P., Jourdren, H.: MPC-MPI: an MPI implementation reducing the overall memory consumption. In: Ropo, M., Westerholm, J., Dongarra, J. (eds.) EuroPVM/MPI 2009. LNCS, vol. 5759, pp. 94–103. Springer, Heidelberg (2009). https://doi.org/10.1007/978-3-642-03770-2_16

15. Pezzi, G.P., Cera, M.C., Mathias, E., Maillard, N., Navaux, P.O.A.: On-line scheduling of mpi-2 programs with hierarchical work stealing. In: 19th International Symposium on Computer Architecture and High Performance Computing (SBAC-PAD 2007), pp. 247–254 (October 2007). https://doi.org/10.1109/SBAC-PAD.2007.36

16. Ravichandran, K., Lee, S., Pande, S.: Work stealing for Multi-core HPC clusters. In: Jeannot, E., Namyst, R., Roman, J. (eds.) Euro-Par 2011. LNCS, vol. 6852, pp. 205–217. Springer, Heidelberg (2011). https://doi.org/10.1007/978-3-642-23400-2_20

17. Sala, K., et al.: Improving the interoperability between mpi and task-based programming models. In: Proceedings of the 25th European MPI Users' Group Meeting, EuroMPI 2018, Association for Computing Machinery, New York (2018). https://doi.org/10.1145/3236367.3236382

18. Subramaniam, S., Eager, D.L.: Affinity scheduling of unbalanced workloads. In: Proceedings of the 1994 ACM/IEEE Conference on Supercomputing, pp. 214–226. IEEE Computer Society Press, Los Alamitos, CA, USA (1994). http://dl.acm.org/citation.cfm?id=602770.602810

19. Thoman, P., Jordan, H., Pellegrini, S., Fahringer, T.: Automatic OpenMP loop scheduling: a combined compiler and runtime approach. In: Chapman, B.M., Massaioli, F., Müller, M.S., Rorro, M. (eds.) IWOMP 2012. LNCS, vol. 7312, pp. 88–101. Springer, Heidelberg (2012). https://doi.org/10.1007/978-3-642-30961-8_7

20. Virouleau, P., Broquedis, F., Gautier, T., Rastello, F.: Using data dependencies to improve task-based scheduling strategies on NUMA architectures. In: Dutot, P.-F., Trystram, D. (eds.) Euro-Par 2016. LNCS, vol. 9833, pp. 531–544. Springer, Cham (2016). https://doi.org/10.1007/978-3-319-43659-3_39

Particle-In-Cell Simulation Using Asynchronous Tasking

Nicolas Guidotti[1]($\boxtimes$), Pedro Ceyrat[1], João Barreto[1], José Monteiro[1],
Rodrigo Rodrigues[1], Ricardo Fonseca[2,3], Xavier Martorell[4],
and Antonio J. Peña[4]

[1] INESC-ID, Instituto Superior Técnico, Universidade de Lisboa, Lisbon, Portugal
`nicolas.guidotti@tecnico.ulisboa.pt`
[2] IPFN, Instituto Superior Técnico, Universidade de Lisboa, Lisbon, Portugal
[3] DCTI/ISCTE-IUL, Lisbon, Portugal
[4] Barcelona Supercomputing Center (BSC), Barcelona, Spain

Abstract. Recently, task-based programming models have emerged as a prominent alternative among shared-memory parallel programming paradigms. Inherently asynchronous, these models provide native support for dynamic load balancing and incorporate data flow concepts to selectively synchronize the tasks. However, tasking models are yet to be widely adopted by the HPC community and their effective advantages when applied to non-trivial, real-world HPC applications are still not well comprehended. In this paper, we study the parallelization of a production electromagnetic particle-in-cell (EM-PIC) code for kinetic plasma simulations exploring different strategies using asynchronous task-based models. Our fully asynchronous implementation not only significantly outperforms a conventional, synchronous approach but also achieves near perfect scaling for 48 cores.

Keywords: Manycore parallelism · Task-based programming · Asynchronous parallelism · Particle-in-cell · Kinetic plasma simulations

1 Introduction

As the number of processing units in multicore processors increases, so does the overhead for running parallel applications on these systems. Many alternative programming models have been proposed to facilitate the software development, while achieving higher application efficiency. Among them, task-based programming has long been hailed for its good load-balancing features, and has reached the mainstream with its adoption on OpenMP (`task` directive). Since task constructs are inherently asynchronous, they have the potential to prevent synchronization points in the code. Such synchronization can cause idle periods in processors, hence reducing performance and efficiency of HPC applications. Moreover, programming using tasks is increasingly being used as a means to facilitate the development on heterogeneous systems [10].

L. Sousa et al. (Eds.): Euro-Par 2021, LNCS 12820, pp. 482–498, 2021.
https://doi.org/10.1007/978-3-030-85665-6_30

Despite the strong potential of the task-based paradigm, its effective advantages are far from being well understood when applied to the non-trivial programs that comprise real-world HPC applications. This paper contributes to a better assessment of the advantages and limitations of tasks with data dependencies when used to parallelize the important class of particle-mesh applications. The case used for our study is a plasma physics kinetic simulation, based on an electromagnetic particle-in-cell (EM-PIC) method. This method is widely used for modeling many relevant plasma physics scenarios, ranging from high-intensity laser-plasma interaction to astrophysical shocks [6].

This paper makes two main contributions. As a first contribution, we propose different task-based implementations of a bare-bones version of the OSIRIS EM-PIC code [18], called ZPIC. The different versions explore the task-based paradigm to different extents – ranging from its most basic use to advanced features such as data dependencies. The suite of parallel implementations is available as open source to the community[1], and constitutes a useful benchmark to evaluate future advances in task-based programming tools and HPC hardware.

As a second contribution, we experimentally evaluate these different implementations with realistic simulation workloads (namely, Laser Wakefield Accelerator and Collision of Plasma Clouds) on a shared-memory multicore processor. Our results show that a fully asynchronous implementation (*i.e.*, using only data dependencies for synchronization) is able to achieve near perfect scaling for 48 cores, despite the unbalanced conditions. This impressive result is accomplished while retaining the code simplicity of task-based programming.

The remainder of this paper is organized as follows. Section 2 provides background on task-based programming models and on EM-PIC methods. Section 3 describes the proposed parallel implementations. Section 4 presents our experimental evaluation. Section 5 surveys related work. Finally, Sect. 6 presents final remarks and perspectives for future work.

2   Background

2.1   Shared Memory Programming

Under a shared memory model, a computational system is composed of processors that share the same memory space. Shared memory systems support many different programming paradigms but developers tend to prefer high-level programming models, such as those based on directives, seeking high coding productivity. In this paper, we focus on the widely-used OpenMP API as well as the OmpSs tasking model.

OpenMP [24] is a popular application programming interface (API) for expressing parallelism in shared-memory systems. The directives provided by OpenMP allow a simple and incremental parallelization approach from sequential code. The two main work sharing directives are `for` and `sections`. The former allows to distribute loop iterations across threads (data parallelism) and

---

[1] https://github.com/epeec/zpic-epeec.

the latter allows to define chunks of code that can run concurrently by different threads (functional parallelism). However, a simple use of these directives can easily assign different amounts of work to the different threads, creating a load imbalance that can lead to idle CPU time due to the synchronization of the different processors [15]. In version 3.0, the task directive was introduced, which allowed a more dynamic assignment of work to the threads. With tasks, the programmer only needs to identify units of independent work, leaving the decision about when to schedule their execution by an available thread to the runtime system. To enforce cross-task coordination (for instance, to ensure that a given segment of code only starts executing after a set of preceding tasks have finished), directives such as taskwait are provided.

More recently, OpenMP 4.0 extended the task construct to allow for defining data dependencies among tasks. The in clause prevents a task from being scheduled before the variables specified in the clause are available. The threads that produce these variables will in turn specify this information with the out clause, meaning that the former thread will only start after all of these have finished. It is also possible to specify an inout dependency. The data dependencies among the tasks define a data-flow graph whose operations are executed asynchronously as the necessary data becomes available. These clauses may also be used to reduce the number of synchronization directives among tasks, since the dependencies may be used to guarantee mutual synchronization implicitly. Data dependencies in OpenMP tasks were introduced after the SMPSs programming model [16], a precursor of OmpSs [11]. Since then, different task-related improvements have been studied within OmpSs, such as accelerator offloading [10] or task-parallel reductions [13]. Several of those are already adopted by the OpenMP standard, while some others are under current active discussion. Besides OmpSs and OpenMP, there are other programming models that support tasking, such as StarPU [7], Cilk [9], Intel TBB [1], and High Performance ParalleX (HPX) [22].

Initially, our intention was to focus only on the OpenMP tasking model, however current implementations do not fully support all types of data dependencies. This is the case of mutexinoutset (commutative in OmpSs), which allows mutual dependencies between tasks, but without a predefined order of execution. For this reason, all task-based implementations of this paper were developed in OmpSs-2, the second generation of the OmpSs programming model.

2.2   Kinetic Plasma Simulations

Electromagnetic particle-in-cell (EM-PIC) codes such as OSIRIS [19] have found widespread use in modeling the highly nonlinear and kinetic processes that occur in several relevant plasma physics scenarios, ranging from astrophysical settings to high-intensity laser plasma interaction. In an EM-PIC code, the full set of Maxwell equations is solved on a grid using currents and charge densities calculated by weighting discrete particles onto the grid [26]. Each particle is then pushed to a new position and momentum via the self-consistently calculated fields. Therefore, to the extent that quantum mechanical effects may

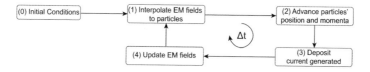

Fig. 1. Main stages in an EM-PIC simulation (adapted from [30]).

be neglected, an EM-PIC code makes no physics approximations and is ideally suited for studying complex systems with many degrees of freedom. For the analysis in this paper, a simplified version of OSIRIS called ZPIC [32] was considered. ZPIC is a purely sequential, bare-bones EM-PIC code implementing exactly the same algorithm as OSIRIS, and maintains all the core features of the latter. Therefore, the ZPIC code is relatively simple yet accurate, allowing an easy exploration of different programming models and parallel platforms.

The main simulation loop of EM-PIC methods is usually divided into four stages [30], as depicted in Fig. 1. In ZPIC, the field interpolation stage (1) is done using a bi-linear interpolation with the field values from the previous iteration, which are then used for the calculation of the Lorentz force acting on each individual particle. The particle advance stage (2) determines the next position and momenta, by integrating equations of motion using a leapfrog scheme [30] and the Boris method [6], making this method second order accurate in time. Using the particle motion calculated in the previous stage, the next stage in ZPIC (3) determines the electric current density on the grid using an exact charge conserving method [31]. The code may apply a digital filter on the current density to reduce short wavelength noise. As a last stage (4), using the current density that was just calculated, the code advances the EM fields in time using a finite-difference time-domain technique on a Yee mesh [6,30].

Also note that the EM-PIC algorithm described here is an implementation of the more general class of particle-mesh algorithms suited for (relativistic) kinetic plasma simulations. In this class of algorithms, the interaction of a large set of particles (bodies) is mediated by fields deposited on a finite mesh, instead of using a direct interaction between the particles. This allows for the algorithm complexity to scale with $\simeq N_p$ (the number of particles) rather than $\simeq N_p^2$ while retaining correct results as long as short range (*i.e.*, shorter than the mesh cell size) interactions do not dominate. This large computational gain makes this class of algorithm extremely popular in many fields, and, while this paper focuses on EM-PIC, the results presented here can be readily applied to any other particle-mesh code.

3   Parallel EM-PIC Implementations

We propose a diverse set of implementations, each covering a relevant point in a vast design space. We start with a natural parallelization of the original ZPIC code, which does not exploit tasks, and remains close to the original program structure. We then depart to task-based implementations, exploring different tasking features.

3.1 Parallel For-Based Implementation

This initial implementation, which we call `zpic-parallel-for`, is the most incremental approach to the original ZPIC code. We use OpenMP's `for` directive to naturally exploit the inherent data parallelism of the the original loop structure of the (sequential) ZPIC code.

Recalling the four main stages of the EM-PIC code (Fig. 1), the first three stages are implemented as a single loop that iterates over all the particles in the simulation. Each iteration interpolates the EM fields at the particle position (stage 1), advances the its momentum and position (stage 2) and then deposits the generated current in the grid (stage 3). Considering that the particles in EM-PIC implementation do not interact directly, but rather through the grid, each particle can be advanced independently (stages 1–2). Therefore, the most natural way to parallelize these three stages is to distribute the particles evenly among the threads with an OpenMP `for` directive (*i.e.*, a particle-based decomposition). However, since all threads share the same global buffer with the grid quantities (electric current and EM fields), two or more threads can advance closeby particles and try to deposit their currents in the same cell, causing a data race. A simple solution is to update the electric current atomically. However, according to our experiments, this approach often results in poor performance. Instead, we created per-thread copies of the electric current buffer, so that each thread can deposit the current in its copy without interfering with the others threads. After all particles (from all threads) have advanced in a given iteration, the program combines all the copies into a single buffer using OpenMP's reduction mechanism. Depending on the grid size, the number of time steps and plasma density, this global large-scale reduction can severely limit the scalability of the `zpic-parallel-for`.

Once stages 1–3 are complete, the program assigns a range of rows in the global grid to each thread (again, using OpenMP's `for` directive), whose EM fields are updated in parallel. There are no data races in this stage of the simulation.

In this implementation, there are several global synchronization points to ensure that either the electric current or the EM fields are updated completely (*i.e.*, in the entire simulation space) before proceeding to the next stage of the simulation. Therefore, if some threads happen to receive a higher load in a given simulation stage, they will straggle, forcing other threads to linger at the synchronization point.

Since the global reduction and synchronization are hard to avoid in a particle-based decomposition, we must change our parallelization strategy to improve the program scalability and efficiency. We describe this approach next and how it can be complemented by a tasking model.

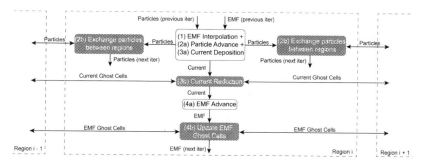

Fig. 2. Data flow (arrows) between the main tasks (round boxes) for one region within a single time step. A spatial decomposition requires additional tasks (in gray) for exchanging data between neighbor regions.

3.2 Task-Based Implementations

In the tasking model, we define work units as `tasks` and rely on the runtime to schedule tasks to the threads rather than resorting to parallel `for` loops to assign work (*e.g.*, particles or grid rows) to threads. Furthermore, by overdecomposing the problem (*i.e.*, creating more concurrent tasks than the available cores), we expect the runtime to mitigate load imbalances by dynamically assigning new tasks to threads that become idle after having completed a previous task.

The success of this strategy depends on the programmer's ability to minimize the synchronization restrictions associated with each spawned task. Ideally, we would like to minimize scenarios where a task needs to synchronize globally (*i.e.*, with all the other concurrent tasks), and replace them with local synchronization (*i.e.*, a task needs to coordinate its actions with a few concurrent tasks).

In the case of ZPIC, the limited scalability and the presence of global synchronization points made us abandon the natural particle-based decomposition for stages 1–3. Instead, we adopt a spatial decomposition for the entire simulation loop, similar to many state-of-the-art EM-PIC codes [14,19,21]. In this approach, the simulation space is split into *regions* alongside the y axis (*e.g.*, a row-wise decomposition). Each region stores both the particles inside it and the fraction of the grid they interact with, allowing both the particle advance and field integration to be performed locally.

However, implementing this spatial decomposition is more complex. Particles can exit their assigned region and must be transferred to an adjacent region. Each region must also be padded with ghost cells (extra rows of cells at the top and bottom of the assigned region, which are copies of neighbor regions), so that the thread processing the region can access grid quantities outside its boundaries. In both cases, the communication and synchronization of a given task then become limited to the couple of tasks that manage the adjacent regions. (Note that, due to simulation conditions, a particle can only move to a neighbor cell at each time step.)

Table 1. Features of each task-based implementation.

Version	Synchronization	Data race	Asynchronous?
zpic-tasklike	Barriers	Reduction	No
zpic-reduction-sync	Data Dependencies (Barrier at the end)	Reduction	Partial
zpic-commutative-sync	Data dependencies (Barrier at the end)	Commutative	Partial
zpic-reduction-async	Data dependencies	Reduction	Full
zpic-commutative-async	Data dependencies	Commutative	Full

Tasks can be synchronized in two ways: with explicit barriers or data dependencies. The latter can be more efficient if the data dependencies are defined in a way that prevents data races and allows for a more efficient task scheduling. Then, the runtime can schedule tasks as soon as their dependencies are satisfied. Unrelated tasks will be executed asynchronously.

Figure 2 shows the tasks for a single region and the data flow between them. Each iteration of the simulation loop begins with the particle advance, in which a task advances all particles within a given region (stages 1–3). However, two tasks can advance particles near the boundaries of a neighbor region and deposit the current in the same cell, causing a data race (similarly to Sect. 3.1). One solution is to store the electric current in local buffers and perform a reduction operation to obtain the final current. Differently from Sect. 3.1, the reduction is only required for ghost cells and can be executed completely in parallel.

Another solution is to use a global buffer and synchronize access to this buffer through data dependencies. This buffer synchronization requires an inout clause creating a mutual data dependency between tasks handling adjacent regions. The way the runtime solves this dependency loop is by executing the tasks in order of their creation. In our case, this would create a sequential execution of all tasks. To avoid this, we use the commutative clause of OmpSs, allowing threads to advance particles in adjacent regions in any order, but not at the same time.

After calculating the final electric current, the next set of tasks advances the electromagnetic fields in each region (stage 4). At the end of the simulation loop, each regions updates the values of the EM fields in their ghost cells.

From the same base algorithm and spatial decomposition, we implemented variants of the code to test the different tasking features. Table 1 provides a brief comparison between the different versions. In the tasklike variant, an OpenMP parallel for loop dynamically assigns each region to a thread, one at a time. The thread then executes all the tasks of the associated region. In this case, the tasks from different regions are synchronized through for-loop barriers. All the other variants are implemented in OmpSs. The async suffix indicates that tasks are synchronized exclusively by data dependencies and the program execution is completely asynchronous. In the sync variant, in turn, a barrier at the end of

```
#pragma oss task \
    inout(E[0; size]) \
    inout(B[0; size]) \
    in(J[0; size])
void emf_advance(...);

for(i = 0; i < n_regions; i++)
    emf_advance(...);
```

```
void emf_advance(...);

#pragma omp parallel for
for(i = 0; i < n_regions; i++)
    emf_advance(...);
```

Listing 1. The electromagnetic fields advance in the tasking (left) and parallel `for` (right) paradigms.

each time step ensures that all the tasks have completed before executing the next time step.

As stated before, a major problem in a spatial decomposition with fixed regions is load imbalance. In some simulations, the particle movement will cause some regions to have a higher plasma density than the others, even if the initial distribution is uniform. Hence, some tasks will take much longer than others to complete. As a solution, we overdecompose the simulation space in more regions (thus, more tasks) than the number of available threads. The created tasks are then dynamically distributed to the threads as a way to balance the load among them. The balance granularity is determined by the region size and smaller regions often lead to smoother load distributions. Smaller regions may also result in a better cache usage as the working set of each (smaller) task may now fit in the L1 cache. Naturally, the cost of an overdecomposition is the additional communication and synchronization between regions. In a shared-memory environment, the communication between regions consists in copying data from one memory position to another, which is a fairly cheap operation as long as the region is reasonably sized. According to our experiments (Sect. 4.3), ZPIC performs best when using 2–3× as many regions as the number of cores. Both SMILEI [14] and PSC [21] uses a similar load balancing technique.

3.3 Code Complexity

Regardless of the target programming model, a spatial decomposition (Sect. 3.2) is more complex to implement than a particle-based decomposition (Sect. 3.1). In a spatial decomposition, the program has to split the simulation space into multiple regions (each one with separate buffers), treat each region individually and handle all the communication between them. In contrast in a particle-based decomposition, we directly exploit the inherent data parallelism of the `for` loops of the original sequential implementation. Both strategies are common in parallel EM-PIC codes.

Considering the same decomposition, both tasking and parallel `for` paradigms have similar code complexity (Listing 1), with less than 1% difference in terms of lines of code. However, a **task** directive may carry additional information in the form of data dependencies. The runtime then uses these dependencies to synchronize and schedule the tasks, in a way that is transparent to the programmer. In contrast, all synchronization points in a parallel `for` need to be explicitly defined by the programmer.

4 Evaluation

The main goal of our evaluation is to study how the proposed parallel implementations of ZPIC scale when used to simulate realistic large-scale problems. By doing that, we assess whether the virtues of the task-based paradigm, especially when complemented with data dependencies, effectively translate to relevant performance gains.

4.1 Experimental Methodology

All programs were compiled with GNU GCC 10.1 (OpenMP v4.5) with the -O3 optimization level. For OmpSs programs, we used the OmpSs-2 2020.06 release version with GCC as the back-end compiler. The results were obtained on a computational node composed of two Intel Xeon Platinum 8160 CPUs with 24 physical cores @2.10 GHz (total of 48 cores) and 96 GB of RAM, running SUSE Linux.

The presented results are the average across five runs. We observed a maximum standard deviation of 1.7%. The speedup was calculated based on the execution time of the original, sequential implementation. There is only one thread running in each CPU core.

To evaluate the performance and correctness of all parallel implementations, we used three types of simulations, which we summarize next.

Laser Wakefield Accelerator [28] (LWFA). In this scenario, a high intensity, short duration laser pulse propagates through an initially uniform plasma. The interaction of the laser with the plasma leads to the formation of a wake trailing the laser pulse, which has an intense longitudinal electric field that can be used to accelerate charged particles, including particles from the background plasma itself (Fig. 3, above). In this test case, there is only one plasma species consisting of electrons (the ions are assumed to form an immobile neutralizing background), and the simulation EM fields are initialized with the field values of the laser. The simulation grids were 2000×512 cells, and the particles were initialized with 16 particles per cell. The simulation was run for 4000 time steps, and used a compensated binomial filter for the current. A moving simulation window follows the laser as it propagates through the plasma.

Collision of Plasma Clouds [20] (Weibel). In this case, ZPIC models two plasma clouds moving perpendicular to the simulation plane. One of the clouds is made of electrons and the other is made of positrons. These clouds start with the same initial density and temperature, but move in opposite directions. This system is susceptible to the so called Weibel instability, that leads to the generation of magnetic field and to the filamentation of the plasma clouds (Fig. 3). This test case used a grid size of 512×512 cells, with each of the plasma species using 256 particles per cell, uniformly distributed. The simulation runs for 500 time-steps.

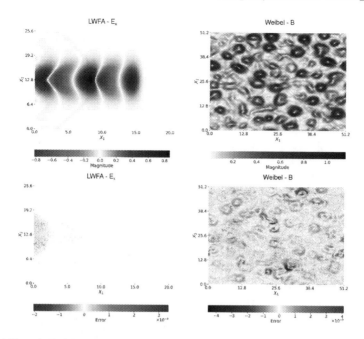

Fig. 3. (Above) Field report for the last time step in both LWFA and Weibel simulations. (Below) Relative error difference between the results of the `zpic-reduction-async` implementation and the sequential baseline, for both LWFA and Weibel simulations.

Uniform Plasmas. We also benchmark our implementation against an isolated, infinite, uniform plasma in two scenarios: a `cold` plasma, where all particles are initialized at rest, and a `warm` plasma, where particles are initialized from a thermal distribution with a width $u_{th} = 0.01c$. There are no initial flow velocity or EM fields. These scenarios are ideal for peak performance benchmarks, as particle density is expected to remain uniform over the simulation space, and there is limited (`warm`) to no (`cold`) particle motion over the simulation. These instances were used exclusively on the weak scaling test.

4.2   Validation of the Parallel Implementations

To validate the parallel implementations, we compare the last report of the magnetic field map generated by each of the parallel implementations and the original ZPIC, and then calculate the differences between them. The maximum relative error observed is on the order of 10^{-4}. Figure 3 (below) illustrates this with the `zpic-reduction-async` implementation.

The discrepancies between the sequential baseline and other implementations are related solely to the electric current deposition algorithm because the order in which the current for each particle is accumulated on the grid changes (when introducing concurrency), leading to different roundoff errors. The max-

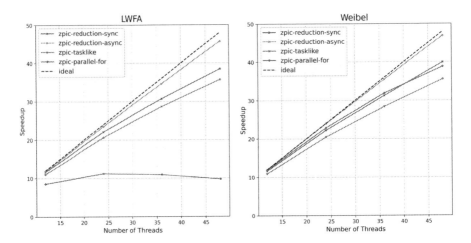

Fig. 4. Scalability comparison among all reduction-based implementations.

imum error observed for this number of iterations is on par with what is to be expected if we were to randomize the position of the particles in the buffer in the serial implementation and, given that both implementations use exactly the same analytical formalism, cannot argue that one implementation more accurately models the system than the other. This discrepancy can be significantly reduced by performing the calculations in double precision. However, it should again be noted that our implementation has no effect on the numerical stability of the PIC method and that it has no bearing in the macroscopical physical results.

4.3   Results

As our first experiment, we compare the strong scaling between all reduction-based implementations of ZPIC (Fig. 4). In this experiment, we fix the number of regions at 144 (which determines the number of concurrent tasks spawned at any given stage of the simulation) – which clearly over-decomposes the problem, given that there are only 48 cores available. We evaluate the impact of changing the number of regions later.

Considering that the Weibel simulation has a high plasma density, the cost of `zpic-parallel-for`'s reduction is amortized over a large number of particles. This diluted cost, combined with the fine-grain parallelism of OpenMP `for` loops, leads to good performance. The opposite happens in the LWFA simulation: the reduction is very expensive compared to the amount of work assigned to each thread (there are $\sim 16\times$ less particles per thread than in the Weibel simulation). Since the cost of this operation increases with the number of threads (and corresponding copies), `zpic-parallel-for` scales very poorly in the LWFA simulation, even having negative scaling over 24 cores.

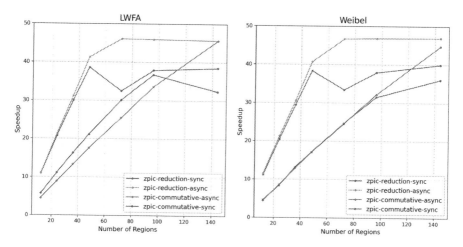

Fig. 5. Performance comparison between task-based implementation of ZPIC for different number of regions.

After changing from a particle-based to a spatial decomposition, the performance of the program is no longer dependent on the cost of the reduction operation, since this operation is restricted to the ghost cells and can be performed completely in parallel. As a result, there is only a 1–2× speedup difference between the LWFA and the Weibel simulation for any `reduction` variant and `zpic-tasklike`. At the same time, the program now explores more coarse-grain parallelism (each thread processes a set of regions instead of iterations in a loop) compared to `zpic-parallel-for`.

The performance of the task-based implementations depends on the synchronization method. Since `zpic-tasklike` relies on frequent and costly global barriers, this version has the worst performance among them. Replacing these barriers with data dependencies not only improves the runtime's load balancing capabilities but also lowers the synchronization costs. Combined with an overdecomposition, `zpic-reduction-sync` is able to match or surpass `zpic-parallel-for` even in its best case, whereas a fully asynchronous implementation (`async` variant) achieves near-perfect scaling for 48 cores with a maximum speedup of 46.89× for Weibel and 45.67× for LWFA. The `commutative`-based versions are discussed in the next experiment.

In the next experiment, we analyze the performance impact of the number of regions for different task-based implementations (Fig. 5). We also compare the difference between the `reduction` and `commutative` solutions.

In the `reduction`-based implementation, all regions can be processed in parallel, since they have separate, local buffers. In contrast, the `commutative` clause prevents two or more tasks from advancing the particles in adjacent regions, avoiding race conditions during the current deposition. As the regions are processed in an interleaved manner, the `commutative` variant only has half of the task throughput of the reduction-based implementation. Due to lower through-

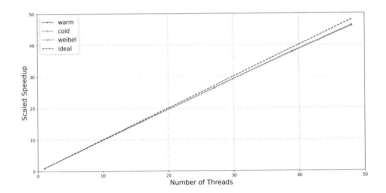

Fig. 6. Weak scaling for the best performing implementation of ZPIC.

put and the extra restrictions, the performance of the `commutative`-based implementation is usually worse than the `reduction` equivalent, except when employing a high number of regions (*e.g.*, 144 regions).

With less than 48 regions (or 96 regions for the `commutative` variant), the program is unable to produce enough tasks to fully utilize the CPU. Even with a single concurrent task per thread, the uneven distribution of plasma across the simulation space causes some threads to be idle while waiting for other threads to finish its assigned task. With an overdecomposition (*i.e.*, more than one region per core), the program is able to generate enough concurrent tasks to maintain a high CPU occupancy. This happens not only because the program is able to maintain a proper load balance by dynamically distributing the tasks, but also because it can constantly generate new tasks that can be fed to the thread pool. Inserting a barrier at the end of the iteration (`sync` variant) interrupts the generation of new tasks, causing some threads to be waiting for the last few tasks of the iteration to finish before advancing to the next iteration. As a result, any `sync` version has negligible performance gains with an overdecomposition.

In both `sync` versions, performance drops when the number of concurrent tasks is not evenly divisible by the number of cores (*e.g.*, at 72 concurrent tasks). In this case, the tasks of the current iteration will be unevenly distributed among threads, leading to a load imbalance. Without the global barrier, the runtime can schedule tasks from the next iteration to fill the load difference. The `commutative` clause imposes additional restrictions to the task scheduling, preventing the program from properly balancing the load across threads.

Finally, we present in Fig. 6 the weak scaling results for the best performing implementation (`zpic-reduction-async`). For this experiment, we used the Weibel simulation as well as two theoretical plasmas (`cold` and `warm`). Using a fixed number of iterations (500) and particles per cell (16×16), we vary the grid size to scale the problem with the number of threads. The LWFA simulation cannot be used in this experiment, since the computational load is mostly concentrated on the small region of the simulation space affected by the laser.

The program performs equally well in all simulations, attaining an efficiency greater than 95% in all experiments. Both `cold` and `warm` plasmas have perfect load distribution, as uniform plasma density remains unchanged throughout the entire simulation. In these theoretical plasmas, the particles remain (almost) static, resulting in very little communication between regions. The `weibel` simulation is completely different: not only can the plasma density vary from one region to another due to the plasma filamentation, but also the particles are rapidly moving throughout the simulation space. Even in these conditions, the program can still maintain an excellent load balance among the threads due to the overdecomposition and dynamic task distribution.

5   Related Work

Tasking has been studied in the context of specific application domains, such as linear algebra [4], human brain simulation [29], graph analytics [2], adaptive mesh refinement [25,27], among others [8,12]. However, only a few papers [25,27] focus on the tasking features that are available since OpenMP 4.0.

Regarding particle-mesh algorithms, which are the focus of this paper, tasking is only scantly studied. Akhmetova et al. [3] used tasking to improve an MPI + OpenMP hybrid EM-PIC code. They introduced the `task` directive (without data dependencies) in existing `for` loops of the particle solver. In contrast, our paper studies the tasking model when applied to the entire EM-PIC algorithm, using data dependencies for synchronization purposes. Koniges et al. [23] propose the use of OpenMP tasking to hide communication in Gyrokinetic Toroidal Simulation (GTS) code. They use OpenMP 3.0, which does not support data dependencies. Anderson et al. [5] ported the 3D Gyrokinetic Toroidal Code (GTC) [17] to HPX [22], exploiting the support of the latter for tasking with data dependencies. In their task-based version, they overdecompose the problem as a way to overlap the communication and balance the load across the CPU cores within a single node.

6   Conclusions

We developed and analyzed a set of task-based implementations of an EM-PIC simulator as a way to contribute to a better understanding of the benefits and limitations of tasking models when applied to the broad class of particle-mesh codes. Our results confirm that tasking, when used with recent data dependencies features, enables the runtime to dynamically schedule highly asynchronous tasks, attaining near ideal scalability even with very irregular workloads. This impressive result is achieved while retaining the simplicity of the tasking model, thus providing the programmer with high coding productivity.

In the future, we plan to investigate tasking in distributed environments by extending our task-based implementation to support either message passing or partitioned global address spaces. In that context, not only can tasks provide a natural way to hide the inter-node communication, but they can also provide a new perspective on the interaction between the two models. Currently, we are extending our task-based implementation to support hardware accelerators, such as GPUs and FPGAs.

Acknowledgements. This work was partially supported by Fundação Ciência e Tecnologia (FCT) under grant UIDB /50021/2020 and by the EPEEC project, which has received funding from the European Union's Horizon 2020 research and innovation programme under grant agreement No 801051.

References

1. Intel® Threading Building Blocks. https://www.intel.com/content/www/us/en/develop/documentation/tbb-documentation/top.html
2. Adcock, A.B., Sullivan, B.D., Hernandez, O.R., Mahoney, M.W.: Evaluating OpenMP tasking at scale for the computation of graph hyperbolicity. In: Rendell, A.P., Chapman, B.M., Müller, M.S. (eds.) IWOMP 2013. LNCS, vol. 8122, pp. 71–83. Springer, Heidelberg (2013). https://doi.org/10.1007/978-3-642-40698-0_6
3. Akhmetova, D., Iakymchuk, R., Ekeberg, O., Laure, E.: Performance study of multithreaded MPI and OpenMP tasking in a large scientific code (2017)
4. Aliaga, J.I., Carratalá-Sáez, R., Kriemann, R., Quintana-Ortí, E.S.: Task-parallel LU factorization of hierarchical matrices using OmpSs. In: IEEE International Parallel and Distributed Processing Symposium Workshops (IPDPSW), pp. 1148–1157 (2017)
5. Anderson, M., Brodowicz, M., Kulkarni, A., Sterling, T.: Performance modeling of gyrokinetic toroidal simulations for a many-tasking runtime system. In: Jarvis, S.A., Wright, S.A., Hammond, S.D. (eds.) PMBS 2013. LNCS, vol. 8551, pp. 136–157. Springer, Cham (2014). https://doi.org/10.1007/978-3-319-10214-6_7
6. Arber, T.D., et al.: Contemporary particle-in-cell approach to laser-plasma modelling. Plasma Phys. Controlled Fus. **57**(11), 113001 (2015)
7. Augonnet, C., Thibault, S., Namyst, R., Wacrenier, P.A.: StarPU: a unified platform for task scheduling on heterogeneous multicore architectures. Concurr. Comput. Pract. Exp. **23**(2), 187–198 (2011)
8. Ayguadé, E., Duran, A., Hoeflinger, J., Massaioli, F., Teruel, X.: An experimental evaluation of the new OpenMP tasking model. In: Adve, V., Garzarán, M.J., Petersen, P. (eds.) LCPC 2007. LNCS, vol. 5234, pp. 63–77. Springer, Heidelberg (2008). https://doi.org/10.1007/978-3-540-85261-2_5
9. Blumofe, R.D., Joerg, C.F., Kuszmaul, B.C., Leiserson, C.E., Randall, K.H., Zhou, Y.: Cilk: an efficient multithreaded runtime system. J. Parallel Distrib. Comput. **37**(1), 55–69 (1996)
10. Bosch, J., Filgueras, A., Vidal, M., Jimenez-Gonzalez, D., Alvarez, C., Martorell, : X.: Exploiting parallelism on GPUs and FPGAs with OmpSs (2017)
11. Bueno, J., et al.: Productive cluster programming with OmpSs. In: Jeannot, E., Namyst, R., Roman, J. (eds.) Euro-Par 2011. LNCS, vol. 6852, pp. 555–566. Springer, Heidelberg (2011). https://doi.org/10.1007/978-3-642-23400-2_52

12. Chasapis, D., et al.: PARSECSs: evaluating the impact of task parallelism in the PARSEC benchmark suite. ACM Trans. Arch. Code. Optim. **12**(4), 41:1–41:22 (2015)
13. Ciesko, J., et al.: Task-parallel reductions in OpenMP and OmpSs. In: DeRose, L., de Supinski, B.R., Olivier, S.L., Chapman, B.M., Müller, M.S. (eds.) IWOMP 2014. LNCS, vol. 8766, pp. 1–15. Springer, Cham (2014). https://doi.org/10.1007/978-3-319-11454-5_1
14. Derouillat, J., et al.: SMILEI: a collaborative, open-source, multi-purpose particle-in-cell code for plasma simulation. Comput. Phys. Commun. **222**, 351–373 (2018)
15. Ding, Y., Hu, K., Wu, K., Zhao, Z.: Performance monitoring and analysis of task-based OpenMP. PLOS ONE **8**(10), 1–12 (2013)
16. Duran, A., Ferrer, R., Ayguadé, E., Badia, R.M., Labarta, J.: A proposal to extend the OpenMP tasking model with dependent tasks. Int. J. Parallel Program. **37**(3), 292–305 (2009)
17. Ethier, S., Tang, W.M., Lin, Z.: Gyrokinetic particle-in-cell simulations of plasma microturbulence on advanced computing platforms. J. Phys. Conf. Ser. **16**, 1–15 (2005)
18. Fonseca, R.A., Silva, L.O., Tsung, F.S., Decyk, V.K., Lu, W., Ren, C., Mori, W.B., Deng, S., Lee, S., Katsouleas, T., Adam, J.C.: OSIRIS: a three-dimensional, fully relativistic particle in cell code for modeling plasma based accelerators. In: Sloot, P.M.A., Hoekstra, A.G., Tan, C.J.K., Dongarra, J.J. (eds.) ICCS 2002. LNCS, vol. 2331, pp. 342–351. Springer, Heidelberg (2002). https://doi.org/10.1007/3-540-47789-6_36
19. Fonseca, R.A., et al.: Exploiting multi-scale parallelism for large scale numerical modelling of laser wakefield accelerators. Plasma Phys. Controlled Fus. **55**(12), 124011 (2013)
20. Fonseca, R.A., Silva, L.O., Tonge, J.W., Mori, W.B., Dawson, J.M.: Three-dimensional weibel instability in astrophysical scenarios. Phys. Plasmas **10**(5), 1979–1984 (2003)
21. Germaschewski, K., et al.: The plasma simulation code: a modern particle-in-cell code with load-balancing and gpu support. **1310**, 7866 (2015)
22. Kaiser, H., Heller, T., Adelstein-Lelbach, B., Serio, A., Fey, D.: HPX. In: A Task Based Programming Model in a Global Address Space, vol. 14, pp. 1–11. ACM Press, Eugene (2014)
23. Koniges, A., et al.: Application acceleration on current and future cray platforms. Proc. Cray User Group Meeting (2009)
24. OpenMP Specification. https://www.openmp.org/specifications/
25. Prat, R., Colombet, L., Namyst, R.. : In: Combining task-based parallelism and adaptive mesh refinement techniques in molecular dynamics simulations, New York, NY, USA (2018)
26. Pukhov, A.: Three-dimensional electromagnetic relativistic particle-in-cell code VLPL. J. Plasma Phys. **61**, 425–433 (1999)
27. Rico, A., Sánchez Barrera, I., Joao, J.A., Randall, J., Casas, M., Moretó, M.: On the benefits of tasking with OpenMP. In: OpenMP: Conquering the Full Hardware Spectrum, pp. 217–230 (2019)
28. Tajima, T., Dawson, J.M.: Laser electron accelerator. Phys. Rev. Lett. **43**, 267–270 (1979)
29. Valero-Lara, P., Sirvent, R., Peña, A.J., Labarta, J.: MPI+OpenMP tasking scalability for multi-morphology simulations of the human brain. Parallel Comput. **84**, 50–61 (2019)

30. Verboncoeur, J.P.: Particle simulation of plasmas: review and advances. Plasma Phys. Controlled Fus. **47**(5A), A231 (2005)
31. Villasenor, J., Buneman, O.: Rigorous charge conservation for local electromagnetic field solvers. Comput. Phys. Commun. **69**(2), 306–316 (1992)
32. ZPIC documentation. https://github.com/zambzamb/zpic/blob/master/doc/Documentation.md, Accessed 05 Sept 2019

Multicore and Manycore Parallelism

Exploiting Co-execution with OneAPI: Heterogeneity from a Modern Perspective

Raúl Nozal[(✉)] and Jose Luis Bosque

Department of Computer Science and Electronics, Universidad de Cantabria,
Santander, Spain
{raul.nozal,joseluis.bosque}@unican.es

Abstract. Programming efficiently heterogeneous systems is a major challenge, due to the complexity of their architectures. Intel oneAPI, a new and powerful standards-based unified programming model, built on top of SYCL, addresses these issues. In this paper, oneAPI is provided with co-execution strategies to run the same kernel between different devices, enabling the exploitation of static and dynamic policies. On top of that, static and dynamic load-balancing algorithms are integrated and analyzed. This work evaluates the performance and energy efficiency for a well-known set of regular and irregular HPC benchmarks, using an integrated GPU and CPU. Experimental results show that co-execution is worthwhile when using dynamic algorithms, improving efficiency even more when using unified shared memory.

Keywords: Heterogeneous computing · Parallel computing · Co-execution · Load balancing · SYCL · oneAPI · DPC++ · Scheduling · HPC

1 Introduction

The future of computing cannot be understood without heterogeneous computing [24], due to its excellent cost/performance ratio and energy efficiency. This facilitates the acceleration of a wide range of massively data-parallel applications, such as deep learning [14], video processing [8,22] or financial applications [4]. However, hardware heterogeneity complicates the development of efficient and portable software, especially when specialized components require their own programming models. In this context, some of the hot topics being researched are: supporting single source programming, improving the usability and efficiency of memory space, distributing computation and data among different devices, and load balancing [3,16–21,25].

Programming models have become more abstract and expressive. OpenCL emerged as an open standard programming model for writing portable programs across heterogeneous platforms [10]. However, it has a very low level of abstraction and leaves to programmers the partitioning and transferring of data and

© Springer Nature Switzerland AG 2021
L. Sousa et al. (Eds.): Euro-Par 2021, LNCS 12820, pp. 501–516, 2021.
https://doi.org/10.1007/978-3-030-85665-6_31

results among the CPU and devices. On the other end, proposals based on compiler directives have been developed, such as OpenACC [9], and later extensions of OpenMP [23], leaving all this work to the compiler, but limiting both the expressiveness and performance. Moreover, market trends and industrial applications indicate a strong predominance of languages such as C++, favoring higher level alternatives. For instance, SYCL is a cross-platform abstraction layer that builds on OpenCL, enabling the host and kernel code to be contained in the same source file with the simplicity of a cross-platform asynchronous task graph [11].

In this context, Intel has developed oneAPI, a unified programming model to facilitate the development among various hardware architectures [7]. It provides a runtime, a set of domain-focused libraries and a simplified language to express parallelism in heterogeneous platforms. It is based on industry standards and open specifications, offering consistent tooling support and interoperability with existing HPC programming models. The oneAPI's cross-architecture language Data Parallel C++ (DPC++) [2], based on SYCL standard for heterogeneous programming in C++, provides a single, unified open development model for productive heterogeneous programming and cross-vendor support. It allows code reuse across hardware targets, while permitting custom tuning for a specific accelerator. Some of the features provided comprise optimized communication patterns, automatic dependency tracking, runtime scheduling and shared memory optimizations, between others.

This article addresses a new challenge in improving the usability and exploitation of heterogeneous systems, providing oneAPI with the capacity for *co-execution*. This is defined as the collaboration of all the devices in the system (including the CPU) to execute a single massively data-parallel kernel [15,16,20,25]. However, it is a hard task for the programmer and needs to be done effortless in order to be widely used. In this way, the expression and abstraction capabilities of oneAPI, such as portability and single-source style, will be exploited to obtain codes that will be easier to implement and maintain. To efficiently exploit the computing capacity of all devices, a series of workload balancing algorithms are implemented, both static and dynamic, obtaining good results with both regular and irregular applications. Experimental results show that co-execution is worthwhile from the point of view of performance and energy efficiency as long as dynamic schedulers are used, and even more if unified memory is applied.

Although oneAPI release is very recent, it has quickly attracted the attention of industry and the scientific community working with heterogeneous systems. A SYCL-based version of the well-known Rodinia benchmark suite has been developed in [12], using Intel oneAPI toolkit. Christgau and Steinke [5] use both the compatibility tool *dpct* of oneAPI, as well as SYCL extensions for the CUDA base code of the easyWave simulator. A study of the performance portability between different Intel integrated GPUs using oneAPI is presented in [13], where a computationally intensive routine is derived from the Hardware Accelerated Cosmology Code (HACC) framework. A debugger based on GDB for SYCL programs that offload kernels to CPU, GPU, or FPGA emulator devices, has been developed as part of the oneAPI distribution [1].

As far as we know, the only work that addresses co-execution with oneAPI is [6]. The authors extend the Intel TBB *parallel_for* function to allow simultaneous execution of the same kernel on CPU and GPU. They implement three schedulers on top of oneAPI, static, dynamic and adaptive LogFit. The main differences with our work are that we provide a pure oneAPI architecture (without TBB) and present a rich variety of kernels, both regular and irregular, which reveal differences in the behavior of schedulers.

The rest of the paper is organized as follows. Section 2 describe the issues that motivate this work while in Sect. 3, the co-execution architecture and its design decisions are exposed. The methodology used for the validation is explained in Sect. 4, while the experimental results are shown in Sect. 5. Finally, Sect. 6 highlights the most important conclusions and future work.

2   Motivation

Intel oneAPI uses the host-device programming model, where the host offloads compute-heavy functions, called kernels, to a set of hardware accelerators, such as GPUs and FPGAs. Its runtime is able to manage complex applications composed of a set of kernels, even if they have dependencies between them, through a Directed Acyclic Graph (DAG). The assignment of a kernel to a particular device can be done by the programmer, so it is determined at compile time, or let oneAPI choose the device at runtime. In either case, a kernel can only be scheduled to a single device when the dependencies are satisfied.

In this context, the only possibility of co-execution is for the programmer to split the work into several kernels, as many as there are devices in the system. Also, data partition and workload distribution must be done manually. Furthermore, the compiler must detect that these kernels are independent and schedule them simultaneously. This complicates the co-execution and, therefore, the exploitation of the whole system to solve a single kernel.

Even if the programmer is willing to face this extra effort, an additional problem arises with workload balancing. Since the division of the workload is done at compile time, it is necessarily static. That is, the portion of work assigned to each device is pre-fixed at the beginning of execution. This partitioning works well for regular applications, where the execution time of a data set depends only on its size [25]. The programmer needs to estimate off-line how much workload to allocate to each device so that both finish at the same time, thus obtaining a balanced execution, as seen in the left part of Fig. 1, for the Gaussian kernel. In this case the kernel execution time is 5 s on the CPU and 2 s on the GPU, which means that the GPU has 2.5× the performance of the CPU. Therefore, assigning the work to devices proportionally to their computing capabilities, a balanced distribution is obtained and the execution time is reduced to approximately 1.5 s.

However, it is well known that static scheduling cannot adapt to the irregular behavior of many applications, leading to significant load imbalances [16]. In these applications, the processing time of a data set depends not only on its size, but also on the nature of the data. Thus, different portions of data of the same

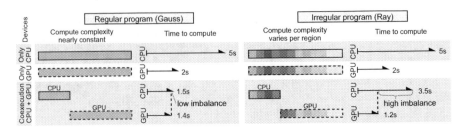

Fig. 1. Static co-execution for regular and irregular programs.

size can generate different response times. This is shown in the right part of Fig. 1, which presents the execution of a Raytracer application on two devices. The darker shades of grey refer to more computationally intensive data areas. Performing the same static balancing as in the regular case, it has coincided that the most computationally heavy regions have fallen on the CPU (slower device). This resulted in a significant imbalance, with the CPU taking 3.5 s while the GPU took only 1.2 s. This situation can only be addressed with dynamic balancing algorithms that allocate portions of work to the devices on demand.

This paper addresses both of these problems. On the one hand, it is proposed to provide oneAPI with mechanisms that allow the implementation of co-execution without additional effort for the programmer. On the other hand, it provides the oneAPI scheduler with a set of dynamic load balancing algorithms to squeeze the maximum performance out of the heterogeneous system, even with irregular applications.

3   Co-Execution Based on OneAPI

The approach to achieve co-execution focuses on using the DPC++ compiler and runtime, hereafter referred to as oneAPI for simplicity. The proposed *Coexecutor Runtime* is built on top of oneAPI as a runtime library to allow the parallel exploitation of multiple hardware accelerators that facilitate the implementation of workload balancing algorithms.

This approach has several architectural and adaptive advantages. Firstly, the design and implementation are based on open standards, both C++ and SYCL, following easily recognizable architectural patterns. Secondly, since it is drawing on previous standards such as OpenCL, it facilitates the adaptation for a whole repertoire of libraries and software generated over a decade, helping to benefit from co-execution. Thirdly, it serves as a skeleton upon which to apply different strategies and workload balancing algorithms for using oneAPI and SYCL. Finally, as it is designed from a sufficiently standardized and abstract approach, it allows the adaptation and extension to execution engines and proposals created by other manufacturers, both compilers and accelerator drivers.

To provide oneAPI with co-execution depends mainly on the correct detection of a potential concurrent execution path by the compiler and the runtime. This materializes a parallel execution of several tasks of the DAG, thanks to the existence of totally independent hardware resources. To achieve good results, it is necessary to use dynamic strategies, currently not available in oneAPI. In addition, it is important to implement workload balancing algorithms to obtain the best possible performance. Both aspects are explained below.

3.1 Dynamic Co-execution

The strategy proposed for dynamic co-execution is to promote multithreaded management architectures based on the runtime of oneAPI. The *Coexecutor Runtime* enhances the isolation between execution devices, since one of the key points is to make it easier for the compiler to detect disjoint memory structures as well as the independence between queues and tasks. In addition, since oneAPI offers a sufficiently sophisticated and complete memory model, the management architecture must be adapted to favor both buffer management and the possibility of exploiting unified memory (USM).

To define the proposal, three perspectives are considered, the execution model, from the memory point of view and the last one, the relationship of the *Coexecutor Runtime* with the runtime of oneAPI, as it is explained in Sect. 3.2.

The *execution model* is shown in Fig. 2a, representing the interaction of the runtime as part of the execution process of an application. Execution is blocked from an application point of view, although internally it works asynchronously.

The *Director* configures the *Coexecution Units* and manages both the *Commander* and its communication with the rest of the entities. The *Scheduler* is instantiated and plugged in with a policy established by the programmer, using one of the schedulers explained in Sect. 3.2. The *Commander* is responsible of packaging the work, emitting tasks and receiving events, as part of the computation workflow with the *Coexecution Units*. This process is termed as *Commander loop*, and it follows the scheduling strategy defined by the *Scheduler*.

Regarding the *Coexecutor Runtime* internal workflow, the *Director* instantiates and configures oneAPI primitives and structures necessary both for the operation with oneAPI runtime and used by the *Scheduler* itself, among which are work and queue entities, execution contexts and mapping of memory structures

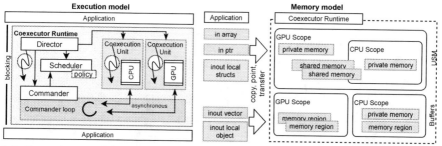

(a) Execution model as part of a blocking section of an application.

(b) Memory model example for USM and SYCL buffers when using CPU and GPU.

Fig. 2. Coexecutor Runtime considering CPU-GPU dynamic co-execution.

between the application and the runtime. In parallel, the management threads of the *Coexecution Units* initialize the communication mechanisms within the runtime, as well as the request of devices and their configuration with oneAPI. The communication is bidirectional between *Commander* and each *Coexecution Unit*, since it is co-executed with an independent scheduler that handles the decisions. As soon as there is a *Coexecution Unit* ready to receive work and the management thread has finished the initial phase, it establishes communication with the *Commander loop*. As the rest of the devices are completing their initialization, they incorporate into the loop, where the scheduling phase starts.

The *memory model* is presented in Fig. 2b. It shows the separation between structures and memory containers, taking into account the two types of strategies used: USM or buffers of SYCL, although the *Coexecutor Runtime* supports the combination of both during the co-execution. On the left of the figure are shown the structures, C++ containers and memory pointers used by the application, while the right outlines the view of the runtime. The *Director* and its *Coexecution Units* handle the allocations and configuration of the memory space with oneAPI, and the programmer only has to request the use. The runtime will distribute them in the oneAPI memory model, either by transferring pointers, copying memory regions or sharing unified memory blocks.

Two ways of operating with oneAPI memory environments are distinguished. If USM is used, the *Coexecutor Runtime* provides two scopes: a larger (upper) one for a device (GPU) and a smaller (lower) for another (CPU). This way, the memory spaces initialized by the GPU are reused in the CPU using oneAPI primitives. On the other hand, if SYCL buffers are used, the scope of each device will manage independent buffers with memory regions that will be part of a higher container or structure. Therefore, favoring the recognition of disjointed memories by the compiler. Private memory allocations can be made in both memory models, in the form of buffers and variables, where each field is controlled independently by each *Coexecution Unit* and its oneAPI's scopes.

Finally, both ways of operating can be combined, since could be parts that use the USM model and others that rely on buffers and variables. *Coexecutor*

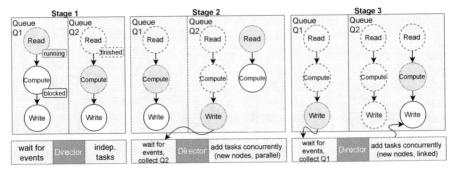

Fig. 3. Example of interaction with the DAG from oneAPI's perspective while running a dynamic approach with two queues.

Runtime will reuse the scope of each device to map any C++ containers and memory sections, each of which will be governed by a memory model.

The interaction between the *Coexecutor Runtime* and oneAPI is shown in Fig. 3. Three stages are presented during the execution of the runtime, with two different queues Q1 and Q2. It starts from a situation where the runtime has established two independent parallel execution queues, due to the existence of two separate underlying architectures. The nodes of each queue are managed by the runtime and its DAG, and they can be in execution (blue), blocked waiting for resources (white) or finished (gray with a dashed line). The *Director* waits for events related to the DAG or performs independent tasks, such as resource management, receiving and sending notifications, status control or work reparation, some of which are essential within the *Scheduler*.

By switching to the stage 2, it can be distinguished how the Q2 is able to process nodes more efficiently, so the *Director* collects results of the write operation and enqueues new nodes of the DAG to the same queue, overlapping computation and communication. Collection operations are dependent on the memory model, the type of operations (explicit or implicit) and the amount of bytes used, thus they could be fast (unified memory) or slow (mixed models or transfer large blocks). Finally, in the third stage, the end of the Q1 is represented with the output data collection while in the Q2 a next writing task is added. This is linked to the branch created in stage 2, as soon as its computation task has started, distributing the DAG management among different time periods.

3.2 Load Balancing Algorithms

To enable dynamic policies to squeeze all the computing capacity out of the heterogeneous system, the *Scheduler* component is introduced, as it is shown in Fig. 2a. It configures the behavior of the load balancer, the distribution and division of the work packages, as well as the way to communicate with the different execution devices.

Figure 4 depicts the relationship of the *Coexecutor Runtime* with the runtime of oneAPI, all of it involved as part of the *Commander loop*. The *Coexecutor*

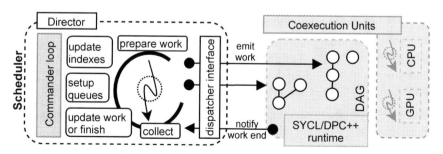

Fig. 4. Commander's loop where the scheduling strategy is performed to coordinate the behaviors of the Coexecution Units.

Runtime internal communication is performed between the management threads, either those associated with the devices (right) or the global manager, usually associated with the *Director* (left). This view simplifies the runtime of oneAPI and its internal DAG management, being considered as a single entity, part of the *Coexecution Units* (right). The *Director* performs a set of periodic actions, as a loop managing events and operations, among which are: preparing the next job to be issued; collecting completed jobs; updating pending jobs; preparing and reusing the queue and command groups as well as other oneAPI primitives; and updating the indexes, ranges and offsets of memory entities.

Every time a work package is prepared, the runtime adds a task in the DAG. Similarly, with the completion of a job, *Commander* receives the notification to collect and merge the output data, if needed. This operation can be lightweight in case of using USM or using implicit operations, delegating more responsibility to oneAPI. The emission and reception of work is requested through a dispatch interface, as a way of unifying requests. Finally, when there are no more pending jobs, the *Commander* will notify the *Director* to close and destroy the primitives and management objects to return control to the application.

As a result of the proposed architecture based on the designed dynamic co-execution model, three algorithms are implemented in the *Scheduler* [15,16,18]. The *Static* algorithm divides the kernel in as many packages as devices are in the system, minimizing the number of host-devices interactions. The size of each package is proportional to the relative computing speed of each device. Its drawbacks are that it is difficult to find a suitable division and that cannot adapt its behavior dynamically to irregular applications. It has a minimum management inside the *Scheduler* component, because it only runs as many iterations in the loop of events as devices are co-executing.

Regarding the strictly dynamic strategies, the *Dynamic* algorithm divides the data in a number of packages of similar size, which are assigned to the devices on demand, as soon as they are idle. This allows it to adapt to the irregular behavior, but increments the overhead communication between host and devices. On the other side, *HGuided* starts with large packages and decreases their size as the execution progresses. The size of the initial packages is proportional to the computing capacity of the devices. Therefore, it reduces the number of synchronization points while retaining most of its adaptiveness. Considering these dynamic policies inside the *Scheduler*, it is not possible to know in advance the quantity of iterations, because it will depend on each execution parameters, as well as the number and type of devices. These operations increase the management overhead due to the operations related to the update of indexes and ranges, as well as the division of the problem into independent regions. Finally, concerning the differences in the operations carried out by *Commander*, *Dynamic* will simplify the number of instructions involved in the calculation of work packages compared to *HGuided*. This is explained since the latter performs a more sophisticated algorithm that takes into account certain conditions, including the computing power of each device. However, the calculation overheads of the latter are compensated by the efficiency of its workload distribution policy.

```
1   coexecutor_runtime<hg> runtime;
2   runtime.config(CounitSet::CpuGpu, coexecutor_runtime::dist(0.35));
3   runtime.launch(data.size(), [&](coexecutor_unit *counit, package pkg) {
4     sycl::buffer<int, 1> buf_input(data.data() + pkg.offset,
5                                    sycl::range<1>(pkg.size));
6     counit->dispatch([&](sycl::handler &h) {
7       auto R = sycl::range<1>(pkg.size);
8       auto input = buf_input.get_access<sycl::access::mode::read_write>(h);
9       h.parallel_for(R, [=](sycl::item<1> it) {
10        auto tid = it.get_linear_id();
11        input[tid] = input[tid] * datav;
12      });
13    });
14  });
```

Listing 1: Coexecutor Runtime computing SAXPY with a dynamic algorithm using simultaneously CPU and GPU.

3.3   API Design

Coexecutor Runtime has been designed to offer an API that is flexible as well as closely linked to the SYCL standard, favoring reuse of existing code and slightly higher usability. Listing 1 shows a simple example of use when computing the SAXPY problem simultaneously exploiting both CPU and GPU. The code fragment where the runtime is used is shown, so the initialization of the problem and its data, as well as the subsequent usage, are omitted.

Line 1 instantiates the *coexecutor_runtime* prepared to compute a program using the HGuided balancing algorithm. In the next line, it is configured to use both the CPU and GPU, giving a hint of the computational power of 35% for the CPU in proportion to the GPU. This value will leverage the algorithm to further exploit co-execution efficiency. Next, the co-execution scope associated with the problem is provided (lines 3 to 14), where a lambda function captures by reference the values used. This scope is executed by each of the *Coexecution Units*, and therefore, they must establish independent memory reservations (or shared, if shared virtual memory is exploited), using the values provided by the runtime itself through the *package* class. Line 6 opens an execution scope, associated to the kernel computation for each device. In lines 7 and 8 a read and write access is requested for the previous memory region (buffer *accessors*), indicating the execution space based on the given package size. Finally, lines 9 to 11 show the data-parallel execution, traversing the indicated execution space (R) and using the *accessors* and variables needed (*datav, input*).

In the line immediately following what is shown in the example, the problem will have been computed simultaneously using both devices. In addition, the data resulting from the computation will be in the expected data structures and containers (vector *input* of C++).

Table 1. Benchmarks and their variety of properties.

Property	Gauss	Matmul	Taylor	Ray	Rap	Mandel
Local work size	128	1,64	64	128	128	256
Read: Write buffers	2:1	2:1	3:2	1:1	2:1	0:1
Use local memory	No	Yes	Yes	Yes	No	No
Work-items ($N \times 10^5$)	262	237	10	94	5	703
Mem. usage (MiB)	195	264	46	35	6	1072

4 Methodology

The experiments to validate *Coexecutor Runtime*[1] have been carried out in a computer with an Intel Core i5-7500 Kaby Lake architecture processor, with 4 cores and an integrated GPU Intel HD Graphics 630. The GPU is a Gen 9.5 GT2 IGP, with 24 execution units. An LLC cache of 6 MB is shared between CPU and GPU.

To accomplish the validation, 6 benchmarks have been selected, which represent both regular and irregular behavior, as described in Sect. 2. *Gaussian*, *MatMul* and *Taylor* correspond to regular kernels, while *Mandelbrot*, *Rap* and *Ray Tracing* are irregular ones. Taylor, Rap and Ray are open source implementations, while the rest belong to the AMD APP SDK, being all ported to oneAPI. Table 1 presents the most relevant parameters of the benchmarks, providing enough variety to validate the behavior of the runtime.

To guarantee integrity of the results, the values reported are the arithmetic mean of 50 executions, discarding a previous first one to avoid warm-up penalties. The standard deviation is not shown because it is negligible in all cases.

The validation of the proposal is done by analyzing the co-execution when using four scheduling configurations in the heterogeneous system. As summarized in Sect. 3.2, Static, Dynamic and HGuided algorithms are evaluated, labelled as St, Dyn and Hg, respectively. In addition, the dynamic scheduler is configured to run with 5 and 200 packages. Finally, two different memory models have also been tested: unified shared memory (USM) and SYCL's buffers (Buffers).

To evaluate the performance of the runtime and its load balancing algorithms, the total response time is measured, including kernel computing and data transfer. Then, two metrics are calculated: imbalance and speedup. The former measures the effectiveness of load balancing, calculated as $\frac{T_{GPU}}{T_{CPU}}$, where T_{GPU} and T_{CPU} are the execution time of each device. The speedup is computed as $S = \frac{T_{GPU}}{T_{co-exec}}$, because the GPU is the fastest device for all the benchmarks.

Finally, energies are measured using RAPL counters, giving the total consumption in *Joules*. The metric used to evaluate the energy efficiency is the Energy-Delay Product (EDP).

---

[1] https://github.com/oneAPI-scheduling/CoexecutorRuntime.

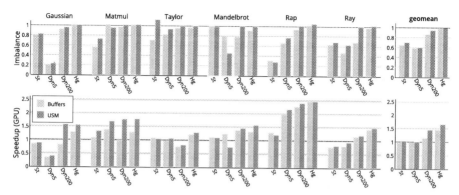

Fig. 5. Balancing efficiency (top) and speedups (bottom) for a set of benchmarks when doing CPU-GPU co-execution.

5 Validation

5.1 Performance

The imbalances and speedups achieved with CPU-GPU co-execution are shown in Fig. 5. The abscissa axes show the benchmarks, each one with four scheduling policies and two memory models, as defined in Sect. 4. Moreover, the geometric mean for each scheduling policy is shown on the right side. Regarding balancing efficiency, the optimal is 1.0, where both devices finish simultaneously without idle times. Any deviation from that value means more time to complete for one device compared with the other. Generally, the imbalance is below 1.0 due to the overheads introduced by the CPU when computing, as a device, and managing the runtime resources, as the host. It rarely completes its computation workload before the GPU finishes, since the latter requires more resource management by the host, increasing the CPU load.

The main conclusion that is important to highlight is that co-execution is always profitable from a performance point of view, as long as it is done with dynamic schedulers, and even more if using unified memory (*USM*), as the geometric mean summarizes for these benchmarks and scheduling configurations.

Analyzing the different load balancing algorithms, it can be seen that the Static offers the worst performance, even in regular applications where it should excel. This is because the initial communication overhead caused by sending a large work package, leads to a significant delay at the beginning of the execution, strongly penalizing the final performance.

Regarding dynamic algorithms, they provide good results in general, especially when the *USM* memory model is used. However, they have the drawback that the number of packages for each benchmark has to be carefully selected. A very small number of packages can lead higher imbalances causing a performance penalty, as can be seen in Gaussian, Mandelbrot or Ray, in the case of Dyn5. At the other extreme, a very large number of packages increases the communication overhead, impacting negatively on performance, as in Gaussian with

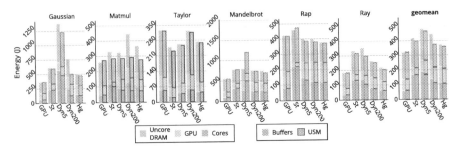

Fig. 6. Energy consumption by cores, GPU and the other units of the package with the DRAM consumption.

Buffers. In between, there is a tendency that the greater the number of packages, the better the balancing. This is an expected behavior because the packages are smaller and their computation is faster, giving less chance of imbalance in the completion of both devices. This is an interesting behavior since the *Coexecutor Runtime* is delivering high performance when using dynamic strategies due to the low overhead of the *Commander loop* when managing packages and events.

The HGuided algorithm offers the best scheduling policy, thanks to its balancing efficiency near to 1. It yields the best performance in all the analyzed benchmarks, with speedups values ranging from 2.46 in Rap to 1.48 in Ray. Moreover, it does not require any a priori parameters, which simplifies its use for the programmer.

Considering the memory models, there is a general improvement in balancing and performance when using *USM* compared with *Buffers*. It can be observed than *USM* performs much better than *Buffers* on regular kernels and with dynamic strategies, but this difference practically disappears on irregular kernels.

Finally, it is important to highlight the relationship between the imbalance and the speedups obtained. Although generally less imbalance indicates better performance, this does not have to be the case if the imbalance is not very high and more amount of work has been computed by the faster device. This is the case of Ray when using *Buffers*, since more work is computed by the GPU.

5.2   Energy

Fig. 6 presents the energy consumption, with each bar composed of up to three regions representing the energy used by: the CPU cores, the GPU and the rest of the CPU package together with the DRAM (*uncore + dram*).

Considering the average energy consumption, using only the GPU is the safest option to ensure minimum energy consumption. This is because the energy savings achieved by the reduction in execution time thanks to co-execution, is not enough to counteract the increase in power consumption caused by the use of CPU cores. However, there are also benchmarks such as Taylor and Rap where co-executing does improve power consumption over GPU, and others where co-execution and GPU-only have similar energy consumption, such as MatMul.

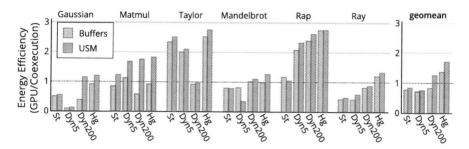

Fig. 7. Energy Efficiency compared with GPU (more is better).

Regarding the schedulers, there is a clear correlation between performance and energy consumption. Therefore, the algorithms that offer the best performance in co-execution are also the ones that consume the least energy. On the contrary, the schedulers that cause a lot of imbalance by giving more work to the CPU, spike the energy consumption, due to the higher usage of CPU cores, like Gaussian and Mandelbrot with Dyn5, and RAP with Static.

Another very interesting metric is energy efficiency, which relates performance and energy consumption. In this case it is represented by the ratio of the Energy-Delay Product of the GPU with respect to the co-execution, presented in Fig. 7. Therefore, values higher than 1.0 indicate that the co-execution is more energy efficient than the GPU.

Looking at the geometric mean, it can be concluded that co-execution is 72% more energy efficient than the GPU execution, using the HGuided scheduler and the USM memory model. Furthermore, this metric is indeed favorable to co-execution in all benchmarks studied, reaching improvements of up to 2.8x in Taylor and RAP. Thus, while co-execution consumes more energy in absolute terms on some benchmarks, the reduction in execution time compensates for this extra consumption, resulting in a better performance-energy trade-off.

5.3   Scalability

The results presented above refer to problem sizes that need around 10 s in the fastest device (GPU). This section presents a scalability analysis of the runtime, varying the size of the problems. To this aim, Fig. 8 shows the evolution of the execution time of each benchmark with respect to the size of the problem, in different configurations: CPU-only, GPU-only and co-executing. Also, with the two memory models: *Buffers* and *USM*.

The most important conclusion to be drawn is that, in all the cases studied, there is a turning point from which co-execution improves the performance of the fastest device. For very small problem sizes, the overhead introduced by the runtime cannot be compensated by the performance increase provided by the co-execution. These points are more noticeable in Gaussian, Mandelbrot and Ray, because the differences in computing capacity between CPUs and GPUs are much more pronounced (13.5x, 4.8x y 4.6x, respectively). Regarding memory

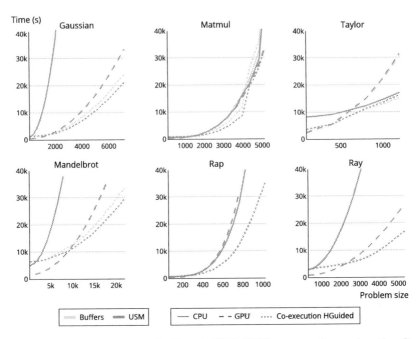

Fig. 8. Scalability for CPU, GPU and CPU-GPU coexecution using the Coexecutor runtime with its HGuided scheduling policy.

models, it is important to note that there are only substantial improvements between *USM* and *Buffers* in Gaussian, Matmul and Mandelbrot. This is because they are the benchmarks which use more memory, as can be seen in Table 1. These improvements become greater as the size of the problem increases.

Matmul is a special case, since by increasing the size of the problem, a point is reached where co-execution obtains the same performance as the GPU-only. A detailed analysis of the hardware counters indicates how the LLC memory suffers constant invalidations between CPU and GPU. Temporary locality of the shared memory hierarchy is penalized when co-executing with very large matrices, because the GPU requests memory blocks aggressively.

6   Conclusions

Hardware heterogeneity complicates the development of efficient and portable software, due to the complexity of their architectures and a variety of programming models. In this context, Intel has developed oneAPI, a new and powerful SYCL-based unified programming model with a set of domain-focused libraries, facilitating the development among various hardware architectures.

This paper provides co-execution to oneAPI to squeeze the performance out of heterogeneous systems. The *Coexecutor Runtime* overcomes one of the main challenges in oneAPI, the exploitation of dynamic decisions efficiently. Three load balancing algorithms are implemented on this runtime, showing the behavior in a set of regular and irregular benchmarks.

Furthermore, a validation of performance, balancing efficiency and energy efficiency is carried out, as well as a scalability study. The results indicate that co-execution is worthwhile when using dynamic schedulers, specifically when using HGuided algorithm and unified memory. All achieved due to efficient synchronization, architecture design decisions, computation and communication overlap, and the underlying oneAPI technology and its DPC++ compiler and runtime.

It is important to emphasize that the co-execution has been validated with CPU and integrated GPU, but the proposed runtime is also capable of using other types of architectures that will be incorporated into oneAPI. Therefore, in the future, the co-execution runtime will be extended to evaluate new heterogeneous devices, such as FPGAs and discrete GPUs. In addition, workload schedulers that can take advantage of the benefits offered by this programming model will be designed, thanks to the results presented in this paper.

Acknowledgment. This work has been supported by the Spanish Ministry of Education (FPU16/ 03299 grant), the Spanish Science and Technology Commission under contract PID2019-105660RB-C22 and the European HiPEAC Network of Excellence.

References

1. Aktemur, B., Metzger, M., Saiapova, N., Strasuns, M.: Debugging sycl programs on heterogeneous architectures. In: International Workshop on OpenCL, IWOCL. ACM (2020)
2. Ashbaugh, B., et al.: Data parallel c++: Enhancing sycl through extensions for productivity and performance. In International Workshop on OpenCL, IWOCL. ACM (2020)
3. Beri, T., Bansal, S., Kumar, S.: The unicorn runtime: efficient distributed shared memory programming for hybrid cpu-gpu clusters. IEEE Trans. Parallel Distrib. Syst. **28**(5), 1518–1534 (2017)
4. Castillo, E., Camarero, C., Borrego, A., Bosque, J.L.: Financial applications on multi-cpu and multi-gpu architectures. J. Supercomput. **71**(2), 729–739 (2015)
5. Christgau, S., Steinke, T.: Porting a legacy cuda stencil code to oneapi. In: Proceedings of IPDPSW, pp. 359–367 (2020)
6. Constantinescu, D.A., Navarro, A.G., Corbera, F., Fernández-Madrigal, J.A., Asenjo, R.: Efficiency and productivity for decision making on low-power heterogeneous cpu+gpu socs. J. Supercomput. (2020)
7. Intel Corporation. Intel® oneAPI programming guide (2020)
8. Costero, L., Igual, F.D., Olcoz, K., Tirado, F.: Leveraging knowledge-as-a-service (kaas) for qos-aware resource management in multi-user video transcoding. J. Supercomput. **76**(12), 9388–9403 (2020)
9. Farber, R.: Parallel Programming with OpenACC, 1st edn. Morgan Kaufmann Publishers, San Francisco (2016)
10. Gaster, B.R., Howes, L.W., Kaeli, D.R., Mistry, P., Schaa, D.: Heterogeneous Computing with OpenCL - Revised OpenCL 1.2 Edition. Morgan Kaufmann, San Francisco (2013)

11. Khronos® SYCL^{TM} Working Group. SYCL^{TM} specification: Generic heterogeneous computing for modern c++ (2020)
12. Jin, Z.: The rodinia benchmark suite in SYCL. Technical report, Argonne National Lab. (ANL), IL (United States) (2020)
13. Jin, Z., Morozov, V., Finkel, H.: A case study on the haccmk routine in sycl on integrated graphics. In: Proceedings of IPDPSW, pp. 368–374 (2020)
14. Lin, F.-C., Ngo, H.-H., Dow, C.-R.: A cloud-based face video retrieval system with deep learning. J. Supercomput. **76**(11), 8473–8493 (2020). https://doi.org/10.1007/s11227-019-03123-x
15. Nozal, R., Bosque, J.L., Beivide, R.: Towards co-execution on commodity heterogeneous systems: Optimizations for time-constrained scenarios. In: 2019 International Conference on High Performance Computing & Simulation (HPCS), pp. 628–635. IEEE (2019)
16. Nozal, R., Bosque, J.L., Beivide, R.: Enginecl: usability and performance in heterogeneous computing. Fut. Gener. Comput. Syst. **107**(C), 522–537 (2020)
17. Nozal, R., Perez, B., Bosque, J.L., Beivide, R.: Load balancing in a heterogeneous world: Cpu-xeon phi co-execution of data-parallel kernels. J. Supercomput. **75**(3), 1123–1136 (2019)
18. Pérez, B., Bosque, J.L., Beivide, R.: Simplifying programming and load balancing of data parallel applications on heterogeneous systems. In: Proceedings of the 9th Workshop on General Purpose Processing using GPU, pp. 42–51 (2016)
19. Pérez, B., Stafford, E., Bosque, J.L., Beivide, R.: Energy efficiency of load balancing for data-parallel applications in heterogeneous systems. J. Supercomput. **73**(1), 330–342 (2016). https://doi.org/10.1007/s11227-016-1864-y
20. Shen, J., Varbanescu, A.L., Lu, Y., Zou, P., Sips, H.: Workload partitioning for accelerating applications on heterogeneous platforms. IEEE Trans. Parallel Distrib. Syst. **27**(9), 2766–2780 (2016)
21. Shin, W., Yoo, K.H., Baek, N.: Large-scale data computing performance comparisons on sycl heterogeneous parallel processing layer implementations. Appl. Sci. **10**, 1656 (2020)
22. Toharia, P., Robles, O.D., Suárez, R., Bosque, J.L., Pastor, L.: Shot boundary detection using zernike moments in multi-gpu multi-cpu architectures. J. Parallel Distrib. Comput. **72**(9), 1127–1133 (2012)
23. Vitali, E., Gadioli, D., Palermo, G., Beccari, A., Cavazzoni, C., Silvano, C.: Exploiting openmp and openacc to accelerate a geometric approach to molecular docking in heterogeneous HPC nodes. J. Supercomput. **75**(7), 3374–3396 (2019)
24. Zahran, M.: Heterogeneous computing: here to stay. Commun. ACM **60**(3), 42–45 (2017)
25. Zhang, F., Zhai, J., He, B., Zhang, S., Chen, W.: Understanding co-running behaviors on integrated cpu/gpu architectures. IEEE Trans. Parallel Distrib. Syst. **28**(3), 905–918 (2017)

Parallel Numerical Methods and Applications

Designing a 3D Parallel Memory-Aware Lattice Boltzmann Algorithm on Manycore Systems

Yuankun Fu[1] and Fengguang Song[2]($\boxtimes$)

[1] Purdue University, Indianapolis, IN, USA
fu121@purdue.edu
[2] Indiana University-Purdue University, Indianapolis, IN, USA
fgsong@cs.iupui.edu

Abstract. Lattice Boltzmann method (LBM) is a promising approach to solving Computational Fluid Dynamics (CFD) problems, however, its nature of memory-boundness limits nearly all LBM algorithms' performance on modern computer architectures. This paper introduces novel sequential and parallel 3D memory-aware LBM algorithms to optimize its memory access performance. The introduced new algorithms combine the features of single-copy distribution, single sweep, swap algorithm, prism traversal, and merging two temporal time steps. We also design a parallel methodology to guarantee thread safety and reduce synchronizations in the parallel LBM algorithm. At last, we evaluate their performances on three high-end manycore systems and demonstrate that our new 3D memory-aware LBM algorithms outperform the state-of-the-art Palabos software (which realizes the Fuse Swap Prism LBM solver) by up to 89%.

Keywords: Lattice Boltzmann method · Memory-aware algorithms · Parallel numerical methods · Manycore systems

1 Introduction

Computational Fluid Dynamics (CFD) simulations have revolutionized the design process in various scientific, engineering, industrial, and medical fields. The current Reynolds averaged Navier-Stokes (RANS) methods can solve steady viscous transonic and supersonic flows, but are not able to reliably predict turbulent separated flows [28]. Lattice Boltzmann method (LBM) is a young and evolving approach to solving these problems in the CFD community [2]. It originates from a mesoscale description of the fluid (based on the Boltzmann equation), and directly incorporates physical terms to represent complex physical phenomena, such as multi-phase flows, reactive and suspension flows, etc. Besides, many *collision models* have been developed for LBM to improve its stability to the second order of numerical accuracy when simulating high Reynolds number flows [2].

© Springer Nature Switzerland AG 2021
L. Sousa et al. (Eds.): Euro-Par 2021, LNCS 12820, pp. 519–535, 2021.
https://doi.org/10.1007/978-3-030-85665-6_32

However, it is challenging to achieve high performance for LBM algorithms, since LBM has large data storage costs and is highly memory-bound on current architectures [24]. Driven by our prior work [5] to merge multiple collision-streaming cycles (or time steps) in 2D, this study aims to augment the memory-awareness idea to support parallel 3D LBM to optimize data re-utilization. Although it might seem to be straightforward to move from the 2D space to 3D space, it is significantly much more difficult to design an efficient 3D memory-aware LBM algorithm. In this paper, we target solving the following three main challenges. (1) As geometries change from 2D to 3D, the required data storage increases from $O(N^2)$ to $O(N^3)$, meanwhile data dependencies of the lattice model becomes much more complicated. There exist single-copy distribution methods to reduce data storage cost by half, but they require following a particular traversal order. Can we combine the best single-copy distribution method with our idea of merging multiple collision-streaming cycles to design a 3D memory-aware LBM with higher performance? (2) If the combination is possible, since normal 3D tiling [21] does not apply to this case, how to additionally explore the spatial locality? (3) When designing the parallel 3D memory-aware LBM, a non-trivial interaction occurs at the boundaries between threads, how to guarantee thread safety and avoid race conditions? Although some existing works use wavefront parallelism to explore the temporal locality, they insert frequent layer-wise synchronizations among threads every time step [11,27]. In this paper, we aim to reduce the synchronization cost among parallel threads.

To the best of our knowledge, this paper makes the following contributions. First, we design both sequential and parallel 3D memory-aware LBM algorithms that combine five features: single-copy distribution, loop fusion (single sweep), swap algorithm, prism traversal, and merging two collision-streaming cycles. Second, we present a parallelization method to keep the thread safety on the intersection layers among threads and reduce the synchronization cost in parallel. At last, two groups of experiments are conducted on three different manycore architectures, followed by performance analysis. The first group of sequential experiments (i.e., using a single CPU core) shows that our memory-aware LBM outperforms the state-of-the-art Palabos (Fuse Swap Prism LBM solver) [17] by up to 19% on a Haswell CPU and 15% on a Skylake CPU. The second group evaluates the performance of parallel algorithms. The experimental results show that our parallel 3D memory-aware LBM outperforms Palabos by up to 89% on a Haswell node with 28 cores, 85% on a Skylake node with 48 cores, and 39% on a Knight Landing node with 68 cores.

2   Related Work

Existing research on designing efficient LBM algorithms mainly focuses on optimizing memory accesses within one time step of LBM due to its iterative nature. For instance, a few LBM algorithms (e.g., swap [13,25], AA [1], shift [19], and esoteric twist [6], etc.) retain a single copy of the particle distribution data (i.e., "single-copy distribution"), and optimize the memory access pattern in the LBM streaming kernel, but each of the algorithms needs to follow a set of constraints (e.g., swap requires predefined order of discrete cell velocities [9], AA requires distinguishing between even and odd time steps, shift requires extra storage [9], esoteric twist requires only one version of the LB kernel [29], etc.) [26] uses a moment-based representation with extra distribution pseudo domain to further reduce the storage cost. Some works hide the inter-process communication cost on multicore accelerators [3], and achieve large-scale parallelization on HPC systems [20] and GPU [1]. [31] introduces a cache oblivious blocking 3D LBM algorithm, but it has an irregular parallelism scheme due to its recursive algorithm design. In summary, the above methods focus on optimizations within one time step. Differently, our 3D memory-aware LBM aims to adopt the efficient single-copy distribution scheme, and design new methodologies to merge two collision-streaming cycles to explore both temporal and spatial data locality at the same time for achieving higher performance.

Another category of works manages to accelerate LBM by wavefront parallelism, which generally groups many threads to successively compute on the same spatial domain. [11] presents a shared-memory wavefront 2D LBM together with loop fusion, loop bump, loop skewing, loop tiling, and semaphore operations. But due to its high synchronization cost incurred by many implicit barriers in wavefront parallelism, their parallel performance has only 10% of speedup on average. [7] presents a shared-memory wavefront 3D LBM with two-copy distributions, and does not use spatial locality techniques such as loop fusion and loop blocking. [27] presents a shared-memory wavefront 3D Jacobi approach together with spatial blocking. It uses two-copy distributions and has simpler 6-neighbors dependencies (rather than the 19 or 27 neighbors in 3D LBM). [12] combines the wavefront parallelism with diamond tiling. By contrast, our 3D memory-aware LBM does not use the wavefront parallelism, but judiciously contains three light-weight synchronization barriers every two collision-streaming cycles. In addition, we partition the simulation domain and assign a local sub-domain to every thread, rather than all threads work on the same sub-domain in wavefront parallelism. In each sub-domain, each thread in our algorithm computes multiple time steps at once, rather than one thread computes one time step at a time in wavefront parallelism. In addition, each of our threads also utilizes prism techniques to optimize spatial locality. This strategy in particular favors new manycore architectures, which tend to have increasingly larger cache sizes.

Modern parallel software packages that support LBM can be classified into two categories based upon their underlying data structures. One category adopts matrix-based memory alignment at the cell level (e.g., Palabos [10], OpenLB [8], HemeLB [14], HemoCell [30]). Since neighbors can be easily found through simple index arithmetics in this case, they are more suitable for simulations with dense geometries. The other category adopts adjacent list data structures (e.g., Musubi [15], waLBerla [4], HARVEY [20]). They are often used for simulating domains with sparse and irregular geometries, but their cells require additional memory of pointers, and double the memory consumption in the worst case. In this study, we choose the widely-used and efficient matrix-based data structure in the LBM community, and select the state-of-the-art Palabos library as the baseline, since Palabos provides a broad modeling framework, supports applications with complex physics, and shows high computational performance.

[18] designs a locally recursive non-locally asynchronous (LRnLA) conefold LBM algorithm, which uses recursive Z-curve arrays for data storage, and recursively subdivides the space-time dependency graph into polytopes to update lattice nodes. However, our work uses a more directly accessible matrix-based data storage and has a regular memory access pattern. Besides, our prism traversal can independently or integrate with merging two time steps to operate on the lattice nodes, while [18] operates on the dependency graph.

3   Baseline 3D LBM Algorithm

The baseline 3D LBM algorithm in this paper is called *Fuse Swap LBM* as shown in Algorithm 1, which involves three features: single-copy distribution, swap algorithm, and loop fusion. We choose the swap algorithm [13] since it is relatively simpler than the other single-copy distribution methods, and is more efficient to use simple index arithmetic to access neighbors in the matrix-based memory organization. The swap algorithm replaces the copy operations between a cell and its neighbors in the streaming kernel by a value swap, thereby it is in-place and does not require the second copy. But when combining it with loop fusion, we must guarantee that the populations of neighbors involved in the swap are already in a post-collision state to keep thread safety [9].

The work-around solution is to adjust the traversal order of simulation domains with a predefined order of discrete cell velocities [9]. Thus each cell can stream its post-collision data by swapping values with half of its neighbors pointed by the "red" arrows (1–9 directions for D3Q19 in Fig. 1a), if those neighbors are already in post-collision and have "reverted" their distributions. We define this operation as *"swap_stream"*. The *"revert"* operation in Fig. 1b lets a cell locally swap its post-collision distributions to opposite directions. To make the Fuse Swap LBM more efficient, Palabos pre-processes and post-processes the boundary cells on the bounding box at line 2 and 7, respectively, so that it can remove the boundary checking operation in the inner bulk domain. Thus Algorithm 1 is divided into three stages in every time step as follows.

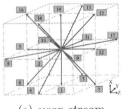

(a) *swap_stream*

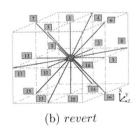

(b) *revert*

(c) Three stages computation.

Fig. 1. Two operations and three stages computation used in sequential 3D fuse swap LBM. (Color figure online)

Algorithm 1. 3D Fuse Swap LBM

1: **for** iT = 0; iT < N; ++iT **do**
2:   Stage I: *collide* and *revert* on the bounding box, i.e., 6 surfaces of cuboid $(1,1,1)$ to (lx, ly, lz)
     // Stage II: bulk domain computation
3:   **for** iX = 2; iX ≤ $lx - 1$; ++iX **do**
4:     **for** iY = 2; iY ≤ $ly - 1$; ++iY **do**
5:       **for** iZ = 2; iZ ≤ $lz - 1$; ++iZ **do**
6:         *collide* & *swap_stream* on (iX, iY, iZ) to half of its neighbors
7:   Stage III: *boundary_swap_stream* on the bounding box

---

4 The 3D Memory-Aware LBM Algorithm

4.1 Sequential 3D Memory-Aware LBM

We design and develop the sequential 3D memory-aware LBM (shown in Algorithm 2), based on the latest efficient Fuse Swap LBM, by adding two more features: merging two collision-streaming cycles to explore the temporal locality, and introducing the prism traversal to explore the spatial locality. Figure 2 shows an example on how to merge two collision-streaming cycles given a $4 \times 4 \times 4$ cube:

1. Figure 2a shows the initial state of all cells at the current time step t. Green cells are on boundaries, and blue cells are located in the inner bulk domain.
2. In Fig. 2b, we compute the first *collide*, *revert* and *boundary_swap_stream* row by row on the bottom layer iX = 1. After a cell completes the first computation, we change it to orange.
3. In Fig. 2c, we compute the first *collide* and *boundary_swap_stream* row by row till cell (2,2,1) on the second layer iX = 2.
4. In Fig. 2d, cell (2,2,2) completes its first *collide* and *swap_stream*, so we change it to red since they are inner cells. Then we observe that cell (1,1,1) is ready for the second *collide*, so we change it to yellow.
5. In Fig. 2e, we execute the second *collide* and *boundary_swap_stream* on cell (1,1,1), and change it to purple.

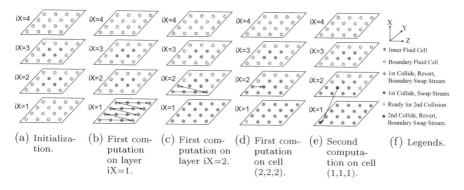

(a) Initialization.　(b) First computation on layer iX=1.　(c) First computation on layer iX=2.　(d) First computation on cell (2,2,2).　(e) Second computation on cell (1,1,1).　(f) Legends.

Fig. 2. 3D sequential two-step memory-aware LBM on a $4 \times 4 \times 4$ cube lattice.

To further increase data reuse, we optimize the algorithm's spatial locality by designing a "prism traversal" method, since the shape of this traversal constructs a 3D pyramid prism or a parallelpiped prism. We use an example to explain its access pattern in a $4 \times 16 \times 16$ cuboid with stride $tile = 4$. Figure 3a–d are the four separate 16×16 layers of the cuboid from bottom to top. The cells with the same number on the four layers construct a *prism* (e.g., the cells with number 1 in Fig. 3a–d construct a pyramid-shape "Prism 1"). In each prism, we still firstly go along Z-axis, then along Y-axis, and upward along X-axis at last. Then we traverse prism-wise from Prism 1 to Prism 30. Finally, if a cuboid is much larger than this example, the majority of prisms are "parallelpiped" shapes like Prism 9 and 10 in Fig. 3e. The reason why the planar slice of a prism is either triangles or parallelograms is due to the *swap_stream* operation. When cutting Fig. 1a (*swap_stream*) along the Y-Z plane, we have a planar slice as shown in Fig. 3f. We observe that a cell (star) swaps with its lower right neighbor (orange) at direction 9. In other words, when the orange cell swaps with the upward row, its neighbor "shifts" one cell *leftward*. Similarly, if cutting Fig. 1a (*swap_stream*) along the X-Y plane, when a cell swaps data with the upward row, its neighbor "shifts" one cell *forward*. Thus when we traverse *tile* number of cells on Z-axis at row iY, they can swap with *tile* number of cells but shifted one cell leftward at row $iY+1$, thereby we get parallelograms in Fig. 3a–d. When the shift encounters domain boundaries, we truncate the parallelograms and get isosceles right triangles or part of parallelograms. At last, we can safely combine "prism traversal" with merging two collision-streaming cycles, since the cell at left forward down corner has been in a post-collision state and ready to compute the second computation when following the above traversal order.

Algorithm 2 presents the sequential 3D memory-aware LBM. Lines 6–10 traverse the domain prism-wise with stride $tile$. Lines 11–14 merge two time steps computation. The first *stream* starting from the bottom layer iX = 1 in Line 10

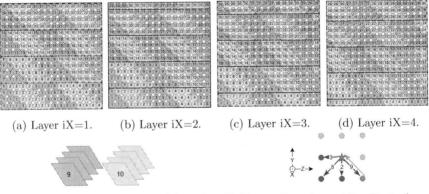

(a) Layer iX=1.   (b) Layer iX=2.   (c) Layer iX=3.   (d) Layer iX=4.

(e) Prism 9 and 10 are parallelpiped shape. Layer iX=4 is on the top.

(f) Planar slice when cutting Fig.1a (swap stream operation) along Y-Z plane.

Fig. 3. Sequential 3D prism traversal on a $4 \times 16 \times 16$ cuboid box.

Algorithm 2. 3D Sequential Memory-aware LBM

1: tile := stride of the prism traversal
2: **for** iT = 0; iT < N; iT += 2 **do**
3: **for** outerX = 1; outerX ≤ lx; outerX += tile **do**
4:   **for** outerY = 1; outerY ≤ ly + tile - 1; outerY += tile **do**
5:    **for** outerZ = 1; outerZ ≤ lz + 2* (tile - 1); outerZ += tile **do**
6:     **for** innerX=outerX; innerX ≤ MIN(outerX+tile-1, lx); ++innerX, ++dx **do**
7:      minY = outerY - dx; maxY = minY + tile - 1; dy = 0; /* forward shift */
8:      **for** innerY=MAX(minY, 1); innerY ≤ MIN(maxY, ly); ++innerY, ++dy **do**
9:       minZ = outerZ - dx - dy; maxZ = minZ + tile - 1; /* leftward shift */
10:       **for** innerZ=MAX(minZ, 1); innerZ ≤ MIN(maxZ, lz); ++innerZ **do**
           /* (1) First computation at time step t. */
11:        adaptive_collide_stream(innerX, innerY, innerZ);
           /* (2) Second computation at time step t + 1. */
12:        **if** innerX > 1 && innerY > 1 && innerZ > 1 **then**
13:         adaptive_collide_stream(innerX-1, innerY-1, innerZ-1);
           /* (3) Second computation of neighbors at certain locations. */
14:        boundary_neighbor_handler(innerX, innerY, innerZ);
15: Second collide, revert & boundary_swap_stream on the top layer iX = lx.
16: **function** boundary_cell_comp(iX, iY, iZ)
17: collide, revert, & boundary_swap_stream on (iX, iY, iZ) to half of its neighbors;
18: **function** adaptive_collide_stream(iX, iY, iZ)
19: **if** (iX, iY, iZ) is on the boundary **then**
20:   boundary_cell_comp(iX, iY, iZ);
21: **else**
22:   collide & swap_stream on (iX, iY, iZ) to half of its neighbors;
23: **function** boundary_neighbor_handler(iX, iY, iZ)
     // Handle the second computation of (iX, iY, iZ)'s neighbors at certain locations.
24: **if** iZ == lz **then** // (iX, iY, iZ) is the last cell of a row.
25:   boundary_cell_comp (iX-1, iY-1, iZ);
26: **if** iY == ly && iZ > 1 **then** // (iX, iY, iZ) is in the last row of a layer.
27:   boundary_cell_comp(iX-1, iY, iZ-1);
28: **if** iY == ly && iZ == lz **then** // (iX, iY, iZ) is the last cell on a layer.
29:   boundary_cell_comp (iX-1, iY, iZ);

---

is necessary due to the data dependency for the second computation. In particular, the if-statement in Line 13 ensures that the cell to compute at time step $t+1$ is in a post-collision state, no matter using D3Q15, D3Q19, D3Q27 or extended lattice models. For simplicity, Lines 16–29 define three helper functions.

4.2 Parallel 3D Memory-Aware LBM

To support manycore systems, we choose OpenMP [16] to realize the parallel 3D memory-aware LBM algorithm[1]. Figure 4 illustrates its idea on a $8 \times 4 \times 4$ cuboid, which is evenly partitioned by two threads along the X-axis (*height*). Then each thread traverses a $4 \times 4 \times 4$ sub-domain with prism stride *tile* = 4. Line 4 in Algorithm 3 defines the start and end layer index of each thread's sub-domain, thus the end layers *myEndX* are "*intersections*" (e.g., layer 4 and 8). Figure 4a shows the initial state at time step t. In addition, the parallel 3D memory-aware Algorithm 3 consists of three stages: Preprocessing, Sub-domain computation, and Post-processing.

---

[1] [23] states that when the minimum effective task granularity (METG) of parallel runtime systems are smaller than task granularity of large-scale LBM simulations, all of these runtime system can deliver good parallel performance.

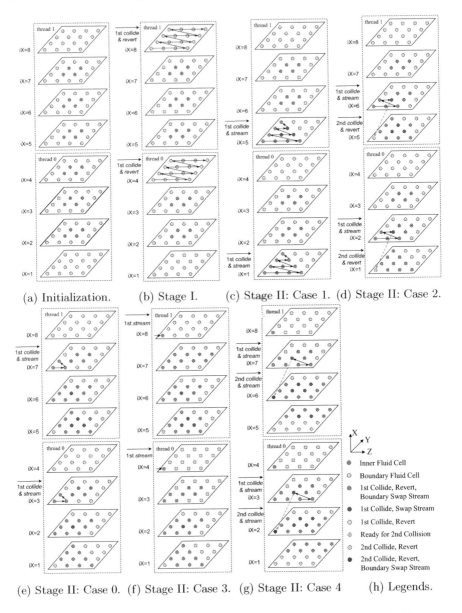

(a) Initialization.   (b) Stage I.   (c) Stage II: Case 1.   (d) Stage II: Case 2.

(e) Stage II: Case 0.   (f) Stage II: Case 3.   (g) Stage II: Case 4   (h) Legends.

Fig. 4. Parallel 3D two-step memory-aware LBM on a $8 \times 4 \times 4$ cuboid.

1. **Stage I (Preprocessing)** *line 5 in Algorithm 3*: In Fig. 4b, thread 0 and 1 compute the first *collide* and *revert* on the "intersection" layers 4 and 8, respectively, and then change them to pink.
2. **Stage II (Sub-domain computation)** handles five cases from step 2 to 7. In *case 0 (lines 15–17 in Algorithm 3)*, when thread 0 and 1 access the cells

---

Algorithm 3. Parallel 3D Memory-aware LBM

1: **for** iT = 0; iT < N; iT += 2 **do**
2:   **#pragma omp parallel default(shared){**
3:   $sub\_h = lx/nthreads$; // height of each thread's sub-domain
4:   myStartX = $1 + thread\_id \times sub\_h$; myEndX = $(thread\_id + 1) \times sub\_h$;
   /* Stage I: First collide & revert on the intersection layer. */
5:   collide & revert on all $ly \times lz$ cells on layer iX = myEndX;
6:   **#pragma omp barrier**
   /* Stage II: Main computation in each thread's sub-domain. */
7:   **for** outerX = myStartX; outerX $\leq$ myEndX; outerX += tile **do**
8:    **for** outerY = 1; outerY $\leq ly$ + tile - 1 ; outerY += tile **do**
9:     **for** outerZ = 1; outerZ $\leq lz$ + 2 * (tile - 1); outerZ += tile **do**
10:      **for** innerX=outerX; innerX$\leq$MIN(outerX+tile-1, myEndX); ++innerX, ++dx **do**
11:       minY = outerY - dx; maxY = minY + tile - 1; dy = 0; /* forward shift */
12:       **for** innerY=MAX(minY, 1); innerY$\leq$MIN(maxY, ly); ++innerY, ++dy **do**
13:        minZ = outerZ - dx - dy; maxZ = minZ + tile - 1; /* leftward shift */
14:        **for** innerZ = MAX(minZ, 1); innerZ $\leq$ MIN(maxZ, lz); ++innerZ **do**
       // Case 0: First collide & stream on the first row and column of each layer except the intersection layers.
15:         **if** innerX != myEndX && (innerX == 1 or innerY == 1 or innerZ == 1) **then**
16:          First boundary_cell_comp(innerX, innerY, innerZ);
17:          **continue;**
       // Case 1: First collide & stream on layer myStartX:
18:         **if** innerX == myStartX **then**
19:          First adaptive_collide_stream(innerX, innerY, innerZ);
       // Case 2: First collide & stream on myStartX + 1; Second collide & revert on myStartX:
20:         **else if** innerX == myStartX + 1 **then**
21:          First adaptive_collide_stream(innerX, innerY, innerZ);
22:          Second collide & revert on (innerX-1, innerY-1, innerZ-1);
23:          Handle the second collide & revert of neighbors at certain boundary locations;
       // Case 3: First stream on layer myEndX; Second collide & stream under one layer:
24:         **else if** innerX == myEndX **then**
25:          First adaptive_stream(innerX, innerY, innerZ);
26:          Second adaptive_collide_stream(innerX-1, innerY-1, innerZ-1);
27:          boundary_neighbor_handler (innerX, innerY, innerZ);
       // Case 4: first collide & stream on other layers; Second collide & stream under one layer:
28:         **else**
29:          First adaptive_collide_stream(innerX, innerY, innerZ);
30:          Second adaptive_collide_stream(innerX-1, innerY-1, innerZ-1);
31:          boundary_neighbor_handler(innerX, innerY, innerZ);
32:   **#pragma omp barrier**
   /* Stage III: second collide & stream on the intersection; then second stream on the layer myStartX. */
33:   adaptive_collide_stream at all $ly \times lz$ cells on layer iX = myEndX;
34:   **#pragma omp barrier**
35:   stream at all $ly \times lz$ cells on layer iX = myStartX;
36:   **}**

---

on the first row and column of each layer except the "intersection" layers, we execute the first *boundary_cell_comp* on them and change them to orange.

3. Figure 4c shows *case 1 (lines 18–19 in Algorithm 3)*. When thread 0 and 1 access the cells on layer *myStartX* (iX = 1 & 5), respectively, we execute the *adaptive_collide_stream* on them to compute at time step t, and then change the boundary cells to orange and the inner cells to red.

4. Figure 4d shows *case 2 (lines 20–23 in Algorithm 3)*. When thread 0 and 1 are on layer *myStartX* + 1 (iX = 2 & 6), respectively, we execute the first *adaptive_collide_stream* at time step t and change boundary cells to orange and inner cells to red. Meanwhile, cell (5,1,1) and (1,1,1) have collected the

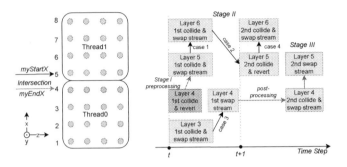

Fig. 5. Handle thread safety on intersection layers.

data dependencies to *collide* at time step $t+1$, we execute the second *collide* and *revert* but without *stream* on them, and change to light purple.

5. Figure 4e shows that when continuing traversal in Prism 1, thread 0 and 1 are on layer iX = 3 & 6. Since the cells traversed in this figure are in the first row and column, case 0 is used here, otherwise, case 4 is used.

6. Figure 4f shows *case 3* (*lines 24–27 in Algorithm 3*). When thread 0 and 1 are on the intersection layers (iX = 4 & 8), we execute the remaining first *stream* at time step t due to preprocessing in Stage I. Then if cells under one layer (iX = 3 & 7) collect their data dependency at time step $t+1$, we execute the second *adaptive_collide_stream* on them.

7. Figure 4g shows *case 4* (*lines 28–31 in Algorithm 3*). When thread 0 and 1 are on the other layers of sub-domain, we conduct the first *adaptive_collide_stream* on (innerX, innerY, innerZ) at time step t, and then the second *adaptive_collide_stream* on (innerX-1, innerY-1, innerZ-1) at time step $t+1$. Then we call *boundary_neighbor_handler* to compute the neighbors of (innerX, innerY, innerZ) at certain locations at time step $t+1$.

8. **Stage III (Post-processing)** *lines 33–35 in Algorithm 3*: Firstly, since Stage I and case 3 have completed the first computation on intersection layers, we wrap up the second *collide* and *stream* on intersections. Secondly, since case 2 have executed the second *collide* and *revert* on the first layers *myStartX* of each sub-domain, the second *stream* remains to be executed.

How to Handle Thread Safety near Intersection Layers: We aim to keep thread safety and minimize the synchronization cost during parallel executions. To this end, we need to carefully design the initial state of each thread so that the majority of computation stays in each threads' local sub-domain. The left part of Fig. 5 shows the view of Fig. 4 along X-Z axis, and layer 4 is the intersection layer that partitions two threads' sub-domains. The right part shows the data dependencies near the intersection layer in two time steps. In the figure, the red block represents Stage I of Algorithm 3, yellow blocks Stage II, and green blocks Stage III. The arrows indicate that data are transferred from layer A to B by using a procedure (or B depends on A). There are three non-trivial dependencies requiring to handle thread safety near intersection layers. (1) Since the swap algorithm only streams data to half of the neighbors under one layer, the *swap_stream* on layer 5—the first layer of thread 1's sub-domain—should be delayed after the *revert* on layer 4 in thread 0's sub-domain. Thus, in Stage I, we pre-process *collide* and *revert* at time step t but without *stream* on layer 4, since *stream* on layer 4 depends on the post-collision on layer 3, which has not been computed yet. (2) In Stage II, the second *swap_stream* on layer 6 called by the case 4 procedure should be delayed after the second *revert* but without *swap_stream* on layer 5. This is because thread 1 cannot guarantee that thread 0 has completed the second *swap_steam* on layer 4. To keep thread safety, *swap_stream* on layer 5 is delayed to Stage III. (3) Thus, in Stage III, the second *swap_stream* on layer 5 is delayed after the second *swap_stream* on layer 4. Above all, since the major computation happens in Stage II of each thread's sub-domain, we avoid the frequent "layer-wise" thread synchronizations that occur in the wave-front parallelism. Besides, we only synchronize at the intersection layers every two time steps, hence the overhead of three *barriers* of Algorithm 3 becomes much less.

5   Experimental Evaluation

In this section, we first present the experimental setup and validations on our 3D memory-aware LBM. Then we evaluate its sequential and parallel performance.

5.1   Experiment Setup and Verification

The details of our experimental hardware platforms are provided in Table 1. To evaluate the performance of our new algorithms, we use the 3D lid-driven cavity flow simulation as an example. The 3D cavity has a dimension of $lz \times ly \times lx$, and its top lid moves with a constant velocity v. Our 3D memory-aware LBM algorithms have been implemented as C++ template functions, which are then added to the Palabos framework. For verification, we construct a *cavity* with the same procedure, and then separately execute four algorithms on it, i.e., Palabos solvers $fuse()$ and $fuse\_prism()$ for N time steps, and our memory-aware algorithms $two\_step\_prism()$ and $two\_step\_prism\_omp()$ for $N/2$ time steps. Then, we compute the velocity norm of each cell and write to four separate logs. At last, we verify that our algorithms produce the same result as Palabos for guaranteeing software correctness.

5.2   Performance of Sequential 3D Memory-Aware LBM

The first set of experiments with 3D cavity flows compare the sequential performance of four different LBM algorithms, which are the Fuse Swap LBM (with/without prism traversal), and the Two-step Memory-aware LBM (with/without prism traversal). For simplicity, we use the abbreviations of fuse LBM, fuse prism LBM, 2-step LBM and 2-step prism LBM, respectively. The problem input are

Table 1. Details of our experimental platforms.

Microarchitecture	Bridges at PSC	Stampede2 at TACC	
	Haswell'14	Skylake'17	Knight Landing'16
Intel CPU product code	Xeon E5-2695v3	Xeon Platinum 8160	Xeon Phi 7250
Total # Cores/node	28 on 2 sockets	48 on 2 sockets	68 on 1 socket
Clock rate (GHz)	2.1–3.3	2.1 nominal (1.4–3.7)	1.4
L1 cache/core	32 KB	32 KB	32 KB
L2 cache/core	256 KB	1 MB	1 MB per 2-core tile
L3 cache/socket	35 MB	33 MB (Non-inclusive)	16 GB MCDRAM
DDR4 Memory (GB)/node	128 (2133 MHz)	192 (2166 MHz)	96 (2166 MHz)
Compiler	icc/19.5	icc/18.0.2	
AVX extension	AVX2	AVX512	

3D cubes with edge size $L = 64$–896. Every algorithm with a prism stride configuration is executed five times, and the average MFLUPS (millions of fluid lattice node updates per second) is calculated. For the "prism" algorithms, different prism strides (ranging from 8, 16, 32,..., to 448) are tested, and we select the best performance achieved.

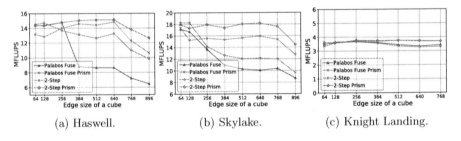

(a) Haswell.   (b) Skylake.   (c) Knight Landing.

Fig. 6. Sequential performance using four LBM algorithms on three types of CPUs.

Figure 6 shows the sequential performance on three types of CPUs. When we use small edge sizes (e.g., $L = 64, 128$), 2-step LBM is the fastest. But when $L \geq 256$, 2-step prism LBM performs the best and is up to 18.8% and 15.5% faster than the second-fastest Palabos (Fuse Prism LBM solver) on Haswell and Skylake, respectively. But since KNL does not have an L3 cache, 2-step prism LBM is only 1.15% faster than Palabos (Fuse Prism LBM solver).

We observe that the performance of algorithms without prism traversal starts to drop when $L \geq 384$. Since the swap algorithm streams to half of its neighbors on its own layer and the layer below, $23.9 \, MB/layer \times 2 \, layers = 47.8 \, MB$ (when $L = 384$), which exceeds the L3 cache size (35 MB per socket on Haswell). Thus we need to use spatial locality by adding the feature of prism traversal. Consequently, on Haswell and Skylake, fuse LBM is improved by up to 71.7%

and 58.2%, respectively, 2-step LBM is improved by up to 28.6% and 50.4%, respectively. When only adding the feature of merging two steps, 2-step LBM is faster than Palabos (Fuse) by up to 53.3% on Haswell and 20.5% on Skylake. Hence, we conclude that both prism traversal and merging two steps significantly increase cache reuse on the large domain.

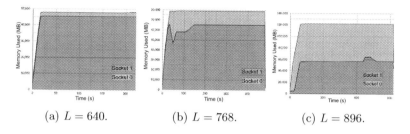

(a) $L = 640$.   (b) $L = 768$.   (c) $L = 896$.

Fig. 7. Memory usage on two sockets of a Haswell node.

In Fig. 6, we observe that the performance of all algorithms starts to drop when $L \geq 768$ on Haswell and $L = 896$ on Skylake. To find out the reason, we use Remora [22] to monitor the memory usage on each socket of the Haswell node. As L increases from 640 to 896, the memory usage on socket 1 (red area) in Fig. 7a–c has enlarged from 2.4 GB to 63.9 GB. When memory usage exceeds the 64 GB DRAM capacity per socket on the Haswell node, foreign NUMA memory accesses are involved, thus the sequential performance reduces. Similar results also happen on the Skylake node. However, because the KNL node only has one socket, the performance on KNL does not drop.

5.3   Performance of Parallel 3D Memory-Aware LBM

Given N cores, Palabos LBM solvers partition the simulation domain evenly along three axes by $N_z \times N_y \times N_x = N$ MPI processes, which follows the underlying memory layout of cells along the axis of Z, then Y, and X at last. But our 3D memory-aware LBM partitions a domain only along X-axis by N OpenMP threads. Hence, Palabos LBM solvers have a smaller Y-Z layer size per core than our algorithm and have closer memory page alignment especially for a large domain. To exclude the factor caused by different partition methods, when the input of Palabos LBM solvers still uses cubes, 3D memory-aware LBM will take two different inputs. Firstly, it takes the input of the "equivalent dimension" of those cubes, such that a thread in our algorithm and a process in Palabos will compute a sub-domain with the same dimension after the respective partition method. Secondly, it simply takes the identical input of those cubes.

Figure 8 shows the strong scalability of three LBM algorithms on three types of compute nodes. The input of Palabos LBM solvers use cubes with edge size L from small to large. Table 2 gives an example of the equivalent input used by 3D memory-aware LBM when Palabos LBM solvers use a cube with $L = 840$

Table 2. Equivalent input used by 2-step prism LBM when the input of Palabos LBM solvers is a cube with $L = 840$ on a Haswell node.

Cores	1	2	4	6	8	10	12	14	20	24	28
lx (height)	840	1680	3360	5040	3360	8400	5040	11760	8400	10080	11760
ly (width)	840	840	420	420	420	420	420	420	420	420	420
lz (length)	840	420	420	280	420	168	280	120	168	140	120

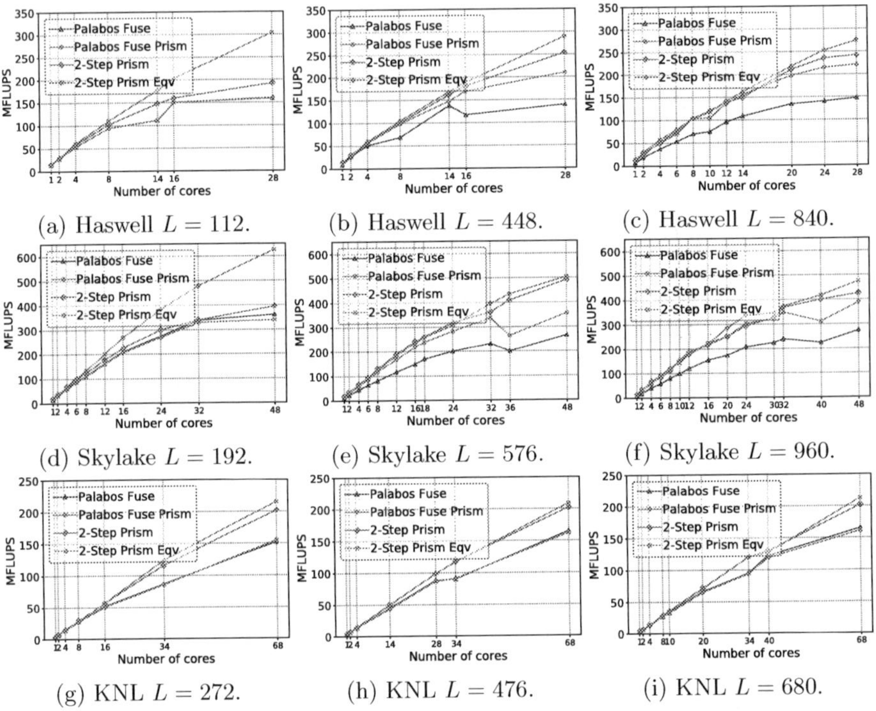

(a) Haswell $L = 112$.

(b) Haswell $L = 448$.

(c) Haswell $L = 840$.

(d) Skylake $L = 192$.

(e) Skylake $L = 576$.

(f) Skylake $L = 960$.

(g) KNL $L = 272$.

(h) KNL $L = 476$.

(i) KNL $L = 680$.

Fig. 8. Strong scalability performance on three types of compute nodes. "2-step prism eqv" = Parallel 3D memory aware LBM takes the equivalent input of cubes.

on a Haswell node. We observe that the 2-step prism LBM scales efficiently and always achieves the best performance in all cases. (1) When using the equivalent input of cubes, for small scale cubes (with $L = 112, 192, 272$) in Fig. 8a, d and g, 3D memory-aware LBM (green legend) is faster than the second-fastest Palabos (Fuse Prism) (orange legend) by up to 89.2%, 84.6%, and 38.8% on the Haswell, Skylake, and KNL node, respectively. Missing L3 cache on KNL prevents the similar speedup as other two CPUs. In Fig. 8b, e and h, for the middle scale cubes (with $L = 448, 576, 476$), it is still faster than Palabos (Fuse Prism) by up to 37.9%, 64.2%, and 28.8% on three CPU nodes, respectively. Due to unbalanced number of processes assigned on three axes, we observe that the performance of

Palabos Fuse and Fuse Prism drop on some number of cores. In Fig. 8c, f and i, for the large scale cubes (with $L = 840, 960, 680$), it is still faster than Palabos (Fuse Prism) by up to 34.2%, 34.2%, and 31.8%, respectively. (2) When using the identical input of cubes, although our 3D memory-aware LBM has larger Y-Z layer sizes, it is still faster than Palabos (Fuse Prism) but with less speedup than before, i.e., by up to 21.1%, 54.7%, and 30.1% on three CPU nodes, respectively. The less speedup suggests our future work to partition a 3D domain along three axes to utilize closer memory page alignment on smaller Y-Z layer size.

6 Conclusion

To address the memory-bound limitation of LBM, we design a new 3D parallel memory-aware LBM algorithm that systematically combines single copy distribution, single sweep, swap algorithm, prism traversal, and merging two collision-streaming cycles. We also keep thread safety and reduce the synchronization cost in parallel. The parallel 3D memory-aware LBM outperforms state-of-the-art LBM software by up to 89.2% on a Haswell node, 84.6% on a Skylake node and 38.8% on a Knight Landing node, respectively. Our future work is to merge more time steps on distributed memory systems and on GPU.

References

1. Bailey, P., Myre, J., Walsh, S.D., Lilja, D.J., Saar, M.O.: Accelerating lattice Boltzmann fluid flow simulations using graphics processors. In: 2009 International Conference on Parallel Processing, pp. 550–557. IEEE (2009)
2. Coreixas, C., Chopard, B., Latt, J.: Comprehensive comparison of collision models in the lattice Boltzmann framework: theoretical investigations. Phys. Rev. E **100**(3), 033305 (2019)
3. Crimi, G., Mantovani, F., Pivanti, M., Schifano, S.F., Tripiccione, R.: Early experience on porting and running a Lattice Boltzmann code on the Xeon-Phi coprocessor. Procedia Comput. Sci. **18**, 551–560 (2013)
4. Feichtinger, C., Donath, S., Köstler, H., Götz, J., Rüde, U.: WaLBerla: HPC software design for computational engineering simulations. J. Comput. Sci. **2**(2), 105–112 (2011)
5. Fu, Y., Li, F., Song, F., Zhu, L.: Designing a parallel memory-aware lattice Boltzmann algorithm on manycore systems. In: 30th International Symposium on Computer Architecture and High Performance Computing, pp. 97–106. IEEE (2018)
6. Geier, M., Schönherr, M.: Esoteric twist: an efficient in-place streaming algorithms for the lattice Boltzmann method on massively parallel hardware. Computation **5**(2), 19 (2017)
7. Habich, J., Zeiser, T., Hager, G., Wellein, G.: Enabling temporal blocking for a lattice Boltzmann flow solver through multicore-aware wavefront parallelization. In: 21st International Conference on Parallel Computational Fluid Dynamics, pp. 178–182 (2009)
8. Heuveline, V., Latt, J.: The OpenLB project: an open source and object oriented implementation of lattice Boltzmann methods. Int. J. Mod. Phys. C **18**(04), 627–634 (2007)

9. Latt, J.: Technical report: How to implement your DdQq dynamics with only q variables per node (instead of 2q), pp. 1–8. Tufts University (2007)
10. Latt, J., et al.: Palabos: parallel lattice Boltzmann solver. Comput. Math. Appl. **81**, 334–350 (2020)
11. Liu, S., Zou, N., et al.: Accelerating the parallelization of lattice Boltzmann method by exploiting the temporal locality. In: International Symposium on Parallel and Distributed Processing with Applications, pp. 1186–1193. IEEE (2017)
12. Malas, T., Hager, G., Ltaief, H., Stengel, H., Wellein, G., Keyes, D.: Multicore-optimized wavefront diamond blocking for optimizing stencil updates. SIAM J. Sci. Comput. **37**(4), C439–C464 (2015)
13. Mattila, K., Hyväluoma, J., Rossi, T., Aspnäs, M., Westerholm, J.: An efficient swap algorithm for the lattice Boltzmann method. Comput. Phys. Commun. **176**(3), 200–210 (2007)
14. Mazzeo, M.D., Coveney, P.V.: HemeLB: a high performance parallel lattice-Boltzmann code for large scale fluid flow in complex geometries. Comput. Phys. Commun. **178**(12), 894–914 (2008)
15. Musubi (2021). https://geb.sts.nt.uni-siegen.de/doxy/musubi/index.html
16. OpenMP (2021). http://www.openmp.org
17. Palabos (2021). https://palabos.unige.ch/
18. Perepelkina, A., Levchenko, V.: LRnLA algorithm ConeFold with non-local vectorization for LBM implementation. In: Voevodin, V., Sobolev, S. (eds.) RuSCDays 2018. CCIS, vol. 965, pp. 101–113. Springer, Cham (2019). https://doi.org/10.1007/978-3-030-05807-4_9
19. Pohl, T., Kowarschik, M., Wilke, J., Iglberger, K., Rüde, U.: Optimization and profiling of the cache performance of parallel lattice Boltzmann codes. Parallel Process. Lett. **13**(04), 549–560 (2003)
20. Randles, A.P., Kale, V., Hammond, J., Gropp, W., Kaxiras, E.: Performance analysis of the lattice Boltzmann model beyond Navier-Stokes. In: 27th International Symposium on Parallel and Distributed Processing, pp. 1063–1074. IEEE (2013)
21. Rivera, G., Tseng, C.W.: Tiling optimizations for 3d scientific computations. In: Proceedings of the 2000 ACM/IEEE Conference on Supercomputing, SC 2000, p. 32. IEEE (2000)
22. Rosales, C., et al.: Remora: a resource monitoring tool for everyone. In: Proceedings of the 2nd International Workshop on HPC User Support Tools, pp. 1–8 (2015)
23. Slaughter, E., et al.: Task bench: a parameterized benchmark for evaluating parallel runtime performance. In: International Conference for High Performance Computing, Networking, Storage and Analysis, SC 2020, pp. 1–15. IEEE (2020)
24. Succi, S., Amati, G., Bernaschi, M., Falcucci, G., et al.: Towards exascale lattice Boltzmann computing. Comput. Fluids **181**, 107–115 (2019)
25. Valero-Lara, P.: Reducing memory requirements for large size LBM simulations on GPUs. Concurrency Computat. Pract. Exp. **29**(24), e4221 (2017)
26. Vardhan, M., Gounley, J., Hegele, L., Draeger, E.W., Randles, A.: Moment representation in the lattice Boltzmann method on massively parallel hardware. In: Proceedings of the International Conference for High Performance Computing, Networking, Storage and Analysis, SC 2019, pp. 1–21 (2019)
27. Wellein, G., Hager, G., Zeiser, T., Wittmann, M., Fehske, H.: Efficient temporal blocking for stencil computations by multicore-aware wavefront parallelization. In: 33rd Annual IEEE International Computer Software and Applications Conference, vol. 1, pp. 579–586. IEEE (2009)
28. Witherden, F.D., Jameson, A.: Future directions in computational fluid dynamics. In: 23rd AIAA Computational Fluid Dynamics Conference, p. 3791 (2017)

29. Wittmann, M., Zeiser, T., Hager, G., Wellein, G.: Comparison of different propagation steps for lattice Boltzmann methods. Comput. Math. Appl. **65**(6), 924–935 (2013)

30. Zavodszky, G., van Rooij, B., Azizi, V., Alowayyed, S., Hoekstra, A.: Hemocell: a high-performance microscopic cellular library. Procedia Comput. Sci. **108**, 159–165 (2017)

31. Zeiser, T., Wellein, G., Nitsure, A., Iglberger, K., Rude, U., Hager, G.: Introducing a parallel cache oblivious blocking approach for the lattice Boltzmann method. Prog. Comput. Fluid Dyn. Int. J. **8**(1–4), 179–188 (2008)

Fault-Tolerant LU Factorization
Is Low Cost

Camille Coti, Laure Petrucci, and Daniel Alberto Torres González[✉]

LIPN, CNRS UMR 7030, Université Sorbonne Paris Nord,
99, avenue Jean-Baptiste Clément, 93430 Villetaneuse, France
{camille.coti,laure.petrucci,torres}@lipn.univ-paris13.fr

Abstract. At large scale, failures are statistically frequent and need to be taken into account. Tolerating failures has arisen as a major challenge in parallel computing as the size of the systems grow, failures become more common and some computation units are expected to fail during the execution of a program. Algorithms used in these programs must be scalable, while being resilient to hardware failures that will happen during the execution. In this paper, we present an algorithm that takes advantage of intrinsic properties of the scalable communication-avoiding LU algorithms in order to make them fault-tolerant and proceed with the computation in spite of failures. We evaluate the overhead of the fault tolerance mechanisms with respect to failure-free execution on both tall-and-skinny matrices (TSLU) and square matrices (CALU), and the cost of a failure during the execution.

1 Introduction

Current High Performance Computing (HPC) systems have been growing for three decades and continue to grow. Now that exascale is around the corner (with the announcement of machines such as El Capitan and the EuroHPC machines), a set of challenges have been identified to be addressed for exascale [16, 22, 29]. Fault tolerance is one of them [8].

The *Top500* ranks the 500 world's most powerful supercomputers (that submit a score). The November 2020 Top500[1] rank includes 5 machines that feature more than a million of cores, and all the 500 machines listed have more than 10 000 cores. Hence, large-scale computing is no longer reserved to a handful of specialized machines, but accessible in many computation centers.

As the number of processors and nodes is increasing, HPC systems become more prone to failures [28]. Failures can arise anytime, stopping partially or totally the execution (crash-type failures) or providing incorrect results (bit errors). In this paper, we focus on failures in the fail-stop model: processes work normally until they stop working completely. Failure detectors utilized in HPC use this model, such as [5].

The challenge for fault-tolerance in HPC presents two aspects: keep the overhead on failure-free execution low and recover the execution after a failure with

---

[1] https://www.top500.org/lists/2020/11/.

© Springer Nature Switzerland AG 2021
L. Sousa et al. (Eds.): Euro-Par 2021, LNCS 12820, pp. 536–549, 2021.
https://doi.org/10.1007/978-3-030-85665-6_33

as little overhead as possible. In other words, the cost of fault tolerance and the cost of failures must remain low.

In this paper, we consider fault tolerance for a computation kernel for dense linear algebra: the LU factorization. It is a basic operation for a wide range of applications, such as solving systems of linear equations, matrix inversion or fast computation of a matrix's determinant. In particular, we examine the so-called *Communication-Avoiding* algorithm for LU factorization: CALU [21]. Such algorithms minimize inter-process communications, making them particularly interesting on current systems where the ratio between computation speed and communication speed is more and more in favor of computation speed.

These algorithms trade communications for computation. Hence, they introduce a specific shape in the algorithmic patterns, and a form of (partial) redundancy in the computation. In this paper, we propose to exploit these algorithmic and algebraic properties to introduce fault tolerance with little modification in the critical path.

Contributions. This paper provides three main contributions: 1) presentation of a fault tolerance algorithm for LU, in CALU and in TSLU, including the tournament pivoting algorithm used in TSLU; 2) evaluation of the overhead of this algorithm during failure-free execution; 3) evaluation of the cost of a failure on the overall execution time.

Outline. We first give an overview of the related literature and previous works on this topic in Sect. 2. Then, Sect. 3 describes our algorithms without and with fault-tolerance. Section 4 presents a performance evaluation of these algorithms. Finally, Sect. 5 provides concluding remarks and perspectives.

2   State of the Art

Fault tolerance has been identified as a major challenge to address towards exascale [8,16,22,28,29,31]. Indeed, a study on the pre-production phase of the the Blue Waters computer shows that the mean time between failures (MTBF) of this machine is only a few hours [27].

Approaches for fault tolerance in parallel applications can usually be classified into two categories: system-level fault tolerance and application-level fault tolerance. Most approaches for system-level fault tolerance rely on rollback recovery: a snapshot of the state of the processes is saved and can be used later to restart after a failure; the consistency of the application is restored using a distributed algorithm. A survey of the basic algorithms can be found in [17]. These techniques have been compared in practice in, for example, [7,11,25]. They have been improved drastically these last 10 years, for example using a combination of replication and machine learning [3], reducing the size of the snapshots to store in iterative methods using lossy compression [30] and bounding the error [15], asynchronous message replay [26], machine-learning [14], and finding the optimal period between two checkpoints [1,24].

The other approach consists in tolerating failures at application-level. The run-time environment must be able to survive failures and support the rest of the application in spite of failures, while allowing to restart processes in the desired semantics. For instance, FT-MPI can replace the failed process, leave a hole in the communicator or add an additional process at the end of the communicator [18]. More recently, the ULFM specification released by the working group of the MPI Forum defines a set of MPI routines to support, as the name suggests, User-Level Failure Mitigation [4].

These interfaces allow the design of fault-tolerant applications. For instance, matrix operations can use partial checksums on the grid of processes and take advantage of algebraic properties on these checksums [6,23]. An approach for stencil-based applications consists in using in-memory checkpointing [19] while masking the effects of the failure in order to progress seamlessly on the surviving processes [20]. Some specific applications can take advantage of their computation patterns, such as weather forecast [2].

This paper focuses on computation kernels for dense linear algebra and, in particular, the LU factorization. Recent advances on parallel algorithms for computing matrix factorization use a (proven) minimal number of inter-process communications [13,21]. It has been shown that the tree-based algorithm used in TSQR can be taken advantage of for fault tolerance [9] and some algebraic properties of the update of the trailing matrix can be exploited to obtain a fault-tolerant QR factorization [10]. This approach is promising in the sense that it introduces little modification in the critical path, and practical experiments showed a small overhead. In this paper, we extend this approach to the LU factorization, which, unlike QR, requires a pivoting phase and has a completely different trailing matrix update. Moreover, we conduct an experimental evaluation of the cost of failure recovery, which was not done for QR.

3   LU Factorization Algorithms

This section describes our new fault-tolerant algorithms. We focus on LU factorization and, in particular, the right-looking, panel-update algorithm.

3.1   TSLU and FT-TSLU

The LU factorization of a tall-and-skinny matrix A is the cornerstone of the LU factorization of a general matrix. It can also be used alone by applications involving a few vectors in a high-dimension space: matrix A has M rows and N columns, where $M \gg N$. In this case, the parallel algorithms use a 1D data decomposition: columns are distributed between processes that hold the full lines. The communication-avoiding LU factorization algorithm used on a 1D data decomposition is called *Tall and Skinny* LU (TSLU).

TSLU uses two consecutive reduction-like operations to compute the LU factorization of a tall-and-skinny matrix. The first phase consists of finding *pivot rows* in order to improve the numerical stability of the overall computation. This operation, known as *tournament pivoting* in communication-avoiding LU, aims at finding at low communication cost the best b row-pivots that can be used to factor the entire matrix A and put them on the final matrix U. This technique gives good performance because it depends primarily on the size of the rows in A and uses a minimal number of inter-process communications.

Algorithm 1: TSLU	**Algorithm 2:** FT-TSLU
Data: Sub-matrix $A_{i,0}$	**Data:** Sub-matrix $A_{i,0}$
1 s = 0 ;	1 s = 0 ;
2 $myrank = i$;	2 **if** *I am a spawned process* **then**
3 $U_{i,s} = $ LU$(A_{i,0})$;	3 $\lfloor U_{i,s} = $ update(s) ;
4 **while** !done() **do**	4 **else**
5 $j = $ myPartner(s) ;	5 $\lfloor U_{i,s} = $ LU$(A_{i,0})$;
6 **if** $myrank < j$ **then**	6 **while** !done() **do**
7 $| f = $ recv$(U_{j,s})$;	7 $j = $ myPartner(s) ;
8 **else**	8 $f = $ sendRecv$(U_{i,s}, U_{j,s})$;
9 $| f = $ send$(U_{i,s})$;	9 **if** FAIL $== f$ **then**
10 $\lfloor$ break;	10 $\|$ restoreFailed$(s, U_{i,s})$;
11 **if** FAIL $== f$ **then**	11 $\lfloor$ continue;
12 $\lfloor$ return;	12 $A_{i,s} = $ concatenate$(U_{i,s}, U_{j,s})$;
13 $A_{i,s} = $ concatenate$(U_{i,s}, U_{j,s})$;	13 $s = s + 1$;
14 $s = s + 1$;	14 $U_{i,s} = $ LU$(A_{i,s})$;
15 $\lfloor U_{i,s} = $ LU$(A_{i,s})$;	15 $\lfloor$ backup$(U_{i,s})$;
/* Process 0 (the root of the tree) owns the final $U_{i,s}$ */	16 $L_i = A_{i,0} \setminus U_{i,s}$;
16 broadcast$(U_{i,s}, root = 0)$;	17 **return** $L_i, U_{i,s}$;
17 $L_i = A_{i,0} \setminus U_{i,s}$;	
18 **return** $L_i, U_{i,s}$;	

The second phase is the factorization itself (see Algorithm 1). If the matrix A is distributed on t processes $P = \{P_0, P_1, \ldots, P_{t-1}\}$, each process computes the LU factorization of its local submatrix; then at each step s, half of the processes send their submatrix $U_{i,s}$ to processes at distance 2^s (line 9), that receive it (line 7) and concatenate it with their local $U_{j,s}$ (line 13). The sender is done with its participation to this part of the computation. When exiting the while loop, process 0 holds the final $U_{i,s}$. It broadcasts it to the other processes (line 16) and each process computes its local part of the L_i matrix.

Neighbor selection is made with function *myPartner(s)* (line 5). It assigns a new partner j to the local process i at step s. The value can be assigned as:

$$j = \begin{cases} i + 2^s, \text{if } i \mod 2^{s+1} == 0 \\ i - 2^s, otherwise \end{cases}$$

where i, j represent process ranks and s the step number.

The computation of TSLU follows a tree-based communication pattern in which a process's computation depends on the data computed by all the sub-tree rooted on this process. If a process fails, its sibling process cannot get the data it needs to proceed with the current step and the next ones; therefore, the computation cannot be recovered.

Knowing these shortcomings of TSLU, we introduce a Fault-Tolerant TSLU algorithm (FT-TSLU). FT-TSLU relies on a fault-tolerant run-time environment to detect crash-type process failures at run-time and restore the communicators. When an error is detected, the failed processes are respawned, the communicator used by processes to exchange information is repaired and the current computation is recovered. Examples of such behavior are illustrated in Fig. 1.

In order to be able to recover the computation, the algorithm keeps track of the states of the matrices computed at each step (except the last one), storing them over the results generated at the previous step, thus enabling all the processes to share their previous known results with a restored process if necessary. Algorithm 2 shows how fault tolerance can be achieved on the FT-TSLU algorithm, making some modifications over the TSLU original algorithm.

The basic pattern is similar to its non-fault-tolerant version. The main difference is that instead of having a sender and a receiver (the sender ending its participation after the communication), processes *exchange* local $U_{i,s}$ intermediate matrices (line 8) and, owning the same concatenated matrix, compute the same intermediate $U_{i+1,s}$. As a result, intermediate computations are replicated taking advantage of processes that would have otherwise been idle.

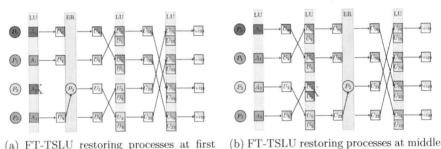

(a) FT-TSLU restoring processes at first step

(b) FT-TSLU restoring processes at middle step

Fig. 1. FT-TSLU execution examples with $t = 4$ processes and one error at different steps in the algorithm.

3.2   CALU and FT-CALU

The *Communication-Avoiding LU* [21] (CALU) algorithm factors a wider (potentially but not necessarily square) matrix A into the product of two matrices L and U by iterating over block-column sub-matrices called *panels* (Fig. 2a).

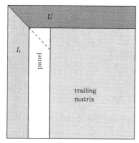 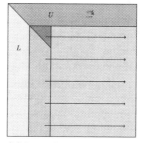 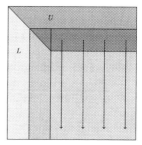

(a) Panel/update: select a panel, compute its LU factorization

(b) Broadcast the Π_{ij} and L_{ij}; pivot A_{ij} with Π_{ij} and $U_{ij} = L_{ij} \setminus A_{ij}$

(c) Update the trailing matrix: $A_{ij} -= L_{ij}U_{ij}$

Fig. 2. CALU

A panel is the leftmost block-column sub-matrix formed by non-processed sub-blocks. Since a panel can be seen as a tall and skinny matrix, CALU uses TSLU to calculate the LU factorization of each panel.

CALU can rely on a 2D data distribution (or a 2D block cyclic one). Processes belonging to the same column are in charge of decomposing the panel corresponding to their column number. During the pivoting step, the permutation matrices are broadcast on the process line to swap the whole lines of the matrix. Then, after a panel decomposition, every process involved in the calculation broadcasts its resulting $L_{i,j}$ sub-block on its row communicator to allow other processes to update the trailing matrix at the right of the panel (Fig. 2b). Then the processes on the upper row update the upper $U_{i,j}$ sub-blocks of the matrix by solving the linear system $U_{i,j} = L_{i,i} \setminus A_{i,j}$ and broadcast the result on their column communicator to enable others processes to update the remaining $A_{i,j}$ sub-blocks, doing the local operation $A'_{i,j} = A_{i,j} - L_{i,j} \times U_{i,j}$ (Fig. 2c). At this stage, CALU can take the next leftmost panel on the recently updated trailing matrix and repeat the same procedure iteratively on the trailing matrix. Algorithm 3 describes how the steps of the CALU algorithm are executed.

But the most significant changes reside in the new added functions to fully correct the failed processes, as can be seen in lines 3, 10 and 15 of Algorithm 2:

- *update(s)*: when a process p has been re-spawned, it must receive from another process the current state of the $U_{p,s}$ matrix, as well as the current step s.
- *restoreFailed(s, $U_{p,s}$)*: when a crash has been detected, all surviving processes try to restore the failed ones, sending the step s in which the error has occurred and the $U_{p,s}$ matrix. Here it must be noted that all processes do not hold the same information, so every process is able to share its own previous results only with its previous partners. When previous partners of a process are part of the surviving ones, then another processing branch has been lost and new processes must be spawned from the initial step.
- *backup($U_{p,s}$)*: performs a backup operation of the $U_{p,s}$ matrix, overwriting the previous results.

Figure 1 illustrates when failed processes are detected (*ER gray bar*) and how they are re-spawned at different steps.

At each successful data exchange the level of redundancy doubles. the number of failures that can be supported is $T_{failures} = 2^s - 1$, where s is the step number.

Algorithm 3: CALU	**Algorithm 4: FT-CALU**
Data: Square Matrix A	**Data:** Square Matrix A

```
Algorithm 3: CALU
Data: Square Matrix A
 1  while stillHasPanel() do
 2    if computing a panel then
 3      Panel = nextPanel() ;
 4      L_{i,j}, U_{i,j} = TSLU(Panel) ;
 5      BCAST(L_{i,j},row_i) ;
 6    else if comput. upper U_{i,s} then
 7      BCAST(L_{i,j},row_i) ;
 8      U_{i,j} = L_{i,j} \ A_{i,j} ;
 9      BCAST(U_{i,j},column_j) ;
10    else if updating A_{i,j} then
11      BCAST(L_{i,j},row_i) ;
12      BCAST(U_{i,j},column_j) ;
13      A_{i,j} = A_{i,j} - L_{i,j} × U_{i,j} ;
14    updateStage() ;
15  return L_{i,j},U_{i,j};
```

```
Algorithm 4: FT-CALU
Data: Square Matrix A
 1  if I am a spawned process then
 2    A_{i,j} = readBackup() ;
 3    updateStage() ;
 4  while stillHasPanel() do
 5    if computing panel then
 6      Panel = nextPanel() ;
 7      L_{i,j}, U_{i,j} = FTTSLU(Panel) ;
 8      backup(L_{i,j}) ;
 9      BCAST(L_{i,j},row_i) ;
10    else if comput. upper U_{i,s} then
11      BCAST(L_{i,j},row_i) ;
12      U_{i,j} = L_{i,j} \ A_{i,j} ;
13      backup(U_{i,j}) ;
14      BCAST(U_{i,j},column_j) ;
15    else if updating A_{i,j} then
16      BCAST(L_{i,j},row_i) ;
17      BCAST(U_{i,j},column_j) ;
18      A_{i,j} = A_{i,j} - L_{i,j} × U_{i,j} ;
19      backup(A_{i,j}) ;
20    if FAIL == f then
21      restoreFailed(current stage) ;
22      continue;
23    updateStage() ;
24  return L_{i,j},U_{i,j};
```

In lines 1, 3, 4, 5 and 14 new functions are used:

- *stillHasPanel()*: returns true if there are still panels to decompose; returns false otherwise.
- *nextPanel()*: returns the next panel.
- *TSLU(Panel)*: executes the TSLU algorithm over the panel, as described in Algorithm 1.
- *BCAST($L_{i,j}, row_i$)*: broadcast the given sub-block on the specified communicator, that could be a row or column communicator.
- *updateStage()*: updates the current stage of the algorithm; i.e., the row and column currently being processed.

As with TSLU, we have designed a fault-tolerant version of CALU: FT-CALU. As far as possible, FT-CALU exhibits the same fault-tolerance characteristics as FT-TSLU: little modifications of the critical path of the algorithm, crash-type process failures detection at run-time, re-spawning all the failed processes at once, communicator and matrix state repairing in order to proceed with the rest of the execution. It relies on the fact that CALU is based on broadcast operations, that replicate the data over the processes of a communicator.

In order to have little impact on the memory footprint, it keeps track of the results obtained at the end of an operation backing up intermediate results on the local media storage device (HD, SSD, etc.). For example, when a process ends the decomposition of a panel with FT-TSLU or when a trailing matrix sub-block has been calculated, each process stores its corresponding sub-block, replacing the results saved from a previous operation over the sub-block. This way, if a process restoration takes place, every process can have access to its last successful result and continue the execution with correct updated information. Algorithm 4 shows how fault tolerance can be achieved on CALU adding some new functions, used in lines 2, 7, 15 and 21:

- *readBackup()*: when a process has been re-spawned, it must perform a read operation of the last saved sub-block.
- *FTTSLU(Panel)*: executes the FT-TSLU algorithm over the panel, that is described in Algorithm 2.
- *backup($L_{i,j}$)*: performs a backup operation of the given sub-block, overwriting the previous results.
- *restoreFailed(current stage)*: performs a dead process restoration on the process grid.

The FT-CALU restoration algorithm proposed in this work has been designed to allow all the processes in the global communicator to detect errors at the same point in the algorithm, independently from the task a process is in charge of; thus, at the end of a broadcast and backup operation all processes can detect which processes have crashed and start the restoration procedure. This way, as with FT-TSLU, we are able to tolerate the possible errors that may appear in the CALU panel factorization and trailing matrix update, including the CALU upper panel update and the remaining trailing matrix update.

Both Algorithms 3 and 4 seem very similar in their communication patterns. In fact, both algorithms use the same process grid and the same initial distribution/partition of matrix A. The main difference between them resides in the backup and restore operations executed just after the information distribution ends. Note that every process involved in the grid calculates, updates and distributes only its corresponding $A_{i,j}$ sub-block on the row and column it belongs to. If a process has already performed its computation, it waits until the remaining working processes finish all their computations. This way, some processes will execute FT-TSLU and others will not; some processes will update a sub-block in the trailing matrix and others will not. Although not all processes have the same tasks to run, they execute at least one dense operation (panel decomposition, a linear solving, matrix multiplication) during the execution of the algorithm and thus the computation load is more evenly distributed. Thus, we can take advantage of the parallel resources.

4   Experiments

We implemented the algorithms described in Sect. 3 and evaluated their performance on the Grid'5000 platform. We used the *Gros* cluster, which has 124 nodes, each of which featuring one Intel Xeon Gold 5220 CPU, 18 cores/CPU, 96GB of RAM, two SSDs of 447GB and a 894GB SSD, and 2 x 25Gb Ethernet NICs. The nodes run a Debian 9.2 Linux-based operating system, and the code was compiled using gcc 8.3 with the -O3 optimization flag. We used OpenMPI 4.1.0 for non-fault-tolerant executions and ULFM 4.1.0u1a1 for the fault-tolerant ones, and OpenBLAS 0.3.8. Input matrix sizes used for testing are 32768×32768, 65536×65536 and 100200×100200, using the OpenBLAS DLARNV subroutine with uniform distribution to randomly generate them. Every experiment was run 10 times and the plots presented in this section present the average values and standard deviation of the largest input matrix.

Failures are injected by sending a SIGKILL signal to the processes. In this case, the operating system sends closing notifications on the TCP sockets used by the run-time environment and the failures are detected immediately. In real life, this cannot happen when a failure occurs and we need to rely on a more advanced failure detection mechanism [5]. Although there exist more realistic techniques to inject failures, we chose not to use them in order to isolate the *algorithmic* cost from the *system* cost, and evaluate the performance of our algorithms separately from some system-specific costs.

4.1   TSLU

Figure 3 compares the execution times of our implementation of TSLU and FT-TSLU. Both of them scale as the number of processes increases. We can see that the failure-free execution time of the fault-tolerant and the non-fault-tolerant versions are similar: the overhead due to the modifications of the communication pattern to introduce fault tolerance are negligible, and OpenMPI and ULFM give similar performance in this context. As expected, failures introduce an overhead. However, we can see that this overhead is very small.

4.2   CALU

Figure 4 compares the execution times of our implementation of CALU and FT-CALU. Likewise, they scale well and the relative overhead of our fault-tolerance mechanisms is very small. It must be noticed that the impact of a failure on the total execution time is very small, like with FT-TSLU. This result shows that exploiting intrinsic redundancies that exist is CALU is a good approach to recover from failures and proceed with the rest of the execution.

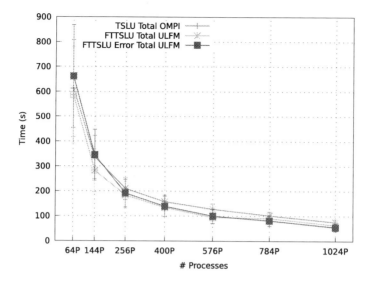

Fig. 3. Comparison of the execution times of TSLU, matrix size 100200 × 100200

When an error is detected and a new process is spawned, the recovery step involves data exchanges to restore the state of the failed process before the crash. This recovery time is presented in Fig. 5: we can see it increases slightly as the number of processes increase, because of the synchronizing operations on the communicator.

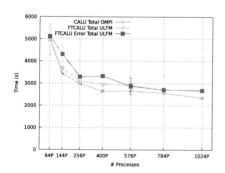

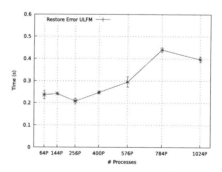

Fig. 4. (FT-)CALU execution time, matrix size 100200 × 100200

Fig. 5. FT-CALU recovery time, matrix size 100200 × 100200

Figure 6 presents a comparison of our FT-CALU executions with all tested matrix sizes. As expected, scalability swiftly increases as the amount of processes increase as well as the matrix size, specially failure-free executions. When a failure occurs, performance looks minimally hit compared against a failure-free FT-CALU execution.

In general, the overall performance increases with the number of processes. As expected, the scalability and the performance per process increase as the size of the matrix increases and the algorithms' good parallelism properties get satisfying performance on the parallel platform, for both fault-tolerant and non-fault-tolerant version of TSLU and CALU.

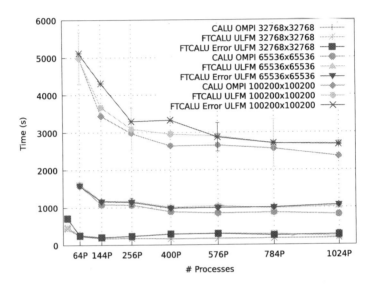

Fig. 6. Comparison of the scalability of FT-CALU for different matrix sizes.

5   Conclusions and Perspectives

In this paper, we have presented an algorithm to perform the LU factorization of a dense matrix in parallel in a context of crash-type failures. The need for fault-tolerant parallel applications has arisen during the last decade and is considered as a major challenge on the road to exascale [16,31]. The algorithms presented here can be used in two contexts: as a computation kernel, guaranteeing the user that if a failure happens during the factorization it will be dealt with automatically, or implementing this algorithm in a fault-tolerant application that calls an LU factorization.

We exploited structural properties of the communication-avoiding LU factorization algorithm [21] in order to introduce intrinsic redundancies upon failures in order to restore the state of the failed processes and minimize the amount of computation required to resume computation. We applied these ideas to the LU factorization of a tall-and-skinny matrix (TSLU) and of a regular matrix. The robustness of the algorithm for TSLU was previously modeled and proved in [12].

We measured the overhead of the fault tolerance mechanisms introduced in the algorithm on the execution time of failure-free executions and the total cost of a failure during the execution. Since our algorithms introduce little modification of the critical path, the overhead on failure-free execution is not significant. The cost of a failure on the total execution time is very important in a context where failures can happen at any time and must not be significantly harmful for the computation. We have seen that the overhead caused by a failure is very small and does not have any significant impact on the execution time.

Therefore, we have seen that our approach based on exploiting intrinsic (partial) redundancies in this communication-avoiding algorithm is sound, both since it has little impact on the failure-free performance and the existence of (partial) intermediate results that new processes can start from allows for a quick post-failure recovery.

The conclusions from this paper are encouraging and open perspectives for applying this approach to other computation kernels, for dense and sparse linear algebra.

Acknowledgement. Experiments presented in this paper were carried out using the Grid'5000 testbed, supported by a scientific interest group hosted by Inria and including CNRS, RENATER and several Universities as well as other organizations(see https://www.grid5000.fr).

The authors would like to thank Julien Langou for the discussions on the numerical stability of the computation of the L matrix.

References

1. Aupy, G., Benoit, A., Hérault, T., Robert, Y., Dongarra, J.: Optimal checkpointing period: time vs. energy. In: Jarvis, S.A., Wright, S.A., Hammond, S.D. (eds.) PMBS 2013. LNCS, vol. 8551, pp. 203–214. Springer, Cham (2014). https://doi.org/10.1007/978-3-319-10214-6_10
2. Benacchio, T., et al.: Resilience and fault-tolerance in high-performance computing for numerical weather and climate prediction. Int. J. High Perform. Comput. Appl. (2020)
3. Benoît, A., Cavelan, A., Cappello, F., Raghavan, P., Robert, Y., Sun, H.: Coping with silent and fail-stop errors at scale by combining replication and checkpointing. J. Parallel Distrib. Comput. **122**, 209–225 (2018)
4. Bland, W., Bouteiller, A., Herault, T., Hursey, J., Bosilca, G., Dongarra, J.J.: An evaluation of user-level failure mitigation support in MPI. In: Träff, J.L., Benkner, S., Dongarra, J.J. (eds.) Recent Advances in the Message Passing Interface, pp. 193–203. Springer, Berlin (2012). https://doi.org/10.1007/978-3-642-33518-1_24
5. Bosilca, G., et al.: Failure detection and propagation in HPC systems. In: SC 2016: Proceedings of the International Conference for High Performance Computing, Networking, Storage and Analysis, pp. 312–322 (2016)
6. Bosilca, G., Delmas, R., Dongarra, J., Langou, J.: Algorithm-based fault tolerance applied to high performance computing. J. Parallel Distrib. Comput. **69**(4), 410–416 (2009)
7. Bouteiller, A., Herault, T., Krawezik, G., Lemarinier, P., Cappello, F.: MPICH-V project: a multiprotocol automatic fault-tolerant MPI. Int. J. High Perform. Comput. Appl. **20**(3), 319–333 (2006)

8. Cappello, F., Geist, A., Gropp, W., Kale, S., Kramer, B., Snir, M.: Toward exascale resilience: 2014 update. Supercomputing frontiers and innovations **1**(1), 5–28 (2014)

9. Coti, C.: Exploiting redundant computation in communication-avoiding algorithms for algorithm-based fault tolerance. In: 2016 IEEE 2nd International Conference on Big Data Security on Cloud (BigDataSecurity), IEEE International Conference on High Performance and Smart Computing (HPSC), and IEEE International Conference on Intelligent Data and Security (IDS), pp. 214–219 (2016). https://doi.org/10.1109/BigDataSecurity-HPSC-IDS.2016.59

10. Coti, C.: Scalable, robust, fault-tolerant parallel QR factorization. In: 2016 IEEE International Conference on Computational Science and Engineering (CSE) and IEEE International Conference on Embedded and Ubiquitous Computing (EUC) and 15th International Symposium on Distributed Computing and Applications for Business Engineering (DCABES), pp. 626–633 (2016). https://doi.org/10.1109/CSE-EUC-DCABES.2016.250

11. Coti, C., et al.: Blocking vs. non-blocking coordinated checkpointing for large-scale fault tolerant MPI. In: SC 2006: Proceedings of the 2006 ACM/IEEE Conference on Supercomputing, p. 18 (2006)

12. Coti, C., Petrucci, L., Torres Gonzalez, D.A.: Fault-tolerant matrix factorisation: a formal model and proof. In: 6th International Workshop on Synthesis of Complex Parameters (SynCoP) 2019 (2019)

13. Demmel, J., Grigori, L., Hoemmen, M., Langou, J.: Communication-optimal parallel and sequential QR and LU factorizations. SIAM J. Sci. Comput. **34**(1), 206–239 (2012). https://doi.org/10.1137/080731992

14. Dey, T., et al.: Optimizing asynchronous multi-level checkpoint/restart configurations with machine learning. In: 2020 IEEE International Parallel and Distributed Processing Symposium Workshops (IPDPSW), pp. 1036–1043. IEEE (2020)

15. Di, S., Cappello, F.: Optimization of error-bounded lossy compression for hard-to-compress HPC data. IEEE Trans. Parallel Distrib. Syst. **29**(1), 129–143 (2017)

16. Dongarra, J., et al.: The international exascale software project roadmap. Int. J. High Perform. Comput. Appl. **25**(1), 3–60 (2011)

17. Elnozahy, E.N.M., Alvisi, L., Wang, Y.M., Johnson, D.B.: A survey of rollback-recovery protocols in message-passing systems. ACM Comput. Surv. **34**(3), 375–408 (2002). https://doi.org/10.1145/568522.568525

18. Fagg, G.E., Dongarra, J.J.: FT-MPI: fault tolerant MPI, supporting dynamic applications in a dynamic world. In: Dongarra, J., Kacsuk, P., Podhorszki, N. (eds.) EuroPVM/MPI 2000. LNCS, vol. 1908, pp. 346–353. Springer, Heidelberg (2000). https://doi.org/10.1007/3-540-45255-9_47

19. Gamell, M., et al.: Evaluating online global recovery with fenix using application-aware in-memory checkpointing techniques. In: 2016 45th International Conference on Parallel Processing Workshops (ICPPW), pp. 346–355 (2016)

20. Gamell, M., et al.: Exploring failure recovery for stencil-based applications at extreme scales. In: Proceedings of the 24th International Symposium on High-Performance Parallel and Distributed Computing, pp. 279–282. HPDC 2015, Association for Computing Machinery, New York (2015). https://doi.org/10.1145/2749246.2749260

21. Grigori, L., Demmel, J.W., Xiang, H.: CALU: a communication optimal LU factorization algorithm. SIAM J. Matrix Anal. Appl. **32**(4), 1317–1350 (2011). https://doi.org/10.1137/100788926

22. Gropp, W., Snir, M.: Programming for exascale computers. Comput. Sci. Eng. **15**, 27 (2013)

23. Huang, K.H., Abraham, J.A.: Algorithm-based fault tolerance for matrix operations. IEEE Trans. Comput. **100**(6), 518–528 (1984)
24. Jones, W.M., Daly, J.T., DeBardeleben, N.: Impact of sub-optimal checkpoint intervals on application efficiency in computational clusters. In: Proceedings of the 19th ACM International Symposium on High Performance Distributed Computing, pp. 276–279 (2010)
25. Lemarinier, P., Bouteiller, A., Herault, T., Krawezik, G., Cappello, F.: Improved message logging versus improved coordinated checkpointing for fault tolerant MPI. In: 2004 IEEE International Conference on Cluster Computing (IEEE Cat. No. 04EX935), pp. 115–124. IEEE (2004)
26. Losada, N., Bouteiller, A., Bosilca, G.: Asynchronous receiver-driven replay for local rollback of MPI applications. In: 2019 IEEE/ACM 9th Workshop on Fault Tolerance for HPC at eXtreme Scale (FTXS), pp. 1–10. IEEE (2019)
27. Martino, C.D., Kalbarczyk, Z., Iyer, R.K., Baccanico, F., Fullop, J., Kramer, W.: Lessons learned from the analysis of system failures at petascale: the case of blue waters. In: Proceedings of the 2014 44th Annual IEEE/IFIP International Conference on Dependable Systems and Networks, DSN 2014, pp. 610–621. IEEE Computer Society, Washington (2014). https://doi.org/10.1109/DSN.2014.62
28. Reed, D., Lu, C., Mendes, C.: Reliability challenges in large systems. Future Gener. Comput. Syst. **22**(3), 293–302 (2006). https://doi.org/10.1016/j.future.2004.11.015
29. Shalf, J., Dosanjh, S., Morrison, J.: Exascale computing technology challenges. In: Palma, J.M.L.M., Daydé, M., Marques, O., Lopes, J.C. (eds.) VECPAR 2010. LNCS, vol. 6449, pp. 1–25. Springer, Heidelberg (2011). https://doi.org/10.1007/978-3-642-19328-6_1
30. Tao, D., Di, S., Liang, X., Chen, Z., Cappello, F.: Improving performance of iterative methods by lossy checkponting. In: Proceedings of the 27th International Symposium on High-performance Parallel and Distributed Computing, pp. 52–65 (2018)
31. Thakur, R., et al.: MPI at exascale. In: Procceedings of SciDAC 2010 (2010)

Mixed Precision Incomplete and Factorized Sparse Approximate Inverse Preconditioning on GPUs

Fritz Göbel[1([☒])], Thomas Grützmacher[1], Tobias Ribizel[1], and Hartwig Anzt[1,2]

[1] Karlsruhe Institute of Technology, Karlsruhe, Germany
fritz.goebel@kit.edu
[2] University of Tennessee, Knoxville, USA

Abstract. In this work, we present highly efficient mixed precision GPU-implementations of an Incomplete Sparse Approximate Inverse (ISAI) preconditioner for general non-symmetric matrices and a Factorized Sparse Approximate Inverse (FPSAI) preconditioner for symmetric positive definite matrices. While working with full double precision in all arithmetic operations, we demonstrate the benefit of decoupling the memory precision and storing the preconditioner in a more compact low precision floating point format to reduce the memory access volume and therefore preconditioner application time.

Keywords: Mixed precision · Preconditioning · Incomplete Sparse Approximate Inverse · Factorized Sparse Approximate Inverse · GPUs

1 Introduction

The solution of large sparse linear systems $Ax = b$ is a ubiquitous problem in scientific computing applications, with iterative solvers like Krylov subspace methods being often the tool of choice. In practice, these iterative solvers are usually combined with preconditioners to improve their convergence behavior. In particular for ill-conditioned matrices A, transforming the linear system with an appropriate preconditioner M into an equivalent, (left-)preconditioned system $MAx = Mb$ can lead to great convergence and runtime improvements.

An efficient preconditioner is an approximation $M \approx A^{-1}$ such that MA has a lower condition number than A and the Krylov method needs fewer iterations to converge. For this approach to be efficient in the execution-time metric, the overhead of generating and applying the preconditioner has to be smaller than the runtime improvement from accelerated convergence. Most Krylov methods allow for a high degree of parallelization, so considering the increasingly large amount of parallel resources available on modern manycore CPUs and GPUs, efficient preconditioners do not only need to provide good approximation properties, but also take advantage of massively parallel hardware.

© Springer Nature Switzerland AG 2021
L. Sousa et al. (Eds.): Euro-Par 2021, LNCS 12820, pp. 550–564, 2021.
https://doi.org/10.1007/978-3-030-85665-6_34

The (left) Incomplete Sparse Approximate Inverse (ISAI) preconditioner [7] computes a sparse approximation M on the inverse of A by ensuring the ISAI-property $(MA - I)_S = 0$ holds on a given sparsity pattern S, which is commonly chosen based on the sparsity pattern of A. The ISAI preconditioner offers a lot of parallelism in the generation phase, as every row of the preconditioner can be computed independently, and its application is a simple sparse matrix-vector product (SpMV).

In scientific simulations, very often one wants to solve symmetric positive definite (spd) linear systems. Among the most efficient solvers for spd problems is the Conjugate Gradient (CG) method. Unfortunately, the ISAI preconditioner, as well as other sparse approximate inverse preconditioners generally do not preserve the symmetry of the input matrix [7,11]. However, a slight modification turns the ISAI preconditioner into the Factorized Sparse Approximate Inverse preconditioner (commonly referred to as FSPAI) as presented in [12]. Being an approximation to the exact Cholesky factorization, the FSPAI preconditioner preserves the spd-ness of the system matrix in the preconditioner, and therewith can be used in conjunction with the CG method to solve the preconditioned system. The downside is that applying the FSPAI preconditioner requires two SpMV operations per iteration instead of one when using ISAI preconditioning.

On modern hardware architectures, the performance of sparse linear algebra kernels is typically limited by memory bandwidth, less so by compute power. That is, the memory access volume in combination with the main memory bandwidth determines the execution time of an algorithm. To address this bottleneck, Anzt et al. [6] proposed to decouple the memory precision format from the arithmetic precision format via a *memory accessor*, practically compressing all data in memory before and after performing arithmetic operations in the processor registers. They propose to perform all arithmetic operations in the natively-supported IEEE 754 double precision format, but to use more compact and imprecise formats to store and read the numerical values. As long as the object can tolerate some compression-induced rounding errors, using this strategy can significantly reduce the runtime of memory-bound algorithms. In this work, we adopt the strategy of decoupling the memory precision from the arithmetic precision and a memory accessor implementation [3] available in Ginkgo [2] for ISAI and FSPAI preconditioning. We always compute and apply the preconditioners in double precision, but utilize the memory accessor to use a lower precision format for the memory operations.

For introducing the idea of mixed precision ISAI and FSPAI preconditioning, presenting the respective software realizations, and demonstrating the practical benefits in a performance analysis on high-end GPUs, the rest of this paper is structured as follows. In Sect. 2 we revisit the ISAI algorithm as presented in [7]. Section 3 describes the extension of this approach to FSPAI preconditioners for spd problems as introduced in [12]. We present an efficient GPU-implementation of the preconditioner generation in Sect. 4.1 before explaining how we make use of mixed precision in the preconditioner application with a memory accessor in Sect. 4.2. In Sect. 5, we demonstrate the practical usability and performance advantages in an experimental evaluation using various test problems from the SuiteSparse Matrix Collection [1]. We summarize our results and give an outlook on future research in Sect. 6.

2   Incomplete Sparse Approximate Inverses for General Matrices

A popular technique for preconditioning sparse linear systems is based on incomplete factorizations: We can approximate the factorization $A \approx L \cdot U$ with sparse triangular factors L and U with only a subset of the fill-in that is usually introduced by a full LU factorization. This incomplete factorization is required to be exact only on a certain sparsity pattern $\mathcal{S}$ (e.g. the sparsity pattern of A^k for ILU(k)), meaning

$$(LU)_{ij} = A_{ij} \quad \forall (i,j) \in \mathcal{S}. \tag{1}$$

A bottleneck in using incomplete factorization preconditioners on parallel architectures is that the generation of the triangular factors is an inherently sequential process, with a long critical path and parallelism only existing in the form of smaller sets of unknowns that can be computed independently (level scheduling [14]). Applying an incomplete factorization preconditioner involves solving two triangular systems via forward and backward substitution, which again exposes very limited parallelism. The *Incomplete Sparse Approximate Inverse* (ISAI [7]) algorithm was initially suggested to accelerate the application of incomplete factorization preconditioners. It replaces the forward and backward triangular solves by a matrix-vector multiplication with the approximate inverses of L and U. The approximation is called *incomplete* since we again require the inverse to be exact only on a limited sparsity pattern S. While replacing forward and backward substitution with the ISAI application greatly accelerate the application phase of incomplete sparse approximate inverse preconditioners, the bottleneck of computing the incomplete factorizations in the first place remains. However, the ISAI can also be computed for general matrices. This allows generating the ISAI preconditioner for the system matrix itself, therewith skipping the factorization generation and further reducing the preconditioner application cost to one SpMV per iteration.

Building on the incompleteness property (1), for a given sparsity pattern $\mathcal{S}$, we define the ISAI property as

$$(MA - I)_{\mathcal{S}} = 0 :\Leftrightarrow (MA - I)_{i,j} = 0 \quad \forall (i,j) \in \mathcal{S}. \tag{2}$$

In the following, we will assume that the preconditioner sparsity pattern is given by a power of A, i.e. that $\mathcal{S}(M) = \mathcal{S}(A^k)$ for some $k \in \mathbb{N}$. With $\mathcal{I} := \{j \mid (i,j) \in \mathcal{S}(M)\}$ being the sparsity pattern of the i-th row of M, the ISAI property (2) can be rewritten as

$$\sum_{k \in \mathcal{I}} m_{ik} a_{kj} = \delta_{ij} \quad \text{for all } j \in \mathcal{I}. \tag{3}$$

This equation is equivalent to the linear system $M(i, \mathcal{I})A(\mathcal{I}, \mathcal{I}) = I(i, \mathcal{I})$ where I is the $n \times n$ identity matrix. To compute the preconditioner M, we transpose the requirement and solve n (typically small) independent linear systems $\tilde{A}x_i = b$ with $\tilde{A}_i = A^T(\mathcal{I}, \mathcal{I})$ and $b = I(\mathcal{I}, i)$, $i = 1, ..., n$. For convenience, we provide the algorithmic description for computing the ISAI preconditioner for a general matrix A by solving n independent linear systems via the Gauss-Jordan-Elimination in Listing 1.1.

Listing 1.1. Algorithm computing the (left) ISAI preconditioner for an $n \times n$ square matrix A on a given sparsity pattern $\mathcal{S}$.

```
1   % Parallel For-Loop
2   for i=1:n
3       % Extract nonzero indices of i-th row of A.
4       I = nonzero_indices(A(i,:));
5       small_dense = transpose(A)(I, I);
6       % The right hand side is composed of the relevant
7       % entries of the i-th unit vector.
8       b = identity(n);
9       b = b(I, i);
10      % Solve small systems with Gauss-Jordan-Elimination.
11      x = small_dense \ b;
12      M(i,I) = transpose(x);
13  end
```

Note that for the preconditioner to be well-defined, all $\tilde{A}_i$ need to be non-singular. This is a strong requirement that is not fulfilled in general for non-symmetric matrices A. At the same time, our experimental evaluation in Sect. 5 reveals that in practice, this strategy succeeds for many systems, providing significant convergence improvement.

3   Factorized Sparse Approximate Inverses for SPD Matrices

We have seen that computing the ISAI preconditioner for general matrices requires all $\tilde{A}_i$ systems to be non-singular. While this requirement is fulfilled for an spd matrix A, the preconditioner matrix M resulting from applying the ISAI Algorithm (Listing 1.1) to an spd matrix is generally not again spd. In consequence, it is not possible to use the general ISAI preconditioner in combination with a CG solver that heavily relies on the spd property. A workaround is to compute an approximation to the (unknown) exact Cholesky factor $A = CC^T$. As we will review next, this *Factorized Sparse Approximate Inverse* (FSPAI [12]) preserves the spd-ness of the system matrix in the preconditioner.

For that, let $A = CC^T$ be the exact Cholesky factorization of A. Computing an ISAI of C on the sparsity pattern of the lower triangular part of A, $\mathcal{S}(\text{tril}(A))$ requires computing a matrix L with

$$LC = I \text{ on } \mathcal{S}(\text{tril}(A)). \tag{4}$$

Obviously, with C being unknown, this is not possible. However, multiplying C^T to (4) from the right yields

$$LCC^T = LA = C^T \text{ on } \mathcal{S}(\text{tril}(A)). \tag{5}$$

With $\mathcal{S}(C)$ only containing nonzero entries on the lower triangular part, this only puts restrictions on the main diagonal of L. While the diagonal entries of C are generally not available information, (5) is equivalent to computing an ISAI of A on $\mathcal{S}(C)$ up to diagonal scaling. Imposing the diagonal part of the ISAI condition (2) on the complete spd preconditioned system $LCC^T L^T = LAL^T$ yields the requirements

$$(LA)_{i,j} = 0, (i,j) \in \mathcal{S}(\text{tril}(A)), \quad i \neq j \text{ and} \tag{6}$$
$$(LAL^T)_{i,i} = 1, \quad i = 1, ..., n \tag{7}$$

for computing the FSPAI of A. Given the similarity between the ISAI and the FSPAI conditions, the FSPAI preconditioner can be computed efficiently with a modified ISAI implementation that appends diagonal scaling, see Listing 1.2. The computed triangular matrix L can then be used to transform the original system into a preconditioned system while preserving the spd property:

$$L^T LAx = L^T Lb. \tag{8}$$

In practice, the FSPAI preconditioner can thus be implemented in the CG iterative solver as two matrix-vector multiplications with the FSPAI preconditioner L and L^T, respectively.

Listing 1.2. Algorithm computing an FSPAI preconditioner for a $n \times n$ spd matrix A on the sparsity pattern of tril(A).

```
1  L = isai(A); % on S(tril(A))
2  D = diag(L);
3  D = 1 ./ sqrt(D);
4  L = D * L;
```

4   Mixed Precision Incomplete and Factorized Approximate Inverse Preconditioners on GPUs

4.1   Generating the ISAI and FSPAI Operators

As discussed in Sect. 2, all rows of the preconditioner matrix M can be computed in parallel. For rows containing only a few nonzeros, the corresponding linear systems are of small size and can be solved efficiently via Gauss-Jordan elimination [5]. For rows containing many nonzeros, this approach quickly becomes unattractive due to the exploding computational cost and dense storage requirements of the Gauss-Jordan elimination. Therefore, we distinguish between "short" and "long" rows, treating them differently in the preconditioner generation.

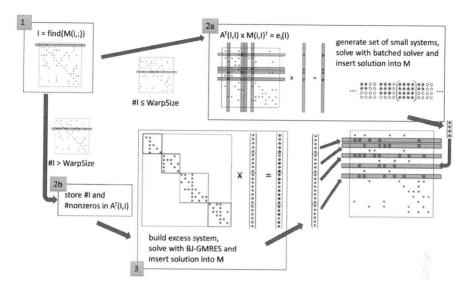

Fig. 1. Preconditioner generation of an ISAI preconditioner matrix M for a square, non-symmetric matrix A. The considered sparsity pattern for M is chosen to equal the sparsity pattern of A. For visualization purposes, the warp size is presumed to be 4.

To compute the ISAI of a matrix A stored in CSR format, the GPU implementation visualized in Fig. 1 launches one warp of size `WarpSize` (32 threads for NVIDIA GPUs) per row of A. The number of nonzeros in each row can simply be derived as the difference of the consecutive row pointer entries. Depending on the nonzero count, the computation of the values in this row is handled via a direct or an iterative method:

(a) $\leq$ `WarpSize` nonzeros: **Batched Gauss-Jordan Elimination with row pivoting**. The warp extracts the small local linear system into shared memory, each thread handling one row. After solving the local system via batched Gauss-Jordan elimination [5], the solution is written out to the preconditioner matrix.

(b) $>$ `WarpSize` nonzeros: **Block-Jacobi preconditioned GMRES.** The warp records the row id and the nonzero count for later processing.

To extract the rows and columns belonging to the small local system, we use an in-register implementation of the *MergePath* parallel merging algorithm [10] to find matching entries (i, j) between the current preconditioner row i and all corresponding rows j defining the extracted block. This strategy storing the block in row-major order for efficient processing via the Gauss-Jordan elimination avoids the otherwise necessary transposition of the local system matrix in shared memory.

After this step, all short rows of the preconditioner have been computed, and the algorithm has to process the long rows. Using the row IDs and the nonzero counts, we generate a block-diagonal "excess system" matrix placing all local systems as a block on the main diagonal. This excess system is then approximately solved via a GMRES solver preconditioned with a block-Jacobi preconditioner, therewith making use of the excess system's inherent block structure. Finally, the solution is again split up and scattered into the corresponding preconditioner rows. Even though this strategy allows for also handling rows with nonzero counts larger than the warp size, this approach becomes unattractive for systems containing many nonzeros in a row, as then, the different blocks contain many redundancies as they were extracted from matching parts of A. We note that when working on triangular sparsity pattern, e.g. when computing an FSPAI preconditioner for an spd matrix, reordering can help to reduce the number of nonzeros accumulated in a single row, see Fig. 2.

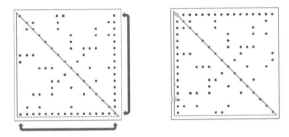

Fig. 2. For the FSPAI operating on the lower triangular part of the system matrix, reordering can help balancing of nonzero entries across the rows.

In general, any sparse matrix format can be used to store the ISAI or FSPAI preconditioners. However, the preconditioners are most efficient if all rows contain a similar number of nonzero elements and no row requires the generation of an excess system. On GPUs, matrices with such a "balanced" nonzero distribution can be handled efficiently via the ELL format. This format enforces all rows to have the same number of nonzeros by explicitly storing zero values for padding. Once a uniform row length is enforced, the ELL format allows for efficient SIMD processing, enabling the ELL SpMV to achieve much higher performance than the CSR-based SpMV [8]. Therefore, after generating the ISAI and FSPAI preconditioners, we convert them to the ELL format to allow for efficient SpMV processing in the preconditioner application.

4.2 Mixed Precision Preconditioner Application

The preconditioner application is among the most expensive operations within most Krylov solvers, aside from the multiplication with the system matrix itself. So to improve the runtime of the preconditioner application, we employ a mixed precision technique that has previously been used successfully for block-Jacobi preconditioning [9]: Since preconditioners are just an approximation to the inverse system matrix, it is often possible to add small rounding errors by storing their entries in a lower precision format. Due to the typically memory-bound performance characteristics of sparse numerical linear algebra kernels, a reduction in the memory footprint of the preconditioner storage translates almost directly into a performance improvement of the preconditioner application. When using such low precision storage, we have to consider two aspects: 1) The rounding errors introduced by lower storage precision can cause the preconditioner itself to lose regularity, which may prevent convergence of the overall Krylov method; 2) The computations themselves must still be performed in high precision, otherwise we would lose precision in the iteration vectors and, due to the preconditioner application becoming a non-constant linear operator, would require the use of a flexible Krylov solver [4].

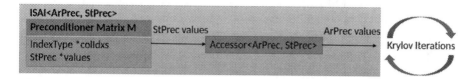

Fig. 3. The *memory accessor* converts STPREC values to ARPREC on the fly, reducing memory movement.

The implementation of mixed precision operations in the Ginkgo library makes use of the so-called *memory accessor* [3] to provide a uniform interface decoupling the storage precision from the arithmetic precision used to perform computations. We consider three different configurations for the preconditioner storage and application: While always performing computations in IEEE 754 double precision, we store the preconditioner values in double (FP64), single (FP32) or half precision (FP16). The corresponding preconditioners are denoted by ISAI<ARPREC, STPREC> and FSPAI<ARPREC, STPREC>, where ARPREC indicates the precision format used in the arithmetic operations and STPREC indicates the precision format used for storing the preconditioner. The *memory accessor* reads STPREC values from memory and converts them to ARPREC values on the fly before applying the preconditioner matrix, see Fig. 3.

For the full implementation of the discussed preconditioners, we refer to the Ginkgo github repository[1].

5   Numerical Experiments

In this section, we evaluate the performance of the mixed precision ISAI and mixed precision FSPAI preconditioners storing the numeric values in lower precision while performing all arithmetic in double precision. This means that the

---

[1] https://github.com/ginkgo-project/ginkgo/pull/719.

preconditioner generation is the same for all precision combinations. The objective of our experiments is to study the effect using a lower precision memory format in the preconditioner application has on the numerical stability and runtime of Krylov methods. Thus, we compare and validate our mixed-precision preconditioners against the full (double) precision versions of the same preconditioners and refrain from repeating experiments showing their general validity (see [7,12]). For the experimental evaluation, we use test matrices of moderate size (more than 20,000 rows; less than 50,000,000 nonzeros) that generally have a low nonzero-per-row ratio. We list the selected non-symmetric and spd test matrices along with some key properties in Tables 1 and 2 in the Appendix. In the experimental evaluation, we first investigate the general ISAI preconditioner in the context of a BiCGSTAB method solving non-symmetric problems. Afterward, we assess an FSPAI-preconditioned CG solver for the spd problems. If not specifically stated otherwise, we use a relative residual stopping criterion of $\frac{\|b-Ax\|}{\|b\|} < 10^{-7}$ and a hard iteration limit of 20,000 iterations for BiCGSTAB and 10,000 iterations for CG, respectively. We always use an all-zero initial guess and a right-hand side of all ones.

5.1   Hardware Setup

The GPU we use in our experiments is a NVIDIA V100 PCIe with 16 GB of main memory, a memory bandwidth of 900 GB/s, and a theoretical peak performance of 7 TFLOPS in double precision [13]. All code and functionality necessary to reproduce the results are publicly available via the benchmark suite of the Ginkgo open source library [2]. The CUDA toolkit version 10.2 was used to compile Ginkgo and the kernels generating and applying the preconditioners.

5.2   General ISAI

To evaluate the preconditioner quality of the general ISAI algorithm, we use a preconditioned BiCGSTAB solver for the 39 non-symmetric test-matrices listed in Table 1. In all these cases, an ISAI preconditioner stored in double precision is able to reduce the number of BiCGSTAB iterations. To assess the preconditioner quality degradation introduced by rounding the numeric values to lower precision, we visualize in the top plot in Fig. 4 the ratio between BiCGSTAB preconditioned with mixed precision ISAI and BiCGSTAB preconditioned with double precision ISAI. We recall that the mixed precision ISAI preconditioners preserve double precision in all arithmetic operations, but employ either single precision or half precision for the memory operations (denoted with ISAI<FP64,FP32> and ISAI<FP64,FP16>, respectively). The mixed precision ISAI employing single precision for the memory operations preserves the convergence of the BiCGSTAB solver for all problems, introducing a convergence delay of more than 3% only for the EPB3 problem. Conversely, ISAI<FP64,FP16> fails to preserve the preconditioner quality for about half the problems.

    Ignoring the potential convergence delay, we visualize in the center of Fig. 4 the mixed precision ISAI speedup over the double precision ISAI. We note that

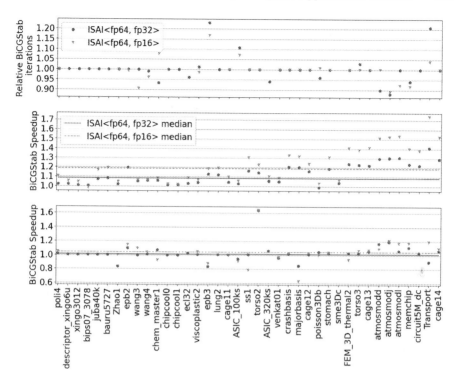

Fig. 4. *Top*: Relative iteration counts for BiCGSTAB using lower precision preconditioner storage compared to double precision. Cases where half precision use results
in lower iteration counts are related to rounding effects. *Center*: Speedup of a single mixed precision ISAI application vs. double precision. The speedup ratios ignore
the quality degradation of the preconditioner when using low precision storage. *Bottom*: BiCGSTAB speedup when using an ISAI preconditioner stored in lower precision
instead of a double precision ISAI. Missing dots indicate the loss of convergence when
using the mixed precision ISAI variant. The horizontal lines display the median among
all values without loss of convergence. BiCGSTAB runtimes do not include the preconditioner generation. *Note*: The matrices are sorted according to their nonzero count
along the x-axis.

the format conversion between memory precision and arithmetic precision is
completely hidden behind the memory access, and all speedups are a direct result
of the reduced memory footprint. While generally growing with the number of
nonzero entries, the speedup reflects the intertwined relation between nonzeros,
precision format, cache size, and the interplay of sparsity pattern and vector data
reuse. As expected, the speedups are generally larger when using half precision
storage, making this an attractive choice if the numerical properties allow for it.

The center of Fig. 4 not only ignores the potential numerical breakdown of an
ISAI preconditioner when rounding to lower precision, but also the fact that the
preconditioner application accounts only for a fraction of a BiCGSTAB solver

iteration. On the bottom of Fig. 4, we quantify the actual savings rendered to the total execution time of a BiCGSTAB iterative solver when replacing a double precision ISAI with its mixed precision variant. We note that additional BiCGSTAB iterations are hardly compensated by faster ISAI application, but for mild convergence variations, the speedups of the mixed precision ISAI preconditioner translate to moderate runtime reduction of the overall BiCGSTAB solver.

5.3   FSPAI

To evaluate the mixed precision FSPAI preconditioner, we use the spd test matrices listed in Table 2. Most of these problems are arising from 2D or 3D finite element discretizations.

The top plot in Fig. 5 indicates that the FSPAI preconditioner quality is barely affected from storing the preconditioner values in lower precision. Using the FSPAI<FP64,FP16> variant, the CG solver fails for the CRYSTM03

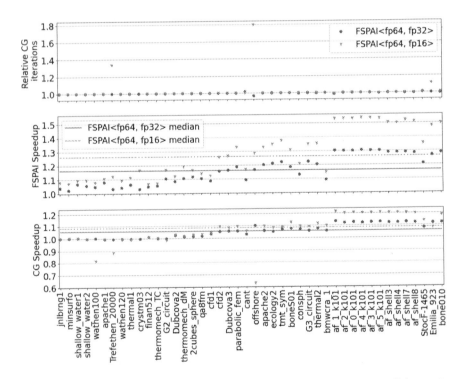

Fig. 5. *Top*: Relative iteration counts for CG using lower precision preconditioner storage compared to double precision. *Center*: Speedup of a single mixed precision FSPAI application vs. double precision. The speedup ratios ignore the quality degradation of the preconditioner when using low precision storage. *Bottom*: CG speedup when using an FSPAI preconditioner stored in lower precision instead of a double precision FSPAI.

problem and the convergence degrades for four additional problems. At the same time, the convergence is only mildly delayed for all other problems. The FSPAI<FP64,FP32> provides the same preconditioner quality as the double precision FSPAI preconditioner.

The center plot of Fig. 5 visualizes the mixed precision FSPAI performance, indicating a clear relation between the nonzero count and the speedup over the double precision FSPAI. For single precision storage, we can accelerate the preconditioner application by up to 1.3×, for half precision storage, this number grows to up to over 1.5×. Across the 46 test problems, we see a median performance improvement of 14% for FSPAI<FP64,FP32> and 27% for FSPAI<FP64,FP16>, respectively.

The bottom plot in Fig. 5 reflects how the mixed precision FSPAI speedups translate into mild but consistent performance benefits for the CG solver. We observe that the overall CG execution time is reduced by up to 20% (median: 8%) when using FSPAI<FP64,FP16> and up to 13% (median: 4%) when using FSPAI<FP64,FP32>, respectively.

6   Summary and Outlook

In this paper, we proposed mixed precision incomplete sparse approximate inverse preconditioners and mixed precision factorized sparse approximate inverse preconditioners that decouple the memory precision from the arithmetic precision and store the preconditioner information in a more compact low precision format. Investigating the numerical effects, we observed that the mixed precision preconditioners are often able to preserve the convergence improvement of their full precision counterparts. We also developed a high performance GPU implementation of the mixed precision preconditioners that achieve speedup ratios corresponding to the memory volume savings. Employing the mixed precision preconditioners into Krylov solvers, we demonstrated that these speedups translate into a mild acceleration of the iterative solution process. Though the runtime savings are incremental, we are convinced that the approach we take can serve as a blueprint for other algorithms, and that the production-ready mixed precision sparse approximate inverse preconditioners we provide can become an attractive building block in the configuration of high performance Krylov solvers. In future work, we will investigate the use of non-standard precision formats that can render higher speedups and focus on designing a cheap mechanism that protects the mixed precision preconditioners from numerical breakdown.

Acknowledgments. This work was supported by the US Exascale Computing Project (17-SC-20-SC), a collaborative effort of the U.S. Department of Energy Office of Science and the National Nuclear Security Administration and the "Impuls und Vernetzungsfond" of the Helmholtz Association under grant VH-NG-1241. This research used resources of the Oak Ridge Leadership Computing Facility, which is a DOE Office of Science User Facility supported under Contract DE-AC05-00OR22725.

Appendix

Table 1. Nonsymmetric test problems along with key properties and BiCGstab iterations. The preconditioners are double precision (<FP64,FP64>) or mixed precision (<FP64,FP32> or <FP64,FP16>). Iteration counts marked with "x" indicate convergence failure.

Non-symmetric test matrices

Name	#rows	#nonzeros	BiCGSTAB	+ISAI<FP64,FP64>	+ISAI<FP64,FP32>	+ISAI<FP64,FP16>
poli4	33,833	73,249	36	19	19	19
descriptor_xingo6u	20,738	73,916	16,441	17	17	x
xingo3012	20,944	74,386	18,901	17	17	x
bips07_3078	21,128	75,729	5,455	17	17	x
juba40k	40,337	144,945	x	17	17	x
bauru5727	40,366	145,019	x	17	17	x
Zhao1	33,861	166,453	62	25	25	25
epb2	25,228	175,027	672	165	165	164
wang3	26,064	177,168	392	226	226	205
wang4	26,068	177,196	866	206	204	198
chem_master1	40,401	201,201	801	402	375	433
chipcool0	20,082	281,150	x	161	161	x
chipcool1	20,082	281,150	x	151	151	x
ecl32	51,993	380,415	x	486	467	x
viscoplatic2	32,769	381,326	x	1,897	1,919	1,871
epb3	84,617	463,625	x	3,431	4,225	4,009
lung2	109,460	492,564	x	78	78	x
cage11	39,082	559,722	32	14	14	14
ASIC_100ks	99,190	578,890	x	28	31	30
ss1	205,282	845,089	12	7	7	7
torso2	115,967	1,033,473	55	11	11	11
ASIC_320ks	321,671	1,316,085	x	51	48	x
venkat_01	62,424	1,717,792	x	57	57	57
crashbasis	160,000	1,750,416	293	42	42	42
majorbasis	160,000	1,750,416	144	22	22	22
cage12	130 228	2 032 536	25	14	14	14
poisson3Db	85,623	2,374,949	387	275	264	277
stomach	213,360	3,021,648	x	36	36	36
sme3Dc	42,930	3,148,656	x	17,603	x	x
FEM_3D_thermal2	147,900	3,489,300	551	26	26	26
torso3	259,156	4,429,042	309	69	71	69
cage13	445,315	7,479,343	30	15	15	15
atmosmodd	1,270,432	8,814,880	513	268	241	268
atmosmodj	1,270,432	8,814,880	498	276	243	246
atmosmodl	1,489,752	10,319,760	329	155	155	143
memchip	2,707,524	13,343,948	x	407	383	373
circuit5M_dc	3,523,317	14,865,409	x	16	16	x
Transport	1,602,111	23,487,281	4,355	1,215	1,467	1,263
cage14	1,505,785	27,130,349	23	15	15	15

Table 2. Symmetric positive definite test problems along with key properties and CG iterations. The preconditioners are double precision (<FP64,FP64>) or mixed precision (<FP64,FP32> or <FP64,FP16>). Iteration counts marked with "x" indicate convergence failure.

Name	#rows	#nonzeros	CG	+FSPAI<FP64,FP64>	+FSPAI<FP64,FP32>	+FSPAI<FP64,FP16>
jnlbrng1	40,000	199,200	100	54	54	54
minsurfo	40,806	203,622	59	39	39	39
shallow_water1	81,920	327,680	12	7	7	7
shallow_water2	81,920	327,680	23	13	13	13
wathen100	30,401	471,601	228	22	22	22
apache1	80,800	542,184	1,550	1,025	1,025	1,029
Trefethen_20000	20,000	554,466	770	3	3	4
wathen120	36,441	565,761	229	27	27	27
thermal1	82,654	574,458	1,384	666	666	666
crytm03	24,696	583,770	91	9	9	x
finan512	74,752	596,992	37	8	8	8
thermomech_TC	102,158	711,558	60	7	7	7
G2_circuit	150,102	726,674	5,198	682	682	682
Dubcova2	65,025	1,030,225	167	121	121	121
thermomech_dM	204,316	1,423,116	60	7	7	7
2cubes_sphere	101,492	1,647,264	x	6	6	6
qa8fm	66,127	1,660,579	59	10	10	10
cfd1	90,656	1,825,580	1,727	874	874	873
cfd2	123,440	3,085,406	7,083	1,991	1,992	1,991
Dubcova3	146,689	3,636,643	170	118	118	118
parabolic_fem	525,825	3,674,625	1,366	1,177	1,177	1,177
cant	62,451	4,007,383	9,452	5,423	5,525	5,440
offshore	259,789	4,242,673	x	311	302	559
apache2	715,176	4,817,870	4,458	1,868	1,868	1,868
ecology2	999,999	4,995,991	5,896	3,167	3,167	3,166
tmt_sym	726,713	5,080,961	3,389	2,067	2,067	2,067
boneS01	127,224	5,516,602	2,331	1,012	1,013	1,013
consph	83,334	6,010,480	x	1,618	1,609	1,618
G3_circuit	1,585,478	7,660,826	8,442	824	824	824
thermal2	1,228,045	8,580,313	5,079	2,560	2,559	2,561
bmwcra_1	148,770	10,641,602	x	6,709	6,725	6,700
af_0_k101	503,625	17,550,675	x	8,739	8,739	8,742
af_1_k101	503,625	17,550,675	x	7,495	7,413	7,427
af_2_k101	503,625	17,550,675	x	9,051	9,052	9,052
af_3_k101	503,625	17,550,675	x	7,099	7,101	7,094
af_4_k101	503,625	17,550,675	x	9,335	9,360	9,334
af_5_k101	503,625	17,550,675	x	9,184	9,148	9,145
af_shell3	504,855	17,562,051	1,967	882	882	879
af_shell4	504,855	17,562,051	1,967	882	882	879
af_shell7	504,855	17,579,155	1,963	882	881	881
af_shell8	504,855	17,579,155	1,963	882	881	881
StocF-1465	1,465,137	21,005,389	x	5,062	5,109	5,089
Emilia_923	923,136	40,373,538	x	5,004	5,014	5,547
bone010	986,703	47,851,783	x	8,437	8,421	8,508

References

1. Suitesparse matrix collection. https://sparse.tamu.edu
2. Anzt, H., et al.: Ginkgo: a high performance numerical linear algebra library. J. Open Source Softw. **5**(52), 2260 (2020). https://doi.org/10.21105/joss.02260
3. Anzt, H., Cojean, T., Grützmacher, T.: Technical report: Design of the accessor. LLNL Report LLNL-SR-818775, January 2021
4. Anzt, H., Dongarra, J., Flegar, G., Higham, N.J., Quintana-Ortí, E.S.: Adaptive precision in block-jacobi preconditioning for iterative sparse linear system solvers. Concurrency Comput. Practice Exp. **31**(6), e4460 (2019)
5. Anzt, H., Dongarra, J., Flegar, G., Quintana-Ortí, E.S.: Batched gauss-jordan elimination for block-jacobi preconditioner generation on gpus. In: Proceedings of the 8th International Workshop on Programming Models and Applications for Multicores and Manycores, PMAM 2017, pp. 1–10. Association for Computing Machinery, New York (2017). https://doi.org/10.1145/3026937.3026940
6. Anzt, H., Flegar, G., Grützmacher, T., Quintana-Ortí, E.S.: Toward a modular precision ecosystem for high-performance computing. Int. J. High Performance Comput. Appli. **33**(6), 1069–1078 (2019). https://doi.org/10.1177/1094342019846547
7. Anzt, H., Huckle, T.K., Bräckle, J., Dongarra, J.: Incomplete sparse approximate inverses for parallel preconditioning. Parallel Comput. **71**, 1–22 (2018). https://doi.org/10.1016/j.parco.2017.10.003
8. Bell, N., Garland, M.: Implementing sparse matrix-vector multiplication on throughput-oriented processors. In: Proceedings of the Conference on High Performance Computing Networking, Storage and Analysis. SC 2009. Association for Computing Machinery, New York (2009). https://doi.org/10.1145/1654059.1654078, https://doi.org/10.1145/1654059.1654078
9. Flegar, G., Anzt, H., Cojean, T., Quintana-Ortí, E.S.: Customized-precision Block-Jacobi preconditioning for Krylov iterative solvers on data-parallel manycore processors. ACM Trans. Math. Softw. (2020). under review. Available from the authors
10. Green, O., McColl, R., Bader, D.A.: GPU merge path: A GPU merging algorithm. In: Proceedings of the 26th ACM International Conference on Supercomputing, ICS 2012, pp. 331–340. ACM. https://doi.org/10.1145/2304576.2304621
11. Grote, M.J., Huckle, T.: Parallel preconditioning with sparse approximate inverses. SIAM J. Sci. Comput. **18**(3), 838–853 (1997). https://doi.org/10.1137/S1064827594276552
12. Kolotilina, L.Y., Yeremin, A.Y.: Factorized sparse approximate inverse preconditionings i. theory. SIAM J. Matrix Anal. Appl. **14**(1), 45–58 (1993). https://doi.org/10.1137/0614004
13. NVIDIA Corp.: Whitepaper: NVIDIA TESLA V100 GPU ARCHITECTURE (2017)
14. Saad, Y.: Iterative Methods for Sparse Linear Systems, 2nd edn. SIAM (2003)

Outsmarting the Atmospheric Turbulence for Ground-Based Telescopes Using the Stochastic Levenberg-Marquardt Method

Yuxi Hong[1], El Houcine Bergou[2], Nicolas Doucet[3], Hao Zhang[3],
Jesse Cranney[3], Hatem Ltaief[1], Damien Gratadour[3], Francois Rigaut[3],
and David Keyes[1(✉)]

[1] King Abdullah University of Science and Technology,
Thuwal, Kingdom of Saudi Arabia
`david.keyes@kaust.edu.sa`
[2] Mohammed VI Polytechnic University, Ben Guerir, Morocco
[3] Australian National University, Canberra, Australia

Abstract. One of the main challenges for ground-based optical astronomy is to compensate for atmospheric turbulence in near real-time. The goal is to obtain images as close as possible to the diffraction limit of the telescope. This challenge is addressed on the latest generation of giant optical telescopes by deploying multi-conjugate adaptive optics (MCAO) systems performing predictive tomography of the turbulence and multi-layer compensation. Such complex systems require a high fidelity estimate of the turbulence profile above the telescope, to be updated regularly during operations as turbulence conditions evolve. In this paper, we modify the traditional Levenberg-Marquardt (LM) algorithm by considering stochastically chosen subsystems of the full problem to identify the required parameters efficiently, while coping with the real-time challenge. While LM operates on the full set data samples, the resulting Stochastic LM (SLM) method randomly selects subsamples to compute corresponding approximate gradients and Hessians. Hence, SLM reduces the algorithmic complexity per iteration and shortens the overall time to solution, while maintaining LM's numerical robustness. We present a new convergence analysis for SLM, implement the algorithm with optimized GPU kernels, and deploy it on shared-memory systems with multiple GPU accelerators. We assess SLM in the adaptive optics system configurations in the context of the MCAO-Assisted Visible Imager & Spectrograph (MAVIS) instrument for the Very Large Telescope (VLT). We demonstrate performance superiority of SLM over the traditional LM algorithm and the classical stochastic first-order methods. At the scale of VLT AO, SLM finishes the optimization process and accurately retrieves the parameters (e.g., turbulence strength and wind speed profiles) in less than a second using up to eight NVIDIA A100 GPUs, which permits high acuity real-time throughput over a night of observations.

Keywords: Non-linear optimization problems · Stochastic Levenberg-Marquardt · GPU computing · Adaptive optics · Computational astronomy · Real-time processing

© Springer Nature Switzerland AG 2021
L. Sousa et al. (Eds.): Euro-Par 2021, LNCS 12820, pp. 565–579, 2021.
https://doi.org/10.1007/978-3-030-85665-6_35

1   Introduction

Outsmarting the Atmospheric Turbulence. A Multi-Conjugate Adaptive Optics (MCAO) system is an essential component for the current and next generation of telescopes, i.e., the Very Large Telescope (VLT) and the Extremely Large Telescopes (ELTs). MCAO is responsible for real-time compensation of the effect of atmospheric turbulence, which would otherwise significantly degrade image quality. MCAO operates by controlling one or several Deformable Mirrors (DM) based on one or several Wave-front Sensor (WFS) measurements in real-time. In order to obtain the best performance, MCAO controllers require knowledge of time-varying parameters, such as the atmospheric turbulence strength and the wind velocity (bi-dimensional). All three variables vary with altitude. Due to the system dimensions of VLTs/ELTs, it remains a challenge to identify these parameters under real-time constraints. The Learn and Apply (L&A) [13] method is a promising technique to meet this demand. The *Learn* phase performs the identification of the three atmospheric turbulence parameters for each altitude layer. The *Apply* phase uses these parameters to activate the control system that drives the DM actuators in real-time, typically at the kHz rate.

The performance of an MCAO system is limited by the accuracy of the atmospheric parameters available to the MCAO controller. It is critical to identify these parameters faster than they are expected to evolve. The typical time over which these parameters evolve significantly varies between two to twenty minutes (with some exceptional cases) [16]. Therefore, the whole cyclic process of acquiring profiling data and executing the L&A pipeline must fit within a total time budget of a few seconds. This is significantly smaller than the period of validity of these parameters, which are essential to drive the MCAO system. While the duration of the acquisition process cannot be compressed in time since one needs to accumulate enough data from the underlying stochastic process to reach a minimum level of convergence, the time-to-solution for both L&A steps have to be shortened as much as possible to comply with this stringent time envelope constraint. In fact, within the L&A method, the *Learn* phase is the major bottleneck, thus improving its time-to-solution is a crucial step towards the real-time identification of atmospheric turbulence parameters. The current state-of-the-art implementation [11] allows for a time-to-solution in the order of minutes for VLT scale systems with a reduced set of system parameters.

Leveraging Stochastic Method for Computational Astronomy. Our goal of real-time performance for MCAO system in VLTs/ELTs is met by using a minibatch version of the Levenberg-Marquardt method – Stochastic Levenberg-Marquardt (SLM). This is an example of an active theme in scientific computing with a practical value: the convergence of big data optimization and high performance computing, which is driven by expanding problem sizes. The hardware architectural trend of packing more compute power in devices, whose memory capacity and memory bandwidth per processing unit cannot keep up, puts an algorithmic premium on shrinking the working datasets. The reduced datasets may then reside higher in the memory hierarchy and closer to the processing units, thus increasing the arithmetic intensity and shrinking the time overhead (and possibly energy consumption) due to data movement. The traditional LM method has proven useful in existing MCAO schemes, however, its relevance to the controller turns out to be limited due to its burdensome execution time relative to the temporal evolution of the parameters identified. The SLM method further improves performance and is able to finish the *Learn* phase in less than a second using 8 NVIDIA A100 GPUs, while maintaining LM robustness in parameter identification, in the context of the MCAO-Assisted Visible Imager & Spectrograph (MAVIS) instrument [25] for the Very Large Telescope (VLT). This performance achieved by using SLM method enables astronomers to effectively overcome the prohibitive dimensionality found when identifying atmosphere turbulence at the scale of MCAO systems for VLTs/ELTs.

The contributions of the paper are as follows. We design the SLM method and present its convergence analysis. We deploy a new GPU-based SLM implementation and measure the performance on various NVIDIA GPU generations. We highlight the performance superiority of SLM over traditional LM as well as existing first-order methods using different sizes of samples. Last but not least, we assess the quality of the optical image formation obtained by SLM under MAVIS specifications.

The remainder of the paper is as follows. Section 2 states the problem and presents related works. Section 3 describes the MCAO challenges and MAVIS dataset features. Section 4 presents a convergence theory for SLM. Section 5 discusses the GPU-based SLM implementation. Section 6 provides a detailed performance analysis of SLM, assesses its numerical convergence and highlights its robustness. Section 7 concludes with a pointer to future work.

2   Problem Statement and Related Work

The identification of turbulence parameters from adaptive optics (AO) telemetry data is a non-linear optimization problem. We first introduce related work in stochastic second-order optimization and then the Levenberg-Marquardt (LM) method application in an AO system. Stochastic sub-sampling variants of Newton method [2,4,5,9,10,12,27] present principled use of second-order information (i.e., the Hessian) to accelerate the convergence while typically using line search techniques to compute the learning rate and ensure global convergence. In general stochastic optimization algorithms using second-order information, a variety of algorithms have been extended to handle access to sub-sampled derivatives: of particular interest to us are the Stochastic LM (SLM) algorithms. The authors in [18,20,24] suggest to use a sub-sampled version of LM for least squares problems. However, they do not provide a complexity analysis for such methods. We consider the following least squares problem:

$$\min_{x \in \mathbb{R}^d} f(x) := \frac{1}{2}\|F(x)\|^2 = \frac{1}{2}\sum_{i=1}^{N} F_i(x)^2, \tag{1}$$

where $f : \mathbb{R}^d \to \mathbb{R}$ and $F_i : \mathbb{R}^d \to \mathbb{R}$, for $i = 1, \ldots, N$ are assumed twice continuously differentiable. The variable N corresponds to the number of samples. The Gauss-Newton method and its globally convergent variants are often the methods of choice to tackle non-linear least-squares problems. The Gauss-Newton method minimizes the problem defined in Eq. (1) by iteratively solving a linearized least squares subproblem of the following form:

$$\min_{s \in \mathbb{R}^d} \frac{1}{2} \|F(x) + Js\|^2, \tag{2}$$

where $J = \nabla F(x)$ with $J \in \mathbb{R}^{N \times d}$. In the case of a full rank Jacobian J, the subproblem (2) has a unique local solution. However, when J is rank deficient the subproblem is ill-posed. Furthermore, the Gauss-Newton method may not be globally convergent, in the sense that its solution depends on the starting point for the minimization. The LM method [8,19,21] was developed to address the Jacobian deficiency and the sensitivity to starting point. At each iteration, it adds a regularization term to Subproblem (2), which becomes

$$\min_{s \in \mathbb{R}^d} \frac{1}{2} \|F(x) + Js\|^2 + \frac{1}{2} \mu^2 \|s\|^2, \tag{3}$$

where $\mu > 0$ is an appropriately chosen regularization parameter. The regularization parameter is updated at every iteration and indirectly controls the size of the step, making Gauss–Newton globally convergent. Several strategies have been developed to update this parameter.

Indeed, this added regularization determines when the Gauss-Newton step is applicable. When it is set to a small value (or even to zero in some LM variants), the update of algorithm corresponds to Gauss-Newton step. When it is set to a large value, the update of the algorithm corresponds to a gradient step. Other variants of the LM algorithm replace the Gauss-Newton subproblem with a random model that is accurate only with a given probability [6,7]. They have also been applied to problems where the objective value is subject to noise [3,22].

In the case of the tomographic AO, the application of LM is first assessed in the Learn & Apply (L&A) method [13]. It is then tested on real telescopes [15] to identify the necessary parameters. The experimental results highlight how LM method is a good optimizer for the atmosphere turbulence identification problem. In the *Learn* phase, the N elements summed in Eq. (1) depend on the AO system configuration and refers to all entries of a covariance matrix (CMM) of the wavefront sensors (WFS) measurements. The matrix involved can be quite large (up to 100K × 100K), requiring 80 GB to store it in double precision.

In this paper, we consider an SLM variant and provide its complexity analysis. Our SLM method uses a random subset of the classical model [18]. This leads to a reduction of the arithmetic complexity and memory footprint, while addressing performance issues encountered for large-scale AO systems.

3   Model and Challenges in Adaptive Optics

When considering the telemetry data of a tomographic AO system (such as the MCAO setting), the relevant atmospheric parameters are embedded into the observed covariance matrix of recent WFS measurements. Since an analytical approximation of this covariance matrix is also available, it is possible to form a least-squares optimization problem to identify a valid set of atmospheric parameters which minimizes the difference between the observed covariance matrix and the analytical one. Details of the actual functions involved can be found throughout the AO literature, e.g., in [14,28]. For simplicity, it is sufficient to consider the analytical model of the measurement covariance matrix as having elements equal to some function M of the atmospheric parameters x:

$$C_{i,j}^{ana} = \sum_{l=1}^{N_l} M_{i,j}(x_l) := M_{i,j}(x), \qquad (4)$$

where $C_{i,j}^{ana}$ is the $(i,j)^{\text{th}}$ entry of the analytical covariance matrix C^{ana}. x_l is the atmospheric parameters of each layer. x_l contains three parameters: turbulence strength and the bi-dimensional wind velocity. From recently obtained measurement data, we can determine the *numerical* covariance matrix as:

$$C^{num} = \frac{1}{N_k} \sum_{k=1}^{N_k} (s_k - \bar{s})(s_k - \bar{s})^T, \qquad (5)$$

where s_k is the measurement vector obtained at time k, N_k is the number of consecutive time samples from which measurements have been obtained, and $\bar{s}$ is the expected value of the measurement vector (typically a zero-vector).

The atmospheric parameters are identified by solving the minimization problem from Eq. (1), where F is defined as the difference between the analytical and numerical covariance matrices:

$$F(x) = vec\left(C_{i,j}^{ana}(x) - C_{i,j}^{num} \right). \qquad (6)$$

The sizes of the matrices involved depend on the AO system dimensioning. In the following, the parameter set for our numerical simulation is based on MAVIS [25] and leads to covariance matrices of size (19584×19584). It is challenging to compute such high dimensional finite-sum problems while enforcing the near real-time constraint. Currently, the standard LM algorithm computes all the samples in this finite-sum problem to determine the gradient and Jacobian. Conversely, the SLM algorithm selects part of the data samples in each iteration to perform the computations, reducing the algorithmic complexity of the standard LM.

4   Complexity Analysis of Our SLM Algorithm

We describe here our proposed SLM method and its complexity analysis using the notation of Eq. (1). Algorithm 1 describes the considered variant, which can be shown to be globally convergent with the classical complexity bound known in the literature for stochastic algorithms (e.g., SGD) and their variants.

We use the following notation in the remainder of the paper $f^k = f(x^k)$, $F^k = F(x^k)$, $J^k = S^k \nabla F(x^k)$, $g^k = \nabla f(x^k) = \nabla F(x^k)^T F^k$, $\tilde{g}^k = \nabla F(x^k)^T S^k F^k$, where $S^k \in \mathbb{R}^{N,N}$ is a diagonal matrix with ones and zeros randomly distributed over the diagonal scaled by the number of nonzero elements divided by N. We note that the scaling used in the definition of the stochastic matrix S^k makes its expectation equal to the Identity matrix I.

Remark 1. Our analysis can be easily generalized to cover more distributions from which to choose S^k. However, for the sake of simplicity and ease of readability of our proofs we limit ourselves to the above-mentioned distribution.

Algorithm 1. SLM algorithm with fixed regularization.

Initialization: : Choose initial x^0. Choose a constant μ. Generate a random index
    sequence $Rand_{seq}$. Choose a data fraction df to decide the samples size used per
    iteration. Record initial $\|\tilde{g}^0\|_\infty$. Choose stopping criteria ϵ.
1: **for** $k = 1, 2, ..., K$ **do**
2:     Get random indices from $Rand_{seq}$
3:     Calculate $J^{k^T} J^k$ and $\tilde{g}^k$ using GPU
4:     If $\|\tilde{g}^k\|_\infty / \|\tilde{g}^0\|_\infty \le \epsilon$, exit algorithm
5:     Solve linear system: $(J^{k^T} J^k + \mu I)\delta x = \tilde{g}^k$
6:     Update x^{k+1}: $x^{k+1} = x^k - (J^{k^T} J^k + \mu I)^{-1}\tilde{g}^k = x^k - \delta x$
7: **end for**

In Algorithm 1, the data fraction (*df*) is the ratio between the amount of selected data and the total data. We first state the general assumptions (several of which are classical) that we use for the convergence analysis of Algorithm 1.

Assumption 1. *($\mathcal{L}$-smoothness) The function f is $\mathcal{L}$ smooth if its gradient is $\mathcal{L}$-Lipschitz continuous, that is, for all $x, y \in \mathbb{R}^d$,*

$$f(x) \le f(y) + \nabla f(y)^T (x - y) + \tfrac{\mathcal{L}}{2}\|x - y\|^2.$$

Assumption 2. *(Boundness of stochastic gradient) The stochastic gradient is bounded by $G > 0$, that is, $\mathbb{E}\left[\|\tilde{g}^k\|\right]^2 \le G^2$.*

The latter inequality implies $\mathbb{E}\left[\|\tilde{g}^k\|\right] \le G$ (using Jensen's inequality).

Assumption 3. *The function F Jacobian is bounded by $\kappa_J > 0$, that is,*

$$\mathbb{E}\left[\|\nabla F(x^k)\|\right] \le \kappa_J.$$

The latter Assumption implies $\mathbb{E}\left[\|J^k\|\right] \le \kappa_J$, independently from S^k.

Lemma 1. *(Unbiasedness of stochastic gradient) The stochastic gradient is unbiased. That is, $\mathbb{E}\left[\tilde{g}^k | x^k\right] = g^k = \nabla f(x^k)$.*

Proof. Directly from the fact that $\mathbb{E}\left[S^k\right] = I$.   □

Lemma 2.

$$\left(J^{k^\top} J^k + \mu I_d\right)^{-1} = \frac{I_d}{\mu} - \frac{1}{\mu^2} J^{k^\top} \left(\frac{1}{\mu} J^k J^{k^\top} + I_p\right)^{-1} J^k$$

Proof. Direct by application of the Sherman-Morrison-Woodbury formula.   □

Note that $J^k \in \mathbb{R}^{p \times d}$, p is minibatch size, d is parameter size, $I_d \in \mathbb{R}^{d \times d}, I_p \in \mathbb{R}^{p \times p}$, I_d and I_p are Identity matrices.

Lemma 3. *Let Assumptions 3 and 2 hold, and*
$A := \left\| \nabla f^{k^\top} \frac{1}{\mu^2} J^{k^\top} \left(\frac{1}{\mu} J^k J^{k^\top} + I\right)^{-1} J^k \tilde{g}^k \right\|$, *then* $\mathbb{E}\left[A|x^k\right] \le \frac{1}{\mu^2}\kappa_J^2 G^2$.

Proof.

$$A \le \frac{1}{\mu^2} \left\|\nabla f^k\right\| \left\|J^k\right\|^2 \left\|\left(\frac{1}{\mu} J^k J^{k^\top} + I\right)^{-1}\right\| \left\|\tilde{g}^k\right\| \le \frac{1}{\mu^2}\kappa_J^2 G \left\|\tilde{g}^k\right\|.$$

Notation A is introduced due to page width limit. Now, by taking the conditional expectation and using Assumption 2, we get the desired result.   □

Lemma 4. *Let Assumption 2 hold, then* $\mathbb{E}\left[\left\|(J^{k^\top} J^k + \mu I)^{-1}\tilde{g}^k\right\|^2 |x^k\right] \le \frac{G^2}{\mu^2}$.

Proof.

$$\left\|(J^{k^\top} J^k + \mu I)^{-1}\tilde{g}^k\right\|^2 \le \left\|(J^{k^\top} J^k + \mu I)^{-1}\right\|^2 \left\|\tilde{g}^k\right\|^2 \le \frac{\left\|\tilde{g}^k\right\|^2}{\mu^2}.$$

Now, by taking the conditional expectation and using Assumption 2 we get the desired result.   □

Theorem 1. *Let Assumptions 1, 2 and 3 hold. Let $K > 0$, $\mu_0 > 0$ and $\mu = \mu_0\sqrt{K+1}$, then*

$$\frac{\sum_{k=0}^{K} \mathbb{E}\|\nabla f^k\|^2}{K+1} \le \frac{D}{\sqrt{K+1}}, D := \mu_0 f^0 + \frac{2\kappa_J^2 G^2 + \mathcal{L}G^2}{2\mu_0}.$$

Proof. From the $\mathcal{L}$-smoothness of the function f we have

$$
\begin{aligned}
f^{k+1} \quad &\le \quad f^k - \nabla f^{k^\top}(x^{k+1} - x^k) + \frac{\mathcal{L}}{2}\|x^{k+1} - x^k\|^2 \\
\overset{\text{By Algo 1 line (6)}}{=} \quad &f^k - \nabla f^{k^\top}\left(J^{k^\top} J^k + \mu I\right)^{-1}\tilde{g}^k + \frac{\mathcal{L}}{2}\left\|(J^{k^\top} J^k + \mu I)^{-1}\tilde{g}^k\right\|^2 \\
\overset{\text{By Lemma 2}}{=} \quad &f^k - \frac{1}{\mu}\nabla f^{k^\top}\tilde{g}^k + \frac{1}{\mu^2}\nabla f^{k^\top} J^{k^\top}\left(\frac{1}{\mu} J^k J^{k^\top} + I\right)^{-1} J^k \tilde{g}^k \\
+ \quad &\frac{\mathcal{L}}{2}\left\|(J^{k^\top} J^k + \mu I)^{-1}\tilde{g}^k\right\|^2,
\end{aligned}
$$

which after taking the conditional expectation and by using Lemmas 1, 3 and 4, we get $\mathbb{E}[f^{k+1}|x^k] \leq f^k - \frac{1}{\mu}\|\nabla f^k\|^2 + \frac{\kappa_J^2 G^2}{\mu^2} + \frac{\mathcal{L}G^2}{2\mu^2}$, which after taking the expectation (by using tower property [1]) we get $\mathbb{E}[f^{k+1}] \leq \mathbb{E}[f^k] - \frac{1}{\mu}\mathbb{E}[\|\nabla f^k\|^2] + \frac{2\kappa_J^2 G^2 + \mathcal{L}G^2}{2\mu^2}$. By rearranging the terms and multiplying by μ we get $\mathbb{E}[\|\nabla f^k\|^2] \leq \mu\left(\mathbb{E}[f^k] - \mathbb{E}[f^{k+1}]\right) + \frac{2\kappa_J^2 G^2 + \mathcal{L}G^2}{2\mu}$. By summing the latter inequality over k from 0 to K and dividing by $K + 1$ we get

$$\frac{\sum_{k=0}^K \mathbb{E}\|\nabla f^k\|^2}{K+1} \leq \frac{\mu\left(f^0 - \mathbb{E}[f^{K+1}]\right)}{K+1} + \frac{2\kappa_J^2 G^2 + \mathcal{L}G^2}{2\mu}.$$

By replacing μ in the last inequality by $\mu_0\sqrt{K+1}$ and by using that $\mathbb{E}[f^{K+1}]$ is lower-bounded by 0, we get the desired result.   □

Corollary 1. *Let Assumptions 1, 2 and 3 hold. Let $K > 0$, $\mu_0 > 0$ and $\mu = \mu_0\sqrt{K+1}$, then*

$$\min_{k\in\{0,\dots,K\}} \mathbb{E}[\|\nabla f^k\|^2] \leq \mathcal{O}\left(\frac{1}{\sqrt{K+1}}\right).$$

Proof. Directly from Theorem 1.   □

This corollary guarantees the convergence trend, i.e., the minimum square of the gradient norm decreases by $\mathcal{O}\left(\frac{1}{\sqrt{K+1}}\right)$ over K iterations. This is the classical complexity bound known in the literature for the stochastic methods, like SGD and its variants.

5   Implementation Details and Performance Optimizations

We implement the SLM method, as described in Algorithm 1, and deploy it on a shared-memory system equipped with multiple GPUs using *C++* and *CUDA* programming models. This densely populated GPU computer system is typical of hardware configurations deployed in remote telescope locations, where power is a scarce resource. We generate ahead the random index sequences used by SLM during the iterative process. We can decompose SLM into four parts: the computation of the stochastic approximated Hessian and Gradient (i.e., $J^{k^\top} J^k$ and $\tilde{g}^k$), the local and global reduction step, the linear system solve, and the parameter update. The time of solving the linear system and updating the parameters is negligible given the small parameter vector length seen in the MAVIS configuration. These two parts may become a bottleneck for other AO settings, which can be addressed with standard vendor optimized numerical libraries. The time for the local and global reduction step may increase with the number of GPUs. The local reduction is first performed on each GPU in an embarrassingly parallel fashion. The global reduction is done on the host side, which requires data movement across the slow PCIe interconnect. The most time-consuming part is the execution of the stochastic approximated Hessian and Gradient (HG) kernel on multiple GPUs. We develop a new GPU-based HG implementation as follows. The HG kernel first fetches the random index and calculates the Jacobian by adding a small perturbation on different parameters every time. Then, HG performs reduction on gradient and approximated Hessian–$J^T J$.

We use two following optimizations to improve the HG kernel performance.

Block Random Index. If we randomly select the index of all entries, non-coalesced memory access will immediately become a performance bottleneck. In order to achieve coalesced memory access, we group contiguous indices of the covariance matrix CMM into a set of blocks. We set the block size to 1024 so that we ensure high occupancy on the GPU. We save the first index of each block. We randomly select the start index of these blocks and map each index block to a physical CUDA block on the GPU.

Reduction Optimization. Atomic operations are used to perform the reductions [11]. The performance can be further improved by using reduction on shared-memory first. We split the reduction stage into two substages. We rely on the NVIDIA collective primitive library *CUB* for reduction inside the block and then fall back to only a single thread to access the global memory for reduction. This reduction takes advantage of the GPU memory hierarchy to maximize bandwidth.

We expose the minibatch size as an additional parameter to tune performance and accuracy. This minibatch size is determined by the product of the data fraction (df) and the total dataset size.

6   Performance Results and Numerical Assessment

6.1   Experimental Settings

In order to assess performance scalability and portability, we use three NVIDIA DGX systems densely populated with GPUs, each with two-socket 20-core Intel(R) Xeon(R) Broadwell CPU E5-2698 v4 @ 2.20 GHz. Each DGX system is equipped with eight P100, V100 and A100 NVIDIA GPUs connected to the host via PCIe. The DGX systems with V100 and A100 GPUs have their respective GPUs interconnected via *NVLINK* while the P100 DGX system relies on PCIe device-to-device communications. We use double precision arithmetic with *CUDA* 11.0 and the MAVIS configuration in all experiments. The CMM matrix size is 19584 × 19584. There are therefore approximately 200M samples and 200K index blocks all in all. We discretize the altitudinal direction into ten layers for the atmosphere turbulence model, which is able to meet the typical demand of the AO system on VLTs. This 10-layer model is generally accepted by the astronomy community and recommended by the European Southern Observatory (ESO) for the design study of VLT instruments. It also delivers a good trade-off between computational efficiency and model complexity for the MAVIS instrument, as currently observed during its preliminary design phase. For each layer, we are interested in the three parameters, i.e., the atmospheric turbulence strength and the bi-dimensional wind velocity, making a total of 30 parameters to retrieve.

6.2   HG Kernel and SLM Benchmarks

We first benchmark the two optimization techniques introduced in Sect. 5.

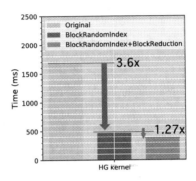

Fig. 1. Performance impact of the optimization techniques on HG using single A100 GPU with $df = 0.1$.

Figure 1 highlights a 3.6X and an additional 1.27X performance improvement acceleration on single A100 GPU using data fraction $df = 0.1$ with *Block Random Index* and *Block Reduction*, respectively. We then assess the performance scalability of our optimized stochastic HG kernel using three data fractions (i.e., three minibatch sizes) on all GPU systems. Figure 2 shows strong scaling (top row), speedup and parallel efficiency (middle row), and weak scaling (bottom row). The kernel shows close to ideal speedup when data fraction is large, e.g., $df = 0.1$. We observe a decent speedup in large data fraction and across the architectures. The parallel efficiency decreases as the data fraction becomes smaller, since GPUs are running out of work and cannot maintain high occupancy. We also observe how HG weak scales as we increase the number of GPUs. Moreover, the HG kernel is able to capture the computational power trend across NVIDIA GPU generations. The parallel efficiency is relatively the lowest on 8 A100 GPUs, given the high theoretical throughput achieved by this generation over the previous ones.

Figure 3 shows the overall SLM time breakdown (top row) and strong scaling results with speedup and parallel efficiency (bottom row) using a single SLM iteration on different DGX systems. The local and global reduction time slightly increases with the number of GPUs but the stochastic HG kernel timing accounts for most of the elapsed time.

6.3   End-to-End AO Simulation Results

We use an end-to-end simulation of the turbulence + telescope + AO system to validate the qualitative performance on MAVIS system configuration, in terms of

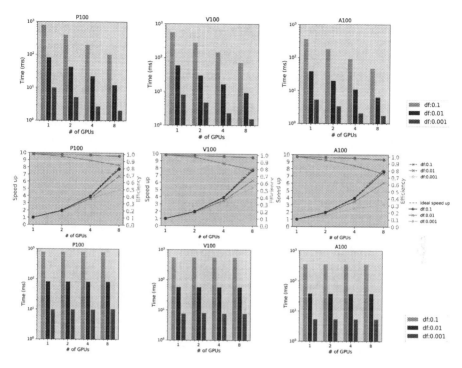

Fig. 2. Strong scaling (top row), speedup (middle row) and weak scaling (bottom row) of HG kernel on different NVIDIA GPU architectures.

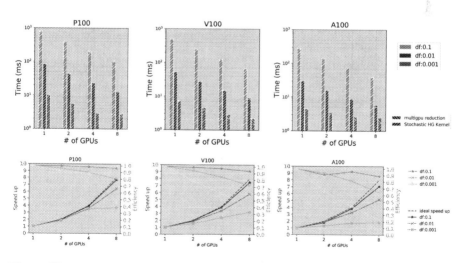

Fig. 3. SLM time breakdown (top row) and strong scaling results (bottom row) using a single iteration on different NVIDIA GPU architectures.

Strehl Ratio (SR), obtained with the estimated turbulence profile under a realistic operational scenario. The SR is widely used in the ground-based astronomy community as an image quality indicator of the AO performance. We compare the SLM method against the LM method used in [11] and other first-order stochastic methods such as SGD [26], Adam [17], and MomentumSGD [23]. We use one A100 GPU with $\mu = 10^{-6}$ and $\epsilon = 10^{-5}$. For the stochastic methods, we set a maximum execution time of 10 s. For the LM method, we let it run until it reaches ϵ. We choose a learning rate of 0.5 for the first-order methods to ensure that they all converge. All methods start from the same initial point, where all other parameters are zero except the atmosphere turbulence of the ground altitude layer. It is set to 1.0 given the fact that the first layer is usually the main contributor (typically more than half of the total turbulence strength).

We are interested in the normalized gradient norm $\|\tilde{g}\|_\infty$ and the convergence result of SLM. We set the data fraction to $df = 0.001$ because this is the smallest one we have seen in our experiments that does not sacrifice the image quality in terms of SR. Figure 4 (left) first recalls the main results of the complexity analysis, as seen in Sect. 4. It demonstrates how our experiments are aligned with the theory by showing the same convergence trend $\mathcal{O}\left(\frac{1}{\sqrt{K+1}}\right)$ in the gradient norm over K iterations. Figure 4 (middle) shows then the normalized gradient norm $\|\tilde{g}\|_\infty$ versus time when $df = 0.001$. The normalized gradient norm $\|\tilde{g}\|_\infty$ of our SLM method drops the fastest among all other methods. The table in Fig. 4 summarizes the SR and time to solution of all data fraction we use. The SR using the true atmosphere turbulence is 25.57%. A difference of the SR that is larger than 1% is considered significant enough to perturb the image quality. Although the SR of LM result is 25.60%, it takes LM more than a minute to get the results. We can also see that Adam and SLM are close to the SR using a true atmosphere profile, while SGD and MomentumSGD fall behind. In fact, none of the three first-order methods are able to reach ϵ. We stop their executions after 10 seconds and check their respective SRs. It is also worth pointing out that even if Adam fails to reach ϵ, it still gets a good SR. However, in a real mode

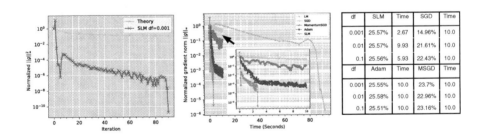

Fig. 4. Theory convergence and SLM $df = 0.001$ vs Iteration. (left); Normalized $\|\tilde{g}\|_\infty$ when $df = 0.001$. (middle); Strehl Ratio in percentage (the higher the better) and time to solution. (right); Time unit: seconds. MSGD: MomentumSGD. True parameters SR: 25.57%. LM result SR: 25.6%.

of operation, we can only monitor the normalized gradient norm $\|\tilde{g}\|_{\infty}$ as the ultimate indicator for a good SR since it is impossible to conduct slow End-to-End simulations with the real-time SLM operation. Furthermore, although the SLM time per iteration is faster with $df = 0.01$ than $df = 0.1$, the overall SLM procedure performs more iterations with the latter than the former. All in all, SLM is able to achieve the best time to solution $df = 0.001$, while reaching a decent SR.

Figure 5 compares the LM method with the SLM method in reaching the plateau of optimal SR using 8 A100 GPUs. The SLM method reaches optimal SR plateau in 3–4 iterations, in less than a second. On the other hand, the LM method needs around 10 s and 25 iterations to reach the plateau. The reason that the SR does not change in the first few iterations of LM is it may not update the parameters in every iteration. We only plot the partial timeline of each method to reach the steady state for SR. The total time to solution of SLM using 8 A100 GPUs with each data fraction is 0.227 s ($df = 0.001$), 1.814 s ($df = 0.01$) and 0.683s ($df = 0.1$). LM is 11.89 s.

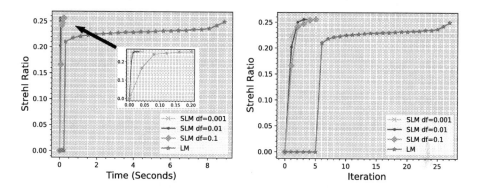

Fig. 5. SR of LM and SLM methods vs time and iteration using 8 A100 GPUs.

6.4 Performance Impact of Data Fraction

To better understand the limits of SLM method, we present here the impact of data fraction on SR. We test SLM on data fraction 10^{-3} (191776 samples), 10^{-4} (19177 samples), 10^{-5} (1917 samples). The SR of each data fraction is 25.56%, 22.8%, and 15.8%. The results show when we decrease data fraction from 10^{-3}, it will weaken the AO performance. A small data fraction implies a larger variance of stochastic gradient, which may lead to deviate far from the optimal solution. We find that $df = 10^{-3}$ balances both performance and quality of the atmosphere profile for this application.

7 Conclusion

We develop a Stochastic Levenberg-Marquardt (SLM) method for solving a large-scale optimization problem that is critical for identifying in real-time the atmospheric turbulence parameters used for the control of AO on ground-based telescopes. Our SLM method utilizes a subset of the dataset to estimate the gradient vector and Jacobian in order to reduce per-iteration cost. We introduce a complexity and convergence analysis for the SLM method. We create an optimized stochastic HG kernel for SLM methods that permits to accelerate the computation on systems equipped with GPUs. We compare the SLM method against the LM method and several state-of-the-art first-order methods. We are able to finish the *Learn* phase in seconds using the MAVIS [25] system configuration. We assess the obtained Strehl Ratio using end-to-end numerical simulations and observe no notable loss in quality of the optimization results. These results correspond to a significant improvement that overcomes the typical performance limitations in tomographic AO systems. With the advent of new generations of optical telescopes, such as the Extremely Large Telescopes, we believe our SLM approach stands as a software technology enabler to ensure real-time operations without compromising the Strehl Ratio metric. In future work, we intend to study other AO system configurations and further assess the SLM limitations. While this paper focuses on NVIDIA GPUs, we are also interested in porting our SLM framework to AMD and the forthcoming Intel GPUs for broadening the support of hardware solutions.

Acknowledgements. The authors would like to thank NVIDIA for remote hardware access.

References

1. Law of Total Expectation. https://en.wikipedia.org/wiki/Law_of_total_expectation, Accessed 17 Feb 2021
2. Agarwal, N., et al.: Second-order stochastic optimization for machine learning in linear time. J. Mach. Learn. Res. **18**(116), 1–40 (2017)
3. Bellavia, S., Gratton, S., Riccietti, E.: A Levenberg-Marquardt method for large nonlinear least-squares problems with dynamic accuracy in functions and gradients. Numer. Math. **140**, 791–824 (2018)
4. Berahas, A.S., et al.: An investigation of Newton-sketch and subsampled Newton methods (2017)
5. Bergou, E., Diouane, Y., Kunc, V., Kungurtsev, V., Royer, C.W.: A subsampling line-search method with second-order results (2020)
6. Bergou, E., Gratton, S., Vicente, L.N.: Levenberg-Marquardt methods based on probabilistic gradient models and inexact subproblem solution, with application to data assimilation. SIAM/ASA J. Uncertain. Quantif. **4**, 924–951 (2016)
7. Bergou, E., et al.: A stochastic Levenberg-Marquardt method using random models with application to data assimilation (2018). arXiv:1807.02176v1
8. Bergou, E., et al.: Convergence and iteration complexity analysis of a Levenberg-Marquardt algorithm for zero and non-zero residual inverse problems. **185**, 927–944 (2020)
9. Bollapragada, R., et al.: Exact and inexact subsampled Newton methods for optimization. IMA J. Numer. Anal. **39**(2), 545–578 (2019)
10. Byrd, R.H., et al.: On the use of stochastic Hessian information in optimization methods for machine learning. SIAM J. Optim. **21**(3), 977–995 (2011)

11. Doucet, N., et al.: Efficient supervision strategy for tomographic AO systems on e-elt. instituto de astrofisica de canarias (2017). https://doi.org/10.26698/ao4elt5. 0099, http://hdl.handle.net/10754/666385

12. Erdogdu, M.A., Montanari, A.: Convergence rates of sub-sampled Newton methods. In: Advances in Neural Information Processing Systems, pp. 3052–3060 (2015)

13. Vidal, F., Gendron, E., Rousset, G.: Tomography approach for multi-object adaptive optics. J. Opt. Soc. Am. A **27**(11), A253–A264 (2010)

14. Gendron, É., et al.: A novel fast and accurate pseudo-analytical simulation approach for MOAO. In: Adaptive Optics Systems IV, vol. 9148, p. 91486L. International Society for Optics and Photonics (2014)

15. Gendron, E., et al.: Final two-stage MOAO on-sky demonstration with CANARY (2016). https://doi.org/10.1117/12.2231432

16. Jia, P., et al.: Modelling synthetic atmospheric turbulence profiles with temporal variation using gaussian mixture model. Monthly Notices Roy. Astron. Soc. **480**(2), 2466–2474 (2018)

17. Kingma, D.P., Ba, J.: Adam: a method for stochastic optimization. In: International Conference on Learning Representation (ICLR) (2015)

18. LeCun, Y.A., Bottou, L., Orr, G.B., Müller, K.-R.: Efficient BackProp. In: Montavon, G., Orr, G.B., Müller, K.-R. (eds.) Neural Networks: Tricks of the Trade. LNCS, vol. 7700, pp. 9–48. Springer, Heidelberg (2012). https://doi.org/10.1007/978-3-642-35289-8_3

19. Levenberg, K.: A method for the solution of certain problems in least squares. Quart. Appl. Math. **2**, 164–168 (1944)

20. Liew, S.S., et al.: An optimized second order stochastic learning algorithm for neural network training. Neurocomputing **186**, 74–89 (2016)

21. Marquardt, D.: An algorithm for least-squares estimation of nonlinear parameters. SIAM J. Appl. Math. **11**, 431–441 (1963)

22. Moré, J.J.: The Levenberg-Marquardt algorithm: implementation and theory. In: Watson, G.A. (ed.) Numerical Analysis. LNM, vol. 630, pp. 105–116. Springer, Heidelberg (1978). https://doi.org/10.1007/BFb0067700

23. Polyak, B.T.: Some methods of speeding up the convergence of iteration methods. USSR Comput. Math. Math. Phys. **4**(5), 1–17 (1964)

24. Ren, Y., Goldfarb, D.: Efficient subsampled Gauss-Newton and natural gradient methods for training neural networks (2019)

25. Rigaut, F., et al.: Toward a conceptual design for MAVIS. In: Adaptive Optics for Extremely Large Telescopes, vol. 6 (2019)

26. Robbins, H., Monro, S.: A stochastic approximation method. In: The Annals of Mathematical Statistics, pp. 400–407 (1951)

27. Roosta-Khorasani, F., Mahoney, M.W.: Sub-sampled Newton methods. Math. Program. **174**(1–2), 293–326 (2019)

28. Zhang, H., et al.: Predictive learn and apply: MAVIS application-learn. In: Adaptive Optics Systems VII, vol. 11448, p. 114482C. International Society for Optics and Photonics (2020)

GPU-Accelerated Mahalanobis-Average Hierarchical Clustering Analysis

Adam Šmelko[1]([⊠]) ⓘ, Miroslav Kratochvíl[1,2] ⓘ, Martin Kruliš[1] ⓘ,
and Tomáš Sieger[3] ⓘ

[1] Department of Software Engineering, Charles University, Prague, Czech Republic
smelko@ksi.ms.mff.cuni.cz
[2] Luxembourg Centre for Systems Biomedicine, University of Luxembourg,
Esch-sur-Alzette, Luxembourg
[3] Department of Cybernetics, Faculty of Electrical Engineering, Czech Technical
University in Prague, Prague, Czech Republic

Abstract. Hierarchical clustering is a common tool for simplification, exploration, and analysis of datasets in many areas of research. For data originating in flow cytometry, a specific variant of agglomerative clustering based Mahalanobis-average linkage has been shown to produce results better than the common linkages. However, the high complexity of computing the distance limits the applicability of the algorithm to datasets obtained from current equipment. We propose an optimized, GPU-accelerated open-source implementation of the Mahalanobis-average hierarchical clustering that improves the algorithm performance by over two orders of magnitude, thus allowing it to scale to the large datasets. We provide a detailed analysis of the optimizations and collected experimental results that are also portable to other hierarchical clustering algorithms; and demonstrate the use on realistic high-dimensional datasets.

Keywords: Clustering · High-dimensional · Mahalanobis distance · Parallel · GPU · CUDA

1 Introduction

Clustering algorithms are used as common components of many computation pipelines in data analysis and knowledge mining, enabling simplification and classification of huge numbers of observations into separate groups of similar data. Atop of that, a hierarchical clustering analysis (HCA) captures individual relations between clusters of data in a tree-like structure of dataset subsets (a *dendrogram*), where each subtree layer corresponds to a finer level of detail. The tree structure is suitable for many scenarios where the definition of clusters is unclear, such as in interactive analysis of noisy data where the assumptions of non-hierarchical algorithms (such as the requirement for apriori knowledge of cluster number of k-means) are not available. Remarkably, the dendrogram

© Springer Nature Switzerland AG 2021
L. Sousa et al. (Eds.): Euro-Par 2021, LNCS 12820, pp. 580–595, 2021.
https://doi.org/10.1007/978-3-030-85665-6_36

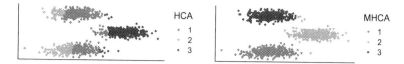

Fig. 1. Mahalanobis-based clustering (MHCA, right) captures the prolonged ellipsoid clusters better than commonly used hierarchical clustering (HCA, left)

output form of HCA provides an ad-hoc dataset ontology which has proven more intuitive for data inspection than the outputs of many other common clustering methods that yield unstructured results.

Here, we focus on hierarchical clustering applications on datasets that originate in flow cytometry, a data acquisition method that allows to quickly measure many biochemical properties of millions of single cells from living organisms. Its widespread use has reached many diverse areas of science including immunology, clinical oncology, marine biology, and developmental biology. The size of the obtained datasets is constantly growing, which naturally drives the demand for fast data processing and advanced analysis methods [11]. From the plethora of developed algorithms, clustering approaches allow easy separation of the measured single cell data into groups that usually correspond to the naturally occurring cell populations and types. Hierarchical clustering improves the result by capturing and revealing more detailed relations between different types of cells.

A dataset from flow cytometry is usually represented as a point cloud in a multidimensional vector space, where each point represents a single measured cell and each dimension represents one measured 'property', typically a presence of some selected surface proteins. Recent hardware development has allowed simple, cheap acquisition of high-quality datasets of several million cells and several dozen of dimensions.

One of the issues in the analysis of this vector space is that the relations between individual dimensions are rather complex, and utilization of simple Euclidean metrics for describing data point similarity is rarely optimal. Fišer et al. [6] have demonstrated the viability of specialized hierarchical clustering analysis method that uses Mahalanobis distance (MHCA) that captures cell clusters of ellipsoid shapes, which are common in cell populations (demonstrated in Fig. 1). Although this approach has proven to detect various elusive dataset phenomena, its scalability remained a concern. In particular, the high computational cost of Mahalanobis distance makes the straightforward implementation on common hardware practically useful only for datasets of up to approximately 10^4 cells.

1.1 Contributions and Outline

In the domain of clustering, algorithm performance has often been successfully improved by proper reimplementation for GPU hardware accelerators [4,8,10]. However, the computation of the MHCA is relatively irregular and rather complex, making the usual acceleration approaches ineffective.

As the main contribution of this paper, we describe our adaptation of MHCA for contemporary GPUs. In particular, we describe a data structure that can be used to accelerate HCA algorithms on GPUs in general, and provide additional insight about efficiency of the specific parts of MHCA algorithm. We subjected the implementation to comprehensive experimental evaluation and compared it with the existing implementation of MHCA to measure the achieved speedup. Finally, we made the implementation available as open-source[1], making it useful for both biological research and further experiments with parallelization of HCAs.

The mathematical and algorithmic overview of MHCA clustering is presented in Sect. 2, Sect. 3 describes our proposed GPU implementation. We summarize the experimental evaluation in Sect. 4. Section 5 puts the our research in proper context with prior work and Sect. 6 concludes the paper.

2   Hierarchical Clustering with Mahalanobis Distance

In this section, we review the necessary formalism and show the Mahalanobis average-linked hierarchical clustering algorithm. The input dataset is a set of points in d-dimensional vector space, here assumed in $\mathbb{R}^d$, which is a common representation for cytometry data [13]. The algorithm produces a binary tree of *clusters* where each resulting cluster is a subset of the input dataset of highly similar ('close' by some metric in the vector space) points.

Mahalanobis distance [12] is defined between a point x and a non-singleton set of compact points P as

$$\delta_M(x, P) = \sqrt{(x - \bar{P})^T (\mathbf{cov}P)^{-1}(x - \bar{P})},$$

where $\bar{P}$ is the centroid (mean) of the set P, and the entries of the covariance matrix are computed as

$$(\mathbf{cov}P)_{ij} = (|P| - 1)^{-1} \cdot \sum_{p \in P} (p_i - \bar{P}_i) \cdot (p_j - \bar{P}_j).$$

One can intuitively view Mahalanobis distance as an Euclidean distance from the cluster centroid that also reflects the shape and the size of the cluster. In particular, in a space that has been linearly transformed so that the covariance matrix of the cluster is a unit matrix, Euclidean and Mahalanobis distance coincide, as shown in Fig. 2.

The MHCA algorithm can be described in steps as follows:

1. *Initialization*: Construct an 'active set' of numbered clusters $P_{1,2,...,n}$, each comprising one input element (data point) as $P_i = \{e_i\}$ for each $i \in \{1...n\}$ where $\{e_1, ..., e_n\}$ denotes the input dataset.
2. *Iteration*: Until the active set contains only a single item, repeat the following:

---

[1] https://github.com/asmelko/gmhc.

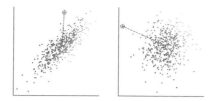

Fig. 2. Mahalanobis distance (left) can be perceived as Euclidean distance (right) in a linearly transformed space where the cluster is perfectly 'round'.

   (a) Compute pairwise dissimilarities of all clusters in A, select the pair (P_r, P_s) with lowest dissimilarity. Output pair (r, s).

   (b) Update the active set by removing P_r, P_s and adding $P_{n+i} = P_r \cup P_s$, where $i > 0$ is an iteration number.

3. *Result*: the binary tree is specified by the trace of $n - 1$ pairs (r, s).

Properties of the output depend mainly on the exact definition of the dissimilarity function used in step 2.a. The common choices include the common 'single' linkage (minimum pairwise distance between the 2 points in different clusters), 'complete' linkage (maximum distance), 'average' linkage (mean distance across clusters), 'centroid' linkage (distance of cluster centroids), and others. The used distance is usually a metric in the vector space, such as Euclidean. The choice of the dissimilarity calculation methods is critical for obtaining results suitable for given analysis; the available methods have been therefore been subjected to much optimization [14].

2.1 Mahalanobis Dissimilarity

Fišer et al. [6] proposed the *full Mahalanobis distance* as a dissimilarity function for HCA as an average of all Mahalanobis distances across clusters, as $\text{FMD}(P_i, P_j) = (|P_i| + |P_j|)^{-1} \left(\sum_k \delta_M((P_i)_k, P_j) + \sum_k \delta_M((P_j)_k, P_i) \right)$. While this construction is intuitively correct and allows the clustering to precisely capture various dataset phenomena that are common in cytometry, the definition opens many inefficiencies and border cases that need to be resolved:

- Mahalanobis distance may be undefined for small clusters because the covariance matrix is singular or nearly-singular. This can be resolved by a complete or partial fallback to robust distance measures, as detailed in Sect. 2.2.
- Because the Mahalanobis distance of a fixed point to a cluster *decreases* when the cluster size increases (e.g., as a result of being merged with another cluster), the minimal dissimilarity selected in the step 3 of the algorithm may sometimes be smaller than the previously selected one. A correction is thus needed to keep the dissimilarity sequence properly monotonic, giving uncluttered, interpretable dendrogram display [5].
- The amount of required computation is significantly higher than with the other linkages (dissimilarity functions), requiring additional operations for

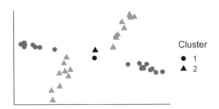

Fig. 3. An example of two clusters for which the CMD fails to satisfactorily approximate the FMD (centroids are plotted in black).

computing the inverted covariance matrix and covariance-scaled Euclidean distances. We mitigate this problem by massive parallelization with GPU accelerators, as detailed in Sect. 3.

The computation of the 'full' average Manalanobis distance is unavoidably demanding, requiring many matrix-vector multiplications to compute distances between all points of one cluster and the opposite cluster. Following the variations of Euclidean dissimilarity measures for HCA, a *centroid-based Mahalanobis distance* may be specified to use only the average of the distance to the centroids of the other cluster, as $\mathrm{CMD}(P_i, P_j) = \frac{1}{2}\left(\delta_M(\bar{P}_i, P_j) + \delta_M(\bar{P}_j, P_i)\right)$. The result may be viewed as a fast approximate substitute for the full variant because the simplification removes a significant portion of the computational overhead and still produces sound results in many cases. The difference between CMD and FMD is highly pronounced only when the centroids of the clusters are near, but their respective covariances differ, as visualized in Fig. 3. Fortunately, such situations are quite rare in clustering of realistic datasets.

2.2 Singularity of Cluster Covariance Matrix

In early iterations of MHCA, the clusters consist of only a few points. Covariance matrix of a small cluster is likely singular, which means it is impossible to compute its inverse required by the Mahalanobis distance measure. Furthermore, even for more points the covariance matrix may be nearly singular, and using its ill-conditioned inverse will yield inaccurate results and numeric floating-point anomalies (such as negative distances or infinities).

To solve this problem, Fišer et al. [6] proposed the following approach: If the number of elements in a cluster relative to whole dataset size is lower than a threshold, the covariance matrix of such cluster is transformed so it can be inverted, and handled in a numerically safe manner. We will denote the used threshold as the *Mahalanobis threshold*, and categorize the clusters as *sub-threshold* and *super-threshold cluster*, depending on their size being below and above the Mahalanobis threshold respectively.

We later explore the following *subthreshold handling methods* for managing the problematic covariance matrix values:

- MAHAL smoothly pushes the vectors of the covariance matrices of the sub-threshold clusters towards a unit sphere, so that the space around the clusters is not excessively distorted (or projected).
- EUCLIDMAHAL enforces unit (spherical) covariance vectors of the sub-threshold clusters (thus enforcing Euclidean distances). Despite the simplicity and effectiveness, the hard thresholding may lead to a non-intuitive behavior; for example, the merging of a pair of large elliptical clusters that are just above the threshold may be prioritized over a pair of more similar but sub-threshold clusters.
- EUCLID enforces unit covariances of all clusters *only until the last sub-threshold cluster is merged*. This option usually leads to a viable formation of compact clusters, but completely ignores the possible intrinsic structure of several super-threshold clusters.

2.3   Complexity and Parallelization Opportunities of MHCA

A straightforward serial implementation of MHCA (such as the implementation in mhca R package[2]) works with iterative updates of the dissimilarity matrix. Let us examine in detail the time complexity of the individual algorithm steps on a dataset that contains n points of d dimensions:

First, the algorithm constructs a dissimilarity matrix in $\mathcal{O}(d \cdot n^2)$, and identifies the most similar cluster pair in $\mathcal{O}(n^2)$. Then a total of $n - 1$ iterations is performed as such:

- a covariance matrix of the merged cluster is computed ($\mathcal{O}(d^2 \cdot n)$) and inverted ($\mathcal{O}(d^3)$),
- the dissimilarity matrix is updated ($\mathcal{O}(d^2 \cdot n)$), and
- the new most similar cluster pair is identified ($\mathcal{O}(n^2)$).

The total complexity is thus $\mathcal{O}(d \cdot n^2 + (n-1) \cdot (d^2 \cdot n + d^3 + n^2))$. Assuming $d \ll n$, the asymptotic complexity can be simplified to $\mathcal{O}(n^3)$. Since we cache the unchanged dissimilarity matrix entries, the memory complexity is $\mathcal{O}(n^2)$.

In an idealized parallel execution environment (PRAM model with concurrent reads and infinite parallelism), we could improve the algorithm to perform faster as follows: All cluster dissimilarity computations (including the later dissimilarity matrix update) can be performed in parallel in $\mathcal{O}(d^3 \cdot \log n)$, using parallel reduction algorithm for computing the covariance sums. The most similar cluster pair can be selected using a parallel reduction over the dissimilarity matrix in $\mathcal{O}(\log^2 n)$. The total required time would thus be reduced to $\mathcal{O}(d^3 n \log^2 n)$ (again assuming $d \ll n$), using $\mathcal{O}(n^2)$ memory.

While this suggests two main ways of performance improvement for the massively parallel GPU implementation, the specifics of the current GPUs pose problems for such naive parallelization approach:

---

[2] https://rdrr.io/github/tsieger/mhca.

- Parallelization of any single covariance matrix computation will improve performance only if the covariance matrix is sufficiently large, otherwise the performance may be reduced by scheduling overhead and limited parallelism.
- Scanning of the large dissimilarity matrix is parallelizable, but is hindered by relatively small amount of available GPU memory and insufficient memory throughput.

In the following section, we address these problems with optimizations that make the computation viable on the modern accelerators. In particular, we show that the computation of a covariance matrix can be divided into many independent parts, thus exposing sufficient parallelization opportunities, and we demonstrate a technique for efficient caching of intermediate contents of the dissimilarity matrix to reduce the memory footprint and throughput requirements of the algorithm.

3   GPU Implementation

Memory handling optimizations form the essential part of our GPU implementation of MHCA, here called *GMHC* for brevity. Most importantly, we address the tremendous memory requirement of storing the dissimilarity matrix ($\mathcal{O}(n^2)$) for large n. We replace this matrix with a special *nearest-neighbor array*, which provides similar caching benefits, but requires only $\mathcal{O}(n)$ memory. This saving in memory volume is redeemed by a slightly higher computational complexity; however, the measured improvement in scalability warrants this trade-off.

Definition 1 (Nearest neighbor array). *For clusters $P_1, \ldots, P_n$ and a symmetric dissimilarity function d, the* nearest neighbor array N *contains $n - 1$ elements defined as*

$$N_i = \operatorname{argmin}_{j > i} d(P_i, P_j).$$

Maintaining a nearest neighbor array in the HCA computation allows us to reduce the amount of distance computations performed after each update. In particular, when a cluster pair (P_i, P_j) is merged into new cluster P_m, only elements with values i and j have to be recomputed, along with the new value for N_m

This is enabled by the symmetry of d, which allowed us to ensure that the contents of the nearest neighbor arrays at some index *only depend on clusters with higher indices*. If we set the new index m to be smaller than all existing indices in the array (i.e., $m = 1$, shifting the rest of the array), the newly appearing cluster can not invalidate the cached indices for the original array, and only the entries that refer to the disappearing clusters i, j need to be recomputed. In consequence, if an already present cluster P_k was to form the most similar pair with the new cluster P_m, this information would be present the $\operatorname{argmin}_{k > m}$ computation, and stored in N_m instead of N_k.

In an optimistic scenario, the above optimization can be used to limit the number of elements that need to be updated in each iteration by a constant number, which leads to a major increase in overall performance. This constant limit is supported by empirical observations on realistic datasets with around 1 million of objects, where the number of triggered updates was rarely over 50. Further, we reduce the need for recomputation by caching several 'nearest' neighbors for each entry of N:

Definition 2 (Neighbor buffer). *A sorted list of L nearest neighbor indices (respectively to the $\mathrm{argmin}_{j>i}$ in Definition 1) stored for each item in N is called a neighbor buffer.*

To ensure the efficiency of the process, we split the update of neighbor buffers to two parts: First, when (P_i, P_j) is merged into P_m, all buffers are filtered and values i and j are removed (i.e., replaced with dummy values). On recomputation, all empty buffers (including newly formed N_m) are filled with indices of nearest L neighbors, while the partially filled buffers are left intact. This allows us to reuse the intermediate results of the computation of an N array entry for as much as L recomputations that involve the cluster.

The complexity of updating the nearest neighbor array element i for the neighbor buffer of size L on m clusters, using a pair dissimilarity computation of complexity $\mathcal{O}(\delta)$, is $\mathcal{O}((m - i) \cdot (\delta + L))$. The reduced amount of index updates thus trades off for index update complexity, depending on L. The optimal choice of L is discussed later in Sect. 4.2.

3.1   Algorithm Overview

The hierarchical clustering of n initial clusters is a series of $n - 1$ iterations, such that in each iteration two clusters are merged into one. Before the first iteration, the nearest neighbor array N must be initialized. Each subsequent iteration comprises the following compact steps:

1. Scan the neighbor array and fetch the most similar cluster pair
2. Create a new cluster by merging the cluster pair
   - Compute its corresponding centroid and covariance matrix
   - Transform and invert the covariance matrix
3. Update the neighbor array (only required if $n \geq 3$)

The individual parts of the algorithm may be scheduled and executed dynamically, ordered only the data dependencies as displayed in Fig. 4. Mainly, this allows us to split the update of the neighbor array into update of the neighbors of old clusters (i, j) and the update of the newly created cluster. Naturally, the individual steps are internally implemented as data-parallel operations as well.

In GMHC, we control the iteration loop from the host code, while the work of each update step is implemented within a CUDA kernel. Our code employs CUDA streams [1] to efficiently implement the execution overlaps, creating some high-level task parallelism in the process. In the rest of this section, we detail the implementations of the individual CUDA kernels.

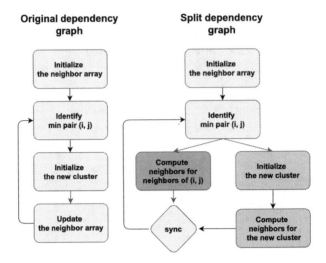

Fig. 4. The original graph of dependencies and the proposed split dependency graph, where blue and yellow boxes can be executed concurrently. (Color figure online)

3.2 Cluster Merging and Covariance Computation

Covariance matrix $\mathbf{cov}P$ of cluster P (and its inversion) is computed only when a cluster is formed; in our case when two clusters are merged. In GMHC, we iterate over all data points $x \in P$ and each item $(\mathbf{cov}P)_{ij}$ is computed as a sum of centered products of x_i and x_j (following the definition from Sect. 2). As the most pressing issue, the performance of this process depends on fast finding of data points x that belong to the cluster in the array of all data points.

A possible straightforward solution, storing an array of assigned points for each data cluster so that the assigned points can be accessed in a fast and compact way, would require dynamic memory allocation or manual apriori over-allocation, and many data moving operations. We settled for a more compact solution with an assignment array that stores a cluster indices for each data point. Although that does not require data copying, both the cluster merge and the retrieval of one cluster points will take $\mathcal{O}(n)$ time. Fortunately, the two operations can be performed by a single parallel scan of the assignment array in this case.

Covariance Kernel Implementation. The covariance kernel takes advantage of the symmetry of a covariance matrix and computes only its upper triangle. Additionally, extra parallelism can be obtained by slicing the computation of the covariance matrix from Sect. 2 over individual data point contributions $\mathbf{S}^x$, as $\mathbf{cov}P = (|P| - 1)^{-1} \sum_{x \in P} \mathbf{S}^x$, where $\mathbf{S}^x_{ij} = (x_i - \bar{\mathbf{x}}_i) \cdot (x_j - \bar{\mathbf{x}}_j)$.

The kernel is implemented as a loop over all data points. A whole CUDA warp is assigned one data point and computes the intermediate $\mathbf{S}^x$. These are then added together in a two-step reduction—all intermediate states within a

CUDA block are reduced using shared memory, which is then followed by a global reduction performed by a separate kernel launch that outputs the totals in a single covariance matrix.

Notably, the covariance matrices of single-point clusters are not computed; rather, they are assigned a default unit matrix.

3.3   Inverse Covariance Storage Optimization

The Mahalanobis distance requires inversion of the covariance matrix, which needs to be computed from the results of the previous step. We use `cuSolver` library[3] for implementing the matrix inversion, namely the routines `potrf` and `potri`.

The inverted matrix is subsequently transformed to better suit the Mahalanobis distance formula, and to eliminate redundant computations later in the process. In particular, we rewrite the Mahalanobis formula for inverse covariance matrix M as a quadratic form

$$x^T M x = \sum_{i=1}^{d} \sum_{j=1}^{d} m_{ij} x_i x_j = \sum_{i=1}^{d} m_{ii} x_i^2 + \sum_{i=1}^{d} \sum_{j>i}^{d} 2 m_{ij} x_i x_j,$$

allowing us to store only the upper-triangular part of the matrix, pre-multiplied by 2.

3.4   Maintenance of Nearest Neighbor Array

GMHC implements 2 similar processes for the neighbor array initialization and update, differing mainly in the granularity of the task size. We thus only focus on the update implementation.

First, specific simplified version of kernel for computing the distances is used for cases when the covariance matrix is unit, falling back to efficient implementation of Euclidean distance. The decision which kernel to execute is done in the host code, depending solely on the selected subthreshold handling method (explained in Sect. 2.2) and the size of the two involved clusters. The decision is formalized in Table 1.

Table 1. The host-side selection of the neighbor-distance kernel

Subthreshold handling method	Sub/sub	Sub/super	Super/super
EUCLID	euclid	euclid	maha
EUCLIDMAHAL	euclid	maha	maha
MAHAL	maha	maha	maha

---

[3] https://docs.nvidia.com/cuda/cusolver/index.html.

The Neighbor Array Update Kernel. The update operation of nearest neighbor buffer array entry N_i is defined as finding L nearest clusters with index greater than i, and storing their ordered indices into N_i neighbor buffer. We split this operation in two parts, each handled by a separate kernel:

1. Compute distances between all relevant cluster pairs concurrently.
2. Reduce the results into a single nearest neighbor buffer entry.

The execution of the first step differs between the Euclidean and the Mahalanobis neighbor computation. While the former parallelizes trivially with one thread computing one distance value, the complex computation of Mahalanobis distance executes faster if the whole warp cooperates in one distance computation.

The precise operation needed to compute the Mahalanobis distance is a vector-matrix-vector multiplication. To evaluate the formula from Sect. 3.3, we utilize the fuse-multiply-add intrinsic instructions to accumulate the results of the assigned work into their privatized buffers, which are subsequently reduced using fast warp-shuffle instructions.

In the second step, which selects the nearest L indices, is the same for both distance measures. We use a three-level implementation: At the first level, the threads accumulate local minima of small array slices into their registers. At the second level, each thread block utilizes the shared memory to efficiently exchange data and compute block-wise minima. The third level collects the resulting minima and performs the same final reduction on a single thread block (thus efficiently utilizing intra-block synchronization). The second and the third level could be fused together if the atomic instructions were used to synchronize data updates explicitly; however, we observed the improvement was negligible and preferred to reduce the design complexity instead.

This whole neighbor buffer 'refill' operation is performed concurrently for every index in the nearest neighbor array that needs to be updated. Our implementation executes a separate CUDA grid for each update, which reduces implementation complexity but still allows the grids to run concurrently and utilize the entire GPU.

4   Experimental Results

We have subjected our implementation of GMHC to extensive experimental evaluation, measuring the effect of main design choices in the algorithm. In this section, we present the most important results and we put them in proper context, particularly with respect to parameter selection and scaling.

4.1   Benchmarking Methodology and Datasets

The experiments were performed on two systems—a high-end server equipped with NVIDIA Tesla V100 SXM2 (32 GB) and a mainstream PC with NVIDIA

GeForce GTX 980 (4 GB). Both systems used Linux CentOS 8 with CUDA Toolkit (11.2).

We used the original MHCA clustering implementation by Fišer et al. [6] as a baseline, which is, to our best knowledge, the only other publicly available MHCA implementation. The baseline algorithm is written in C as strictly sequential without explicit utilization of SIMD instructions; but it properly utilizes the highly-optimized `Blas` library for most heavy computation. It was benchmarked on a high-end server with Intel Xeon Gold 5218 CPU, clocked at 2.3 GHz (with 64 logical cores) and 384 GB RAM (the same as the high-end server used for benchmarking GMHC). We stress that the comparison between CPU and GPU implementation is not entirely objective, and the test results should be perceived more as a measure of overall data capacity improvement than of the implementation quality. We did not test MHCA on the mainstream PC platform, because of the enormous $\mathcal{O}(n^2)$ memory requirements totaled to hundreds of gigabytes in our benchmarks.

As testing data, we used several high-dimensional datasets originating in mass cytometry [15], namely the `Nilsson_rare` (44K data points, 14 dimensions), `Levine_32dim` (265K data points, 32 dimensions) and `Mosmann_rare` (400k data points, 15 dimensions). For brevity, we report only a subset of the measured results, but these should generalize well to other data. In particular, we did not observe any significant data-dependent performance differences.

In all experiments, we measured the wall time of the total algorithm execution. The experiments were performed multiple times to prevent random deviations in measurement; we display mean values of the measurements. Because the experimental evaluations on both mentioned GPUs behaved consistently with no surprising differences on any particular hardware, we present mainly the results from Tesla V100 SXM2 GPU unless stated otherwise.

4.2   Experiment Results

First, we evaluated the scalability of the GMHC implementation depending on the size of the dataset. The inputs of different sizes were achieved by randomly sub-sampling the Mosmann dataset. Figure 5 shows the wall time for each sub-threshold method, revealing that the performance scales sub-quadratically with data size. Notably, the optimized implementations of EUCLID and EUCLIDMA-HAL scale about 10× better than full MAHAL for this dimensionality.

The tradeoff between Euclidean and Mahalanobis computation in the first two methods can be further controlled by setting the threshold value t, controlling whether a cluster is considered small or large, and in turn, deciding the dissimilarity metric to use. Figure 6 summarizes the performance gains for various setting of this threshold.

In the figure, $t = 0$ forces all methods perform dissimilarity measurements using the Mahalanobis distance. When we increase t only very slightly to 0.01, the EUCLID method time decreases dramatically and stays almost the same in the remainder of t range. This is often caused by small sub-threshold clusters that are propagated to the very end of the clustering, which postpones the switch to

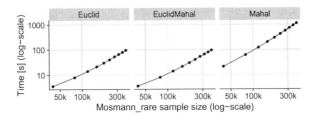

Fig. 5. Comparison of the subthreshold distance computation method performance.

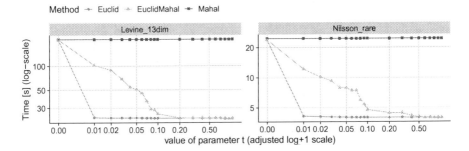

Fig. 6. Clustering time of subthreshold methods with varying Mahalanobis threshold value on two different datasets.

the Mahalanobis distance. On the other hand, the EUCLIDMAHAL method shifts its wall time smoothly towards the EUCLID method as t increases, which is a consequence of the first super-threshold cluster appearing later in the process.

To determine the optimal value of the nearest neighbor buffer size, we benchmarked the clustering of datasets with a range of parameters L (Fig. 7).

Curiously, the observed results show that while $L = 1$ is optimal for EUCLID and EUCLIDMAHAL, it performs worst for MAHAL method. This is a consequence of the used distance function in dissimilarity measurements—for the EUCLID and EUCLIDMAHAL method, where the Euclidean distance function dominates, the time difference for performing smaller number of neighbor updates did not balance the increased time complexity of a single update. The MAHAL method works optimally with $L = 2$; as the L increases further, the performance starts to decrease again.

Similarly, the optimal value of L increases for higher-dimensional datasets, which we tested on Levine_32dim data (detailed results not shown). In particular, for Mahalanobis distance, we measured the same optimal value $L = 2$ with much greater performance gain (over 30%) against $L = 1$ than on the Mosmann dataset. We expect that the optimal value of L will continue to increase with the dimensionality of the dataset in case of the MAHAL method. On the other hand, the Euclidean-based methods kept their optimum at $L = 1$.

Finally, we compared the performance of GPU implementation of MHCA to the CPU baseline, to estimate the outcome for practical data analysis scalability.

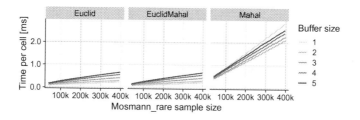

Fig. 7. Comparison of neighbor buffer sizes for subthreshold methods ($t = 0.5$)

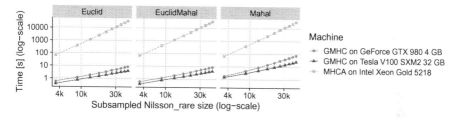

Fig. 8. GMHC and MHCA comparison on Nilsson dataset with default $t = 0.5$.

Figure 8 indicates an overall performance increase by up to 1400× in case of the MAHAL method and by up to 8000× in case of mixed-Euclidean methods. When comparing performance on the older 'gaming' GTX 980 GPU, the speedups were around 400× and 4000×, respectively. In summary, modern GPUs have been able to accelerate the MHCA task by more than three orders of magnitude, which is consistent with the effects of parallelization applied to many other clustering algorithms.

5   Related Work

The original version of MHCA clustering for flow cytometry by Fišer et al. [6] used a MATLAB implementation to analyze datasets of around 10^4 multi-dimensional data points. Due to the limited scalability and interoperability with modern data analysis environments, a C version of the algorithm has been implemented within R package mhca and enhanced with the possibility of assuming apriori clusters for approximation, to reduce the unfavorable $\mathcal{O}(n^3)$ time complexity for large datasets. That allowed the authors to process datasets of around 10^6 data points within an interactive environments [9].

Despite of the performance advancement, the approximation in the method did not retain the sensitivity required to detect various small clusters of interest (i.e., small cell populations), such as the 'minimum residual disease' cells crucial for diagnosis of acute myeloid leukemia [6]. Similar approximations are used in many other clustering methods to gain performance at the cost of precision justifiable in a specific domain; including the 2-level meta-clustering approach of FlowSOM [7], and advanced approximate neighborhood graph structure of FastPG [2].

Acceleration of HCAs on GPUs has been explored by several authors: Chang et al. [3] discuss hierarchical clustering of gene mRNA levels assayable by DNA microarray technology. Their GPU code computes matrix of pairwise distances between genes using Pearson correlation coefficient as one of the present metrics, and utilized a special property of data to effectively perform single-linkage over the present matrix. Zhang et al. [16] used similar clustering methodology, but employed GPU texture elements for the data representation of gene expression profile HCA. Both acceleration methods resulted in performance increase between 5× to 30× on datasets of 10^4 data points.

6   Conclusions

We have presented an implementation approach for Mahalanobis-average linkage hierarchical clustering algorithm, which utilizes modern parallel GPU accelerators to increase its performance. In the benchmarks, our GPU implementation GMHC has achieved over $10^3×$ speedup on practical datasets over the current CPU implementations, which enabled scaling of the MHCA algorithm to large datasets produced by current data acquisition methods.

Together with the open-source implementation, we have provided a new high-performance building block for dataset analyses which should support the growing demand for fast data analysis methods not only in cytometry, but also in other areas of data analysis dealing with irregularly shaped Gaussian clusters.

The implementation structure detailed in the paper has allowed us to streamline the utilization of parallel hardware for accelerating general hierarchical clustering algorithms. We expect that the proposed data structures will be ported to support acceleration of dissimilarity measures in other hierarchical clustering methods, providing a solid building block for future acceleration of data mining and knowledge discovery.

Acknowledgements. This work was supported by Czech Science Foundation (GAČR) project 19-22071Y, by ELIXIR CZ LM2018131 (MEYS), by Charles University grant SVV-260451, and by Czech Health Research Council (AZV) [NV18-08-00385].

References

1. CUDA C++ Programming Guide (2021). https://docs.nvidia.com/cuda/cuda-c-programming-guide
2. Bodenheimer, T., et al.: Fastpg: fast clustering of millions of single cells. bioRxiv (2020)
3. Chang, D.J., Kantardzic, M.M., Ouyang, M.: Hierarchical clustering with cuda/gpu. In: ISCA PDCCS, pp. 7–12. Citeseer (2009)
4. Cuomo, S., De Angelis, V., Farina, G., Marcellino, L., Toraldo, G.: A gpu-accelerated parallel k-means algorithm. Comput. Electric. Eng. **75**, 262–274 (2019)
5. Everitt, B., Skrondal, A.: The Cambridge dictionary of statistics, vol. 106. Cambridge University Press, Cambridge (2002)

6. Fišer, K., et al.: Detection and monitoring of normal and leukemic cell populations with hierarchical clustering of flow cytometry data. Cytometry Part A **81**(1), 25–34 (2012)
7. van Gassen, S., et al.: Flowsom: using self-organizing maps for visualization and interpretation of cytometry data. Cytometry Part A **87**(7), 636–645 (2015)
8. Gowanlock, M., Rude, C.M., Blair, D.M., Li, J.D., Pankratius, V.: Clustering throughput optimization on the gpu. In: 2017 IEEE International Parallel and Distributed Processing Symposium (IPDPS), pp. 832–841. IEEE (2017)
9. Kratochvíl, M., Bednárek, D., Sieger, T., Fišer, K., Vondrášek, J.: Shinysom: graphical som-based analysis of single-cell cytometry data. Bioinformatics **36**(10), 3288–3289 (2020)
10. Kruliš, M., Kratochvíl, M.: Detailed analysis and optimization of cuda k-means algorithm. In: 49th International Conference on Parallel Processing-ICPP, pp. 1–11 (2020)
11. Lugli, E., Roederer, M., Cossarizza, A.: Data analysis in flow cytometry: the future just started. Cytometry Part A **77**(7), 705–713 (2010)
12. Mahalanobis, P.C.: On the generalized distance in statistics. National Institute of Science of India (1936)
13. Shapiro, H.M.: Practical Flow Cytometry. John Wiley & Sons, Hoboken (2005)
14. Shirkhorshidi, A.S., Aghabozorgi, S., Wah, T.Y.: A comparison study on similarity and dissimilarity measures in clustering continuous data. PloS one **10**(12), e0144059 (2015)
15. Weber, L.M., Robinson, M.D.: Comparison of clustering methods for high-dimensional single-cell flow and mass cytometry data. Cytometry Part A **89**(12), 1084–1096 (2016)
16. Zhang, Q., Zhang, Y.: Hierarchical clustering of gene expression profiles with graphics hardware acceleration. Pattern Recogn. Lett. **27**(6), 676–681 (2006)

High Performance Architectures and Accelerators

PrioRAT: Criticality-Driven Prioritization Inside the On-Chip Memory Hierarchy

Vladimir Dimić[1,2(✉)] , Miquel Moretó[1,2] , Marc Casas[1,2] ,
and Mateo Valero[1,2]

[1] Barcelona Supercomputing Center (BSC), Barcelona, Spain
{vladimir.dimic,miquel.moreto,marc.casas,mateo.valero}@bsc.es
[2] Universitat Politècnica de Catalunya (UPC), Barcelona, Spain

Abstract. The ever-increasing gap between the processor and main memory speeds requires careful utilization of the limited memory link. This is additionally emphasized for the case of memory-bound applications. Prioritization of memory requests in the memory controller is one of the approaches to improve performance of such codes. However, current designs do not consider high-level information about parallel applications. In this paper, we propose a holistic approach to this problem, where the runtime system-level knowledge is made available in hardware. Processor exploits this information to better prioritize memory requests, while introducing negligible hardware cost. Our design is based on the notion of critical path in the execution of a parallel code. The critical tasks are accelerated by prioritizing their memory requests within the on-chip memory hierarchy. As a result, we reduce the critical path and improve the overall performance up to 1.19× compared to the baseline systems.

1 Introduction

The growing gap between the processor and memory speeds, often referred to as the *Memory Wall* [39], has been one of the important factors driving the design of modern computing systems. In the last decades, DRAM chips have become more complex, introducing multiple levels of parallelism to allow for a higher bandwidth between the processor and the memory. On the processor side, several components, such as caches and prefetchers, serve to provide higher effective bandwidth and reduced latency between the cores and the memory subsystem. The interface between the processor and the main memory, the memory controller, is also an important point for optimization.

Early memory controller designs adopted simple request ordering algorithms from queuing theory, such as *first come-first served*, which was further improved to take into account the *row buffer* locality [32]. Multi-core processors introduce new challenges to memory request scheduling. It is necessary to take into account the priority of threads, avoid starvation and ensure forward-progress of

© Springer Nature Switzerland AG 2021
L. Sousa et al. (Eds.): Euro-Par 2021, LNCS 12820, pp. 599–615, 2021.
https://doi.org/10.1007/978-3-030-85665-6_37

all co-running threads [23, 25–27]. However, these proposals lack the awareness of the global impact of prioritization decisions on the execution of parallel applications. The relatively short-term knowledge available by observing hardware-level behavior is not always enough to achieve the best performance improvements.

Taking a look at the software level reveals that modern parallel computer systems are becoming more difficult to program due to their increasing complexity. Modern programming models aid a programmer in creating well-performing parallel applications by offering simple ways to describe parallel constructs. For example, task-based parallel programming models introduce the notion of a *task* as a sequential part of the application that can run simultaneously with other tasks [6, 16, 22]. A programmer specifies these tasks and their dependencies using pre-defined annotations. The correct execution and synchronization of the tasks are handled by the runtime system library. Thus, the runtime system contains by design the information about the parallel code and the underlying hardware, and therefore can serve as an interface between these two layers. The usefulness of runtime system-level information in the context of HPC applications and hardware has been extensively studied [1, 4, 5, 7, 10, 11, 19, 24, 38].

In this paper, we further explore the opportunities to exploit the high-level information about a parallel application inside the hardware. In particular, we focus on the notion of critical paths in the context of task-parallel codes. We define *critical tasks* as the tasks belonging to the critical path of the execution. Following the definition of the critical path, reducing the duration of these tasks reduces the execution time of the whole parallel code. Previous works have exploited task criticality to improve scheduling on heterogeneous systems [7] as well as for power management [5]. These proposals, however, do not target generic chip-multiprocessors as they depend on asymmetric processor design and voltage-frequency scaling, respectively. In addition, they focus only on runtime systems and core designs, without targeting the memory hierarchy.

To overcome these shortcomings, we design PrioRAT, a general solution for all modern chip-multiprocessors. We follow a holistic approach where the runtime system knowledge is used in hardware to drive the prioritization algorithm. Specifically, we exploit the notion of task criticality, motivated by the discussion in the previous paragraph. During the execution, the runtime system computes tasks' criticality and provides it to the underlying hardware. Then, on-chip hardware resources make use of this information to prioritize the memory requests coming from the critical tasks. As a result, the critical tasks have their memory requests served faster, which reduces their duration and, thus, improves the performance of the whole parallel application by reducing the length of the critical path.

This paper makes the following contributions:

– We extend scheduling algorithms inside the shared on-chip components to consider memory request criticality. Task criticality is estimated by the runtime system using existing methods and is forwarded to the hardware via the well-supported memory mapped registers, which does not require changes to the processor's ISA.

- We evaluate the performance of PrioRAT on a cycle-accurate microarchitectural simulator using a set of characteristic workloads from the high performance computing (HPC) domain. PrioRAT outperforms the baseline system without prioritization by up to 1.19× in terms of execution time.

The remaining of this document is structured as follows. Section 2 provides the context for our work and introduces the intuition behind memory request prioritization. Section 3 explains our proposal in detail. Section 4 describes the experimental setup, while Sect. 5 presents the results of the evaluation. Finally, Sect. 6 describes related work and Sect. 7 concludes this paper.

2   Background and Motivation

Since the introduction of the first multi-core processor at the very beginning of this century, the importance producing well-performing parallel codes has been recognized. Many programming models have been designed to ease the development process of parallel applications [6,16,17,22,28]. Some of these programming models are based on task-based parallelization. A way to improve the performance of a task-parallel application is to identify the critical path in the execution and reduce its duration. There are many works devoted to identification [3,12,20] and acceleration of the critical path [5,7–9,14,36].

On the hardware level, the increasing gap between processor and memory speeds warrants giving a special attention to improving the utilization of the main memory resources. Some previous works propose reordering DRAM commands to achieve higher throughput [29,32,37]. However, they do not target multi-core processors. Other solutions focus on ensuring fair share of memory resources among all the threads [25–27]. Another family of scheduling algorithms considers the criticality of each memory request [15]. These proposals try to improve the performance of each thread independently by accelerating requests that have most negative impact on the execution time.

However, such designs do not consider the high-level notion of the critical path at the application level. In certain parallel codes, it is possible to sacrifice the performance of non-critical tasks by giving priority to critical tasks in order to reduce the critical path and, thus, the overall execution time.

To illustrate the effects of critical task prioritization, we develop a synthetic application that performs a strided access to an array. The stride is a configurable parameter used to indirectly tune the pressure on the caches and main memory by controlling the reuse of the accessed cache lines. The application is split into tasks and each task accesses its portion of the input array. Tasks are split in two groups: (i) critical tasks, which are artificially serialized to simulate a critical path, and (ii) non-critical tasks, which can run in parallel with other tasks.

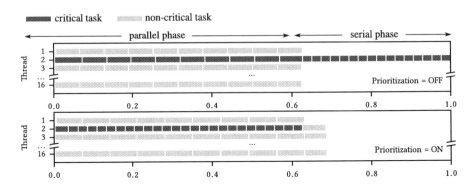

Fig. 1. Execution traces of the synthetic benchmark in the baseline configuration (top) and prioritized configuration (bottom).

We configure the benchmark to run with 24 critical and 150 non-critical tasks, each accessing an array of 256 KB with a stride of 16. This is equivalent to one access per cache line and achieves the highest memory contention in our simulated environment. We simulate two executions of the benchmark on a cycle-accurate simulator modeling a 16-core processor with a three-level cache hierarchy and main memory[1]. The first run is performed on a baseline system without prioritization, while in the second execution, we prioritize the memory requests issued by the critical tasks. Figure 1 shows the traces of these two executions. Each trace displays the tasks and their duration during the execution (x-axis) and the thread where they execute (y-axis). Time is normalized to the execution on the baseline configuration and both traces have the same time scale. Critical and non-critical tasks are colored differently.

In the baseline configuration (see Fig. 1, top), we observe the serialization of critical tasks and its negative impact on the total execution time – more than 30% of the execution time is spent running only serial code. We also note that during the parallel phase, the critical tasks execute slower compared to the last third of execution. This is a result of the high memory contention caused by the concurrent execution of many tasks in the parallel phase.

The bottom part of Fig. 1 shows the trace when memory requests issued by critical tasks are given priority in the shared on-chip resources. The effects of the prioritization are clearly manifested through the reduced duration of the critical tasks. The non-critical tasks execute slower than in the baseline configuration, but the whole application finishes faster because the critical path is reduced.

This example clearly demonstrates the importance of having a high-level notion of the application within the hardware as it enables better decisions at hardware level. With these conclusions in mind, we develop PrioRAT, a solution that exploits the runtime system information about a task-based parallel code to guide prioritization of memory requests inside the on-chip memory hierarchy.

---

[1] Section 4 describes the experimental setup in detail.

3   PrioRAT: Criticality-Driven Prioritization within the On-Chip Memory Hierarchy

PrioRAT is a holistic approach to prioritization in the on-chip memory hierarchy driven by the application-specific information available at the runtime system level. The runtime system library detects a critical path in an execution of a parallel application and marks the tasks belonging to the critical path as *critical*. In hardware, we add a bit to each request to signal its criticality. The queues in the on-chip memory hierarchy are extended to prioritize critical requests (also called *prioritized requests*). Depending on the way the task criticality is exploited, we define two PrioRAT configurations:

- PR.static is a configuration where certain cores are configured to always issue prioritized memory requests. The runtime system is aware of the cores' configuration and schedules critical tasks onto prioritized cores.
- PR.dynamic is an approach where the runtime system controls whether each core issues prioritized requests depending on the criticality of a task scheduled on a given core. This approach requires an interface between the processor and the runtime system to enable switching of the configuration of the core.

In both configurations, the shared resources in the on-chip memory hierarchy, i.e., the last-level cache (LLC) and the memory controller, and the interconnect are extended to handle the prioritization of requests within their queues. In the following sections, we explain in detail the modifications to all relevant components necessary to implement PrioRAT.

3.1   Programming Model and Runtime System Support

We build PrioRAT on top of the existing parallel task-based programming model, OpenMP [28]. OpenMP is a directive-based programming model, where a programmer defines units of parallelism, such as tasks and loop iterations and defines dependencies between tasks. The runtime system library handles the scheduling of the defined tasks and loops on a multi-threaded machine. Internally, the runtime system tracks tasks using a Task Dependency Graph (TDG), which is constructed following the programmer-provided dependency information and implicit synchronization primitives. We use Nanos++ [2] as the runtime system that supports OpenMP-compatible task-parallel applications.

Inside Nanos++, we exploit an existing algorithm, called *bottom-level*, that analyzes the TDG and identifies a critical path of the execution by observing the distance of each task from the bottom of the TDG. This distance is updated on every insertion of a new task into the TDG by traversing the TDG from the bottom to the root. After the update, the root node stores the length of the longest path to the bottom level. The algorithm determines the critical path by following the longest path(s) along the way from the root to the bottom level. There may be several paths that satisfy this condition. In that case, the runtime system exposes to the user two configuration options: (i) choosing one random

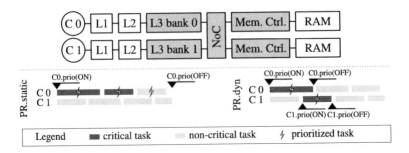

Fig. 2. Top: Overview of a dual-core system implementing PrioRAT. Colored components employ priority queues to prioritize memory requests. Bottom: Examples of executions of two PrioRAT configurations.

such path as the critical path, or (ii) marking all such paths as critical. The second option may result in more critical tasks compared to the first one.

The task criticality information is used by the runtime system to enable memory request prioritization inside the hardware. Depending on the PrioRAT configuration, the runtime system interacts differently with the processor, which is illustrated at the bottom of Fig. 2.

PR.static is a static configuration where each core is set up to either always or never issue prioritized requests. The processor configuration is exposed to the runtime system via command line arguments or environmental variables. The scheduler within the runtime system assigns tasks to the cores taking into account task's criticality and whether a core issues prioritized requests. Critical tasks are preferentially scheduled on prioritized cores, while non-critical tasks can be scheduled on any core, depending on their availability.

In *PR.dynamic*, the task criticality information is provided to the processor cores by the runtime system using memory-mapped registers. Before each task begins execution, the runtime system signals to the core the criticality of that task. A core that executes a critical task issues high priority memory requests.

3.2   Hardware Extensions

This section introduces the micro-architectural extensions necessary to implement PrioRAT. The top of Fig. 2 shows an overview of a system implementing PrioRAT, consisting of a dual-core processor connected to main memory. The hardware extensions for our proposal implement the following functionalities: (i) indicate to a core whether to prioritize memory requests of the currently-running task, (ii) flag memory requests as critical or non-critical and carry that information through the memory hierarchy, and (iii) prioritize requests in the memory hierarchy. We explain each feature in detail in the remaining of this section. As mentioned before, both PrioRAT configurations rely on exactly the same hardware extensions.

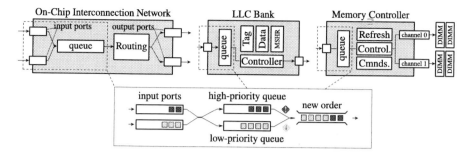

Fig. 3. Request prioritization inside shared on-chip components.

Awareness of Task Criticality in the Core. We add to each core a memory-mapped register, called *crit.reg*, which designates the priority of the memory requests issued by the currently-running task. In our implementation, the size of this register is one bit. In *PR.static*, each core is configured to always issue either high-priority or low-priority requests, i.e., the value of this register is constant for the duration of the application. It is the responsibility of the runtime system to carefully schedule tasks to utilize statically defined prioritization of the corresponding memory requests. In *PR.dynamic*, the runtime system updates the value stored in *crit.reg* to hold the criticality of the task scheduled to run on the corresponding core. This is illustrated in Fig. 2 using runtime system functions `Ci.prio(ON)` and `Ci.prio(OFF)`, which switch on and off the request prioritization for a given core `i`, respectively.

Assigning a Priority to Memory Requests. When issuing a request to the L1 cache, the core flags the request with criticality information stored in the *crit.reg*. This information is carried with the request along its way through the memory hierarchy. Since we model priority with two values, we require only one bit of information to be attached to each request. This adds a negligible overhead to the existing wires and logic in the on-chip memory hierarchy.

Memory Request Prioritization. To implement request prioritization within the shared on-chip resources, we extend the queues that hold incoming requests before they get processed. PrioRAT implements a double-queue design, where each queue holds either high or low priority requests, as shown in Fig. 3. When selecting the next request for processing, the requests in the high-priority queue are preferred over the request from the low-priority queue. In the case of inter-connection network and the LLC, the prioritization happens in the queue that holds incoming requests.

Memory controllers, on the other hand, already implement algorithms for request prioritization in order to exploit parallelism offered by DRAM chips. In order to take into account the request criticality in the memory controller, we extend the existing request scheduling policy, *First Ready-first come first served*

(FR-FCFS). PrioRAT is independent of the baseline scheduling policy as it only adds another sorting criterion. This policy schedules first the request that hit in the already open rows in the DRAM chip. If no such request exists, the ordering is done in *first come - first served* manner. We augment this policy with the task criticality information. To preserve the performance benefits of exploiting row hits, we consider the criticality only after there is no request satisfying the row hit condition. For the requests of the same criticality we use the FCFS ordering.

To offer higher memory bandwidth to the cores, many modern processors make use of multiple memory controllers. The PrioRAT design does not require any synchronization between memory controllers as the prioritization is done independently in each controller. Thus, PrioRAT can be directly applied to such processors without any modification.

3.3 Discussion

Support for Simultaneous Multi-Threading (SMT). Modern processors implement support for simultaneous multi-threading in order to better utilize the resources of superscalar out-of-order cores. In such systems, one physical core can execute two different threads. In the context of our work this means that two tasks of different criticality can share the same core. To ensure the correct prioritization of critical requests in an SMT processor, we would extend the input queue of the L1 cache in the same way as described for the LLC earlier in this section. The core would also be equipped with a *crit.reg* per thread.

Ensuring Fairness. PrioRAT's mechanism for memory request prioritization needs to ensure fair scheduling of tasks and applications. Within one application's tasks, it is the responsibility of the runtime system to ensure correct task and request prioritization. Well-known mechanisms for preventing starvation of non-prioritized requests can be employed in the shared resources' queues. On multi-programmed systems, it is necessary to ensure that one application does not starve other applications. For example, a "rogue" runtime system could make all tasks of a single application critical and therefore get an unfair share of hardware resources. To solve this issue, the operating system could, for example, enforce quotas for critical tasks or requests per application. Similar schemes are already proposed in previous works, which we briefly describe in Sect. 6. An alternative solution would be to integrate the algorithms for task prioritization within the operating system and, therefore, guarantee the their integrity.

Alternative Algorithms for Task Priority Estimation. PrioRAT hardware design is orthogonal to the algorithm to detect task criticality. We consider an existing algorithm to calculate task criticality based on the application's critical path, as described in Sect. 3.1. The critical path is calculated by considering the TDG's structure and the tasks' distance from the bottom of the TDG. An alternative TDG-based approach could also consider the task duration when calculating critical path. For example, it might be a better idea to prioritize a

Table 1. Benchmark details.

Benchmark	Abbrev.	Input parameters
Array scan	Scan	174 arrays of 256 KB; total array size 68.5 MB
Blackscholes	BS	16M options, 512K block size, 5 iterations
Conj. Grad	CG	matrix qa8fm, 16 blocks, 97 iterations
Cholesky	Chol	16×16 blocks of 256×256 elem. (matrix 4096×4096 elem.)
Fluidanimate	Fluid	native: 5 frames, 500,000 particles
Heat-Jacobi	Heat	8192×8192 resolution, 2 heat sources, 10 iterations
Molec. Dyn	MD	2000 atoms, periodic space, stretch phase change
miniAMR	AMR	64K max. blocks, 16×16×16 block, 2 objects, 40 variables
prk2-stencil	PRK2	8192 elem. per dimension, 1024 block size, 5 iterations
LU Decomp.	LU	12 blocks of 512×512 elem.
Specfem3D	Spfm3D	147,645 pts., 2160-elem. mesh, 125 GLL int. pts. per elem.
Sym. Mat. Inv.	SMI	8×8 blocks of 1024×1024 elem. (matrix 8192×8192 elem.)

Table 2. Parameters of the simulated system.

CPU	16 OoO superscalar cores, 192-entry ROB, 2.2 GHz, issue width 4 ins/cycle
Caches	64B line, non-inclusive, write-back, write-allocate
L1	private, 32 KB, 8-way set-associative, 4-cycle latency, split I/D, 16-entry MSHR
L2	private, 256 KB, 16-way set-associative, 13-cycle latency, 16-entry MSHR
L3	shared, 16 MB, 16-way set-associative, 68-cycle latency, 256-entry MSHR
Memory	120 ns latency; 2 channels, each with the effective bandwidth of 4.3 GB/s
	128-entry buffer in the memory controller

single long-lasting task compared to several chained short tasks. However, such approach requires a way to estimate task duration, which can be achieved via profiling, a heuristic based on code analysis or given as a hint by a programmer. Some proposals [5] employ static annotations of task priority introduced by a programmer. However, this requires good a knowledge of the code structure and potential previous profiling. While hand-tuned hints can provide better final criticality estimation, they are less practical than dynamic solutions which are able to adapt to different scenarios, input sets and platforms.

4   Experimental Methodology

Benchmarks. To evaluate PrioRAT we use a set of benchmarks that covers common applications running on HPC systems implemented in a task-based programming model. The list of selected benchmarks with their corresponding input parameters is shown in Table 1. The synthetic benchmark described in Sect. 2, Scan, is also used in the evaluation.

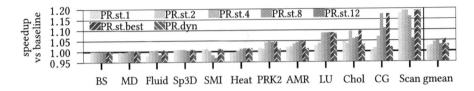

Fig. 4. Speedup of PR.static and PR.dynamic compared to the baseline.

Simulation Setup. We use TaskSim, a trace-driven cycle-accurate architectural simulator [30,31]. TaskSim simulates in detail the execution of parallel applications with OpenMP pragma primitives [28] on parallel multi-core environments. The simulated system mimics an Intel-based processor and consists of 16 cores connected to main memory. We model a superscalar out-of-order cores with a detailed three-level cache hierarchy. Each core has two private cache levels, L1 and L2, while the L3 is shared. We use a main memory model with an effective bandwidth of 8.6 GB/s and latency of 120 ns. All relevant parameters of the simulated system are shown in Table 2.

5   Evaluation

5.1   Performance Evaluation

This section presents the overall performance of the two PrioRAT configurations for all evaluated benchmarks using the environment described in Sect. 4. Figure 4 shows the speedup of various PrioRAT configurations per benchmark compared to the execution on the baseline system. The following paragraphs explain the results for all evaluated configurations.

PR.static. First, we observe speedups achieved by a range of PR.static configurations. We consider configurations having 1, 2, 4, 8 and 12 prioritized cores in a 16-core system. These configurations are denoted as PR.st.X, where X is the number of prioritized cores. Some of the benchmarks, such as MD, Heat, AMR and LU, perform better when running on systems with more prioritized cores. In such configurations, there is a higher chance for all critical tasks to be prioritized. Moreover, sometimes it is beneficial to also accelerate some non-critical tasks, especially if that does not significantly penalize the performance of other non-prioritized tasks. On the other hand, some benchmarks, such as Fluid, SMI, Chol and Scan, achieve the best speedups when using less prioritized cores, i.e., 2, 4 or 8 cores. These codes have long critical paths and, therefore, do not benefit from prioritizing too many non-critical tasks. On average, the best performing PR.static configuration is PR.st.8, which performs 4.6% faster than the baseline. The best speedup of 1.19× is observed for Scan.

In addition, we define PR.st.best, which is the best-performing PR.static configuration per benchmark. On average, this configuration is 5.9% faster than the

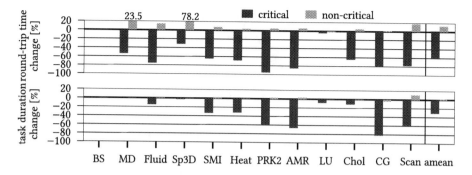

Fig. 5. Impact of request prioritization on request round-trip time (top) and task duration (bottom) for PR.dynamic

baseline. This shows that in scenarios where per-benchmark tuning is possible, application specific PR.static configuration can achieve better performance than a statically defined configuration.

PR.dynamic. Finally, we evaluate PR.dynamic, denoted PR.dyn in Fig. 4. On average, this configuration outperforms the baseline by 3.0%. With 8 out of 12 benchmarks, this configuration achieves similar speedup as PR.st.best. In Chol, it achieves lower speedups due to scheduling artifacts that cause non-critical tasks to be scheduled for execution shortly before a critical task starts executing. This leads to a situation where all cores are busy executing non-critical tasks, while a critical task is waiting in a ready queue.

To better understand the performance gains, we observe the behavior at the microarchitectural level. The prioritization of critical requests reduces their round-trip time from the core to the memory subsystem and back, at the expense of the increased round-trip time for non-critical requests. This effect is demonstrated on the upper plot in Fig. 5, which shows the round-trip time only for requests that arrive to the main memory (i.e., the LLC misses).

Since critical memory requests observe reduced round-trip time, the critical tasks spend less time waiting for memory operations and therefore can execute faster. This finally results in a shorter execution time of the critical path, which may improve the overall performance of an application. These effects are shown at the bottom of Fig. 5, which shows change in the duration of critical and non-critical tasks compared to the baseline configuration. We can observe that the critical path is significantly reduced in many applications.

However, this does not result in drastic performance improvement, as shown in Fig. 4. The reason for such behavior is as follows. We use a critical path detection algorithm based on the structure of a TDG. It does not consider the duration of tasks, but rather the number of tasks on the path from the starting to the ending node. In addition, when the critical path is accelerated in PrioRAT, other non-critical tasks may become the new critical path (from the point of view of execution, not the TDG). Nevertheless, even with an infinite reduction of the

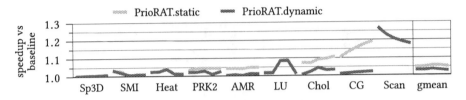

Fig. 6. Impact of memory latency (60 ns, 80 ns, 100 ns, 120 ns and 140 ns) on PrioRAT's performance. Benchmarks with low speedups are omitted for clarity. Geometric mean includes the omitted benchmarks.

critical path's length and a perfect scheduling algoritm, the achieved speedup is limited by the non-prioritized tasks. Only in the cases of LU and Chol, critical tasks stay in the critical path after the prioritization, which makes the reduction in critical path duration directly observable in overall performance gains.

5.2   Performance Sensitivity to Memory Latency

The evaluation presented so far is based on experiments using a memory latency of 120 ns, as explained in Sect. 4. Since memory latency varies across different systems, we explore how PrioRAT performs in systems with memory latencies ranging from 60 ns to 140 ns. Figure 6 shows the performance of the two PrioRAT configurations for the mentioned memory configurations. We do not show the results for the three benchmarks achieving lowest speedups, i.e., BS, MD and Fluid. The geometric mean is calculated taking into account all benchmarks, including the omitted ones. The results show that, for some benchmarks, the performance of PrioRAT varies across systems with different memory latencies. This is pronounced for LU, Chol, CG and Scan. Chol and CG perform better with PrioRAT in systems with higher memory latencies because prioritization in these systems makes more impact compared to the low-latency systems. The opposite behaviour is noticed for Scan. Due to a very high memory contention in this benchmark, most of the request round-trip time is spent waiting for a response from DRAM. Since prioritization only impacts the time requests spend in the queue waiting to be served, we conclude that prioritization has less effect in high-latency systems. We expect such behaviour to be rare in real codes. On average, we notice that PrioRAT performs equally across systems with different memory latencies.

5.3   Hardware Cost of PrioRAT Implementation

PrioRAT requires minor extensions in the core, the shared caches, the interconnect and the memory controllers, as explained in Sect. 3.2. The size of the *crit.reg* is one bit per core. In case of SMT support (see Sect. 3.3), PrioRAT requires one one-bit register per hardware thread. Inside the shared components, i.e., the caches, the interconnect and the memory controllers, we use double-queue to prioritize requests, which we design to be the same total size as the corresponding queue in the baseline system. Therefore, only added cost is a simple logic for scheduling requests into the two queues based on the request criticality. Finally, to enable passing criticality information with request, the structures that hold requests and corresponding communication lines are extended with one bit. All described extensions introduce negligible overhead in area compared to the baseline system.

6   Related Work

Acceleration of the Critical Path. In the context of fork-join programming models, the notion of a critical path applies to the slowest thread in a parallel region. Accelerating such threads has been studied for heterogeneous chip multiprocessors [21,35]. In the context of task-based programming models, critical path is often defined as the longest path from the starting until the final node in a task-dependency graph. The critical path detection has been extensively researched [3,12,20]. CATS [7] and CATA [5] are methods to accelerate critical paths targeting task-based programming models. CATS and CATA can only be implemented in heterogeneous systems or systems with support for dynamic voltage scaling, respectively. PrioRAT does not have these shortcomings and is applicable to any modern multi-core processor.

Scheduling in the Memory Controller. FCFS (First Come – First Served) is the simplest memory controller scheduling algorithm that considers only request arrival time. FR-FCFS (First Ready FCFS) [32] improves the FCFS algorithm by taking into account the locality of the row buffers inside DRAM chips to reduce costly *activate* and *precharge* actions. Many other previous works optimize the ordering of DRAM commands in order to improve memory bandwidth [29,37].

Multi-core processors introduce new challenges, such as avoiding unfairness and starvation. FQM [27], STFM [26], PAR-BS [25] and ATLAS [23] are some of the many techniques that try to achieve fairness among threads by prioritizing requests inside memory controllers. Since these static schemes do not always achieve the best performance for a wide range of applications, researchers have proposed many adaptive scheduling algorithms. BLISS [34] prioritizes applications that are more sensitive to memory interference. Ipek et al. [18] propose an adaptive memory controller scheduling scheme based on reinforced learning. Hashemi et al. [15] identify that, so called, *dependent* cache misses are an important contributor to performance degradation when on-chip contention is present. This scenario occurs when an instruction causing a cache miss also depends on another instruction that results in a miss. Prioritizing such misses results in a reduced waiting time for the second miss.

However, the mentioned proposals focus only on the information visible to the core, which is generally observed on relatively short time intervals of several thousands of CPU cycles. Such fine-grained observations cannot capture the macro trends in the whole application as well as the impact of prioritization on the overall performance. Our scheme is driven by the runtime-provided knowledge on task criticality. Such approach significantly simplifies the hardware and enables better long-term decisions inside the on-chip resources.

Exploiting Criticality in Hardware. Subramaniam et al. [33] evaluate the impact of criticality information in the optimizations of on-chip components, such as the L1 data cache and the store queue. Ghose et al. [13] utilize the load criticality to augment the FR-FCFS scheduling policy in the memory controller. Both of these solutions observe criticality on the instruction level, contrary to our approach that uses task-level criticality. Moreover, they require precise predictors of criticality which comes with additional hardware cost in each processor core. PrioRAT utilizes runtime-provided information and does not introduce complex and expensive hardware predictors.

7   Conclusions

In this paper we present PrioRAT, a runtime-assisted approach for prioritization of memory requests in the processor. PrioRAT exploits the high-level information about the application, contrary to many state-of-the-art proposals. Our approach relies on the runtime system library to detect the critical path in a task-parallel application and forward task criticality information to the underlying hardware. The processor uses the knowledge of the task criticality to guide the prioritization of the memory requests inside the shared on-chip memory hierarchy.

We evaluate PrioRAT on a set of representative HPC codes. The extensive evaluation shows that PrioRAT outperforms the baseline system by up to $1.19\times$ in terms of the execution time. Further analysis demonstrates a high impact of the prioritization on the request service time and task duration. Therefore, we demonstrate the importance of the availability of application-level knowledge inside the on-chip components.

Acknowledgements. This work has been partially supported by the Spanish Ministry of Science and Innovation (PID2019-107255GB-C21/AEI/10.13039/501100011033), by the Generalitat de Catalunya (contracts 2017-SGR-1414 and 2017-SGR-1328), by the European Union's Horizon 2020 research and innovation program under the Mont-Blanc 2020 project (grant agreement 779877) and by the RoMoL ERC Advanced Grant (GA 321253). V. Dimić has been partially supported by the Agency for Management of University and Research Grants (AGAUR) of the Government of Catalonia under Ajuts per a la contractació de personal investigador novell fellowship number 2017 FI_B 00855. M. Moretó and M. Casas have been partially supported by the Spanish Ministry of Economy, Industry and Competitiveness under Ramon y Cajal fellowship numbers RYC-2016-21104 and RYC-2017-23269, respectively.

References

1. Alvarez, L., Vilanova, L., Moreto, M., Casas, M., Gonzàlez, M., et al.: Coherence protocol for transparent management of scratchpad memories in shared memory manycore architectures. In: ISCA 2015, pp. 720–732 (2015). https://doi.org/10.1145/2749469.2750411

2. Barcelona Supercomputing Center: Nanos++ Runtime Library (2014). http://pm.bsc.es/nanox

3. Cai, Q., González, J., Rakvic, R., Magklis, G., Chaparro, P., González, A.: Meeting points: using thread criticality to adapt multicore hardware to parallel regions. In: PACT 2008 pp. 240–249 (2008). https://doi.org/10.1145/1454115.1454149,

4. Casas, M., Moretó, M., Alvarez, L., Castillo, E., Chasapis, D., Hayes, T., et al.: Runtime-aware architectures. In: Euro-Par 2015, pp. 16–27 (2015). https://doi.org/10.1007/978-3-662-48096-0_2

5. Castillo, E., Moreto, M., Casas, M., Alvarez, L., Vallejo, E., Chronaki, K., et al.: CATA: criticality aware task acceleration for multicore processors. In: IPDPS 2016, pp. 413–422 (2016). https://doi.org/10.1109/IPDPS.2016.49

6. Chamberlain, B., Callahan, D., Zima, H.: Parallel programmability and the chapel language. Int. J. High Perf. Comput. Appl. **21**(3), 291–312 (2007). https://doi.org/10.1177/1094342007078442

7. Chronaki, K., Rico, A., Badia, R.M., Ayguadé, E., Labarta, J., Valero, M.: Criticality-aware dynamic task scheduling for heterogeneous architectures. In: ICS 2015, pp. 329–338 (2015). https://doi.org/10.1145/2751205.2751235

8. Liu, C.-H., Li, C.-F., Lai, K.-C., Wu, C.-C.: A dynamic critical path duplication task scheduling algorithm for distributed heterogeneous computing systems. In: ICPADS 2006, vol. 1, p. 8 (2006). https://doi.org/10.1109/ICPADS.2006.37

9. Daoud, M., Kharma, N.: Efficient compile-time task scheduling for heterogeneous distributed computing systems. In: ICPADS 2006, vol. 1, pp. 11–22 (2006). https://doi.org/10.1109/ICPADS.2006.40

10. Dimić, V., Moretó, M., Casas, M., Ciesko, J., Valero, M.: Rich: implementing reductions in the cache hierarchy. In: ICS 2020, p. 13 (2020). https://doi.org/10.1145/3392717.3392736

11. Dimić, V., Moretó, M., Casas, M., Valero, M.: Runtime-assisted shared cache insertion policies based on re-reference intervals. In: Euro-Par 2017, vol. 10417, pp. 247–259 (2017). https://doi.org/10.1007/978-3-319-64203-1_18

12. Du Bois, K., Eyerman, S., Sartor, J.B., Eeckhout, L.: Criticality stacks: identifying critical threads in parallel programs using synchronization behavior. In: ISCA 2013, pp. 511–522 (2013). https://doi.org/10.1145/2485922.2485966

13. Ghose, S., Lee, H., Martínez, J.F.: Improving memory scheduling via processor-side load criticality information. In: ISCA 2013, pp. 84–95 (2013). https://doi.org/10.1145/2485922.2485930

14. Hakem, M., Butelle, F.: Dynamic critical path scheduling parallel programs onto multiprocessors. In: IPDPS 2005, p. 7 (2005). https://doi.org/10.1109/IPDPS.2005.175

15. Hashemi, M., Ebrahimi, E.K., Mutlu, O., Patt, Y.N.: Accelerating dependent cache misses with an enhanced memory controller. In: ISCA 2016, pp. 444–455 (2016). https://doi.org/10.1109/ISCA.2016.46

16. Intel Copropration: Intel® Cilk™ Plus Language Extension Specification (2013)

17. Intel Copropration: Intel® Thread Bulding Blocks (2020)

18. Ipek, E., Mutlu, O., Martínez, J.F., Caruana, R.: Self-optimizing memory controllers: a reinforcement learning approach. In: ISCA 2008, pp. 39–50 (2008). https://doi.org/10.1109/ISCA.2008.21
19. Jaulmes, L., Casas, M., Moretó, M., Ayguadé, E., Labarta, J., Valero, M.: Exploiting asynchrony from exact forward recovery for due in iterative solvers. In: SC 2015 (2015). https://doi.org/10.1145/2807591.2807599
20. Joao, J.A., Suleman, M.A., Mutlu, O., Patt, Y.N.: Bottleneck identification and scheduling in multithreaded applications. In: ASPLOS 2012, pp. 223–234 (2012). https://doi.org/10.1145/2150976.2151001
21. Joao, J.A., Suleman, M.A., Mutlu, O., Patt, Y.N.: Utility-based acceleration of multithreaded applications on asymmetric CMPs. In: ISCA 2013, pp. 154–165 (2013). https://doi.org/10.1145/2485922.2485936
22. Kale, L.V., Krishnan, S.: CHARM++: a portable concurrent object oriented system based on C++. In: OOPSLA 1993, pp. 91–108 (1993). https://doi.org/10.1145/165854.165874
23. Kim, Y., Han, D., Mutlu, O., Harchol-Balter, M.: ATLAS: a scalable and high-performance scheduling algorithm for multiple memory controllers. In: HPCA 2010, pp. 1–12 (2010). https://doi.org/10.1109/HPCA.2010.5416658
24. Manivannan, M., Papaefstathiou, V., Pericas, M., Stenstrom, P.: RADAR: runtime-assisted dead region management for last-level caches. In: HPCA 2016, pp. 644–656 (2016). https://doi.org/10.1109/HPCA.2016.7446101
25. Mutlu, O., Moscibroda, T.: Parallelism-aware batch scheduling: enabling high-performance and fair shared memory controllers. IEEE Micro 29(1), 22–32 (2009). https://doi.org/10.1109/MM.2009.12
26. Mutlu, O., Moscibroda, T.: Stall-time fair memory access scheduling for chip multiprocessors. In: MICRO 2007, pp. 146–160 (2007). https://doi.org/10.1109/MICRO.2007.40
27. Nesbit, K.J., et al.: Fair queuing memory systems. In: MICRO 2006, pp. 208–222 (2006). https://doi.org/10.1109/MICRO.2006.24
28. OpenMP Architecture Review Board: OpenMP Technical Report 4 Version 5.0 Preview 1 (2016)
29. Peiron, M., Valero, M., Ayguadé, E., Lang, T.: Vector multiprocessors with arbitrated memory access. In: ISCA 1995. pp. 243–252 (1995). https://doi.org/10.1145/223982.224435
30. Rico, A., Cabarcas, F., Villavieja, C., Pavlovic, M., Vega, A., Etsion, Y., et al.: On the simulation of large-scale architectures using multiple application abstraction levels. ACM Trans. Archit. Code Optim. 8(4), 36:1–36:20 (2012). https://doi.org/10.1145/2086696.2086715
31. Rico, A., Duran, A., Cabarcas, F., Etsion, Y., Ramirez, A., Valero, M.: Trace-driven simulation of multithreaded applications. In: ISPASS 2011, pp. 87–96 (2011). https://doi.org/10.1109/ISPASS.2011.5762718
32. Rixner, S., Dally, W.J., Kapasi, U.J., Mattson, P., Owens, J.D.: Memory access scheduling. In: ISCA 2000, pp. 128–138 (2000). https://doi.org/10.1145/339647.339668
33. Subramaniam, S., Bracy, A., Wang, H., Loh, G.H.: Criticality-based optimizations for efficient load processing. In: HPCA 2009, pp. 419–430 (2009). https://doi.org/10.1109/HPCA.2009.4798280
34. Subramanian, L., Lee, D., Seshadri, V., Rastogi, H., Mutlu, O.: The blacklisting memory scheduler: achieving high performance and fairness at low cost. In: ICCD 2014, pp. 8–15 (2014). https://doi.org/10.1109/ICCD.2014.6974655

35. Suleman, M.A., Mutlu, O., Qureshi, M.K., Patt, Y.N.: Accelerating critical section execution with asymmetric multi-core architectures. In: ASPLOS 2009, pp. 253–264 (2009). https://doi.org/10.1145/1508244.1508274

36. Topcuoglu, H., Hariri, S., Wu, M.-Y.: Performance-effective and low-complexity task scheduling for heterogeneous computing. IEEE Trans. Parallel Distrib. Syst. **13**(3), 260–274 (2002). https://doi.org/10.1109/71.993206

37. Valero, M., Lang, T., Llabería, J.M., Peiron, M., Ayguadé, E., Navarra, J.J.: Increasing the number of strides for conflict-free vector access. In: ISCA 1992, pp. 372–381 (1992). https://doi.org/10.1145/139669.140400

38. Valero, M., Moretó, M., Casas, M., Ayguade, E., Labarta, J.: Runtime-aware architectures: a first approach. Supercomput. Front. Innov. **1**(1) (2014). https://doi.org/10.14529/jsfi140102

39. Wulf, W.A., McKee, S.A.: Hitting the memory wall: implications of the obvious. ACM SIGARCH Comput. Arch. News **23**(1), 20–24 (1995). https://doi.org/10.1145/216585.216588

Optimized Implementation of the HPCG Benchmark on Reconfigurable Hardware

Alberto Zeni[1,2](✉), Kenneth O'Brien[1], Michaela Blott[1],
and Marco D. Santambrogio[2]

[1] Research Labs, Xilinx Inc., Dublin, Ireland
{alberto.zeni,kenneth.o'brien,michaela.blott}@xilinx.com
[2] Politecnico di Milano, Milan, Italy
marco.santambrogio@polimi.it

Abstract. The HPCG benchmark represents a modern complement to the HPL benchmark in the performance evaluation of HPC systems, as it has been recognized as a more representative benchmark to reflect real-world applications. While typical workloads become more and more challenging, the semiconductor industry is battling with performance scaling and power efficiency on next-generation technology nodes. As a result, the industry is turning towards more customized compute architectures to help meet the latest performance requirements. In this paper, we present the details of the first FPGA-based implementation of HPCG that takes advantage of such customized compute architectures. Our results show that our high-performance multi-FPGA implementation, using 1 and 4 Xilinx Alveo U280 achieves up to 108.3 GFlops and 346.5 GFlops respectively, representing speed-ups of 104.1× and 333.2× over software running on a server with an Intel Xeon processor with no loss of accuracy. We also demonstrate that the FPGA-based solution achieves comparable performance with respect to modern GPUs and an up to 2.7× improvement in terms of power efficiency compared to an NVIDIA Tesla V100. Finally, a theoretical evaluation, based on Berkeley's Roofline model demonstrates that our implementation is near optimally tuned on the Xilinx Alveo U280.

Keywords: Reconfigurable architectures · High performance computing · Benchmark testing

1 Introduction

The High Performance LINPACK (HPL) benchmark [1] is one of the most widely regarded tool for the ranking of supercomputers. HPL gained prominence as a performance metric because of the strong correlation between its measurements and the real world application performance. As a consequence, system vendors thrived on releasing designs that would increase HPL performance. However, HPL rankings are no longer closely correlated to real-world applications, especially in the High Performance Computing (HPC) context, which hosts a growing variety of application domains which do not focus on HPL-like dense linear

© Springer Nature Switzerland AG 2021
L. Sousa et al. (Eds.): Euro-Par 2021, LNCS 12820, pp. 616–630, 2021.
https://doi.org/10.1007/978-3-030-85665-6_38

algebra. In this context, the High Performance Conjugate Gradient (HPCG) benchmark [2] has been designed to more closely correlate with prominent real world applications based on memory bound sparse linear algebra problems. Similar to HPL, HPCG is a tool for ranking computer systems and intended to be complementary to HPL. The benchmark solves a sparse system of partial differential equations, based on a simple additive Schwarz symmetric Gauss-Seidel preconditioned conjugate gradient problem, and produces a performance score which can be used to rank systems. Concurrently, modern HPC applications continue to demand more computing capability than what current processors can deliver. Thus there is a performance gap between the demand for computational power and what can be achieved [3]. This forces us to search for new architectural solutions as we are reaching the end of Moore's Law [4]. One solution is to use hardware accelerators to offload compute-intensive tasks from the main processor. Some examples of hardware accelerators are Graphic Processing Units (GPUs) and Field Programmable Gate Arrays (FPGAs). FPGAs in particular, have recently proven to be a much more efficient architecture compared to CPUs, both in terms of performance and power consumption [5–7]. To demonstrate the usefulness, performance and efficiency of these approaches, in this paper we propose a multi-node FPGA implementation of the HPCG Benchmark, which aims to highlight the advantages of using reprogrammable devices in the context of HPC applications. Our main contributions in this paper are:

- We present the first high-performance, single and multi-FPGA implementation of the HPCG benchmark, which achieves significant improvements over leading versions on state-of-the-art CPUs and comparable performance to GPU implementations with no loss of accuracy.
- We applied the Roofline Model to the HPCG implementation on the Xilinx Alveo U280 and underlying hardware, and demonstrated that performance is near-optimal.
- We implemented the kernels inside of the benchmark with several numerical precisions to show the performance achievable by the FPGA technology in different contexts.

The paper is organized as follows: Sect. 2 provides an overview of the software algorithms in HPCG and a description of the basic FPGA architecture, while Sect. 3 provides an overview of the related work. Section 4 illustrates our implementation and optimizations. In Sect. 5 we illustrate our experimental results, and validate our results using the Berkeley Roofline model. Finally, Sect. 6 summarizes our contributions and outlines future work.

2   Background

In this section we describe in detail the structure of the HPCG benchmark, and also provide an overview of the FPGA architecture. The HPCG benchmark is fundamentally a boundary condition solver for partial differential equations using the additive Schwarz Preconditioned Conjugate Gradient (PCG) method

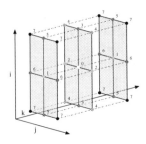

Fig. 1. 27-Point stencil operator of the HPCG benchmark. This stencil is represented inside of the benchmark as the non-zero variables inside the matrix used in the solver.

[2]. The application generates a problem data set, which includes all necessary data structures and a sparse matrix representation. The sparse linear system used in the benchmark is based on a simple elliptic partial differential equation discretized with a 27-point stencil on a regular 3D grid as seen in Fig. 1. The user can decide to divide the problem into smaller subsets corresponding to a local domain of size $N_x \times N_y \times N_z$. The benchmark automatically detects the number of processors at runtime. Then it decomposes them into $P_x \times P_y \times P_z$, where $P = P_x P_y P_z$ is the total number of processors. This creates a global domain $G_x \times G_y \times G_z$, where $G_x = P_x N_x$, $G_y = P_y N_y$, and $G_z = P_z N_z$. The matrix structure is intended to facilitate the problem setup and validation of the solution, and has to be preserved. During the initial setup and validation phases, the benchmark may call a set of user-defined optimizations, which allow for analysis of the matrix, reordering of the matrix rows, and transformation of data structures. Next, the benchmark calls the reference software solver and stores the final residual result. Then, the optimized FPGA benchmark is executed for one cycle and the result of this cycle is used to compute how many iterations of the benchmark are required to match the residual obtained in software. Finally, the optimized FPGA benchmark is executed for the correct number of iterations and its result is checked for correctness. The objective of the PCG algorithm is to solve a linear system. To do so the benchmark iterates a number of different operations whose objective is to stress the memory bandwidth of the system:

- Vector Dot Product Multiplication (DP) which are used to compute coefficients for the various vector update operations.
- Vector updates in the form of a slightly modified vector addition (WAXPBY).
- Vector operations in the form of the application of a preconditioner based on the Symmetric Gauss-Seidel Smoother (SYMGS). The process is based on two sweeps: a forward sweep (update local elements in row order) and backward sweep (update local elements in reverse row order). This data dependency constraint makes the SYMGS routine difficult to parallelize and is the main challenge of the benchmark.
- Sparse Matrix Vector Multiplication (SPMV). The pattern of data access is similar to a sweep of SYMGS, however, the rows can be processed in parallel since there are no data dependencies between rows.

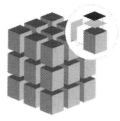

Fig. 2. 3D decomposition of the HPCG problem. Each of MPI process is responsible for each section. Each of the MPI processes syncs up with all of it's neighbors and exchanges the required information before proceeding to the next step.

The original software implementation of HPCG uses a combination of MPI and OpenMP as the underlying programming model and detects the number of MPI processors at runtime and builds a 3D decomposition of the problem, as seen in Fig. 2. Since the jobs on large supercomputers go through a batching system and the number of available nodes may vary due to downed nodes, it is useful that the software is able to adjust to the available resources. This way, one can use all of the available cores on all the available machines, at the expense of the overhead that MPI introduces to sync the results over multiple MPI processes. In our design we kept the structure of the MPI communication as close to the original as possible, but we also reduced the overhead significantly, as we execute all of the benchmark operations on FPGA. With this in mind, instead of dividing the problem by the number of available processes, our implementation divides the problem by the number of FPGAs available. By doing this, we are able to evenly distribute the problem over the FPGAs, thus increasing the level of parallelism, while still keeping the impact of the MPI overhead very low.

2.1 Field Programmable Gate Arrays

An FPGA is an array of logic blocks (cells) placed in an infrastructure of interconnections, which can be programmed at three distinct levels: the function of the logic cells, the interconnections between cells, and the inputs and outputs. Every logic block contains a Look-Up Table (LUT), a register and a multiplexer (MUX), and it can perform different functions, depending on how the Static Random Access Memory (SRAM) is programmed. Modern FPGA also implement high level functionality fixed into the silicon to improve performance. Examples of these include multipliers, generic Digital Signal Processor (DSP) blocks, embedded processors, high speed I/O logic and embedded memories. The processing functionality of FPGAs can be customized at logic port level, while other architectures such as GPU and CPU can only be programmed using their static instruction set. The circuit may be described in a number of programming languages such as hardware centric Register Transfer Level (RTL) or higher level C++ dialects such as High Level Synthesis (HLS), which we have leveraged in this work.

3   Related Work

This section provides an overview of the HPCG implementations present in the state of the art. The main difference between the HPL and HPCG benchmarks is that HPL focuses on dense matrix-matrix multiplications, while HPCG solves a symmetric sparse matrix operations. These differences translate into a massively different footprint in arithmetic intensity, positioning HPCG as a more realistic alternative to HPL, and therefore making it a better candidate for representing real world applications on modern supercomputers [2,8]. In recent years, there has been a race towards fine-tuning HPL and porting to different architectures, showing that sometimes topping the Top500 does not necessarily imply having good performance with HPCG. A key example is the Sunway TaihuLight supercomputer, which is still one of the fastest HPL machines in the world, but scores poorly performance in HPCG [9]. Park et al. [10] presented the effort performed by Intel for optimizing both shared memory implementation and mitigating MPI communication overhead. Phillips et al. showed an optimized implementation of the benchmark on GPU and also evaluated its performance in [11]. The work performed by the RIKEN team on the K computer presented in [12] and the work of Ruiz et al. presented in [13], focused on system specific optimizations of the benchmark. Other evaluations of HPCG on recent architectures can be found in [14] for the Tianhe-2 supercomputer and in [15] for the NEC SX-ACE. It is also worth mentioning the importance of the work by Marjanovic et al. [16] for modeling performance and Vermij et al. [17] for both performance analysis and power efficiency. It is not a surprise that the FPGA architecture is gaining momentum in the HPC community [18]. Several research projects have promoted and evaluated the performance of various FPGA-based platforms for HPC [19,20]. Although FPGAs have gained popularity in recent years, an FPGA version of the HPCG benchmark is currently absent from the literature. Our implementation aims to show the performance of the FPGA architecture, rather than the performance of a specific system. We focused on optimizing the interaction of the FPGA with the system, keeping all of the computation of the benchmark on the FPGA, thus making it easily repeatable and easily adaptable when new FPGAs are released.

4   HPCG Implementation

Our design shows how the FPGA's flexibility can be useful in multiple practical scenarios, thus it focuses on providing the best solution of the global HPCG problem, rather than focusing on implementing a single kernel. To achieve a higher degree of parallelism, we optimize the data communication process by reducing the data traffic between the FPGAs and host machines while maintaining the same MPI structure of HPCG when using multiple FPGAs. In this section, we describe the design of our solution and its various optimizations.

4.1   Single FPGA Implementation

We reduce the PCIe communication by storing all of the data required by the kernels on the FPGA only once and enabling kernel to kernel streaming from the on-board High Bandwidth Memory (HBM) memory. Moreover, we exploit the HBM memory modules present on the Xilinx Alveo U280 to achieve better memory bandwidth. To exploit memory burst when reading the data on the FPGA, we organized the data into packets of 512 bits, corresponding to the maximum transfer per clock cycle supported by the memory interface. We implemented all the different kernels inside the benchmark in our design: **Dot Product Multiplication (DP), Sparse Matrix Vector Multiplication (SPMV), Symmetric Gauss-Seidel Smoother (SYMGS) and Vector Vector Coefficient Multiplication (WAXPBY)**. To fully exploit memory bandwidth on our target board, each kernel has ten independent Compute Units (CUs) that work in parallel and connect to all the memory channels available. The SYMGS kernel is called by the pre-smoother and post-smoother processes and it represents the major time consumer in HPCG. In the software implementation the SYMGS smoother routine begins by calling communicating boundary elements of the local matrix with neighbor processors. Because all of the computation happens on the FPGA, we can skip this communication step. The kernel then reads the input vector from HBM and updates them in row order. This kernel exploits the particular representation of the sparse matrix inside the benchmark to achieve better performance. As previously mentioned, the sparse linear system used in the benchmark is based on a 27-point stencil and so each row of the sparse matrix always has 27 randomly distributed non-zero elements at most. Knowing this, we flattened the matrix using the Compressed Sparse Row (CSR) compression format to exploit better memory bandwidth when reading it from HBM, as seen in Fig. 3. By doing this, we parallelize the computation of the smoother update on the vector by scheduling a number of Processing Elements (PEs) equal to the number of variables inside one packet of 512 bits, which depends on the size of the datatype. The update operation is performed in pipeline, so every time a block is read, the previous one is being processed. Once all these updates have been processed, we have to perform the same operation but in reverse row

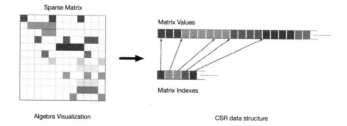

Fig. 3. Compressed row format implemented within the benchmark. The matrix is flattened so that it can be accessed linearly and no random memory access is required to read the non-zero variables.

order. During the first sweep, we can compute only one packet per clock cycle per CU, as the width of the memory ports is 512 bits. To avoid this limitation in the backward pass, we cache the data on the Ultra Ram (URAM) of the FPGA so we can access data faster. By doing this, we are able to avoid reading from off-chip memory and so we implemented more PEs in the backward pass, speeding up the process significantly, especially in the case of double precision operations where memory bandwidth is very limited (Fig. 4).

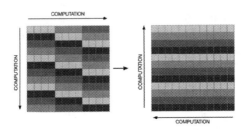

Fig. 4. Visual representation of the computation of the SMYGS kernel, with different degrees of parallelization in the forward and backward sweep. Squares of the same color in the same row are executed in the same iteration.

The DP kernel implements our parallel design of vector dot product. We read the two input vectors that are streaming from the previously executed kernel, and we pipeline the computation of the product with the reading process. After each packet of 512 bits has been computed, we perform a partial parallel reduction with the partial results, and we store this result inside of a circular buffer to avoid resource contention. Once all the packets have been computed, the CU performs a final parallel reduction using the partial results in the circular buffer and produces the final result of the DP. To group all the previous results and avoid PCIe communication, we implemented a simple compute unit that acts as a bridge between the CUs of DP and the ones from WAXPBY. This compute unit performs a parallel reduction of the ten different results coming from the DP compute units and broadcasts the result to all of the WAXPBY CUs. Each of these CUs take two vectors and two coefficients as inputs, and output a single vector. This kernel performs very similarly to vector addition, but it also multiplies the two vectors by the coefficients before computing the sum of the two. The data organization is consistent with the DP kernel, each CU implements again a number of PEs that work in parallel. The SPMV kernel implements the sparse matrix multiplication of the benchmark. The operations that this kernel has to perform are very similar to the SYMGS kernel, but because no back sweep is necessary, the structure of SPMV is actually simpler. To avoid PCIe communication, we keep the data of the sparse matrix on the HBM blocks of our target board. We multiply each non-zero variable of the flattened matrix to the corresponding vector value, then we store each of this results in a circular buffer, to avoid resource contention. During the multiplication process we compute the final result of the row multiplication using a parallel reduction. Finally,

Table 1. Percentage of the resource utilization of our design on the Xilinx Alveo U280

Kernel	FF	LUT	DSP	BRAM	URAM
WAXPBY	10.42%	10.49%	16.84%	44.64%	0.00%
SPMV	6.67%	10.29%	2.11%	7.94%	0.00%
DP	3.19%	4.95%	2.44%	29.76%	0.00%
SYMGS	11.46%	31.48%	66.60%	4.96%	84.38%
TOTAL	31.75%	57.22%	87.99%	87.30%	84.38%

once the benchmark reaches the end of the iterations, the result produced by our implementation is compared to the software version and the results are validated. Table 1 shows the resource utilization percentage of our design on our target board, the Xilinx Alveo U280. The main limitation of our implementation is currently memory bandwidth, as we utilize all of the available banks of HBM for our implementation. Therefore, we are not able to fully utilize the available computational resources. We observe that our main limitation after HBM is represented by the DSPs. DSPs are the primary resource available on the FPGA that can compute floating point operations, and because we compute a lot of operations in parallel we are very close to using all the available ones on the FPGA. We can also observe that URAM and Block Random Access Memory (BRAM) utilization are close to 90% too, this is due to the fact that we implement a lot of circular buffers to avoid resource contention and PCIe communication, so we use these resources to store the data locally on the board. Moreover, it is important to note that even though we utilize most of the FPGA resources, they are not always used at any given time. To avoid reconfiguring the FPGA during the benchmark execution when switching kernels and exploit kernel to kernel streaming, we program all the kernels only once using a single bitstream. Also, since the HBM bandwidth represents our current bottleneck, we do not sacrifice parallelization when doing this but instead, save valuable time every time a different kernel needs to be executed.

4.2 Multiple FPGA Implementation

To implement the benchmark on multiple FPGAs we implemented a load balancer that handles the computation by scheduling the dimension of the subset for each FPGA. The host organizes the inputs accordingly to the number of available machines with FPGAs. The pre-processing of the inputs occurs as in the single device implementation, the load balancer divides the inputs evenly into different groups and then assigns them to the FPGAs. Once the division of the inputs is completed, the host allocates the necessary memory on the different FPGAs, enabling each FPGA to execute its set of operations independently. To enable the execution of the benchmark on multiple FPGAs some synchronization is required to ensure that all the FPGA nodes have the correct inputs. The communication between FPGAs happens through MPI on the host machines.

To simplify the structure of our implementation, we kept some of the checkpoints of the original software implementation. First, when multiple FPGAs are available, our load balancer identifies the ones that are ready for execution and launches the benchmark organizing the inputs accordingly. Once the kernel execution reaches a checkpoint, e.g. after the DP algorithm, we retrieve the data required from the FPGAs through PCIe and broadcasts it to all the other host that then communicate with the FPGA boards. Because we are currently limited by the PCIe interface, we need to avoid synchronization as much as possible. To synchronize data we put checkpoints where the existing syncing CUs are. These CUs serve as broadcaster of results to all the other CUs inside the FPGA in the single board implementation. In the case of the multi-FPGA implementation the CUs also interact with the host and then proceed execution.

5   Performance Evaluation

In this section, we describe the experimental settings used to evaluate the design of our HPCG implementation and present our performance results. The design of the architecture has been described using C++ and Xilinx Vitis 2020.1. We benchmarked the architecture using OpenCL profiling events that provide an easy to use API to profile the code that runs on the FPGA device. To validate our results we first compare our design of HPCG against the software version of the benchmark executed on CPU and GPU. We evaluate the performance of our implementation considering power consumption and show its performance when using different levels of data precision. To compare our design against other implementations we left the problem generation of the benchmark untouched. We execute the benchmark over 30 times and we present an average of the results to take into account any variance in the problem generation. The results were collected on four servers each with 384 GB of DDR4 RAM, an Intel Xeon Gold 6234 processor and a Xilinx Alveo U280 at the Xilinx Adaptive Compute Cluster (XACC) located at ETH Zurich. To compare against the GPU implementation we took the results of this implementation from the official HPCG website[1].

5.1   Experimental Results

Figure 5 shows the performance improvement of our implementation using a single FPGA compared to the original software implementation of HPCG using 16 threads on an Intel Xeon server. Details of the obtained results are highlighted in Table 2. Our FPGA implementation is able to support different problem size dimensions, like the software implementation. Note that the performance of our design remains roughly constant over different problem dimensions, this is due to the fact that the FPGA does not introduce overhead in the computation of the problem and that the level of parallelization remains the same regardless of the problem dimensions. In our test case the CPU was able to perform marginally

---

[1] https://www.hpcg-benchmark.org/software/index.html.

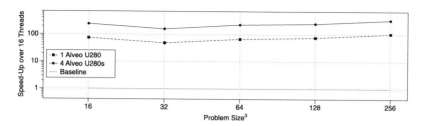

Fig. 5. FPGA HPCG Speed-Up over the original software version of HPCG for different problem size (log-log scale). Platform with 4 Xilinx Alveo U280s.

Table 2. Performance in GFLOPS of FPGA-HPCG on the Alveo U280 against original software version of HPCG.

Problem size	FPGA HPCG 1 Alveo U280	FPGA HPCG 4 Alveo U280s	Software HPCG Intel Xeon
16^3	106.1	339.5	1.43
32^3	107.1	342.7	2.19
64^3	103.9	332.5	1.53
128^3	107.2	343.0	1.4
256^3	108.3	346.6	1.03

better with a problem of size 32^3, thus the little dip seen in Fig. 5 for this particular problem dimension. Observe that our implementation attains speed-ups ranging from 48× to 104× when compared to software for our single FPGA implementation on our target board, the Xilinx Alveo U280. We chose this board to test our implementation since the performance of the benchmark drastically benefits from the usage of HBM given that the focus of HPCG is to stress the memory bandwidth of the system. Figure 5 also shows the performance of our implementation when using multiple Xilinx Alveo U280 FPGAs. Computing time scales well, however, the communication with multiple FPGAs introduces an overhead that increases with the number of FPGAs. This is mainly due to the PCIe communication rather than MPI, as the number of variables that need to be sent to all the machines for synching is very limited, as we previously explained. We compare our performance to modern GPUs such as the NVIDIA P100 and NVIDIA V100, but also compare our results to the NVIDIA K40 and NVIDIA M40, that are widely deployed and still relevant boards whose performance are still listed by the HPCG. Table 3 shows the performance of our implementation on FPGA against the optimized versions of HPCG on GPU. Results show that our design attains significant speed-ups with respect to the NVIDIA K40 and NVIDIA M40, from 2.6× to 3.2× respectively, and attains similar performance to the NVIDIA P100. The Xilinx Alveo U280 and the NVIDIA P100 boards have similar memory bandwidth, and also have a chip manufactured using a similar node process. Additionally, we can observe that our design on the Alveo

Table 3. Performance of HPCG when using different computing architectures solving the same problem of size 256^3.

Platform	GFLOPS	GFLOPS/W
Intel Xeon	1.03	0.0079
NVIDIA Tesla K40	33	0.1404
NVIDIA Tesla M40	41.5	0.1660
NVIDIA Tesla P100	100	0.5780
NVIDIA Tesla V100	145.9	0.5955
Xilinx Alveo U280	108.3	1.6164

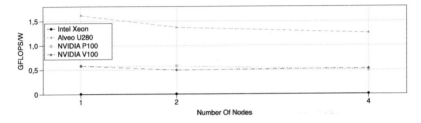

Fig. 6. Comparison of the power efficiency of our FPGA-based HPCG implementations when using our multiple nodes. Problem Size $= 256^3$.

U280 achieves roughly 75% of the performance of the V100 in terms of Giga Floating Point Operations Per Second (GFLOPS). Moreover our implementation shows a significant improvement when power consumption is taken into account; our design on the Alveo U280 achieves significant improvements in terms of GFLOPS/W of 2.7× and 204× with respect to the NVIDIA Tesla V100 and the Intel Xeon implementations respectively. Because we compute all the kernels on the FPGA we do not need to communicate between the various threads as the original software version of HPCG. Also the communication between the various boards happens only after certain kernels, thus we can avoid a lot of the MPI communication that is present in the original version of the benchmark. By reducing the impact of the MPI communication, our design attains up to 49.4× speed-up when using 4 Alveo U280s when compared to the software version. In Fig. 6 we can observe that our design performs significantly better with respect to all the other implementations when we use GFLOPS/W as a performance metric. In our case our FPGA we measured 67W on average to operate when computing the kernel, while the NVIDIA P100 and NVIDIA V100 require 173W and 245W respectively. To measure the power consumption of the GPU boards we used the NVIDIA System Management Interface (SMI) while for the FPGA we utilized Xilinx Board Utility. We can also observe the impact of the PCIe communication in our implementation in Fig. 7 as the efficiency is lowered when using multiple FPGAs because of this overhead. To comply with the rules of the benchmark all of the operations within HPCG need to be performed using double

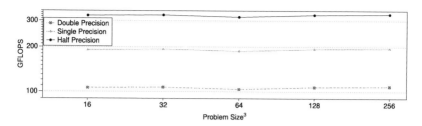

Fig. 7. Comparison of our FPGA-based HPCG implementation when using different degrees of precision running on a single Alveo U280 (log-log scale).

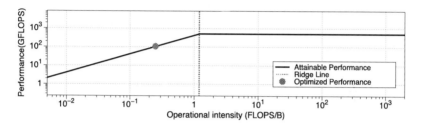

Fig. 8. Roofline analysis for our HPCG kernels on the Xilinx Alveo U280.

precision data. The original software implementation of the HPCG benchmark is not programmed to compute operations at a lower precision, as its focus is to stress the memory bandwidth of the system. To prove the effectiveness of the FPGA architecture in doing operations with reduced precision we also implemented the benchmark using single and half precision variables as seen in Fig. 6. The number of the PEs we can schedule doubles every time the bitwidth of the variables is cut in half. We can observe that the performance of our reduced precision implementation scales nearly linearly with the precision used.

5.2   Results Validation

The Roofline model [21,22] is a visually-intuitive method to understand the performance of a given kernel based on a *bound and bottleneck* analysis approach. The Roofline model characterizes a kernel's performance in billions of instructions (GFLOPS, y-axis) as a function of its operational intensity (OI, x-axis). We use *Operational Intensity* as the x-axis and, given that our kernel performs only double operations, use billions of float operations per second (GFLOPS) as the y-axis. *Operational Intensity* is defined as instructions per byte of memory traffic, which measures traffic between the caches and memory.

On one Xilinx Alveo U280 FPGA, 9024 Digital Signal Processors (DSPs) are available, which are the modules of the FPGA that compute floating points operations. To compute the theoretical maximum of double GFLOPS for the FPGA we first calculated how many resources of the FPGA were used to compute a double precision Multiply-Accumulator (MAC) operation which accounts for two FLOPS. Each MAC operation uses 8 DSPs, which means that we can perform a number of operations in parallel equal to $2*9024/8 = 2256$, the maximum frequency of the FPGA to fully exploit the HBM is 225 MHz, as such the theoretical maximum double performance is $(2256)/(1/225MHz) \times 10^{-9} = 507.6$ double GFLOPS. Peak performance is upper bounded by both the theoretical FP64 peak rate and the peak memory bandwidth, which define the red line in the plot. The results show the operational intensity of our kernel on the HBM of the FPGA, indicating that we are bound by the bandwidth of the HBM (Fig. 8). This can be explained by the operational intensity of the HPCG benchmark which is low by design, as the benchmark contains only memory bound kernels. Note that the optimized performance of our algorithm still touches theoretical ceiling, showing that our implementation represents a near-optimal implementation of the HPCG benchmark as it is limited only by the memory bandwidth of the HBM present on the FPGA.

6   Conclusions and Future Works

Our work presents the first multi-FPGA implementation of the HPCG Benchmark. Our implementation demonstrates runtime improvements of up to 333× using four FPGAs, compared with the original CPU algorithm. Additionally, results show improvements in power efficiency up to 408× compared to the same implementation, and a 2.7× improvement with respect to HPCG run on the NVIDIA V100. We also show that our implementation achieves comparable performance to the GPU implementation of HPCG running on a NVIDIA P100. We also show how our implementation performs when using different data precision, showing how our implementation could be useful in other real-world application scenarios. Finally, we demonstrate that our implementation results in near optimal performance for the Xilinx Alveo U280 evaluating our results using the Berkeley Roofline Model. Future work will focus on reducing the impact of the PCIe interface on the performance of the benchmark. To enable linear performance improvements with increasing FPGA counts, we plan to implement direct FPGA to FPGA communication using the on-board networking ports. We will also open-source all the code regarding this implementation in the near future.

Acknowledgments. We acknowledge the Xilinx University Program for providing access to the Xilinx Adaptive Compute Cluster (XACC) at ETH Zurich.

References

1. Dongarra, J.J., Luszczek, P., Petitet, A.: The linpack benchmark: past, present and future. Concurrency Comput. Pract. Experience **15**(9), 803–820 (2003)
2. J. Dongarra, P. Luszczek, and M. Heroux, "Hpcg technical specification," Sandia National Laboratories, Sandia Report SAND2013-8752, 2013
3. Shalf, J.M., Leland, R.: Computing beyond moore's law. Computer **48**(SAND-2015-8039J), 14–23 (2015)

4. Theis, T.N., Wong, H.-S.P.: The end of moore's law: a new beginning for information technology. Comput. Sci. Eng. **19**(2), 41–50 (2017)
5. Jiang, W., et al.: Accuracy vs. efficiency: Achieving both through fpga-implementation aware neural architecture search. In: Proceedings of the 56th Annual Design Automation Conference 2019 (2019)
6. Zeni, A., Crespi, M., Di Tucci, L., Santambrogio, M.D.: An fpga-based computing infrastructure tailored to efficiently scaffold genome sequences. In: 2019 IEEE 27th Annual International Symposium on Field-Programmable Custom Computing Machines (FCCM), IEEE (2019)
7. Di Tucci, L., O'Brien, K., Blott, M., Santambrogio, M.D.: Architectural optimizations for high performance and energy efficient smith-waterman implementation on FPGAs using OpenCL. In: Design, Automation & Test in Europe Conference & Exhibition (DATE), 2017. IEEE (2017)
8. Dongarra, J., Heroux, M.A.: Toward a new metric for ranking high performance computing systems. Sandia Report, SAND2013-4744 **312**, 150 (2013)
9. Dongarra, J.: Sunway taihulight supercomputer makes its appearance. Natl. Sci. Rev. **3**(3), 265–266 (2016)
10. Park, J.: Efficient shared-memory implementation of high-performance conjugate gradient benchmark and its application to unstructured matrices. In: SC 2014: Proceedings of the International Conference for High Performance Computing, Networking, Storage and Analysis. IEEE (2014)
11. Phillips, E., Fatica, M.: A cuda implementation of the high performance conjugate gradient benchmark. In: Jarvis, S.A., Wright, S.A., Hammond, S.D. (eds.) PMBS 2014. LNCS, vol. 8966, pp. 68–84. Springer, Cham (2015). https://doi.org/10.1007/978-3-319-17248-4_4
12. Kumahata, K., Minami, K., Maruyama, N.: High-performance conjugate gradient performance improvement on the k computer. Int. J. High Perform. Comput. Appl. **30**(1), 55–70 (2016)
13. Ruiz, D., Mantovani, F., Casas, M., Labarta, J., Spiga, F.: The hpcg benchmark: analysis, shared memory preliminary improvements and evaluation on an arm-based platform (2018)
14. Zhang, X., Yang, C., Liu, F., Liu, Y., Lu, Y.: Optimizing and scaling HPCG on Tianhe-2: early experience. In: Sun, X., et al. (eds.) ICA3PP 2014. LNCS, vol. 8630, pp. 28–41. Springer, Cham (2014). https://doi.org/10.1007/978-3-319-11197-1_3
15. Egawa, R., et al.: Performance and power analysis of SX-ACE using HP-X benchmark programs. In: 2017 IEEE International Conference on Cluster Computing (CLUSTER). IEEE (2017)
16. Marjanović, V., Gracia, J., Glass, C.W.: Performance modeling of the HPCG benchmark. In: Jarvis, S.A., Wright, S.A., Hammond, S.D. (eds.) PMBS 2014. LNCS, vol. 8966, pp. 172–192. Springer, Cham (2015). https://doi.org/10.1007/978-3-319-17248-4_9
17. Vermij, E., Fiorin, L., Hagleitner, C., Bertels, K.: Boosting the efficiency of HPCG and graph500 with near-data processing. In: 2017 46th International Conference on Parallel Processing (ICPP), IEEE (2017)
18. Sundararajan, P.: High performance computing using fpgas, Technical Report. Available Online 2010: Technical report (2010) www.xilinx.com/support
19. Dimond, R., Racaniere, S., Pell, O.: Accelerating large-scale HPC applications using FPGAs. In: 2011 IEEE 20th Symposium on Computer Arithmetic, IEEE (2011)
20. Herbordt, M.C., et al.: Achieving high performance with FPGa-based computing. Computer **40**(3), 50–57 (2007)

21. Williams, S., Waterman, A., Patterson, D.: Roofline: an insightful visual performance model for multicore architectures. Commun. ACM **52**(4), 65–76 (2009)
22. Muralidharan, S., O'Brien, K., Lalanne, C.: A semi-automated tool flow for roofline anaylsis of opencl kernels on accelerators. In: First International Workshop on Heterogeneous High-performance Reconfigurable Computing (H2RC 2015) (2015)

Author Index

Printed in the United States
by Baker & Taylor Publisher Services